Marriage and Alternatives:

Exploring Intimate Relationships

Marriage and Alternatives:
Exploring Intimate Relationships

Roger W. Libby
State University of New York at Albany

Robert N. Whitehurst
University of Windsor, Canada

Scott, Foresman and Company
Glenview, Illinois
Dallas, Tex.
Oakland, N.J.
Palo Alto, Cal.
Tucker, Ga.
London

The editors would like to express appreciation to Carolynne Kieffer, Charles Cole, Lonny Myers, Gordon Clanton, and Brian Gilmartin for their enthusiasm, prompt response, and caring support during the development of this book. We also wish to thank Elizabeth Havelock, Donna Dempster, Ronald Mazur, and Sandra Browning for their critical comments and encouragement. Additional thanks are due to Walter Dinteman, Ralph Croston, and Christine Bowman of Scott, Foresman and Company.

Library of Congress Cataloging in Publication Data

Main entry under title:

Marriage and alternatives.

  Bibliography: p. 397.
  1. Marriage. 2. Unmarried couples.
3. Sex customs. 4. Group sex. I. Libby,
Roger W. II. Whitehurst, Robert N.
HQ734.M385   301.42   76-28704
ISBN 0-673-15050-X

2 3 4 5 6 7–ALP–83 82 81 80 79 78 77

To those who choose to explore intimacy within and beyond marriage.

The Contributors

Jessie Bernard, Ph.D., is resident scholar and professor emerita of sociology at Pennsylvania State University and has been a Fellow of the National Institute of Education in Washington, D.C. She is the author or coauthor of many books and articles on marriage and the family, parenthood, and sex roles. Among her many published works are *The Future of Marriage*, *The Sex Game*, and *The Future of Parenthood*.

Gordon Clanton, Ph.D., is a lecturer in the sociology department at San Diego State University. He is coeditor of *Face to Face to Face: An Experiment in Intimacy*, a study of a three-person group marriage based on the diaries of the participants, and of *Jealousy*, an interdisciplinary anthology of research and reflection.

Charles Lee Cole, Ph.D., is associate professor of family relations in the department of family environment at Iowa State University in Ames. He is serving currently as director of the Cohabitation Research Project, and he is a marriage counselor in private practice.

Joan M. Constantine is a certified family therapist in private practice with the Center for Family Change in the Boston area. Trained at the Boston Family Institute, she co-leads experiential workshops dealing with alternative life-styles, sex, family systems, and jealousy. She is coauthor with Larry Constantine of *Group Marriage: A Study of Contemporary Multilateral Marriage*, a book based on their longitudinal study of group marriages.

Larry L. Constantine is a certified family therapist in private practice with the Center for Family Change in the Boston area. Trained at the Boston Family Institute, he is active in education and research at the Boston State Hospital, and he also does corporate therapy. He and Joan Constantine co-lead experiential workshops dealing with alternative life-styles, sex, family systems, and jealousy.

Sandra Coyner, Ph.D., is assistant professor of history and social science at Syracuse University in New York. A feminist scholar with interests in women's studies and the women's liberation movement, she is currently writing a book comparing images of women in Victorian England and images of women in America in the mid-fifties.

John F. Cuber, Ph.D., is professor emeritus of sociology at Ohio State University, where he still teaches part-time. A prolific writer, he has published thirteen books, one of which is *The Significant Americans* (Peggy Harroff, coauthor), and over fifty articles. He also wrote the first book on marriage counseling, *Marriage Counseling Practice*, published in 1947.

Martin Duberman, Ph.D., is distinguished service professor of history at Lehman College, City University of New York. He is the author of *Charles Francis Adams, 1807–1886*, which was awarded the Bancroft Prize for History in 1962, and of *James Russell Lowell*, which was a nominee for the National Book Award in 1966. He is a playwright as well as a historian, and his documentary play, *In White America*, won the 1963-64 Vernon Rice Drama Desk Award. In 1971, Mr. Duberman received a prize from the American Academy of Arts and Letters for his contributions to literature.

Anna K. Francoeur received her M.A. in history from New York University. A member of the Groves Conference on Marriage and the Family, she has taught at the college and high-school levels and is coauthor with her husband, Robert T. Francoeur, of *Hot and Cool Sex: Cultures in Conflict* and *The Future of Sexual Relations*, an anthology of readings.

Robert T. Francoeur, Ph.D., is a certified sex educator and professor of human sexuality at Fairleigh Dickinson University. He holds a B.A. in English and philosophy, an M.A. in Roman Catholic theology, an M.S. in biology, and a Ph.D. in biology. He has written numerous articles and nine books on human sexuality, alternate life-styles, and futurism, including *Utopian Motherhood: New Trends in Human Reproduction; Eve's New Rib: Twenty Faces of Sex, Marriage, and Family; Hot and Cool Sex: Cultures in Conflict;* and *The Future of Sexual Relations*.

Brian G. Gilmartin, Ph.D., has been visiting assistant professor of family development at Virginia Polytechnic Institute and State University. He has conducted the most extensive study of swinging yet accomplished.

Peggy Harroff is a free-lance writer with an A.B. in sociology from Ohio State University. She is coauthor of three articles and of the book *The Significant Americans* with her husband, John F. Cuber.

John S. Kafka, M.D., is clinical professor of psychiatry and behavioral sciences at the George Washington University School of Medicine as well as training and supervising analyst at the Washington Psychoanalytic Institute. He also serves as a psychiatric consultant to the National Institute of Mental Health.

Carolynne Kieffer is a doctoral candidate in social psychology in the department of sociology at the University of Missouri-Columbia. She holds a master's degree in family relations from Florida State University. She is active in the National Council on Family Relations and in the Groves Conference on Marriage and the Family.

Jacquelyn J. Knapp, Ph.D., is a clinical psychologist in Daytona Beach, Florida. She has published articles on her research into the attitudes of marriage counselors toward alternative life-styles as well as on her in-depth study of sexually open marriages.

Roger W. Libby, Ph.D., is research associate in sociology at the State University of New York at Albany. He has been research director of The Institute for Family Research and Education at Syracuse University and visiting assistant professor of family development at the University of Georgia. He has written or edited several books including *Renovating Marriage: Toward New Sexual Life-Styles* and *Sexuality Today and Tomorrow*. His articles have appeared in such journals as *The Journal of Social Issues*, *Archives of Sexual Behavior*, and *The Pacific Sociological Review*.

David Mace, Ph.D., is professor of family sociology at the Bowman-Gray Medical School. A founder of the Marriage Guidance Council in England, he is also, with his wife Vera Mace, a cofounder of the Association of Couples for Marriage Enrichment, Inc.

Vera Mace, M.A., is a cofounder of the Association of Couples for Marriage Enrichment. She is a coauthor with David Mace of numerous articles and books on marriage and the family, including *Marriage East and West* and *We Can Have Better Marriages If We Really Want Them*.

Ronald Mazur is a health educator at the University Health Services of the University of Massachusetts at Amherst where he is also director of the Peer Sex Education Program. He holds a Master of Divinity degree and is ordained as a Unitarian-Universalist minister. He is one of the writers of the Unitarian sex education booklet *About Your Sexuality*. In addition to publishing articles, he is the author of two books, *Commonsense Sex* and *The New Intimacy: Open-Ended Marriage*.

John McMurtry, Ph.D., is professor of philosophy at the University of Guelph in Canada. He is a well-known athlete and has published articles on sports and on philosophy.

Lonny Myers, M.D., is a clinician and director of medical education for the Midwest Population Center in Chicago. She is serving as chairman of the midwest region of the American Association of Sex Educators, Counselors, and Therapists (AASECT) and is coauthor of *Adultery and Other Private Matters: Your Right to Personal Freedom in Marriage*.

Robert Rimmer holds an M.A. degree from Harvard University and is the author of many popular novels such as *The Harrad Experiment*, *Proposition 31*, *Thursday, My Love*, *The Rebellion of Yale Marratt*, and *The Premar Challenge*. He has several nonfiction books also, including *Adventures In Loving* and *You and I . . . Searching for Tomorrow*. He resides in Quincy, Massachusetts. Through his writing he has been a key proponent of innovative alternative life-styles.

Della Roy, Ph.D., is professor of material science at Pennsylvania State University. She is coauthor, with her husband Rustum Roy, of the book *Honest Sex*.

Rustum Roy, Ph.D., is professor of solid state chemistry at Pennsylvania State University. With his wife Della Roy he has been active in radical Christian movements. He is currently involved with professional work on the interrelationship between science and human values.

Robert G. Ryder, Ph.D., is a psychology professor and dean of the school of home economics and family studies at the University of Connecticut. He was formerly chief of the family development section of the National Institute of Mental Health. He is the author of many articles that evolved from his longitudinal research on marriage and the family conducted at the National Institute of Mental Health.

Pepper Schwartz, Ph.D., is assistant professor of sociology at the University of Washington, Seattle, and coauthor or coeditor of two books, *Women at Yale: Liberating a College Campus* and *The Sexual Scripts: The Social Construction of Female Sexuality*. Her current research concerns bisexuality.

Robert N. Whitehurst, Ph.D., is professor of sociology at the University of Windsor, Canada. He is the author of many articles and coeditor of two books prior to this volume: *The New Sexual Revolution* and *Renovating Marriage: Toward New Sexual Life-Styles*. He has conducted research on alternative life-styles and changing female-male relations.

Foreword

Marriage and Alternatives: Exploring Intimate Relationships seductively invites comparison with its predecessor, *Renovating Marriage.* Comparisons, however, do not appear in the same way to all evaluators, because crucial idiosyncratic factors emerge from the several contexts within which the opinions arise. Young people, as a rule, do not (and probably never did) orient themselves to sexual matters in the same manner as do older people. In spite of the simplistic and overused application of the developmental model of marriage and family study, with its emphasis on "stages" and "tasks," we still need to call attention to the basic idea that age and status position foster crucial differences in the "realities" which are perceived. A person who has been divorced, and one who has never been divorced, despite conscientious efforts to understand others' positions, rarely perceive the same problems and the same solutions in the man-woman world. Nor, as a rule, do a parent and a nonparent. Nor does one who has "made it," at least reasonably well, in the quest for fulfillment as husband, or wife, or parent see marriage, the roles, and success and failure in the same way as does one for whom the lights have failed. Then, too, ideological stances build fences around perceptions, even of what the publicly known facts are and, more importantly, what such facts mean. No facts "speak for themselves"—not to mention that very often the facts themselves are in dispute. Not only is the quest for intimacy a varied one, intimacy itself means very different things to different people. A comfortable and secure traditional conservative does not—possibly cannot—experience the same cognitive world as does a philosophical radical or an avowed individualist. A broadly educated person tends to have widely different perceptions and orientations from those of a person of narrowly circumscribed exposure to the ever expanding panorama of ideas, alternatives, and human experiences.

In writing this Foreword we make no claim, therefore, to complete objective orientation to the ideas it embraces, despite efforts to do so. Our evaluations, like those of the several contributors, grow out of *our* background, ages, and social position. We are both "older people," divorced and remarried, with adult children, both trained as sociologists, but not exclusively so, and have worked together professionally for more than a decade and a half. We both share a commitment to the concept of pluralism in life-styles and an abhorrence of coercion and brainwashing for or against *any* particular life-style. Our own innovations have been cautious and few, but through counseling and close friendships we have experienced a wide exposure to various—even radical—alternate life-styles. Both personally and professionally, then, we bring to this evaluation an appreciation, but not necessarily a total endorsement, of the innovative life-styles in this book.

It is to be expected, too, that readers of this book, and other critics, will not all share the same perspectives, advocate the same changes, or assess history in the same way as the contributors to this book do. But this book deals with ideas which any educated person should at least be exposed to, no matter what his or her personal persuasions. This is particularly important in these times, when a mind-boggling pluralism pervades the relationships of man and woman, parent and child. Each of the several prospectuses in this book has a logical and factual and historical perspective which will make good sense to some people and little to others. Probably because it is impossible to say anything about marriage in these times which will be unanimously accepted, there has emerged a plethora of suggestions and this book effectively elaborates many of them.

Like *Renovating Marriage*, this book breaks with the trite, genteel "value free" tradition of so many social scientists. One always knows what Libby and Whitehurst, and their several collaborators, advocate on each of the issues considered. While they do not always stand exactly together, they share one basic, pervasive stance, namely, that the worlds of men and women, parents and children are in sore need of radical rescripting.

The foregoing need not be taken to mean that everyone, or even a majority, feels any such pressing need for radical renovation of marriage, parenthood, or premarriage roles, despite the last two decades or so of continuous bombardment by innovative literature. Yet, obviously, for some who are seriously discontented with one or another aspect of the traditional scheme of things and who are idealistic about the prospects for viable change, there appears to be an urgent need for sharp departure from the existing monolithic code, rather than the merely somewhat modified ideologies and practices of many of our contemporaries. The ideas and experiences of the sexual—life-style innovators and proponents are the stuff of this book. And to many readers it will appear to be heady stuff indeed. Whether it will turn out to be reliable prophecy for better personal fulfillment and for improved social structure, or will turn out to be merely the fervent wishes of a sincere, sensitive, and creative few, only time will tell.

The intentions of *Renovating Marriage* have been carried forward faithfully in *Marriage and Alternatives*. Additional topics of importance are treated, for example, singlehood as a life-style, sexually open marriages, the interconnectedness of women's liberation and sexual liberation, bisexuality, children in the innovative life-styles, and a clear and more explicit examination of the quest for intimacy. The textual content is also embellished by an updated and well-selected bibliography. And the counter-epilogue by the Maces is by no means the least of the balancing.

In a time of increasing interest and acceptance of innovations in life-style, this book is a worthwhile contribution to the dialogue. Reading it will bring hope to some; it will frighten others. Its credibility and its plausibility will vary widely. But it will put no one to sleep!

Mt. Gilead, Ohio

John F. Cuber
Peggy B. Harroff

Contents

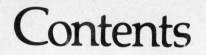

Introduction

It is no secret that emotional closeness, touching and caressing, sexual fulfillment, and intellectual sharing compose the most basic human needs and desires. A full, rich life includes achieving intimacy with others, whether such intimate experiences occur within or beyond various styles of marriage. With the increasing mobility of the nuclear family, the intimacy needs from one's spouse and relatives must be supplemented with an intimate network (Stoller, 1970) of people who provide an expanded sense of both "family" and "community" through shared experiences with close social interaction.

Intimacy and love are difficult to define in ways that are meaningful in shared communication. Definitions of intimacy and love reflect the values and life-style biases of people who are searching for closeness. For some, monogamous, sexually exclusive marriage provides the bulk of intimacy needs, while for others various needs for intellectual, physical, and emotional aspects of intimacy are met through what Carolynne Kieffer refers to as a "patchwork" or a *combination* of intimate relationships which include three major dimensions: breadth (range of activities), openness (self-disclosure of deep-seated emotions), and depth (sharing core aspects of oneself) (see Kieffer, Chapter 18).

Definitions of intimacy and love (whether sexual or not) identify the warp and woof of various alternative expressions of self through marriage and alternatives to marriage. Explorations into intimacy require an awareness of the range of choices of life-styles which might best meet one's intimacy needs at each stage in the process of social and sexual interaction over a lifetime. The social environment, the opportunity for intimacy, and the ability to introspect and reflect on life-styles which seem to be most fulfilling at *each* stage of what may be called the *intimacy career* (which includes and overlaps with the sexual and/or marital careers, and with the occupational career) influence the design of one's patchwork of intimate others. One of the major themes of this book is the quest for intimacy.

Marriage: Panacea for All Personal, Sexual, and Social Problems?

The search for intimacy usually involves the assumption that companionate-equalitarian monogamous marriage will provide "the good life" where all of one's needs for security and intimacy will be satisfied through constant sharing and togetherness (or, what Nena and George O'Neill have called the "couple front" in *Open Marriage*, 1972) for an entire lifetime. Richard Udry has aptly described the typical view of marriage:

Americans believe in marriage above all. They marry earlier, remain unmarried less often, and remarry after divorce more frequently and more rapidly than people of any other industrialized nation. They look to their marital relationship for their greatest satisfaction in life (1971, p. 2).

Following exchange theory in social psychology, everyone tries to maximize rewards and minimize costs in their relationships, be these marital or nonmarital. We are in the market for the best deal we can find, so we can share in the good life. This search for the best deal is a part of our capitalistic, competitive society. The quest for intimacy may include discarding relationships and/or life-styles which fail to meet a person's expectations for emotional and sexual satisfaction. Somehow, North Americans expect that marriage (specifically monogamy) will *provide* this good life, and they won't have to *create* it. To these people marriage is seen as the answer to all personal, sexual, and social deficiencies. Somehow the sense of inner security and self-acceptance and love of oneself and the existential view of intimate relationships as adjuncts to personal intimacy seem to get lost in an obsessive reaching out to others to satisfy one's personal needs for intimacy. This situation is analogous to Abraham Maslow's (1954) need hierarchy where he contended that one must meet one's basic needs (hunger, sex, etc.) before trying to achieve self-actualization (or personal intimacy and the development of intimate relationships which extend beyond *needs*). In order to describe and analyze the range of alternative life-styles in which intimacy can be achieved, we must take a critical look at monogamy and its alternatives.

It is likely that all but two to three percent of the younger generation will marry sometime—and most at an early age. Does this mean marriage is successful? Or happy? Does it mean that the human desire for intimacy, love, sex, warmth, and individual growth can be fulfilled in a traditional monogamous marriage? Does the experience of marriage match up to the high expectations people generally have for it?

The rising divorce rate alone is a clear indicator that for many people marriage has not worked. Romantic stereotypes, media images, and thoroughly ingrained preconceptions too often pave the way for severe disillusionment, disappointment, and a sense of personal failure. The beautiful myths and high hopes for marriage do not easily translate from fantasy into reality.

Traditional monogamous marriage, with its assumptions of sexual exclusivity—and for many spouses, emotional exclusivity—has long been the sole model for expressing sexuality and satisfying the need for intimate relationships. Partly because it has been so universal in American society, traditional monogamy has escaped close scrutiny and continual reassessment. Because marriage was a given it was not a subject of research, and consequently there is a lot we do not yet know about marriage or intimate relationships. As a first step toward understanding or evaluating marriage, we must begin to examine some of the misconceptions, myths, and stereotypes of the institution and compare these myths to the realities. Only then can we attempt to improve marriage and validate alternatives.

The Myths and Realities of Monogamy

As pointed out above, *one myth is that all of one's personal, sexual, and social needs can be met through monogamous marriage.* The myth of monogamous bliss is sobering to confront in light of the realities of expecting too much from one intimate relationship, and then experiencing dissatisfaction when the monogamous expectations for constant intimacy are not realized. *Two additional related myths are that marriage is a static state where all needs will be satisfied, and that time will strengthen these expectations through an exclusive relationship.* While newly wedded people may maintain the honeymoon romance for a while, empirical studies indicate that it is the rare couple that is able to *maintain* such an ecstatic state of intimacy within an exclusive marriage forever. As Jessie Bernard indicates (see Chapter 8), it is probable that most couples must eventually choose between permanence in their marriage and exclusivity over their marital career. These two values (permanence and exclusivity) are usually in conflict. Thus, young couples often opt for exclusive intimacy—sexual ground rules until they realize that they are not achieving all of their emotional and/or sexual needs in marriage, and then they must decide whether to open up their marriage in various areas (marriages are not open *or* closed in the dichotomous sense, but are open *and* closed in specific areas such as emotional caring for others) to maintain permanence, or to remain exclusive and not fully satisfied.

One myth has it that we will love each other more after years of marriage—yet the reality is often otherwise, as shown by the use of strategic threats such as: "If you don't stop running around with other women, I'll divorce you, and I've told my mother so." Permanence is a typical gauge for "success" in a chosen life-style or relationship. However, the expectation that permanence will accompany monogamous marriage with rigid boundaries excluding other intimates is not often materialized in real life. There is a ring of truth to the cartoon where the bride turns brightly to her husband and says: "Darling! Our first marriage!" The serially monogamous marital system we've created with an increasing divorce rate and with much frustration and confusion is not what most people have expected from marriage. The realities of sexual and mental "infidelities" must be considered in light of the monogamous image.

Many Americans blame the individuals involved for marital unhappiness or "failure," rather than focusing attention on the social structure or differing needs and desires of individuals (different people have variant levels of expectations, and the same individuals vary in their needs and expectations over time). However, the young (and sometimes older) couple who are "in love" usually fail to realize that their intimacy needs and desires may change over time, and that others may become a part of their patchwork of intimate relationships. For example, if one marital partner changes and takes on new interests and there are not enough shared activities to maintain the original expectations for marital intimacy, opening up the marriage or divorce may result.

If all marriages were permanent and maintained high levels of intimacy, we would not have an increasing divorce rate, and empirical studies would indicate that more spouses are happy with their marriages. Permanence can result from continued growth and adjustment to change in a relationship and to social change, but static views or role expectations in any relationship are the death knell to permanence. Marriage and other intimate relationships must be viewed, then, as processes rather than as static states where people supposedly exist in a vacuum from personal, relational, and societal change.

Another myth is that exclusivity will come easily and naturally (see Schwartz, Chapter 15). Ira Reiss (1973) and Roger Libby (1977) have observed that the broadening range of choices of sexual life-styles prior to marriage affect marital choices and ground rules. We cannot isolate habits learned before marriage (such as multiple sexual and emotional relationships) from the probability that similar practices will recur after marriage (see Libby, Chapter 4, for an elaboration of this theme). As illustrated in Chapter 6, most extramarital sexual behavior is probably "cheating" and unknown to the spouse, who wears blinders with rationalizations or naive beliefs such as "My spouse wouldn't do something like *that!*" While there is some cultural lag, permissive changes in premarital and nonmarital sexual attitudes and behavior are being reflected in postmarital patterns of marriages based on increased freedom and less possession and jealousy. Extramarital sex (EMS) is a fact of North American sexual behavior. Most is probably still seen as infidelity or adultery, but this book will also explore other marital concepts where sex with others is viewed as consistent with marital goals (thus, *comarital sex* or *CMS*). As Jessie Bernard (Chapter 8) points out, infidelity must be redefined when the ground rules of marriage change and become more personalized.

Elsewhere Bernard has stated:

Whether or not such relations are more frequent . . . a trend toward acceptance is unmistakable. . . . A conception of marriage which tolerates, if it is not actually sympathetic with, extramarital relations is on its way, and provision for sexual varietism is almost standard in male blueprints for the future. The time is not far off when this desideratum of husbands' marriages may also be achieved (1972, p. 24).

How do marital partners react to EMS if it is not agreed upon? Is exclusivity of sexual intimacy within monogamous marriage a realistic expectation in today's world with increasing opportunities for additional intimate relationships? Obviously, there are no pat answers to these questions, for all married people. The variety of marital definitions (from monogamous to open marriage) and the multitude of situations, differences in people, and changes in the same people over time make sweeping generalizations impossible. However, most North Americans conceive of sexual relationships beyond marriage (EMS) as adultery and therefore morally bankrupt. Cultural attitudes are probably becoming slightly more accepting of EMS, although we have no definitive data from large, random, and national samples (beyond global public opinion surveys which are too insensitive to the issues to allow any valid generalizations).

Reactions to a spouse's extramarital "affairs" may range from uncontrollable anger to acceptance to happiness (if the experience enhanced the spouse and the marriage). It is not unusual to hear spouses exclaim: "I'd kill him (or her) if I caught him playing around." It seems that the horror of a spouse engaging in sexual intercourse with another is justification to feel that the spouse is no longer fit to live! The symbolic meaning of EMS is often interpreted as a threat to marriage. Fear is a strong emotion, and along with its closely related emotion of jealousy, fear provides a basis for not expanding erotic and emotional perimeters to include others beyond the pair bond.

Our perceptions of reality are contingent on the socialization experiences we have had (reinforcements or punishments for expressing various values or engaging in specific behaviors). Definitions of love and intimacy and behavioral expressions of these concepts differ, then, according to what we have learned from our experiences in relationships and from the images presented in the mass media and other cultural representations of what it means to be intimate, to love, and to be loved. Philosophers, psychologists, sociologists, novelists, theologians, and others differ in their views of various kinds of intimacy and love. For example, Erich Fromm (1956) claims that erotic love *must* be exclusive, and that humans *cannot* love several people *sexually* at the same time, while Bob Rimmer's concept of love, rather than being a game of subtraction as with Fromm, is a multiplying experience where the more people one loves, the more one is capable of loving (although there are limits, see Rimmer, Chapter 24). As Gerhard Neubeck puts it:

Forsaking all others has never been a realistic expectation, and, based on the assumption that there always will be others, couples can explore what the possibilities for themselves and each other should be: when, where, and how the additional individuals can be incorporated into the basic and nourishing unit. They must change more overtly so that their marriages will permit them to be less exclusive (1969, p. 189).

The author of *The Joy of Sex* (1972) and *More Joy* (1974), Alex Comfort, favors experiments with networks of sexually intimate relationships. He states:

. . . we are dishonest because we have a society that is supposed to be monogamous but in fact practices serial polygamy. Most people have been married more than once, and adultery is universally tolerated. Open marriage would simply legitimize what we already live (*Time*, January 8, 1973, p. 35).

Perceptions about open marriage will be discussed in later chapters.

Image Versus Reality: An Elaboration of an Old Theme

Social images or stereotypes do not always fit with behavioral realities and emotional feelings. The area of intimate life-styles is certainly no exception; two people may appear to be monogamous because they live together and are married, but what they *do* or what they *agree to* in their marital "contract" (whether written or verbal) is often private and therefore not obvious to neighbors, friends, relatives, employers, or others. The "secret society" of intimate relationships is a fascinating reality which is nearly untapped by behavioral scientists. The contrast between what we *say* we do and what we *really* do is often not revealed, but the gap nevertheless exists.

It is very likely that many so-called monogamous, sexually exclusive marriages are far from what they appear in that a "contract" has been negotiated between the spouses for some variety of comarital intimacy or open marriage. While such contracts may not be written or legal, they are nevertheless real and active in situationally defining what a couple agree is appropriate emotional and sexual sharing with others. As Susan Edmiston states in her *Ms.* magazine article "How to Write Your Own Marriage Contract":

. . . writing . . . a contract may seem a cold and formal way of working out an intimate relationship, but often it is the only way of coping with the ghosts of 2,000 years of tradition lurking in our definitions of marriage (1972, p. 67).

Whenever someone introduces into a conversation the fact that they are married, or about to marry, the ensuing dialogue as well as certain modifications in the behavior of the others makes obvious a number of current stereotypes of the meaning of marriage. It is commonly assumed, for instance, that everyone knows what marriage means and that everyone accepts the image of a monogamous, sexually exclusive marriage as a reality for all couples who have any claim to being happily married. The symbolic wedding bands clearly indicate the exclusivity of the "love" relationship with no sanction for any extramarital sex. In recent years, however, social change and new realities have been eating away at, and appear to counter, this romanticized image of marriage. Americans are being forced to take another look at marriage with an eye to potentially renovating and redefining these relationships so that one has a range of permissible patterns of intimate life-styles from which to choose to design one's own patchwork of intimate others.

The double standard which allows men more freedom to enter multiple sexual relationships (to have a more expanded patchwork of sexually intimate experiences) is slowly passing. The women's liberation movement, increased female employment (economic independence), and an increasing range of options to monogamous marriage and motherhood support greater bargaining power for women in their selection of intimate life-styles. This will probably be evident in a trend towards more women initiating divorce and entering another life-style by expanding their intimate network of relationships; this view is supported by Dressel and Murray's (1976) analysis of changing family and marital behavior.

A long list of studies on marital happiness and unhappiness would seem to sum up marriage as a relatively poor situation for women. Traditionally the wife must understand and cater to the husband far more than the husband must cater to the wife. Women consistently evaluate their marriages lower than do their husbands. Aided by the mass media, a new consciousness is apparent among women—a consciousness of their inferior status in traditionally defined marital roles, including the sexual role (see Coyner, Chapter 14). After reading reports of the research conducted by Masters and Johnson, women seem to be asking more stridently for their emotional and sexual needs to be met. Of course, husbands are not always so happy either—both members of the couple may be mutually disillusioned.

Once the woes of marriage are recognized, one might ask: Is communication the problem? Are most marital problems "solved" by open, honest communication? No, communication is not the only important ingredient in marriage. Spouses can communicate well and still feel hostile toward each other or fail to meet each other's needs. In many cases, spouses simply do not share similar goals, or one or both spouses may have changed their goals during the marriage and now find the relationship no longer adequate. While selective communication may be one key to a happy marriage (there appears to be a fine line between honesty and insensitivity) (see Myers, Chapter 22), there are some inadequacies it cannot make up for.

The double standards of male versus female, single versus married, and heterosexual versus homosexual are some examples of the kind of dichotomous pigeonholing which define our perceptions of intimacy in one or more relationships (see Mazur, Chapter 13 for an elaboration of these double standards). The lack of "fit" between social images and what people *really* do and feel reflects the irrelevance of many social policies, laws and sanctions to the fulfillment of human potential for intimacy. This view is concurred with by John Pflaum (1972), who contends:

In a society of suffering, people cling to one another in non-productive social relationships fearing that otherwise they will be abandoned. Sufferers contract alliances intended to provide emotional defenses against isolation. These relationships are negative in origin and will persist only as long as both partners are motivated by their anxieties. Marriage and other exclusive arrangements may be better than the screaming loneliness of four walls, but they are a shadow of existence and symptomatic of a poorly designed social structure (1972, p. 115).

The lack of familial support for nonmonogamous life-styles is clear from Gilmartin's research on swingers (see Chapter 10). In spite of the rather weak social and legal support system for alternatives to monogamy, we live in a pluralistic society with subcultural groups which offer some support for those who are experimenting with various intimate life-styles. Gilmartin's emphasis on friends as supporting individuals for nonmonogamous couples offers some hope (relating to friends who support one's choices). Of course, the degree of social or emotional support from others depends to some extent on how *public* one is about entering into a nonmonogamous life-style which stresses the extension of one's self to more than one significant other. Even though some people are not terribly bothered unless the intimates become *sexual* intimates, the patchwork concept by Kieffer (Chapter 18) allows for intimate relationships which may be either sexual or platonic. Alternative life-styles exist, but how many are not very visible to the public eye? The definition of the range of intimate alternatives to monogamy, along with some redefinitions of marriage, comprise the bulk of this book.

The Visibility and Viability of Alternatives: The Emergence of Choice

One goal of this book is to expose alternative avenues to intimacy, and to make these alternatives more viable as real options for those in search of intimacy. Although we assume that monogamous marriage can and does meet the intimacy needs of many people, it is clear that one's intimate network of friends, lovers, and others is sometimes difficult to classify with one term, forcing a range of definitions of marriage. We, the editors, are in full agreement with Carl Rogers, who emphasizes the importance of experimenting with alternatives to marriage and the family as we've known them. He states:

Marriage and the nuclear family constitute a failing institution, a failing way of life. No one would argue that these have been highly successful. We need laboratories, experiments, attempts to avoid repeating past failures, exploration into new approaches. . . . Unheralded and unsung, explorations, experiments, new ways of relating, new kinds of partnerships are being tried out, people are learning from mistakes and profiting from successes. They are inventing alternatives, new futures, for our most sharply failing institutions, marriage and the nuclear family (1972, p. 212).

People vary in their needs, desires, fantasies, potentials, and the opportunity to select various intimate life-styles, and people vary in all of these over time. *No one pattern of intimates and no one concept of marriage is appropriate for all people.* Everyone is not suited to marriage—of *any* style. Indeed, there are those who should remain single, and many more who should avoid the responsibility of parenthood. We are advocating democratic pluralism in this book—the *choice* to live a life-style of your own making without interference from those who tend to make others' lives their business. We agree with former Federal Communications Commissioner Nicholas Johnson in his view that "The choice you'll never know is the choice you'll never make. Many Americans are not sufficiently informed of the alternatives to make an intelligent choice of the life they most want" (1972, p. 16). Specifically, we advocate clear thinking and the right to try out what pleases you rather than try to live by the mores of another age. Just as people differ in their personalities, needs, and goals, so must marriage vary for those who choose to marry. To attempt to fit all married people into the monogamous mold is to expect the impossible. It is no small wonder that the romanticized idea of satisfying all emotional and sexual needs in one relationship for a lifetime fails the test of reality soon after the honeymoon, and it is not surprising that an increasing proportion of married people "cheat" or seek divorce as an escape from marital disillusionment.

Countless Americans are—and have for some time been—experimenting with alternatives to traditional monogamy, but they have been given few guidelines and little help in this search by the mass media, church, or other social institutions or groups. Some experimenters are finding social support for their life-styles through such books as Rimmer's *The Harrad Experiment* (1966), the O'Neills' *Open Marriage* (1972), Rogers' *Becoming Partners* (1972), and the Lobells' *John and Mimi* (1973). But other supports are needed. While some people experimenting with various alternative life-styles are relatively public about their choice, many others fear negative feedback or recriminations for nonconformity.

Various alternative life-style groups and social movements such as the women's liberation movement, the human potential movement, population groups, humanist organizations, and the American Civil Liberties Union offer social and legal support to those who choose to develop and live alternatives to sexually exclusive monogamous marriage. Even though there are socially acceptable intimate relationships beyond marriage, the taboo on sexual intimacy outside marriage is still strong, particularly when one or more married people are involved, or if the motivation and meaning of sexual intimacy is something other than an exclusive, procreative, or "love" relationship lasting a lifetime.

Although there are more questions than answers about the multitude of intimate life-styles, we will pursue some tentative answers and pose questions which researchers, policy-makers, and laypersons might consider.

Finding Some Answers: Questions, Research, and Theory

There are many questions which social scientists must pursue about marriage and its alternatives, about intimacy, and about the personal and social implications of specific life-styles. Social scientists have barely begun to investigate intimate relationships, and innumerable questions about these alternatives need answering so people can make more intelligent choices, and so social policies, laws, and social institutions and groups can be more informed about the problems and joys of various explorations into intimate experiments in living.

Some important questions follow: What is the symbolic meaning and effect of other relationships on marriage (specifying whether or not the other relationships are sexual, to what extent they are intimate, clandestine, or open, etc.)? To answer such questions, we must first ask what *style* of marriage one has. As Reiss (1973) contends, only then can we intelligently discuss the effects of EMS or CMS on individual spouses, on couples, and on other intimates who relate to either or both spouses.

We also need to determine to what extent sexual intimacy is a communication of affection and a pleasant experience in the array of intimate lifestyles. We must ask how sex affects friendships. Why are some people alienated from conventional marriage expectations, while others accept them? What do youth feel about marriage and emerging alternatives to marriage? How do women fit into specific alternatives which include increased emotional and sexual freedom? How is intimacy (whether sexual or not) dealt with in open marriages, swinging groups, creative singles (as defined by Libby in Chapter 4), communes, group marriages, and other alternatives? What about jealous feelings—how do such feelings differ by intensity of intimate others, whether the other relationships are sexual or not, primary or secondary, etc.? What are the differential experiences of those who have primary, coprimary (equally important), secondary, and transitory intimate and/or sexual relationships? How are jealous feelings handled in each of these kinds of relationships? What is the relationship between fantasy and reality about sexual-intimate relationships beyond the primary pair bond? What is the relationship between attitudes, behavioral intentions, and actual intimate behavior? What distinctions can be made between marriages or other intimate relationships where the "contracts" were changed to accommodate sexual freedom, and marriages or other relationships (such as cohabitation) which were entered with some provision for sexual freedom? How will changing marital styles affect children and the nuclear family (see Chapter 17)?

A related list of questions concerning singlehood appears in Chapter 4, but most of those questions have broader application to other alternatives as well. For example, what is the nature of the process of selecting a given intimate network or life-style? What role models guide one to make choices, and upon what basis are choices reevaluated over time? More specifically, how do specific reference groups, attitudes, situations, opportunity structures, significant others, and various mass media affect the choices and the relative viability of each of the alternatives? What is the interrelationship between specific components of intimacy (breadth, openness, and depth for intellectual, physical, and emotional aspects of a relationship)? What are the proportions of people who either select or fall into (see Whitehurst, Chapter 21) various life-styles? What are the *crucial events* and *turning points* which lead to *role transitions* and changing commitments as one moves in and out of various social situations, occupations, cities, new social networks, and into and out of accompanying life-styles? What interpersonal experiences (such as encounter groups) are helpful in maintaining emotional stability and nurturing personal growth and self-actualization as opposed to anomie for specific life-styles? When comparing what people *say* they feel and do with what they *really* do, are they honest with others and with themselves about their happiness?

The questions could go on endlessly, but it remains for social scientists to study emerging intimate-sexual life-styles. Such research will be accomplished by people who care about the future of marriage and alternatives. In order to answer the questions posed in this Introduction as well as in other chapters, social scientists will have to utilize multiple research methods of data collection such as participant observation, in-depth interviews over time with the same people, and other methods designed to sensitize and develop theories which explain and predict the process and outcomes of each alternative, given specific social support systems. Descriptive research without a theoretical basis can offer little insight into the answers to the questions posed here. For example, analysis of perceived costs and rewards associated with given role definitions for particular life-styles and the relationship between these perceptions and emotional and behavioral realities requires the utilization of exchange theory, role theory, and aspects of symbolic interaction, reference group, and labeling theory. Even though these theories have been evolving in social psychology for several years, marriage and family researchers have been somewhat slow to use these theories and to develop them as they apply to content areas.

The lack of theoretically and methodologically sophisticated research on intimacy in its many shapes and forms is reflected in the largely descriptive and often moralistic textbooks used in marriage and family courses. Such texts have typically presented and ratified the traditional courtship and monogamous marriage model, with little serious consideration of variant views of marriage and alternatives. Only in recent years have textbook authors begun to mention alternative marital and sexual life-styles. Once the mass media portrayed some life-styles deviating from the monogamous model, textbook writers had little choice but to cite at least some of the professional and popular literature on these increasingly visible alternatives. It is a bit curious that social scientists waited for journalists to expose intimate alternatives to monogamy before acknowledging or researching these realities. Once the media depict a variant life-style (such as open marriage or bisexuality), social scientists recognize the potential professional gains to be accomplished by being one of the first to research these "new" life-styles (which may actually have existed in some form for a long time but lacked social visibility and exposure). And yet, textbooks still have not dealt comprehensively with the range of intimate life-styles. Only a handful of researchers have made inroads into the study of intimate alternatives to monogamy; and most of their efforts have lacked a theoretical basis and adequate samples and methods.

More sophisticated research with a sound theoretical basis *could* offer guidelines for intimate relationships of a higher quality than are now common—whether such intimacy exists within or beyond marriage. Perhaps some readers of this book will undertake careers in social science to close the gap between social realities and stereotyped images concerning the nature of intimacy. In the meantime, this book includes the most contemporary insights into intimacy with its various components and intricacies in the form of alternative life-styles and a reconceptualization of marriage.

What This Book Offers

This book is an expression of concern about marriage and other intimate relationships. As such, it is intended to be a springboard to further dialogue and research about marriage and alternatives in a society with a clear range of intimate life-styles. The basic issues of "why intimacy?" and "what life-styles offer the most rewards in terms of intimacy for different individuals?" underlie the development of the entire book. We do not intend to put yet one more nail in the coffin of marriage, nor do we intend to make the spurious argument that marriage and the family are on the way out as cultural institutions.

In contrast to Masters and Johnson's book, *The Pleasure Bond* (1975), this book really *does* offer "a new look at sexuality and commitment," as well as intimacy and its many expressions. Masters and Johnson's book viewed sexually exclusive monogamous marriage as a universal good for the human condition, but they did not consider the gamble of monogamy along with the risks of open marriage and other alternatives to monogamy (see Libby, 1976, for a review of *The Pleasure Bond*). This book makes no claim that every person should adopt any particular intimate life-style. *Emotionally exclusive monogamy is considered legitimate for those who select it, but patchworks of intimates are also considered for monogamous couples who choose to remain sexually exclusive, thus modifying traditional marriage to suit the needs and desires of monogamous couples in a highly mobile and often alien society.* The following quotation, used with the permission of one of the author's graduate students, illustrates the possibility of renegotiating the boundaries or role expectations when it comes to sexual behavior in and out of marriage.

Personally, the result of having some boundaries or spaces clearly understood and negotiated with my spouse results in a paradox: Boundaries give way to freedom. Openness builds trust, and I can experience more true, loving concern for him because I am both free to care, and free to make a commitment. Clarity in this area enables me to be clear, open, negotiating with significant others in my life. I have experienced close sexual relationships with others while being married (for what relationship is not sexual?), and each relationship has had its own unique expression of the feelings in that particular relationship (Brewster, 1976).

The above introspective statement expresses the complex relationship between freedom, commitment, trust, sensitivity, responsibility, and intimacy, and it forces a serious analysis of the symbolic meanings attached to various touching and sexual behaviors. *What makes a relationship intimate? What is sexual as opposed to sensual? How do the answers to these questions affect the achievement of intimacy and self-actualization?* These are questions that Maslow surely would still want to consider in light of the emergence of alternative life-styles.

As a part of the exploration of marriage and other intimate arrangements, we hope to open up marriage so it can thrive, not as a decrepit monolith, but as a set of multiple possibilities for those seeking to enrich their intimate relationships. Freed of old myths, we can discover what women, men, and intimacy are about.

This book is not meant to be a blueprint for the future. It only attempts to get at relevant questions and issues by pulling together the ideas, opinions, and research data of a broad range of investigators.

In part one of the book, the contributors analyze and critique marriage from three differing perspectives. Part two presents a range of alternatives to marriage and nontraditional variations of marriage. Among the choices described and evaluated are singlehood, living together (cohabitation), extramarital and comarital sex (from affairs to open marriage and swinging), and group marriage. The impact of the counterculture on marriage is also explored. The third part of the book considers the question, "Alternatives for whom?" Here the influence of the women's and alternative life-styles movements on intimate relationships is explored, and the meaning of alternatives is compared for women and men, adults and children, and for heterosexuals, homosexuals, and bisexuals. In the final section, we look at some suggestions and possibilities for the future of intimate relationships. An epilogue and counter-epilogue then offer contrasting views about the viability of marriage and alternatives.

Given the limitations of available research and theory, and assuming that there are different ways of legitimately *knowing* about social-sexual-in-

tworks, this book presents insights from sociology, psychology,
y, theology, literature, drama, history, and other disciplines. It is
ocial scientists to study *human potential for intimacy* rather than
search to mundane problems on a "functional" level. This requires
g a *maximal* model of human relating rather than focusing on a
odel of meeting basic needs. Somehow the joys and peak experi-
h Maslow envisioned get lost in the shuffle to survive economi-
ionally, and in other ways. Perhaps readers of this book will seek
ways to self-growth and thereby become role models for others
so seek more meaningful experiences through the exciting explo-
timate relationships.

—**Roger W. Libby**

Marriage and Alternatives:
Exploring Intimate Relationships

Part 1.

Traditional Monogamous Marriage

In these first three chapters, John McMurtry, Robert Whitehurst, and Della and Rustum Roy examine traditional monogamy from a historical-Marxist perspective, a sociological viewpoint, and a humanistic position. Although McMurtry and Whitehurst offer no real alternatives to traditional marriage (short of a major overhaul of our economic and social systems), the Roys offer a more concrete plan of action for both premarrieds and post-marrieds. These chapters establish an underlying theme for the rest of the book in that they raise questions about the pragmatic validity of monogamy for everyone in the culture today. Not only does the reader find in these chapters that monogamy does not and cannot work very well today for everyone, but there are also a number of glimpses into why this is so.

McMurtry shows some limitations of monogamy in light of the changing function of the nuclear family. He also shows how this form of marriage conforms to the basic outlines of a property structure which benefits the corporate state system instead of individuals.

Whitehurst examines some assumptions about the nature of sex, marriage, and monogamy. His perspective involves an analysis of the ways the current social structures and norms tend to support outcomes other than traditional monogamy. His conclusions are not very optimistic. He sees continued change, but no real set of supportive structures emerging to bolster either traditional monogamy or alternatives.

The Roys begin by analyzing monogamy and evaluating the effect of the sexual revolution and other social changes on monogamy. Continuing, they show that the single, divorced, widowed, young, and old are often left without a sense of community and lacking social-sexual and emotional supports. The Roys' humanistic approach to these problems includes the establishment of communities based on a quasi-religious set of assumptions about the nature of caring and the exercise of loving concern for one another.

It is obvious from these introductory chapters that real monogamy is not at all like the idealized stereotypes presented in love stories and supported by religious ideology. It is, rather, an amalgam of responses to a social situation, defined from the past but demonstrated to be unworkable for many people in the present. Like the chapters that follow throughout this book, the introductory chapters describe, critique, and analyze an intimate life-style, probing for the underlying assumptions that shape individuals' most intimate relationships. No solutions are provided and only extremely tentative and uncertain graspings at the future are attempted. Clearly, we need more critical questioning, research, and action if we are to move beyond the present impasse in which monogamy is less than satisfactory for many, but norms and guidelines for alternatives are lacking.

1.
Monogamy: A Critique
John McMurtry

The author reviews the principles underlying our monogamous style of marriage and criticizes the assumption that monogamy is natural and superior to other forms of long-term intimate sexual relationships. He pursues the logical problems inherent in the arguments for monogamy and adds a listing of other possibly inhibiting and destructive outcomes related to the strict practice of traditional monogamy.

McMurtry argues that marriage is essentially a relationship of mutual ownership, with marital partners laying claim to one another sexually as private property. He relates this to the capitalist system and concludes that monogamy is more important as a stabilizer of the social system than as a provider of benefits for monogamous partners or their children. McMurtry also suggests that the institution of marriage is unlikely to change drastically unless there is significant change, too, in the larger social order.

"Remove away that black'ning church
Remove away that marriage hearse
Remove away that man of blood
You'll quite remove the ancient curse."
　　　　　—William Blake

Almost all of us have entered or will one day enter a specifically standardized form of monogamous marriage. This cultural requirement is so very basic to our existence that we accept it for the most part as a kind of intractable given: it is dictated by the laws of God, Nature, Government, and Good Sense all at once. Though it is perhaps unusual for a social practice to be so broadly underwritten, we generally find comfort rather than curiosity in this fact and seldom wonder how something could be divinely inspired, biologically determined, coerced, and reasoned out all at the same time. We simply take for granted.

Those in society who are officially charged with the thinking function with regard to such matters are no less responsible for this uncritical acceptance than the person on the street. Psychoanalysts traditionally regard our form of marriage as a necessary restraint on the anarchic id and no more to be queried than civilization itself. Lawyers are as undisposed to questioning the practice as they are to criticizing the principle of private property. (This is appropriate, as I shall later point out.) The clergy formally perceive the relationship between man and wife to be as inviolable and insusceptible to

"Monogamy: A Critique" by John McMurtry from The Monist (October 1972), Vol. 56, No. 4.
© 1972 by the Open Court Publishing Co. Reprinted by permission.

question as the relationship between the institution they work for and the Christ. Sociologists standardly accept the formalized bonding of heterosexual pairs as the indispensable basis of social order and perhaps a societal universal. Politicians are as incapable of challenging it as they are the virtue of their own continued holding of office. And philosophers (at least the English-speaking philosophers), as with most issues of socially controversial or sexual dimensions, ignore the question almost altogether.

Even those irreverent adulterers and unmarried couples who would seem to be challenging the institution in the most basic possible way, in practice, tend merely to mimic its basic structure in unofficial form. The coverings of sanctity, taboo, and cultural habit continue to hold them with the grip of public clothes.

Principles of Traditional Monogamy

"Monogamy" means literally "one marriage." But it would be wrong to suppose that this phrase tells us much about our particular species of official wedlock. The greatest obstacle to the adequate understanding of our monogamy institution has been the failure to identify clearly and systematically the full complex of principles it involves. There are four such principles, each carrying enormous restrictive force and together constituting a massive social-control mechanism that has never, so far as I know, been fully schematized.

To come straight to the point, the four principles underlying monogamy are as follows:
1. The partners are required to enter a formal contractual relationship
   a. Whose establishment demands a specific official participant as well as certain conditions of the contractors (legal age, no blood ties, etc.), and a standard set of procedures;
   b. Whose governing terms are uniform for all and exactly prescribed by law; and
   c. Whose dissolution may only be legally effected by the decision of state representatives.

The ways in which this elaborate principle of contractual requirement is restrictive are obvious. One may not enter into a marriage union without entering into a contract presided over by a state-investured official.[1] One may not set any of the terms of the contractual relationship by which one is bound for life. And one cannot dissolve the contract without legal action and costs, court proceedings, and in many places actual legislation. (It is the one and only contract in all English-speaking law that is not dissoluble by the consent of the contracting parties.) The extent of control here—over the most intimate and putatively "loving" relationships in all social intercourse—is so great as to be difficult to catalog without exciting in oneself a sense of disbelief.

Lest it be thought there is always the real option of entering a common-law relationship free of such encumbrances, it should be noted that these relationships themselves are subject to state regulation, though of a less imposing sort. Second, and much more important, there are very formidable selective pressures against common-law partnerships such as employment and job discrimination, exclusion from housing and lodging facilities, special legal disablements,[2] loss of social and moral status (consider such phrases as "living in sin," "make her an honest woman," etc.), family shame and embarrassment, and so on.

2. The number of partners involved in the marriage must be two and only two (as opposed to three, four, five, or any of the almost countless other possibilities of intimate union).

This second principle of our specific form of monogamy (the concept of "one marriage," it should be pointed out, is consistent with any number of participating partners) is perhaps the most important and restrictive of the four principles we are considering. Not only does it confine us to just one possibility out of an enormous range, but it confines us to that single possibility which involves the least number of people, two. It is difficult to conceive of a more thoroughgoing mechanism for limiting extended social union and intimacy. The fact that this monolithic restriction seems so natural to us (if it were truly "natural" there would be no need for its rigorous cultural prescription by everything from severe criminal law[3] to ubiquitous housing regulations) simply indicates the extent to which its hold is implanted in our social structure. It is the institutional basis of what I will call the "binary frame of sexual consciousness," a frame through which all our heterosexual relationships are typically viewed ("two's company, three's a crowd") and in light of which all larger circles of intimacy seem almost inconceivable.[4]

3. No person may participate in more than one marriage at a time or during a lifetime (unless the previous marriage has been officially dissolved by either one partner's death or successful divorce).

Violation of this principle is, of course, a criminal offense (bigamy) which is punishable by a considerable term in prison. Of various general regulations of our marriage institution, this one has experienced the most significant modification: not, indeed, in principle, but in the considerable flexibility of its "escape hatch" of divorce. The ease with which this escape hatch is opened has increased considerably in the past few years (the grounds for divorce being more permissive than previously) and it is in this regard most of all that the principles of our marriage institution have undergone formal alteration. The changes are in plumbing rather than in substance.

4. No married person may engage in any sexual relationship with any person whatever other than the marriage partner.

Although a consummated sexual act with another person alone constitutes an act of adultery, lesser forms of sexual and erotic relationships[5] may also constitute grounds for divorce (i.e., cruelty) and are generally proscribed as well by informal social convention and taboo. In other words, the fourth and final principle of our marriage institution involves not only a prohibition of sexual intercourse per se outside one's wedlock (this term deserves pause), but a prohibition of all one's erotic relations whatever outside this bond. The penalties for violation here are as various as they are severe, ranging from permanent loss of spouse, children, chattel, and income to job dismissal and social ostracism. In this way, possibly the most compelling natural force towards expanded intimate relations with others[6] is strictly confined within the narrowest possible circle for the whole of adult life (barring delinquency). The sheer weight and totality of this restriction is surely one of the great wonders in the history of institutional control.

Defenses for Marriage

With all established institutions, apologetics for perpetuation are never wanting. Thus it is with our form of monogamous marriage.

Primary Justifications

Perhaps the most celebrated justification over the years has proceeded from a belief in a supreme deity who secretly utters sexual and other commands to privileged human representatives. Almost as well known a line of defense has issued from a conviction, similarly confident, that the need for some social regulation of sexuality demonstrates the need for our specific type of two-person wedlock. Although these have been important justifications in the sense of being very widely supported, they are not—having other grounds than reason—susceptible to treatment here.

If we put aside such arguments, we are left I think with two major claims. The first is that our form of monogamous marriage promotes a profound affection between the partners which is not only of great worth in itself but invaluable as a sanctuary from the pressures of outside society. Since, however, there are no secure grounds whatever for supposing that such "profound affection" is not at least as easily achievable by any number of *other* marriage forms (i.e., forms which differ in respect to one or more of the four principles), this justification conspicuously fails to perform the task required of it.

The second major claim for the defense is that monogamy provides a specially loving context for child upbringing. However, here again there are no grounds at all for concluding that it does so as effectively or any more effectively than other possible forms of marriage. (The only alternative type of upbringing to which it has apparently been shown to be superior is non-family institutional upbringing, which of course is not relevant to the present discussion.) Furthermore, the fact that at least half the span of a normal monogamous marriage *involves no child upbringing at all* is disastrously overlooked here, as is the reinforcing fact that there is no reference to or mention of the quality of child upbringing in any of the prescriptions connected with it. In brief, the second major justification of our particular type of wedlock scents somewhat too strongly of red herring to pursue further.

Restrictions

There is, it seems, little to recommend the view that monogamy specially promotes "profound affection" between the partners or a "loving context" for child upbringing. Such claims are simply without force. On the other hand, there are several aspects to the logic and operation of the four principles of this institution which suggest that monogamy actually *inhibits* the achievement of these desiderata. Far from uniquely abetting the latter, it militates against them in three ways:

1. Centralized official control of marriage (which the Church gradually achieved through the mechanism of canon law after the fall of the Roman empire[7] in one of the greatest seizures of social power in history) necessarily alienates the partners from full responsibility for and freedom in their relationship. "Profound closeness" between the partners is thereby expropriated—at least partly—rather than promoted, and "sanctuary" from the pressures of outside society is prohibited rather than fostered.

2. Limitation of the marriage bond to two people necessarily restricts, in perhaps the completest way possible consistent with offspring survival, the number of adult sources of affection, interest, material support, and instruction for the young. The "loving context for child upbringing" is thereby dessicated rather than nourished, providing the structural conditions for such notorious and far-reaching problems as sibling rivalry for scarce adult attention[8] and parental oppression through exclusive monopoly of the child's means of life.[9]

3. Formal exclusion of all others from erotic contact with the marriage partner systematically promotes conjugal insecurity, jealousy, and alienation by

   a. Officially underwriting a literally totalitarian expectation of sexual confinement on the part of one's husband or wife; which expectation is, *ceteris paribus,* inevitably more subject to anxiety and disappointment than one less extreme in its demand and/or cultural-juridical backing;[10]

   b. Requiring so complete a sexual isolation of the marriage partners that, should one violate the fidelity code, the other is left alone and susceptible to a sense of fundamental deprivation and resentment;

   c. Stipulating such a strict restraint of sexual energies that there are habitual violations of the regulation. These violations *qua* violations are frequently if not always attended by willful deception and reciprocal suspicion about the occurrence or quality of the extramarital relationship; anxiety and fear on both sides of permanent estrangement from partner and family; and/or overt and covert antagonism over the prohibited act in both the offender (who feels "trapped") and the offended (who feels "betrayed").

Further Restrictions

The disadvantages of the four principles of monogamous marriage do not, however, end with inhibiting the very effects they are said to promote.

There are further shortcomings:

1. The restriction of marriage union to two partners necessarily prevents the strengths of larger groupings. Such advantages as the following are thereby usually ruled out:

    a. The security, range, and power of larger socioeconomic units;

    b. The epistemological and emotional substance, variety, and scope of more pluralist interactions;

    c. The possibility of extra-domestic freedom founded on more adult providers and upbringers as well as more broadly based circles of intimacy.

2. The sexual containment and isolation which the four principles together require variously stimulates such social malaises as

    a. Destructive aggression (which notoriously results from sexual frustration);

    b. Apathy, frustration, and dependence within the marriage bond;

    c. Bad faith, lack of spontaneity, and distance in relationships without the marriage bond;

    d. Sexual fantasizing, perversion, fetishism, prostitution, and pornography in the adult population as a whole.[11]

Taking such things into consideration, it seems difficult to lend credence to the view that the four principles of our form of monogamous marriage constitute a structure beneficial either to the marriage partners themselves or to their offspring (or indeed to anyone else). One is moved to seek for some other ground of the institution, some ground that lurks beneath the reach of our conventional apprehensions.

Marriage as Ownership

The essence of our marriage institution, the basic principle that underwrites all four restrictions, is this: *the maintenance by one man or woman of the effective right to exclude indefinitely all others from erotic access to the conjugal partner.*

The first restriction creates, elaborates on, and provides for the enforcement of this right to exclude. And the second, third, and fourth restrictions together ensure that the said right to exclude is, respectively, not cooperative, not distributed simultaneously or sequentially, and not permissive of even casual exception.

In other words, the four restrictions of our form of monogamous marriage together constitute a state-regulated, indefinite, and exclusive ownership by two individuals of one another's sexual powers. Marriage is simply a form of private property.[12]

That our form of monogamous marriage is another species of private property should not surprise us.[13] The history of the institution is so full of suggestive indicators—dowries, inheritance, property alliances, daughter sales (of which women's wedding rings are a carry-over), bride exchanges, legitimacy and illegitimacy—that it is difficult not to see some intimate connections between marital and ownership ties. We are better able still to apprehend the ownership essence of our marriage institution when in addition we consider

1. That until recently almost the only way to secure official dissolution of consummated marriage was to be able to demonstrate violation of one or both partner's sexual ownership (i.e., adultery);
2. That the imperative of premarital chastity is tantamount to a demand for retroactive sexual ownership by the eventual marriage partner;
3. That successful sexual involvement with a married person is prosecutable as an expropriation of ownership—"alienation of affections"—which is restituted by cash payment;
4. That the incest taboo is an iron mechanism which protects the conjugal ownership of sexual properties, both the husband's and wife's, from the access of affectionate offspring, and the offsprings' (who themselves are future marriage partners) from the access of siblings and parents; [14]
5. That the language of the marriage ceremony is the language of exclusive possession ("take," "to have and to hold," "forsaking all others and keeping you only unto him/her," etc.), not to mention the proprietary locutions associated with the marital relationship (e.g., "he's mine," "she belongs to him," "keep to your own husband," "wife stealer," "possessive husband," etc.).

Maintenance of the Capitalist Order

Of course, it would be remarkable if marriage in our society were not a relationship akin to private property. In our socioeconomic system we relate to virtually everything of value by individual ownership—that is, by the effective right to exclude others from the thing concerned. [15] That we do so as well with perhaps the most highly valued thing of all—the sexual partner's sexuality—is only to be expected. Indeed it would probably be an intolerable strain on our entire social structure if we did otherwise.

This line of thought deserves pursuit. The real secret of our form of monogamous marriage is not that it functionally provides for the needs of adults who love one another or the children they give birth to, but that it serves the maintenance of our present social system. It is an institution which is indispensable to the persistence of the capitalist order, [16] in the following ways:

1. A basic principle of current social relations is that some people legally acquire the use of other people's personal powers from which they may exclude other members of society. This system operates in the workplace (owners and hirers of all types contractually acquire for their exclusive use workers' regular labor powers) and in the family (husbands and wives contractually acquire for their exclusive use their partner's sexual properties). A conflict between the structures of these primary relations—as would obtain were there a suspension of the restrictions governing our form of monogamous marriage—might well undermine the systemic coherence of present social intercourse.
2. The fundamental relation between individuals and things which satisfy

their needs is, in our present society, that each individual has or does not have the effective right to exclude other people from the thing in question.[17] A rudimentary need is that for sexual relationship(s). Therefore the object of this need must be related to the one who needs it as owner or not owner (i.e., via marriage or not-marriage, or approximations thereto) if people's present relationship to what they need is to retain—again—systemic coherence.

3. A necessary condition for the continued existence of the present social formation is that its members feel powerful motivation to gain favorable positions in it. But such social ambition is heavily dependent on the preservation of exclusive monogamy in that

   a. The latter confines the discharge of primordial sexual energies to a single unalterable partner and thus typically compels the said energies to seek alternative outlet, such as business or professional success;[18]

   b. The exclusive marriage necessarily reduces the sexual relationships available to any one person to absolute (nonzero) minimum, a systematic promotion of sexual shortage which in practice renders hierarchical achievement essential as an economic and "display" means for securing scarce partners.[19]

4. Because the exclusive marriage necessarily and dramatically reduces the possibilities of sexual-love relationships, it thereby promotes the existing economic system by

   a. Rendering extreme economic self-interest (the motivational basis of the capitalistic process) less vulnerable to altruistic subversion;

   b. Disciplining society's members into the habitual repression of natural impulse required for long-term performance of repetitive and arduous work tasks; and

   c. Developing a complex of suppressed sexual desires to which sales techniques may effectively apply in creating those new consumer wants which provide indispensable outlets for ever increasing capital funds.

5. The present form of marriage is of fundamental importance to

   a. The continued relative powerlessness of the individual family, which, with larger numbers, would constitute a correspondingly increased command of social power;

   b. The continued high demand for homes, commodities, and services which, with the considerable economies of scale that extended unions would permit, would otherwise falter;

   c. The continued strict necessity for adult males to sell their labor power and adult females to remain at home (or vice versa), which strict necessity would diminish as the economic base of the family unit extended;

   d. The continued immense pool of unsatisfied sexual desires and energies in the population at large, without which powerful interests and institutions would lose much of their conventional appeal and force;[20]

e. The continued profitable involvement of lawyers, priests, and state officials in the jurisdictions of marriage and divorce and the myriad official practices and proceedings connected thereto. [21]

If our marriage institution is a linchpin of our present social structure, then a breakdown in this institution would seem to indicate a breakdown in our social structure. On the face of it, the marriage institution is breaking down—enormously increased divorce rates, nonmarital sexual relationships, "wife swapping," the *Playboy* philosophy, and communes. Therefore one might be led by the appearance of things to anticipate a profound alteration in the social system.

But it would be a mistake to underestimate the tenacity of an established order or to overestimate the extent of change in our marriage institution. Increased divorce rates merely indicate the widening of a traditional escape hatch. Nonmarital relationships imitate and culminate in the marital mold. "Wife swapping" presupposes ownership, as the phrase suggests. The *Playboy* philosophy is merely the view that if one has the money, one has the right to be titillated, the commercial call to more fully exploit a dynamic sector of capital investment. And communes—the most hopeful phenomenon—almost nowhere offer a *praxis* challenge to private property in sexuality. It may be changing. But as Karl Marx observed, "History weighs like a nightmare on the brains of the living."

Afterword

After five years' engagement with the impact and problems raised by my article "Monogamy: A Critique," I am moved to report the following observations in counterpoint to it:

1. There is a crucial *asymmetry* between the principles of capitalism and of institutionalized monogamy not noted in my article (which only indicates points of symmetry).

   The crucial asymmetry in question is this: Capitalism promotes accumulation of (money) property without limit whereas institutionalized monogamy prohibits the accumulation of (sexual) property beyond a single holding. Otherwise put, the principles of capitalism make for radical inequality of ownership, whereas the principles of institutionalized monogamy make for utter equality of ownership. (It is this observation, brought to my attention by my wife Cynthia, which has led elsewhere to the general claim—against Marx—that there are spheres of ownership in "capitalist" society which are structurally independent of the laws of capital.)

2. My article fails to draw an important ethical distinction between extramarital erotic relations which develop conjugal union (e.g., by deepening it and/or broadening it to include others) and extramarital erotic relations which derogate from conjugal union (e.g., mere "affairs" which alienate the marriage partners from each other through concealment, lies, and so on, and/or lead nowhere so far as extending this union).

   Now I think this ethical distinction is clearly implicit in the article's general endorsement of the principle of inclusiveness, and general repudiation of the principle of exclusiveness. However, that this implicit positioning has not been sufficient to render the article's opposition to mere "affairs" clear has been made evident to me by a number of readers who have imagined that it validates their shallow extramarital liaisons: that is, extramarital liaisons which neither deepen nor broaden the conjugal union but rather the opposite. Hence in view of this misunderstanding, I would like to emphasize now that I regard all such superficial and divisive connections as intolerable to a genuine marriage union and constitutive of its divorce whether legally recognized or not. Though, I might add here, there may still seem to be cases of erotic play outside a marital union which are just *neutral* with respect to it, which seem simply to fall outside this ethical distinction I have pressed altogether—cases of sheer sexual sportiveness which on the face of it need no more develop or detract from a marriage than running with another in the sun. Yet even here, I cannot help wondering whether the nonpossessive love which must be realized in such cases does not in fact involve a very deep development of the conjugal union, and as such render in the end these cases, too, within the range of the ethical distinction I have drawn.

Reference Notes

1. Any person who presides over a marriage and is not authorized by law to do so is guilty of a criminal offense and is subject to several years imprisonment (see, for example, Canadian Criminal Code, Sec. 258).

2. For example, offspring are illegitimate, neither wife nor children are legal heirs, and husband has no right of access or custody should separation occur.

3. "Any kind of conjugal union with more than one person at the same time, whether or not it is by law recognized as a binding form of marriage—is guilty of an indictable offence and is liable to imprisonment for five years" (Canadian Criminal Code, Sec. 257, 1aii). Part 2 of the same section adds: "Where an accused is charged with an offence under this section, no averment or proof of the method by which the alleged relationship was entered into, agreed to or consented to is necessary in the indictment or upon the trial of the accused, nor is it necessary upon the trial to prove that the persons who are alleged to have entered into the relationship had or intended to have sexual intercourse."
Here and elsewhere, I draw examples from Canadian criminal law. There is no reason to suspect the Canadian code is eccentric in these instances.

4. Even the sexual revolutionary Wilhelm Reich seems constrained within the limits of this "binary frame." Thus he says (my emphasis): "Nobody has the right to prohibit his or her partner from entering a temporary or lasting sexual relationship with someone else. He has only the right *either to withdraw or to win the partner back."* (See Wilhelm Reich. *The Sexual Revolution* [T. P. Wolfe, trans.]. New York: Farrar, Strauss and Giroux, 1970, p. 28.) The possibility of sexual partners extending their union to include the other loved party as opposed to one partner having either to "win" against this third party or to "withdraw" altogether does not seem even to occur to Reich.

5. I will be using "sexual" and "erotic" interchangeably throughout the article.

6. It is worth noting here that (*a*) man has by nature the most "open" sexual instinct —year-round operativeness and variety of stimuli—of all the species (except perhaps the dolphin); and (*b*) it is a principle of human needs in general that maximum satisfaction involves regular variation in the form of the need object.

7. "Roman Law had no power of intervening in the formation of marriages and there was no legal form of marriage. . . . Marriage was a matter of simple private agreement and divorce was a private transaction." (See Havelock Ellis. *Studies in the Psychology of Sex* [vol. II, part 3]. New York: Random House, 1963, p. 429).

8. The dramatic reduction of sibling rivalry through an increased number of adults in the house is a phenomenon which is well known in contemporary domestic communes.

9. One of the few other historical social relationships I can think of in which persons hold thoroughly exclusive monopoly over other persons' means of life is slavery. Thus, as with another's slave, it is a criminal offense "to receive" or "harbour" another's child without "right of possession" (Canadian Criminal Code, Sec. 250).

10. Certain cultures, for example, permit extramarital sexuality by married persons with friends, guests, or in-laws with no reported consequences of jealousy. From such evidence, one is led to speculate that the intensity and extent of jealousy at a partner's extramarital sexual involvement is in direct proportion to the severity of the accepted cultural regulations against such involvements. In short such regulations do not prevent jealousy so much as effectively engender it.

11. It should not be forgotten that at the same time marriage excludes marital partners from sexual contact with others, it necessarily excludes those others from sexual contact with marital partners. Walls face two ways.

12. Those aspects of marriage law which seem to fall outside the pale of sexual property holding—for example, provisions for divorce if the husband fails to provide or is convicted of a felony or is an alcoholic—may themselves be seen as simply prescriptive characterizations of the sort of sexual property which the marriage partner must remain to retain satisfactory conjugal status—a kind of permanent warranty of the "good working order" of the sexual possession. What constitutes "the good working order" of the conjugal possession is, of course, different in the case of the husband and in the case of the wife. There is an *asymmetry* within the marriage institution which, I gather, women's liberation movements are anxious to eradicate.

13. I think it is instructive to think of even the nonlegal aspects of marriage, for example its sentiments, as essentially private property structured. Thus the preoccupation of those experiencing conjugal sentiments with expressing how much "my very own," "my precious," the other is—that is, with expressing how valuable and inviolable the ownership is and will remain.

14. I think the secret to the long mysterious incest taboo may well be the fact that in all its forms it protects sexual property—not only conjugal (as indicated above), but paternal and tribal as well. This crucial line of thought, however, requires extended separate treatment.

15. Sometimes—as with political patronage, criminal possession, *de facto* privileges, and so forth—a *power* to exclude others exists with no corresponding "right" (just as sometimes a right to exclude exists with no corresponding power). Properly speaking, thus, I should here use the phrase "power to exclude," which covers "effective right to exclude" as well as all nonjuridical enablements of this sort.

16. It is no doubt indispensable as well—in some form or other—to any private property order. Probably (if we take the history of Western society as our data base) the more thoroughgoing and developed the private property formation is, the more total is the sexual ownership prescribed by the marriage institution.

17. Things in unlimited supply—like, presently, oxygen—are not of course related to people in this way.

18. This is, of course, a Freudian or quasi-Freudian claim. "Observation of daily life shows us," says Freud, "that most persons direct a very tangible part of their sexual motive powers to their professional or business activities." (See Sigmund Freud, *Dictionary of Psychoanalysis* [Nandor Fodor and Frank Gaynor, eds]. New York: Fawcett Publications, Premier Paperback, 1966, p. 139).

19. It might be argued that exclusive marriage also protects those physically less attractive persons who—in an "open" situation—might be unable to secure any sexual partnership at all. The force of this claim depends, I think, on improperly continuing to posit the very principle of exclusiveness which the "open" situation rules out (e.g., in the latter situation, X might be less attractive to Y than Z is and yet X not be rejected, any more than at present an intimate friend is rejected who is less talented than another intimate friend).

20. The sexual undercurrents of corporate advertisements, religious systems, racial propaganda and so on are too familiar to dwell on here.

21. It is also possible that exclusive marriage protects the adult-youth power structure.

2.
The Monogamous Ideal and Sexual Realities

Robert N. Whitehurst

Whitehurst examines some of the ordinary assumptions which accompany our North American views of sexuality in terms of the maintenance of monogamy. The Bible, pornography, youth sexuality, sex education, sexual deviancy, marriage, and monogamy are discussed from a structuralist-change viewpoint.

The author's conclusions suggest that monogamy, though not dying, does not—indeed cannot—work, except as an ideal in this culture. North American society today has few of the qualities that would allow monogamy to flourish. We are no longer a simple, stable society governed by extended family, kin, the church, or a tightly knit community. Whitehurst suggests that it would be rational therefore to recognize some of the variant life-styles now around us in underground form and to test their validity more openly.

The relationship between sex acts and marriage is changing, probably very rapidly. However, some old assumptions which do not reflect much of the reality of many people whose sex lives are not consonant with a monogamous ideal still persist. The model for understanding today's interactions is, unfortunately, an idealization and nostalgic embellishment of a past that may never even have resembled the ideal. As a step toward fuller comprehension of sex in our culture, this article will take up some of the commonly held assumptions that purport to help us understand sexuality and then discuss some of the reasons why monogamy cannot be a completely successful ideal today.

Assumptions About Sexuality

1. The Bible Is Against Sex. Probably the most pervasive underlying guide or model for ideas about sexuality held by Jews, Christians, and even atheists in North America today is the Bible. The assumptions made about Biblical edicts on the subject of sex could do with much closer scrutiny than they are usually given.

First, the Bible is not entirely either antisexual or prosexual in any of the usual meanings of these positions. If anything, it is actually both, and depending on exegetic sources used it can be held to be either. What are generally stressed in Christian North America, though, are those teachings of the Bible that are *definitely antisexual* in tone (Whitehurst, 1971, pp. 1-16).

There is an additional difficulty in using the Bible as the chief guide to sexual morality—aside from the fact that it can be read to support conflicting points of view with a little bit of something for everyone. A great number of people see the Bible as nothing more than an interesting historical document, as a literature of a romantic nomadic tribe, or at best as a general guide to behavior and ethics that are not specifically relevant to life today. Fundamentalism, perhaps like colonialism, is probably in for hard times due to lack of adherents (it remains to be seen whether certain youthful revival-type activities are more than passing fancies and fadlike behavior of the young.) [1]

2. Pornography Is Bad. The assumption is made by many that certain literature, films, and pictorializations of sex are bad and evil and will contaminate (but to what end?) the minds of youth and others; there is also a related assumption that avoidance of pornographic material somehow helps one achieve purity. This is at best a highly doubtful assumption and has been well discussed elsewhere (Sagarin, 1971, pp. 105-14). The Scandinavian experience casts doubt on the evils of pornography and the data we have on the sales of such material in North America casts doubt on the serious interest of youth in this market. Anyway, if purity of mind implies refraining from thinking about sex, it is doubtful whether many of us could be called "pure of mind"—or would want to be. Prurient interests are not the sole focus of any group, any religion, or any age. Rather, all have buried inside them some of the best and some of the worst—and pornography is at most only a weak indicator of the real meaning of lives of most people and often an extremely unimportant part of it all.

3. Youth Sexuality Is Rampant. Older people, forgetting much of their past and remembering their sexual present (or in many cases, their fantasy life of the present) project their own hang-ups and problems onto youth and assume that all youth are sexual athletes. Much of the difficulty that arises between youth and parents involves subtle sexual overtones, unresolved parental difficulties, and problems of relationships that become defined as youth-sex problems. One youth put it aptly, claiming "Parents have dirty minds." Sexuality may play a much smaller role in youthful lives than parents seem to think. This is an area much in need of good research. Unfortunately, it is an area that is likely to remain essentially untouched because of its sensitivity and difficulty in conducting such research.

4. Sex Education Is Mostly Unnecessary. Related to the above assumption is the idea that *youth will act out experimentally* what they learn about in the classroom. There is no way that current sex education practice can be defended as adequate or good, but this does not mean it is unimportant. Of course, in a sexually repressive society, *no* sex education would be more consistent with society's images than the vapid kind to which most youth are currently exposed (Potter, 1968). Unless we become used to the idea that children are sometimes sexual, but not obsessed with sex as some adults are, we cannot do an adequate job of sex training or education. Only in terms of the plumbing aspects of sex can we do much, but the real problem lies in learning interpersonal competence and a sense of operable values—things which we seem unable or unwilling to deal with realistically.[2] A corollary involves the notion that it is better to give little or no information about sex until the individual nears adulthood. This highly questionable assumption is unique in that we do not hold other spheres of learning in the same light. Society seems to presume ignorance to be the preferred state in this one area until suddenly "maturity" makes people able to handle sexual problems—indeed a dubious bit of logic.

5. Deviants Are Sick. Persons who are nonmonogamous, homosexual, or otherwise in violation of the code of this ethically fractured culture are often held to be sick and in need of psychiatric or other therapeutic treatment. This concept may indeed be some kind of step forward in western man's way of explaining the source of illness and deviation, but it is probably not correct in many cases. Obviously, such an attitude is not productive of life-styles viable in today's world. We feel ourselves enlightened if we no longer feel that some people are inhabited by devils or evil spirits as our ancestors once felt. We little realize that we are being just as mystical, although we now have a new set of vested interests—psychiatry instead of the church. We have substituted neuroses for demons and now have psychiatrists, but we still have a long way to go to fully understand human behavior. Sociologists often note that it is as important to study the society that produces and labels deviants as it is to study deviants themselves. To conclude that all who vary from the monogamous ideal are sick may be a useful approach for a society pursuing social solidarity of its citizens, but it is inconsistent in a presumably free and open democratic pluralist society, since it fails to validate the experience of a large minority. Such a judgment may not only be harmful, but it also is misleading and only a sometime truth.

6. Good Marriage Means Good Sex. As an outgrowth of the "love conquers all" philosophy, we are culturally led to believe that sex is best in a monogamous marriage where "true love" exists. Although this may often be true, it may just as often be untrue. An analysis of the role of husband (or wife) and lover in an extramarital affair might be revealing and cause some to find a real variance with stereotypes in terms of their own experience.

Lonny Myers describes the variance that can occur in the relationship between good and bad marriage and good and bad sex.[3] It is obvious that the folklore supports the notion that only in marriage can a satisfying sex life be obtained. Anything that tends to lend support for another ethic would be downplayed or ignored by those whose interests are protected by the maintenance of conventional monogamous forms. If we could establish the actual correlation between good sex and good marriage, we might find that there is no direct relationship. It is obviously possible to have perfectly horrid sex either in or out of marriage, or to have perfectly good sex in either situation. However, it is probable that some good sex occurring outside of marriage is marred by culturally derived self-definitions that label it *bad*.[4]

7. Monogamy Is Best and Is the Highest Form of Marriage. This assumption involves cultural absolutism, now more frequently held to be a naive and unpopular attitude to take in thinking about ourselves. We now understand that there are few absolutes in the world and to assume that monogamy has been somehow sanctified by a higher power as a desired end state may yet require a more full examination. This notion involves ideology and not science. As fewer people yield to dogma and more begin to take on other and broader perspectives, the monogamy assumption—at least as an absolute for everyone—is under heavy attack. Monogamy is no doubt "best" for most people today because of the current sanctions and cultural restrictions on our knowledge. Other forms may be proved just as viable—or more so—in the future. Only openness and freedom to construct other forms will provide the context for the acquisition of this knowledge.

8. Monogamy Works. Of all the assumptions discussed above, none is more likely to be held by so many people and less likely to be true in its usually construed sense than the idea that monogamy works. The data on marriage, extramarital sex, and male-female relations in general in this culture tend to support the notion that we pay lip service to the monogamous ideal but in fact do maintain a significant variety of other sexual life-styles. The spate of recent books on the topic probably reflects market conditions; it also is a reflection of a vast disquiet in marriage as it operates today.[5] As for the reasons why monogamy does not work, we must understand some of the sociological reasons why it is naive to expect monogamy to be a fully workable solution to the problem with marriage today. The following discussion suggests *that there are few facilitating factors present in our culture that would make monogamy a viable life-style for everyone.* In fact, given present trends as noted below, we might expect that monogamy will become less often the preferred mode of adaptation, at least as a lifetime option for many people.

The Trouble with Monogamy

Table 1 should help to clarify the problematic status of monogamy today. Social factors and trends affecting monogamy will be discussed separately following Table 1.

As an idea, monogamy is beautiful to behold in its pristine philosophical purity; however, it is a little difficult to put the ideal into practice. In terms of the variables discussed above, the weaknesses of monogamy essentially stem from structural problems in society, not from the neurotic immaturity of its citizens. Most people respond to structures pretty much (but not entirely) as given. If there are loopholes and snags and new possibilities in the system, they will be maximized by those who feel the opportunity for change is there.

When community solidarity breaks down and the eyes of the townspeople no longer count as controllers of behavior, marriage as a monolithic institution is also likely to change. Monogamy—like most social conventions—is held together by external controls and internal restraints. The family as an extended group, as well as the nuclear family, no longer has as much power or influence on behavior as it once had. It obviously relinquishes control over the individual to other agencies earlier and more completely than once was the case.

Urban anonymity provides ample opportunities for experimentation in a setting of great variety, enhanced by the leisure of affluence. Sexual salesmanship also promotes alternatives by creating dissatisfaction with self and

Table 1.

Factors Inhibiting the Persistence of Monogamy as a Dominant Form

Factor:	Effect on Monogamy:
1. Weakened social control agencies	Makes family, community, religion ineffective as social control groupings. Sanctioning power becomes weak.
2. Urban life-style of anonymity, freedom, variety, alternatives	Leads to experimentation, search for meaning, and a sense of being detached and alienated.
3. Ethic of sexual abstinence before marriage	Leads to exaggeration of the role of sex in life, tends to force people to question vitality of their own sex lives, may further lead to dissatisfaction and experimentation.
4. Selling by sex	Makes people susceptible to media influence, associates sex with consumerism, and develops obsessive concern over sex.
5. Open opportunity for practice of variations	Broadens experimentation base, allows relatively free practice of alternate forms.
6. Affluence	Creates increased leisure, search for newness, kicks, and leads to experimentation.
7. Equality ethic	Frees women to establish a new style of relating to men, enhancing probability of new social forms.
8. Social crises	Lead to an ethic of wanting experience now, little sense of future reward, and impulse gratification.
9. Youth revolt	Leads to irreverence toward elders and their institutions, including marriage.
10. Alienation	Leads to attempts to recapture a sense of community, fellowship with others on a broader base than the old monogamous model.
11. Rampant immorality in corporations, government, etc.	Makes for sense of relative nonsinfulness of those who seek alternatives to marriage and extramarital sex.
12. Increasing premarital sex and nonmarital living	Legitimizes breaking societal norms, broadens sexual contacts before marriage, creates strains in narrowing sexual access after marriage—result may be dissatisfaction and seeking more sexual contacts outside of marriage.

spouse. When coupled with other factors, such as our repressive premarital abstinence ethic and the decrease in deferred gratifications, we should not expect the end result to be strong loyalty to the institution of marriage as now structured. [6] Rampant immorality in big corporations and big governments, including lying and cheating to achieve goals and bribery, deception, and a host of questionable enterprises, cannot be a positive model for other institutions, namely the institution of marriage. There is probably much spillover of moral relativism from the outside world into personal life.[7] Carried into marriage styles, the presumed sins of extramarital sex seem truly insignificant beside some of the wrongdoing exposed daily in the press and television. If this suggested listing is seen at all as reflecting the realities of our world, one might well ask: Why are so many still behaving monogamously? If we knew the real answer to the question, it may be that true monogamy is simply one more myth that we continue to accept unquestioningly and that the reality is at extreme variance with the myth.

The Persistence of the Monogamous Ideal

If our previous assessment of the assumptions and the problems in contemporary monogamy are somewhere near correct, we must conclude that there is a tremendous disparity between what North Americans profess to believe and the reality of what they practice. Further, they must continually labor under some strain if our listing of inhibiting factors reveals anything about current social structures. There are several possibilities, all of which might be held as open hypotheses until better evidence is in. It is possible that the life-style we once knew is really flying apart and that the current state of marriage is just one more indicator of our inability to get it all together. It is possible that we are so steeped in ignorance that no matter what happens we will protect ourselves with myths which will persist and alter only imperceptibly with time. We may become a complex schizoid culture which can hold so many contradictions and irreconcilable opposites that we cannot comprehend or describe them. The most preferable possibility is that we are becoming a true pluralistic democracy in which people can live out a variety of life-styles that suit them. The dim outlines of such a happy possibility are scarcely discernible. In any event, it is fairly clear that we are faced with some kind of transitional period in which our assumptions do not match very well with the social facts about sex and marriage.

Monogamy persists in part because we have no other strongly held norms that can take its place. It is so security-inducing (like a pill that doesn't cure the disease, but only lessens the pain) that we do not know how to get along without it. If we ever raise a generation of youth secure in themselves and detached from institutions that provide the forms of security with which we are familiar, monogamy might be replaced with another dominant form or set of forms of marriage. That time is not yet with us. In the meantime, we can look forward to even greater disruption in marriage since the old sources of stability are not likely to return. Alternate forms will likely, at least for some time to come, reflect our old sexual norms and hang-ups, making it difficult to arrive at viable alternatives. If we remain as adroitly schizoid as our past tendencies would suggest, we may well be able to accommodate everyone into the system and learn to live in ignorance, with pluralism, or with some variety of both.

With such a myriad of expectations, emerging norms, potential modes of expression in life-styles, and variety of options open to youth today, there is little doubt that the future will be interesting, though confusing. Monogamy does not work if we use the cultural definition of the term. But it keeps on going, refuses to die (at least as an idea and an ideal), and is not likely to be replaced in the foreseeable future by anything nearly as popular. Monogamy does not work except in a minimally pragmatic sense; but this means we can begin to choose our life-styles. Such luxury of choice is pretty new in a world that until recently offered no such options, except for the idle rich and other privileged minorities.

Whether sex occurs in or out of marriage may be less important to the coming generation who appear less concerned with legal status than with moral rationales in terms of what is happening in their lives. All kinds of orientations can be brought to both marital and nonmarital relationships (Whitehurst, 1970, pp. 27-8). Our traditional and narrow concern for sex occurring only within monogamy is being transcended by new norms and new people. The task is to make newer orientations productive of human growth. Whether we will be unable to more closely approximate this ideal as monogamy changes and our concepts broaden is an unanswered question.

Monogamy and Culture

Given the structural interpretation of monogamy as described previously, it is possible to have an operable monogamous ideal in a culture in which people only experience sex with the married partner under certain rigid conditions. These conditions involve fairly stable folk-type societies, held together by religious norms and sanctions, supported by the extended family and community (Murdock, 1949, p. 10). Murdock notes that the four functions fundamental to human social life and always fulfilled by the family in every culture are: sexual, economic, reproductive, and educational. The case can be made that in North American society, each of these functions is either being altered or phased out. Sexual functioning solely within marriage has been already well intruded upon, the economic function has long since changed, and with increased female employment opportunities, a serious question about the economic functions and interdependence of males and females is an open issue. Much the same comment can be made about families as educational functionaries. This leaves the function of *reproduction* as probably the last stronghold of marital partners. Given the currently high illegitimacy rates, adoptive procedures opening up, and potential ability to produce children without families (at least without fathers), it is possible that even this function will drop out.

Folk cultures also quite regularly have ritual holidays on which the norms concerning adultery are held in abeyance for a period. These folk festivals where norms are set aside ordinarily act as a safety valve to keep people monogamous at other times. Folk cultures do not sell with sex—indeed they tend not to become obsessed at all by the subject since it assumes a much more natural and normal place in their daily lives. Youth are often not restrained in premarital sexuality, and are certainly not asked to extend the period of sexual abstinence into adulthood. All these factors are different in our mass, urbanized society. We can still hold our monogamous ideal, but to make it work requires the supportive help of a number of other institutions and organizations. This we do not have. To expect most people in our society to act monogamously is to fly in the face of the structural realities and opportunities to respond otherwise. In a loose-knit culture in which the family recedes in importance, it is logical to expect higher alienation rates and more departure from conventional norms governing the sexual behavior of adults. It is possible, of course, to hold on to a belief that things remain the same, that is, that monogamy really still prevails. The social functions of myth-maintenance are well known in simpler societies, but in complex ones like ours, more people must insist on applying their critical evaluations to our own folk norms, including monogamy. Although sociological awareness does not make for instant freedom, it is a step toward open dialogue and future change—perhaps even to a more integrative, fulfilling, and less limited life-style.

Reference Notes

1. Recent resurgence of the "Jesus-freaks" may be as much a reflection of the movement's willingness to co-opt the essence of the rock concert, and to develop a more respectable "Woodstock" experience for youth as it is an indicator of real commitment to Christianity. This is not to gainsay a continued interest in religion on the part of these individuals, but the question remains whether the original impetus was a felt need for more religion or the possibility of extending and legitimizing other youth culture activities.

2. These values might involve valuing oneself as a sexual person, feeling good that bodies provide pleasure, including the value of touching others as a sensual and sexual experience that is normal, fulfilling, and good. See Lester A. Kirkendall and Roger W. Libby, "Interpersonal Relationships—Crux of the Sexual Renaissance," in *Journal of Social Issues* (April 1966), pp. 45-62.

3. See discussion in this volume by Lonny Myers, Chapter 22.

4. Jessie Bernard has observed a similar tendency in self-definitions of comparative happiness among single and married women. See also, Jessie Bernard, "Marriage, His and Hers," in *Ms.* (December 1972), pp. 46-47.

5. Among some suggested authors would be: Bernard, 1972; Francoeur, 1972; O'Neill & O'Neill, 1972; Hunt, 1969; Neubeck, 1969; Gordon, 1972; Otto, 1971; Skolnick & Skolnick, 1971; and Fullerton, 1972.

6. Widespread violation of premarital sex norms is not likely to be conducive to fulfillment of the rigid expectation that one will remain monogamous after marriage.

7. This is only an interesting hypothesis, since no data seem to be available to relate the spillover effect of moral relativism. If it does affect extramarital sexuality, it would no doubt be easier to make the case that sexual deviance can be positive—the pursuit of wars, shady business practices, and other deviancy of this sort more usually cannot be seen in a positive light except by strange twists of logic.

3.
Is Monogamy Outdated?
Rustum Roy and Della Roy

The authors argue that traditional monogamy needs opening up in order to meet the needs of men and women today. They identify several elements of change in the social environment that are necessitating change in the institution of marriage, and they evaluate some existing nontraditional models of marriage.

The Roys take a radical Christian humanist approach, calling for institutional reforms that would promote a sense of community—that sense of belonging which is often missing from life today. The Roys also suggest some immediate modifications of the marriage institution, including training and education for marriage, trial engagements/marriages, broadened supports for single people, and more humane termination of marriages.

Monogamy: Where We Stand Today

The total institution of marriage in American society is gravely ill. This statement does not apply to the millions of sound marriages where two people have found companionship, love, concern, and have brought up children in love. But it is necessary to point to the need for *institutional* reforms, even when the personal or immediate environment may not appear to need it. Yet many refuse to think about the area as a whole because of personal involvement—either their marriage is so successful that they think the claims of disease exaggerated, or theirs is so shaky that all advice is a threat. Is the institution then so sick? Consider for example:

Year after year in the United States, marriage has been discussed in public and private session with undiminished confusion and increasing pessimism. Calamity always attracts attention, and in the United States the state of marriage is a calamity.

These are the words with which W. H. Lederer and D. Jackson open their book *The Mirages of Marriage.* Vance Packard in *The Sexual Wilderness* summarizes a recent major survey thus: "In other words, a marriage made in the United States in the late 1960's has about a 50:50 chance of remaining even nominally intact."

Clifford Adams concludes from an Identity Research Institute study of six hundred couples that while the divorce rate is numerically at 40 percent in this nation, and in some West Coast highly populated counties the *real* divorce rate is running at 70 percent, in fact 75 percent of marriages are a

"Is Monogamy Outdated?" This article first appeared in THE HUMANIST Mar./Apr. 1970 and is reprinted by permission.

"bust." And Lederer and Jackson report that 80 percent of those interviewed had at some time seriously considered divorce. So much for the statistics. Qualitatively the picture painted by these and other researchers is even bleaker but needs no repeating here.

There is no doubt then about the diagnosis of the sickness of marriage taken as a whole. Yet no person, group, magazine, or newspaper creates an awareness of the problems; no activist band takes up the cause to *do* something about it. Some years ago, we participated in a three-year-long group study and development of a sex ethic for contemporary Americans, and we found this same phenomenon: that serious group study and group work for change in the area of sex behavior is remarkably difficult and threatening, and hence rare. Thus, we find an institution such as monogamous marriage enveloped by deterioration and decay, and unbelievably little is being done about it on either a theoretical basis or detailed pragmatic basis.

For this there is a second major reason: Marriage as an institution is partly governed by warring churches, a society without a soul, a legal system designed for lawyers, and a helping system for psychiatrists who almost by their very mode of operation in the marriage field guarantee its failure. Consequently, marriage is oscillating between tyrannical repression and equally tyrannical expression.

By *traditional monogamy*, we refer to the public's association with the term, i.e., marriage to one person at a time; the centrality of the nuclear family; the restriction of all overt sexual acts and nearly all sexually tinged relationships and heterosexual relations of any depth to this one person before and after marriage; expectation of a lifetime contract; and a vivid sense of failure if termination is necessary. John Cuber and Peggy Harroff in *The Significant Americans* have called this "the monolithic code," and it is based on precepts from the Judaic and Christian traditions. All working societies are structured around such codes or ideals, no matter how far individuals may depart from the norms and whether or not they accept the source of such "ideals."

How does change in a code or ideal come about? When the proportion of the populace living in conflict with their own interpretation of the monolithic code, and "getting away with it," reaches nearly a majority, then *new* ideals must evolve for the social system to remain in equilibrium. We are convinced that although no *discontinuous* change in the ideals of a culture is possible, traditional monogamy as an ideal may be altered *in a continuous fashion* in order to respond to the needs of men and women today.

Traditional monogamy was *one* interpretation of the Judeo-Christian tradition. We are convinced that for widespread acceptability, any new ideals must be interpretable in terms of Judeo-Christian humanism, the basic framework of mainstream "Americanism," and the most explicit humanism so far developed. Such an interpretation is neither difficult nor likely to encounter much resistance from the many other contemporary American humanisms which have not swung far from the parent Protestant humanism. But the importance of such an interpretation for middle-class America is crucial. If a new monogamous ideal is to evolve, it must be acceptable to middle America—liberated, affluent, but waspish at heart.

Elements of Change

Social institutions are the products of particular social environments, and there must be a finite time lag when an institution appropriate for one situation survives into a new era in which the situation has changed drastically. It is clear that traditional monogamy is caught precisely in this overlap of two radically different situations. It is important to identify precisely the particular problem-causing elements of change in the environment.

1. The sexual revolution has made it infinitely more difficult to retain monogamy's monopoly on sex.

We live in an eroticized environment which is profoundly affecting many institutions. The change towards greater permissiveness and its effect on the sexual climate can be summed up in the aphorism, "What was a temptation for the last generation is an opportunity for this." Underneath it all are the measurable, real, physical changes—the advent of prosperity, mobility, and completely controlled conception.

Parallel to physical changes are vast social changes. The eroticization of our culture oozes from its every pore, so much so that it becomes essentially absurd to expect that all physical sexual expression for a fifty-year period will be confined to the marriage partner. Moreover, this eroticization escalator shows no sign of slowing down, and its effect on various institutions will be even more drastic in the future. Following are some illustrations.

The influence of the literature, the arts, the media, and the press on the climate for any institution is profound, and marriage is no exception. Caught between the jaws of consumer economics in a free-enterprise system and the allegedly objective purveyors of accurate information (or culturally representative entertainment), human sexuality has become the most salable commodity of all. Perform, if you will, the following simple tests. Examine the magazine fare available to tens of millions of Americans; spend a few hours browsing through . . . something like *Cosmopolitan*. If you are serious, visit a typical downtown bookshop in a big city and count the number of pictorial publications whose sole purpose is sexual titillation. Next try the paperbacks available to most Americans through drugstores, supermarkets, and airports. Does *one* speak of the beauty and wonder of uniting sex to marriage? Go see ten movies at random. Will one of them rail against sexual license? Thus the mass media have had a profound effect on the American people's marriage ideals. They especially confuse those whose fast-held "traditions," speaking through emasculated school, bewildered Church, and confused home, still prompt them to try to affirm a traditionally monogamous system. Yet some have mistakenly denied that there is a causal relation between the media and our rapidly changing value systems. Worst of all, very few of those who urge the freedom of access to more and more sexual stimuli work to legitimize, socially and ethically, a scheme for increased sexual outlets.

2. There is a vast increase in the number and variety of men-women contacts after marriage, and no guidelines are available for behavior in these new situations.

Of the sexual dilemmas which our present-day culture forces upon the "ailing" institution of traditional monogamy, premarital sexual questions now appear very minor. For all intents and purposes premarital sexual play (including the *possibility* of intercourse) has been absorbed into the social canon. We foresee in the immediate future a much more serious psychological quandary with respect to extramarital or comarital sexual relations of all levels of intensity. The conflict here is so basic and so little is being done to alleviate it, that it is only surprising that it has not loomed larger already. Traditional monogamy as practiced has meant not only one spouse and sex partner at a time but essentially only one heterosexual *relationship*, of any depth at all, at a time. We have shown above that our environment suggests through various media the desirability of nonmarital sex. Further, our culture is now abundant in opportunity: time, travel, meetings, committees, causes, and group encounters of every stripe bringing men and women together in all kinds of relationship-producing situations. Our age is characterized by not only the opportunity but by the necessity for simultaneous multiple relationships. One of the most widely experienced examples is that chosen by Cuber and Harroff in their study of the sex lives of some "leaders" of our society. They noted the obviously close relationship of such men with their secretaries with whom they work for several hours a day. But the same opportunity now exists for millions of former "housewives" returning to work after children are grown. They too are establishing new heterosexual friendships and being treated as separate individuals (not to mention as sex objects) after ten or fifteen years.

3. Traditional monogamy is in trouble because it has not adjusted itself to find a less hurtful way to terminate a marriage.

From the viewpoint of any philosophy that puts a high value on response to human need and the alleviation of human suffering, the mechanisms available for terminating marriage are utterly unacceptable. Traditional monogamy involves a lifetime commitment. Anything that would necessitate termination short of this must, therefore, be a major failure. "Divorce, American Style" demands so much hurt and pain and devastation of personalities that we must try to temper the hurt it causes to human beings. We must take as inescapable fact that about half of all the marriages now existing will, and probably should, be terminated. The question is, what way of ending marriages would minimize total human suffering? In seeking a solution, we must avoid the pitfall of considering the relief of the immediate pain of one or two persons to be the greatest and single good. Full consideration must always be given to all the "significant others"—children, parents, friends—and to the long-range effects on society. The institution of traditional monogamy will increasingly come under attack while it is unable to provide better means to terminate a contract than those now in use.

4. Traditional monogamy does not deal humanely with its have-nots—the adult singles, the widowed, the divorced.

Statistically speaking there are in America more involuntarily single persons above age twenty-five or thirty than there are racial minorities who had no choice but to accept their culturally disadvantageous skin color. The latter have had to bear legal and social affronts and suffer the subtle and possibly debilitating psychological climate of being thought unacceptable in certain surroundings. But they share this disability with voiceless single persons in a marriage-oriented society. Our society proclaims monogamy's virtue at every point of law and custom and practice, as much as it says white is right. Biases, from insurance rates to adoption requirements, subtle advertisements, and Emily Post etiquette all point to traditional monogamy as the acceptable form of society. Unbelievably, this barrage goes on unopposed in the face of some tens of millions of persons outside the blessed estate. Monogamy decrees that the price of admission into the complex network of supportive relationships of society is a wedding band. Yet it turns a blind eye to the inexorable statistical fact that only a third of those women who are single at thirty-five, a tenth of those at forty-five, and a twentieth of those at fifty, will ever wear that symbolic band. Is access to regular physical sexual satisfaction a basic human right on a plane with freedom or shelter or right to worship? For effective living in our world every human being needs individuals as close friends and a community to belong to. Traditionally, monogamous society has ruled, *ipso facto*, that tens of millions of its members shall have no societally approved way of obtaining sexual satisfaction. Much worse, because sexual intimacy is potentially associated with all heterosexual relationships of any depth, the unmarrieds must also be denied such nonsexual relationships.

Here, surely, every humanist must protest. For it is the humanist's social ideal—that the greatest good of human existence is to enjoy deep interpersonal relationships and as many of these as is compatible with depth—that is contravened by traditional monogamy's practice. Moreover, there is less provision today for single women to develop fulfilling relationships than there was a generation or two ago. The larger family then incorporated these losers in the marital stakes into at least a minimal framework of acceptance and responsibility.

Levels of Change: Individual, Community, and Society

Any vision of a better future for society presupposes, consciously or unconsciously, a value system and basic assumptions about the nature of humankind. A theory of humanity and life must precede a theory of monogamy. Our view of the nature of humanity is the Judeo-Christian one. People were meant to live *in community*. The normative ideal for every person is that he or she live fully known, accepted, and loved by a community of significant others. In this environment individual creativity and creative individuality will be realized to the maximum extent, and each person can serve society best.

In this spectrum we have, as yet, not even mentioned marriage—and intentionally so. There is a crucially important hierarchy of values, in which the individual's needs and the community's good are vastly more important than the "laws" or preferred patterns of marital behavior. Indeed, these "laws" must be tested empirically by the criterion of how well they have been found to meet the individual-community-society needs most effectively. It is important to see that the humanist is not committed, prima facie, to *any* particular pattern of men-women relationships.

Marriage, monogamous or polygamous, fits somewhere between the individual and community levels of social organization. Unfortunately, in many cultures the institution of marriage and the stress on the family has generally militated against, and sometimes destroyed, the community level of relationship.

This has not always been so—not even in America. The "larger family" of maiden aunts and uncles and grandparents, and occasional waifs and strays, has been a part of many cultures including that of the rigidly structured joint-family system in India and the plantation system of the American South. Tribal cultures abound. In the Swiss canton or settled New England town the sinews of community are strong enough to make them fall in between the extremes represented above and lying, perhaps, closer to the former. There is an inverse correlation between the complexity of a highly developed society and the strength of community channels and bonds. It is in the technology-ruled society where we find men and women turning to the intimacy of marriage to shield them from further impersonalization when the second level of defense—the community level—has disintegrated through neglect. But monogamous marriage is altogether too frail an institution to carry that load also. A typical marriage is built frequently of brittle and weak members held together by a glue of tradition rapidly deteriorating under the onslaught of a half-dozen corroding acids—mobility, prosperity, permissiveness, completely controlled conception, and continuously escalating eroticization.

There is no question that the first and essential step in the evolution of monogamy is the recovery of the role of community in our lives. It appears to us, however strange a conclusion it seems, that precisely because our world has become so complex, depersonalization is an essential, ineradicable fact of our lives in the many public spheres. This requires, then, a radical restructuring of the private sphere to provide the supports we have found missing in the traditional monogamous pattern. To know and accept ourselves deeply we need to be known and accepted. And most of us are many-sided polyhedra needing several people to reflect back to ourselves the different portions of our personalities. With changing years and training and jobs this need grows instead of diminishing. Thus, it comes about that humanists have a great deal to contribute to their fellows.

Our proposed modification of monogamy, then, has the reemphasis of community as one of its primary goals. This is hardly novel, but it has been the conclusion of every group of radical Christian humanists trying to reform society for hundreds of years. And it was the New World which provided for them a unique opportunity to attempt the radical solutions. Hence we have, dotted across America, the record and/or the remnants of hundreds of experiments in radical community living.

Today we believe that society's hope lies in working at both ends of the game—the basic research and the development. We need to become much more active in optimizing or improving present marriage in an imperfect society—changing laws, improving training, providing better recovery systems, etc. But alongside of that, we need to continue genuine research in radically new patterns of marriage. This can only be carried out by groups or communities. Further, we need experimentation not only by those groups that are removed from the day-to-day world, but also by groups nearer the mainstream that may devise solutions that can be models for reform of the urban bourgeois culture.

Marriage-in-Community: Some Models

We cannot here do justice to a discussion of possible models for radical new patterns of marriage-in-community. Instead, we wish only to emphasize the importance of such experimentation and its neglect, in our supposedly research-oriented culture, by serious groups concerned for society. It is hardly a coincidence that the yearning for community should figure so prominently in all utopian schemes for remaking society. The contemporary resurgence is described in B. F. Skinner's *Walden Two* or Erich Fromm's *Revolution of Hope* and Robert Rimmer's *Harrad Experiment*. It is being attempted in groping, unformed ways in the "hippie" and other city-living communes, and is being lived out in amazingly fruitful (yet unpublicized) models in the devoutly Christian Bruderhof communities in the United States and Europe, and in the Ecumenical Institute in Chicago. And in rereading the details of the organization of the hundreds of religious communities we find that they have an enormous amount to teach us, on many subjects from psychotherapy to patterns for sexual intercourse.

Probably the most important lesson for contemporary America, however, is that communities survive and thrive and provide a creative framework for realizing the human potential if their central purpose is outside themselves and their own existence. The second lesson is that wherever many persons are involved, *some* discipline and order are absolutely essential.

Were it not for the sheer prejudice introduced by a misreading of Judeo-Christian tradition, and its bolstering by the unholy alliance of state-and-church Establishment, we may well have learned to separate potential from pitfall in various patterns of communal living. The Mormon experience with polygamy is not without its value for us, and Bettelheim has helped shake the prejudice against nonparent child rearing drawing on data from the kibbutzim. Rimmer, perhaps, through his novels *The Rebellion of Yale Marratt* and *Proposition 31*, has reached the widest audience in his crusade for a variety of new marital patterns. He has dealt sensitively, and in depth, with the subtle questions of ongoing sexual relations with more than one partner—the threat of which is perhaps the most difficult taboo against communal life for most educated Americans. From some dozens of histories in personal and "marathon" encounter situations, we believe that Rimmer's portrayal of typical reactions is remarkably accurate. Most middle-class, educated Americans above thirty-five have been so schooled into both exclusivity and possessiveness that no more than perhaps 10 percent could make the transition into any kind of structured nonexclusivity in marriage. But for the younger group, especially those now in college, the potential for attempting the highly demanding, idealistic, disciplined group living of some sort is both great, and a great challenge. It is here perhaps by setting up contemporary-style communities of concern and responsibility that young humanists can make one of their greatest contributions to society at large.

Modifications for Today

No company survives on its fundamental research laboratory alone, although many cannot survive long without one. Each needs also a development group that keeps making the minor changes to its existing products in order to eliminate defects in design and to meet the competition or the change in customer needs. So too with marriage. While "far out" research must proceed on new patterns, we must simultaneously be concerned with the changes that can modify traditional monogamy to meet its present customer needs much more effectively—that is to say, humanely.

Our society is pluralist in many of its ideals. The first and most important change in society's view of marriage must also be the acceptance of the validity of a range of patterns of behavior. The education of our children and of society must point to ways and points at which, *depending on the situation*, it is right and proper to make this or that change. Indeed, we can doubtless describe the era we are entering as one of "situational monogamy"—that is, traditional monogamy can still be upheld as the ideal in many circumstances, but, in specific situations, modifications are not only permitted but required.

Institutionalizing Premarital Sex

Premarital sexual experience is now rather widely accepted, covertly if not overtly, throughout our society. Especially when we use the word "experience" instead of "intercourse," the studies from Kinsey to Packard support a very substantial increase in necking and petting including petting to orgasm. The trend toward "keeping house together" in college and beyond is also spreading like wildfire. We see here an opportunity within relatively easy reach for a simple evolution of the monogamous ideal.

Almost all analysts believe that postponing marriage by two or three years and making it more difficult—with some required period of waiting or even waiting and instruction—would be very beneficial. Traditional marriage in its classical form enjoined a "decent" (six months to two years) engagement period partly for the same reason. One of the main drives toward early marriage is that there is no other way to obtain regular sexual gratification in a publicly acceptable manner. By one simple swish of tradition, we can incorporate all the recent suggestions for trial marriages, "baby" marriages, etc., and cover them all under the decent rug of the "engagement." These would be engagements with a minor difference: In today's society they would entitle a couple to live together if they desire, and sleep together—*but not to have children.* Thus, engagement would become the first step that entitles one to legal sex—publicly known sex with contraceptive devices. By no means need this become the universal norm. Pluralism of marital patterns should start here, however. Many parents and various social groups may still urge their members to restrict engagements to a noncoital or nonsexual level of intimacy; but even here they would do well to legitimize some advanced level of sexual activity and by so doing they would probably protect their marriage institution more effectively.

Along with the engagement-including-sex concept could be introduced the idea of "training" for marriage. Everyone falls for the training gimmick. Driver education, often taken after three years of driving, is still useful, and is induced by the lowered insurance rates. Similarly if society required a course in "marriage education" before granting a license, another important step in improving the quality of marriage would have been achieved.

Expanding the Erotic Community in the Postmarital Years

With the engagement-including-sex, we have broken the premarital half of monogamy's monopoly on sex. It is our judgment that for the health of the institution it will become necessary in America in the next decade to break the second half also—postmarital sexual expression. (Recall that our theory demands that we seek to maximize the number of deep relationships and to develop marriages to fit in with a framework of community.) To do this we are certain that the monopolistic tendencies of relationships must be broken, and hence the question of sexual relations cannot be bypassed. We believe that in the coming generation a spectrum of sexual expression with persons other than the spouse are certain to occur for at least the large majority, and possibly most persons. If monogamy is tied inextricably with postmarital restriction of all sexual expression to the spouse, it will ultimately be monogamy which suffers. Instead, monogamy should be tied to the much more basic concepts of fidelity, honesty, and openness, which are concomitants of love of the spouse, but which do not necessarily exclude deep relationships or various degrees of sexual intimacy with others. In the studies and counseling experience of many, including ourselves, there is no evidence that all extramarital sexual experience is destructive of the marriage. Indeed, more and more persons testify that creative comarital relationships and sexual experience can and do exist. But most persons need guidelines to help steer them from the dangerous to the potentially creative relationships, and to provide help on the appropriateness of various sexual expressions for various relationships.

A few practices are crucial:

1. *Openness:* Contrary to folklore, frank and honest discussions at *every stage* of a developing relationship between all parties is the best guarantee against trouble. We know of husbands who have discussed with their wives possible coitus with a third person, some to conclude it would be wrong, others, unwise; others to drop earlier objections, and still others to say it was necessary and beautiful. We know of wives to say it was necessary and beautiful. We know of wives who have said a reasoned "no" to such possibilities for their husbands and kept their love and respect; and many who have said "yes" in uncertainty and have found the pain subsides. Openness is not impossible.
2. *Other-centeredness:* Concern for *all* the others—the other woman or man, the other husband or wife, the children—must be front and center in reaching decisions on any such matters.
3. *Proportionality:* Sexual expressions should be proportional to the depth of a relationship. This leads, of course, to the conclusion that most coitus and other intimate expressions should only occur with very close friends. This conclusion is questioned by many, but essential for our theory.
4. *Gradualism:* Only a stepwise escalation of intimacy allows for the open discussion referred to above. Otherwise such openness becomes only a series of confessions.

It is important to discover the value of self-denial and restraint. It is incumbent on individuals to demonstrate, while accepting other patterns, their ability to maintain loving, warm relationships with both single and married persons of the opposite sex and of limiting the sexual expression therein in order, for example, to conserve psychic energy for other causes.

Providing a Relationship Network for Singles

It is principally because of the fear of sexual involvement that single people are excluded from married society. In the new dispensation, a much more active and aggressive policy should be encouraged to incorporate singles within the total life of a family and a community. She or he should be a part of the family, always invited—but not always coming—to dinner, theaters, and vacations. The single person should feel free enough to make demands and accept responsibility as an additional family member would. The single woman, thus loved and accepted by two or three families, may find herself perhaps not sleeping with any of the husbands but vastly more fulfilled as a woman. No couple should enter such relationships unless the marriage is secure and the sexual monopoly not crucially important: Yet all concerned couples should be caused to wonder about their values if their fear of sexual involvement keeps them from ministering to such obvious need. The guidelines for decisions, of course, are the same as those above. We know of several such relationships, many but not all involving complete sexual intimacy, that have been most important in the lives of the single persons. Recently, we have observed that our present society makes it very difficult for even the best of these relationships to continue for a lifetime. And we see the need for developing acceptable patterns for altering such relationships creatively after the two- to five-year period which often brings about sufficient changes to suggest reappraisal in any case. The dependent woman often becomes confident and no longer needs the same kind of support; the independent one becomes too attached and becomes possessive enough to want exclusivity. The mechanisms we discuss under divorce should no doubt operate here as well.

Legalizing Bigamy

It may appear as a paradox, but in keeping with the theory above and the pluralist trend of society, it is almost certainly true that contemporary style monogamy would be greatly strengthened if bigamy (perhaps polygamy-polyandry) were legalized. This would provide a partial solution to the problems dealt with in the last two sections; moreover, it would do it in a way that is least disturbing to the monogamous tenor of society. The usual living arrangements of most persons would be unaffected if one woman in twenty had two husbands in the house; or one man in ten had two wives—sometimes in different cities and frequently in different houses.

There is a substantial unthinking emotional resistance to legalizing bigamy based partly on a supposed, but incorrect, backing from Christian doctrine. There is, however, no biblical injunction sanctifying monogamy: The Christian humanist is not only free to, but may be required to, call for other patterns. Indeed, after World War II the Finnish Church is reported to have been on the verge of endorsing bigamy because women so outnumbered men at the time. However, the ratio of women to men equalized sooner than expected, and the plan was abandoned.

In the next decade, the ratio of women to men is expected to get as high as seven to five in the country, and it is higher in the highest age brackets. Various gerontologists have suggested the legalization of bigamy for the aged, and the capacity for social change in our society is so weak that perhaps bigamy will have to be legalized first under Medicare! It is indeed difficult to see why bigamy should not be legalized, once the doctrinal smokescreen were to be exposed for what it is.

Making Marital Difficulties and Divorce Less Destructive

A reform of the total system of marriage *must* provide for a much less destructive method for terminating one. The first change required in our present ideal is to recognize that a good divorce can be better than a poor marriage. We can continue to affirm the importance of the intention of the lifelong commitment, but we must begin to stress the quality of the commitment and the actual relationship as a higher good than mere longevity.

Early detection of trouble makes repair easier and surgery less likely. If we take our automobiles to be inspected twice a year to be safe on the highways, is it too much to expect that the complex machinery of a marriage could be sympathetically "inspected" periodically to keep it in the best working condition? Here the church and the university can help by showing the need for, and providing such "inspections." Conceivably a biennial or triennial marriage marathon or weeklong retreat utilizing the newest insights of encounter groups could be made normative for all marriages. Such check-ups would in some cases catch the cancer early enough, and in others indicate the need for surgery.

In any case, a failing marriage needs to be treated by a person or persons who are neutral on the value of divorce itself, committed to the goal of maximizing human potential, and not determined to preserve marriage for its own sake. We believe that a team of a marriage counselor and, where appropriate, younger clergymen or another couple who are close friends can, over a period of several months, help the husband and wife arrive at a wise decision most effectively. The use of a fixed-length trial period for either separation or continuance, after specific changes, with an agreed upon evaluation at the end of the period has proved its real value in all the cases where we have seen it used. Our own experience has been that many of the worst situations are avoided if the couple can keep channels open to their closest friends—always working with them together. Two helpful changes need to occur here. First, it should be made much more acceptable to talk openly and seriously about marital tensions with close friends; and second, we should all learn the principle of never giving any personal information about absent third parties except when we think it can specifically do some positive good.

For ordinary divorce, it is difficult to see what the professional psychiatrist or lawyer-as-adviser can contribute. [Rather than working toward reconciliation or compromise, these professionals tend to promote extreme polarization and hostility by ignoring the well-being of one of the two partners.] In any case, neither paid adviser nor loving friend can prevent the tragedy that results when John, married to Mary, has become deeply attached to Alice. But this tragedy need not be compounded by bitterness, anger, and self-justification in the name of helping. We do know of couples divorcing and parting as friends—persons who *love* each other to the best of their ability, and yet, after sober, agonizing months of consideration, decide to separate. We know that that is the way it must happen in the future.

Conserving Ideals: Changing the Marriage Service

Because our psychological conditioning is affected, even by every minor input, we can help preserve the monogamous *ideal* by bringing in honesty at the high points in its symbol-life. This would mean, for instance, minor alteration of the traditional marriage service, and not necessarily to water down its commitments. Thus, everyone recognizes the value of a lifelong commitment. But to what should that commitment be? To preserving a marriage when we know that half will fail and make all involved guilty over it? Why not, rather, a lifelong commitment to loving and speaking the truth in love? One can be true to this even if separation occurs. Why should not the marriage service make the closest friends—best man, maid of honor, etc., who have essentially trivial roles in the ceremony—take on a real commitment to become the loving community for the couple, covenanting to communicate regularly, stand by them always, but also to speak admonition in love whenever they see it needed. Even such a small beginning would symbolize the fact that each couple enters not only into a marriage but also into a much needed community.

The rebellion of the young reflects only intuitively their alienation from a science-technology-dominated world which they have not the discipline to understand. The need for new and revitalized institutions that would provide every kind of support to individuals could not be greater. Inexorable logic points to the centrality of community in any such attempts. Yet no American, indeed Western, sociologist or psychologist of any stature (always excepting Skinner) has paid any serious attention to the structuring of revitalized institutions. We attribute this largely to their ignorance of the primitive Christian roots of their own heritage, and see in it the great loss to contemporary humanism of the insight and experimental data from the bold humanist experimenters of the last century. However, it is unlikely that in the permissive society it will be possible to demand the minimum discipline required for a community to cohere. What changes can we really hope for on the basis of present observations? On the basis of emotional reactions and capacity for change in attitudes to men-women relationships, sexual patterns, or marriage, which we have observed even in the most secure and highly motivated persons, we can only be discouraged and pessimistic. Always here and there the exception stands out: concerned persons acting out love in new ways demanded by new situations. We agree with Victor Ferkiss when he says in *Technological Man:*

There is no new man emerging to replace the economic man of industrial society or the liberal democratic man of the bourgeois political order. The new Technology has not produced a new human type provided with a technological world view adequate to give cultural meaning to the existential revolution. Bourgeois man continues dominant just as his social order persists while his political and cultural orders disintegrate.

"Bourgeois man" will persist, as will traditional monogamy. But for humanists, there is no release from the mandate to try to alter traditional monogamy to make it better serve human needs, for "we are called upon to be faithful, not to succeed."

Part 2.

Intimate Alternatives to Marriage:
Beyond Sexual Exclusivity

The next nine chapters of this book explore a variety of intimate alternatives to monogamous marriage, including singlehood, unmarried cohabitation, extramarital and comarital sex, open marriage, swinging, and group marriage. As social norms shift and the range of legitimate life-styles broadens, these alternative life-styles will be viable options for a growing population.

In an article about singlehood, Roger Libby challenges the stereotypes about singles and develops several models that are useful in analyzing and better understanding singlehood and the choice of that life-style or others. Libby also critically reviews the literature on singles and moves toward developing a theory of singlehood.

In his article on cohabitation, or living together unmarried, Charles Cole reviews the major concepts and findings in this area and draws them together in an effort to provide a theoretical framework for future research. Cole provides an insightful view into the process involved in establishing a cohabitation relationship and points up some similarities and differences between marriage and cohabitation.

Roger Libby shows in Chapter 6 that extramarital sexuality takes many forms, many of which do not conform to common preconceptions about sexual behavior outside the marital dyad. His thorough review of the literature includes a sorting out of the definitional issues and a discussion of the symbolic meanings of extramarital and comarital sex in marriage today.

Gordon Clanton approaches the problem of intimacy in the modern world from yet another angle: He examines the mass media's portrayal of extramarital and comarital sexuality. His typology of extramarital sex is based on the extent to which the spouse knows about and approves of an extramarital involvement. As Clanton suggests, the impact of the media on sexual attitudes and behavior urgently needs more in-depth research.

In an article full of questions about the choices we will have to make in the future, Jessie Bernard speculates about the relative importance we will assign to exclusivity and permanence in marriage. She also analyzes the differences in the meanings of infidelity and adultery, stressing that infidelity is a complex concept having different meanings in different relationships.

Although open marriages that provide for extramarital sex are not the norm in North America, the Knapp and Whitehurst studies of sexually open marriages indicate that there are some couples who are willing to risk this openness and who find it rewarding. This research is important for the understanding it can offer of a broad range of future marriages, particularly since we seem to be moving toward what Farber has called the "permanent availability" model for sexual relationships.

Although swinging has apparently seen a decline in the past few years, the activity is still alive and perhaps flourishing in some quarters. Gilmartin not only compares swinging couples with nonswingers in his research, but he also raises questions of a theoretical nature that have implications for relationships beyond the narrow context of swinging. The problems of shared meanings and value congruence for spouses are brought out, with Gilmartin noting that what people do is significant only insofar as we comprehend their definitions of what they are doing.

The Constantines' descriptions of group marriage reveal yet another adaptation and response to the search for an alternative to the small nuclear family and traditional marriage. The Constantines conclude that sexuality is not the key to success for group marriages, but that interpersonal relations and the ability to resolve interpersonal problems are of greater importance.

Drawing on a large study of married couples, Kafka and Ryder have pulled out information on nonconforming counterculture couples, reporting how they escape and sometimes return to conventionality. A "psychology of plenty" mentality, which appeared to govern the counterculture's vision of the world at the time of this data collection, seems to be a key to understanding whether people accepted or rejected the conventional wisdom regarding sex and marriage. In the face of uncertain economic futures, this article remains an exclamation point and question mark, raising questions about the future based on the recent behavior of a group who may still be moving toward yet new adaptations to other life-styles.

4.
Creative Singlehood as a Sexual Life-Style: Beyond Marriage as a Rite of Passage

Roger W. Libby

Being single means being alone in our society, and it generally connotes a negative state of being. In this article, Roger Libby challenges the assumption that singlehood is an undesirable life-style, justifiable only as a stage toward monogamous marriage which transforms two lonely singles into vibrant and joyous marital companions. Instead, Libby sees singlehood as a positive option for many individuals—an option they may actively choose or reject and choose again at various stages in the sexual career and for any number of reasons. He emphasizes the creative aspects of singlehood and the advantages of carving out a life-style to meet one's individual needs in lieu of conforming to a preconceived monogamous model.

Libby begins by raising the issue of who is single, and he considers the many forms that creative singlehood may take. After critically reviewing much of the demographic, empirical, and journalistic literature about singlehood, he presents some theoretical models that describe singlehood and illustrate the continuous process of evaluating and choosing singlehood or other sexual life-styles. Libby ends by suggesting directions for future research into singlehood.

Single people have received little attention in research, theories, and scholarly analysis of social scientists. Family sociologists have either ignored singles or relegated them to boring, out-of-date discussions of dating, court-ship, and mate selection as steps toward marriage and parenthood. The neglect is blatant in that the number of adults between twenty-five and thirty-four who have never been married increased by 50 percent between 1960 and 1975 (U.S. Bureau of the Census, 1960, 1975). About half of those aged eighteen to thirty-nine are unmarried, and typically about a third of a woman's adult life is spent as a single person (U.S. Bureau of the Census, 1970). There are more women than men who are single at any given time, but as will be

"Creative Singlehood as a Sexual Life-Style: Beyond Marriage as a Rite of Passage," copyright © 1977 by Roger W. Libby.

This article is based on a presentation at the Connecticut College symposium, "Current and Future Intimate Life-Styles," November 13-14, 1975. The theoretical models were created with Molly Laird, who was also a valuable resource person for many of the ideas. The author also wishes to acknowledge the following for their comments on various drafts of this article: Judith Long Laws, Bernard Murstein, Gilbert Nass, Kathy Everly, Donna Dempster, Ronald Mazur, Sharon Rucker, Bob Thamm, Gordon Clanton, Bob Whitehurst, Elizabeth Havelock, Sterling Alam, Carolynne Kieffer, Shirley Nuss, and Norman Bell.

seen in this paper single men appear to be less happy as a group than single women. Since most writing on singles has been journalistic or descriptive social science unrelated to any well-developed theory, little is understood about singlehood as a sexual life-style.

The stereotype of the Joe Namath kind of swinging single and the opposing stereotype of the frustrated and miserable single person (as in George Gilder's *Sexual Suicide* and *Naked Nomads*) obscure the realities of singlehood. These polarized images which surface in the mass media and in everyday interaction blind social scientists and others to the range of life-styles being lived or contemplated by singles. Furthermore, the bulk of descriptive research on premarital sex and on cohabitation among college students has not informed social theory concerning singlehood. This is because the college years are too early to identify singlehood as an active choice rather than a premarital stage in the monogamous model. The same may be true of the post-college singles subculture which has received attention in the mass media.

Computer dating, singles' bars, career orientations in urban areas, and even a singles' church (*Newsweek*, June 12, 1972) offer opportunities for single people to socialize and work together; but in many if not most singles' social functions, the end goal is still to find a partner to live with or to marry. We are socialized in a couple-oriented society where at least 90 percent are expected to (and in fact do) marry.

However, at any one time about a third or more Americans are unmarried, separated, or in some way "unattached." Census figures do not allow for a precise delineation of living arrangements such as cohabitation, but the high divorce rate, the rise in the average age of first marriage, and the apparent longer period between divorce and remarriage (when remarriage occurs) provide a demographic basis for speculation about the dissolution of couples and emergence of singlehood as a life-style. It is also important to take into account divorced, separated, and widowed people when discussing singlehood as a sexual life-style. It may be significant, for example, that widowhood is increasing more for women than for men. This is because men are older when they marry than are women, and women tend to live longer; this creates stiffer competition among women for marital partners (Glick, 1976, personal discussion).

Singlehood is beginning to emerge as a positive option to marriage and other couple images. Social and ideological support for singlehood as a choice, rather than as a residual category for the unchosen and lonely, has come from the women's liberation movement, from the alternative life-styles and human potential movements, and from such groups as Zero Population Growth (ZPG), Planned Parenthood, and the National Organization for Non-Parents (NON). In addition, discrimination against singles in the tax structure has lessened (1972 Tax Reform Act, Dullea, 1975).

Ira Reiss (1973) has noted a trend toward increased legitimacy of choice of sexual life-styles and toward greater permissiveness in attitudes and behavior in heterosexual relationships prior to and after marriage. Murray

Straus (letter to author, November 1975) has proposed the hypothesis that the more sexually restrictive a society, the more singleness will be defined in negative ways (because marriage is necessary to make sex legitimate). And yet, family sociology has not investigated singlehood as an important life-style or satisfactorily analyzed various social sanctions for and against singlehood.

This article will attempt to bring us one step nearer to a clear conceptualization of the costs and rewards of choosing singlehood as a sexual life-style. The focus will be on the roles and position of single people over their sexual lives or "careers." I will discuss definitional issues first; then review the available literature; present some theoretical models; and finally suggest questions for future research.

Definitions: Who Is Single?

In both the professional and popular literature, single people have been inconsistently defined. While some researchers would simply limit singles to never marrieds, others include divorced, separated, and widowed people who are not cohabiting with a sexual partner. Others incorporate legal, social, and personal dimensions into the definition, such as age, intention to remain single or to marry, acceptance or nonacceptance of multiple sexual and emotional relationships, living arrangement, means of financial support, involvement in primary (even if not exclusive) sexual relationships, and the budgeting of time between one or more people and other obligations. Some distinguish between the labels *unmarried*, *single*, and *unattached.* Others simply state that singlehood, like marriage, is a state of mind rather than a legal status or a label conferred by others. Some define singlehood in terms of marriage (thus the stages "premarital" and "postmarital"), while others view singlehood as a choice rather than a stage. Although the definition of "single" may seem obvious to some, the definitional issues are complex.

Rather than defining singlehood in any narrow way, I will consider the whole range of sexual life-styles that potentially fall within the single category. In this context, singlehood might be a choice for some, or a stage leading to marriage or remarriage for others. It might also be a stage leading to cohabitation, which could in turn lead to marriage. On the other hand, marriage may be seen as an interim stage, with divorce and singlehood emerging as choices at later stages. My emphasis is on the *process* and on the concept of a sexual career involving different choices made at different stages in the life cycle. *Yesterday's choice could be today's stage in transition to tomorrow's new choice.*

To go further with this conceptualization of sexual career choices, there are costs and rewards involved with any choice. Those who *choose* to be single do so after evaluating the relative costs and rewards of other life-styles which are realistic options. The existence of a theoretical choice is not the same as having the option to make that choice, or to openly act on one's preferences. For example, one may want to have multiple sexual partners, and one may visualize this as a choice, but unless there are partners available and willing, along with a network of people and social institutions to support such a life-style, the option does not actually exist.

Before continuing to define singlehood, perhaps it would help to say what a single person *is not. For the purposes of this paper, "creative singlehood" is not legal marriage or cohabitation. A creatively single person is not emotionally, sexually, or financially dependent on one person; psychological and social autonomy are necessary to be defined as single* (Margaret Adams, 1971). If one person allows another to monopolize the majority of his or her time to the near exclusion of others as sexual partners, that person would not be considered single. A single person is committed to various leisure and occupational relationships, but does not make an exclusive commitment which precludes other emotional and sexual experiences.

Singlehood is a state of availability. This definition rules out those who are totally or mostly dependent on a relationship which demands conformity to the monogamous model, but it could include separated and divorced people, regardless of whether they are parents. This definition, then, goes beyond legal categories to focus on self-definitions and on the social identities acquired through labeling.

Although a person may be single either by choice or from the lack of opportunity to find a suitable partner, I will stress those creative singles who choose to remain single, and who choose not to cohabit or limit sexual behavior to one person. A single person may be eighteen or seventy-five, but this paper will emphasize the upper-middle-class college graduates in urban areas who are involved in professional careers and have a rather open opportunity structure for relating sexually with multiple partners. Although single people may change their life-styles at any point after reevaluating their particular situations, I will emphasize those who have chosen creative singlehood instead of cohabitation, sexual celibacy, marriage, or communal living. Being single need not mean being alone, but some time alone is assumed here. Furthermore, having primary and/or coprimary (equally primary) intimate relationships, as well as secondary and transitory relationships, would not necessarily conflict with singlehood.

There are *degrees* of singlehood, as I will illustrate later. One may be more single one month than another but still not move outside the single status. Or, one may be single, choose to cohabit or marry, and perhaps choose to later divorce and become single again. In this sense singlehood and other choices are *reclaimable* statuses or identities. One has the option of repudiating a current identity or reclaiming an earlier status.[1]

The strong emphasis on marriage as the final outcome of the dating-courtship script has essentially made singlehood a "deviant" choice. In spite of increased acceptance of premarital and nonmarital intercourse, for many *marriage is a rite of passage to legitimize sexual expression.* The emerging legitimization of singlehood as a sexual life-style flies in the face of the traditional view of premarital relationships leading to marriage. In Chapter 3 of this book, Roy and Roy identify reasons for the emphasis on marriage and offer a suggestion for social policy. They state:

It is principally because of the fear of sexual involvement that the singles are excluded from married society. In the new dispensation, a much more active and aggressive policy should be encouraged to incorporate single persons within the total life of a family and a community.

The fear of intimate or sexual relationships with married people is an underlying factor which contributes to the isolation of many singles from community life. A single person's availability to others is a critical factor affecting his or her identity.

Singlehood can change along various dimensions as one moves through the life cycle. A single person's role responsibilities and rights depend on familial, economic, and other considerations; commitment may shift from singlehood to some form of coupling and back again in response to other factors in one's life (Gilbert Nass, letter to author, October 1975). Roles shift in that they are defined by the self and by various reference groups and significant others. As social acceptance of singles increases and a social support system evolves, the roles attached to the single position will multiply. Institutionalized support for the sexual conduct of available single people may be minimal currently, but it is growing, particularly in large cities where the proportion of singles is high.

This brings me to some basic concepts which underlie creative singlehood and other multiple relationship life-styles. The social scripting of sexual and sex role behavior (or alternative sexual life-styles) is based on the following assumptions:

1. There is an eternal, erotic, emotional attraction between people, and a permanent availability of people to each other for emotional and sexual expression regardless of marital or living arrangements or sex. Bernard Farber (1964) predicted a trend away from the orderly replacement of marriage partners (lifetime monogamy) toward a more free-floating permanent availability. He stated: "Permanent availability implies that the basic needs of the individual may change . . . and that meeting personality needs at an early age may not suffice to maintain the marriage" (1964, p. 168).
2. There is an emerging autonomy of sexual expression apart from marriage, the family, and reproduction, so that the individual, not the couple or a larger entity, is the lowest common denominator when considering the meaning of sexual conduct (Jetse Sprey, 1969).
3. There is increasing visibility and viability of sexual life-styles (called the legitimacy of sexual choice by Ira Reiss, 1973); the full range of choices is receiving increased social support so that realistic options are increased.
4. We live in a secretive society where people can do as they wish without negative social sanctions if they are relatively discreet (open opportunity structure).
5. Change in one aspect of a culture or in one stage of a sexual career (such as increased sexual intercourse before marriage) affects change in other institutional arrangements or stages (such as the ground rules for sexual behavior for married partners). New definitions of coupling (such as sex-

ual friendships outside a primary relationship as in sexually open marriage) force a new look at singlehood.

6. Sexual behavior cannot be isolated or compartmentalized from the rest of a relationship. Nonsexual motives for sexual behavior and sexual motives for nonsexual behavior make compartmentalization of sex from various emotions, desires, expectations, and fantasies impossible.

The above assumptions give support to creative singlehood, and they encourage multiple sexual and emotional relationships for all categories of single and coupled people. The assumptions also feed into the social scripts for two contrasting sexual life-styles described in Table 1 (Libby, 1976). After looking at these two social scripts, I will comment on the relevant empirical, theoretical, and journalistic literature on singles.

A Selective Review of the Literature on Singles

The purpose of this review is to present the essence of what is now known or suspected about singles. Demographic data on age trends for first marriage, divorce rates, and similar descriptive information will be briefly covered. Then the few relevant empirical studies of singlehood as a chosen life-style will be described, and some journalistic literature will be discussed.

Demographic Data

Paul Glick (1975) and Jessie Bernard (1975) have presented some of the most current statistics on the delay in marriage and the increase in divorce, single parenthood, and various living arrangements for never married and other unattached people. It is difficult to predict whether marriage rates will continue to decline. We do know, though, that the average age of first marriage for women increased from twenty to twenty-one between 1960 and 1974, and the age increase for men during that period was from about twenty-two plus to twenty-three. Single men and women are delaying marriage and choosing to remain single longer. The proportion of women aged twenty to twenty-four remaining single has increased from 28 percent in 1960 to 40 percent in 1974 (U.S. Bureau of the Census, 1974). The figures for men are obscured by the movement of men in the armed forces.

Glick notes several reasons for the increase in age at marriage for women. About three times more women were enrolled in college in 1972 compared to in 1960, and the increase in employment for that period was greater for women than for men. Also, women at their peak marrying age (twenty-one) have outnumbered men at their peak marrying age (twenty-three) in any given year. Because the peak is about two years earlier for women than for men born the same year, there is a younger but larger group of women competing for partners from the smaller and older group of men. This situation, which Glick calls the "marriage squeeze," will probably exist until the average age of marriage for men and women equalizes.

Table 1.
Two Social Scripts for Sexual Relationships

	"Primrose Path" of Dating	Branching Paths of "Getting Together"
Fifth to Sixth Grade	Structured heterosexual activities; spin the bottle type of activity; having one boyfriend or girlfriend.	Unstructured activities, with no emphasis on marriage or relating to one member of the opposite sex. Interest-orientation rather than obsession with one opposite sex person.
Seventh to Ninth Grade	Group dating and dating with parents as chaperone figures. Parents drive car, etc. Sneaking around with opposite sex. Emphasis on meeting personal needs and acceptance from peers by conforming to their expectations.	No parental imposition of monogamous expectations. Nonpossessive, equalitarian relationships with no emphasis on dichotomy of sexual and nonsexual relationships.
High School	Double dating and single dating in cars with exclusive expectation once one dates a person a few times (going with one person, or "going steady").	"Getting together" *rather than* dating, with female initiating relationships as much as male and paying and driving car as much as male does.
After High School	• Work and continue monogamous dating, or date more than one person, or go to college and do same, or marry monogamously. Static, rigid role expectations for female and male. • Stress physical levels of intimacy as a basis for sexual morality. Sex viewed as economic ownership, meeting one's personal security needs, and as exclusive. If live together, it is sexually exclusive. • Divorce, tolerate unhappy "marriage," or for a minority, live happily ever after in a sexually and emotionally exclusive monogamous marriage. • Remarriage and divorce, or a repeat of the above (serial monogamy with "cheating" on the side by both spouses). • Emphasis on the weakness of the participants in marriage when unhappiness or divorce occurs, rather than questioning the monolithic image of marriage as "the answer" for anyone who chooses to marry. • Disillusionment with marriage for many. Searching for the "good life," but confused as to how to find it. Conflict between images in the mass media and what the local minister is preaching. Enter the therapist . . . who may or may not help. . . . What next?	• Stress qualities and common interests in relationships as a basis for decision making about sex and other relationship concerns. • Touching and sensuality encouraged. Sex only in mutually appropriate and mutually discussed situations. Sex as one language in some relationships with a range of symbolic meanings —from mutual pleasure (or horniness), to friendship, to love (love not seen as exclusive but as multiple following Robert Rimmer in *The Harrad Experiment*, and other novels). • If live together, relationship is sexually and emotionally nonexclusive. • Creative singlehood, or if marriage, some similar kind of open-ended arrangement such as the alternatives described in this book. • A *decision* to be open or closed in various areas of marriage, with the ongoing process of renegotiation of the marital contract. Marriage as a process rather than a static set of promises. • Various open marriages with comarital or satellite relationships viewed as supportive of the pair bond rather than as a threat to it. • Swinging—from recreational to utopian. • Group marriage. • Communal living with or without sexual sharing. • Compartmentalized marriage—with "night off" from marriage. • If divorce, joy rather than sadness (creative divorce). • Synergy: 1 + 1 = more than 2. (See O'Neill & O'Neill, 1972.)

NOTE: It is not uncommon for those socialized in the traditional script to later decide to take on different roles and to adopt one of the emerging alternatives to the monogamous image or the cheating reality . . . so some switching back and forth between scripts prior to and after marriage(s) is common. The above scripts are two *ideal types* on a continuum rather than actual dichotomies. However, many people still fit the traditional extreme of the "primrose path."

As Margaret Adams (1971) explained, the economic autonomy that college degrees and employment provide is critical to the emergence of singlehood as a life-style for women.[2] Both Glick (1975) and Adams (1971) consider the women's liberation movement to be a contributing social force supporting singlehood for women. Glick concludes that the postponement of marriage and childbearing by women appears to be part of a trend toward choosing alternatives to marriage, and he feels women may both try and like alternatives, including singlehood (Glick, 1975, p. 4).

The census data make it difficult to reflect on singlehood as a sexual life-style because living arrangements are not precisely delineated. "Living alone" and "living with nonrelatives" does not distinguish singlehood beyond a legal status; one might be cohabiting, monogamous, or creatively single. Since a sexual career may include frequent changes in living arrangements, more frequent data collection and/or accurate biographical information on individuals is necessary to chart role transitions. Although Jessie Bernard (1975) used census data to describe changing life-styles from 1970 to 1974, she admittedly could only speculate about their meaning and trends in sexual and living arrangements. Nevertheless, Bernard's and Glick's data tentatively indicate that marriage is becoming less popular.

The decreasing popularity of marriage appears dramatic when one observes the linear increase in divorce rates. There were over one million divorces in 1975 in the U.S.—6 percent more than in 1974. In contrast, the marriage rate dropped 4 percent that year, to roughly 2.1 million (U.S. Bureau of the Census, 1976). Glick and Norton (1973) estimate that one in three marriages for women thirty years old has ended or would end in divorce. After comparing marriage and divorce rates over a seven-year span, Ivan Nye (personal discussion with author, February 1976) predicted that national statistics on divorce will soon reach the levels of such states as California and Washington, where about 50 percent of first marriages, and even more remarriages, end in divorce. Since divorce is more prevalent among the remarried (Nye & Berardo, 1973, p. 529), it would appear that people will be spending more of their adult lives in some single status.

Furthermore, we cannot assume that those who do not divorce are happily married. The marriage and family literature (including longitudinal studies) reveals that only about 10 to 20 percent of marriages are self-reported as happy throughout most of the marriage, and wives report less satisfaction than husbands. Also, more men than women remarry; five-sixths of divorced men and three-fourths of women aged thirty-five to forty-four remarry (Glick, 1975). Apparently the double standard of aging, whereby women tend to be considered less attractive sooner than men (Susan Sontag, 1972), and the larger proportion of women to men with increasing age account for such a sex differential in remarriage rates. Since women tend to be less satisfied with marriage, it may also be that they are less anxious to remarry. The relaxation in divorce laws (although many so-called "no-fault" laws are not as the label implies, Weitzman, 1974) and the decreasing social stigma of divorce make singlehood a more viable alternative for both sexes. In spite of the increased economic independence of women through increased employment, women still appear to have more liabilities such as children and fewer assets to bargain for remarriage. Finally, it appears that the period between divorce and remarriage is increasing for young people of both sexes.[3] Even though most divorced people still remarry, an increase in the time interval after divorce, which has been about three years, may indicate a trend toward postmarital singlehood without remarriage for a growing population.

Empirical Studies

In addition to demographic statistics, studies of attitudes about marriage contribute to predictions about future life-style choices. Although the social psychology literature indicates that attitudes alone are not very accurate predictors of behavior, when considered with behavioral intention and selected situational, reference group, and social support variables, attitudes do contribute to the prediction of behavior (Fishbein & Ajzen, 1975; Acock & DeFleur, 1972). Peter Stein (1973) collected data on a population of college students (N of nearly 500, with a response rate of 75 percent of the college's class of 1973). He found that 3 percent of freshman women did not expect to marry as compared to 8 percent of senior women. Most impressive was his finding that 40 percent of senior college women did not know whether or not they should marry, and 39 percent of seniors felt that traditional marriage is becoming obsolete (Stein, 1973). Yankelovitch (1972) has noted a similar increase in disillusionment with marriage among college student samples over the years.

Whitehurst (see Chapter 19) and White and Wells (1973) have also studied university students' attitudes toward various life-styles. These investigators concluded that some changes were in the making but that dramatic, widespread changes in life-style choices should not be expected. Twelve percent of Whitehurst's three hundred nonrandomly selected students felt that monogamy is dying; of these 88 percent were single. Whitehurst found that 58 percent agreed it is possible to love (including sexually) more than one person at a time, but more marrieds than singles felt this way.[4] The implications of such beliefs for extramarital and comarital sex, as well as for eventual divorce and choice of singlehood or remarriage, are obvious. Furthermore, less than half intended to have conventional marriages like those of their parents, and nearly a fifth would be willing to try group living arrangements. Generally, then, Whitehurst's student subjects perceived some need for change in conventional monogamous marriage.

In the past few years, some research directly concerned with singlehood and sexuality has been undertaken. Stein (1975) conducted in-depth interviews with ten women and ten men (median ages of thirty-five and twenty-nine, respectively). All but two subjects had been married or involved in some type of exclusive sexual relationship prior to choosing a nonexclusive single life. Stein purposefully limited his sample to those who were nonexclusive, who did not plan to marry in the near future, and who did not hope to live with one person in an exclusive relationship in the near future. Thus, singles in this sample were defined as those who were sexually available to multiple partners after having experienced exclusivity. This is an obvious bias; one would expect such a sample to strongly endorse singleness, due in part to their previous unhappiness in exclusive relationships. Not surprisingly, Stein's sample felt that exclusive and/or marital relationships restricted human growth. One wonders what would be reported by other types of singles including those who had never experienced an exclusive relationship, or those who had been involved in an open marriage, communal living, group marriage, or some other alternative to traditional monogamous marriage or exclusive cohabitation.

Stein identifies some of the pushes and pulls toward and away from singlehood and monogamous marriage. Stein rightly points up the need for an ideology to make singlehood more viable as an option to marriage, and he identifies the lack of control which single people have over their existence (due to economic exploitation by such businesses as singles' bars, for instance). Stein's list of pulls toward singlehood (which might more precisely be called rewards from an exchange theory view) includes career opportunities, variety of experiences, self-sufficiency, sexual availability, exciting life-style, freedom to change and experiment, mobility, sustaining friendships, and supportive relationships such as men's and women's groups, group living, and specialized groups. Pushes toward singlehood (or costs associated with other life-styles) include suffocating one-to-one relationships, obstacles to self-development, boredom, unhappiness and anger, role playing, and conforming to expectations of others. Some other pushes toward singlehood could be poor communication with a mate, sexual frustration, lack of friends, isolation and loneliness, limitations on mobility and possible experiences, and influence of or participation in the women's movement (Stein, 1975, pp. 493-4). Stein also lists pulls and pushes toward marriage, most of which involve economic, emotional, and sexual security, and the influence of parents.

While Stein's study does offer some insights into one segment of the singles population, it also has several limitations. First, Stein did not present his findings in the context of any well-developed theoretical framework. In addition, he refers to singlehood as an emerging social movement (a response to sources of discontent, a set of goals, and a program to implement the goals, as defined by Killian, 1973). This claim is not justified; it would be more accurate to conceive of singlehood as one of several intimate life-styles receiving increased social and legal support from the human potential, women's liberation, and population control social movements. A more comprehensive treatment of Stein's study is available in his book, *Single* (1976). Stein's ideas for future research, presented in his article and book, are likely to spur more systematic and theortetically based empirical investigations into singlehood.

Fishel and Allon (1973) carried out an extensive ethnographic study of singles' bars. They utilized participant observation and open-ended interviews with one hundred people in eight singles' bars in New York City. Their conceptualization of single people was consistent with those of Stein and of such singles' publications as *Single Magazine*. Being single meant not being married or living together and not being engaged, pinned, or going steady. Taking the self-definitions of the participants in the bars, a "constant, steady relationship" implied attachment and not singlehood. There were some who were married or suspected of being married who frequented the singles' bars. For these people, the researchers concluded that singlehood was situational—that one could appear single and behave according to that social image. Actual interaction patterns were stressed and a situational definition of singlehood used. However, coupling was found to be a primary goal of participants in the singles' bars—success was often measured by achieving coupling and leaving singlehood behind. In this sense, singlehood as choice or stage is a critical research question.

Fishel and Allon's research is based in social theory, largely drawing on Georg Simmel's sociability theory of interaction patterns and Irving Goffman's analysis of interaction. The researchers concluded that singles' bars were full of those seeking companionship as an answer to their self-estrangement and isolation from others. The picture was one of disillusionment with self and others, dissatisfaction with the prescribed role playing in the singles' bar, and a sense of boredom which the participants hoped to replace with excitement, ego support for being attractive, and some semblance of intimacy with others.

Fishel and Allon's findings are consistent with another study of singles in Chicago by Starr and Carns (1973). A nonrandom availability sample of seventy single people was interviewed in 1970 and 1971; all in the sample were college graduates in their early to mid-twenties who had done graduate work and then moved to the big city to work. None had been married and most had no previous conception of the singles scene. The relative ease in meeting people during college had not been experienced in the urban single life.

The frequency with which the subjects went to singles' bars dropped off the longer they lived in the social context of urban singlehood; this was particularly true of women. Single men were often in search of instant sex, and many had sex with women of lower social status. Men were more sexually oriented, while women tended to be interested in friendship and permanent relationships. Starr and Carns found that singles' bars, neighborhood apartment living complexes, and parties did not offer much in the way of companionship or satisfactory ways to meet people. The majority of cross-sex friendships resulted from having been introduced to someone when at work (usually to someone who did not work in the same office). The researchers viewed the work world as the most significant context in which singles could develop a strong sense of self. The carefree swinging singles image was not supported. The contrast between the relatively happy singles in Stein's select sample in New York City and those in the samples collected by Starr and Carns and by Allon and Fishel is suggestive of the broad range of life-styles and degrees of singlehood.

The process of adjusting to a new single life includes relating to old and new friends and meeting companions for intimacy and sex. Yet the traditional sociological research on friendship patterns fails to include sexual expression as a dimension of some friendships. For example, Booth and Hess (1974) failed to deal directly with the issue of sex in friendship in their data collection on eight hundred middle-aged and elderly urban residents. Booth and Hess apparently assumed that friendship by definition excludes sex. Ramey and other investigators have shown this to be false. Friendship studies should consider the full range of friendship types rather than narrowing their observations to conform with their narrow world views (implications for the sociology of knowledge are rampant).

Research on personality characteristics and adjustment to marital or nonmarital life gives some clues to the viability of singlehood for women as compared to men. Spreitzer and Riley (1974) carried out a secondary analysis of a sample of 2454 applicants for social security benefits. The median age of the sample was fifty-five, and less than 3 percent were under thirty-five (1974, p. 534). They found that higher intelligence, education, and occupation were associated with singlehood for females, while single males tended to have poor interpersonal relations with parents and siblings (1974, p. 541).

Several other studies compare singlehood and marriage in terms of relative adjustment and happiness for men and women. Genevieve Knupfer, Walter Clark, and Robin Room (1966) found that single men were more antisocial and maladjusted than married men. They also concluded that single women aged thirty and over were less depressed, neurotic, passive, and maladjusted than their married counterparts. In agreement with the conclusions of Knupfer et al., Jessie Bernard (1972) summarized four studies and concluded that single men were less happy than married men. Luther Baker's (1968) results similarly supported those of Knupfer et al. He found that never married women without children had above average personal and social adjustment based on the national norms established for the California Test of Personality. Finally, Lenore Radloff's (1974) study of depression indicated that single women were less depressed than divorced or separated women, but that single men were more depressed than divorced or separated men.

In contrast to the above, Norval Glenn (1975) found that married persons of both sexes reported greater global happiness than any category of unmarried persons, and that the difference in happiness between marrieds and unmarrieds was greater for females than for males. The Glenn study utilized self-report data from 1972, 1973, and 1974 social surveys of the U.S. conducted by the National Opinion Research Center. Glenn's study suggests that the data from the above researchers should be cautiously interpreted; however, as Bernard (1975) has noted, the self-reported global happiness of the married women in Glenn's study may be suspect, partly due to the social desirability of reporting greater happiness than is actually felt. Bernard concludes that such data tend to obscure "the dismal picture of the mental health of married women so convincingly documented in the research literature" (1975, p. 600).

The conclusion to be drawn from most available data is that marriage is probably better for men than it is for women. Existing studies of the relative adjustment and happiness of single women and men do not warrant sweeping conclusions about the dire state of single men as argued by journalists such as George Gilder, but it does seem that single women are happier than single men.[5] Perhaps this pattern will change as more men become independent and liberated; male dependency on mother and then on wife as pseudo-mother may account for the greater unhappiness of single men.

Journalistic Reports

Journalists, on the other hand, have carried out some more thorough (though not methodologically precise) investigations of singlehood than have social scientists. One journalistic investigation of singlehood is the now classic study of the world of the formerly married by Morton Hunt (1966). In that study Hunt identified a broad range of life-styles for formerly married people—from the "abstainers" to the "addicts." It is significant that Hunt's book is still in print ten years later, and that he has been asked to carry out a new study to update his earlier book. For the updated study, Morton and Bernice Hunt collected questionnaire data on a nonrandom, availability, mail-in sample of separated and divorced people in order to compare parents with nonparents. They looked at the process of adjusting to a new single life, including relating to old and new friends, meeting companions for intimacy and sex, and planning to remain single or to remarry.

Studies on increased premarital and extramarital sex, though only indirectly relevant to singlehood, indicate support for Sprey's (1969) argument that there is an increasing autonomy of sex from marriage, the family, and parenthood. Daniel Perlman's (1974) study, for example, documents the rise in sexual activity among unmarried college students. He found that his liberal sample reported both high self-esteem and more coital partners when compared with subjects of earlier studies by Stratton and Spitzer (1967) and by Reiss (1966). It remains for future research to identify how much of what is commonly called premarital or extramarital sex is really nonmarital and thus part of the single life.

Between the extreme images of the swinging and always elated single and the desperately lonely, suicidal single lies a continuum of single people with joys and sorrows similar to those of people electing other life-styles. Since Martin Panzer's article, "No World for a Single," appeared in *Coronet Magazine* (April 1955), singlehood as a choice rather than a residual category of undesirables has become a reality for some. As the article suggests, it may be that most single people are not happy; this is the view of George Levinger who notes that more do not opt for singlehood because they "need deep attachments that go beyond the 'modular man' [or woman] syndrome implied as normative by Toffler" (letter to author, November 1975). Levinger noted that his research with University of Massachusetts students "indicates that almost none would look forward to a future in which he or she remains permanently single." Of course, the attitudes expressed by a sample of college sophomores may not be adequate predictors of the later behavior of this same group.

Similarly, Jeanette Ames McIntosh and Gilbert D. Nass (1975) studied

109 females at Wheelock College, and it was found that 5 percent were willing or very willing to remain unmarried throughout their lives. As Wheelock has a fairly conservative student body, it might be hypothesized that more liberal samples would yield larger minorities who desire lifelong singlehood. Furthermore, it is possible that the proportion of women selecting singlehood along with careers will increase over time.

We are left, then, with the impression that singlehood (like marriage) is not a lifelong commitment for most people. Choices are usually replaced by new choices. After all, singlehood could not be a binding choice, for to whom would one be bound by such a choice? To oneself? Perhaps theoretical choices vary more than real options, but we will not really know the range of either choices or options without more comprehensive, theoretically grounded research. In the meantime, social scientists leave speculation and descriptive studies to journalists, for the most part, just as they previously left the study of sex to Kinsey, a zoologist. One wonders how long social scientists will wait to study the realities of the twentieth century.

One journalist (Phyllis Raphael, 1975) has argued that twentieth century woman's dilemma is whether to marry or not, but that she need not worry about sex since it is available to the single person who wants it. Raphael feels that most people want to be married and that they attempt to act on that want. Furthermore, she argues that people are what they *do* rather than what they *say* they do. As simple as this may seem, it indicates the importance of comparing attitudes, behavioral intentions, and reported behavior with actual interactive behavior. Such comparison is essential if we are to determine how satisfied people really are with various life-styles.

A Theoretical Approach to Singlehood

It will be helpful to consider singlehood within a theoretical framework. Four figures have been developed as aids in presenting theoretical models of different aspects of singlehood. The first figure presents various dimensions of singlehood and a continuum of degrees of singlehood. The second figure depicts the transitions in relationships over time. The third and fourth figures describe the process of evaluation and reevaluation of life-style decisions. The theoretical approach taken here integrates elements from symbolic interaction, role, and exchange theories.

The degrees and dimensions of singlehood presented in Figure 1 are some of the many considerations that enter into decisions made about sexual life-styles and role transitions. They help define the relative rewards and costs associated with decisions. However, Figure 1 is limited in that it does not identify the process of role and exchange transactions over a sexual career. (These factors are dealt with in the remaining figures.) Before explaining Figure 1, the relevance of exchange theory will be discussed.

As Libby and Carlson (1976) indicate, the relative costs and rewards of any relationship or decision in a relationship include not only observable rewards and punishments, but inner feelings, motives, and other less tangible but extremely important emotional and cognitive states. For example, one

Figure 1.
Degrees and Dimensions of Sexual Life-Styles

Decentralized commitment and interdependency

Degrees:	Dimensions:
Creative Singlehood	

→Singlehood as choice with multiple relationships which are temporary and secondary	Living alone or with roommates
	Financial independence
→Singlehood as choice with multiple relationships which are both primary and secondary, but not temporary	Sexual independence
	Emotional independence
	Self as determinant of budgeting of time

Cohabitation

→Open primary relationship with mutual intentions to enter open cohabitation or open marriage	Open cohabitation (with or without legal marriage)
→Open cohabitation or open marriage	Financial interdependence
	Sexual interdependence
	Emotional interdependence
	Primary but not exclusive relationship(s) to budget time

Exclusive Monogamous Model

→Closed cohabitation	Exclusive cohabitation (with or without legal marriage)
→Premarital courtship (exclusive)	
→Serial monogamy	Financial dependence
→Permanent monogamy	Sexual dependence
	Emotional dependence
	Primary and exclusive relationship to budget time together (constant togetherness or couple front)

Centralized commitment and dependency

NOTE: The dotted lines with arrows indicate feedback loops to other life-styles if one chooses to or is forced to leave a particular life-style. The continuum from creative singlehood to the exclusive monogamous model does *not* assume a regular progression. People do not necessarily go from top to bottom of the figure; one may stop at any point, or skip life-styles (they may begin with traditional premarital courtship and end with serial monogamy or permanent monogamy, skipping cohabitation). The arrows indicate the entry points into the various life-styles.

factor which contributes to a person's perception of fairness in relationships is the relative degree of interdependence (with reciprocity) or dependency. Usually dependency entails an unbalanced interaction with one person both incurring greater costs than the other person and being less satisfied with the relationship. As will be explained, such a lack of reciprocity usually results in a reevaluation of the relationship (see Figure 3, although some people remain in relationships with little apparent profit.

There are several ways to conceptualize a sequence of interactions and decision making in terms of exchange theory. Thibaut and Kelley (1959) used reward-cost matrices to depict the possible outcomes of social interaction. Outcomes are evaluated through comparison levels (CL) which are "the lowest level of outcomes a member will accept in the light of available alternative opportunities" (such as other more attractive people to relate to), and by comparison level for alternatives (CL alt.), which is "the standard the member uses in deciding whether to remain in or leave the relationship" (or, when comparing other relationships or potentials for relationships with current relationships) (Thibaut & Kelley, 1959, p. 21). Decisions are based on the assumption that people enter and remain in relationships (or life-styles) only as long as the relationships and life-styles are evaluated by the interactants to be profitable (profit in exchange terms is rewards minus costs).

Secord and Backman (1974) have pointed out that changes occur in the perception of rewards and costs for any given relationship:

Rewards and costs may change as a function of (1) past exchanges which shift reward-cost values of current behaviors, (2) changes in the characteristics of the dyad members occurring through training, education, or other experiences, (3) changes in external circumstances that introduce new rewards and costs or modify the values of old ones, (4) sequential factors in the relation itself, such as the augmentation of satisfaction in current relations as a result of previously rewarding experiences in the dyad, and (5) associations with other behaviors having different reward-cost values (Secord & Blackman, 1974, p. 234).

Reward-cost benefits in one's relationships are illustrated by the categorization of sexual life-styles in Figure 1. Reading down from "singlehood" to "permanent monogamy" one can see the lessening degrees of autonomy from others. Choosing singlehood may include multiple relationships of a transitory nature, or more intense and enduring bonds (such as primary relationships). The "Dimensions" section of Figure 3 identifies some of the costs and rewards associated with various sexual life-styles. The range of life-styles is collapsed into three major prototypes: creative singlehood, cohabitation, and monogamy. These three prototypes are useful in comparing the partitioning of one's time, money, emotions, and sexual expression in various life-styles. Many people, of course, are in gray areas outside these prototypes involving some different combination of the dimensions.

Figure 2 was created to illustrate the sequential effects of rewards and costs in relationships over time. The reevaluation of the relative costs and rewards of relationships over time is central to the exchange theory conceptualization used as a basis for explaining and predicting transitions in relation-

Figure 2.

Transitions in Relationships Over Time

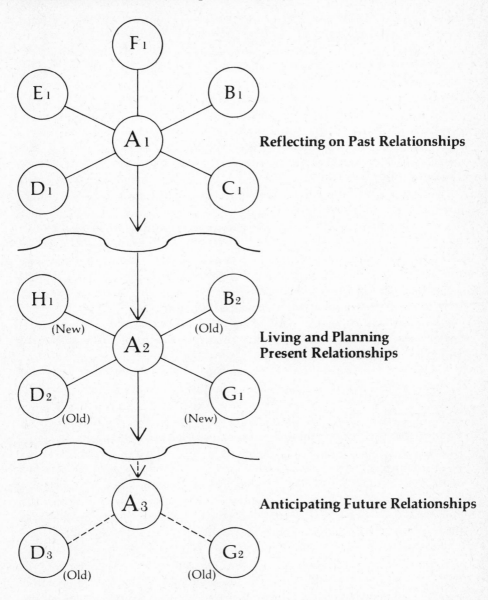

Reflecting on Past Relationships

Living and Planning Present Relationships

Anticipating Future Relationships

Note:

Person A₁ (past) is traced to the present (A₂) and the future (A₃). Person A forms relationships with Persons B–G at one stage or another. The biography of relationships can be used to reflect on one's past, to analyze the present configuration of old and new relationships, and to hypothesize about future relationships. Some relationships might be primary, coprimary, secondary, transitory, or simply acquaintanceships. According to exchange theory, reflecting on past relationships, living with present relationships, and anticipating future relationships all influence the perception of relative costs and rewards of relationships.

ships. Thibaut and Kelley (1959) and others have published various interpretations of exchange theory (sometimes called interpersonal attraction or equity theory) which have recognized the importance of the sequential effect of past decisions on present and future decisions about relationships. Without considering sequential effects from past exchanges in a matrix of relationships, one cannot identify satiation of a given stimulus situation (for example, when one is bored with the same person doing the same things). A researcher must be aware of present and past exchanges as well as the matrix of likely outcomes for a particular exchange. In the sexual realm this means one must be aware of past and present exchanges with sexual, emotional, and ego values. To do this we need a biographical and current analysis of the relative costs and rewards associated with the myriad of relationships in each person's life. Such data could be collected over time, or from retrospective accounts (Libby & Carlson, 1976). It is imperative to carry out a sequential analysis in order to explain—let alone predict—the nature of decisions leading to role transitions.

The implications for exchange outcomes for competing sexual choices appear in Figure 2, where a sample overview of the development and demise of a person's relationships over time is provided. The costs and rewards associated with each relationship change as the individual's personal and social situations, expectations, needs, and desires change; this affects whether the person maintains or abandons various relationships. Some patterning of role expectations and behaviors can usually be identified through such a natural history analysis of one's relationships over time, and projecting into the future may be possible.

Figure 3 illustrates the reevaluation of current relationships. A person in the reevaluation stage of potential "unbonding" must consider the rewards and costs of the various life-style options. When and if a person selects singlehood, there are both pulls and pushes which affect the new single identity. The process of coupling, dissolution of coupling (or unbonding), and identification of "crucial events" and "turning points" (Turner, 1970, pp. 12-13) resulting in role transitions and transformations in choices of life-styles appears in Figure 3. As can be seen in the figure, ongoing decisions about roles, needs, and self-identities involve a series of role bargains where discrepancies between actors' sexual and emotional expectations and behavior contribute to perceived costs and rewards for various role behaviors.

When there are discrepancies and crucial events concerning identities, needs, or role definitions in a relationship, the actors typically consider hypothetical alternative relationships or life-styles. Hypothetical comparisons may be complemented by actual comparative experiences with others serving as role models to consider alternative roles and ways of interacting and making commitments. After reentering the interactional space of the troubled relationship, the actors (Persons A and B) must decide whether to leave the relationship, change it, or continue living with unfulfilled needs. The hypothetical process of role-need-identity-taking with peers and significant others as models or mirrors of the self aids in weighing the costs and rewards of put-

Figure 3.

Reevaluation of Role Expectations for a Relationship

Key
C. E. = Crucial Event
A = One Person
B = Another Person

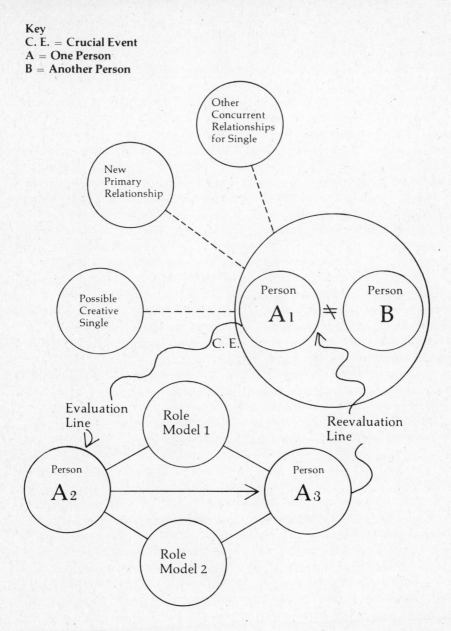

NOTE:
Here we can see Person A's evaluation of needs and possible roles and future identities prompted by difficulty in the relationship with Person B. Among the options are to stay in the present relationship or to become creatively single. Person B may go through an evaluation process similar to that illustrated for Person A.

ting energy into the troubled relationship. For example, Figure 3 would allow us to hypothesize that Person A and Person B have a primary relationship (it might be two cohabiting people, two single people, or a married couple). Due to various crucial events, one or both people may be unhappy enough to reevaluate the worth or the nature of the relationship. The evaluation line indicates that Person A is exposed to others who can serve as role models. These role models (possibly close friends or even movie stars) provide a basis to compare the costs and rewards being experienced in the relationship with Person B, with the costs, rewards, and role expectations connected with the roles of the models.[6] The reevaluation line leading back to the primary relationship symbolizes the comparison of alternative relationships (as shown by the role models) with the present troubled primary relationship. Person A and Person B then decide whether to continue their relationship as it is, to change their role expectations, or to uncouple. The outcome could be other primary relationships, or a series of secondary relationships. Uncoupling may lead to creative singlehood or to recoupling with another person or the same person. The lack of a set of static role expectations forces continual reevaluation of the relative costs and rewards in all relationships. But whatever the outcome, the reevaluation process occurs after crucial events lead to comparisons with role models.

If the outcome of someone's reevaluation of a relationship results in a possible single, that person has further role choices for relationships in his or her sexual career, as shown in Figure 4. The person can move into the status of a single and then become a cohabitor after meeting someone. Or the person can marry someone after orbiting (searching) for a partner. A third alternative is to meet several people and become a creative single. These three major types of role choices in a transitional stage are depicted in Figure 4.

Figure 4 illustrates bonding and unbonding and transitions to various sexual life-styles. Satisfactory bonding is illustrated in the top half of the figure, while the dotted vertical lines to the bottom half show the weakening of bonds in a given life-style (the unsatisfactory state as with Person A in Figure 3 and how one may launch into another life-style after breaking the previous bond(s).

The possible *transitions* (through orbiting) in role bonding (or coupling) over a sexual career are shown in Figure 4. Individuals may select singlehood, cohabitation, or monogamous marriage at various times. The three life-styles in Figure 4 (creative singlehood, cohabitation, and monogamous marriage) are only examples (or prototypes) from the larger range of life-style choices which could be described. For example, single people don't have to have four separate bonds at one point in time; some may have three bonded relationships, and others may have none.

As one example of the process of role transitions, a single person could orbit and enter any of the three types of life-styles (or bonds) and then (possibly due to bad experiences) launch out into orbit again in search of another relationship or another life-style. Any entry into a given choice may in turn be followed by another launching into the orbit of life-styles and reentry into

Figure 4.

Transitions in Role Bonding

Key
P. S. = Possible Single
A = One Person
B = Another Person

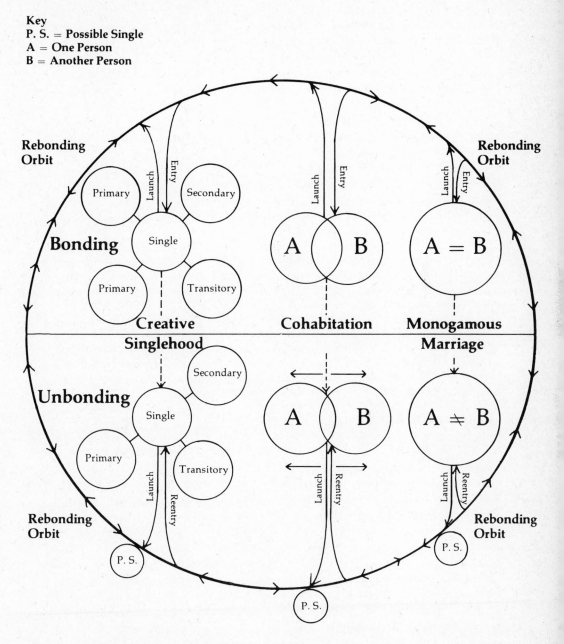

NOTE:
In the lower half of the circle, the single person may launch into orbit seeking a new bond after losing a primary relationship; the cohabitors may launch into orbit because they have grown apart; and the married couple may seek new bonds due to dissatisfaction with their relationship.

another life-style with greater promise of rewards. The nature of the entry and launching process depends in part on one's comparison level for alternatives.

Individuals vary in their ability and willingness to tolerate an unhappy relationship. Further variation between people can be seen by comparing those with short-term and long-term (career) sexual orientations. Short-term people typically make more frequent role transitions and live mainly in the present, while long-term career people carefully chart out their future and have a higher tolerance threshold for costs in everyday interaction in intimate relationships. People learn habits, and while these can change, it appears that old patterns of behavior tend to reemerge. Such patterns influence future decisions and negotiations and can contribute to explanations and predictions of role and life-style choices.

Implications for the nature and length of dyadic relationships and alternative life-styles abound. Farber's (1964) permanent availability model has direct relevance to the continuing demise of lifelong monogamous marriage as the *only* option in everyday commitment and interaction patterns. As Farber explains:

. . . depending as it does upon the tentativeness of interpersonal relations, permanent availability suggests that family relationships are capricious and as a result of this capriciousness, people cannot have much confidence in long-run plans. Short-run planning in family life is more consistent with the view of marriage as a voidable relationship and remarriage as a perennial possibility than is long-run planning. To have confidence in long-range planning, individuals must regard their social relations as relatively stable and orderly. Career orientation implies that family relations are predictable over long periods of time. Career [i.e., long-term] orientation is therefore more consistent with orderly replacement from one generation to the next than is role orientation (1964, p. 306).

Farber's model leads me to the conclusion that people will launch out of both monogamous marriage and cohabitation arrangements increasingly more frequently. Even though creative singlehood cannot be viewed as a lifelong choice for most, it appears to offer an attraction for an increasing proportion of people who are dissatisfied with other more traditional choices involving sexual exclusivity and other restrictions often in conflict with the need to be free. Figure 4 represents the entry and launching process; it may be that more people will be in orbit (far out?) as they make short-term commitments to a life-style and then seek happiness through quick role transitions to other choices. Toffler (1970) predicted that we would move toward a series of transitory and casual sexual relationships or encounters; these could be illustrated in Figure 4, as could the option to remain in a given life-style such as cohabitation or monogamy for longer periods of time. Future research may reveal that the pleasure of new sexual and emotional experiences, along with the comfort and affection of long-term love relationships which are minus the hassles of cohabitation, will be a strong "pull" toward creative singlehood in the future.

Some Research Questions

Currently there are many more questions than answers about singlehood as a sexual life-style. Some examples of research questions include:

1. How do the happiness, adjustment, and interaction-commitment patterns of singles vary by size of city; by ratio of women to men; by marital status, such as never married, separated, or divorced; by parenthood or nonparenthood; by education, occupation, and income; and by migration patterns?

2. How do those who select singlehood make such a choice? Who are their role models? How do variant time periods affect modeling effects and role transitions? How do specific reference groups, attitudes, situations, significant others, and various mass media affect the choice and relative viability of singlehood? What are the key social supports and negative sanctions for singlehood?

3. What is the interrelationship between the various dimensions of singlehood (financial, sexual, emotional, time budgeting, career orientation, etc.)?

4. What are the proportions of people who either select or "fall into" the various life-styles in Figure 1? What is their relative happiness, controlling for sex and age?

5. To what extent do various samples of people from all marital categories view creative singlehood as moral, appropriate, or as a threat to marriage? How do social labels mesh with self-definitions of singles?

6. What are the crucial events and turning points which lead to role transitions and changing commitments as one moves in and out of various social situations, occupations, cities, new social contacts, etc.? How does the single experience vary by sex, age, biographical history, and current social situation? How does the opportunity structure vary in terms of meeting and maintaining relationships? Who is best and worst suited to creative singlehood and why?

7. What are the correlates leading to high self-acceptance as opposed to high self-esteem? Do singles commonly distinguish between these two self-concepts? Why are some single by choice and others by default? How do these two groups differ?

8. What interpersonal experiences (such as encounter groups) are helpful in maintaining emotional stability and personal happiness and combating anomie?

9. When one chooses singlehood, is the choice binding to anyone? To the self? What is the nature of personal commitments to singlehood? Is singlehood viewed as a temporary state or as a commitment for an extended period of time? What differences are there between those who see singlehood as a temporary state and those who have no intention of changing their life-style?

10. To what extent is singlehood a state of mind? Do married and cohabiting

people consider themselves to be at least part-time single? On what basis? How do their claims relate to their actual interactive behavior?

11. When comparing what singles say they feel and do with what they really do, are they honest with others and with themselves about their happiness?

12. What are the differential experiences of those who have primary, coprimary, secondary, and transitory sexual relationships as singles? How are short-term and long-term commitments defined in various kinds of friendships and other sexual and nonsexual relationships? If distinctions are made between commitments to sexual and nonsexual friends or acquaintances, on what basis are such distinctions made, and what are the implications for intensity and permanence of these relationships?

The questions could go on, but the challenge before social scientists is to pose more theoretically grounded questions, to develop theoretically based hypotheses, and to carry out studies that will indicate how theories should be modified in light of data. Retrospective life histories (as recommended by Stein, 1975), combined with longitudinal and cross-sectional studies should yield valuable data on what it means to be single in urban and suburban America. In-depth interview studies of single people with a broad range of personal, family, and social backgrounds, and engaged in a variety of personal and professional pursuits should provide a basis for comparisons, explanations, and ultimately for some predictions about the future of creative singlehood. Interview studies will have to be complemented by participant observation studies carried out in the single's work world, restaurants, bars, hotels, and clubs, as well as in other social settings which cater to a mixture of single and married people. Analyses of attitudes, feelings, and behaviors in such a range of public settings with the use of multiple research methods such as interviews and participant observation should yield results which have some theoretical value. Large attitude and opinion surveys (such as that by *Psychology Today* on happiness, October 1975) could also contribute to knowledge, if not theory, about the costs and rewards associated with the single life as compared with marriage.

Perhaps in the end we will find that single people are not as different in their goals as many would contend. It may be that most people, regardless of life-style or marital status, really just want to be happy and seek pleasure. Creative singles may be saying that they don't need marriage or cohabitation to find sexual and emotional happiness. For those who choose creative singlehood, marriage is not a necessary rite of passage for legitimizing one's sexual identity.

Reference Notes

1. The concept of reclaimable identities was arrived at with Ronald Mazur (letter to author, October 1975).
2. Also, as Gordon Clanton has suggested to the author (letter, January 1976), we may find that with greater affluence more people will choose to remain single. There may be an economic

threshold operating; as a society we can only sustain single people to the extent that we have the housing, jobs, and social support for singlehood.

3. This is not yet a demonstrated fact (Paul Glick, discussion with author, 1976), but I believe this trend will be documented in the near future.

4. Jessie Bernard's discussion of younger couples stressing exclusivity and older couples opting for permanence without exclusivity is relevant here. See Chapter 8.

5. Commenting on this article, Gilbert Nass offered a contrasting point of view. He stated: "Single life may not be better for single women than single men. In fact, given society's bias in favor of men, the male bachelor has much more going for him. However, in a world in which the advantages lie with married men, the man who is single is more likely to be among the population who can't take advantage of this good deal because of personal handicaps (there are exceptions of course). Thus, it is probably the better selection of single women over single men that causes them to function better despite an environment geared toward men. As Knupfer, et al. (1966) point out, a well-adjusted woman may be unmarried because no one asks her—the same cannot be said for single men."

6. Elizabeth Havelock and Bob Whitehurst have suggested (letter, January 1976) that married people view single people as role models, too. Their observation is that marrieds both vicariously identify with the "swinging singles" image, and at the same time pity singles for their isolation and assumed loneliness. The married may find the freedom of the single person appealing, but at the same time the single person may view the married person as happy because of the companionship of the marital partner. These contrasting images of the costs and rewards associated with both singlehood and marriage perpetuate the existence of both as choices.

5.
Cohabitation in Social Context

Charles Lee Cole

Interest in the phenomenon of unmarried cohabitation has increased steadily over the past several years. Cole's article brings the reader up to date by providing both a review of the literature and a further elaboration of the dynamics of cohabitation.

An extensive review of the social psychology of relationship processes shows that cohabitants do not plan ahead in terms of contracting relationships, that they maintain strong affective bonds, and that there are some predictable patterns in decision making in the dyad. In part, the decision-making patterns reflect some basic sex-role biases as well as the desire to continue to dominate in certain spheres that were held as individual responsibilities before the cohabitation period began. Cohabital dissolution tends to follow similar patterns to marital dissolution.

In closing, Cole points out some major questions for future research. He also speculates about trends in cohabitation and comments on its meaning for the courtship and marriage patterns of the future.

Heterosexual cohabitation is not a new phenomenon. Trost (1975), Clatworthy (1975), Berger (1971), Kieffer (1972), and Whitehurst (1973) point out that data on cohabitation indicate that the custom of heterosexual mates living together without legal sanction is well documented throughout history. In American society alone, common-law marriage statutes that encompass many situations in which unmarried couples cohabit without legal contract are still legally recognized in fifteen states. For a discussion of the legal aspects of cohabitation, see Stein (1969) and Drabkin (1974).

Furthermore, data collected by the U.S. Census Bureau (Bernard, 1975) indicate that more individuals are living with unrelated individuals of the opposite sex than ever before. Glick (1975) notes that Census reports (U.S. Bureau of Census, 1964, 1973) indicate that in 1970 eight and a half times as many adults as in 1960 reported that they were living with an unrelated adult partner of the opposite sex. Thus, it is increasingly evident that many individuals today have life-styles that do not necessitate legal marriage. See Chapter 4 of this book for a discussion of creative singlehood as an alternative life-style.

Although cohabitation has been practiced in some form in a variety of

"Cohabitation in Social Context," © Charles Lee Cole, 1977.

The author would like to thank Anna Cole, who is a marriage counselor in private practice, Ames, Iowa, for critically reviewing this chapter. The author also wishes to acknowledge the assistance of Donald Bower, of the University of Georgia, who has been the project coordinator on the Cohabitation Research Project since 1974.

cultures throughout history, sociological research in this area has traditionally been limited. In fact, the literature on cohabitation to date has been mainly comprised of journalistic accounts in the popular press (e.g., *Newsweek*, 1966; *Esquire*, 1967; Grant, 1968; McWhirter, 1968; Schrag, 1968; *Time*, 1968; Block, 1969; Karlen, 1969; Rollin, 1969; Sheehy, 1969; *Life*, 1970; Hunt, 1971; Coffin, 1971; Lobsenz, 1973, 1974; Proulx, 1973; Peer, 1973; Sheraton, 1973; and Otten, 1974). Many of these journalistic accounts are little more than sensationalistic attempts to capitalize on the novelty of the life-style. They are usually based upon very small samples and focus on subjective accounts that are little more than case studies. In some instances the accounts reflect prejudices and constitute ideological ax-grinding (usually tainted with conservative values and labeling cohabitation as a deviant behavior).

Social scientists interested in cohabitation are attempting to develop collaborative networks whereby researchers can pool their efforts in order *(a)* to design research instruments that will facilitate collecting reliable data and *(b)* to develop conceptual models and research hypotheses for the future. The 1973 Groves Conference on Marriage and the Family, held in Myrtle Beach, South Carolina, marked the beginning of an ongoing effort to hold workshops periodically for the purpose of collectively working toward sociological and social phychological explanations of the cohabitation phenomenon. The *Cohabitation Research Newsletter* is a recent vehicle for disseminating cohabitation research.

Research reports published to date in professional journals have been primarily descriptive (Arafat & Yorburg, 1973; Berger, 1971; Clatworthy, 1975; Cole, 1976; Henze & Hudson, 1974; Hudson & Henze, 1973; Johnson, 1973a; Lyness, Lipetz, & Davis, 1972; Macklin, 1972, 1974; Peterman, Ridley, & Anderson, 1974; Smith & Kimmel, 1970; Thorman, 1973; Trost, 1975; and Wells & Christie, 1970). In addition, a number of graduate theses have been written on cohabitation (Bower, 1974, 1975; Gavin, 1973; Johnson, 1968; Kieffer, 1972; Lautenschlager, 1972; Montgomery, 1972; Mosher, 1974; Secrest, 1975; and Storm, 1973). The thrust of most of this research has been on describing cohabitation as a social phenomenon. Few attempts have been made either to conceptualize the meaning of cohabitation as a life-style or to place it into the larger realm of emerging alternative life-styles. Hennon (1974) is one of the few researchers who have attempted to apply sociological theory to cohabitation; he views cohabitation as an example of a variant life-style that can be systematically conceptualized in terms of a social systems model. Chapter 4 in this book provides an excellent example of the application of social exchange theory and symbolic interactionism to the decision-making process in choosing a life-style.

In this article I will focus on cohabitation as a variant life-style option that can be evaluated in terms of its relative costs and rewards. I will critically review key studies on cohabitation and propose ways in which to sharpen the conceptual focus of future research in order to develop theory that will help illuminate the meaning of the life-style.

In Quest of a Theoretical Model

One of the critical concerns of social scientists is the development and application of theoretical models to explain social phenomena. In this chapter I will utilize elements of social exchange theory and symbolic interactionism in much the same vein as Libby does in Chapter 4, i.e., as conceptual tools to provide explanations as well as descriptions of the cohabitation phenomenon. For example, Macklin's (1972, 1974) discussion of the advantages and disadvantages of cohabitation can be conceptualized as rewards (advantages) and costs (disadvantages). By using rewards and costs as the key concepts, I can generate propositions from existing research data that will explain the relative influence of specific types of costs and rewards on the outcomes of various relationships. Chapter 4 provides a more complete discussion of how principles from symbolic interactionism, role, and exchange theory can be utilized to construct models that have heuristic value in explaining a variety of emerging alternative life-styles, such as cohabitation. Detailed models will not be developed in this article, but suggestions will be made at various points in the discussion as to how models might be applied.

What Is Cohabitation?

Cohabitation has not been systematically defined in a conceptual sense or operationalized for empirical inquiry. There are many implicit and explicit meanings attached to the term *cohabitation.* Some researchers (e.g., Trost, 1975) suggest that the term *cohabitation* be applied to married as well as unmarried couples. Trost (1975, p. 677) notes that the term *syndyasmos* was suggested by Löcsei (1970) for referring to both married and unmarried cohabitation. The term *syndyasmos* means those varieties of enduring living arrangements between men and women. Explicit in Löcsei's (1970) definition of *syndyasmos* is the notion that it applies to both legalized and nonlegalized pair-bond relationships. A common feature in many researchers' nominal definitions (e.g., Nasholm, 1972; Claesson, Lindgren, & Lindth, 1973; and Hickrod, 1972) is the notion of a heterosexual couple sharing a common living facility for the purpose of meeting certain family functions. The specific family functions included vary from researcher to researcher. Some researchers limit the primary family functions to the economic and sexual functions; others may include additional functions such as childbearing and socialization. Still others qualify the sexual function by suggesting that it may or may not be part of the relationship matrix. Implicit in these definitions is the notion that cohabitation involves a heterosexual dyadic relationship. Table 1 lists various specific definitions used in cohabitation surveys.

American researchers [1] have generally agreed that the concept of cohabitation be nominally defined in terms of a heterosexual couple consistently sharing a living facility without a legal contract. Macklin (1972) was the first to use the time dimension as a key component in classifying cohabitation relationships. She noted that her fairly inclusive definition would give researchers a more complete picture of the many varieties of cohabitation that

Table 1.

Definitions of Cohabitation and Closely Related Concepts From Selected Studies

Researcher(s)	Definition
Arafat and Yorburg (1973)	"living together relationship with a member of opposite sex"
Bower (1974, 1975) and Cole and Bower (1974)	"a heterosexual couple 'consistently' sharing a living facility without legal contract"
Claesson, Lindgren, and Lindth (1973)	"man and woman live together, with or without children, and fulfill family functions without formally marrying"
Clatworthy (1975)	"a heterosexual couple 'consistently' sharing a living facility without legal contract, . . . if the couple feel they are living together then they are. . ."
Cole (1973a, 1974)	"share bedroom and/or bed with someone of the opposite sex for four or more nights a week for three or more consecutive months, . . . a heterosexual couple 'consistently' sharing a living facility without legal contract"
Guittar and Lewis (1974); Lewis, Spanier, Storm, and LeHecka (1975); and Storm (1973)	"two people of the opposite sex who live together in a common residence for at least 75 percent of the time (about five days and nights out of the week)"
Henze and Hudson (1974)	"two unrelated persons of the opposite sex living together without being legally married"
Hickrod (1972)	"two non-related members of the opposite sex sharing common habitat duties and responsibilities of housekeeping, with or without sexual relationships and with or without any marriage ceremony"
Johnson (1968, 1973a)	"the relationship between an unmarried couple is similar to what has been called a 'common-law union' "
Kalmback (1973)	"share bedroom and/or bed with someone of the opposite sex for four or more nights for three or more consecutive months"
Kieffer (1972)	"the quasi-marital relationship between a male and a female who are not married to each other by legal ceremony or by common law and who occupy the same dwelling unit as a residence on a more or less regular basis. The relationship is assumed for an indefinite period of time and does not assume legal status with its consummation, as in common-law. The noncontractual nature of consensual cohabitation distinguishes it from the contractual cohabitation of marriage"
Lautenschlager (1972)	"two persons of the opposite sex living together in a relatively permanent manner similar in many respects to marriage but without legal or religious sanctions"
Lyness, Lipetz, and Davis (1972)	"the situation where a man and a woman who are not married to each other nor by common-law arrangement occupy the same dwelling"
Macklin (1972, 1974)	"share a bedroom and/or bed with someone of the opposite sex to whom not married for four or more nights a week for three or more consecutive months "
Montgomery (1972, 1973)	"when two cross-sex individuals live together in what is essentially a full-time way and they define themselves as a couple"
Nasholm (1972)	"two adult persons of different sex living together under marriage-like conditions in the same household without having officially confirmed their relationship through marriage"
Peterman, Ridley, and Anderson (1974)	"are now or have ever lived with someone of the opposite sex"
Shuttlesworth and Thorman (1974)	"am or have been living with a person of the opposite sex to whom not married"
Smith and Kimmel (1970)	"single students of opposite sex living together, usually in off-campus apartments"
Trost (1975)	"living together under marriage-like conditions but without a marriage"

exist on the college campus and elsewhere. Macklin (1972) proposed the following typology of cohabitation:

Type A— Relationships involving sharing a bed or bedroom for at least four nights a week for three or more consecutive months.

Type B— Relationships involving sharing a bed or bedroom less than four nights a week for three or more consecutive months.

Type C— Relationships involving sharing a bed or bedroom for four or more nights a week for less than three consecutive months.

Type D— Relationships involving sharing a bed or bedroom for less than four nights a week for less than three consecutive months.

Other researchers (e.g., Clatworthy, 1975; Lyness et al., 1972; Peterman et al., 1974; Henze & Hudson, 1974) have not utilized the time dimension as a critical criterion in distinguishing types of cohabitation. Many researchers (e.g., Henze & Hudson, 1974; Peterman et al., 1974; Thorman, 1973; Clatworthy, 1975; and Lyness et al., 1972) have utilized self-definitions of cohabitation in which the actors define their relationship as living with someone of the opposite sex. This makes it difficult to differentiate between long-term, ongoing relationships and short-term, transitory relationships. Trost (1975, p. 677) proposes using a "phenomenological definition, which means that . . . cohabitation is used for the phenomenon of living together under marriage-like conditions but without a marriage." Trost's definition is consistent with many of the other European researchers' definitions (e.g., Nasholm, 1972; and Claesson et al., 1973) in that it implies that cohabitors share many of the same marital and family functions as do married couples. None of these European researchers explicated the nature of the marriage-like functions clearly enough to clarify the nature of pair bonding.

I view the cohabitation relationship as a special type of primary relationship in which the partners meet socioemotional, sociosexual, sociophysical, and socioeconomic needs and maintenance functions. My view implies that the cohabitation relationship involves a relatively large degree of interpersonal commitment in order to meet interpersonal need and support system functions. As O'Neill and O'Neill (1972a, 1972b) have observed, it is difficult if not impossible for one primary relationship to meet all of a person's needs. Kieffer (see Chapter 18) further suggests that intimacy needs are ordinarily met by multiple significant others in varied types of relationships. However, the sociological literature on primary relationships and small groups indicates that the participants in a small group have to be well integrated into the group for the group to operate as a significant support system. This does not rule out, of course, the possibility of the individuals moving in and out of significant social relationships of a primary group nature. As Libby (see Chapter 4) points out, an individual has a variety of options for meeting interpersonal needs during the course of his or her lifetime. Libby implies that cohabitation as a life-style might well be considered transitional for many individuals.

In this article, my definition of cohabitation is *a more or less permanent relationship in which two unmarried persons of the opposite sex share a living facility without legal contract.* Implicit in my definition is the notion of the time dimension which Macklin (1972) suggests is important. Common-law marriages might be subsumed under this definition of cohabitation if we assume that the nature of the consensual union is voluntary and not legally binding by written or unwritten contracts between the partners. The qualifier, "not legally binding by written or unwritten contracts between partners," is important since a large number of long-term cohabitants report that they have negotiated some type of interpersonal contract that specifies formation, maintenance, and dissolution contingencies.

How Widespread Is Cohabitation?

As Trost (1975) notes, the answer to the question, "How widespread is cohabitation?" is dependent upon what is meant by cohabitation. Using the definition I proposed above, I would consider all heterosexual partners who are not legally married to each other and who consistently share a common living facility with each other as cohabiting. This definition will allow me to use census data as well as campus survey data to estimate how prevalent the phenomenon of living together outside of marriage is both in the United States and in some of the Scandinavian countries as well.

Based upon data from the 1970 U.S. census (U.S. Bureau of Census, 1973) approximately .2 percent (143,000 unmarried couples) of the adult population (based upon persons eighteen years of age and older) are living with a partner of the opposite sex to whom they are not legally married. This statistic (143,000 unmarried couples) can be thought of as a crude estimate of the number of unmarried couples cohabiting as of the 1970 census in the United States. It is very probably a conservative estimate since college student populations would not systematically be represented in that census figure. Safire (1973) notes that the incidence of cohabitation is not restricted to the younger generation. She points out that cohabitation is increasingly prevalent among the middle-aged who are separated or divorced as well as among the elderly who are widowed. Bernard (1975) notes that living with nonrelatives is more prevalent among men than women who are separated (5.4 percent of the women and 25.6 percent of the men) and divorced (6.1 percent of the women and 17.8 percent of the men). Slight differences also were observed among single women and men who were living together with unrelated individuals (7.3 percent of the women and 8.1 percent of the men). It is uncertain from these data what percent of the cases involving individuals living with nonrelatives and unrelated individuals involves cohabitation as defined in this chapter. Bernard (1975) points out, however, that one can speculate that many of the unmarried individuals (including single never married as well as divorced) who are living with unrelated individuals may be living together with a member of the opposite sex in cohabitation.

Perhaps the most complete data, even though unrepresentative of the

Table 2.

Prevalence of Cohabitation on American College Campuses Based Upon Selected Cohabitation Surveys

Researcher(s)	Time of Study	Region of Country and Campus Type	Number of Respondents and Sample Type	Male/Female Ratio		Housing Policy Permits		Percentage of Cohabitation
				M	F	Off-Campus Housing	24-Hour Visitation	
Arafat and Yorburg (1973)	1971	Northeast Large Urban Univ.	765 (Convenience)	58%	42%	Yes	N.A.	20%
Clatworthy (1975)	1973	Mideast Large State Univ. (Urban Area)	—	—	—	Yes	Yes	22%
Cole (1973a)	1973	Mideast Small Liberal Arts College (Rural Area)	190 (Stratified-Random)	51%	49%	Some	Yes	17%
Cole (1974)	1974	Mideast Small Liberal Arts College (Rural Area)	163 (Stratified-Random)	53%	47%	No	Restricted (except Srs.)	9%
Huang (1972)	1971	Midwest Large State Univ. (Urban Area)	643 (Convenience)	45%	55%	Yes	Yes	12%
Henze and Hudson (1974)	1972	Southwest Large State Univ. (Urban Area)	291 (Random)	57%	43%	Yes	Yes	23%
Lautenschlager (1972)	1972	West Coast Large State Univ. (Urban Area)	519 (Convenience)	54%	43%	Yes	Yes	25%
Macklin (1974)	1972	Northeast Large Private Univ. (Small City)	299 (Stratified-Random)	65%	35%	Yes	Yes	31%
Peterman, Ridley, and Anderson (1974)	1972	Northeast Large State Univ. (Small City)	1099 (Stratified-Random)	66%	34%	Yes	Yes	33%
Shuttlesworth and Thorman (1974)	1972	Southwest Large State Univ. (Urban Area)	431 (Convenience)	60%	40%	Yes	Yes	36%

U.S. population as a whole, are on college students who are cohabiting. (See Table 2.) At least nine college campuses have been surveyed about the incidence of cohabitation. Some of the surveys (Cole, 1973a, 1974; Henze & Hudson, 1974; Macklin, 1974; Peterman et al., 1974) are based upon probability samples and thus can be thought to be more representative of their respective campuses than can the nonprobability sample-based surveys (Arafat & Yorburg, 1973; Lautenschlager, 1972; and Shuttlesworth & Thorman, 1974). As Macklin (1974) notes, the incidence of nonmarital cohabitation on the college campus varies from less than 10 percent of the student body to more than 33 percent. Furthermore, she notes (1974, p. 55) that the reported incidence of cohabitation on the college campuses surveyed is dependent upon "a variety of factors: the schools' geographic locations, housing and parental regulations and their enforcement, the male-female student ratio, the researchers' sampling methods and their definition of cohabitation" (1974, p. 55). Macklin further notes that in her study of the Cornell campus the cohabitation rates varied by class standing and sex, with 54 percent of the female seniors and 27 percent of the male seniors cohabiting as opposed to 27 percent of the female sophomores and 13 percent of the male sophomores. She explains the male-female differential in cohabitation rates as a function of the opportunity structure since the male-female ratio on the Cornell campus gives females an almost two to one advantage in selecting potential partners. The increase in cohabitation rates by class standing indicates a general trend toward intimacy escalating with age.

It is possible to generate a number of propositions about the incidence of cohabitation on the basis of data from campus surveys. Take, for example, the opportunity structure that is comprised of factors such as sex ratios, university housing facilities and policies, economic resources and independence, etc. Each of these factors could be used as an independent variable in constructing empirically verifiable hypotheses that predict that the incidence of cohabitation will be greater in environments that have a sex ratio favorable to partner selection opportunity, that have open housing and twenty-four-hour visitation policies, and where the individuals command a measure of economic independence.

Political pressure and social policy in the society at large no doubt have an effect upon the incidence of cohabitation. Hayner (1966) notes that in Mexico the rate of unmarried cohabitation was one fifth as high as the legal marriage rate (20 percent of the couples living together were unmarried) in 1950. Trost (1975) notes that the Mexican government succeeded in encouraging an estimated 240,000 unmarried couples to get married officially and legalize their relationships in response to a governmental "Wedding Days" proclamation. These data suggest that one might generate propositions about the incidence of cohabitation as being a function of social policy and political action. One such proposition would be that the incidence of cohabitation will vary inversely with the amount of political pressure applied through social policies to encourage marriage.

Sweden and Denmark provide converse examples to Mexico; social policies and societal sanctions have become liberalized in these Scandinavian countries and provide greater opportunity for cohabitation without fear of social stigma. Trost (1975) reports that, according to a 1974 national sample survey in Sweden, 12 percent of the couples living together were cohabiting out of wedlock. Furthermore, Trost (1975) hypothesizes that as the marriage rate decreases, the rate of nonmarital cohabitation increases. He cites two countries that are evidencing this trend, Sweden and Denmark, thus providing empirical support for his hypothesis.

Relationship Adjustment Processes

Social interaction between cohabitant partners suggests that each partner takes the other into account and continually adapts and adjusts to the social situation as he or she subjectively defines it. Research has identified several social processes applicable to cohabitation including dyadic formation, decision making, relationship maintenance, conflict and change, and dissolution. These processes, of course, are not unique to cohabitation and apply at a general level to all social relationships. Their consideration here, however, is necessary if one is to obtain a clearer view of the dynamics of living in a cohabitation relationship.

Dyadic Formation

How does a couple initiate a cohabitation relationship? Research by Macklin (1972, 1974), Cole (1973a, 1974), Clatworthy (1975), Johnson (1968), Kieffer (1972), and Storm (1973) suggests that most couples do not make a conscious decision to live together but rather tend to gradually drift together as a result of spending increasing amounts of time together. The pattern usually starts with the partners spending one night a week together, moves on to their adding a second and then a third night a week, until one of them gradually finds it more convenient to move more clothes and personal items over to the other's room or apartment, and ends with their moving in and living together. At the point in the process when the partners move in together, the social reality of their relationship undergoes a significant change that calls for a new subjective assessment of that relationship. They must now redefine their social situation to account for the fact that they are cohabiting. This redefinition frequently is accompanied by a reassessment of their feelings toward their partner as well as their own self-concept. If the partners perceive that cohabiting provides them with a favorable reward-cost ratio, they will likely continue to live together. Some of the possible rewards include more frequent sexual opportunities and feeling a sense of satisfaction from the companionship and emotional support afforded by living with someone of the opposite sex.

Research on cohabitation among college students indicates that few relationships are formed as a result of overt planning and action. In fact, very few partners even reveal their personal expectations of what the relationship is hoped to be and/or to become before they actually move in together. Part of this could be due to the fact that they are in an anomic, highly transitory stage in their lives. College students lack culturally sanctioned role models to guide them in forming their interpersonal relationships. It is also likely that they have learned through past relationships that one can be hurt, which is a cost, when relationships are being negotiated through the bargaining process (Blau, 1964; Scanzoni, 1972). Covert bargaining to enter a cohabitation relationship may be viewed as a means of attempting to minimize the cost, or the hurt, if the partner does not reciprocate. By not fully disclosing personal expectations, the partners are operating at a low degree of cost commitment that provides them with a safety valve for ending the relationship if they feel that the reward-cost ratio is below their minimal acceptance level (comparison level). The tenuous nature of the initial commitments made in the bargaining process is evidenced by the fact that a majority of student partners choose to maintain their old room in the beginning stages of their relationship just in case it does not work out. Having this type of safety valve to retreat to can also be viewed as keeping one's alternatives open, assuring more options and thus providing credits that can be cashed in at some future time.

Cole (1976) proposes that cohabiting couples develop *interpersonal existential commitments* to each other and their relationship. Interpersonal commitments promote future transactions, self-other investments, and dyadic cohesion. Johnson (1973a, p. 396) prefers the term *personal commitment*, which he defines as "the extent to which an actor is dedicated to the completion of a line of action." Johnson's notion of personal commitment implies that the individuals entering a cohabitation relationship are bonded together only to the degree that both partners are determined to develop an enduring relationship for as long as it takes to fulfill the expected purpose(s) of living together.

Tentative results of my own research (Cole & Bower, unpublished longitudinal research in progress) reported in Bower's thesis (1975) suggest that most cohabitants considered their relationship as strong, affectionate, and excluding outside dating when they began to live together. Similar results are cited in research by Macklin (1972) and Shuttlesworth and Thorman (1974), while Kalmback (1973) found that the largest portion of her sample (46 percent) began cohabitation with a strong, affectionate, nonexclusive relationship. Based upon data on the degree of commitment they had to the relationship at the time they began cohabiting, I found that only a minority of cohabitants were committed to marry their partner (6 percent) or to definitely work hard to develop a lasting relationship (7 percent). The majority were committed to stay together as long as the relationship was mutually satisfying (38 percent) or personally enjoyable (31 percent). Almost one fifth (18 percent) of the cohabitants I interviewed entered the relationship with no stated commitment to make it permanent. These data suggest that most cohabitants will invest time and energy in a relationship as long as the rewards (satisfactions and enjoyments) outweigh the costs (sacrifices). Bower (1975) reports that the majority of cohabitants (both male and female) indicated that they benefited from their relationship in the sense that they increased their understanding of what was involved in a relationship. The experience will also shape their expectations for future relationships.

Clatworthy (1975) notes that cohabitants felt that the most important characteristics one could have in order to successfully cohabit were maturity and self-confidence. My own research has shown that the couple's emotional maturity and self-esteem determine their ability to communicate feelings and needs.

Decision Making

Little research has been done on the decision-making patterns and processes of cohabiting couples. My own data (based upon unpublished research in progress)[2] suggest that fairly complex decision-making patterns are established among long-term cohabitors. For example, among the forty couples that I had in-depth interviews with after a year or more of cohabitation, the majority (75 percent) evidenced segmentalized decision making, where primary decision-making responsibility was allocated to one partner more than the other or both. In many cases, decision-making responsibility was based upon the individual partner's background, interests, and competencies. For instance, if one partner owned the car prior to cohabitation, he or she would most likely be the person primarily responsible for decisions regarding its maintenance and care. The couples I interviewed usually made decisions on the basis of who was most involved in a particular area or affected by the outcome of the decision. All of the couples indicated that some of the decisions were made jointly. I observed that females were responsible for more sectors than were males. It is unclear whether or not this greater female responsibility is indicative of traditional sex-role inequality where the woman is frequently relegated a disproportionate share of the responsibility for household tasks and decisions.

Relationship Maintenance

Social relationships that endure for a very long time develop patterns of interaction and a social organization. A social structure eventually emerges with a division of labor for carrying out relationship maintenance tasks. Cohabitants, as do marrieds, frequently divide labor along sex-role lines. At least six studies (Johnson, 1968; Macklin, 1972; Henze & Hudson, 1974; Kieffer, 1972; Danziger & Greenwald, 1974; Cole & Bower, 1974) have suggested that cohabitation is not as equalitarian in the assignment of sex roles and/or household tasks as one might expect. Bower (1975) reports findings on household tasks and responsibilities that reveal perceptual differences on who does what around the house. Table 3 indicates that males perceive gender role equality in the assignment of responsibility for jobs, while their female partners view the situation quite differently. Females perceive themselves to be doing most of the work.

Related to the social structure of the relationship is the issue of boundaries. Cohabiting couples have to establish the relative importance of specific areas of separateness and togetherness. Related to the issue of relationship

Table 3.

Ratings of Selected Relationship Maintenance Jobs, by Sex. (In Percent)

| | Male Responsibility | | | Female Responsibility | |
	Usually	Always	Whoever	Usually	Always
A. **By Male Cohabitants**					
Wash dishes	7	3	61	19	3
Initiate sex	39	8	48	5	—
Handle finances	21	13	40	8	2
Shop for food	5	2	53	23	7
Care for car	23	42	15	2	3
Clean floors	11	3	32	29	5
Cook meals	47	3	31	7	13
Deal with landlord	15	24	23	8	5
Bring in money	11	5	58	5	3
Care for pet	3	3	23	13	7
Pick up around house	13	—	60	21	2
Make minor repairs	52	31	13	—	2
Empty garbage	34	15	37	3	2
Wash clothes	5	3	44	34	10
B. **By Female Cohabitants**					
Wash dishes	10	2	40	35	10
Initiate sex	30	2	64	5	—
Handle finances	11	19	36	6	5
Shop for food	8	2	48	25	5
Care for car	14	40	18	5	10
Clean floors	8	2	33	24	19
Cook meals	3	—	41	40	11
Deal with landlord	11	28	27	3	6
Bring in money	10	23	8	53	7
Care for pet	5	2	20	11	6
Pick up around house	2	—	59	36	3
Make minor repairs	39	19	22	5	—
Empty garbage	27	13	45	2	5
Wash clothes	10	2	37	27	19

NOTE: Some categories add up to less than 100 percent becaust they were not applicable to certain couples.

Adapted from Bower (1975, p. 372)

boundaries is the notion of exclusive versus nonexclusive sharing and intimacy. Tentative findings from Huang (1976) suggest that about 7 percent of her sample of cohabiting couples had agreed to be nonexclusive. For these sexually nonexclusive couples relationship equity and openness are highly valued. Huang further posits that these couples are in quest of new ways of relating to multiple significant others on deeper, more intimate levels. Her data focus upon sexual sharing in a physical sense but fail to examine other socioemotional and sociointellectual components of intimacy. Kieffer, however (see Chapter 18), discusses multiple dimensions of intellectual, physical, and emotional intimacy and how these relate to personal development and relationship maintenance. See O'Neill and O'Neill (1972a) for a discussion of the open marriage model and the closed relationship model which are applicable to cohabitation as well as marriage. Lyness et al. (1972) propose that qualitative relationships are built upon and maintained by mutual trust, respect, willingness to share personal feelings and reciprocity, sexual satisfaction, happiness with the relationship, emotional involvement in the relationship, and commitment.

Communication is vital to keeping the relationship viable for meeting each partner's needs. Bower (1975) reports that effective communication is more significantly related to the female's than the male's adjustment to their relationship. Bower's report is consistent with much of the earlier marriage literature (Luckey, 1960; Stuckert, 1963), which points out that it is important for marital satisfaction that the wife accurately perceive her husband, but not important in itself that the husband understand his wife. This suggests that, in the past and to some degree at present, women have made the adjustments to a relationship. More recent research on marital adjustment (Bienvenu, 1970), however, has consistently shown communication to be highly important for both wives and husbands.

Conflict and Change

One of the most critical areas of adjustment in any social relationship is conflict management. Hennon (1974) notes that cohabiting couples negotiate conflict on the basis of ground rules that emerge from interaction. The ground rules may include such things as when and how the partners will negotiate differences. The rules generally include a set of parameters that will govern how much time and energy each partner can realistically be expected to invest for a specific conflict resolution. The conflict management approach to cohabitation adjustment assumes that conflict is a natural process that is vital for producing change within the relationship, implying a dynamic rather than a consensus model. Open communication facilitates learning and the adoption of new modes of negotiating conflict situations. I view conflict resolution as an adaptive process rather than the outcome of a zero-sum game that suggests that one party has to lose in order for the other party to win. In terms of exchange theory, if one partner wins a disproportionate amount of the time, the relationship is out of balance. If the losing partner perceives that his or her comparison level for alternatives provides more attractive options, then the exchange relationship will be terminated. Reciprocity is the key in an exchange relationship such as cohabitation. In order for cohabitation to be maintained, it is critical that the dynamics of conflict resolution be relatively balanced, allowing each partner at least a minimal level of satisfaction with how the conflicts are resolved.

Dissolution

What happens when cohabitation relationships fail to meet the interpersonal needs of individuals? In the majority of cases the relationship will be dissolved. It is evident from the data on commitment that most student co-habitants view the relationship as important and worth continuing only as long as it provides mutual satisfaction and enjoyment which they feel is re-warding enough to work for through their investment of self.

Macklin (1974), Clatworthy (1975), and Shuttlesworth and Thorman (1974) note that cohabitation is usually viewed as a positive experience. Even in the cases where the relationship dissolved, most cohabitants felt they had gained something important from the experience. Shuttlesworth and Thorman (1974) report that over 80 percent of the cohabitants in their sample felt that the experience gave them deeper self-understanding and in general fostered their emotional growth. It is difficult to ascertain how dur-able cohabitation relationships are over time. Kieffer (1972, 1976) suggests that 65 to 70 percent of her cohabiting couples reported that they intended to stay together in a cohabitation relationship or move into a legal marriage. Kieffer cautions, however, that there are differences in behavioral intentions and actualities. Macklin's (1974) data indicate that many cohabitation rela-tionships are relatively durable; about 20 percent of her sample of cohabi-tants at Cornell had previously experienced a cohabitation relationship of at least three months' duration that had dissolved by the time of her study.

Cohabitation dissolution and divorce are similar in that the partners go through many of the same processes of postrelationship adjustment. Wise-man (1975) thinks of the divorce process as a series of stages ranging from denial, loss, and depression, to anger and ambivalence, to reorientation and the creation of a new identity, and finally on to the acceptance of the new life-style and achieving a new level of functioning. In another paper (Cole, 1976) I discuss how these same processes apply to cohabitation dissolution as well.

Limitations, Issues, and Directions for Research

A critical assessment of the literature on cohabitation reveals problems in the areas of conceptualization, measurement, and sampling. Few studies have adequately drawn from sociological and social psychological theory in formulating theoretical models to explain the social significance of the co-habitation life-style. The work done prior to the 1973 Groves Conference Workshop on Cohabitation (see Reference Note 1) is very difficult to inter-pret with regard to what is meant by cohabitation and its prevalence. A wide variety of labels were used to refer to the phenomenon of an unmarried het-erosexual couple sharing a common bedroom. There were also about as many definitions and measures of cohabitation (refer back to Table 1) as there were studies. Most work since the workshop has attempted to use uni-form labels and operational measures of the phenomenon. Since most re-search to date has been limited to a few college communities, it is difficult to generalize beyond the campuses surveyed. Less than six of the surveys dis-cussed in this article drew their respondents from probability samples. Sam-ples composed of a class of students in family studies or any other specialized area tell us little about the larger university community. Therefore, we must concede that our data bases for understanding and explaining cohabitation are very limited.

Research (Cole & Bower, 1974; Lewis, Spanier, Storm, & LeHecka, 1975) suggests that more attention needs to be given to distinguishing between the types of cohabitation. Couples differ in their motives for entering the relationship. Johnson (1973b) suggests that at least three types of cohabitation are analytically distinguishable: (1) cohabitation before marriage which serves as a prelude to marriage; (2) quasi-marriages and common-law relationships, practicing marriage without obtaining a license and/or going through a wedding ceremony; and (3) cohabitation as an alternative lifestyle.

Since cohabitation involves a pair-bond relationship, it is important to focus upon the couple as the unit of analysis. This can be accomplished by developing unit measures that reflect both partners' perspectives (Cole, 1973). A variety of behavioral observation techniques, such as simulation gaming (as recommended by Straus, 1971), interaction over revealed differences from partners observed in conjoint interviews (as recommended by Strodbeck, 1951), etc., could be used to obtain data on pair-bond interaction patterns and processes, communication styles, conflict management and resolution patterns and processes, as well as power and decision-making patterns and processes. Data obtained from direct behavioral observations could then be combined with retrospective life histories (as recommended by Stein, 1975) and questionnaire data to develop a more complete picture of the dynamics of cohabitation.

The cohabitation relationship, like all relationships, changes over time and thus must be studied longitudinally. Paneled studies could be used with age and relationship-type[3] cohorts followed over time. Although the costs of paneled studies are great, the payoff in terms of our understanding of the complexities of relationship processes would be even greater. Paneled studies would need to employ control groups of married couples and, possibly, individuals engaged in multilateral relationships as well in order to determine which relationship processes are unique to cohabitation and which also are characteristic of marital dyads and/or more complex intimate relationships. Such research would call for a national probability sample, and it will be a long time before adequate funding can be secured for a project of that scope. Therefore, it is important for cohabitation researchers now to pool their limited resources, to do cooperative and collaborative research (as suggested by Macklin, 1974), and to work toward building a reliable data base.

In order to understand the meaning and social significance of cohabitation as a life-style, the five broad questions that follow must be answered in the near future. The first three questions have been modified from Libby's chapter on creative singlehood to apply to cohabitation. The last two questions stem from research by Macklin (1974), Peterman et al. (1974), Henze and Hudson (1974), Lyness et al. (1972), Johnson (1973b), and Cole.

1. How do cohabitants' happiness, adjustment, and interpersonal commitment patterns vary over time and by locality, past relationship his-

tories (whether they have cohabited before, been married before, lived alone without intimate relationships before, lived in a commune before, lived in a multilateral relationship, lived with a member of their own sex), education, occupation, income and social status, race, migration patterns, sexual orientation and history (whether they are heterosexual only, have been homosexual but are now heterosexual only, or bisexual now formerly homosexual, bisexual formerly heterosexual, have always been bisexual, the number of sexual partners and experiences they have had, etc.), cohabitation type (whether they define the relationship as leading to marriage, a substitute for marriage, or an alternative life-style), and age?

2. What proportion of the population is currently cohabiting or has ever cohabited by each of the relationship types, age, sex, race, religion, ethnicity, locality, and socioeconomic status?

3. How do those who select cohabitation make such a choice by age, sex, relationship type, religion, ethnicity, locality, socioeconomic status, past relationship histories, and sexual orientations and histories? Who serves as a role model for cohabitants and how do role models change over time? What are the effects of specific reference groups, significant others, attitudes and values, mass media, etc., on the choice of cohabitation? What is the relative viability of the life-style? What are the key social support systems that operate to enhance the viability of cohabitation? And what are the key negative sanctions that impede the growth and development of the life-style?

4. What factors lead to a positive cohabitation experience (as measured by such things as emotional maturity, self-concept, interpersonal relationship skill competence, life satisfaction, relationship adjustment, and interpersonal commitment) by age, sex, relationship type, education and student status, race, religion, ethnicity, locality, and socioeconomic status? How and for whom is cohabitation beneficial (as measured by changes in levels of emotional maturity, self-concept, interpersonal competence, life satisfaction, relationship adjustment, and interpersonal commitment) and why?

5. What are the interrelationships over time between rates of the various types of cohabitation, marriage rates, divorce rates, singlehood, parenthood, level of societal complexity, and social policies governing interpersonal life-style choice?

Trends and Speculations

Cohabitation is becoming normative on a number of college campuses as a part of a new courtship pattern. This new pattern values the experience of intimate sharing (involving the whole relationship, not just the sexual aspects) with someone of the opposite sex as a means of exploring new levels of self-awareness and emotional growth. It remains to be seen whether or not cohabitation will fulfill the expectations of those subscribing to the new courtship pattern's value system. Campus cohabitation is characterized as a relatively intense dyadic experience based upon a deep level of emotional involvement and interpersonal commitment (Macklin, 1974).

It is highly likely that the incidence of cohabitation will steadily increase as the opportunities for more freedom in the selection of residence and room-mates become more widespread. Many campuses already have coed dorms and generally enforce few, if any, restrictions on off-campus housing, twenty-four-hour visitation, etc. Even on campuses where housing policies are restrictive, there is evidence of students desiring the option to cohabit. As social forces peel away the last elements of in loco parentis from the college campus, it is likely that university policies regarding sexual morals, housing, etc., will become more liberal.

Perhaps the conservative elements of society will attempt to inhibit the liberalization of housing policies on college campuses. It is probable that con-servative pockets will continue to exist in those regions of the country where fundamentalist religious groups are the strongest. Knowledge of social change within the United States would lead me to believe that the two coastal areas would be the innovators and lead the trend while the South and Mid-west would lag behind. Tentative evidence on rates of cohabitation on college campuses across the nation suggests such a pattern.

If campus cohabitation continues to be viewed as primarily a premarital behavior in the context of a new courtship pattern, it will likely have little im-pact upon the institution of marriage. One of the things that will probably happen, however, is that the age at marriage for first marriages will go up. It is also possible that the divorce rate for first marriages in the first years of marriage will go down as a result of cohabitation serving as a screening de-vice to lower the probability of mismatched mates marrying. Theoretically, the cohabitation period would allow the partners to work through many of the dyadic adaption and adjustment processes that couples who married without first having lived together would have to go through. These empiri-cal speculations must be closely examined if we are ever going to understand the impact of premarital cohabitation upon subsequent marital behavior.

In the event that campus as well as noncampus cohabitation becomes in-creasingly viewed as an alternative life-style, the marriage rates for first mar-riages would drop. This would have implications for the institution of the family as we know it today. Furthermore, if the family shrank in importance within our society, it would imply changes in other institutions. It would most surely necessitate changes in social policy, which is primarily based upon the assumption that the vast majority of people live in nuclear families. That assumption, although widespread, is already erroneous. The 1970 Cen-sus (U.S. Bureau of Census, 1973) reports that only 37 percent of the Ameri-can population resides in a nuclear family unit, which is defined as a bread-winner husband/father and a homemaker wife/mother and their dependent children residing in a common dwelling. Another probable change would be a reduction in the birth rate since most cohabiting couples who view their rela-tionship as an alternative life-style report that they desire to remain childless. Childlessness too would have implications for other areas of society. The economy would have to shift more toward marketing adult consumer goods and services since there would be less demand for children's consumer items.

At present, however, it does not appear likely that a large proportion of the cohabiting population will be living life-styles that radically deviate from the institution of marriage as we know it today. I do not anticipate cohabitation replacing marriage as a social institution. It seems to me that the greatest impact of cohabitation will be upon the courtship institution with some, at present undetermined, incidental effect upon the institution of marriage.

Implications for Personal Decision Making

Cohabitation is but one avenue for achieving intimacy. It is clear that the desire for intimacy has been a strong motivational force for many individuals to enter cohabitation relationships. Cohabitation, like many other alternative life-styles, requires a relatively high level of interpersonal commitment if it is to be a truly meaningful relationship. A meaningful relationship requires personal competency in dyadic formation as well as relationship maintenance skills, such as being able to effectively communicate, negotiate in decision making and conflict management, etc. A positive self-concept seems to be essential for both mastering interpersonal relationship skills and for attaining personal growth in highly intimate relationships. As Kieffer notes (Chapter 18), the world of alternative life-styles is no place for naive people.

Reference Notes

1. Macklin (1974) notes that a variety of labels have been used to refer to an unmarried heterosexual couple sharing a common bedroom. Some of the terms used include: *living together* (Lyness et al., 1972); *living together unmarried* (Whitehurst, 1973); *two-step marriage* (Mead, 1966); *companionate marriage* (Lindsey, 1926); *unmarried college liaisons* (Whitehurst, 1969); *live-ins* (Clatworthy, 1975); *trial marriage* (Berger, 1971); *consensual unions* (Lautenschlager, 1972); *consensual cohabitation* (Kieffer, 1972); and perhaps the most commonly agreed upon label, *cohabitation* (Macklin, 1972, 1973, & 1974; Johnson, 1968, 1973; Kieffer, 1972; Montgomery, 1973; Henze & Hudson, 1974; Cole, 1973; Bower, 1974, 1975; Peterman et al., 1974). The fact that cohabitation has been defined differently by various researchers makes it difficult to make meaningful comparisons between various studies that use different definitions and/or labels. In order to make some sense out of available research data, a group of researchers organized an ad hoc research task force at the 1973 Groves Conference on Marriage and the Family. Out of that workshop came the following definition of cohabitation: "A heterosexual couple consistently sharing a living facility without legal contract." "Consistently sharing" implies that the relationship is continuous and not an on and off affair of short duration. "Without legal contract" means that it is a consensual cohabitation (as suggested by Kieffer, 1972) that is distinguishable from marriage and/or common-law marriage.

2. Cole and Bower are doing longitudinal research on cohabitation that involves following cohabiting couples through several years of their relationships. The project is complex and among its many objectives is to study relationship processes and to develop indicators of relationship quality based upon data that will compare couples living together in cohabitation pair-bond relationships with those who eventually marry and with those who subsequently split up. We are interested in finding out in more detail what, if any, relationship processes are different for couples who continue living together and those who marry. We are attempting to collect data on as many couples as possible from all areas of the country and representative of as many age groups and social classes as well as racial and ethnic backgrounds as possible. To facilitate our data collection, we have relied heavily upon help from professional colleagues teaching and practicing as counselors in a variety of settings. If you would be interested in helping us in our research, please write the author, Dr. Charles L. Cole, Project Director, Cohabitation Study, c/o Department of Family Environment, LeBaron Hall, Iowa State University, Ames, Iowa, 50011.

3. By "relationship-type" I mean whether this is the first or one of a number of cohabitation experiences and how the individuals define their relationship—as a prelude to marriage, substitute for marriage, or as an alternative life-style.

6.
Extramarital and Comarital Sex:
A Critique of the Literature
Roger W. Libby

The following article offers an extensive review of the literature on extramarital and comarital sex. First the definitional problem and the semantics of emerging sexually liberated marriages are dealt with. Then Libby reviews and comments on the findings of studies beginning with Kinsey (excluding swinging and open marriage studies which are examined in Chapters 9 and 10) and ties in nonmarital and premarital trends with behavior after marriage. Key studies after Kinsey are reported in detail and some theoretical notions are introduced to provide an overview of sex after marriage. Libby also describes the cross-cultural research on extramarital sex and comments on the theoretical and methodological problems of various studies.

A major concern of this chapter is the conflict between the ground rules of marriage styles and the sexual desires of the participants in marriage. Flirtation is discussed from the points of view of those who see it as "making love without meaning it" and those who view it as behavior that no longer has relevance today. The symbolic meaning of extramarital and comarital relationships is explored in depth, with full recognition of Sprey's theory of the increasing autonomy of sexuality from marriage, the family, and parenthood. Finally, the future of marriage is examined in the context of research and theory.

An Overview

Recent books, movies, and dramatic productions indicate how extreme the curiosity and obsession with extramarital sexual behavior has become. Books such as *Adultery and Other Private Matters* by Lonny Myers and Hunter Leggitt (see Chapter 22), *The New Intimacy: Open-Ended Marriage* by Ronald Mazur (see Chapters 13 and 23), *Playing Around; Women and Extramarital Sex* by Linda Wolfe, *The Complete Handbook for a Sexually Free Marriage* by John and Mimi Lobell, *The Affair* by Morton Hunt, *Open Marriage* by Nena and George O'Neill, and *Extramarital Relations* by Gerhard Neubeck illustrate the range of symbolic meanings and motives attached to sexual intercourse beyond the marital dyad. Combine the effects of the above-mentioned popular books with other media such as novels (*Thursday, My Love* by Robert Rimmer and *Couples* by John Updike), movies

---

Excerpts from SEXUAL BEHAVIOR IN THE HUMAN MALE (1948) and SEXUAL BEHAVIOR IN THE HUMAN FEMALE (1954) by A. C. Kinsey, et al., are reprinted by permission of the Institute for Sex Research, Indiana University.

("Bob and Carol and Ted and Alice" and nearly every "adult" movie thereafter), and Broadway plays ("Promises, Promises" was one of the earliest of a long line of sexual plays, with the off-Broadway play "Let My People Come" being the epitome of a sexual musical), and one cannot help but be cognizant of the strong societal interest in the many emotions and scripts for various kinds of extramarital experiences. As Neubeck (1969) emphasizes, it is quite natural that there be an eternal attraction between the sexes. Such an attraction is played to the hilt in the mass media, for example in the popular soap operas on television. These "soaps" offer viewers the opportunity to identify with the joys and sorrows of those having extramarital love affairs and other kinds of romantic and casual sexual involvements outside the socially sanctioned marital relationship.

While many married people confine their desires to the world of fantasy, others brave the threat of the cultural stigma of "sinner" or "cheater" in order to enter into extramarital sexual relationships. It can be assumed that there are now emerging styles of marriage based on a greater acceptance of freedom to have other sexual relationships.

Several sociocultural trends support marriages which include sexual freedom in their "ground rules." The gradual passing of the double standard, the changing concept of female sexual expression, the wider availability of effective contraceptives, and greater opportunity to carry on a discreet affair (thanks to urbanization, modern transportation, and the permissiveness of the mass media) all contribute to changing conceptions of marriage. *Marriage* in this culture does not and will not always mean *monogamy*, and to some couples a form of "monogamous nonpromiscuous pluralism" (Mazur, 1968) is acceptable. The trend to a more permissive courtship system is another sociocultural trend supporting changing marital patterns. It would seem that marriage cannot stand alone in a time of social change in terms of motivations for nonmarital and premarital sexual relationships, appropriate sexual expression in various kinds of relationships, and the increased openness surrounding sexual behavior in the mass media and the mass culture. Indeed, Whitehurst's (1966) hypothesis that extramarital sex may be an extension of normal behavior has relevance to marriage and the sanctioning of extramarital relationships in the present and near future.

Before proceeding to review and critique the literature, let us discuss definitions for some of the words related to the subject of this article, as well as the need for research.

The Definitional Issues

Without standard definitions of concepts which describe styles of marriage it is confusing for the reader to understand the connotations of terms such as *extramarital* and *comarital*. Additionally, commonly accepted definitions of marriage are assumed to adequately describe marriage in the entire society. The assumption has been that the term *marriage* is equated with monogamy and exclusivity in the spousal dyad. One goal of this article is to dispel such generalizations about marriage, and to emphasize the emergence of other concepts of marriage. To accomplish this goal, we must view marriage as more than a legal or church-sanctioned relationship. What does it mean when two people are said to be married to each other? It implies that these people intimately agree on certain ground rules and expectations (or at least profess to), and that the quality of commitment to each other is such that they are engaged in a primary and centrally important relationship. However, to be married does not necessarily mean to be possessed by another or to be committed to an exclusive relationship.

Similarly, to label all sex outside a marriage relationship as *extramarital* is to cloud the nature of other sexual relationships and to say nothing about the acceptance or lack of acceptance of such behavior within the ground rules of a marriage. While the most general description of sex outside marriage could be *extramarital*, different types of sexual expression outside marriage must be distinguished by the use of more precise language. Thus, the motivations and quality of an extramarital liaison may differ from the motivations and quality of a comarital liaison. Roy and Roy (see Chapter 3) used the term *extramarital* to connote "situations which are not as clearly noncompetitive." They distinguished comarital from extramarital relationships by stating that comarital sex does not have the pejorative meanings that terms such as *adultery, extramarital*, or *unfaithfulness* tend to have. The Roys defined comarital as:

Any man-woman relationship, and/or sexual expression thereof, which exists alongside of and in addition to a marriage relationship. Such relationships are basically not competitive with the marital relationships; they may have a neutral or even a positive effect on it (1968, p. 98).

Comarital as defined by the Roys does not necessarily mean that both spouses participate in or have the freedom to participate in outside relationships. Thus, the Roys discussed wives who "come to terms with their husbands' comarital relationships . . ." (p. 105), which could well indicate that the wives were inactive outside of marriage. Later they confused the issue by stating that comarital sex is "symmetrical" for both spouses (p. 106).

Apparently cognitive awareness by spouses of comarital sex is not necessary in the Roys' definition of comarital sex. They mentioned that a discovery may lead to "a new and real warmth and gratitude toward the spouse—who may even be unaware of the other relationship" (p. 110). It is unclear how open or how honest one must be with one's spouse to qualify for honest sex, or comarital sex as defined by the Roys. Concepts such as *responsible* are not clearly spelled out. It would seem that the distinction between extramarital and comarital is largely one of acceptance by the spouse, but this is unclear.

The Roys' breakdown of comarital sex into three kinds of relationships is indicative of the broad range of possible interactions under the term *comarital*. One type of comarital relationship is on the strictly recreational level (e.g., swinging); next there is a middle ground where comarital and extramarital are nearly equated in terms of the consequences; and third is the smaller category where spouses engage in comarital sex in an established and rich relationship. All three kinds of comarital sex can be confused by using *swinging* to cover the whole range of relationships described. The Smiths emphasized that *swinging* is a much too broadly used concept to have any real utility (1970, p. 133).

Comarital was somewhat differently conceived by Smith and Smith, since they used the term to refer to

. . . married couples who are either actually involved together in establishing relationships beyond that of the marital dyad for sexual purposes, or to couples in which there is both knowledge of and consent to such relationships regardless of whether the sexual activity includes both partners or is independent to some degree (1970, p. 134).

Additionally, the Smiths would agree with the Roys that comarital sex excludes deceitful sex or sex without consent (p. 134).

For the purposes of this article, *extramarital sexual behavior* includes both traditional, conventional adultery (or *infidelity* or *cheating*) and consensual or comarital sex—two distinct types of EMS. *Comarital sex* includes both sexually open marriage (see Knapp & Whitehurst, Chapter 9) and swinging or mate sharing (see Gilmartin, Chapter 10). If both spouses are involved in comarital sex, they may carry on such behavior separately (as in sexually open marriage), or together (as in swinging). Clanton (Chapter 7) and Gilmartin (Chapter 10) use *consensual adultery* as another way to define comarital sex. I use *extramarital* as a larger rubric for sex beyond the marital dyad. As Christensen has emphasized (letter to the author, January 7, 1975), extramarital sex is the overall generic term and comarital sex is simply a subdivision of extramarital. Thus, extramarital and comarital are not opposing terms, but comarital sex is subsumed as one type of extramarital sex.[1]

Some of the extramarital sex described in this article is impossible to categorize as either comarital or adulterous (cheating), because these distinctions have rarely been made in research. Which label is used often depends on the value judgment attached to the label. Thus, if the labeler disapproves of extramarital sex, negative concepts such as "unfaithfulness," "adultery," and "cheating" may be used. Those who are more accepting of extramarital sex are likely to make distinctions between extramarital, comarital, and adulterous behavior. For the remainder of the article, extramarital sex will be abbreviated as EMS and comarital sex as CMS.

The Need for Research

Although there is much talk about EMS and CMS and a great deal of humorous and serious writing, research on the subject is sparse and lacks depth or breadth. The need for scientific data is profound. Bowman perceived the importance of doing sound research two decades ago:

The student of social relationships wants to know what these extramarital experiences *mean* to the participants, their mates, parents, friends and society in general. One of the firmest beliefs of monogamous ideology is that such 'affairs' are sordid . . . to refer to companionship and the finer sentiments of love in regard to such relationships is to suggest, from the conventional point of view, unjustifiable euphemisms for that which is debased. . . . Yet the problem of meaning cannot be brushed aside so easily, for, to some degree, cultural definitions are self-validating (1949, p. 628).

Bowman's plea for research has not been answered with any in-depth study. Yet he stated his beliefs about the benefits of such research:

If social research should begin to penetrate the moral facade, it would undoubtedly discover a variety of values in sexual intercourse where no attachments significant enough to be called love are involved. The relationship may be that of friendship or casual acquaintance, ephemeral or enduring, leading eventually to love, or hate, or indifference, or continued friendship. Through sexual experience men and women can learn a great deal about one another, not only as sexual objects but as social beings functioning in various roles (1949, p. 631).

In his book, *The Family in Search of a Future* (1970), Herbert Otto related research to the need for understanding and social engineering. He stated:

It is only with the advent of modern anthropological research and sociological theory that man has recognized his institutions, not as eternal verities, but as defined ways of being social. For the first time, he is now free to examine such institutions as marriage and the family with a certain amount of objectivity and to restructure these institutions, not in blind compliance to social pressures and economic sanctions, but in full consciousness of his needs and potentialities . . . (1970, p. 9).

Research is needed as an initial step toward understanding the social and sexual aspects of extramarital relationships which are sanctioned in marriage. Exploratory research must ascertain under what circumstances EMS and CMS are beneficial to individuals and/or to marriages, and when such relationships are a threat to individuals and marriages. To accomplish this, couples who agree on some form of marriage where extramarital sexual expression is sanctioned could be questioned to find out about the "ground rules" of their marriages (what situation and/or relationships are acceptable for extramarital relationships), and the effect of their attitudes and behavior on their self-concepts, their marriages, and their extramarital relationships. Additionally, the relationships between fantasy and actual behavior and between sexual desire and behavior could be explored. An exploratory study designed to generate hypotheses for further research and to develop a typology of styles of marriage which include some provision for extramarital sexual expression (be it petting, intercourse, oral-genital sex or whatever) is much needed. Bowman's (1949) emphasis on the *meaning* of the experience is directly related to the need for such a study. Kirkendall's (1961) emphasis on understanding distinctions between relationships which foster trust, integrity, honesty, communication, and respect, and relations which are exploitative, is crucial to such research.

Review of the Literature

Very little research has been published about extramarital sexual relationships, especially research designed to explore the rationale for extramarital or comarital relationships which are in some way approved in the marital contract.

We have as yet no study of a large random sample to indicate that the majority of Americans do or don't engage in some type of extramarital sexual behavior. Similarly, no data are available that indicate the degrees of rejection, tolerance, agreement, or full encouragement of marital partners becoming involved in other sexual and/or intimate relationships. Extreme caution must be used in generalizing to American marriage or marriage in other cultures until more definitive data are available.

The Kinsey Research

In his classic studies published in 1948 and 1953, Kinsey and his associates included questions about extramarital sexual behavior and attitudes. Since both studies were based on nonrandom samples which were biased toward northern urban populations, one must be careful when generalizing the findings to others. Nevertheless, some insights can be derived from the two studies. In the 1948 volume on males Kinsey indicated that the extramarital topic accounted for more refusals to interview than any other reason (p. 585). He also suggested that those participating in the research ". . . have probably covered up on this more often than any other single item" (p. 585). He concluded that (allowing for cover-up) about 50 percent of married males engage in extramarital intercourse (p. 585). Since Kinsey's average frequencies of intercourse according to age, social class, and so on can be misleading (e.g., the entire history of coital experience can take place in one week out of a year and be reported as once a week), I will summarize some findings here rather than citing exact frequencies.

In general it was found that lower-class males have most of their EMS at younger ages, while the opposite was true for middle- and upper-class males. As Kinsey hypothesized, this difference could relate to the higher incidence of premarital intercourse for lower-class males who may have acquired the "habit" of a variety of partners, while it may take longer for middle- and upper-class males to release their inhibitions. EMS was found to be sporadic, and few long-term affairs were documented. EMS was most common for those from urban areas, and for those who were not religiously devout (pp. 588-9). Kinsey considered sexual variety reasonable and normal for the male, as he concluded that ". . . the human male would be promiscuous in his choice of sexual partners throughout the whole of his life if there were no social restrictions" (p. 589). Kinsey assumed that females are less interested in a variety of partners due to a natural variation in the "conditionability" of the sexes. He attributed this to differences in nervous systems (p. 589). However, evidence from the intervening twenty-plus years provides some basis for concluding that cultural learning rather than inherent differences between the sexes is the deciding factor.

Kinsey stated that EMS occurred whether other sexual outlets were available or not and whether the husband were satisfied at home or not; he concluded that "most of the male's extra-marital activity is undoubtedly a product of his interest in a variety of experience" (p. 590). However, when the wife was not interested in meeting the sexual needs of the husband (as in the wife's refusal of oral-genital contacts), the husband was likely to seek EMS.

Lower-class wives were often tolerant of their husband's EMS as long as they did not learn of the particulars. They seemed to expect some EMS. While EMS was generally less accepted by the middle class, it was found that fewer problems existed in the upper classes because it was usually kept secret. EMS sometimes resulted in marital discord or divorce when it was found out by the wife, but ". . . it is sometimes had with the knowledge of the other spouse who may even aid and encourage the arrangement" (p. 592). From Kinsey's data it would appear that future research on CMS should draw on a middle- to upper-social class sample.

But what does EMS mean? The traditional double standard was noted by Kinsey, but one of his conclusions was as follows:

The significance of extra-marital intercourse may more often depend upon the attitudes of the spouses and of the social groups to which they belong, than upon the effect of the actual intercourse upon the participating individuals. Few difficulties develop out of extra-marital intercourse when the relationships are unknown to anyone but the two persons having the intercourse. . . . Extra-marital intercourse most often causes difficulty when it involves emotional and affectional relations with the new partner who takes precedence over the spouse (p. 593).

Kinsey noted that some men made better sexual adjustments in marriage due to EMS, as did women who found a new partner to be exciting and educational through teaching them how to reach orgasm (p. 593). Kinsey did not collect data on extramarital petting behavior for men, although he did for women. It would be interesting to know more about those men who pet but do not have intercourse extramaritally. This writer agrees with Kinsey that some people probably rationalize that petting is not "infidelity" like actual penile-vaginal penetration may be. Similarities between premarital and extramarital sexual moralities are probable.

In the 1953 study it was found that about 26 percent of the sample of married women had experienced extramarital intercourse by age forty, and that another 16-20 percent had engaged in petting behavior without intercourse (pp. 416, 427). Thus, although there undoubtedly was some cover-up, about 42 percent of the sample reported either extramarital petting or intercourse. It is reasonable to assume that the incidence of petting and intercourse is somewhat higher in the 1970s than in the pre-1953 period when the Kinsey data were collected. But once again, Kinsey did not have a random or representative sample of the entire nation—let alone of the "human female" as his book's title suggests. As with most of the research reviewed in this article, the Kinsey studies made no distinction between kinds of extramarital relationships (i.e., whether most or all of the extramarital sex was adulterous, or whether some of it was actually CMS).

Reiss (1960) noted that petting is related to abstinence before marriage, and that petting may be transitional behavior with the possibility of future cultural acceptance of intercourse. This would also seem to have some relevance to the acceptability of EMS or CMS, although it remains for future research to bear this out. Kinsey contended that extramarital petting was probably increasing, although he had no data to support the rate of increase (p. 426). He indicated that "a considerable amount of public petting is allowed between married adults when coitus would be unacceptable" (p. 426). Research should be designed to make distinctions between various levels of physical intimacy and to note how these intimacies affect individuals and/or marriages in various situations.

Females were most likely to have EMS in their mid-thirties and early forties if they became involved at all. They often preferred younger men (which may be due to the wish to feel young and to the lure of youthful sexual drives). Females who engaged in EMS had as many or more orgasms in EMS as in their marriages (p. 418). This is probably due to the excitement of a new partner and the likelihood of highly responsive females getting involved with EMS. As with premarital intercourse, females with more education were more likely to have EMS. About 31 percent of females in the college sample experienced EMS by age forty (p. 421). Similarly, those born before 1900 were less likely to have EMS, and high incidences were most affected by religious background (p. 424).

Of those women who had EMS, 44 percent did not intend to renew the experience. Additionally, 71 percent of the experienced wives reported no difficulties with their marriages. This is in spite of the fact that 49 percent said their husbands either knew of or suspected the EMS (p. 434). In view of the finding that 29 percent of the females with premarital experience had experienced EMS by the time of the interviews, in comparison with 13 percent of those who had not had such experience, there may well be more EMS as studies continue to indicate an increase in premarital intercourse for females (Freeman & Freeman, 1966; Packard, 1968; Kaats & Davis, 1970; Gagnon & Simon, 1969; Bell & Chaskes, 1970; Christensen & Gregg, 1970; Hall & Wagner, 1972; Zelnik & Kantner, 1972; Eshelman, 1972).[2] Kinsey indicated that females who had premarital intercourse were no more likely to have a variety of extramarital sexual partners than were females with no premarital experience (p. 428). (About 80 percent of those women with EMS experience had one to five partners regardless of the nature of their premarital experience.)

Bell (1963) noted comparisons between sexual behavior before and after marriage:

When we relate our discussion of extramarital sexual behaviour to premarital sexual behaviour, it becomes clear that the stated attitudes and actual behaviour are often in conflict in today's American society. More important, it indicates to the social scientist that the attitudes are not effective deterrents of non-marital coitus and are not incorporated by a number of individuals to the extent that their violation leads to any great guilt or remorse. . . . The lack of agreement between the moral sexual norms and the sexual behaviour of many individuals points up the 'schizoid' nature of sex in America (p. 383).

Kinsey reported several motivations for EMS for females. Females some-times wanted to acquire social status; the desire for sexual variety was an-other motivation. Other reasons included the wishes to accommodate a re-spected friend, retaliate against a spouse's EMS, assert independence from a spouse or social code, and obtain emotional satisfaction and spouse encour-agement (pp. 432-4). Of this latter rationale (which may allow a change from EMS to CMS) Kinsey commented:

There is a not inconsiderable group of cases in the sample in which the husbands had encouraged their wives to engage in extra-marital activities. . . . In some instances it represented a deliberate effort to extend the wife's opportunity to find satisfaction in sexual relations. In not a few instances the husband's attitude had originated in his de-sire to find an excuse for his own extra-marital activity. What is sometimes known as wife swapping usually involves this situation (p. 434—5).

Most of the husbands who sanctioned their wives' EMS did so in ". . . an honest attempt to give them the opportunity for additional sexual satis-faction" (p. 435). Kinsey noted that while EMS sometimes led to marital dif-ficulties and/or divorce, this was not at all inevitable. He stated:

There are strong-minded and determined individuals who can plan and control their extra-marital relationships in such a way that they avoid possible ill consequences. In such a case, however, the strong-minded spouse has to keep his or her activity from becoming known to the other spouse, unless the other spouse is . . . willing to accept the extra-marital activity. Such persons do not constitute a majority in our present-day social organization (p. 433).

The Post-Kinsey Research

Christensen (1962) cited two studies since Kinsey which sampled atti-tudes of British and French women toward EMS. Both studies employed a questionnaire. The British study done by Eustace Chesser (1956) involved six thousand subjects. Most of the females in this sample never desired EMS, and most of those who did desire EMS were those who were the least sexually satisfied and the least happy in marriage. Also, Chesser reported that about a third of married women believed that most men would like to engage in ex-tramarital intercourse even if they were happily married. The second post-Kinsey study cited by Christensen was published by the French Institute of Public Opinion in 1961. Adultery was the only concept of extramarital or comarital sex included, and it was found that almost half of the French women believed that "nearly all men" or "many men" deceive their wives by engaging in adultery. The double standard was evident in that adultery was considered more serious if engaged in by the wife than the husband, and half of the women thought it excusable if a man has a short and casual affair with another woman. Most serious affairs were seen as indicators of loss of love and confidence and of marital breakdown. Over a decade since the French and English studies, and over two decades after Kinsey's studies, the issue of the double standard continues to surface when one discusses extramarital sex, or any sex for that matter. (See Mazur, Chapter 13.)

If Reiss' (1960) observations about the passing of the double standard in courtship are applicable to extramarital and marital relationships, there may be a trend toward more sexual freedom for women as part of the trend toward more social freedom for women. As Bernard (1969) pointed out:

. . . a new kind of woman is emerging . . . and one of the distinguishing characteristics . . . is that she can be casual about sex. In the past she could not. And in the past, therefore, husbands were justified in feeling alarmed if they found out that their wives were engaged in sexual relations with another man. Because otherwise, if it hadn't been a deep relationship, she wouldn't have done so. But for the woman of today this is no longer true. They can be as casual about sexual relations in or out of marriage as men. They can accept sex at some point without conflict. Even a regular extramarital relationship does not faze them or in fact interfere with their marriage (p. 44).

What are the norms of expected conduct? Bernard feels that "The norm is not to be flagrant about it. It is being flagrant about it that violates the rule" (p. 46). This may be truer of older people than of younger people.

It is important to emphasize that youth are likely to have somewhat different visions of what they want in marriage than older adults. Freeman and Freeman (1966) found that 10–25 percent of their national sample of senior college women approved of EMS, and 5–10 percent approved of and practiced intercourse with married men. No comparable data for college men were presented. These findings must be accepted with some caution, as the authors did not go into detail in the explanation of their methods and sample.

Whitehurst hypothesized that ". . . it is possible that the youthful penchant currently in vogue for honesty in interpersonal relations may lead to more, rather than less, adultery . . . a new morality may be emerging which does not preclude EMS but prescribes the rules for it" (1969, p. 137). Whitehurst (see also Chapters 19 and 21) appraised the current situation as far as females are concerned:

. . . an increasing number of females are participating more freely while maintaining good marriages. It is just a fun thing to do and more and more people are finding out they can do it and still stay within the confines of the social order. In some sense, the increase in EMS is a function of the breakdown of the web of social controls, which become ineffective in this type of society. . . .

Consistent with Whitehurst's observations was the rationale for calling the April 1966 issue of the *Journal of Social Issues* "The Sexual Renaissance in America." The web of social controls governing sexual interaction has undoubtedly broken down in other societies. Ira Reiss, the editor of that special issue, explained:

. . . it is . . . true that regardless of what the past approach to sexual relations was in America, we are witnessing today a new interest, a national conversation, a more open attitude, and it is that which I am calling the sexual renaissance. It is the rebirth of an approach to sexuality that surely was present somewhere in our ancestors' past (1966, p. 2).

Neubeck (1969) stressed the necessity of recognizing and understanding extramarital relations. To do this we must go beyond the frequencies offered by Kinsey and ask questions about motivations for EMS and CMS, as well as the kind of social-psychological environment in which such relationships occur. As one of the contributors to the Neubeck book, Whitehurst reported a study which did go beyond mere frequencies of intercourse. The data were based on a small ($N = 112$) nonrandom sample, so caution must be exercised in making generalizations to larger populations. Whitehurst's purpose was to identify some variables which were important in understanding EMS within a sociological perspective. He contended that the monogamous base of society is maintained by boundary-maintenance through language with negative connotations. Thus he stated, "It is no chance happening that the word 'adultery' in our society has a negative connotation, but in some societies it does not" (p. 130). He added, "We have equated adultery often with 'sick, immature, narcissistic, neurotic,' and other names denoting evil" (p. 130). Similarly, one could observe that most of our vocabulary emphasizes the negative aspects of extramarital sexuality. Concepts such as "infidelity," "unfaithfulness," and "the other woman" assume that extramarital relationships are universally bad. It would seem that these concepts would be inappropriate for describing EMS which is sanctioned in marriage (as with CMS).

Whitehurst's study included alienation as a major independent variable. He grouped his sample according to high and low levels of alienation. He stated:

That many currently feel a sense of alienation from conventional institutions and norms might not be surprising in our kind of world. Alienation, when coupled with a relatively high level of opportunity to interact with others, can be expected to create the stuff of extramarital sexual practice (1969, p. 134).

Harper (1967) suggested that while cultural taboos are stronger against EMS than premarital coitus, married people can generally plan opportunities which are less hurried and more discreet. Thus, Whitehurst's thesis was:

. . . the behaviour should be quite frequently expected, and if expected and explained as a socio-structural and cultural problem, it may then be construed much more nearly as normal rather than as abnormal behaviour in the kind of society we now experience (1969, p. 136).

Whitehurst was interested in the upper-middle class because he assumed that family change most often occurs in this class. He found that 80 percent of the extensive extramarital involvement included high-alienation men (p. 139). Using Cuber's classification system, the low-alienation group was more likely to have "vital" or "total" marriages. Most of the men who abstained from EMS did so for religious or moral reasons, or out of a feeling of family responsibility. A majority of the high-alienation group reported that their marital adjustment was reflected in the deviations. Seventy percent of the low-alienation group versus only 30 percent of the high-alienation group had indulged in "some playing around, either at parties, with office help, or others, but no serious sexual involvement" (p. 140). Opportunity was a crucial intervening variable, as 41 percent of the sample stated this was a deciding factor as to whether they engaged in EMS. Whitehurst explained the relevance of opportunity to EMS:

Opportunity appears to be dependent upon the social situation in which the male operates. . . . If reference group support is lacking . . . a male will be less likely to find opportunity unless he is a singular deviant . . . those scoring low in alienation avoid opportunities for EMS by enveloping themselves in a social structure which supports conformity (in some significant sense, this creates an impossibility for deviation extramaritally because of the web of social control with which this kind of person surrounds himself) (p. 140).

Whitehurst was cautious in interpreting his data, but indicated that men who were high in "powerlessness" were more likely to satisfy the need for power over another in an EMS relationship (p. 141). This may relate to the need to "prove" one's masculinity. Additionally, those with EMS experience were more socially isolated and were seeking intimacy apparently in EMS relationships. Since 67 percent of Whitehurst's sample had not had any kind of EMS, the representativeness of upper-middle-class businessmen would not seem to square with the probable reality of a higher proportion of such experience (e.g., as reported by Kinsey). Whitehurst acknowledged this deficiency in his sample, and attributed it to the methodology and/or the "halo effect present in the middle class" (p. 142). He concluded that there is a need for further clarification of the relationship between alienation, social isolation, and powerlessness, as well as opportunity for EMS (p. 144). Since Whitehurst's sample was all male, future research will need to include a comparison between men and women.

A Milestone Study by Cuber and Harroff. The study including both sexes is described in *Sex and The Significant Americans* by Cuber and Harroff (1965). *This study has probably provided more insights into extramarital sexual relationships which are sanctioned in marriages than any other study to date.* Yet the sample was nonrandom and was limited to the upper middle class. The age range (thirty-five to fifty-five) unfortunately did not include young married couples. However, the study is rich in detail from the unstructured in-depth interviews with 437 upper-middle-class Americans. Neubeck recognized the value of the study when he included a chapter by Cuber in his book (1969). In that chapter Cuber pointed out that treating all EMS as *adultery* is misleading, as no distinctions are made between the range of extramarital relationships—from the casual to the intense. He stated: "Such a category contributes nothing but a moralistic label which obscures more discriminating understanding of behaviour" (p. 191).

Cuber and Harroff originally identified five types of marriage. They stated that "infidelity" (Cuber is guilty of universally using the negative terms he later abhors) occurred in all but the "total" marriage, but that it occurred for differing reasons. The marital type which would seem to most closely approximate marriages where extramarital relations are approved would be the "vital" marriage, although EMS is by no means sanctioned in all "vital" marriages. In some "vital" marriages EMS ". . . is not construed as disloyalty or as a threat to continuity, but rather as a kind of basic human right which the loved one ought to be permitted to have—and which the other perhaps wants also for himself" (p. 62).

Cuber (1969) defined three types of marriages with EMS. First, Cuber indicated that EMS may compensate for a defective marriage, and that these marriages are often maintained without love due to the societal emphasis on the value of continuing marriage as opposed to the negative sanctions on terminating marriage (p. 192). In such cases the extramarital relationships may be more like marriage than relationships meeting the legal definition of marriage. The second type of marriage which includes EMS is the discontinuous marriage. Spouses are often separated by occupational or professional roles, or by war, and agree to EMS as long as the relationships are casual and not threatening to the marriage. Type three includes the "true Bohemians." Monogamy (as Americans are *supposed* to practice) is not recognized in this type of relationship, and extramarital relationships are fully sanctioned (pp. 192-3). It is likely that a significant proportion of EMS in the Cuber and Harroff study is actually CMS, although the concept was not used in 1965. This would seem particularly relevant to categories two and three.

What one expects initially from marriage tends to condition the kind of marriage which develops. Cuber and Harroff noted that "Expectations are often interlaced with ambivalence" (p. 68). They added that it was not uncommon for men and women to doubt whether they should give up sexual variety permanently to get married. An example of the frustrations and conflicts between marriage and natural desires is evident with one male interviewee. The man stated:

This tying up of love, marriage, parenthood, and sex into one package is crazy for this century. They're all important, normal, healthy, and essential, really. But just because you love a woman and want her for a mother for your kids doesn't mean to me that you have to give up forever your right to sleep with another woman and enjoy her close companionship. If we hadn't agreed on that before we got married, we'd have stayed single. But the hell of it is that it's easier to agree on it and to act on it than it is to pull it off smoothly. Deep down you also feel that love *ought* to be enough—but then it isn't. It's a mess, isn't it? (p. 69).

Cuber and Harroff included descriptions of irregular and regular extramarital relationships of several varieties. Some were what could be called love affairs and others were continuous sexual relationships. An example of the latter follows:

Sure, I sleep off and on with Ross's secretary. It's not really an affair. Neither of us is exclusive about it. We just like each other that way. . . . Every once in a while we look at each other and sort of know it's about that time again. . . (p. 154).

Cuber and Harroff placed their comments in an interpersonal framework similar to that of Kirkendall (1961). They were concerned about the quality of marriages and extramarital relationships, and how EMS relationships affect various styles of marriage as well as different people. The effects of EMS on the spousal relationship depend heavily on several factors listed by Cuber. These factors include:

. . . whether the adultery is carried on furtively or is known by the spouse; (b) whether the married partners agree to the propriety or expediency of such behaviour; (c) whether one or both participate; and (d) whether the condonement is genuine and based on principle or is simply the result of an ultimatum by one of the two parties (1969, p. 193).

Cuber pointed out that the assumption that EMS is furtive is not validated by the data, for a "considerable number of spouses have 'levelled' with their mates, who cooperate in maintaining a public pretense of monogamous marriage" (p. 193). Additionally, Cuber and Harroff found that "triangles" are not necessarily destructive to marriage, whether the third person is known by the spouse or not. EMS, according to Cuber and Harroff, need not have a detrimental effect on the mental health of the participants or the spouse. This interpretation is based on Cuber and Harroff's nonclinical sample, while studies of counseling patients might yield far different results.

Such is the case in a study by Beltz (1969) where five couples in counseling were interviewed over five years. While Cuber stressed the subjective impressions of reality by the interviewees, Beltz emphasized behaviorist theory. All of the couples in Beltz's small sample had entered monogamous marriage, later altered their "contracts," and then sought marital counseling. Beltz drew the *unwarranted* conclusion that "It does not appear possible, within our cultural setting, to maintain a marriage where extramarital sex is condoned and permitted" (p. 188). Cuber avoided this kind of over-generalization and concluded that the effect of EMS is particular to the situation, the kind of marriage, and the psychological stability of the spouses. As an example of successful comarital sex, a woman in her late forties (with two children and a successful husband) told Cuber and Harroff that she and her husband

. . . live more or less like single people—when something interesting comes along, for either of us, we pursue it. . . . And this doesn't mean we have separate rooms at home—or even beds. Far from it! . . . I'd say my husband and I love each other—we just don't own each other (p. 156).

Consistent with the comarital concept, Cuber and Harroff stated that most of their sample did not hold a double standard, so that if sexual freedom was a part of a marriage, it was true for both spouses.

As for reactive feelings to EMS, Cuber (1969) stated that "Overwhelmingly, these people expressed no guilt with respect to what they were doing . . ." (p. 194). He pointed out that many EMS relationships were deep, meaningful encounters without the feeling that it must last for a lifetime (as in marriage), and that EMS relationships are held together by *will* rather than by *law*. Cuber contended that long-term EMS relationships were often ". . . more psychologically fulfilling than marriage" (p. 196). This observation would seem related to the disillusionment after twenty years of marriage noted by Pineo (1961) in his follow-up of the Burgess and Wallin study. It is quite possible that Americans expect too much from marriage and that, when these expectations are not realized, some of the emotional and sexual needs are met either extramaritally or comaritally.

Studies of EMS and the Social Context. In an investigation of forty couples Neubeck and Schletzer (1962) found that low strength of conscience accompanied sexual involvement, but not fantasy or emotional involvement. Those who were among the low-satisfied group sought fantasy instead of actual sexual or emotional relationships outside marriage. While the study was not extensive, some interesting hypotheses were advanced in the findings. Neubeck and Schletzer stated that "The environs of marriage are obviously too narrow for impulse-ridden individuals . . ." (p. 151). The interviews led the researchers to suggest future research designed to answer such questions as:

> . . . what is the effect of the kind and degree of involvement on the other spouse? . . . what makes for tolerance for the spouse's involvement on the other spouse? . . . after an involvement has taken place, how will the behavior and attitude of the other spouse affect future involvements? (1962, p. 281).

Although primarily a journalist, Morton Hunt published a compilation of his empirical observations and personal insights in *The Affair* (1969). The empirical aspect of the book was not well explained, and although two social scientists carried out the questionnaire study of 360 married people on a national basis, one is left wondering how valid or representative the study is. Hunt also interviewed ninety-one people in free-wheeling tape-recorded interviews. Much like Cuber and others, Hunt advanced some insightful hypotheses, but fell into the same trap of using words loosely (such as "infidelity," "unfaithfulness," and so on). He dealt more specifically with "affairs," which can be defined in several ways. Hunt cited authorities who stated opinions about the value of EMS, but his conclusion is presented in his preface. He stated:

> The evidence . . . clearly shows that in some circumstances an extramarital affair severely damages the marriage, the participants, and even such innocent bystanders as the children; in other circumstances it does none of these things, and is of no consequence; and in still other circumstances it benefits the individual by awakening him to his own emotional needs and capabilities . . . each extramarital act ought to be judged as morally evil, morally neutral, or morally good, according to the totality of the circumstances and the effects on all concerned (p. xv).

Gebhard was quoted by Hunt as predicting the cumulative incidence figures of extramarital intercourse in 1968 as being about 60 percent for males and 35–40 percent for females, which is "change, but not revolution" (p. 11). [3]

Hunt recognized that the cocktail lounge is a favorite haunt for meeting prospective sex partners, especially casual sex partners (p. 75). This is supported by the Roebuck and Spray study (1967), which included data from thirty men and thirty women who were regular patrons of an upper-middle-class cocktail lounge. Roebuck and Spray followed the activities of these sixty people over a two-year period, and conducted a follow-up study two years after the initial study. All who were included in the sample visited the lounge at least once a week. The employees of the lounge (bartenders and cocktail waitresses) were utilized for part of the data collection. The researchers frequented the lounge regularly and gathered additional data by participant-observation. The methodology of the study was much more rigorous than other studies reported in this article. However, no claim could be made for a random sample. The men had incomes above $10,000 and all of the men and the single women believed in God and attended church. Seventy percent of the men were married, while none of the women were married (40 percent of the women were divorced or separated). It was found that 80 percent of the men and women in the sample were considered to be stable, and few were heavy drinkers.

A third method of data collection was interviewing all in the sample several times a year. The cocktail lounge is an ideal setting for obtaining part of a sample, as indicated by Roebuck and Spray's observations:

The popularity of the cocktail lounge . . . stems from the fact that it is a setting in which casual sexual affairs between unattached women and higher-class men can be conducted in a context of respectability. From the standpoint of the patrons, these activities tend to be viewed more in terms of reaffirming social identities than rejecting social norms (p. 393).

The activities were not found to disrupt the family life of the men (p. 395). Married men were not "driven" to the lounge from unhappy marriages. The cocktail lounge as a social organization merely provided the atmosphere for meeting needs of men and women. The single women were not interested in breaking up a home or in marrying the men with whom they had EMS. None of the women married the men they met in the lounge, and none of the men were divorced in the five-year follow-up study (p. 394). [4] As the single women married, they stopped frequenting the lounge and were replaced by other single women wanting social fun and sexual interaction without the game of the courtship relationship. The bartenders and cocktail waitresses were often intermediaries for establishing contact with potential sexual partners. While the men believed in the double standard, they did not exploit the women and maintained friendly relationships with them. The women were not virgins. The men remained "good husbands and fathers . . ." (p. 393). It is probable that most of the married men were "cheating" in terms of their marital contracts, but it is also quite likely that some of the men were behaving within the bounds of propriety according to their wives. The men did not feel guilty, but would feel shame if caught (p. 393), which seems to indicate that most of the men were "cheating." Whether this is true is not clear from the report. The lack of married women in the cocktail lounge studied may be more a reflection of the particular lounge than of cocktail lounges or married women in general.

Studies from Sociology and Social Psychology Since 1970. In contrast to the study of casual sexual relationships in the cocktail lounge, Kafka and Ryder studied nonconventional marriages where the spouses were not possessive toward each other, but encouraged the free expression of affection in a present-oriented rather than a future-oriented way (see Chapter 12). Similarly, Knapp and Whitehurst's studies of sexually open relationships indicate that consensual extramarital (or comarital) sex is not analogous to the adulterous extramarital sex in Roebuck and Spray's cocktail lounge study.

Johnson (1970) reported on the projective, fantasized, and actual EMS for one hundred middle-class, middle-aged couples from the suburbs of one large midwestern city. Unfortunately, he limited his indicators (or motives) for fantasized EMS to nine negative reasons based on "60 case histories involving extramarital sexual relations from the files of a Family Service Agency" (p. 450). Thus, the only reasons for any EMS considered were specific deficiencies in marriage. No distinction was made between EMS and CMS. While it was found that husbands who experienced EMS had lower marital satisfaction than husbands who had not had EMS, general dissatisfaction in the marriage or over the sexual relationship was not as frequently associated with EMS for the wives (pp. 454—5). Thus, 30 percent of the experienced husbands and 60 percent of the experienced wives had high marital adjustment scores. When asked if most men (or women) who were happily married would like to have EMS, 78 percent of the men and 41 percent of the women who had denied experiencing EMS said "yes" (p. 452). Since 20 percent of the husbands and 10 percent of the wives stated that they had experienced EMS, the sample can be considered a conservative one, and the findings must be qualified in light of the biased sample.

Psychology Today reported the results of a sex survey of its readers ($N=20,000$) (Athanasiou, Shaver, & Tavris, 1970) and while no refusal rate could be reported, the extramarital findings are probably somewhat indicative of the attitudes and behavior of a young (the majority were under thirty), liberal, highly educated population. While 80 percent stated that EMS is acceptable in various circumstances, 21 percent would consider EMS permissible if spouses agree. Most (95 percent) reject the idea that EMS is acceptable if nothing is mentioned to the spouse. About 40 percent of the men and 36 percent of the women reported having experienced EMS, but no distinction between EMS and CMS was made. Husbands began having EMS sooner than wives, but women reported about the same frequencies as men once they began EMS (p. 43). The Athanasiou et al. study is probably a good example of the attitude-behavior discrepancy, in that more tend to approve than actually engage in EMS or CMS. It is likely that the lack of opportunity to engage in EMS may be a key variable accounting for the gap between attitudes and behavior.

Social-psychological research has consistently shown attitudes to be fairly poor predictors of behavior. Recent research (Fishbein & Ajzen, 1975, summarize this literature very well) emphasizes the importance of identifying beliefs and behavioral intentions in addition to attitudes when attempting to predict behavior and decisions about behavior. When combining these theoretically distinct but interrelated predictive variables with situations which are specific to the behavior and opportunity to engage in the behavior (in this case extramarital and/or comarital sex), it is likely that more accurate predictions and more thorough explanations of the costs and rewards associated with sexual behavior beyond marriage will be developed. The interaction of social norms about EMS and CMS can be considered along with attitudes, beliefs, and behavioral intentions specific to a given situation where people must decide whether or not to engage in EMS and/or CMS. It is assumed that opportunity to engage in CMS or EMS is limited by social constraints as well as the lack of available, willing partners and accessible locations to carry out sexual desires. Variation in social constraints, partners, places to experience EMS or CMS, and other opportunity variables would seem to intervene between social background, attitudinal, and other predictive variables when EMS and CMS are the relevant dependent variables. The Athanasiou et al. study (1970) is an introduction to the need to specify variables which more precisely identify the social and personal context of the range of extramarital sexual behavior. It is clear that sampling and conceptual differences with studies make comparisons between studies difficult.

Sampling and conceptual differences are obvious when comparing the Athanasiou et al. study (1970) with a study of marriage and family roles by Nye, Carlson, and Berardo (1970). As Carlson (1976) reported, a random sample of 210 Yakima, Washington, couples, (a conservative sample in contrast with the more liberal *Psychology Today* readership), with a response rate of less than 50 percent and a fairly high proportion of people with incomes less than $10,000, yielded the conclusion that over 80 percent of husbands and 85 percent of wives strongly disapproved of extramarital sex under any circumstances. Carlson found that over 92 percent of husbands and 96 percent of wives disapproved of EMS under most or all conditions; almost no double standard was evident, as both spouses disapproved of EMS. There were no items dealing with any kind of CMS in the survey. It appears that the conservative-liberal sample differences and item variation account for the rather strong differences between the *Psychology Today* and Carlson results.

Another recent study which focused mainly on marital coitus but included one question as to whether or not spouses had engaged in EMS was carried out by Edwards and Booth (1976). They selected a stratified probability sample of 294 women and 213 men from census tracts in Toronto. A multiple regression analysis of eighteen social background and marital variables accounted for 12 percent of the variance in wives' engagement in EMS and 21 percent for husbands' likelihood of experiencing EMS (p. 78). The explained variance for marital coitus was only slightly greater; 18 percent and 32 percent of marital coitus was explained by all 18 variables for wives and husbands, respectively (p. 78). EMS was more common among younger than older spouses, and this was particularly true of husbands (which is contrary to other research findings reported in this article). Also contrary to other research was the lack of relationships between occupation, education, religiousness, and urban or rural residence and engagement in EMS (pp. 79-80). An additional contrary finding was that wives who were employed were *less* likely to engage in EMS (p. 80). This makes little sense. In light of this finding, the low relationships in the entire study, the global nature of the questions (only one question was included on extramarital relations), the bias of using physicians to ask questions about sexual behavior, and the lack of any theory, the findings seem very suspect.

Ziskin and Ziskin (1973) note that to believe and practice EMS is not to deny the importance of marriage, it is merely to redefine the ground rules to include CMS. Their informal two-hour interviews with 124 couples in Southern California who practiced some form of comarital sex (open marriage, swinging, etc.) indicated that most were pleased with their marriages, with themselves, and with their other relationships. Nearly 80 percent were aged thirty-five to fifty, and the sample was middle- to upper-middle class, and Caucasian. While the sample was a volunteer sample, utilizing friends, advertisements in the media, etc., it does offer some very tentative insights into the experiences of couples experimenting with comarital sexual relationships. About 40 percent of the sample were swingers.

The Ziskins discuss dating, separate vacations, and relatively durable affairs as types of comarital sex beyond swinging where spouses carry on other relationships with mutual consent in an independent fashion. They note that some couples arrange for free time, which is similar to the fourth compartment discussed by Myers (see Chapter 22). The Ziskins note that in their sample swingers were more likely to experience marital problems from excessive sexual activity with others as compared with those with more independent arrangements. Most couples found that their marital relationship, including the sexual aspect of the marital experience, was enhanced by comarital sexual relationships with others (p. 244). A minimal amount of jealousy was reported, as most were relatively secure in their marriages and were not possessive toward their spouses (p. 245). Contrary to traditional expectations, these people did not spend an inordinate amount of time and energy with other relationships, and their marriages received the bulk of time and energy and remained the central relationship for intimacy and companionship. The authors offer an "extramarital sex contract" in writing as an example of how to make the ground rules clear (though open to renegotiation). They predict that more couples will establish sexually open marriages, but that this need not occur for all or most people, as it is simply one way to pattern a marriage.

In the recent literature, there have been three studies that had samples of over two thousand subjects. The first study includes 2,026 women and men from twenty-four cities and suburban areas. Most of the participants were secured by professional public opinion survey teams who administered questionnaires to groups of sixteen who were called on the phone to discuss sex and then fill out the questionnaires. One in five contacted on the phone agreed to participate in the study. The data were collected in 1972, and then Morton and Bernice Hunt interviewed one hundred people and Morton Hunt anaylzed the data for the Playboy Foundation (1974). Hunt dealt with extramarital sex of the adulterous variety, with swinging, and with group sex, but no items on sexually open marriage were included.

Hunt concluded that there has been an increase in the active incidence of extramarital intercourse among women under age twenty-five over the Kinsey figures of about twenty years earlier. While Kinsey reported that 8 percent of married women had experienced EMS by age twenty-five, 24 percent of Hunt's sample had done so by 1972. If one can legitimately project a linear increase in EMS for this young age group, as well as a future increase in the accumulative incidence, EMS rates for women will continue to rise rather dramatically. It is interesting to note that most (about four-fifths) of both women and men in Hunt's sample do not believe that their spouses know about their extramarital experiences. Hunt also indicated that those who engage in EMS appear to do so at a younger age than was true in Kinsey's study. Although Hunt does not seem convinced, his data (combined with other data and trends discussed in this article and this book) provide a reasonable basis from which to predict a significant increase in the accumulative incidence of extramarital intercourse. To conclude (as Hunt does, 1974, p. 361) that *his data* indicate that only a small minority have tried sexually open marriages, and that even fewer have made them work, is simply not justified. Hunt is probably correct in the 2 percent estimate of those who have been involved in swinging, but he has no data to discuss sexually open marriages or the joys, sorrows, and consequences of such marriages.

In contrast to Hunt's study, Bell, Turner, and Rosen (1975) do have *some* basis to evaluate the relative happiness of those who have engaged in at least one extramarital (though not comarital) experience. Although the 1973 sample included 2,262 married women, they were secured through an availability-snowball technique using professionals in the marriage and family field to ask people to fill out questionnaires and mail them in. About 60 percent of the questionnaires were returned, mainly from those with a high level of education. It was found that 20 percent of those who rated their marriages as good or very good had EMS as compared to 55 percent rating their marriages as fair to very poor. No distinction was made between extramarital sex of the adulterous variety and comarital, or consensual sex. Bell et al. were cautious in their interpretation. They stated:

. . . it must be stressed that while women with low-rated marriages have much higher rates of extramarital coitus there are many women who rate their marriage as very good who also have extramarital coitus, as well as those who rate their marriage as unhappy who also have low rates of extramarital sex. This would suggest that for many women extramarital coitus is influenced by a number of personal or social values that go beyond how they evaluate their marriage. Furthermore the implication is that greater sexual liberality will often suggest for some women sexual experimentation in a variety of ways, including extramarital coitus (1975, p. 383).

Support for my prediction of an increase in EMS can be garnered from the Bell et al. sample, as 26 percent of the married women reported EMS by age thirty-five as compared to the same percentage by age forty in Kinsey's sample two decades earlier. Combined with Hunt's findings, it appears that more women are having EMS and at a younger age. Bell et al. observed that only 16 percent of those women reporting EMS limited the experience to one time, and that a third had EMS more than ten times with each partner.

The most recent addition to North American extramarital sexual data is the *Redbook Magazine* mail questionnaire study of over 100,000 women (October 1975). Although the questions are global and no theoretical framework was utilized, the large sample and recency of the data collection (1974) make this journalistic study worth citing. Of the married women in the *Redbook* sample (mostly young women aged twenty to twenty-nine), about a third already reported engaging in EMS, and 38 percent of those married more than ten years reported EMS. College-educated wives were less likely to engage in EMS until age forty, after which they were more likely to experience EMS. Wives who stayed at home were less likely to have extramarital sexual experience than working wives or wives doing volunteer work outside the home. Forty-seven percent of those working had engaged in EMS (the work environment offering a means to meet and relate sexually with other men). Although those wives reporting EMS were somewhat less happily married, half or more who have had EMS were happily married and sexually satisfied with their husbands. Since the sample was quite young, and since more women are entering the work force, it would appear that this survey adds to existing data to support the generalization that more North American women will experience extramarital sexual relations. One general question on mate swapping indicated that 4 percent had tried swinging, but no questions on sexually open marriage were included. Thus, the only data gathered about comarital sex were concerned with mate swapping.

The realities of EMS and CMS have been analyzed in light of North America thus far. Now I will discuss and analyze some available cross-cultural studies.

Cross-Cultural Research on EMS. Christensen (1962) reported a cross-cultural comparison of the attitudes of Danes, Midwestern Americans, and Intermountain (Mormon) Americans toward "infidelity." Although Christensen's data were limited to traditional "cheating" behavior, he found that Danes of both sexes were more accepting of infidelity than were those in his two American samples.

Christensen's cross-cultural and longitudinal research has contributed much to our understanding of cultural and time variation in extramarital attitudes. As such, his research is an example of the kind of studies needed to develop comprehensive theories explaining and predicting changing sexual attitudes and their relation to sexual behavior. Although Christensen included no conceptualization of CMS, this was because his research was prior to the visibility and popularity of sexually open marriage. Other researchers can now build on his data to further theory about EMS and CMS.

In a ten-year comparison with his 1958 samples, Christensen (1973) studied university students in the same three cultures (Danish, Midwestern, and Intermountain) as well as university students in several other cultures. The samples were drawn nonrandomly from sociology or social science classes, so no statistics were computed. For purposes of longitudinal comparisons, findings relevant to the three cultures above will be discussed here. Denmark was the most permissive about EMS, as was earlier the case with premarital intercourse. Those with premarital sexual experience are the most liberal about EMS, but Christensen points out that this liberal attitude becomes more conservative as people get involved in more committed relationships. Although the attitude-behavior relationship is not directly addressed in this study (as Christensen has done in earlier studies of premarital sex), his conclusion remains to be applied to age cohort samples over time with reported behavior as well as attitudes. He concluded:

... when love is introduced into the equation, and then when there is an additional assumption that the sex partner also is married, percentages approving extramarital coitus go down whether the respondent is thinking of freedom for both sexes or just for the male (1973, p. 205).

It may be that there is a closer relationship between extramarital attitudes, behavioral intentions, and behavior in Denmark than in America and that the liberal Danish attitudes are more reflected in liberal (open) marriages. It must be remembered that Christensen earlier found that people in more traditional cultures go beyond their beliefs with their actual sexual behavior and then feel guilty about it, while those in more liberal cultures would engage in more sex if they had the opportunity, as their attitudes tend to extend beyond their sexual behavior. This presents a somewhat variant way of looking at Christensen's own conclusion about EMS, although the commitment variable may confuse the relationship between extramarital attitudes and behavior.

To be more specific about Christensen's data from college students, American samples did not change much in their attitudes about infidelity in ten years, but the Danish sample in 1968 was considerably more accepting of EMS than were Danes in the 1958 sample. Christensen's 1968 sample of Danes indicated that about 80 percent of the females and 69 percent of the males approved of infidelity "If he or she feels the need for sexual release (with prostitutes or others) during periods of long absence from spouse." In 1958, 29 percent of Danish women and 34 percent of Danish men approved the same statement. Additionally, in 1968 about 75 percent of Danish men and 72 percent of Danish women approved of infidelity "If he or she has fallen in love with an unmarried person," while just over a fourth of Danes approved the same statement in 1958. Similarly, while 68 percent of Danish women and 66 percent of Danish men approved of infidelity "If he or she has fallen in love with another married person" in 1968, 23 percent of women and 22 percent of men in Denmark approved the same statement in 1958. It is clear that extramarital sexual attitudes were much more liberal in 1968 than they were in 1958, and it would appear that the linear increase in liberality of attitude has continued. This liberal attitude is probably evident in extramarital and comarital sexual relationships in Denmark today.

Analogous to the Christensen data (in the sense of limiting the dependent variable to adultery) is a study carried out in Sweden by an opinion institute and reported on by Jan Trost in 1970. The opinion institute sent out interviewers to carry out a government-supported study that asked Swedes, "With how many persons have you had sexual intercourse during the last 12 months?" Trost classified the 2,000 Swedes aged eighteen to sixty who said they had engaged in EMS as having committed adultery. He reported that the opinion institute study found that 5 percent *said* they had experienced EMS. Trost believes that the institute data actually reflect the reality of a very low incidence of EMS in Sweden, but the data are biased in that the study was a survey where a stranger asked global questions and the study was supported by a governmental committee.[5] The 5 percent figure is especially limited when considering that the question was confined to EMS *in the last 12 months.* As noted earlier in this article, attitudes are generally not directly correlated with reported behavior. Christensen's 1968 data (1973) indicate that Danes and then Swedes have the most liberal attitudes about EMS. It is unlikely that there is such a low incidence of EMS (or CMS) in Sweden *even if* the attitudes are more liberal than the behavior. This is particularly true when one considers the accumulative incidence, and it is also relevant that the data collected for this study are now quite old.

Although the full report is not yet available in America, it appears that Zetterberg's data (1966) are the same data used by Trost (1970). In an article by Moskin (1969), portions of the Zetterberg data are cited. In summary, Zetterberg found that young Swedes are having sexual relations with more people and beginning their sexual lives earlier than their parents; 93 percent accept premarital sexual relations when engaged or going steady; 98 percent of the married subjects had premarital intercourse; most men have had as many as five sexual partners, while most women have had one or two partners; the double standard is more accepted by women than by men; 77 percent believe in limiting sex to committed relationships and believe that "promiscuity" is wrong; as Trost reported, 95 percent of married Swedes say they have not engaged in extramarital sex within a year; and 93 percent disapprove of extramarital sex. It remains for future cross-cultural research to include more sensitive methods of data collection, and to provide data on CMS as well as traditional adultery.

A final study of the sexual behavior of Australian women (Bell, 1974) provides an opportunity for cross-cultural comparison with American research by the same author. The study was a volunteer, nonrandom mail questionnaire sample of 1,442 Australian women (with about a 55 percent response rate), with the data collection taking place in 1972 and 1973. This is the first systematic study on sexual behavior of Australian women, and so the findings are important as a basis for comparison with data from other cultures.

Bell reported that 37 percent experienced EMS. The percentages by age group were: twenty-five and under, 25 percent; age twenty-six to thirty, 37 percent; age thirty-one to forty, 45 percent; age forty-one to fifty, 46 percent; and for women over fifty, 17 percent. Bell concluded, "Given the present rates for the women under 30 years of age it would seem reasonable to speculate that when those age groups reach 50 years of age that 50 to 60 percent of them will have had extramarital intercourse" (p. 149). Only 8 percent of those with extramarital experience limited themselves to just one sexual experience with one partner (p. 152).

Bell concluded that Australian women were more likely to report EMS than American women, and they are more likely to have EMS more times per partner than American women. Also, Australian women desire EMS more than American women, and a generally more permissive picture seems apparent in Australia than in America. The meanings of extramarital intercourse remain hazy from Bell's research. It remains for additional research to ascertain the range of symbolic meanings and motives of extramarital sexual behavior. Cross-cultural research utilizing samples from Australia, America, and other cultures would be useful to make further generalizations about the distinctions between extramarital and comarital sex across cultures.

The Meaning of Extramarital Relationships

At least some of the marital styles which support some form of EMS will probably define EMS as a *game*. Thus, Foote's (1954) thesis that sex is a legitimate form of play (where the rules are made by the players) is relevant to at least some EMS. Foote pondered how trust, relaxation, and confidence can be measured in different relationships in various erotic interactions. If sex is fun and it is a game, Americans must learn to separate sex from love in some EMS relationships. Ellis contended that females ". . . who say that they can only enjoy sex when it is accompanied by affection are actually being unthinkingly conformists and unconsciously hypocritical" (1958, p. 68). The extent to which females (as well as males) are able to interact sexually in friendships and acquaintanceships with a range of affection (as well as a range of physical intimacy) needs to be investigated.

While some EMS relationships are games, Neubeck (1969) believes that the games concept may not be needed. He stated:

The 'games' people 'play' strategies and counter-strategies used to gain attention, love and excitement, may no longer be needed. People may explore together what in quantity and quality the marital relationship can stand in regard to additional relations (p. 198).

Neubeck explored the concept of "ground rules" in his book, stressing that there are implicit and explicit rules, and the interpretation of these rules varies from person to person and couple to couple (p. 12). It is a mistake to assume that all married people agree to the same ground rules, or that all married people stick to the same ground rules they had when they entered marriage. Yet as Neubeck contended, ". . . ground rules are hardly ever specifically discussed before marriage, but are nevertheless *assumed* to be the same for both spouses" (p. 13). We don't often consider ground rules until they are broken. Thus, if we agree to strict monogamous marriage (as most Americans probably do), when we find out our spouse is "cheating" we wonder where we went wrong. Yet we have no explicit ground rules to regulate fantasy about sexual relationships outside marriage. How common are fantasized "infidelities"? How does the fantasy life of an individual relate to actual marital and extramarital behavior?

Neubeck stated that we assume marriage to be an exclusive relationship which is entered voluntarily and is permanent (p. 13). Thus, to what extent does a spouse have a right to a private life and to develop other heterosexual relationships? In what situations are other relationships nurturant to marriage as well as satisfying to the self, and when are other relationships a threat to the marriage and/or the self? Neubeck recognized that while marriage is a group situation, the individual also has personal goals (p. 15). Whitehurst

(1969) referred to Bossard's belief in the "trouble" caused by an individual seeking individual development while married. Whitehurst commented: "This is a near-classic restatement of the standard sentiments of Americans about marriage" (p. 133).

Bernard (see Chapter 8) indicated that a choice between exclusivity and permanence may be necessary. She commented:

If we insist on exclusivity, permanence may be endangered. The trend . . . seems to be in the direction of exclusivity at the expense of permanence in the younger years but permanence at the expense of exclusivity in the latter years (1970, p. 99).

The interdependency in a marriage was noted by Neubeck (1969), who based his statements on Kurt Lewin's field theory. One has more freedom in larger groups, which would mean that the marital dyad may be limiting by nature of the number of participants in the group. According to Lewin, marrying is a "symptom" of the desire for the least possible social distance (p. 15). Yet, individuals differ in their needs for free space—and marriage as traditionally defined may not allow enough for needs to be met for some people. Lewin noted that too small a space leads to tension and to the seeking of less confining situations (p. 16). Such movement can result in jealousy if detected or not agreed upon. Intense jealousy is based on the "owning" of a spouse, as well as insecurity or fear about the lack of permanency of the marriage.

How do members of a family react when they find out their mother (wife) or father (husband) has had "boy (girl) friends"? Neubeck noted that ". . . as an extramarital affair becomes known throughout the family, tolerance is needed by the other members as well as by the spouse" (p. 8). It is important that researchers inquire into how spouses handle the issue of explaining or keeping secret their agreement to extramarital freedom in some form to their children, depending on their ages and ability to understand. Due to social pressures and lack of maturity it may be that most parents who agree on extramarital freedom keep these activities from their children—at least until the children are old enough to understand. Those who are seriously committed to swinging or to another form of CMS may or may not explain the virtues of such freedom to their children when they are in late adolescence—the issue remains open.

Neubeck stated propositions which researchers can test:

The greater the need for freedom, the more confining the marriage environment might be, and the subsequent wish to escape from it; the greater the need for the possession of property and subsequent willingness to share property, the greater the jealousy and willingness to be faithful on one's own part (p. 17).

The need for freedom to meet needs outside the marital relationship is related to the rather common expectation that every possible sexual, emotional, and personal need will be (or should be) met by one another in the context of a marriage that lasts for an entire lifetime. Neubeck reacted to this expectation by stating: "This permanent togetherness results in quantitative and qualitative exposure that may lead to satiation, since there is only a finite number of personality aspects available" (p. 18).

It is likely that many have a desire or need to relive their dating days by at least flirting with members of the opposite sex. This playfulness and fun may be difficult to achieve in marriage. Neubeck stated:

If flirtation . . . means 'making love without meaning it,' it is obviously not possible to flirt with a spouse. A spouse is not a candidate for consummation; spouses have already consummated (p. 19).

And yet, according to Decter (1972), flirtation is an activity of the past. Decter argued:

Flirtation . . . has become, in an era which offers no sanction to chastity, an activity fraught with consequence . . . there is no longer by definition such a thing as real flirtation—whose purpose is to denote a relation between a man and a woman in which each offers full tribute to the presumed erotic attractions of the other . . . (1972, p. 51).

Most people probably pretend that monogamy is the only ideal state, but secretly wish for and occasionally participate in and enjoy flirtation, which sometimes leads to physical intimacy. Mazur (1968) commented on flirtation:

The potential dangers of flirting lie not in the activity itself, but in the foolish interpretation of it by insecure and possessive partners who see it as a threat to themselves (p. 25).

The extent to which this is true of married people could be noted by questioning spouses about their flirting behavior and their perception of their spouse's jealousy or lack of jealousy.

In order to determine the meaning of extramarital and comarital relationships, a theoretical approach must be taken. One of the shortcomings of research on EMS and CMS is the lack of any well-developed theoretical framework. This deficiency pervades sex research. Gecas and Libby (1976) develop and apply symbolic interaction theory to sexual behavior, and Libby and Carlson (1973) carry this further by integrating symbolic interaction and exchange theory to view sexual behavior as symbolic exchange where inner feelings and motives are utilized along with overt acts to determine the relative costs and rewards for people involved in various sexual relationships. The motives and meanings may vary for two people in a given sexual relationship (whether in or out of a marriage), and these same people may change (or grow) over time, such that the same motives and meanings for sexual expression change too. One cannot intelligently discuss consequences of EMS or CMS for marriage, individuals, or society without theoretically grounded research which follows people over time. The fact that there are so many different interpretations of data by investigators and others who are exposed to reports of studies, and the fact that predictions vary so much about the future of marriage and alternative marital and sexual life-styles, point to the need for theoretically based research and more precise measurement with multiple methods of data collection to assure validity and generalizability of results.

Current attempts at theory development in the extramarital area have been rather meager, but then current attempts at data collection have been limited also. The interaction between data and theory in social science cannot be avoided in the area of extramarital and comarital sex if generalizations are to be made with some degree of confidence. John Edwards (1973) attempted to summarize the field of extramarital research in the form of empirically based propositions, but his propositions turned out to be largely demographic and fairly limited in being based on data with global variables and with no real conceptualization for any kind of extramarital sex beyond adultery.

Hunt (1974) tends to differ with Whitehurst in the interpretation of EMS as "an extension of normal behavior without strong guilt feelings . . ." (1974, p. 270). Hunt claims that the emphasis on secrecy, disloyalty, and partial abandonment fears, along with the repudiation of marital love, indicate internal conflicts for those involved with EMS (p. 361). One is left wondering why there *must* be inner conflicts or guilt, but Hunt has no data on open marriage or on inner conflicts that can resolve the question.

Two studies of recent vintage do offer some basis to conclude something about the range of symbolic meanings or life-styles which include extramarital and comarital sex. Stein's (1974) innovative study of call girls and their male clients (who are predominantly married) offers fascinating insights (though no real theory) into the meanings of extramarital *and* marital sex and intimacy. Most of the 1,242 males studied (using two-way mirrors and tape recorders and involving 64 call girls) felt something was missing in their marital lives. They felt undernourished emotionally and sexually. They were upper-middle-class men who came to call girls to find more assertive women who would take the lead in social and sexual interaction, who would listen to them, and who would perform erotic acts such as oral sex which they tended not to find at home with their wives. Stein concluded that both sexes are finding that they can enjoy sex without love as long as mutual respect and consideration are present. She observed that sex may be for recreation, to enhance status and ego, for romance, and for other reasons (1974, p. 314). The interviews with the call girls, combined with the conversations between call girls and the men, provided a rather depressing picture of marriage for many of the men. While such a sample is obviously select, it does provide a view of marriage for at least some upper-middle-class men. Studies with nonrandom and select samples give us some of the pieces of the puzzle which some day will provide a theory of the range of marital styles and the realities of the multitude of motives, meanings, and consequences of various extramarital and comarital behaviors.

A very different kind of extramarital (comarital, really) sex is obvious from the research by Ramey (1975a, 1975b) on "intimate friendship" groups. Unlike Stein's men who paid money for brief sexual exchange and reassurances from call girls, Ramey studied 380 upper-middle-class individuals who consider sexual intimacy to be appropriate (or potentially viable) in friendships. He included mostly those with sexually open marriages, but some single people were also involved with intimate friendship relationships. Ramey distinguished between open intimate friendship groups where the emphasis was on being free to relate sexually and emotionally beyond the marital dyad or larger group, and closed intimate friendship groups (which were a minority), where sexual contacts were limited to group members.

Utilizing a volunteer, nonrandom availability sample, Ramey interviewed people and asked them to fill out a survey form as well. The individual, rather than the dyad (or "couple front") or a larger group, was viewed as the basic "building block" of society (1975b, p. ix). Ramey defined "intimate friendships" as his subjects viewed them, which means "open acceptance of *potential* sexual intimacy, rather than . . . sexual involvement" (1975a, p. 520). Practically, one wonders if accepting the definitions of some or even most of such a sample of nonrandom people is really sufficient as a basis to define intimate friendships in such a way. It would seem that a researcher would and should make distinctions between those who believe in a life-style and those who *practice* it (that is, those who have engaged in sexual and emotional relationships on a friendship basis). This distinction was not clearly made by Ramey. It is conceptually rather muddy to group those who contend they *would* do something with those who already have done so, even if most have.

Ramey's investigation reveals that intimate friendships occur with "social contacts, academic contacts, career contacts, and religious contacts" (1975a, p. 522). Students and faculty, those living in cohabitation or communal arrangements, and others may enter into heterosexual, homosexual, or bisexual activities.

Relating specifically to a major theme of this book, Ramey observed:

Love does not occur without intimacy. Intimate friendships are loving relationships in which both the needs of the individual and the desire of the individual to meet the intimate partner's needs before consideration of her/his own are paramount. Intimate friends often refer to one another as lovers or otherwise indicate their love for their intimate friends (1975b, p. 92).

The positive aspects of love and genuine intimacy with and without sex are consequences not always realized in the traditional extramarital affair. Ramey commented that intimate friendships were more honest and rewarding than the way his sample previously lived their lives (1975a, p. 529). He indicated an interest and plan to carry out a national study to determine the extent of intimate friendships in a more identifiable population. Such a study is much needed. In the meantime we must speculate about various kinds of extramarital and comarital relationships, be they adulterous affairs or intimate friendships, from the studies done and reported. We can sometimes make fairly insightful comments about what may be the case by considering the insights from studies which may have a tangential application to the subject, or from the insights from various social theorists, novelists, and others who keep their eyes open and who have observed the secret society of various sexual and intimate interactive behaviors. Symbolic meanings and opportunities to develop intimate relationships according to one's sex, one's spouse, and other variables must be considered to obtain a holistic view of EMS and CMS.

It is probable that the husband often has more freedom to develop heterosexual friendships (as in the work environment) than the wife. Yet Neubeck (1969) has noted that Babchuk and Bates found that both spouses were likely to develop friendships and share confidences with members of the opposite sex (p. 22). Is "faithfulness" only measurable in terms of physical intimacy? Can one be "faithful" to the spouse and have extramarital sexual relationships? Does this depend on the spousal agreement as to what is "faithful," or is the only baseline that of traditional monogamy?

Our culture seems obsessed with the purely physical (and emotional) aspects of extramarital and comarital relationships. Neubeck believes that sexual needs should not be seen as different from other needs when studying marital dynamics (p. 19). But the physical is symbolic for meeting psychological needs as well. As Neubeck observed, "That marriage should serve all the needs of the spouses is built into our marital expectations, yet anyone who examines this proposition realistically is struck with its impossibility" (p. 21). Neubeck goes on to point out that we don't live in isolation, and some needs are met outside the pair bond. The extent to which needs are met outside the pair bond remains to be documented.

Depending on the style of marriage, one's tolerance level is related to various forms of sexual expression. Tolerance level obviously is related to what the spouse perceives to be the *meaning* of the partner's EMS relationships. To use extremes—is it a casual fling or a love affair? Neubeck observed that problems of meaning result from lack of understanding, and that jealousy often results from misinterpretation of meaning. Understanding and communication are thus related to tolerance for EMS.

Neubeck's conclusion remains to be tested empirically. It was:

... it is now clear that marriage can work out successfully for both of the spouses even when it is not an all-inclusive relationship, when either in reality or in fantasy there are other persons who share one's life (p. 24).

It often has been said that "variety is the spice of life." As with food, people differ in their sexual desires and tastes. But is variety of sexual partners necessarily supportive or detracting from marriage? Davis contended that "The role of variety in erotic stimulation places a strain on any stable relationship, including marriage. In short, an orderly integration of the sexual drive with social life taxes to the utmost the normative machinery" (1966, p. 331). But Davis also observed that ". . . adultery does no harm *if* the spouse approves" (p. 334). Kephart (1966) explained that the "safety-valve theory" can be interpreted in two ways—EMS can supplement and therefore support marriage, or it can threaten marriage by "working overtime" (p. 72). Kephart explained that the latter is true, and that the increase in premarital and extramarital sex may "have deleterious effects on the institution of marriage . . ." (p. 72).

The incognito erotic ranking of individuals cited by Zetterberg (1966) most likely relates to the frustrations, conflicts, and jealousies which can accompany extramarital relationships. As Zetterberg emphasized, it is not the sexual as much as the emotional involvement with a third party which violates the privacy taboo (p. 135). But Zetterberg stated that ". . . there are many sexual relations that do not involve any emotional surrender of either party" (p. 141). Researchers need to make comparisons between extramarital and comarital relationships of varying degrees of emotional (as well as erotic) intimacy to ascertain nuances of meaning to the extramarital and marital relationships. It should also be noted whether the incest taboo covers mutual friends of a marital couple or not, as Zetterberg suggested is true (p. 142). Is there a difference in meaning between CMS with a mutual friend and a friend of the spouse having EMS when no relationship exists between the friend and the other spouse?

Research could well utilize Sprey's (1969) conceptual framework which sees sexuality as an emerging autonomous institution which is not tied to reproduction and childrearing (p. 432). The "institutionalization" of sexuality was viewed as a private, but not normless world which is still part of the social order (p. 435). Rather than viewing EMS and CMS as *deviance* or neurotic behavior, this framework allows for an analysis of EMS and CMS relationships in the context of exchange theory. This does not mean that EMS and CMS cannot also be related to marriage, but it means that studying sexual expression in and of itself, along with its symbolic meanings, can be more objective if not universally tied to marriage. To Sprey this involves exchange rules within a game (Sprey is accepting Foote's "sex as play"). If the only baseline for deviance and disorganization is that of traditional reproductive morality, little objective data and explanation can be forthcoming. Sprey noted that lumping all adultery into the meaningless category of deviance does not aid in the study of concepts related to EMS and CMS (p. 438). This does not mean that a structural-functional conceptual framework cannot be employed on another level to understand the effects of EMS and CMS relationships on marriage and the family. It is to be remembered that behavior can be *deviant* in relation to traditional "ideal" norms without necessarily being indicative of disorganization. This is especially true when considering emerging marital styles. The autonomous realm of sexuality postulated by Sprey is consistent with Zetterberg's conceptualization of erotic rankings and a secret society (following Simmel). Sprey's conclusion is appropriate; it seeks to analyze EMS from more than one perspective. He stated:

It is strongly suggested . . . that the study of sexuality—independent of its traditional linkage with procreation—can provide us with a great deal of understanding of what Marcel Mauss has called the conditions under which men, despite themselves, learn to make contracts, to give, and to repay (1969, p. 440).

If Nye, Carlson, and Berardo's (1970) theory is correct, support for Sprey's conceptual framework is forthcoming. They contended:

The trends in societal change are presently toward further differentiation, and since the trend toward the autonomous family is based on increased differentiation, one can predict, with some confidence, a continued trend toward autonomy for family members and a larger proportion of comparatively autonomous families (p. 17).

The Future of Marriage

It is difficult to say whether emerging marital styles will gain strong support in the larger culture. However, it is noteworthy that Sweden is moving toward a more relaxed view of marriage in its legal structure. Marriage will be viewed as a contract of convenience intended to secure parents for children.

Serial monogamy as currently practiced leaves much to be desired. Yet to expect that all should enter monogamous marriage with the romantic expectations of marital bliss in a totally exclusive relationship, is to anticipate human beings who are socialized to happily fit the same mold. The reality is far from the expectation. Rather than happy, many feel disillusioned and caged as animals in the zoo. Cadwallader has stated:

Contemporary marriage is a wretched institution. It spells the end of voluntary affection, of love freely given and joyously received. Beautiful romances are transmuted into dull marriages; eventually the relationship becomes constricting, corrosive, grinding and destructive. The beautiful love affair becomes a bitter contract (1967, p. 48).

Alternative marital structures are explored by Otto (1970), as well as in novels by Rimmer (see Chapter 24). Otto contended that the "functionality of our major institutions can be assessed by asking, 'To what extent is the institution contributing to the development, actualization, and fulfillment of human potential?'" (p. 5). To increase the functionality of marriage Otto advised taking a pluralistic approach to marital structures. He claimed:

This is most appropriate, for we are a pluralistic society—with pluralistic needs. In this time of change and accelerated social evolution, we should encourage innovation and experimentation in the development of new forms and social and communal living (p. 8).

Otto aptly concluded:

What will destroy us is not change, but our inability to change—both as individuals and as a social system. It is only by welcoming innovation, experimentation and change that a society based on man's capacity to love man can come into being (p. 9).

The ability to not only accept but to socially engineer change in marital styles is a task for social and political scientists, among others. This will necessitate not only a change in attitude about marriage and sex, but it will entail a change in traditional conceptions about the roles of social scientists.

To understand, let alone guide, social change, social scientists will have to commit themselves to the study of interpersonal relationships. Family sociologists will have to bury the traditional approach of ratifying the family of yesteryear, and replace the worship of monogamous marriage with an open view of emergent structures (including monogamy as one option) to suit a wide variety of personalities, needs, and life-styles. This means more sensitive theories and methodologies will have to be developed by social scientists who do not fear taking a journey into the "secret society." The challenge is immense, but the rewards for human beings make the effort worthwhile.

Reference Notes

1. Reiss (letter to author, January 22, 1976) prefers to refer to consensual and nonconsensual extramarital sex rather than using the term comarital for consensual extramarital sex, as he feels that much like work outside marriage, any extramarital relationship (whether sexual or not) is *external* to marriage rather than a part of it. This way of defining terms is interesting, but it would seem that relationships which are agreed upon by spouses are included *within* the ground rules and conceptualization of a marriage and are therefore a *part of* or *internal to* that definition of marriage rather than external to it.

Another way of conceptualizing consensual extramarital and comarital sex is to refer to "transmarital sexuality," which Smith and Smith use to include "any sexual activity, interaction, relationship, or ideological scheme which aids and abets the transformation of the institutional superstructure and/or the interpersonal infrastructure of traditional marriage in a way which allows greater relative interpersonal autonomy and independence and fosters a greater capacity for intimacy and sociability" (1974, p. 21). The definitional issue is more than semantic sophistry; the implications have relevance to the way we view the meaning of marriage and the meanings attached to other relationships. In order to renovate marriage and to offer alternatives to monogamy and to any kind of legal marriage, our language will need renovation too.

2. In an unpublished study (1972) of over four hundred randomly selected college students, White found that about 72 percent of the women and 85 percent of the men who were already married reported engaging in premarital intercourse. It is likely that rates of premarital and extramarital intercourse will continue to increase given the availability of contraceptives and the emergence of a more liberal ideology about sexual expression.

3. If a large, random, and national study were undertaken, it would probably reveal that these estimates are low. However, it would most likely take an in-depth interview similar to that of Kinsey to uncover this kind of data.

4. Of course, divorce is only the most blatant indicator of marital failure or unhappiness.

5. My analysis of Trost's statements in Libby and Whitehurst (1973) was criticized by Trost (1974) for assuming that the methodology was not conducive to accurate estimates of extramarital intercourse in Sweden. In my reply to Trost's comments (1974), I indicated that Trost's requests for more specific data from the opinion institute which carried out the study were legitimate, but that the fact that his requests went without response shed further doubt on the validity of the study and the inferences made by Trost about Swedish extramarital sexual behavior. I also expressed the hope that Trost and other researchers from different countries will agree that constructive criticism among social scientists is an important aspect of the pursuit of knowledge and academic excellence. It is true that language problems may account for some of the differences in interpretation of data such as used by Trost here, but it is my view that Trost underestimates the extent and acceptance of extramarital sexual behavior in Sweden. I could be wrong, but future research is needed to resolve the question.

7.
The Contemporary Experience of Adultery: Bob and Carol and Updike and Rimmer

Gordon Clanton

Gordon Clanton approaches the concept of adultery from a fresh per-spective, suggesting that recent developments can be analyzed in terms of a typology based on the extent to which the spouse knows about and approves of an extramarital involvement. Although clandestine *adultery will continue to be statistically more common, Clanton urges researchers to focus on con-sensual adultery, or extramarital sex with the knowledge and the consent of the spouse.*

Clanton defines and discusses three subtypes of consensual adultery: group marriage, open-ended marriage, and recreational adultery (which in-cludes swinging). He illustrates these with material from contemporary fic-tion and film and argues that the popular media offer useful clues for the study of intimate behavior in our culture. He suggests that there is a recipro-cal relationship between media and "real life" and that the media help create a readiness for the behavior they describe—in this case, for a specific form of adultery. Novels and films set the stage for discussion and enable people to sort out their own values and test their own experiences against the possi-bilities conveyed by the media. Although the complex relationships between "nature and art" are difficult to understand from the limited research done on media impact, it is clear that media affect sexual behavior in a number of ways. Increasing adultery (as defined by Clanton), especially consensual adultery, may be one of these outcomes.

A New Kind of Adultery

Dawn[1] is an adulteress. Over the years she has had sexual intercourse with a number of men other than her husband. Her first extramarital adven-ture took place two years after her marriage. Since then she has been in-volved with a dozen or more men—a few frivolously, several in a deep emo-tional way, and one seriously enough to make her question her primary relationship to her husband.

Perhaps atypically, Dawn's husband (David) knew about all the extra-marital involvements either as they were happening or soon thereafter. Al-though there have been some moments of hurt and confusion, both partners affirm Dawn's unusual life-style. They experience little regret and virtually no guilt—and they know the difference between the two. Both of them consciously seek in their relationships with one another and with others an expansion of horizons, a heightening of self-awareness and other-awareness. They are open to what the future will bring. Their lives have no fixed boundaries where friendship and sex are concerned.

Significantly, neither Dawn nor David wishes things were otherwise. They appear to have no desire to limit one another's freedom to relate to others—even if such relating sometimes has a sexual component. They do not regard Dawn's extramarital relations as indicative of weakness in their marriage. Indeed, they believe that it is the security in their marriage which makes possible her openness to extramarital experiences. Apparently none of the dissatisfaction and deception and little of the hurt that goes with adultery as it is traditionally understood mark Dawn's life. She is a good wife and mother; she is a competent professional woman. There is apparently nothing pathological or socially destructive about the way she lives. Hers is a new-style adultery, adultery with the knowledge and approval of her husband, adultery without guilt or regret.

Two important questions are pressed upon us by our encounter with Dawn's story: (1) What is the word *adultery* coming to mean? (2) To what resources does one turn for helpful information and insight about the contemporary experience of adultery? This essay attempts to answer these questions.

The Emergent Meaning of Adultery

When a word about whose meaning there was once essential consensus comes to evoke a rather broad spectrum of mutually exclusive meanings, the word loses its ability to communicate clearly. When this happens either new terms must be invented or old definitions reworked in order that meanings be clear.

Adultery is a word in the midst of such a meaning crisis. Not many years ago there was a general agreement concerning its denotations and connotations. *Adultery* suggested a married person engaging in sexual intercourse with someone other than his or her legal mate. It was expected that the adulterous pair would make every effort to hide their behavior from others—especially from their spouses. Spouses, upon learning of their mate's extramarital adventure, were expected to disapprove, to be hurt and angry, and perhaps to seek (or at least threaten) divorce.

But in the contemporary setting this consensus is less secure. True, for many moderns the word *adultery* still evokes the responses delineated above. But the spectrum of possible understandings has broadened substantially. Some like Dawn and David would now seek to apply the label *adultery* to certain positively valued experiences.

But there are difficulties inherent in such usage. Consider this dictionary definition:

Adultery. The sexual intercourse of two persons, either of whom is married to a third person; unchastity; unfaithfulness.[2]

Note that this definition begins with a value-free description. But then the lexicographer adds: *unchastity; unfaithfulness.* Now a value judgment has been added. Adultery *by definition* seems to involve impurity, infidelity, and lack of virtue.

Yet a growing number of married persons now include extramarital sexual experiences which occur with the knowledge and consent of the spouse as part of their life-styles. Are such extramarital experiences adultery? Yes and no. *Yes* in that they consist of "the sexual intercourse of two persons, either of whom is married to a third person." But *no* in that the persons involved do not view such experiences as impure (unchaste) nor do they make deception of the spouse part of the adulterous gestalt. How appropriate is the word *unfaithfulness* in describing a sexual relationship of which the spouse knows and approves? Has the husband been *unfaithful* if the wife knows what he has done and does not interpret his behavior as unfaithfulness? Clearly, the presumption of a link between *the sexual intercourse of two persons, either of whom is married to a third person* and *unchastity; unfaithfulness* is unwarranted. My own research and that of others is demonstrating that for many persons extramarital intercourse is not necessarily unchaste or unfaithful. Therefore, if the word *adultery* is still to be used, it must be stripped of its negative connotations. *Adultery* must be used neutrally to name a relationship marked by *the sexual intercourse of two persons, either of whom is married to a third person;* if further discriminations are to be made other words will have to be added.

If we wish to be true to etymology (our word *adultery* comes from the Latin *adulterare,* to pollute, to defile), it may not do to speak of "good adultery" or "loving adultery" or "creative adultery." And I have no great urge to quarrel with those who avoid the word *adultery* in reference to positively valued behaviors. But since neologisms (such as comarital sex, multilateral relationships, and the like) create as many definitional problems as they solve and since their very novelty hampers their effectiveness, I have chosen to encourage an expansion of our understanding of the old word *adultery* so that it can be used to label some extramarital sexual experiences which are not unchaste or unfaithful.

A Typology of Adultery

The typology which follows aims at supplying a conceptual frame in which the word *adultery* might be better understood. Here I shall list and briefly describe several different kinds of behavior that might properly be called adultery and suggest how they relate to one another and overlap. Such a typology, hopefully, is not a Procrustean bed—it is not created out of nothing so that encountered bits of behavior can be trimmed or stretched to fit it. Rather, the typology arises out of inductive exploration. The actual behaviors encountered by researchers accumulate until certain generalizations and relationships emerge, and *these* are summed up in a typology. The typology has no value or integrity unless it is helpful in identifying and understanding the real behavior of real people. As such, a typology is a trial balloon, or a way in which a writer says, "Here are the generalizations that seem warranted to me. What do *you* think?" In that spirit I offer the following typology.[3]

As a criterion by which to name and arrange extramarital relationships, I propose we use *the extent to which the spouse knows and approves of the relationship*. If this mode of analysis is adopted, all adulterous acts and relationships can be arranged along a spectrum which runs from *spouse does not know and would not approve* to *spouse knows and approves*.

Clandestine Adultery

Clandestine adultery is the term I propose to describe an extramarital sexual relationship which the adulterer assumes must be kept secret from the spouse. It is expected that if the spouse knew about it, he or she would disapprove. This is the type of relationship that the word *adultery* frequently connotes for most people.[4]

Consensual Adultery

Consensual adultery is the label I propose for extramarital sexual relationships of which the spouse knows and approves. Here the adultery is viewed by both spouses (at least temporarily and experimentally) as part of their life-style—not as an aberration. Although some readers will have difficulty imagining a situation in which one knows and approves of a spouse's adultery, many others will recognize this as something they have done or, at least, have fantasized.[5] Here we are talking about a relatively new style of adultery—adultery without deception, adultery which in the eyes of those involved is not marked by unchastity or unfaithfulness.

Ambiguous Adultery

Of course, not all extramarital relationships can be fitted into one of these two categories. Some display elements of both types. A person may know about the spouse's extramarital involvement but not be able to approve of it; the adultery may then be tolerated as preferable to divorce.[6] Or, she/he may approve of the *idea* of the spouse's other sexual relationships but prefer not to know about the specifics. Sometimes a sincere effort to adapt to a spouse's adulterous experiences is unsuccessful, and consent, though promised, is withdrawn. For these "mixed" types I propose the label *ambiguous adultery*.

These three types may be represented schematically as follows:

CLANDESTINE ADULTERY	AMBIGUOUS ADULTERY	CONSENSUAL ADULTERY

Clandestine and consensual adultery are mutually exclusive polar opposites. In the one case the extramarital relationship is hidden from the spouse in the expectation that he or she would disapprove if he or she knew. In the other—and much less common—case, the extramarital relationship is revealed to the spouse who is expected to approve. The label *ambiguous adultery* is proposed for all those "in-between" situations in which the extramarital relationship is made known to the spouse (intentionally or unintentionally) who then responds (or is expected to respond) with something other than approval, *and* for cases in which some degree of approval of extramarital sex is registered without full knowledge of how that approval will be lived out. Many well-intentioned attempts at consensual adultery are marked by this kind of confusion and pain. Of the married couples I have interviewed who claim to have made consensual adultery a functional part of their relationships, most admit that some of their experiences have been touched by jealousy, misunderstanding, and ambiguity.

Note that these types of adultery are dependent upon the way the married persons understand and mutually define marriage. An adulterous relationship is categorized on the basis of how the spouse responds and how the adulterous partner *expects* the spouse to respond.

For the near future, I submit, research and reflection should be focused on ambiguous and consensual adultery. The "old adultery" we always have with us. Clandestine adultery has been studied and editorialized about at great length. The time has come to devote our research energies to the "frontier aspects" of the contemporary experience of adultery and to the impact of these new forms on marriage in American society.

Subtypes of Consensual Adultery

All consensual adultery is not alike. I submit that there is value in carrying the typology one step further and laying out three subtypes of consensual adultery. Here perhaps the most helpful criteria are *the degree of commitment and the probability of permanence* that mark the adulterous relationship. If these criteria are adopted, three subtypes of consensual adultery emerge and together form a spectrum from *most* commitment and permanence to *least* commitment and permanence as follows:

GROUP MARRIAGE	OPEN-ENDED MARRIAGE	RECREATIONAL ADULTERY

Group Marriage

A *group marriage* is an agreement which links three or more persons in a common projection of a future together, a future marked by spatial propinquity, emotional interdependence, economic sharing, and sexual access to persons in addition to one's legal spouse or primary lover. Group marriage, in other words, is consensual adultery marked by a maximum of commitment and the highest expectation of permanence. [7]

True group marriage is rare but many persons have thought and fantasized about such a venture. Athanasiou and his associates found in their survey of *Psychology Today* readers that

> . . . nine percent are in favor of group marriage and another 16 percent "might be interested." Fewer than half actively disapprove. This topic prompted numerous comments from readers: several said that group marriages strongly appealed to them, but as one put it, they were too "culturally conditioned" to act on the interest. [8]

Catalyst for much of the talk about group marriage is the novel *Proposition 31* by Robert H. Rimmer. Although the four principal characters in the book form a firm and permanent compact—a marriage involving four adults rather than two—most sympathetic readers do not feel drawn to emulate them. But many readers of this book and of Rimmer's other fiction *do* move toward opening their marriages to new possibilities including forms of consensual adultery marked by less commitment and less expectation of permanence than would be the case in group marriage. Group marriage, then, is currently more important as a construct which inspires openness to rethinking and experimentation than as a blueprint for the future of marriage. Discussions about group marriage sometimes inspire experiments with other forms of consensual adultery.

Open-Ended Marriage

One common kind of response to reading, talking, and thinking about group marriage is the unorthodox understanding of marriage and marital fidelity which some observers are beginning to call *open-ended marriage.* This label describes a relationship between spouses in which it is understood that each grants the other the freedom to involve himself or herself in important emotional relationships with others with the understanding that sexual sharing may accompany such involvements. Many couples are resentful of the way in which an orthodox understanding of marriage makes it difficult for married persons to have significant and involving friendships with the opposite sex. Some who have taken the step of affirming the worth of deep extramarital friendships have taken the additional step of refusing to exclude the possibility of sexual sharing in the context of such a friendship. Thus the stage is set for a kind of consensual adultery. The resulting extramarital experiences lack the degree of commitment and the expectation of permanence (and, of course, the spatial propinquity and the economic sharing) that are marks of group marriage, *but* such relationships are marked by significant friendship-type commitments, the sharing of affection as well as of bodies, and the relative permanence of lasting friendship. This kind of relationship is becoming more and more common and deserves the careful attention of social analysts and helping professionals (psychologists, social workers, clergymen, and so on).

Recreational Adultery

Recreational adultery is a general label for extramarital sexual experiences marked by a relatively low level of commitment and by the expectation of relative impermanence. The most widely publicized version of recreational adultery is swinging. Swinging usually involves a couple in an exchange of spouses solely for the purpose of sexual play.[9] Emotional involvements are generally discouraged. Swinging parties afford participants large numbers of potential partners. A growing literature describes this kind of sexual sharing.[10]

There are other forms of recreational adultery in which the marriage partners do not participate together. Included here would be approval of a spouse's sexual experience with a pick-up or a prostitute. What all forms of recreational adultery have in common is this: It is expected that there will be little emotional involvement in the extramarital experience. This is in sharp contrast to the kinds of relationships encouraged by an open-ended marriage.

Needless to say, some marriages in which there is a commitment to consensual adultery are open to many, perhaps to all, of the possible variations described here. There is considerable variety in the contemporary experience of adultery. The typology has been offered in the hope that readers might find it helpful for sorting and grouping—and thus understanding—adulterous relationships of which they have knowledge whether from their own lives, from the lives of others, or from fiction they have read. With this conceptual frame in mind, let us return to the second question which Dawn's story presses upon us: To what resources does one turn for helpful information and insight about the contemporary experience of adultery?

Fiction as a Resource and Reinforcement

Persons who engage in forms of deviant behavior cannot stand alone against the world. (Note: The words *deviant, deviance,* and so on are neutral terms. They carry no implicit value judgment as to the rightness or wrongness of any act or life-style.) Rebels, though their strength may be impressive, require the context of a small community of support. Without the feeling that others share their experience and have the resources to help them understand themselves, the deviants experience unpleasant alienation and anxiety. Dawn and others like her need to know that someone empathizes with them and that there are sources of information and insight relative to the life-style they have chosen.

Truly deviant people seldom have an easy time locating a supportive community and the resources which give meaning to their life-styles, but Dawn's situation had special problems. Her first affair took place in the 1950s. The "sexual revolution" was years away. Adultery was not so common a topic of conversation then as it is now. There was no body of scientific literature to peruse. In fact, had it not been for the Kinsey reports, an adulteress in the Fifties might have believed herself to be the only such person in the world! And, of course, the Kinsey studies revealed only that people *did* commit adultery. There were few hints as to *why* or *how* or *with what results*. Social science had not yet begun its infatuation with human sexuality. Nearly all talk about *constructive adultery* still lay in the future. To be sure, a few well-paid analysts in big cities could deal nonjudgmentally with extramarital sex, but most counselors, clergymen, physicians, and writers of advice columns—even most bartenders and best friends—tended to view all extramarital sex as ill-advised, improper, or downright sinful.

But Dawn discovered that there *were* sources of insight into some of her feelings and behavior. If adultery was being neglected by social scientists and counselors, it was getting considerable attention from fiction writers. So Dawn (and others like her) sought and found perspective on her life-style by reading novels, plays, and short stories of her own and earlier times.

The fiction she read reminded Dawn that she was not alone; it supplied her need for a supportive community. She knew that others had thought about extramarital sex and she understood herself better because of her encounter with their words, thoughts, and images.

Though we are not quite so deprived of support and sources of insight relative to adultery, perhaps we, like Dawn, could move toward a fuller understanding of the phenomenon, and of our fantasies and experiences of it, through the exploration of fictional treatments.

Writers of fiction often treat significant human phenomena long before the phenomena attract the attention of most social scientists, counselors, and the like. Unencumbered by methodological commitments, content to speak of one or two human beings without feeling the need to generalize, happy if they say something about the "human condition" but content if they do not, novelists are free to explore in a way that most scholars are not. The writer of fiction can link together multiple biographies with no concern to obtain a representative sample. The novelist would rather talk about one real man or woman (*real* as only a fictional character can be real) rather than expound on the most carefully constructed ideal type. In this connection Leo Lowenthal has written:

It is the artist who portrays what is more than reality itself. . . . One of the concerns which the creative writer shares with the theoretician is to describe and name new experience. . . . He is neither an articulate recording machine nor an inarticulate mystic but a specialized thinker and it is often only after his creative tasks have been performed that society recognizes its predicaments. . . . It is the task of the sociologist of literature to relate the experiences of the writer's imaginary characters and situations to the historical climate from which they derive. He has to transform the private equation of themes and stylistic means into social equations.[11]

Fictional statements, if they are not always *auto*biographical, are often at least *bio*graphical. A well-crafted novel or short story invites the reader into some kind of identification with one or more characters in a way that the social scientist's careful profile of "the average American" never seems to do. The reader of well-written fiction feels that the adventures have really been lived by someone—even if only in the imagination. And because they have been *lived* rather than merely observed from some value-free afar, the events,

people, and feelings of good fiction supply the reader with support and resources for living his/her own adventures. There may be some value in
seeing fiction, journalism, and hard-data social science as three different vantage points from which to observe the human drama. Our understanding of
what we are will be impoverished if we overlook any of these perspectives.

Three Examples of Relevant Fiction

The following are three socially significant pieces of fiction from the late
1960s; they reflect the emergence of consensual and ambiguous adultery.
Each work is important for different reasons. Together they embrace the
broad spectrum of behaviors which we must now lump together under the
rubric *adultery*. And each, in its own way, contributes to our understanding
of the social, cultural, and ethical meanings of extramarital sex.

John Updike's *Couples*

Couples, by John Updike[12] explores the complex web of adulterous relationships that link eight New England couples in the mid-Sixties. The adultery portrayed is mostly of the old-style clandestine variety, but Updike
clearly believes that secrecy in such matters is inherently unstable. "An affair
wants to spill, to share its glory with the world. No act is so private it does not
seek applause" (p. 124).

But Updike's characters make every effort at deception. The landscape
is littered with deceived spouses, suspicions, rumors, and revelations. The
couples acknowledge in the jokes they make and in the party games they play
the existence of the emotional and sexual bonds which they are not free to
discuss. The intramarital sparring that results is both amusing and agonizing.
For example, one evening after their friends Frank and Janet Appleby have
left, Marcia Smith begins to interrogate her husband Harold and this exchange results:

"Are you sleeping with Janet?"
"Why, are you sleeping with Frank?"
"Of course not."
"In that case, I'm not sleeping with Janet." (p. 149)

But, of course, Marcia and Harold *are* both having affairs (with Frank
and Janet, respectively). In time this becomes known among the four of
them. They acknowledge their adulterous bonds and try to incorporate them
into a conflict-free life-style, but in this they are never wholly successful.
Rather, Updike tells us that a "pattern of quarrel and reunion, of revulsion
and surrender, was repeated three or four times that winter" (p. 171).

Two other couples, the Saltzes and the Constantines, seem to have extramarital experiences with one another that almost fit into the consensual category, but the Saltines (as the other couples name these four) are on the
fringes of Updike's narrative so we are not allowed to fully explore their relationship.

The central figure in *Couples* is Piet Hamema who beds down with no fewer than four other women in addition to his wife Angela. There are two emotionally involving relationships and two less important ones. His affair with Foxy Whitman finally leads to his divorcing Angela and marrying Foxy. Piet suffers a lot. The logistics of deception and the accumulation of guilt complicate his life incredibly. As another novelist, Felix Bastian, has written:

Sexual eccentricity has been interpreted as monstrous evil by the moralists, as a disease by the psychoanalysts, and as a matter of taste by various libertarians. What has been commonly overlooked in these, no doubt, worthwhile exegeses of the phenomenon is its everyday character as a mass of technical difficulties. [13]

Yet Piet seems never to give very serious consideration to abandoning his life-style. Adultery, despite its burdens, is too important to give up. In the words of the *Time* review:

Trapped in their cozy catacombs, the couples have made sex by turns their toy, their glue, their trauma, their therapy, their hope, their frustration, their revenge, their narcotic, their main line of communication and their sole and pitiable shield against the awareness of death. Adultery, says Updike, has become a kind of 'imaginative quest' for a successful hedonism that would enable man to enjoy an otherwise meaningless life. [14]

This notion of adultery as a location of ultimate concern, of adultery as an alternate religion, is borne out through the testimony of Updike's characters. Angela says of Freddy Thorne:

He thinks we're a circle. A magic circle of heads to keep the night out. He told me he gets frightened if he doesn't see us over a weekend. He thinks we've made a church of each other.

Other episodes and images reinforce the link between adultery and ultimate meaning. For Piet, while engaging in adulterous intercourse with Bea Guerin, "Death no longer seemed dreadful" (p. 352). It is not without significance that Piet and his mistress Foxy are the only two of their circle of friends ("except for the Catholics") who go to church. Toward the end of the novel Piet, by then separated from his wife but not yet having moved toward a permanent bond with Foxy, watches an ancient church building burn—"struck by God's own lightning"—and then goes to bed with Carol Constantine.

Adultery, for Updike's characters, is a quest for meaning and adventure but it is a troublesome, even traumatic quest. Marriage is, by its very nature, beset with problems. In fact, says Updike, "Every marriage is a hedged bet" (p. 48). But adultery is no easy way out. There is no escape from the responsibility of relationships. "The first breath of adultery is the freest; after it, constraints apeing marriage develop" (p. 477).

Society, the couples learn, offers no rulebook for adultery. Those who transgress the boundaries of emotional and sexual monogamy must manufacture their own morality and solve their own problems. They are sailing in uncharted waters. Of the adulterous lovers, Piet and Georgene, Updike tells us: "Lacking a marriage or any contract, they had evolved between them a code of mutual consideration" (p. 57).

But despite everyone's best efforts, the complications seem to win again and again. There are two divorces. The Applebys and the Smiths are never quite able to make their foursome work. Freddy Thorne and Carol Constantine are portrayed as pathetically compulsive about their sexuality. At one point Foxy ends her reminiscences of her affair with Piet with this resigned summary: "Adultery. It's so much *trouble*" (p. 343).

Updike leaves it for the reader to decide whether or not it is *worth* the trouble. Perhaps there is nothing more to say.

Without a sacramental view of marriage, adultery becomes just a species of "visiting" or saying *Howdy*, and as a perpetually exciting theme of novels it is surely on the wane. [15]

The adultery in *Couples* carries a lot of freight for the characters of the novel, but ambiguity marks their experiences of one another, and adulterous life-styles prove exceedingly complicated. The reader begins to see something of the sweep and variety of extramarital sexuality, but the novel does not clearly affirm or prescribe. There is no promotion of a philosophy or a program, and few readers, I suspect, will be attracted by Updike's narrative to the life-styles portrayed.

Bob and Carol and Ted and Alice

A very different perspective on extramarital sex is offered in *Bob and Carol and Ted and Alice*, a film with screenplay by Paul Mazursky and Larry Tucker. [16]

Bob and Carol Sanders, affluent young marrieds who like to think even younger, attend an encounter marathon at an Esalen-like retreat center and return home to Beverly Hills feeling transformed and liberated. Their best friends, the somewhat less hip Ted and Alice Henderson, seem unable to appreciate the "new" Bob and Carol.

The Sanders' new commitment to candor does not have to wait long for a test. Bob returns from a business trip and confesses an adulterous encounter to Carol who, after being assured that Bob does not love the girl, affirms both the act and his sharing of it. In fact, Carol is so pleased that Bob is free enough to have such an experience and to tell her about it, so pleased with her own positive response, that she tells Ted and Alice the whole story. They are unable to appreciate it. Alice is devastated by the news and, by it, is confirmed in her own antisexuality. Ted, representing clandestine adultery in his attitudes and in his fantasies, thinks Bob was really dumb to tell Carol. When Bob returns (early!) from his *next* business trip, he finds Carol in bed with the friendly neighborhood tennis pro/stud. After an initial outburst of angry jealousy, Bob too is able to affirm his spouse's adultery and her candor about it.

The film's grand finale is an attempt at an orgy. The two couples, pleasantly drunk, go to bed together. Interestingly, it is the women who take most of the initiative in precipitating this encounter. There is embarrassing silence and a little strained extramarital necking but they do not consummate their being together sexually. In fact, Bob and Ted, with Carol naked in the bed between them, begin to discuss the stock market. The film ends with the foursome still friends but not lovers. Beyond that, it is hinted that Bob and Carol will not again seek sexual experiences outside of marriage. Bob gives voice to the crucial insight:

That's it! What the world needs now is love, not this . . . The trouble with my affair and the trouble with yours, Carol, is just that. There wasn't any *love*. [17]

The "this" which the world doesn't need is the orgy. The liberated young marrieds had worked the approval of consensual adultery into their marriage covenant but they found that when extramarital sex with affection is tried, two things happen: (1) It does not work. (2) The earlier experiments with sex-just-for-fun are seen as failures and that kind of adultery is also ruled out for the future.

Although the film is essentially a slick comedy, it nevertheless offers a few usable insights into the contemporary experience of adultery. Perhaps most important: *Bob and Carol and Ted and Alice* (hereafter, *BCTA*) tells a mass audience that consensual adultery exists. For millions of moviegoers this film was a first vivid testimony to the fact that it might actually be possible for extramarital intercourse, with the knowledge and approval of the spouse, to occur. *BCTA* is not a stag film, not a Scandinavian import, not a low-budget effort aimed at intellectuals and the youth culture. It is commercial cinema featuring established and rising stars. Although its theme has not been treated in such a film before, *BCTA* is not tractarian or evangelistic. Its appearance means simply this: *American mass society is ready to be entertained rather than offended by adultery.*

Adultery, then, need no longer be bitter, painful, and tragic. Adultery can now be *comic*. It can be taken much less seriously than before. The appearance of this kind of film about extramarital sex reflects the arrival of a new sociosexual self-consciousness. Middle America has begun to think about the new-style adultery—adultery in which the spouse is not deceived, adultery which does not necessarily destroy marriages, adultery which (at least experimentally) is incorporated into one's life-style.

In addition to its annunciatory function—and despite its comic format —*BCTA* accurately reports some of the interesting dimensions of the "new adultery." Many persons who have participated in encounter groups and related exercises of the human potential movement have in fact been moved to greater candor about their sexual feelings and more than a few have consciously tried adding extramarital sexuality to their understanding and practice of marriage. This kind of alteration of a couple's understanding of marriage is not always easy; it is often painful and conflict-ridden. Many couples who begin these explorations decide against the radical alternatives and discover a deeper commitment to the conventional pattern.

The film's portrayal of the way in which Bob and Carol work through their sharing of their extramarital experiences makes it look too easy, but it does suggest some of the dynamics of that kind of exchange—and it raises some questions. Does Carol *really* approve of Bob's extramarital adventure or is she just trying to look liberated? Is Bob's response to Carol's experience with the tennis pro a model of mature affirmation or the product of his resolve that he will not be out-Esalened by his wife?

Another tinge of reality is to be seen in the prominence of the *dare* motif in the almost-orgy scene. Even among the "liberated" there are inhibitions to overcome so alcohol and strange combinations of peer pressure are needed to catalyze movement toward the radical alternative.

Many younger viewers and reviewers saw the ending of the film as a cop-out. Although moviegoing America is ready to laugh along with consensual adultery, perhaps we are not yet ready really to affirm it as an option. Maybe the message is that when nice people—and, of course, Natalie Wood and Robert Culp could not play anything but nice people—when nice people flirt with adultery, they decide it is not the ideal course. Not only do they decide not to consummate the spouse-swap, Bob and Carol also seem to renounce their earlier less-involving adulteries. Note that they are not guilt-ridden or remorseful about their extramarital adventures but they do see them as less than ideal. Monogamy wins this round—but the cultural stage has been set for a major film in which the four-handed bedroom scene does *not* culminate in a discussion of the stock market.

Viewers who are put off by the "cop-out" ending should realize that the film is not *essentially* about adultery or mate-swapping except in an illustrative way. The film's main thrust, it seems to me, is this: Bob and Carol are trying to be young, to participate in the youth culture for which they were born a little too early. Their dress and grooming is modified mod. They smoke marijuana and listen to rock music. They involve themselves politically and aesthetically in those things that youth endorse. And yet the final almost-orgy scene is set in Las Vegas, an entertainment center for the middle-aged. The intoxicant with which they ready themselves for their liberation is alcohol, not marijuana. Their decision not to have intercourse is followed by Jackie deShannon singing "What the World Needs Now Is Love." The end of the film is marked not by the driving, sensuous beat of acid rock but rather by the soft sound of what jukebox programs call an "adult hit." Despite their efforts, Bob and Carol do not make it into the youth culture. Not this time.

BCTA depicts the new adultery not as an end in itself but as a part of the new quest for emotional openness and as a part of the age-old quest for youth and youth's prerogatives. If the film tells us that new sexual styles are not really live options for the over-thirties—thus leaving middle-aged viewers secure in their monogamy—perhaps it also tells us that modes of consciousness are emerging which, in time, will alter the way we define and live the man-woman relationship.

Bob and Carol and Ted and Alice is as humorous as *Couples* is pathetic, yet both convey a kind of ambiguity about adultery and a not-yet-knowing about its future. We are living in the transition time, in a time of not being sure, in a time in which—perhaps—we can shape and reshape values and expectations relative to human sexuality. The Updike novel and the Mazursky/Tucker screenplay both leave us wondering whether or not there is reason to hope we might do this wisely and well.

Robert Rimmer's *Proposition 31*

Proposition 31 by Robert H. Rimmer[18] offers several perspectives on the contemporary experience of adultery; the novel has at least something to say about a number of different forms of extramarital relationships.

Horace is married to Tanya and is having an affair with Sylvia. This is a clandestine relationship. Tanya becomes romantically involved with next-door neighbor David. Horace finds out about this liaison and he and Tanya deal with it much as Bob and Carol dealt with one another's adulteries—except that in the Rimmer narrative the agony, while short-lived, is more real. David's wife Nancy proves less resilient; the news of the affair almost destroys her. She runs away threatening divorce and even suicide—the extreme stereotyped responses to the discovery of old-style adultery. But she is pursued by Horace who (1) seduces her and (2) convinces her that the four of them should spend some time together and talk things through. The seduction is facilitated by a convenient and very severe snowstorm which forces Horace and Nancy to share a hotel room. Rather improbable logistical accidents of this sort are common in Rimmer's fiction. The author clearly believes that even after people have begun to liberate themselves intellectually, they may yet need the right circumstances to motivate their actions.

So Horace, professor of sociology and social visionary, convenes a mini-encounter group in a vacation cabin in the wilderness—complete with the books that have made him the self-actualizing person he is. This woodsy cabin scene (part II, chapters 6-9) is the essence of Rimmer. Horace reflects the author's optimism and his conviction that seemingly impossible problems can be solved.

In his enthusiasm, Horace mounted the hearth and jiggled the fire into a roaring flame with a poker. "Leaving Nancy's escapade with Peter Alberti aside, and if my interest in Sylvia had never been discovered, and assuming David's brief fling with his secretary was only a reactive phenomenon, we have just one thing to contend with that makes our marital problems difficult to resolve. Tanya is pregnant and David is the father" (p. 186).

Oh, is *that* all? Rimmer clearly believes that even the thorniest dilemmas can be worked through if mature and secure adults will simply apply themselves and believe that they are, in large measure, masters of their fate and architects of their future. Horace continues:

"Up to the time we discovered one another's infidelities, we were reasonably good friends. I'm not going to pretend that we loved one another. In the past we may have had moments when we actually disliked one another as individuals or as composite married couples.... But, to put it in a nutshell, I think we could learn to love one another" (p. 186).

This is the key. *We could learn to love one another.* Love, for Rimmer, is learned behavior. Horace and Tanya and David and Nancy decide to try building a future together; they set about designing a group marriage. To be sure, there are difficulties and tensions, but they are all managed. There is bitterness, jealousy, and misunderstanding, but none that does not melt away before rational analysis, love's warmth, and the conscious reprogramming of selves.

In time the four evolve a commitment to one another which is so strong that they cannot imagine not living together permanently, and when scandal strikes, all four go to work to legalize group marriage by means of an amendment to the state constitution. The novel ends with the four of them, inseparably bound together, working on that campaign, planning a house that will accommodate their combined families, and celebrating the birth of Tanya's child.

In *Proposition 31* clandestine adultery becomes ambiguous adultery which in turn becomes consensual adultery of the group marriage variety. A subplot involves Nancy and later Horace with a neighborhood swingers' group and thus affords us a glimpse of recreational adultery. But having shown something of the whole spectrum of adulterous possibilities, Rimmer clearly opts for group marriage. Through juxtaposition with other varieties, he seeks to show that group marriage is the highest form of variation on the marital relationship. If both *Couples* and *Bob and Carol and Ted and Alice* ended with a question, *Proposition 31* presumes to supply the answer.

To be sure, *Proposition 31* is "message fiction," a tract, a blueprint for utopia. Rimmer clearly wants his readers to respond with enthusiasm to the model his characters work out. There is even an annotated bibliography at the end of the volume standing ready to guide the reader in his quest for new forms of consciousness and alternate social arrangements.

Many readers of *Proposition 31* and of Rimmer's other utopian novels find the characters unreal. Whether one chooses to describe them as "too strong to be real" or as "one-dimensional," the fact remains that many readers have considerable difficulty identifying with them and are unable to locate such people in their own social worlds. In fairness, two things should be pointed out in this connection: (1) Bob Rimmer himself *is* very much like Horace and other characters in the Rimmer novels; [19] (2) perhaps a self-confessed utopian novelist is entitled to create characters who are more *ideal* than real since by definition *(utopia* means *no place)* the goal is to describe people and institutions which are superior to any in our experience.

Rimmer believes in the power of positive thinking. Perhaps he would applaud Kurt Vonnegut Jr.'s dictum: "We are what we pretend to be, so we must be very careful about what we pretend to be." [20] Rimmer personally dislikes what he calls "breast-beating fiction," fiction which devotes itself exclusively to probing what is wrong with humankind and lamenting our failures. Rimmer's fiction pretends boldly. It pretends that humans are rational, that problems have solutions, that things can get better.

Although he proposes a radical alternative to traditional monogamy, Rimmer is rather conservative in many ways. Group sex and homosexuality are specifically ruled out. [21] The group marriage is a closed system—for people over thirty—with members limiting themselves to emotional and sexual intimacy only with the two members of the opposite sex within the group. (There is almost no mention of important emotional sharing between David and Horace.) Rimmer is clearly not an advocate of an anything-goes morality. He is reaching for an internally consistent *system* of behavior, a system complete with rules and limits and responsibilities.

Despite its flaws, *Proposition 31* is an important book. It has catalyzed much rethinking and inspired many fantasies. Substantial numbers of the young and the not-so-young have subjected the taken-for-grantedness of sexual patterns to new scrutiny because of having read Rimmer. [22] In time someone will write a novel which treats alternatives to monogamous marriage with a little more subtlety and a little less program than Rimmer. But for now, *Proposition 31* fills a vacuum. It is one of a very few books which deal so candidly with the conscious search for a meaningful sexual future.

Some Comparisons

Our three fictional treatments of adultery invite innumerable comparisons and contrasts. Space limitations prevent extended discussion here but the reader may wish to explore, for example, the striking differences between Updike's and Rimmer's understandings of how a "wronged" spouse reacts when the adultery of the mate is discovered. In *Couples* Janet and Harold commit "revenge adultery" when they learn that their spouses have lovers. In *Proposition 31* Horace very self-consciously seduces Nancy, initiates the group marriage discussion, and insists that all four of them can learn to love one another. The contrast between Updike's gloomy vision and Rimmer's optimistic one is also to be seen through parallel reading of the two "showdown" scenes. When, in *Couples*, Ken and Foxy and Piet and Angela gather to discuss Piet and Foxy's adultery, bitterness and dismay prevail. Twin divorces loom as the only option. But in *Proposition 31*, when Horace and Tanya and David and Nancy begin to discuss their future in light of their adulteries, many avenues are explored and the four decide to create their own utopian framework.

A mark which all three of our sources share is the relative affluence of the characters. The adulterers of Tarbox are upper-middle-class folk. The backdrops and artifacts make it clear that Bob and Carol and their friends are even more affluent than Updike's couples. And Rimmer's heroes are not only financially well-off to begin with, they are able to locate benefactors who are willing to dump large quantities of money upon them and their endeavors. [23] We should begin to inquire into the class boundaries and the economic implications of the new adultery—and to ask if such deviant behavior is the prerogative only of the wealthy.

Although the Updike novel is clearly artistically superior to the film and the Rimmer book, the latter two are in many ways more socially and culturally important. *Couples* tells us again what we already knew: Clandestine adultery is complicated and painful and perhaps not worth the trouble. *Bob and Carol and Ted and Alice* announces that adultery might now be comic as well as tragic and that consensual adultery, if not the wave of the future, is at least one of the options with which responsible adults might experiment. *Proposition 31* goes still further. It raises hopes in connection with a radical alternative to the dominant sexual orthodoxy. It puts us in touch with some of our own personal feelings and fantasies and leads us through an exploration of a new model. The Rimmer book brings us to the edge of our future. By unashamedly arguing for his answer, Rimmer forces us to ask ourselves some very important questions. If we dwell too long on the weaknesses of *Proposition 31*, it may be because we are not ready to face those questions.

The great variety of behavior and motivation that marks extramarital relations in our time is just beginning to be appreciated. There are still big gaps which must be filled by sensitive writing and filmmaking—and, of course, it is imperative that social scientists and helping professionals develop appreciation of this variety so that they can make their analytic and therapeutic contributions.

The film and the two novels considered here teach us that while clandestine adultery is still with us, there are, emerging alongside it, new forms of extramarital experience. These new forms are complex and multifaceted and they defy simple labeling as *good* or *bad*. Ambiguous and consensual adultery are entering the corporate consciousness as socially significant forms worthy of the attention of thinking, feeling persons in the process of constructing their own life-styles.

Couples and *Bob and Carol and Ted and Alice* and *Proposition 31* are among the resources of our time for society's ongoing resocialization where sexuality and adultery are concerned. But we are *all* constantly in the business of socializing one another—formally and informally. Our further task consists of pointing out for one another helpful treatments of things that matter and responding compassionately and creatively to the probes and prods of the writers we read. This essay has tried to take some steps in that direction. More important than my typology, more important than my choice of three pieces of relevant fiction, more important than my brief reactions to them, is the contention that something new is happening in our awareness of extramarital sex *and* that novels and films can assist us in sorting out and living with our new possibilities.

Reference Notes

1. Dawn (not her real name) is one of the persons I interviewed for an ongoing study of alternative forms of intimate association.

2. Funk and Wagnall's *Standard Dictionary* (Chicago: Encyclopedia Britannica, 1966).

3. I have chosen, because of space limitations, to restrict myself to a treatment of adultery that is marked by sexual intercourse. It might be interesting to explore very important emotional but nonsexual relationships outside of marriage. Also, nonmarital relationships which have sexual components but which do not involve intercourse are very common and more than worthy of careful inquiry. For the purposes of the present essay, however, I shall treat only extramarital relationships marked by coitus.

4. It must be acknowledged here that there are adulterous relationships which the principals value as *good*, about which they feel no guilt, and which, perhaps, they *wish* they could share with their spouses and others *but* they do not do this because, as they understand it, the spouse(s) could not cope with the revelation. In such cases the criterion I am employing is less helpful than we might wish. It is my opinion, however, that this criterion—the extent to which the spouse knows and approves—is helpful in most cases and so I develop it even while acknowledging that it will not be the best analytic tool in every situation.

5. A full bibliography of materials which treat various forms of spouse-approved adultery would be inappropriate here, but for the reader who wishes to explore such phenomena further, here are some suggestions:

Alfred C. Kinsey et al. *Sexual Behavior in the Human Female* (Philadelphia: W. B. Saunders, 1953). See especially pp. 434 ff. Of the 221 female respondents whose adulteries were discovered or suspected by their husbands, 42 percent reported that no difficulties resulted. Kinsey notes the existence of spouse swapping and other situations in which the husband encourages his wife's extramarital intercourse.

Robert Athanasiou et al. "Sex." *Psychology Today*, July 1970. This survey of 20,000 readers reported that (1) 40 percent of the married men and 36 percent of the married women have committed adultery; (2) 80 percent of the respondents say that extramarital sex could be all right under certain circumstances; (3) the notion that adultery is all right if you do not talk about it is almost totally rejected; (4) 5 percent of the married respondents have participated in spouse swapping and (5) 41 percent of the married men and 22 percent of the married women "are interested in swapping."

Lonny Myers and Hunter Leggitt, "A New View of Adultery." *Sexual Behavior*, February 1972.

For an account of a three-person group marriage based on the diaries of the participants see Gordon Clanton and Chris Downing, eds., *Face to Face* (New York: E. P. Dutton, 1975 and Ballantine Books, 1976).

See also note 10.

6. A survey of 1,212 of its readers in the October 1968 issue of *Ladies Home Journal* suggested that most American women are prepared to forgive their husbands at least one adulterous experience before considering divorce. Seventy-four percent said that a single act of adultery by either partner should only infrequently be a cause of divorce.

7. The notion of *permanence* is conceptually problematic since few of the people actually involved in group marriage are given to the use of language like "for the rest of our lives" or "till death do us part." Perhaps we could say that group marriage has a *relative permanence*. That is: Permanence is the *ideal* toward which the participants move; there is no preset terminal date.

8. Robert Athanasiou et al. "Sex." *Psychology Today*, July 1970, p. 43. This preaction category, the realm of thought, wish, and fantasy, has usually been overlooked by sex researchers. The *Psychology Today* study (wisely, I would argue) invites our attention to this dimension of human sexuality.

9. The terms *mate swapping* and *wife swapping* can refer to any of several forms of consensual adultery—group marriage, open-ended marriage, or swinging—and are not, therefore, terms that can be used with precision.

10. See James R. Smith and Lynn G. Smith, eds., *Beyond Monogamy* (Baltimore: Johns Hopkins University Press, 1974) and Gilbert D. Bartell, *Group Sex* (New York: Wyden, 1971).

11. Leo Lowenthal. *Literature and the Image of Man* (Boston: Beacon, 1963), pp. ix f.

12. Page numbers cited are from John Updike, *Couples* (Greenwich, Conn.: Fawcett Publications, 1968). For Updike's further reflections on sexuality and adultery see his exquisite short story "Eros Rampant" in *Harper's* magazine, June 1968. Also of interest in this connection is an essay on Denis de Rougement entitled "More Love in the Western World" in Updike's *Assorted Prose* (New York: Knopf, 1965).

13. Felix Bastian. *The Enclaves* (Garden City, N.Y.: Doubleday, 1965), p. 23.

14. *Time*, April 26, 1968, pp. 66-7.

15. Personal correspondence from John Updike, December 1970.

16. The screenplay has been adapted into a novel by Patricia Welles (New York: Bantam, 1969). It is very disappointing. The novel reproduces the screenplay dialogue (with very few variant readings) and punctuates it with cliché-ridden descriptive passages and shallow psychologizing. This time the movie is better than the book.

17. Quoted from the novel, p. 184.

18. Page numbers cited are from Robert H. Rimmer, *Proposition 31* (New York: New American Library, 1968). Rimmer has written two other novels which offer utopian perspectives on the sexual dimensions of the human experience. *The Rebellion of Yale Marratt* (New York: Avon, 1964) treats enlightened bigamy, and *The Harrad Experiment* (New York: Bantam, 1967) describes an experimental college at which male and female students are paired off as roommates. Rimmer's views are further elaborated and some reactions to them are registered in *Adventures in Loving* (New York: New American Library, 1973).

19. I base this judgment on my own extended conversations with Rimmer. Others who know him corroborate my estimate.

20. From the introduction to Kurt Vonnegut, Jr., *Mother Night* (New York: Avon, 1961), p. v.

21. Group sex is sexual activity involving more than two persons at the same time. Group sex and group marriage are clearly *not* the same thing. Rimmer is opposed to group sex (see *Proposition 31*, pages 258 ff). He was surprised and upset when the cover of the paperback version of

Proposition 31 announced in bold print: "The author of *The Harrad Experiment* takes group sex one shocking step further."

22. In their book *Group Marriage* (New York: Macmillan, 1973), p. 31, Larry and Joan Constantine report that "almost all of our early contacts [with persons experimenting with group marriage] and most later ones reported that Rimmer's novels . . . played some role in leading to their actual involvement. Most often, the novel served as an object of discussion, an excuse for talking about threatening new ideas rather than as a progenitor."

23. This almost miraculous intrusion of large quantities of money is a mark of all three of Rimmer's utopian novels. A wealthy home builder who is sympathetic to the group marriage idea sets up a five-million-dollar foundation and names Horace its director. Yale Marratt makes *two* fortunes, one in currency speculation and one on the stock exchange *and* is given money by an eccentric but sympathetic millionairess. Harrad College is funded by offstage philanthropy and Sheila Cole (one of the six central characters) inherits a fortune.

8.
Infidelity: Some Moral and Social Issues

Jessie Bernard

This classic article examines the concept of infidelity in our society and the value system that establishes sexual exclusivity and permanence as the key components of a marriage. Bernard then distinguishes between the several types of infidelity and relates age, sex, and class variables to incidence of infidelity and the spouses' ability to tolerate infidelity.

Bernard also examines the problem of meeting normal psychological dependency needs within the framework of marriage in the future. Recognizing that any one person's resources are limited, she questions whether and how people can depend on each other for long-term support when relationships become looser and involve multiple sexual-emotional pairings.

Both exclusivity and permanence are required in marriage as institutionalized in our society. However, they may be incompatible with one another in the kind of world we now live in where men and women are, in Bernard Farber's words, "permanently available." Sapirstein points up the difficulties:

Monogamy began in societies which had strong religious injunctions against infidelity and used every possible device to limit the temptations. Contrast the Chinese peasant dress or the shaved head of the young Hebrew bride with the modern woman who, whether married or not, does all she can to heighten her charms (Sapirstein, 1948, p. 173).

It may be that we will have to choose between exclusivity and permanence. If we insist on permanence, exclusivity is harder to enforce; if we insist on exclusivity, permanence may be endangered. The trend, as we shall note presently, seems to be in the direction of exclusivity at the expense of permanence in the younger years but permanence at the expense of exclusivity in the later years.

Exclusivity is still buttressed and enforced by both religious and secular law; permanence, by personal promises and vows. Sexual relations with anyone other than the spouse is forbidden by the seventh commandment and also by law. Adultery, though rarely prosecuted, is a crime in most states. [1] Society itself is the injured party. [2] Exclusivity is further buttressed by way of divorce legislation: Adultery is universally accepted as a ground for divorce. The spouse is now the injured party. No marital partner has to tolerate it.

"Infidelity: Some Moral and Social Issues" by Jessie Bernard from SCIENCE AND PSYCHO-ANALYSIS, Vol. XVI, THE DYNAMICS OF WORK AND MARRIAGE, edited by Jules H. Masserman. Reprinted by permission of Grune & Stratton, Inc., and the author.

Excerpts from SEXUAL BEHAVIOR IN THE HUMAN FEMALE by A. C. Kinsey, et al., 1953, are reprinted by permission of the Institute for Sex Research, Indiana University.

Infidelity Versus Fidelity

Infidelity, as distinguished from adultery, is the violation of a promise or a vow. Strangely enough, there is no universal, prescribed, or standard vow required of all those entering marriage. The officiating officer seems to have considerable latitude. Some denominations include both a promise and a vow; some only one or the other.[3] Some require a promise to cleave only to one another, some do not. Some require a forsaking of all others; a few do not mention this.[4] But almost every promise and/or vow incorporates permanence. This vow or promise is for keeps, till death parts them. Permanence, in brief, is more emphasized than exclusivity in the marital promises and vows.

The precise meaning of what is promised or vowed—to love, comfort, cherish, and so on—has been elaborated by one pair of commentators. Love, they tell us, means that one will treat the spouse affectionately. Comfort means that one will impart strength, cheer, encourage, gladden, as opposed to dispiriting, distressing, discouraging, saddening, or nagging. And the promise or vow to forsake all others includes more than other men or women as objects of attraction. It may include loving one's mother more than one's spouse, or children more than husband. It includes even imaginary clinging to old flames. Just thinking "If I had only married so-and-so instead of you!" constitutes a breach of this promise. And the fantasy of other sex partners does also (Easton & Robbins, 1938, p. 49). On the basis of this logic, a good case could also be made for including the man who prefers his work to his wife, a situation documented at least for some tycoons and no doubt characteristic of many ambitious professional men also.

Of special interest is the interpretation by two commentators of the promise or vow to forsake all others as not demanding a too rigid definition of exclusivity: "The right of husband or wife to the primary love of the other does not justify an insistence on exclusive possession nor condone jealousy of innocent friendships" (Cuber, unpublished manuscript, p. 50). Satiety and boredom should be avoided; external relationships should be encouraged. To be sure, these commentators are not advocating external *sexual* relationships; but it is interesting that innocent friendships—whatever they may mean—are not forbidden by the marital vows.

When we ask, therefore, what promises or vows are broken by marital infidelity, the answer is that they are promises to love, to honor, to cherish, and to comfort as well as to forsake all others and, in some cases, to cleave to one another. Strictly and narrowly interpreted, then, whenever one or both spouses ceased to love, honor, cherish, or comfort one another, they would be guilty of infidelity in the sense of reneging on a sacred promise. And, indeed, many men and women do in fact interpret infidelity in this way. But for our purposes here the common conception of infidelity, though inadequate, is accepted.

To make a distinction between adultery and infidelity does not mean that there is an inconsistency involved. Any kind of extramarital sexual relations constitutes a violation of the law and hence, by definition, adultery, a crime, an offense against the state. But extramarital relations are not in all cases, as we shall note presently, viewed by the spouse as an offense against him (her) or as infidelity.

Infidelity and Deprivation

If there is no deprivation of a spouse—of promised love, honor, cherishing—has a promise been violated? If a husband's relations with another woman do deprive his wife so that she suffers a real loss—emotional, sexual, or financial—there can hardly be any question that he has violated a promise; he is unfaithful to her. He is, in the popular conception, "cheating on her." Even those who accept extramarital relationships would probably not condone such deprivation of a spouse. But suppose a husband still "cleaves to his wife," that is, continues to live with her, to support her, to assume all his responsibilities toward her, even to love her—perhaps more than ever [5] —so that there is no deprivation. Can he still be accused of infidelity? And vice versa?

We do not know, of course, in what proportion of cases deprivation is present. On the assumption that, if infidelity causes no difficulty in a marriage, there is no deprivation present, we may find one clue in the Kinsey data, which show that so long as spouses did not know about extramarital relationships no damage was reported: "Extra-marital relationships had least often caused difficulty when the other spouse had not known of them. . . . Some of the extra-marital relationships had been carried on for long periods of years without ill effects on the marital adjustments. . . ." Not deprivation to the spouse, but knowledge of the relationship, was the damaging factor. The extramarital coitus had not appeared to do as much damage as the knowledge that it had occurred (Kinsey et al., 1953, p. 433). Othello had taught us this long ago. [6]

But how often, one may legitimately ask, does the spouse know? Among marriages in which the wife had engaged in extramarital relations, the husband was not aware of the situation in about half (51 percent) of the cases; he knew in 40 percent; and suspected in about 9 percent. But even among the 49 percent in which the husband knew or suspected, there was no difficulty reported—and presumably, therefore, no deprivation in about two fifths (42 percent) of the cases. [7] If, as estimated by Kinsey and his associates (1953, p. 434), 71 percent of the marriages in which extramarital relations of wives had occurred had not developed difficulties, the inference seems justified that deprivation was not involved. The wife's extramarital relationship did not deprive the husband [8] —at least not enough to create difficulties.

Forms of Infidelity

To speak, as we have done so far, as though extramarital relationships were all of a kind, simple and unidimensional, is of course misleading. They are of many kinds and assume different forms. It would be possible to draw up a complex systematic matrix inclusive of all combinations of duration, seriousness, and intensity of relationships and discuss each cell individually. Instead, discussion here is limited to seven forms as they have been reported in the literature.

1. Of perhaps least moral and social significance is the kind of relationship which takes the form of coquetry and flirtation—"making love without meaning it"—commonly accepted in many social circles; no seriousness is attached to it by either party or by their spouses. Sapirstein finds a functional use for it:

The normal flirtatiousness and minor conquests which are part of every social gathering give ample opportunities for testing out the old desires. These can be shared and enjoyed together without the necessity of continually proving in the open market one's residual desirability in the romantic chase. While such a compromise is difficult in the framework of our monogamous culture . . . it seems to be one of the few available compensations in this sensitive problem (Sapirstein, 1948, p. 173).

And this kind of relationship may be comprised in the "innocent friendship" which Easton and Robbins (1938, p. 49) believe is not required to be forsaken.

This form of relationship may even include physical embrace or petting. Kinsey and his associates (1953, p. 426) found that "at dinner parties, cocktail parties, in automobiles, on picnics, and at dances, a considerable amount of public petting is allowed between married adults." At the time Kinsey and his associates were gathering their data, 16 percent of their women subjects had engaged in such extramarital petting. Kinsey was of the opinion that this kind of behavior was increasing, though he did not feel he could document such a conclusion from the data.

2. Conceivably more serious is the transient, even fly-by-night, sex-as-play form, a sometime thing that leaves little residue except as it may leave a precipitate of guilt. About 11 percent of the Kinsey female subjects (42 percent of the 26 percent who had engaged in extramarital relations) had limited their experiences to a period of one year or less. Roughly the same proportion had had only one partner. Rather than a regularly spaced pattern, it was "more usual to find several nonmarital contacts occurring in the matter of a few days or in a single week when the spouse is away on a trip, or when the female is traveling and putting up at a hotel, or at a summer resort, or on an ocean voyage, or visiting at a friend's home" (Kinsey et al., 1953, pp. 420-25).

3. Quite different is what Helen Gurley Brown labels "the matinee." This is a purely playful relationship which arises between working men and women who use the lunch hour for their rendezvous at her apartment. The basic rule for such a relationship is "Never become serious." The hazards, beyond that of being found out—for, of course, it must be secret—are that one partner or the other might become bored or fall in love and thus become serious. Either eventuality is fatal to the relationship. In fact, to forestall the likelihood that it may become serious, one of the conditions of success of the matinee is that one or both partners be happily married to others (Brown, 1965, ch. 9).

4. What might be called a quasi-matinee form of infidelity has been re-

ported on by a team of sociologists, a form which they call the cocktail-lounge relationship (Roebuck & Spray, 1967, pp. 388-95). Its salient characteristics, so far as they are relevant here, may be summarized as follows:

The cocktail-lounge model is a semiserious, semicommitted relationship, semistable; that is, it is of more than transitory duration, definitely not a "pick-up" relationship in the usual sense. It tends to occur among fairly high-status individuals. Most of both men and women in the reported study had had at least some college education. The men were in business and professional occupations; most of the women were either college students (20 percent) or secretaries (33 percent). The employees of the cocktail lounge judged most (80 percent) of both the men and the women to be "stable." . . . The "natural history" of such relationships was one in which after a year or two the women marry (or remarry) and leave the system and are replaced by another cohort. The men do not drop out unless they have to leave town or, in some cases, become too old for these activities. In no case was the marriage of the man reported as disrupted (Bernard, 1968a, pp. 69-70).

The men tended to average in their late thirties, the women in their mid-twenties, the medians being thirty-nine and twenty-four respectively.

5. There is, next, the long-lasting pseudomarital form of infidelity, a relationship which Cuber has found to be very similar to conventional marriage:

The dynamics of . . . these relationships . . . break with conventional stereotypes about them which generally run to assertions that such relationships typically follow a cycle which begins in infatuation, has a relatively short decline, ends in disillusionment, a new partner is found, and the cycle is repeated. We found examples fitting this model, to be sure, but typically the cases were otherwise. . . . In the prolonged . . . relationships there is often no more a "cycle" than there is intrinsic to marriage—the relationship is monogamous, continues "until death. . . ." Where there is a cycle in any real sense, it tends to be like the cycle in a goodly number of marriages. These relationships, like marriage, sometimes move from vitality and a strong erotic accent to a more matter-of-fact, comfortable kind of interaction. Surprisingly enough, some have settled into a kind of apathy which makes one wonder why they go on, since there are no institutional obligations involved. But perhaps sentiment and a quiescent kind of attachment may be stronger bonds than external social sanctions (Cuber, unpublished manuscript).

Cuber does not judge these relationships to be any more vulnerable than sanctioned unions. They appear to have powerful intrinsic supports which psychiatrists are in a better position to evaluate than laymen. Even to a layman, however, it is apparent that there must be overriding reasons why the partners in such relationships have not married. The relationship looks very much like polyandrous marriage. Kinsey and his associates (1948, p. 593) reported similar unions among their male subjects. And among the 9 percent of their women subjects who had engaged in extramarital relationships for four or more years, there must have been some of the 11 percent who had had only one partner (Kinsey et al., 1953, p. 425).

6. Fantasied infidelity—relations with an imagined partner or imagined relations with a real person—is certainly far more common than acted-out infidelity, but, according to St. Matthew, no less real. "I say to you that

every one who looks at a woman lustfully has already committed adultery with her in his heart" (Matt. 5:28). Just daydreaming. Even, presumably, looking at the Playmate of the Month. Or at any attractive girl on the street. From this point of view it would be difficult for any man not to be judged guilty of adultery, however conformist his overt behavior might be. Or any woman, either, for that matter, who had been exposed to the seduction of an entertainment world personality. Or either husband or wife who fantasies another partner, real or imaginary, in the sex act.

This fantasy form of infidelity has been given some research attention by a team who interviewed forty suburban couples in business-professional occupations, averaging about thirty years of age (Neubeck & Schletzer, 1962). They included sexual and emotional involvements as well as merely fantasy involvement and correlated their findings with measures of marital satisfaction and of "conscience."[9] They found, expectably enough, that "the less satisfied persons seek . . . satisfaction in fantasy" more than others do, but the same was not true with respect to the conscience variable. Those with high conscience scores were as likely as those with low conscience scores to have fantasy involvement.[10]

This lack of relationship between conscience score and fantasy involvement seems to contradict Sapirstein's conclusions based on his experience with clients:

The inability to face the extramarital urge frequently has a disruptive effect on the marriage. When these feelings are repressed into the unconscious, they almost invariably are associated with hostility to the marital partner. The man may feel that his wife is playing a potentially punishing role toward him for his thoughts of infidelity, and he may begin to resent her. . . . He may be unable to accept this hostility, and live in constant preoccupation and terror about his sexual thoughts (Sapirstein, 1948, pp. 173-4).

Perhaps the seeming conflict between Sapirstein and Neubeck is more apparent than real. The fantasy involvement may be present in almost everyone, but it may be a source of disturbance in only a few.

There seem to be no research reports on the relative frequency of the fantasy of the ideal surrogate lover we are told sometimes takes the place of the actual spouse in the coital act in order to render the experience more palatable.

7. There is a kind of noncoital, nonfantasy relationship which involves a profound sharing of the self with another, not a spouse, that is not adulterous in the legal sense though susceptible to the charge of infidelity. Such a situation was depicted in a recent London and Broadway play in which the wife is—justifiably—more fearful of the Platonic intimacy between her husband and another woman than she would have been of a coital relationship. The kind of relationship which can develop between men and women who work together as a team over a period of time sometimes assumes an emotional interdependence outweighing the marital bonds of either one without supplanting them. These may be among the innocent relationships which, according to Easton and Robbins, are not forbidden by the marital vows. It is

an index of our relative concerns that little research attention has been devoted to this kind of relationship.

Patterns of Infidelity

By the age of forty, about twice as many of the Kinsey male subjects as of the female subjects had engaged in extramarital relations (50 and 26 percent respectively (Kinsey et al., 1953, p. 437).

In the Middle Ages when a man was to be away from his wife for any length of time he clamped her into a chastity belt to protect her, presumably, not only against trespassing males but also against her own carnality. Women reared in our society have presented—at least until recently—a somewhat different picture:

Most males can immediately understand why most males want extra-marital coitus. . . . To most males the desire for variety in sexual activity seems as reasonable as the desire for variety in the books that one reads, the music that one hears, the recreations in which one engages, and the friends with whom one associates socially. On the other hand, many females find it difficult to understand why any male who is happily married should want to have coitus with any female other than his wife (Kinsey et al., 1953, p. 409).

And their specific findings corroborated this conclusion; the patterns with respect to extramarital relationships differed considerably between the sexes.

Before age twenty-five, for example, there was no relation between years of education and active incidence of extramarital relations among women; among men, there was lower incidence among the more educated. After age twenty-five, however, education made little difference among the men, but among women the active incidence was positively related to education—higher, that is, among the better educated. The period of greatest incidence among women was in the age bracket thirty-six to forty (17 percent); among men it was highest in the late teens (35 percent) and declined consistently thereafter. In general, the incidence among men tended to be more regularly spaced; among women, as noted earlier, more sporadic (Kinsey et al., 1953, p. 437).

But far the most interesting finding was one with respect to frequency of coitus per week among those who engaged in extramarital relations. In the early years it was four times greater among the men than among the women (0.4 and 0.1 respectively); in the early thirties, the frequencies were the same for both sexes (0.2). But in the early forties, it was twice as high among women as among men (0.4 and 0.2 respectively) (Kinsey et al., 1953, p. 437). These data suggest that, although women were less disposed to engage in extramarital coitus, when they did, it was with greater frequency.

Infidelity Tolerance

A useful concept for thinking and researching and, hence, ultimately, for counseling, might have to do with the relative tolerance for infidelity which spouses show. For such purposes we might think in terms of a gradient. For example, a spouse might: (1) reject infidelity and divorce the partner, (2) reject the infidelity but not divorce the partner, (3) accept the infidelity grudgingly, under duress, (4) accept the infidelity willingly, or (5) urge or encourage infidelity. Both ends of this continuum have been documented in the literature (Kinsey et al., 1953, pp. 434-5). One's "infidelity tolerance" seems to be related to age, to sex, and to class. Women until now have tended to be more resigned to infidelity than men; about twice as many husbands (51 percent) as wives (27 percent) considered extramarital relations of their spouses as a factor in their divorces (Kinsey et al., 1953, pp. 436-8). The evidence with respect to age is not so clear-cut, but it appears that older men and women firmly anchored in a long-standing marriage tend to hesitate before breaking it up for infidelity. "In time," Kinsey notes, love, jealousy, and morality "seemed less important, and the middle-aged and older females had become more inclined to accept extra-marital coitus, and at least some of the husbands no longer objected if their wives engaged in such activities" (Kinsey et al., 1953, p. 417). The wives of working-class men are often reared in an ethnic tradition which accepts infidelity in young men as a matter of course, as something to bear if not to grin about. In general, the cultural context in which the infidelity occurs seems to be as important as the specific situation itself, if not more so, in determining the level of "infidelity tolerance."

Signs of Change

Despite the prevalence of the several forms of infidelity, the public for the most part still gives lip service to the standard of marital exclusivity.[12] But there are several straws in the wind which suggest that we are veering in a different direction, that attitudes, values, and behavior are changing with respect to this standard. Among these straws in the wind are: (1) the increasing emphasis on the positive aspects of extramarital relationships by researchers; (2) the greater tolerance shown at least by some theologians or ethicists; (3) the position vis-à-vis adultery in current thinking about divorce legislation; and (4) the increase in extramarital relationships among younger women.

1. One of the most interesting indications of change now taking place is the apologia which is becoming fashionable among researchers in discussing extramarital relationships. It has now become the positive, functional aspects which are increasingly emphasized rather than, as in the past, the negative and dysfunctional aspects. Kinsey and his associates (1948, p. 591) noted that the research literature to date was almost uniformly unfavorable in its judgment. "Only an occasional writer suggests that there may be values in such experience which can be utilized for human needs." And in 1953 (p. 431) they pointed out that "certainly any scientific analysis must take into account the fact that there are both advantages and disadvantages to engaging in such activity."

Gerhard Neubeck, on the basis of his research and counseling, has also concluded that there may be a positive function for extramarital relations in many marriages.

Marriage cannot serve to meet all of the needs of both spouses at all times. Many marriage partners define at least implicitly—certainly discretely—what area of satisfaction they will leave to outsiders, and they are not only *not* disturbed that outsiders serve in this capacity but probably relieved that they themselves are not called upon to have to address themselves to each and every need or whim of their mates. In this sense the extramarital relationship becomes supplementary to the marriage relationship (Neubeck, unpublished paper).

The current trend seems sometimes to be, in fact, not only in the direction of tolerance but even, in some cases, of advocacy. Some wives, Sapirstein (1948, p. 174) notes, are relieved to find that the marriage is suffering from nothing more serious than infidelity. "If that's all that is bothering you, go ahead and get it out of your system, but please don't become emotionally involved."

2. This positive evaluation has also found acceptance in the so-called situational school of ethics among some theological thinkers. Thus Joseph Fletcher, professor in the Episcopal Theological School of Cambridge, Massachusetts, writing in the Catholic *Commonweal*, has this to say:

There is nothing against extramarital sex as such, in this ethic, and in *some* cases it is good. . . . The *Christian* criteria for sex relations are positive: Sex is a matter of certain ideals of relationship. These ideals are based upon a certain faith: about God, Christ, the Church, who man is, and his destiny. Therefore, if people do not embrace that faith (and most do not), there is no reason why they should live by it. And most do not. . . . If true chastity means a marital monopoly, then let those who believe in it recommend it by reason and example. Nothing is gained by condemning the unbeliever. Indeed to condemn him is more unjust (immoral) than a sexual escapade (Fletcher, 1966, p. 431).

In this emphasis on sincerity and emotional authenticity, Joseph Fletcher is articulating the creed professed and practiced by a certain segment of the younger population today. They too make a big thing about authentic emotion, about fidelity in the sense of being true to their own inner selves. They object to the games people play and to what they call adult hypocrisy. The enormous emphasis on authentic emotion, on fidelity, on sincerity tends to make the criterion for judging a relationship the way people feel rather than objective sanctions. One is reminded of George Sand's *obiter dictum* that the hours a woman spent with her lover were true and good; the nights she spent with an unloved husband were sinful and bad.

3. Another straw in the wind has to do with the trends in divorce legislation. I had occasion not long ago to review the grounds alleged for divorce over a period of time as an index or measure of our society's legal specifications for marriage. The permitted legal grounds have not changed very rapidly, but the grounds used have tended to change from a frequent use of adultery[13] to a more frequent use of cruelty. Now we are in process of arriving at the concept of the no-fault divorce. Under this new conception, all that is necessary is for a court to find that the marriage has broken down. The

only proof needed will probably be a separation for a specified period of time. Until now—by universally accepting extramarital relations as grounds for divorce—we have demanded fidelity as a legal obligation of both spouses. With the introduction of the no-fault concept of divorce, such fidelity is no longer legally defined as part of marriage. That is, a person who engages in extramarital relationships but does not wish to have a divorce cannot necessarily be divorced for this reason alone. If the spouse wishes a divorce he or she will have to separate himself or herself from the other and prove in this way that the marriage has in fact broken down. The separation, not the extramarital relations, is the proof the court will need to prove that the marriage has broken down. Unless someone wishes to prosecute a man or woman for the crime of adultery, it will disappear from the scene as a legal entity for all intents and purposes.

4. There is, finally, evidence of change in the actual behavior of women over time. Kinsey and his associates reported among their subjects that by age forty, more than a fifth (22 percent) of the women born in the nineteenth century had engaged in extramarital coitus; almost a third (30 percent) of those born in the twentieth century had. At age forty-five, the proportions were 21 and 40 percent respectively. By age twenty-five, only 4 percent of the nineteenth-century women had engaged in such relations; twice as many (8 percent) of those born in the first decade of the twentieth century had; even more, 10 percent, of those born in the second decade had; and 12 percent of those born in the 1920s (Kinsey et al., 1953, pp. 422-4).[14] It would be logical to assume that, for women born in the 1930s and 1940s, the proportion who engaged in extramarital relations by age twenty-five is not less than, let us say, about 15 percent.[15]

The Future: Permanence or Exclusivity?

In the rapidly growing form of nonmarital relationship which young people are evolving today (Bernard, 1968-9), especially on university campuses, there are no vows of permanence. Nor are there any legal sanctions to buttress exclusivity. The emphasis seems to be on fidelity based on authentic emotion. One unpublished study of such relationships by Michael Johnson at the University of Iowa reports great emphasis on exclusivity, at least for the duration of the relationship. Among the findings with respect to twenty-eight couples are the following:

Does living together involve some conception of fidelity? The unmarried couples were asked two questions concerning their attitudes toward "adultery": "Under what conditions do you feel it would be all right for you to sleep with someone other than your partner?" and "Under what conditions do you feel it would be all right for your partner to sleep with someone other than you?" It is interesting to note that the respondents tend to put more restrictions on themselves than do their partners. Thus 48 percent of the males as compared to 39 percent of the females say that under no conditions would it be all right for the male partner to sleep with someone else. But 59 percent of the females as opposed to 44 percent of the males say that under no conditions would it be all right for the female partner to sleep with someone else. Less than a fifth of the respondents would accept such a relationship under any conditions at all. Once again we find the females more likely to be double standard than the males. A somewhat extraordinary discovery is that 11 percent of both males and females are double standard in the direction of more freedom for the female. . . . As for sexual behavior, the females in our sample have more often encountered the opportunity to sleep with someone else, 78 percent having had a chance as opposed to 64 percent of the males. However, when given the chance the male is more likely to take advantage of it (Johnson, 1969).

The young men are theoretically more permissive with respect to women than to themselves, but less "faithful" to their partners than the young women are in the presence of temptation.

But what seems more interesting is a rough comparison with the Kinsey findings of a generation ago. If we equate the Kinsey data on the attitude that extramarital coitus justifies divorce with the Johnson data on the attitude that such relations on the part of one's partner are never justified—admittedly not a completely legitimate equating of statements from a scientific point of view, but suggestive—we arrive at Table 1. The most interesting conclusions are to the effect that more of the young people in the Johnson sample seem to adhere to the standard of exclusivity than of the subjects in the Kinsey sample. The one exception is the attitude of the men toward extramarital relations on the part of women: Here the Kinsey men seem to be more conservative. But a disparity of only 7 percentage points in a comparison in which one set of subjects numbers only twenty-eight cases is not large enough to be unequivocally credited (Cell A, Table 1).

Table 1.

Attitude Toward Infidelity by Conventional Spouses and by Partners in Nonmarital Unions*

	Males in		Females in	
Attitude Toward Infidelity	Conventional Unions, %	Nonmarital Unions, %	Conventional Unions, %	Nonmarital Unions, %
Extramarital relations by wife or partner cause for divorce, or never justified	(A) 51	44	(B) 14	59
Extramarital relations by husband or partner cause for divorce, or never justified	(C) 18	48	(D) 27	39

*SOURCES: Johnson, 1969; Kinsey et al., 1953.

In the other cells the disparities—especially in Cell B and Cell C—are large enough to be taken seriously even in so small a set of cases. The young women in the Johnson sample were far less tolerant of extramarital relations by women than the Kinsey women were—59 percent as contrasted with only 14 percent (Cell B). They were also less tolerant than the Kinsey women of extramarital relations by men (Cell D). The disparity was only a matter of 12 percentage points (39 as compared with 27 percent) and may therefore only hover on the brink of statistical significance. But the disparity of 30 percentage points—48 and 18 percent—seems to me conclusive that the Johnson male subjects were more conservative with respect to extramarital relations of men than were the Kinsey subjects (Cell C).

I add all this up to mean that the women in the relationships which did not promise permanence were more conservative in their attitudes toward extramarital relations both for men and for women than were the women in the Kinsey sample, and that the Johnson sample men were more conservative than the Kinsey men so far as exclusivity for men was concerned. Exclusivity seemed more important than permanence.

A *caveat* is in order. The factor of age may invalidate any reading of the accompanying table. The Kinsey data included more older subjects, and older spouses probably have more "infidelity tolerance" than younger people. Permanence far outweighs exclusivity on their scale of values, as we noted above in our discussion of infidelity tolerance. We may, therefore, be comparing young people with low "infidelity tolerance," in a naturally conservative stage of the union, with older people in a less conservative stage, with high "infidelity tolerance." In any event, in these nonpromiscuous relationships, the relative emphasis seemed to be on exclusivity rather than on permanence.[16]

Jealousy and Insecurity

From a psychiatric standpoint two facets of the problem of infidelity seem to warrant at least cursory mention: male jealousy and female security. Kinsey and his associates made a considerable point of the mammalian origin of male jealousy. "While cultural traditions may account for some of the human male's behavior, his jealousies so closely parallel those of the lower species that one is forced to conclude that his mammalian heritage may be partly responsible for his attitudes" (1953, p. 411). And Edward Westermarck (1922, vol. 1, ch. 9), the great historian of human marriage, was of the opinion that monogamy rested on male jealousy. But Kingsley Davis, a sociologist, argues precisely the opposite point of view. Monogamy, by granting exclusivity to males, gives rise to jealousy. He sees jealousy as an institutional prop for monogamy. "Where exclusive possession of an individual's entire love is customary, jealousy will demand that exclusiveness. Where love is divided it will be divided according to some scheme, and jealousy will reinforce the division" (Davis, 1949, p. 184).[17] I shall not go further into Davis' subtle and sophisticated analysis; this statement does not, obviously, do it justice. But I would like to suggest that jealousy as a prop for monogamous relationships seems to be in process of attrition. How many cases have been treated lately in which jealousy was an important element? How many new plays deal with jealousy? How many movies? Television programs? Books?[18]

If male jealousy has been seen as a major support for sexual exclusivity, anxiety and insecurity have served a similar function among women with respect to permanence. As recently as just a few years ago I was willing to say that extramarital relations had different significance for men and for women. I believed then that a woman could not be casual about such relations, that she was not likely to engage in them unless there was more than a touch-and-go depth to them, that she could not, like men, treat them incidentally. To her they implied a commitment. I am no longer convinced of this. It seems to me now that a new kind of woman is emerging—or, if you will, an old kind is re-emerging[19] —on the scene. And one of the distinguishing characteristics of this woman is that she can be casual about sex, as in the past few women could. If women engaged in sexual relations outside of marriage it was because they were involved; the relation meant a great deal to them. Husbands, therefore, were justified in their alarm when they learned of them. But for many women today this is apparently no longer true. They can accept the sex-as-fun point of view without conflict. Even a regular extramarital relationship does not faze them or, in fact, necessarily interfere with their marriages.[20]

I believe that the increasing economic independence of women has played a part in this change.[21] Much of the terror which gripped women whose husbands were unfaithful to them in the past stemmed from the threat it posed to their economic security. What if the other woman won her husband away from her permanently? There is evidence in both Kinsey's statistical and Sapirstein's clinical data that, when or if she was assured that this was not likely, tolerance of infidelity increased.[22] I am, however, far from believing that economic independence tells the whole story, for there are economically independent women who are as terrified of losing men as the most economically dependent. The prostitute-pimp relationship is only the most extreme example of a situation which can occur in any setting. For psychological dependency must certainly be included in any analysis of infidelity tolerance.

Psychological Dependency Needs

Economic independence is a fairly simple phenomenon, merely a status, not intrinsic to the person who happens to occupy it. But psychological dependency is a personality trait and hence far more complex. Sapirstein (1948), in a book that has greatly influenced my own thinking, analyzed the nature of dependency needs in marriage, showing how normal they were, in men as well as in women, and how essential their fulfillment was. The basic function married partners performed for one another was, he showed, precisely that of satisfying the normal dependency needs that everyone experiences. The countless stresses and strains and threats that life subjects us to find alleviation in the unfailing support which in a good marriage can be depended upon from a spouse. No matter how helpless we may feel confronted by failure and disparagement in our nonmarital roles, we know that we can depend on our spouses to reassure us and build us up. He was writing in terms of threats from outside of the relationship—loss of job or difficulties with the children—which required reassurance from the spouse. But infidelity is a threat within the relationship itself, threatening the spouses with loss or diminution of the very support and reassurance marriage is supposed to supply. If we cannot depend on our spouses for such support, we may, Sapirstein notes, turn to others (1948, p. 170).

In connection with this analysis, I would like to raise a number of questions which psychiatrists are in a better position to deal with than a sociologist.

1. Can you foresee any form of socialization which would obviate the dependency needs which Sapirstein finds so basic in people reared in our society today? If people could be reared in a way that such dependency needs did not exist, what would it do to the nature of the marital bond?

2. If infidelity tolerance in both men and women should increase, what can we expect this to do to the nature of the marital relationship itself? Will it mean marital relationships are so solid, so impregnable, so secure that neither partner feels threatened by infidelity? Or so superficial, so trivial, so expendable, with so little at stake that infidelity really does not matter? Will it mean that there is so little psychological dependency in the relationship that a threat of its loss is only a minor misfortune, not a major catastrophe?

3. The fact that in so many cases infidelity (if not known by the spouse) seemed to cause no deprivation in the spouse raises an old question: How many people can one love or be attached to at the same time? If one is "true"—in one's own fashion—to several persons at once, what is the quality of the relationships? Does anyone really have enough resources to supply the psychological dependency needs of several persons?[23]

4. If infidelity becomes an acceptable practice, will it be possible for spouses to *depend* on one another for the psychological support they need? Or will it deprive them of it? Do you accept the findings on deprivation presented above? *Can* a person supply reassurance to a spouse if involved with someone else?

I am sure a great many other questions have occurred to you. You may even have the answers.

Reference Notes

1. "American law has tended toward the proscription of all extra-marital sexual relationships; but in recognition of the realities of human nature, the penalties for adultery in most states are usually mild and the laws are only infrequently enforced. In five of the states the maximum penalty is a fine. There are three states which attach no criminal penalty at all to adultery, but civil penalties may be involved in these and in many other states. . . . The broadest definitions of adultery and the heaviest penalties are concentrated in the northeastern section of the United States, all ten of those states being among the seventeen which may impose prison terms for a single act of extra-marital coitus. In actual practice, such extra-marital coitus is rarely prosecuted . . ." (Kinsey et al., 1953, p. 429).

2. However, the law is often used for quite different ends than the protection of society. In the summer of 1968, for example, a black minister in Irasburg, Vermont, was arrested on grounds of adultery by the state police. The governor of the state said the state police had "devoted their efforts to a persecution of the Rev. Mr. Johnson," and the whole episode was viewed as evidence of racism (Sheppard, 1966). This incident illustrates the Kinsey statement that "not infrequently the prosecutions represented attempts on the part of neighbors or relatives to work off grudges that had developed over other matters. In this, as in many other areas, the law is most often utilized by persons who have ulterior motives for causing difficulties for the non-conformant individuals. Not infrequently the prosecutions represent attempts by sheriffs, prosecutors, or other law enforcement officers to work off personal or political grudges . . ." (Kinsey et al., 1953, p. 429).

3. The Book of Common Prayer specifies the following promises: "Wilt thou love her, comfort her, honor her, cherish her, and keep her; and forsaking all others, cleave thee only unto her, so long as ye both shall live?" "Wilt thou love him, honor him, inspire him, cherish him and keep him; and forsaking all others, cleave thee only unto him, so long as ye both shall live?" The Protestant Episcopal promise includes: to have, to hold, to love, to cherish; the vow includes, for both partners, to have, live together, love, comfort, honor, keep and forsake all others. The Lutheran promise: to take, plight troth; the vow, to love, have, comfort, honor, keep, and forsake all others. The Presbyterian promise: to promise and covenant to be loving and faithful; the vow, to have, love, honor, live with, cherish. The Baptist promise: to take, have, hold, love, cherish; the vow, to take, love, honor, cherish, and forsake all others. The Methodist promise: to have, hold, love, cherish. The Ian Maclaren Service vow: take, love, cherish, give loyalty; the wife vows to take, love, and honor. The Community Church Service vow: to take, live together, love, honor, trust, serve, be true and loyal. The scriptural service vow: to take, love, cherish, have, hold, forsake all others, cleave to one another (Leach, 1945, 1959).

4. Some include the forsaking in the promise, some in the vow, some in both, some in neither.

5. "There are some individuals . . . whose sexual adjustments in marriage have undoubtedly been helped by extramarital experience. . . . Some women . . . make better adjustments with their husbands. Extramarital intercourse has had the effect of convincing some males that the relationships with their wives were more satisfactory than they had realized" (Kinsey et al., 1948, p. 593). "Sometimes sexual adjustments with the spouse had improved as a result of the female's extramarital experience" (Kinsey et al., 1953, p. 433). These authors cite earlier studies also reporting improved marital relationships after extramarital experiences. Robert A. Harper (1961, pp. 384-91) arrives at the same conclusion. One young man, discussing wife-swapping clubs, rejected the idea that infidelity was involved; the practice often enhanced the marital bonds.

6. I swear 'tis better to be much abus'd
    Than but to know 't a little. . . .
What sense had I of her stol'n hours of lust?
I saw 't not, thought it not, it harm'd not me:
I slept the next night well, fed well, was free and merry;
I found not Cassio's kisses on her lips:
He that is robb'd, not wanting what is stol'n,
Let him not know 't, and he's not robb'd at all. . . .
I had been happy, if the general camp,
Pioners and all, had tasted her sweet body,
So I had nothing known. O, now, for ever
Farewell the tranquil mind! farewell content!
Farewell the plumed troop, and the big wars,
    That makes ambition virtue! O, farewell! (Shakespeare, Othello, act 3, sc. 3)

7. The proportion of cases in which there was serious difficulty when known by the husband was identical—42 percent—to the proportion of cases in which there was no difficulty at all when known (Kinsey et al., 1953, p. 434).

8. The proportion would probably be even higher in the reverse situation, that is, where it was the husband who engaged in the extramarital relations, for women were only half as likely as men to rate spouse's extramarital coitus as a major factor in divorce: 27 percent and 51 percent respectively (Kinsey et al., 1953, p. 438). If, however, the husband were diverting part of a modest family income to another woman, the wife might well feel that she was being deprived.

9. Marital satisfaction was measured on the basis of replies to 15 statements such as "My spouse loves me, confides in me, shows me affection . . . completely, fairly much, somewhat, little, or not at all." Conscience was measured on the Psychopathic Deviate scale of the Minnesota Multiphasic Personality Inventory, a score of 61 or more indicating low conscience and a score of 60 or less, high conscience.

10. The low conscience subjects were, however, more likely than high conscience subjects to show sex involvment.

11. In *The Sex Game* (Bernard, 1968b), considerable attention is devoted to "innocent" relationships.

12. On a television program broadcast January 23, 1966, 88 percent of a national sample said they believed that adultery was wrong for women and about the same number, 86 percent, that it was wrong for men as well. These proportions of the sample were not very much higher than for premarital relations: 76 percent felt them wrong for women and 72 percent for men. More than half (57 percent) considered it wrong even for engaged couples. The conditions under which the questions were administered were not described so we have no way of knowing how much of an incentive there was for overstating a conforming attitude. With respect to extramarital relations, 26 percent of the sample—more men than women—would, it was reported, consider them acceptable under certain circumstances.

13. We know that a considerable proportion of married men and women at some time or other engage in extramarital relations (about half of the men and a quarter of the women), but adultery is rarely alleged in actual divorce. A survey of 1272 readers of the *Ladies Home Journal* in 1968 reported that 74 percent did not think a single act of adultery by either spouse should necessarily be a cause for divorce.

14. The incidence was somewhat higher among educated women after age twenty-five than among less educated. Increasing education over time may therefore tend to accelerate the trend if the relationship between education and extramarital relations continues.

15. The increasing salience of "wife-swapping clubs" and other forms of extramarital relationships may accelerate this trend. I am indebted to Dr. Edward J. Rydman, executive director of the American Association of Marriage Counselors, for one such example, namely, Club Rebel, "formed to serve the sophisticated new generation and . . . dedicated to those who have rebelled at outdated codes and morals . . ." (Personal letter, December 30, 1968).

16. There are other young people to whom neither permanence nor exclusivity is important. They believe in communal living in which everyone has access to everyone else, mutual attraction and affection being the only criteria of acceptability. It is doubtful if this pattern will find many adherents in the immediate future.

17. Davis distinguishes jealousy as a reaction to illegitimate seizure of property from jealousy as the result of deprivation of a love object (Davis, 1949, pp. 178-81). From the point of view of competitive concerns, extramarital sexual relations are more threatening than premarital to men. If a girl who has had premarital relations marries a man, he can assume that, everything considered, he was the best sexual partner. At least he had something that compensated for whatever he may have lacked. But in extramarital sexual relations he has no such reassurance. He is competing with a partner or partners who, for all he knows, may be better performers than he. And, further, a woman who has engaged in premarital sexual relations is more likely than one who has not to engage also in extramarital relations (Kinsey et al., 1953, pp. 427-8).

18. Except, perhaps, in connection with homosexual or Lesbian relationships where the total matrix is so different, where outside support is so equivocal, and where, therefore, normal social processes do not operate.

19. Until fairly recently it was taken for granted in many parts of the world that there would be sexual relations if almost any man and woman were alone together for any length of time.

20. An undoubtedly exaggerated illustration of this trend was presented several years ago in Paris where economically successful wives were taking on young lovers. "All of my friends have young friends nowadays. The oldest . . . is 27. . . . There are so many handsome, eager, virile, appreciative young men in Paris, why should any of us ever again put up with men who are older and more tired?" The woman quoted was a fortyish manager of a beauty salon (Sheppard, 1966).

21. "It's this way," Marianne said. "We are all making money nowadays. We have good jobs and we don't need what your musical comedies call sugar daddies. We can pick and choose and, after all, why not have someone who is young, easy, and amusing?" (Sheppard, 1966).

22. This is not to deny the anguish or the humiliation of knowing that they were less attractive sexually than the other woman. It is one of the hardest defeats in the world to take. It may be ineffable. Women learn to forgive if they have to, but rarely to forget. The wife quoted by Sapirstein (1948, p. 174) who gave her consent to her husband's infidelity still did not want to know when it happened; it would be too hard to bear. "Don't let me know when you do it. I'll be hurt but I'll live through it." The same is true of men, also, of course. Acceptance of this type of defeat has been almost impossible for men to swallow. The law has been lenient if he resorted to violence, even assault and murder. But even among men change has been rapid.

23. In Mormon polygyny there were strictly enforced institutionalized rules forbidding favoritism to any wife, which in themselves were doubtless supportive and reassuring. A man had, so to speak, to "ration" his need-fulfillment efforts.

9.
Sexually Open Marriage and Relationships: Issues and Prospects

Jacquelyn J. Knapp and Robert N. Whitehurst

Knapp and Whitehurst have combined their respective research efforts in this article to identify themes and trends in sexually open marriages and relationships. Generalizing from data on over one hundred respondents in widely scattered areas, they suggest that sexually open relationships may hold promise for achievement of personal growth, expanded intimacies, and more equality in relationships. They feel the very possibility of nonmonogamous marriages seems contingent on recent changes in society towards stressing sexual freedom, equality, and the development of human potential.

Most people who enter sexually open relationships appear actively to seek complexity, novelty, excitement, and increased personal awareness. The respondents report that sexually open relationships are fulfilling in these respects although they tend to be more challenging and frustrating since other people may not understand the choice of this life-style. Sexually open marriage and relationships seem to be ways of attempting to combine elements of stability and security with a primary partner while reaching for some extras in life that add romance and adventure. Although this life-style is not rapidly becoming an alternative of the masses, it has implications for many current marriages and may become accepted in the near future in forms other than the limited variety now in practice.

It is not unusual in the social sciences for researchers exploring a relatively new phenomenon to disagree on definitions or descriptive terms, leading to a bewildering multiplicity. Recently we have experienced an overabundance of sometimes confusing terms such as open marriage, open-ended relationships, intimate friendships, commitment with freedom, self-fulfillment within marriage, opening-up marriage, and so on, all referring to certain types of emerging nontraditional interpersonal living styles.

Particularly confusing is the phrase *open marriage*, coined by Nena and George O'Neill in their best-selling book (1972). Often misinterpreted, their description of open marriage emphasized role equality and flexibility—a peer relationship—and the potential for each spouse to grow separately, rather than suggesting or promoting sexual openness. While the O'Neills did not recommend outside sex, they did not advise people to avoid it either, main-

"Sexually Open Marriage and Relationships: Issues and Prospects." This paper was originally presented at the Conference on Current and Future Intimate Lifestyles, Connecticut College, November 1975. Reprinted by permission of the authors, Jacquelyn J. Knapp and Robert N. Whitehurst.

taining a noncommittal, neutral position that extramarital relationships are not integral to open marriage but *may* be included if the couple has the necessary trust, identity, and open communication. Thus, actualized outside sexual relationships are not necessary for the marriage to be *open*.

In their research the authors found that almost all respondents equated open marriage with *sexually* open marriage in which one or both spouses have openly acknowledged independent outside sexual relationships with satellite partners who maintain their own residences. Such patterns usually but do not necessarily develop out of O'Neill-type open marriage, with role flexibility, equality, open communication, trust, etc., existing in varying degrees. When nonlegally married couples agree to have other nonsecret sexual involvements, their arrangement may be referred to as a *sexually open relationship*. The key characteristic of both sexually open marriages and relationships (SOM/R) is a mutual agreement not to be sexually exclusive but to expand the boundaries of emotional, physical, and social relationships to include other people in addition to the primary mate.

The sparse research that exists on either open marriages and relationships (OM/R) or SOM/R tends to emphasize couples' sexual behavior and its consequences, a bias not unusual in our sex-obsessed society. This paper attempts to present and integrate data and implications from two completed studies on sexually open marriage and relationships and to speculate as to the long-term viability of this nontraditional life-style.

Whitehurst's Study

Whitehurst (1974) examined the self-reported living patterns, attitudes, and feelings of couples involved in both SOR and SOM. A number of social factors were related to the increasing potential for experimentation with alternative marriage forms, particularly sexually open relationships within and without marriage. As morality becomes increasingly relative, the community no longer has unequivocal answers or sanctioning power over social deviants. There are increases in personal alienation, urban anonymity, individual mobility, and open talk of marital variations and sexual freedom. At the same time we have decreasingly effective social controls through the traditional agents of family, religion, and general community. Forces are no longer squeezing people into preordained life-styles, set by outside authorities and sanctioned by these agencies. The resulting normative vacuum allows greater experimentation, reliance on support networks of close friends, and variety-filled living styles, including SOM/R.

Subjects of the Study

Through references from others Whitehurst located and gave questionnaires to thirty-five couples—twenty-three legally married and twelve couples not legally married—who defined their marriages or relationships as sexually open. The data presented are for the total sample since response patterns for the two groups were not significantly different.

Age of respondents ranged from twenty to sixty-two. Their residences, primarily urban and suburban, were in both Canada and all major geographic regions of the United States. Most respondents were upper-middle-class professionals or career people. They were influenced toward SOM/R by the O'Neills' book, Robert Rimmer's novels, liberal friends, therapy groups, and the general dissatisfactions of isolated urban life and conventional marriage. The majority said they were atheists or agnostics, and a significant number were Unitarians or Humanists who viewed living a full life as their sacred obligation. Several couples had had limited group marriage experiences, which lasted only briefly. A distinguishing feature of their current life-style was that all outside dating was done on an individual basis.

Respondents saw SOM/R as a compromise way of living which merged freedom to pursue personal growth and autonomy with commitment and security. Rejecting the restrictiveness of traditional marriage, they sought variety, complexity, romance, and courtship, and even problems to keep things lively. SOM/R appeared a way to have role equality and structure in ongoing evaluations of gender-role performance.

General Characteristics of Sexually Open Marriage and Relationships

As active seekers of utopian ideals and interpersonal complexity, respondents appeared intellectually committed to sexual openness. The complexity sometimes exacted a price in uncertainty, anxiety, and a degree of emotional pain. However, these were not experienced as totally undesirable since they resulted in high levels of communication, mutual problem solving, and ongoing excitement. Tranquility and even stability in the primary relationship were at times traded for personal growth and ego-enhancement from outside relationships. But the emotional discomfort was associated with growth and positive change, according to a "pleasure-pain formula," and therefore accepted.

In addition to the relationship complexities and inevitable anxieties, some other common experiences were significantly increased feelings of self-esteem and an overall positive evaluation of the meaning of SOM/R. Virtually no one had any desire to return to conventional types of relationships. Sexual problems per se were relatively rare. Respondents seemed more natural and less rigid in their views of sex, which was considered fun and vital, than conventional persons who might approach sex less playfully. Few sexual double standards were reported, the women's liberation movement being a major influence and impetus for refining gender roles and equal status arrangements.

Women seemed to have an easier time making outside contacts which led to sexual relationships, and as a result they had more outside partners than the men in the sample. Unlike the North American feminine stereotype, these women were not passive or hesitant to express their ideas, needs, and goals to men who interested them. The male respondents in contrast were more traditional and conservative than the females to begin with and had to do the most changing and adapting to the sexually open life-style. In sum, sexual openness was to some extent favored by the female respondents, who appeared to be the primary benefactors.

As the O'Neills suggested, loyalty and fidelity were redefined in terms of relationship primacy rather than mate ownership or exclusivity. With intimacy extended beyond the primary pair, the mate became the most significant but not the *only* significant other. The result was a paradoxical situation: The primary bond became simultaneously more *and* less important. Contrary to usual Western-type thinking about love and the experience of polarities, these couples reported a concurrent development of both intensification or closeness and a sense of apartness with the primary other. Whether this occurred as a self-fulfilling prophecy or not is unimportant. They believed the primary bond was enhanced by increased freedom. If they experienced themselves as closer to each other, that was their reality, the validity of which cannot be questioned, even though it challenges our cherished belief that love can be good only with one person at a time.

In light of such unconventional views and behavior, it appeared that judgment of the success or failure of sexually open marriages or relationships cannot be based upon pair longevity or lack of stress, conflict, or confrontation between partners. Instead success evaluations must be based upon insiders' views. Evaluations can only be made in terms of overall self- and couple-satisfaction—especially by enhanced self-feelings and a sense of integration with the larger world.

Problems in Sexually Open Marriage and Relationships

The problem most unique to SOM/R seemed to be the limited potential for honest social interaction and friendships beyond the most intimate relationships. Confidants had to be chosen with great care or else there was the risk of exposure and rejection. Many found it painful to have to exclude more conservative friends, relatives, and co-workers from knowledge of the sexually open life-style. It was difficult to accept the fact that their views and behavior probably would be rejected within their own larger social networks.

Although none of the couples had formal written contracts outlining their ground rules, all had verbal agreements which required continuous accommodation and renegotiation. Each couple had to work out their own commitments regarding the options available as they related to others and the degree of openness with which they felt comfortable. Reaching agreement often required intense, honest communication and endurance that Whitehurst speculated would be too difficult for many people conventionally reared in a jealous, possessive, male-dominated society.

Jealousy most often involved fear of loss and lingering feelings of possessiveness or desire to control the mate. Though they worked toward equality, occasionally partners discovered they had a different commitment to or involvement in SOM/R which led to conflict, particularly in regard to sharing free time. The partner "left out" might experience resentment and loneliness. This was usually not a serious problem, however, since most respondents had careers, many interests, strong individual lives, and outside partners of their own to occupy free time.

The women complained that their primary male partners or spouses, in spite of generally heightened communication resulting from the life-style, sometimes backed away from intense emotional discussions and escaped into work, sports, or all-male activities. In addition the women often felt that household division of labor wasn't truly equal; that the men lacked motivation to enlarge their share of the everyday tasks; or that the men frequently had lower standards of neatness and cleanliness.

Sometimes freedom and openness were abused, as in the case of one couple who used outside relationships as a means to escape each other. When the primary relationship bond either was not solidified first or was neglected and SOM/R was used to try to keep the relationship from falling apart, openness did not work to the benefit of the couple. When a person acted out his or her aggressions and hostilities against a primary partner through an intimate relationship with someone else, the process became destructive rather than liberating.

Whitehurst concluded that SOM/R is not advisable for people who are not emotionally equipped to handle freedom, time alone, complex inter-relationships, high intensity communication, or the inevitable struggle of possessiveness versus autonomy.

Benefits of Sexually Open Marriage and Relationships

As mentioned, the problems of SOM/R were viewed as inevitable and accepted or tolerated within a framework of personal growth and relation-ship enrichment. Respondents were enthusiastic in extolling the benefits of the way they lived: Increased openness led to newly discovered feelings about themselves and their relationship to the world; with enhanced self-esteem came increased relationship-esteem and closeness; and as they opened up to new experiences they felt less isolated and more personally fulfilled.

Explicitly or implicitly many evaluated sexual nonexclusiveness for themselves on the basis of questions such as: Is life more fun, interesting, and varied? Do I feel more zest in living? Most answered yes, though few seemed to succeed in achieving total success and stability in a primary rela-tionship with an ego-satisfying outside relationship. Nevertheless, respon-dents expressed no regrets at having entered SOM/R, which they continued to see as a viable mode of life. They placed extremely high value on their per-sonal growth experiences, and were unwilling to return to or move toward a traditional life-style.

Knapp's Study

Within the context of rapid cultural change in the visibility and vocality of sexual nonconformists, Knapp (in press) has hypothesized a movement to-ward increasing rejection of traditional male-female relationships. She con-ceived of SOM/R as a ramification of our moving, as Robert and Anna Fran-coeur suggest, from a *hot-sex culture* to a *cool-sex culture*. [1] The traditional hot-sex marriage is closed and typified by rigid roles, unequal statuses, and possessive exclusiveness, while nontraditional cool-sex marriage is open and promises role flexibility, spouse equality, and open companionships.

Knapp (1974, 1975a, in press) studied seventeen legally married couples who defined their marriages as sexually open. Two initial selection criteria were followed: One or both spouses had had or were currently having outside sexual relationships, and, second, they indicated that they preferred independent functioning rather than exchanging partners as in swinging. As the research progressed it became evident that additional characteristics were common across couples: Emotional involvement with satellite partners was generally accepted; nonspouse partners lived in their own homes; prospective partners did not have to be selected from certain groups or predetermined populations; and goals such as social and intellectual sharing, personal growth, and increasing one's ability to love and communicate were pursued in addition to sexual pleasure.

Subjects of the Study

Knapp's couples, eleven from north central Florida and six from eastern Kansas, were located primarily through referrals from mutual acquaintances. Everyone contacted to participate in the study agreed to do so. Each respondent answered fifty-one open-ended and forced-choice questions regarding personal history, open marriage attitudes, and sexual experiences. Thirty-one respondents also took two personality tests (the Myers-Briggs Type Indicator[2] and the Clinical Analysis Questionnaire[3]); two respondents took only the Myers-Briggs. Because there were no significant areas of difference either in background or sexual experiences and attitudes, results are presented for the total sample rather than the separate Florida and Kansas groups.

Respondents, all Caucasians, averaged just over thirty years of age with a range of twenty to forty-eight years. Fifty percent of their occupations, including that of student, were academically related. Annual income varied from $3,000 to $40,000. Everyone had completed high school, seven had some college, seven had bachelor's degrees, nine had master's degrees, one had attended law school, one was a physician, and four had Ph.D.s. Eighteen were oldest children in their families of origin, and five were single children. The majority reported having no particular religious beliefs in the traditional sense, though they described themselves as concerned with spiritual aspects of being. Ninety-four percent of the females and 88 percent of the males reported having sexual intercourse prior to marriage. Ten of the couples had a combined total of nineteen children, ages two to fifteen. Length of marriage ranged from one to twenty-two years, ten couples having been married from one to five years and four couples between eleven and fifteen years. Five males and two females had been previously married and divorced. Five couples had participated in marriage counseling. Outside sexual relationships had been one of several difficulties leading to counseling for six people with only one female indicating that it had been the primary problem for which she sought help.

Sexual Behavior Patterns in Sexually Open Marriage

All of the wives and fifteen of the seventeen husbands had been or were currently involved in open outside sexual relationships. In eleven of the seventeen couples the wife was first to have outside sexual experience, and in three additional instances she was responsible for arranging a shared first outside experience, together with her husband and close friends.

Wives again prevailed in the extent of outside activity, having eighty-one satellite partners or 57 percent of the combined total while their spouses had sixty partners, 43 percent of the total. The women had more satellite relationships in nine of the marriages, husbands had more in five instances, and three couples had the same number of outside partners. When one partner had considerably more outside contacts than the spouse had, there tended to be more stress in the marital relationship. In one instance when the wife was sexually active outside and the husband had no other relationships it led to severe marital strain based upon the husband's fear of impending loss. In a similar situation, however, the husband agreed with his wife's views of marriage and simply felt too busy himself at that time to get involved in comarital complexities.

About two-thirds of the sample, males and females equally, had primarily experienced deep friendship or affection with their satellite partners; eight additional persons stated their most common experience had been sex with love. Length of relationships varied from a month or less of active sexual involvement to one or two years or more, seventeen people describing long-term relationships with varying degrees of personal commitment to the non-spouse partners.

Most couples emphasized that they did not have to share all the details, thoughts, or feelings about the additional relationships, though they were strongly against lying to the spouse or withholding information when asked for it. They also stressed the importance of treating outside partners, who were sometimes very "inside" in importance, with about the same respect, care, and concern they tried to show for the spouse. It was not unusual for spouses and outside partners to get together to discuss problems or mutual interests or engage in joint decision making.

The respondents' children were mostly under ten years of age. Perhaps because their parents' nontraditional marital style was not very visible, they had not raised any questions that would indicate worry or even curiosity about what their parents were doing when they went out or had friends over. Respondents did emphasize that they wanted to share their feelings and beliefs about marriage as soon as the children were mature enough to understand the deliberate rejection of traditional values and standards, but they had not yet done so.

Ground Rules for Sexually Open Marriage

Informal verbal contracts seemed to evolve as problem areas developed, though three couples had agreed upon sexually open marriage contracts before marriage. The "rule" with the highest priority was honesty in relationships, followed by acceptance of emotional involvements that did not interfere or compete with the primary marital relationship and freedom for each spouse to pursue separate interests. In addition, couples had explicit expectations regarding the need for discretion, time sharing, and avoidance of potentially stressful outside relationships such as those with a close relative of the spouse, with someone obviously emotionally disturbed, or with persons themselves involved in disruptive marriages. It was highly desired that spouses or primary mates of outside partners know and approve of the additional relationship, as usually was the case. Maintaining secret relationships and investing energy in clandestine meetings were generally unacceptable and even repulsive to the respondents, who repeatedly stressed the value of openness in living one's convictions.

Fourteen couples had agreed to a flexible, nongender-based role structure in the family. Household tasks were either performed by those who especially enjoyed doing them or were rotated. Three couples by mutual choice followed traditional divisions of labor, these wives seeming to prefer such an arrangement and not feeling it had been "forced" upon them.

Advantages and Disadvantages of Sexually Open Marriage

The most frequently reported benefits included: better fulfillment of personal needs; the excitement of new experiences, both social and sexual, leading to feelings of increased vitality and enjoyment of sex with the spouse; an eventual lessening of jealousy and possessiveness; freedom and security together; and the opportunity to be fully oneself with no further need for role playing.

Seven respondents could think of no particular disadvantages to SOM as they were living it. Others mentioned jealousy; time-sharing problems, occasional resentment over the importance of an outside partner that had resulted from differing expectations of the various people involved; difficulty finding private meeting places; and living with the realization that one's beliefs or behavior might be threatening or offensive to significant others with differing values.

Twenty-two respondents reported increased satisfaction with their marriages after becoming involved in SOM. Four said there had been no significant changes (things were OK before and OK now), and one husband felt decreased satisfaction. For three couples the question of increased or decreased satisfaction was not applicable since they had decided to have sexually open marriages prior to marriage. Twenty-seven stated they had no desire to return to sexual monogamy and that for them being unmarried might be a better alternative than traditional marriage.

Motivations for Sexually Open Marriage

Twenty-nine persons indicated that they preferred SOM because it enabled them to live their personal philosophies or beliefs. Almost as many said it helped them to meet unfulfilled emotional, physical, intellectual, and social needs, and as a result to reduce pressures in the marital relationship. Since two people can never hope to satisfy all of each other's needs directly related to happiness and well-being, they reasoned that outside relationships (social or sexual) have the potential to relieve pressure within the marriage and provide a broader base for need-fulfillment and happiness. To them marriage which excluded meaningful intimacy with anyone else in the world simply did not make sense. With only two exceptions respondents' awareness of unmet needs and acceptance of a definite philosophy of SOM preceded their outside sexual involvement. This philosophical acceptance was followed by varying degrees of emotional acceptance and intellectual-emotional integration. Manufacturing a philosophy to rationalize already accomplished sexual behavior was not at all typical of this group.

Personality Factors in Sexually Open Marriage

Contrary to some mental health professionals' opinions that persons engaging in extramarital sexual activity may be acting out or displacing hostilities or narcissistic needs or that they are neurotic, immature, promiscuous, maritally maladjusted, or psychopathically deviant in addition to sexually inadequate or aberrant, Knapp (1974) found that on the basis of their scores on the Clinical Analysis Questionnaire her respondents as a group could not be judged as significantly more neurotic, anti-social, or personality disordered than the general population of the United States. If anything, they were less neurotic and less anxiety-prone and more self-assured and nondefensive.

More important in descriptive terms were the results of the Myers-Briggs Type Indicator (MBTI). In brief, the MBTI is a self-report personality inventory which elicits preferences on four dichotomies: Extraversion-Introversion (E-I), Sensing-Intuition (S-I), Thinking-Feeling (T-F), and Judging-Perceptive (J-P). The end result is a "type" of four letters, one from each dichotomy, with corresponding descriptions for each of the sixteen major categories and their subdivisions (Myers, 1962).

Since MBTI data from the seventeen SOM couples are presented in detail elsewhere (Knapp, 1974, 1975b), a brief summary will suffice here. Seventy-two percent of the sample fell into one of three categories: the extroverted intuitive (ENFP, 39 percent), the introverted intuitive (INTJ, 18 percent), and the introverted feeling type (INFP, 15 percent), The preference that all three of those types have in common is intuition (N). Intuitives tend to be individualistic, independent, oriented toward possibilities, high academic achievers, creative, nonconforming, stimulated by complexity and chaos, initiating, inventive, relatively indifferent to what others say and do, imaginative at the expense of observation, and willing to sacrifice present realities for future possibilities. While estimations place the number of intuitives in the general population at about 25 percent, they made up 88 percent of the sample, most closely resembling standardization groups of highly creative artists (Myers, 1962).

The majority of respondents also chose feeling over thinking (i.e., preferring to make judgments on the basis of personal values rather than impersonal logic) and perceptive over judging (i.e., being open, spontaneous, and adaptable rather than exacting, critical, and decisive). They were fairly well-balanced between extroverts and introverts, unlike the general population which supposedly has about 75 percent extroverts. Extraversion-introversion was found to be statistically unrelated to initiation of the first outside sexual activity, though gender of the initiator, female, was highly significant. Interaction of the two variables, E-I and gender, was also found to be insignificant.

Based upon a composite of the group's predominant characteristics as indicated by their MBTI preferences we can hypothesize a modal type of person who is more inclined to try SOM. Such persons would be imaginative; future-oriented; individualistic; willing to take risks to explore possible new ways of relating to others; caring little for convention; and willing to defend personal views and values with determination. Open to new experiences, they would tend to use enthusiasm and idealism to influence others. Rather than being destructively antisocial or lacking in social conscience, they would be deliberately nonconforming, variant rather than deviant, and socially innovative. While not as concerned about socially prescribed morality as the average person, they would be strong believers in their personal ethical systems. If current trends persist, such persons would be females more often than males.

If further research upholds the personality trends observed with this small sample, then certain types of people indeed might be attracted to SOM and be more able to manage such a complex life-style successfully.

Overview of the Two Studies

While the results of these two early studies obviously cannot be generalized to a larger population, they are of considerable value in attempting to acquire a descriptive handle on sexually open marriages and relationships. The combined sample of 104 respondents, forty married and twelve unmarried but pair-bonded couples from across the United States and Canada, provides quite homogeneous data in regard to the participants' backgrounds, motivations, experiences, insights, values, problems, hopes for the future, and rejection of traditional monogamous marriage.

Based upon these data, the authors hypothesize that two polar types of couples may be attracted to a sexually open life-style: (1) those who have high levels of conflict and dissatisfaction in their primary relationships and either are divorce-bound or searching for an alternative to divorce, and (2) those who have established and are maintaining strong, stable, primary relationships in which there is a high degree of mutual affection, respect, understanding, and agreement regarding choice of life-style.

The high-conflict, stressful marriages, a minority in the sample, usually had one spouse, most often the wife, who wanted a sexually open, nontraditional arrangement while the husband preferred a less extreme, more traditional relationship socially and/or sexually. One such husband expressed his preference for "good old-fashioned uncomplicated secret affairs" and found his wife's openness emotionally difficult to handle. In most of the stressful marriages there was also an intellectual-emotional split in acceptance of SOM—in their heads they totally agreed with the philosophy and *wanted* it to work for them, but emotionally their gut-level reactions were fear, anger, and resentment. Role strain and basic personality conflicts, perhaps aggravated by the additional pressure of outside relationships, were also evident, as in one couple where the husband was a traditionalist and strong intuitive thinking type while his wife was a sensing-feeling type who believed strongly in sexual freedom.

As an interesting aside, Knapp received referrals to six couples as potential participants from a colleague in a northern Florida city. Before she could arrange to meet with them and administer the questionnaires most of the couples had separated and were filing for divorce. Had they become involved in the study they might have provided valuable data about divorce-bound couples and their involvement in SOM. As Whitehurst noted earlier, SOM as a Band-Aid usually did not succeed in holding an already shaky marriage together, and if the relationship were fragile or immature to begin with SOM may very well have been the catalyst that blasted it apart.

The majority of the marriages were relatively satisfactory, low-conflict ones, and some could even be labeled exemplary. The latter couples conveyed a sparkle and extraordinary vitality along with other common characteristics: (1) mutual devotion; (2) the ability to integrate outside relationships with the primary one so that each seemed to benefit the others; (3) facility in expressing a cogent philosophy of SOM; (4) nearly equal social/sexual involvement of both spouses in outside relationships; (5) an equal conviction of the rightness of SOM for them so that one spouse did not have to exert pressure on the other to accept a nontraditional marriage; and (6) achievement of intellectual-emotional integration with relative ease. When SOM seemed most successful the couples had not reshaped themselves to fit a non-monogamous marriage style since it suited them as they already were. Prime examples are the couples in which at least one of the spouses had been previously married and resolved never to have a traditional marriage again, forming their open-marriage contracts before the second marriage.

Sexually open marriage appeared to be especially attractive and beneficial to the women in both samples for a number of stated reasons: (1) They acquired essentially equal social/sexual rights with the men, eliminating the usual double standard; (2) The threat of secret affairs was virtually eliminated and open outside relations were seen as much less threatening to family stability and integration since the noninvolved mate retained some input and control; (3) Role structures tended to become flexible so that the women no longer were solely responsible for household maintenance and child care; (4) Having independent outside relationships allowed them to adjust their own social and sexual paces, which often exceeded those of the males; (5) Each person was able to express affection to and receive affection from more sources, a need the women said was often unfulfilled to some extent in their primary relationships; and (6) There was some relief that they no longer had to be the only persons required to satisfy all of their mates' needs. Being the primary initiators and beneficiaries of SOM/R, women thus tended to invest more interest and energy in nourishing and maintaining their nontraditional life-styles than the males, who had relinquished some of their traditional advantages.

Both researchers were struck with the efforts of each couple in their respective samples to achieve a harmonious balance between commitment to the primary relationship and freedom to function independently and experience others outside the primary relationship. Knowing this was a thin line to walk, respondents nevertheless persisted in their search for the best of both worlds, convinced that marriage or nonmarital commitment need not be a social or emotional prison.

Future Outlook

Predictions about the future for SOM/R or any other kind of nontraditional living style must be based upon current trends and consideration of long-term changes in the social climate.

According to the 1970 United States Census (Ramey, 1975), there is evidence that both males and females are postponing first marriages. At the same time, divorces have doubled since 1965, the current rate in Florida being 66 percent, and the number of nonmarried cohabitors in the United States is probably well over six million. With 35 percent of the adult population single, widowed, divorced, or separated, and 60 percent of all married women employed full-time outside the home, only about 18 percent of the population remain in traditional nuclear families, the institutionalized norm in our society. Another ideal, backed by legal sanctions, is sexually monogamous marriage, though evidence would indicate that in actual practice the majority of marriages are nonmonogamous (Kinsey, 1948; Gebhard in Hunt, 1969). Thus, since the end of World War II we have slowly shifted away from our unquestioning adherence to a monolithic value system regarding marital and family behavior and moved toward increasing pluralism or more choices and more freedom in making those choices.

As this trend continues, Whitehurst's earlier observations of a normative vacuum resulting in increased experimentation and variety become even more salient. Given the current trend toward greater variety in marriage and relationship styles, the prominence of SOM/R among all the various alternative styles must be evaluated and then weighed against traditional marriage, which still prevails in the public image as the ideal or prototype.

Whitehurst sees male-female inequality and closed monogamy as still being deeply entrenched in our society by early socialization and custom. Only a select minority of people can presently tolerate negative sanctions imposed by middle-class morality and complex interpersonal stresses. The need exists for considerably more network support through positive sanctions of laws, customs, and community acceptance before SOM becomes more stable and functional. There are indicators, however, especially in the larger cities, that societal barriers may be gradually giving way. With increased visibility and success rates lending support to the viability of SOM, it may eventually become a more prevalent form for a greater segment of the upper middle class. At present, however, it is not seen as likely to replace secret affairs as the favored mode of extramarital sex for the majority of people engaged in nonmonogamous marriage or to be any more important than a number of other unconventional marriage adaptations.

Knapp, in contrast, hypothesizes an increasingly important role for OM and SOM among other alternative styles and in opposition to traditional marriage based upon two of her research conclusions: (1) that more and more women are finally expressing their dissatisfaction with conventional marriage and taking the lead in establishing marriages based upon role equality with options for open outside relationships if desired, and (2) that people with certain definable types of personality are discovering that SOM especially fits their needs and personal philosophies of living. Given our social climate of rapid change and situational morality, it would seem that those who have been square pegs jammed into the round holes of traditional marriage are better able now than ever before to find appropriate reference and membership groups to support their marriage experimentation. Following the emergence of women's liberation, gay liberation, Black power, Chicano power, and the American Indian movement, perhaps the next move out of the closet will be by the marriage liberation movement!

Among the many alternate life-styles, including swinging, group marriages, singlehood, single parenthood, homosexual unions, communal families, cohabitation, and aggregate marriages, open marriage with options for satellite sexual relationships would seem more viable than many others simply based on practicality. For example, group marriage and communal living both require a pooling of resources, an adequately large but low-profile residence, and extremely complex accommodation to the needs and idiosyncrasies of others who are physically present in the household or commune. Swinging, in the group party sense, requires considerable organization and tolerance for exhibitionism and voyeurism. Homosexual marriages have a certain visibility and they risk both legal and community sanctions, still bearing the stigma of sexual perversion and mental illness. In comparison, sexually open marriages have very low visibility, do not require special living arrangements, and are based upon the intactness of the marital unit. Children remain under the primary influence of their parents, and outside relationships may be formed and dissolved without major upsets in living arrangements or property settlements. When it works well, participants combine the security and specialness of the marital commitment with the freedom and individuality required for self-actualization. For these reasons and more, Knapp believes that SOM may become one of the most viable of all the alternatives.

How does this alternative measure against the heavy forces of traditional, male-dominated, publicly monogamous marriage? At present, convention prevails, backed by the religious and educational superstructure of society. Futurists are predicting radical changes in those social forces, however, as technology and population bring about unthought-of changes and adaptations in an increasing spiral. This process may leave marriage as we have known it in a state of relative chaos for some time to come, but out of chaos can emerge diversity and perhaps tolerance for differences. It may not be too iconoclastic to predict increasing openness in alternative living styles with sexually open marriage in the vanguard—while simultaneously realizing that predictability itself has become unpredictable, and the future is anybody's fantasy.

Reference Notes

1. The Francoeurs (see Chapter 20) characterize *hot sex* as "male-dominated, double standarded, intercourse-obsessed, property-oriented, and clearly stereotyped in its sexist images and models." *Cool sex* is described as "egalitarian, single standarded, sexually diffused, and oriented towards intimacy and open, synergistic relations with persons" (Francoeur & Francoeur, 1974; pp. 34 and 39).
2. I. Myers. *Manual for the Myers-Briggs Type Indicator.* Princeton, N.J.: Educational Testing Service, 1962.
3. K. Delhees and R. Cattell. *Manual for the Clinical Analysis Questionnaire,* Champaign, Ill.: 1PAT, 1971.

10.
Swinging: Who Gets Involved and How?

Brian G. Gilmartin

Gilmartin's approach to swinging is unique in several respects. It is the first study of swinging to use a comparison or control group; the variables he analyzes lead to provocative if tentative conclusions about the characteristics of swingers and the nature of sexuality and intimacy-seeking; and his social-psychological interpretation brings new insights into who becomes a swinger and how this occurs.

No other study has so clearly brought out the importance of socialization background variables such as early relationships with parents and kin, political and religious affiliations, and early interest in the opposite sex. Gilmartin also points out the crucial importance of shared meanings and values for swinging couples. His conclusions have significance for those seeking intimacy in both conventional and unconventional relationships.

Sexual mate sharing, or swinging, is a form of comarital sexual behavior. Statistically, relatively few Americans are currently involved in sexual mate sharing: Most scholarly estimates place the figure at about 2 percent of all married couples (see Hunt, 1974). But this seemingly small percentage actually represents approximately 900,000 married couples, nearly all of whom are middle class. In essence, a substantial minority of socially and financially well-off people are involved in swinging.

The term *swinging* refers to that form of sexual behavior which involves legally married spouses sharing coitus and other forms of erotic behavior with other legally married couples in a social context defined by all participants as a form of recreational convivial play. In this article, I will use the terms *swinging, comarital sexual behavior,* and *mate sharing* interchangeably. However, it should be noted that other writers may not do so. (See Libby, Chapter 6, for a discussion of definition issues concerning comarital sex.)

The main purpose of this article is to suggest a theory that might effectively explain how and why some suburban middle-class people develop and sustain a long-term active interest and involvement in sexual mate sharing. The article will first consider the findings of various researchers, particularly in regard to swinging styles and formats. Next, it will present the author's research (Gilmartin, 1976) involving two hundred California couples. Theoretically important concepts which will be highlighted include: (1) nature of the affective relationship with parents and kin during the formative years and in adulthood; (2) the importance of friends, social organizations, and neighbors to people who swing; (3) the political and religious attitudes of swingers; (4) early development of heterosexual-social interests and involvement; (5) access to glamorized but instructive swinging literature; (6) the crucial importance of value congruence between spouses for a true swinging marriage; and (7) some whys and wherefores of marital happiness or failure for swingers.

Selective Review of the Research: Swinging Styles and Formats

There is a counterproductive temptation to pigeonhole so-called deviant persons. Yet, even among a highly deviant category such as swingers, there is an amazing and fascinating variety of behavioral styles and attitudes. Such variations should not be ignored because the social/psychological antecedents and consequences of each style may be markedly different. Although a thorough investigation of swinging types or styles is beyond the scope of this report, I will briefly review the literature on swinging and consider the relevant data and conclusions of other researchers.

Two of the earlier swinging studies cited are the ones by Carolyn Symonds (1968; 1971) and George and Nena O'Neill (1970). Symonds' study was conducted in Southern California while the O'Neills' was done in New York City. Together they provide some very interesting and contrasting perspectives on swinging as practiced in different metropolitan areas. A key finding in both of these reports is that suburban swinging is governed by a markedly different set of norms than swinging in the inner city. Swinging within the city characteristically seems to involve a heavy concentration of single, never married people while suburb swinging tends to be tightly restricted to married couples. Symonds further suggests that urban swinging tends to be much more "utopian" than "recreational," and its participants tend to be more socially and politically active and liberal than those in the suburbs.

In Palson and Palson's (1972) study of 136 swingers, the researchers actually participated in swinging in an intensive eighteen-month study. In addition to participant observation, couples were informally interviewed in conversations which were much the same as typical discussions at swinging parties. The Palsons were primarily interested in the symbolic meanings of swinging as *defined by the participants*. Swingers were found to naturally deal with jealousy through "individuating" behavior, where the ground rules varied to the extent that explicit or rigid rules were difficult to identify. It was important to swingers that everyone enjoy swinging. Swingers went through stages—from the initial curiosity stage to a stage of increased selectivity where uniqueness of the style of interaction developed. Marital compatibility was stressed, and most spouses were mutually supportive if any problems evolved at the parties. Although the Palsons conclude that swinging often solidifies marriages, they predict that alternative sexually free life-styles such as swinging may decrease or disappear in the future if the decline in economic prosperity can be taken as an indicator of a return to more restricted sexual behavior.

In contrast with the Palsons, James and Lynn Smith (1970) estimate that 15 to 25 percent of married couples may become involved in swinging under optimal conditions. The Smiths studied swingers who participated in sexual freedom group parties in the San Francisco area. Much like other swinging literature, they report that swingers tend to be highly educated and low on religious affiliation. Some of their findings, based on their sample of 44 percent married, 32 percent single, and 25 percent divorced people, include: comarital sexual behavior is part of an "emergent subculture complete with jargon, symbols, communication techniques . . ." (1970, p. 133); men usually initiate swinging, but women can handle swinging with less jealousy than men; those who stick with swinging learn to deal with sexual jealousy; jealousy between spouses is less likely with mutual spousal agreement about sexual freedom than with those who engage in conventional adultery; some people at parties observe but don't participate in sexual interaction, particularly those who are beginners at swinging; 60 percent had never been in therapy, and only one person sought therapy because of problems related to swinging; the conformity and strict ground rules reported by Bartell (1971) were not reported by the Smiths; and marriages can be improved by swinging and other forms of comarital sex (which dispels the myth that anyone involved in a deviant sexual life-style has personal or marital problems).

Bell and Silvan (1970) interviewed twenty-five swingers. Observations were also carried out at parties. They described various kinds of swingers, such as "closet swingers" where the group is small (two or three couples) and the closed door policy is common, and open parties or orgies. In agreement with much of the swinging literature, Bell and Silvan found that most swingers view sex as recreational rather than highly emotional, and see swinging as an end in itself, instead of a means to other goals such as status achievement. Unlike the Smiths or the Palsons, Bell and Silvan conclude there are many swingers who choose the activity due to personal psychological problems. In contrast with the Palsons, Bell and Silvan conclude that swinging is likely to increase as society continues to become more liberal in sexual attitudes and behavior.

Cole and Spanier (1972) collected survey data on 579 respondents where only 1.7 percent of the sample in a midwestern town had engaged in swinging. Following the logic of symbolic interaction theory, the subjective definitions of swinging as viewed by the participants was a criterion for swingers' evaluation of the merits or problems of swinging, and the evaluation of marital happiness. Swingers were found to be less controlled by agents of social control (such as one's family). Spanier and Cole (1972) found that almost 7 percent of their sample would consider participation in swinging (given an opportunity to do so). Their research is limited in terms of both the sample (one small midwestern town) and the method (survey research), so as with most swinging research it is difficult to conclude much about swinging from such a study.

Charles Varni (1972) has contributed to the research a description of three types of swinging groups differentiated by their degree of stability, and he has developed a useful typology of swingers based on the degree of emotional involvement they seek in swinging activities. Varni's research primarily involved intensive interviews with sixteen swinging couples in the San Diego, California, area.

Varni describes swinging groups as either very stable, fairly stable, or unstable. The first type is a close-knit, cohesive group with little membership turnover; the fairly stable group has a relatively large number of swingers who are known to one another, a loose organization (sometimes in cliques), and somewhat fluid membership; and the unstable type of group consists of couples who come together for one night only. For many swingers, the very stable group seems to be an ideal. It might be conceived as a group of five to ten couples who are very compatible—ideologically, intellectually, emotionally, and sexually. Swingers preferring an unstable situation were typically older and more anxious about being "found out" by their employers or other influential community figures.

The typology of swingers Varni suggests is a continuum that ranges from those desiring no emotional involvement to those advocating and seeking a deep commitment. Five main steps on the continuum are:

1. *Hard-core swingers*—want no emotional involvement, are not very selective, and often participate in unstable party and one-couple situations.
2. *Egotistical swingers*—experience little emotion, but are fairly selective. Swinging is purely sexual and is compartmentalized from the rest of their lives. Husbands use their wives and wives rarely become devoted to swinging.
3. *Recreational swingers*—socially oriented to fairly stable groups, with both swinging and nonswinging activities with the same group members. Wives are partially used and encouraged by husbands but usually become dedicated swingers.
4. *Interpersonal swingers*—the emphasis is on close emotional relationships with couples who are selected carefully.
5. *Communal swingers*—go beyond interpersonal swingers in advocating some form of group marriage.

An estimate based on Varni's and the author's research would indicate that about 14 percent of swingers are "hard core" or "egotistical"; 43 percent are "recreational"; and another 43 percent are either "interpersonal" or "communal" swingers.

The Present Study: Identifying Characteristics of Swingers

Most of the early research on sexual mate sharing has dealt with matters such as what the sexual ideology and philosophy of swingers is, what their techniques of deviance disavowal and neutralization are, how they meet others of like mind, what they do and talk about at their parties, and what types of sexual mate sharing exist. All of these questions are important for the social psychology of the family and for the study of deviant behavior. But the research has provided almost no viable insights into the question of who among the suburban middle class is likely to be attracted to swinging and who is likely to enter into the experience and form a long-term involvement with the swinging world.

With the hope of discovering some preliminary clues as to *who* becomes a swinger and *how* (developmentally) one does so, this researcher intensively questioned one hundred swinging couples and one hundred nonswinging couples using both written questionnaires and in-person interviews. All of the couples were legally married, middle class, and living in suburban residential areas. All couples in both the swinging and the nonswinging (control) groups lived in private single-family homes. Seventy percent of the couples resided in the San Fernando Valley suburbs of Los Angeles, and 30 percent lived in the East Bay suburbs near San Francisco. Eighty percent of the couples were obtained through the help of the leaders of various swinging clubs, and the remaining 20 percent were obtained through the assistance of individual swinging couples with whom the researcher became acquainted.

The swinging group and the comparison group of nonswingers were matched on such characteristics as age, neighborhood of residence, annual income, level of attained education, and presence or absence of children. The control couples were not advised that the study was to deal with sexual mate sharing; they were instead told that the study was a university-sponsored, government-supported investigation of contemporary suburban family life.

Each husband and wife in both the swinging group and the control group was asked to fill out a detailed questionnaire. Only the questionnaire data were obtained from the controls as these were all that were needed. The swinging couples, on the other hand, were also interviewed at some length. Interviews were always carried out with couples rather than with individuals.

Just under 40 percent of the nonswinging suburbanites who were asked to serve as respondents proved willing to do so. There is reason to believe that volunteers for virtually any kind of study tend to be more liberal, assertive, outgoing, and socially aware than those who are reluctant to volunteer. Such researchers as Maslow and Sakoda (1955) and Martin and Marcuse (1957) have produced evidence of this tendency. In essence, since volunteers tend to be somewhat more liberal than nonvolunteers, the comparison group employed for this study might be viewed as providing a comparatively conservative test of the several research hypotheses. As a group they were probably at least slightly more like the swingers than a truly representative group of nonswinging suburbanites would be.

In general, the swinging couples were very cooperative, and most of those approached were willing to be studied. Many swingers seem to enjoy talking about themselves and their life-styles, particularly when they believe the person with whom they are talking will accept them as they are. It may also be that the more a swinger discusses sexual ideology, the more thoroughly and firmly it is internalized and the more personally confident the swinger becomes.

Affective Relationship with Parents During Formative Years

Because the family unit is the primary agency of social control, any research into the etiology and social context of swinging must carefully examine the nature and quality of relations with kin and particularly with parents.

As children and adolescents, swingers were found to have enjoyed significantly less cordial and less emotionally satisfying relationships with their parents than did the comparison group. Only 39 percent of swinging husbands remembered their childhoods as either happy or very happy; the figure for nonswinging husbands was 65 percent. The comparable percentages for wives were 45 percent (swingers) and 60 percent (nonswingers). On the other hand, 61 percent of swinging husbands recalled their childhoods as unhappy or only fairly happy; only 35 percent of nonswinging husbands said the same thing about their childhoods. The disparity between the two groups of wives was similar.

The respondents were also asked about their degree of remembered happiness during the adolescent years. The findings were almost the same as those obtained for happiness during the childhood years, although in all four groups there was a small drop in the percentage that remembered their adolescent periods as having been happy. This could be expected since adolescence is normally regarded as a period of stress and transition.

For most people, the quality of family life is a powerful determinant of personal happiness. This is especially true in the childhood and adolescent years when the individual must reside with the family and depend on it for the satisfaction of many different strongly felt needs. All children need recognition, respect, and interaction with significant adults. But when this interaction is sparse, unpleasant, or excessively strained, a child's sense of security is likely to remain undeveloped.

Swingers experienced considerably less gratifying relationships with their parents than did controls. Apparently the social distance in many of the swingers' families promoted more psychological differentiation from parents than is normal. Only 40 percent of swinging husbands and 42 percent of the swinging wives agreed with the statement: "My parents always respected me; I always felt free to discuss my problems with them." In contrast, 68 percent of control husbands and 65 percent of control wives agreed with the statement.

Data obtained on the frequency of informal communication in the family of orientation were found to corroborate these results. Only 23 percent of swinging husbands and 32 percent of swinging wives felt they enjoyed informal conversations as children with their parents on a "frequent" basis. The analogous findings for the controls were 36 percent for husbands and 48 percent for wives.

Respondents were also asked whether their parents had subjected them to more or fewer rules and regulations than had parents of friends of the same age and sex. There was a marked tendency among the husband swingers to have felt subjected to fewer rules than the controls. Fully 40 percent of swinging husbands felt that they had been subjected by their parents to fewer rules than their age mates; only 22 percent of control husbands felt this way. On the other hand, the analogous findings for wives revealed no significant differences between swingers and controls. The data suggested that swinging wives may even have been subjected to more rather than fewer rules than control wives.

On items where the respondents estimated how authoritarian their parents were, some similar but not completely consistent findings emerged. Here swingers were more likely than controls to recall their parents as either authoritarian or too permissive. These findings were not statistically significant, but they may suggest that swingers were less likely than similar nonswingers to have been reared in warm, democratic, or responsible-permissive home environments.

The data did strongly suggest, though, that swinging wives and husbands felt more tightly controlled as adolescents by their parents than did controls. Only 48 percent of swinging husbands and 42 percent of swinging wives said they were satisfied at the age of 17 with the amount of freedom and autonomy their parents permitted them. This compares to 69 percent of control husbands and 66 percent of control wives who were satisfied. There is the possibility that the swingers were mainly dissatisfied at age seventeen because they were granted too much freedom and autonomy rather than too little. However, this does not appear likely. The cross-cultural study of Kandel and Lesser (1969) found that adolescents reared in either a "laissez-faire" or an "authoritarian" manner were much more likely than those treated "democratically" to feel too tightly controlled and restricted.

Because modeling occurs, the degree of marital happiness of a mother and father can also have a bearing on the development of deviant tendencies in children. Nevertheless, swinging wives were no more likely than control wives to have had divorced parents. Swinging husbands, on the other hand, were almost three times more likely than control husbands to have had divorced parents. Twenty-nine percent of swinging husbands came from homes broken by divorce compared to only 10 percent of control husbands. In addition, 8 percent of swinging husbands and 6 percent of control husbands said their parents had been separated. These findings were significant at the .01 level of confidence. Inasmuch as wives generally are not the ones to precipitate the original interest and involvement in swinging, the much weaker findings for them on the matter of divorce in the family of orientation might be expected.

Those respondents whose parents had never divorced were asked to rank the happiness of their parents' marriages. Even with the divorced homes eliminated, there was a marked tendency on the part of swinging husbands to perceive their parents as having been less happily married than control husbands perceived their parents. Only 6 percent of swinging husbands saw their parents' marriages as having been "very happy" in contrast to 22.2 percent of control husbands. Among wives, 12.7 percent of swingers and 24.4 percent of controls described their parents' marriages as happy.

Considering that swingers proportionately had relatively strained, unsatisfying relationships with their parents during childhood and adolescence, it might be expected that swingers and nonswingers would differ regarding their current relations with parents and kin. It might also be expected that as adults they would interact with relatives significantly less often than would the controls. Swingers were indeed found to interact significantly less often with their relatives and kin than controls.

Moreover, while swinging is generally viewed as deviant by most middle-class Americans, it is likely that it is seen as even more deviant for women than for men. Our culture has long had a double standard of sexual behavior both before and after marriage. When a married woman with children involves herself in sexual mate sharing, it might well call forth strong negative sanctions. Moral revulsion on the part of relatives might be expected which would adversely affect the woman's kin relationships. Women's traditionally close ties to the family (by virtue of their roles and the way in which they are socialized) might be severed because of disapproval of variant moral standards.

Swingers of both sexes reported significantly less interaction with relatives than controls, and the disparity between groups was greatest among the women. Among the nonswinging controls, only 25 percent of wives and 35 percent of husbands interacted with their relatives less often than once in three months. The comparable figures for swingers were 52 percent for wives and 47 percent for husbands. While significant for both sexes, these findings were particularly strong for wives. Fully 46 percent of nonswinging wives saw their relatives at least a few times per month compared to only 21 percent of swinging wives.

Even when we confine our attention to couples whose relatives reside within the same immediate metropolitan area, swingers still interacted with kin less often than controls. Among the wives living near their kin, 42 percent of nonswingers saw their relatives once or more per week compared to only 21 percent of swingers. Only 14 percent of control wives living geographically close to their kin saw them less often than once per month; in contrast, about four out of ten swinging wives saw their kin this infrequently. The analogous findings for husbands were not statistically significant, but they were in the expected direction.

Given the relative lack of communication and mutual respect there seems to have been in the childhood homes of swingers, it might be expected that swingers would continue as adults to agree less with their parents than the controls do with theirs on issues of personal importance. The data convincingly bear out this expectation. Commonly, even people who as adolescents had comparatively poor relations with their parents change considerably as they become parents themselves. Some 82 percent of swingers in this sample were parents, but there is no indication that this had brought them closer emotionally to their own parents. For example, 42 percent of control husbands and wives felt that they presently agreed "a very great deal" with their parents about ideas, values, and opinions which they deem important in life. The comparable percentages for mate-sharing swingers were 8 and 11 percent for husbands and wives, respectively. On the other hand, 47 percent of swinging husbands and 45 percent of swinging wives report "very little if any agreement" with their parents about major issues; only 12 percent of control husbands and 14 percent of control wives felt the same way. Similarly strong differences between swingers and controls were found concerning emotional closeness to their mothers. These differences were particularly noteworthy for wives; 42 percent of control wives, compared to only 14 percent of swinging wives, presently feel emotionally close to their mothers.

Finally, the respondents were asked to describe the importance of their relatives to them in their overall scheme of things. As expected, wives were less likely than husbands to view relatives as "unimportant." But swingers of both sexes were significantly more likely than controls to view their relatives as being "unimportant." Only 28 percent of control husbands and 12 percent of control wives viewed relatives as "unimportant;" for swingers, the analogous findings were 46 percent for husbands and 27 percent for wives.

On the basis of these findings, it seems *the usual emotional dependency which prevails between children and their parents never became firmly established in the families of orientation of most swingers.* This is critical because it is the strong emotional bond between individuals and their families that makes the family system an extremely powerful social control agent. Since that bond and the strong controls did not develop effectively for most swingers, they acquired quite early in life a sense of personal freedom that permitted the exploration of deviant alternatives for self-expression and coping with life's stresses. Most people, because of their deeply internalized norms, are affected by the attitudes and perspectives of their parents in ways of which they are scarcely even aware. A close emotional bond greatly facilitates the degree and thoroughness with which norms are internalized. It is in this manner that the range of behavioral alternatives for most people becomes effectively narrowed. This is not to suggest that people on very good terms with their parents never deviate from any of their parents' normative ideas. They are, however, likely to deviate from far fewer of them (and to a lesser degree) than those who are not on such good terms with their parents.

Presumably because of the relatively cool and emotionally aloof home life swingers experienced as children, they were strongly motivated at an early age to turn to the peer group for most of their emotional gratification. Despite some shortcomings as parents, parents of swingers were perceived to be quite sociable. Indeed, they were commonly recalled as having been deeply involved with their adult friends. Given these tendencies among the parents of swingers, the young preswinger had seldom if ever been without a good sociability model upon which to pattern personal behavior. The presence of such sociability models (even though they were recalled as having been far more "adult-centered" than "child-centered") probably militated against the selection of many other forms of deviance which tend to be practiced alone.

Relationships with Friends, Social Organizations, and Neighbors

The fact that the family has the individual in its "clutches" long before any other system has, renders it especially potent as a social control institution. However, given that the most powerful social control usually occurs in situations where it is least perceived and in which the individual most enjoys spending time, it is clear that relations with chosen friends constitute an important consideration in a study of nonconformity.

Numerous studies have pointed out that people who are relatively isolated from relatives also tend to be relatively isolated from friends. However, this study clearly reveals sexual mate sharers to be an exception to this rule. The current lives of mate-sharing husbands and wives do not appear at all socially isolated. In fact, *swingers in the present study were generally found to interact with people in general more often than nonswinging controls, even though the latter interacted significantly more often with relatives than did swingers.* More specifically, 44 percent of swinging husbands and 39 percent of swinging wives were found to visit with their friends "more often than once per week," compared to only 13 percent of control husbands and 21 percent of control wives. At the other extreme, only 4 percent of swinging husbands said they visit with friends only once per month or less often; the analogous findings for control couples were 40 percent for the husbands and 26 percent for the wives.

Further analysis revealed that number of years in swinging had no effect on frequency of social involvement with friends. The question arises, however, as to whether the friends with whom swingers interacted were primarily fellow swingers. This does not seem to be the case. Interview data from swinging couples suggest that most mate-sharing respondents developed an early dependency on the peer group for a variety of satisfactions, many of which they could not get from their parents. Moreover, the average swinging couple only gets together with fellow swingers about once every two weeks, while 74 percent of swinging couples visit with friends once or more per week. Fully 59 percent of the swinging wives viewed friends as being of greater personal importance than relatives and kin; only 26 percent of control wives felt the same way. Among husbands the differences were equally great; 79 percent of swingers but only 42 percent of controls felt that friends were of greater importance than relatives.

Involvement with clubs and social organizations is commonly used by sociologists as an indicator of the strength of a group's bonds with its community. The degree of social participation especially affects subjective personal happiness (see Phillips, 1967). For these reasons, the respondents in this study were asked how many formal social organizations in their community they belonged to in the past year, and how many meetings of such clubs and organizations they normally attended each month. Informal swinging groups that might meet within the community were ruled out for these items.

No significant differences were found for either husbands or wives in the number of meetings of clubs and formal social organizations attended each month. This fact is of considerable theoretical importance, as it suggests that for at least the swingers of this sample, mate-sharing behavior is not associated with withdrawal from community involvement. In fact, even when attention was focused only on membership in the local P.T.A. no significant differences emerged. Though the data lack statistical significance, it is interesting to note that the differences favored the swingers for both husbands and wives (except for wives' membership in the P.T.A.). For example, more control husbands than swinging husbands typically attend no meetings of clubs or formal organizations during a month.

In addition, swinging husbands belonged to significantly more community clubs and formal social organizations than control husbands. As the analogous findings for wives were not found to be statistically significant, these results may not be reliable. It should be noted though that 36 percent of control wives belonged to no clubs or formal social organizations over the past year; this compared to only 27 percent of swinging wives. The highly significant analogous findings for husbands were 55 percent for controls and 29 percent for swingers. These findings are in marked contrast to those of Bartell (1971) who found swingers to be relatively inactive in community affairs. The fact that swingers in the present study were contacted through swinging clubs may have introduced a bias in the direction of "joiners."

Besides relatives and chosen friends, neighbors constitute another group which has traditionally been very important as a source of informal social conviviality. However, unlike friends, neighbors are not deliberately chosen; people end up with a collection of neighbors as a direct function of where they happen to live. It might be expected that swingers would perceive neighbors as a kind of threat. A substantial fraction of swingers did indicate that they frequently worried about the possibility of relatives dropping in unannounced at the wrong time. Friendly relationships with neighbors would greatly increase the likelihood of being inopportunely surprised by visitors.

Informal relationships with neighbors were looked at, and not surprisingly 61 percent of swinging husbands characteristically get together socially with neighbors less than four times per year. This was true of only 43 percent of nonswinging husbands. The analogous findings for wives were 62 percent for swingers and 36 percent for nonswingers. The fact that almost twice as many swinging wives as control wives were employed outside the home could account for some of this difference; the less often a woman is home, the less often she is likely to see her neighbors. However, the marked difference between the two groups of husbands, all of whom were employed, suggests that swingers tend to be highly selective in terms of their patterns of friendship and peer relations.

Political and Religious Affiliations

Swingers had weaker ties than nonswingers to all the major institutions of social influence and control. This is not to suggest that swingers do not have political or religious attitudes and values. They do have such values, and frequently these are very strongly and deeply felt. But swingers do not seem to want direct personal involvement in the conventional political or religious institutions any more than they seem to want it in the extended family kin group.

Data were obtained on the political affiliations of respondents; and the most striking difference between swingers and nonswingers was that far fewer swingers were found to be affiliated with *any* political party. Among swingers 33 percent of husbands and 34 percent of wives classified themselves as "independents" compared to only 9 percent of control husbands and 11 percent of control wives. In addition, 28 percent of swinging husbands and 22 percent of swinging wives checked that they were "uncommitted and not interested in politics," compared to only 3 percent of control husbands and 5 percent of control wives. These differences regarding political party affiliation would tend to suggest a sense of detachment and even a feeling of exasperation on the part of many swingers with conventional party politics.

Respondents were asked a number of questions about specific political and social values. Among the issues these questions dealt with were unconditional amnesty for draft resisters, civil disobedience, the women's liberation movement, zero population growth, availability to high school aged adolescents of reliable contraception, freedom of adolescents to use their own parental home bedrooms for premarital coitus and/or "living together unmarried," the legitimacy of conscription and of unconditional obedience to the dictates of political leaders, the rights of young people to wear long hair and to dress in accordance with their tastes, etc. The percentage differences between the swingers and the controls on approval or rejection of a given political or social idea were often more than fifty or sixty points.

A representative example of the swingers' liberal-humanitarian tendency can be seen in the way in which they responded to the statement: "We should be patriotic toward the human race, *not* toward any particular nation." Fully 58 percent of swinging husbands registered strong agreement, compared to only 20 percent of control husbands. Only 16 percent of swinging husbands disagreed, compared to 44 percent of control husbands. Among wives the differences between the two groups were also sharp.

In essence, swingers seemingly tend to be more "freedom oriented" than nonswingers. And this strong freedom orientation is reflected in their detachment from conventional institutions. However, as an interesting and pertinent sidelight, when it comes to the issue of population control, swingers seem to be more willing than nonswingers to have some of their freedom taken away. The question was raised: "In light of the current situation of uncontrolled population growth and the many severe problems that it creates, no couple anywhere should be legally permitted to procreate more than two children." Fifty-seven percent of swinging husbands and 48 percent of swinging wives agreed with the statement compared to only 26 percent of control husbands and 24 percent of control wives. Zero population growth advocates have argued that actual freedom goes down as population size and density go up. Swingers are more willing to have some of their freedoms taken away in the interest of population control than most middle-class residents tend to be, while the latter are more responsive than swingers to arguments favoring nationalism and patriotism and to the renunciation of individual freedom for the benefit of these values. In short, it may be false and misleading to assert that swingers and other types of nonconformists tend to be entirely in favor of freedom in all its many forms, or that most middle-class suburbanites tend to favor restrictive controls in all areas of life lest their society become overrun by anarchy. Different groups tend to favor different sets of freedoms and restrictions. But in line with their attachment to conventional institutions, nonswinging controls were far more conventional and traditional in terms of the kinds of social controls they endorsed.

The most traditional of all social institutions other than the family is religion, and as expected, *swingers are even more detached from organized religion than they are from the political and kinship institutions.* However, the break from religion was not complete for most swingers. As with ties to politics, swingers seem to have rejected and renounced ties to the *traditional* or *conventional* religions; they do not seem to have rejected all beliefs that could be considered religious.

There were no statistically significant differences between swingers and controls in recalled frequency of attendance at organized religious services at the age of fifteen. Roughly half of both swingers and controls remembered having attended religious services weekly or more often. Looking at the denomination in which the respondents were born and reared, there were similarly no meaningful differences between swingers and controls—except with regard to the "no organized religion or agnostic" category. Thirteen percent of swinging husbands and 8 percent of swinging wives were reared with no organized religion or as agnostics, compared to 1 percent of control husbands and none of the control wives. Former membership in all of the other organized religions and denominations revealed no differences between the two groups.

As present-day adults, swingers differ markedly from controls in frequency of attendance at organized religious services. Sixty-eight percent of swinging husbands and 52 percent of swinging wives never attend religious services; this compares to only 27 percent of control husbands and 25 percent of control wives. Only 7 percent of swinging husbands and 3 percent of swinging wives currently attend services on a weekly basis compared to 25 percent of the control husbands and 29 percent of control wives.

Religious institutions have long had a powerful influence upon life in America. However, as powerful an institution of social control as religion is, its influence is mediated largely through the family rather than through the efforts of religious functionaries. It is the parents who introduce their children to religious services and Sunday school and who later exercise coercion to ensure their attendance. Similarly, it is the parents who interpret and impart religiously based values and knowledge on an intimate, primary-group basis day after day. Thus it should come as no surprise that people who develop a degree of emotional estrangement from parents and kin are likely to do so also with respect to the family's religious institution. It may also be that swinging couples view most churchgoers as being highly materialistic and fundamentally *non*spiritual in orientation; they may see weekly church attendance as an attempt by others to conform to "middle-class" community expectations rather than as an attempt to fulfill genuine spiritual needs.

Early Heterosexual Orientation and Involvement

We have seen how swingers are significantly more likely than non-swingers to be emotionally and intellectually detached from such major conventional social institutions as relatives and kin, politics, and religion. While such detachment can go a long way toward prompting and enabling a person to consider and explore nonconformist solutions to the problems of everyday life, it does not provide any clear clues as to why a person might hit upon the *specific* form of nonconformist deviance of sexual mate sharing. The comparative early dating and sex histories of the respective samples of this study provide such a clue.

The respondents were asked to indicate the grade in school when they first felt a strong romantic interest in an opposite-sex age mate. According to Broderick (1966, 1972), the large majority of children have strong romantic interests and attachments as early as the third grade. Yet the differences between the swingers and the nonswingers are strong and convincing. Thirty-one percent of swinging husbands and 37 percent of swinging wives had felt strong romantic interests as early as the kindergarten through third-grade level; this compared to only 11 percent of control husbands and 9 percent of control wives. Only 16 percent of swinging husbands and 24 percent of swinging wives were at the eighth-grade level or older when they first felt a strong romantic interest; the analogous figure for the controls was 44 percent for both husbands and wives. These differences were significant far beyond the .001 level.

Of particular relevance to the foregoing are two of Broderick's (1972) findings. First, the earlier children became romantically interested and emotionally attached to age mates of the other sex, the more socially skilled and competent they were, and the more same-sex friends they were likely to have. Second, Broderick found that 43 percent of children who developed early romantic interests did not have cordial, rewarding relations with their parents. In comparison, only 15 percent of those who did not develop such early romantic interests had troubled relationships with their parents. The reader will recall the earlier finding that swingers tend to interact with chosen friends significantly more frequently than controls, and that they were quite well skilled socially. The reader should further recall the closer attachment and involvement of controls with their relatives, particularly their mothers and fathers. From these data and from those of Broderick, *it would appear that early learning of the emotional gratifications from heterosexual-social interaction is one of the key preconditions for selecting erotic forms of deviance over other forms of deviance.*

The speed with which the various stages of social-heterosexual involvement were passed was also significantly greater for swingers than for controls. For example, among husbands 68 percent of swingers had had their first date by the age of 14, compared to only 48 percent of controls. Among wives 61 percent of swingers had started dating by the age of 14, compared to only 44 percent of controls. Eighteen percent of control husbands and wives had waited until at least age seventeen before they started dating; among the swingers only 9 percent of husbands and 8 percent of wives waited this long.

Respondents were also asked how many dates they averaged during a typical month during their junior year of high school. This type of question, of course, has an equal bearing upon the matter of social skills and upon the relative absence of social-heterosexual interaction anxiety as it has upon romantic or sexual needs, interests, and desires. With this in mind, 36 percent of swinging husbands and 48 percent of swinging wives averaged at least five dates during a typical month when they were juniors; the comparable figures for nonswingers were 18 percent for husbands and 27 percent for wives. It is interesting to note, however, that 18 percent of swinging husbands and wives averaged *no* dates per month at this time; but among nonswingers, 26 percent of husbands and 30 percent of wives were not dating.

The swingers had "gone steady" with a significantly greater number of persons before they married than had controls, and they started going steady earlier. Thirty-five percent of swinging husbands and 51 percent of swinging wives had gone steady by the age of fifteen; among controls only 20 percent of husbands and 38 percent of wives had started this early. Forty percent of swingers said they had "been in love" four or more times before first marriage compared to only 7 percent of controls.

Swingers were also considerably more likely than controls to recall social activities with the opposite sex as being more important to them than social activities with their own sex. While significant for both sexes, these findings tended to be particularly strong for husbands.

A revealing questionnaire item called for response to the statement: "At the age of 20 or so I could have done without the opposite sex for three or four months at a time if circumstances had forced me, and still have remained basically happy and secure." Fully 46 percent of swinging husbands and 50 percent of swinging wives registered disagreement with this statement, compared to only 20 percent of control husbands and 29 percent of control wives. These findings are highly significant, particularly for husbands. They were somewhat weaker for the wives primarily because 55 percent of swinging wives were already married by the time they were 20; only 36 percent of control wives had married that early.

Indeed, *one of the strongest findings of this study was that swingers tended to marry significantly earlier than controls.* Among the husbands, 39 percent of swingers had married by the time they were twenty compared to only 12 percent among controls. Forty-one percent of control husbands were twenty-five or older when they married, compared to just 23 percent of swinging husbands. Among wives only 4 percent of swingers married at twenty-five years of age or older; this compared to 20 percent of controls.

Two other findings help us to understand the courtship background of swingers. The first of these concerns the age of first sexual intercourse. Among husbands 71 percent of swingers, compared to only 41 percent of controls, had sexual intercourse by age seventeen or younger. Among wives 48 percent of swingers and 22 percent of controls started at seventeen years of age or earlier. Indeed, 40 percent of swinging husbands and 23 percent of swinging wives were fifteen or younger when they started, compared to only

17 percent of control husbands and 4 percent of control wives. For a middle-class American group these figures are clearly quite high. Moreover, only 4 percent of swinging husbands and 1 percent of swinging wives were twenty-two or older when they commenced coitus; the analogous figures for controls were 26 percent for husbands and 31 percent for wives.

The second finding concerns the number of people with whom coitus was experienced fifteen or more times prior to first marriage. Here again very strong differences were obtained between the two groups. *The distinction between swingers and controls was not whether they had experienced premarital coitus, but instead the number of partners with whom they had experienced it.* For example, 38 percent of swinging wives had had premarital coitus fifteen or more times with each of two or more partners, compared to only 13 percent of control wives. Among husbands 41 percent of swingers had had premarital coitus fifteen or more times with *three or more* partners, compared to only 19 percent of controls. At the other extreme just 5 percent of swinging husbands were virgins at marriage compared to 22 percent of control husbands; among wives 14 percent of swingers were virgins at marriage, compared with 40 percent of controls. (In Chapter 6, Libby discusses the relationship between premarital sexual experience and extramarital involvements further.)

In sum, the swingers in this study became romantically interested and involved with the opposite sex significantly earlier in life than nonswingers. They had also started dating earlier and passed through the stages of increasingly intense courtship and sexual involvement both earlier in life and faster than nonswingers. The swingers learned early that boy-girl social relationships offer some of life's great rewards. They developed (and to some extent may have had at the outset of life) a significantly stronger need for social-heterosexual interaction than did the controls. This strong need (in combination with their history of gratifying involvement with the other sex, and their comparatively detached, emotionally cool relations with parents and kin) served to assure that, if they were to move toward deviant or nonconformist roles, these roles would revolve around social-erotic matters rather than around some other activity or interest.

Access to Instructive Swinging Literature

Until the 1970s very few middle-class people had ever heard about sexual mate sharing. Still fewer realized that this sort of social recreational behavior—rare though it was—occurred primarily in middle-class circles. The question therefore arises as to how the phenomenon spread so widely over the past few years. Surely there have always been people in America who possessed the background characteristics of emotional detachment from kin and an early and strong heterosexual interest and involvement. But it seems improbable that until comparatively recently many of these people gravitated toward sexual mate sharing.

Interviews with swinging couples revealed that for 75 percent of swingers the availability of a literature about swinging was a major factor in precipitating the desire to experiment with and explore this activity. Most of the remaining 25 percent had moved from the swinging world of singles (see Libby, Chapter 4) to the swinging world of marrieds; and even these people were heavily influenced by articles and books. Wives very rarely introduced discussion of sexual mate sharing; indeed, none of the wives in this study took the lead. It seems to be the husband's introduction to and awareness of the swinging literature that makes the crucial difference.

The years 1957 to 1960 saw the publication of many popular accounts on the subject of sexual mate sharing. The Roth decision of the United States Supreme Court in 1957 had opened the floodgates for the publication of all kinds of nonpictorial erotica. A representative semipornographic magazine of this period was *Mr.* Every month *Mr.* featured a department comprised of letters that had allegedly been sent in by readers who wanted to share their "wife-swapping" experiences with other interested people (see Wilson & Meyers, 1965). Most of the letters and articles of this early period were fictionalized and highly glamorized accounts designed to make swinging look beautiful, alluring, and highly romantic. In many cases these letters contained well-thought-out ideological and philosophical justifications for swinging which the fictional "wife swappers" written about allegedly shared.

Gradually an increasing number of authentic letters from real people began to appear. By 1960 there was no longer a need for fictionalized accounts, for the letters received from real swingers were richer in content than the original made-up accounts had been.

During this early period most sexually oriented publications were sold only in "adult book stores," although a few of them were also available at the larger newsstands in major cities. Middle-class men away from home on business could kill lonely hours browsing through these materials, and many would sooner or later encounter the glamorized case histories of swinging. For some men, the case histories seemed to provide the sense of direction they had been seeking; they provided a cookbook formula that could be tried, followed, and experimented with. The formula was imperfect and often misleading. But it did present a picture of middle-class husbands and wives with a strong interest in rich, purely erotic experiences. And these people were depicted as satisfying their interest and needs within the context of an ideology which did not threaten the quality or solidarity of marriage and family life. Basically, these materials provided an exciting, well-structured solution to the felt need for sexual variety.

For most people, and for women especially, the need for sex and erotic gratification is socially conditioned from early childhood into being closely associated with at least some of the following: love, romance, close emotional attachment to one partner, marriage, and family life. Preswinging men quite characteristically see themselves as having strong needs for these experiences too. But for them the need for sex is conceptually and emotionally distinct from the need for these other things. Sex for them is a strong need and interest in and of itself.

The marriage relationship of preswingers, no matter how gratifying, had not satisfied erotic needs in a comprehensive manner. Most of the preswinging husbands had dealt with this psychological unrest by engaging in occasional *conventional* (as opposed to consensual) extramarital sex. They would seek the companionship of "call girls" or other women desirous of sexual intercourse. And this was done primarily when the men were far away from home, such as when they were on business trips. Many of these husbands had enjoyed close psychological relationships with their wives and so felt guilty and uneasy about these affairs.

A wide array of swinging literature, including glamorized case histories and advertisements for swinging clubs, could never have been sufficient *by itself* to promote an interest and involvement in swinging. Before such a literature can proliferate, there must be a sizable group of people who are relatively estranged from parents and conventional social control agencies, and who find heterosexual interaction to be immensely gratifying. People with rich premarital sexual histories (such as most swingers in the current sample) are especially attracted to this literature and/or to libertarian-humanistic publications such as *The Los Angeles Free Press* where advertisements for swinging organizations are commonly carried. In short, before a person would move toward swinging there must first be an autonomous state of mind (freedom from the usual controls); a strong, autonomous heterosexual interest; and literature which shows the way. Without the swinging literature (and, later, contact with experienced swingers), potential swingers would very likely never even become aware of comarital sexual behavior. They would have to find some other way of adapting to their situations.

Value Congruence and Socialization of the Spouse

The socialization process for swingers usually involves an effort by the husband to involve the wife in swinging. Most wives are at first very reluctant to try swinging, and only after some successful and satisfactory encounters do some wives come to define swinging as pleasurable. As Whitehurst (1974) has noted, there may be a differential advantage in swinging for women in that ". . . the most significant learning may occur for the female in terms of a positive self-concept, controls over her body, and an increase in general competence and interpersonal certainty about herself." Interestingly, *various studies on sexual mate sharing indicate that once the female begins to enjoy swinging she often becomes more satisfied with it than the male.*

Quite commonly when a husband wishes to interest his wife in swinging he will leave some swinging literature and perhaps some related pornography where she is likely to find it. The wife notices this and characteristically (in line with her socially learned role) reacts with strong negative emotional feelings. This can be called stage one, or the *revulsion* stage. Depending upon the depth and strength of her revulsion, she is likely to glance over the material out of curiosity. This revulsion stage can be relatively short-lived, or it can be permanent, depending upon (1) the strength of the woman's internalized norms, (2) her ties to her own kin family network, (3) how strong her marriage and her emotional attachment to her husband are, and (4) the quality and success of the first one, two, or three swinging encounters. In any case, this stage is likely to be fraught with a considerable amount of open weeping in her husband's presence (an example of role playing rooted in internalized normative expectations) and loud emotional argumentation.

Assuming that the woman's background is not too conservative and that the husband manages to offer primarily intellectual and ideological arguments about why they should at least try swinging (e.g., honesty, openness, sharing sexual variety together as recreation, etc.), she is likely to move slowly toward stage two, or *resistance*. During this stage she begins to learn that some very respectable people like herself swing. The husband may even invite a couple that swings in for a chat. He will perhaps keep his wife in the dark about the sexual behavior of the couple for the first couple of hours. Since the wife will usually have established some rapport with the couple by the time the conversation turns to swinging, she typically finds it impossible to react in a strongly negative or insulting manner. In essence, the apparently normal and appealing nature of the visiting couple has in part neutralized and normalized their deviance for the wife.

The argumentation between husband and wife during this second stage tends to lack the emotional fervor which prevailed during the revulsion stage. The wife reacts primarily with her own intellectual arguments as to why she should not swing. The husband counters these with the appropriate points from the swinging ideology.

The resistance stage can last for several months. If the husband is successful, the wife is likely to move to stage three, or the *resignation* stage. During this stage the wife resigns herself to trying out a swinging party. At this stage the most crucial factor is whether or not the first experience with swinging is pleasant. Those couples adequately familiar with the swinging ideology and alerted to the pitfalls to avoid in getting started will usually avoid serious problems. On the other hand, naive couples may make serious blunders during their first one or two swinging encounters. They may arrange to meet a couple sight unseen at a motel; or they may invite a couple to their home without having previously investigated them. Many of the people interviewed for this study had extremely unpleasant experiences because they violated the principle that one must never commit oneself and one's spouse to a swinging encounter without having first interacted with the couple at a bar or a restaurant or in the company of mutual friends. It seems likely that for many couples such unpleasant experiences could send the wife back from the resignation stage to the revulsion stage, and at the same time reduce the husband's desire to press the issue further.

After resignation the fourth stage for many women is *acceptance*. This stage usually comes after a few favorable swinging experiences. Some swinging wives remain at the acceptance stage while others, after additional swinging experiences, move on to stage five—*enthusiasm*. At this stage they find that they no longer feel guilty and they begin to relish swinging to an even greater extent than their husbands.

Yet for a large number of couples, almost all of whom are comparatively new to the swinging scene, the wives are still very much back at the resignation stage, and many of them fluctuate between resignation and resistance. In essence, these wives simply occasionally "go along" in order to please their husbands or in order to "save" their marriages. It is my contention that the couples for whom this applies cannot be called true swingers, as they have not yet undergone all the necessary attitudinal changes.

Furthermore, one of the major conclusions of this research is that those wives who do get beyond the resignation stage to either the acceptance or the enthusiasm stage tend to have backgrounds very similar to those of their husbands in terms of (1) comparatively unsatisfying formative years in the parental home, (2) emotional detachment and comparative alienation as adults from parents and the family network, and (3) a history of early interest and involvement in social-heterosexual activities and of romantic attachments from an early age and onward. On the other hand, those wives who do not get beyond the resignation stage (even though they may swing from time to time in order to please their husbands) tend to have backgrounds that are comparatively similar to the backgrounds of the control group wives.

A further key characteristic of swinging wives is that they are much more likely than nonswinging wives to work outside the home. Sixty-two percent of swinging wives worked outside of the home compared to only 33 percent of nonswinging control wives. This is despite the fact that 82 percent of swinging wives were also mothers; the analogous figure for control wives was 88 percent.

Working outside the home may be significant in that it is another earmark of autonomy and of nontraditionality for the swinging wives—particularly in that most of them were also mothers. Being out in the work world would also afford them greater opportunity to interact with men and to share with men certain interests, ideas, values, and even personality traits such as assertiveness. In essence, with their greater independence working women could more swiftly encounter and evaluate deviant alternatives.

A swinging relationship in which the husband is enthusiastic but the wife cannot get past the resignation stage is not likely to become a stable, active swinging dyad. Just as a few experiments with homosexual behavior do not necessarily make a person a homosexual, a few swinging experiences are not a sufficient condition to render a couple a true swinging couple. *In the world of swinging, couples function as units;* and in order to be an effective unit the component parts must complement each other; the value systems of the two parts of the dyad must be reasonably congruent or complementary.

The concept of *value congruence between spouses* is commonly referred to in family research. The greater the number of characteristics a husband and a wife have in common, the greater the likelihood that the couple will achieve satisfaction. Behaviors such as comarital sex or premarital sex cannot in and of themselves create conflict and disharmony among people; these behaviors alone cannot cause a relationship to deteriorate.

What can and does matter greatly is what a person thinks and feels about his or her personal behavior, and the degree of congruence between the internalized norms of the spouses. Harmony between mates as to what their values and expectations are for their relationship is of crucial importance. If both mates have similar expectations as to what they want sexually from their relationship, they have a high likelihood of success. Husbands and wives who are not especially happy with each other, or whose normative perceptions of social reality (especially as they relate to sexual mate sharing) tend to be markedly disparate, ought to avoid this form of nonconformist recreation. It could precipitate a deterioration of such a marriage.

Shared Meanings and Other Factors in Marital Happiness

In order for a couple to become a successful swinging dyad, they must have "shared meanings" for the concept of adultery. As a couple and as individuals they must thoroughly transform their understanding of the term, abandoning the conventional meanings. As an illustration, two particularly pertinent questions were asked of each respondent in this study. First, they were asked to react to the following statement: "It is possible to engage in a great deal of extramarital sexual intercourse without being at all unfaithful or genuinely untrue to your marriage partner." Among swingers, 81 percent of husbands and 89 percent of wives registered agreement; among controls the analogous figures were only 15 percent for husbands and 7 percent for wives. The differences may have been even greater except that some of the swingers did not equate comarital sex with "extramarital sexual intercourse." Some of them commented after filling out the questionnaires that swinging to them was not *extra*marital sexual intercourse because it was an experience shared as a couple. Most swingers, however, do see swinging as a type of extramarital sex.

A second item asked for reactions to the statement: "When adultery occurs, it is usually symptomatic of the fact that the marriage is not going well." Again, less than 20 percent of swinging husbands and wives agreed with the statement, compared to almost 80 percent of control spouses.

The matter of shared meanings between husbands and wives has a very important bearing upon the outcome of EMS. This can be seen in the statistical relationship between forms of EMS on the one hand and marital happiness on the other. The respondents were asked to rate their overall marital happiness. Fifty-six percent of swinging husbands and 58 percent of swinging wives rated it as "very happy," compared to 43 percent of control husbands and 49 percent of control wives. Among those who rated it as "happy" were 29 percent of swinging husbands and 23 percent of swinging wives; 33 percent of control husbands and 31 percent of control wives rated it as "happy." At the other end of the ledger only 15 percent of swinging husbands and 19 percent of swinging wives rated their marriages as being either "fairly happy" or "unhappy," compared to 24 percent of control husbands and 22 percent of control wives. These results were not statistically significant, but they did tend to slightly favor swingers in terms of marital happiness.

Such findings become far more interesting when we compare swingers with control couples who had engaged in conventional adultery. Among 34 percent of control couples either the husband or the wife had experienced some conventional EMS. And only 26.5 percent of these control husbands in adulterous unions saw their marriages as "very happy," compared to 51.5 percent of control husbands in nonadulterous unions. Among swinging husbands, the reader will recall, 56 percent rated their marriages as "very happy." At the other end of the spectrum 32.3 percent of control husbands in adulterous unions rated their marriages as only "fairly happy" or "unhappy," compared to 19.7 percent of control husbands in nonadulterous unions and 15 percent of the husbands in swinging unions. Among wives, 41.2 percent of control women in adulterous unions rated their marriages as "very happy," compared to 53.0 percent of control wives in nonadulterous unions; 58 percent of swinging wives, it will be recalled, rated their marriages as being "very happy."

Especially interesting among the foregoing findings is the suggestion that among controls adultery seems to hurt the husbands' satisfaction with their marriages more than it hurts the wives' satisfaction—even though the husbands were usually the adulterers. This suggests that in conventional social settings where *no* form of adultery is regarded as acceptable, the husband's deviance from sexual fidelity may reflect his dissatisfaction and unhappiness with the marriage and the beginning stages of marital disorganization.

Among swingers, however, we are not dealing with a conventional social setting. The internalized norms pertinent to adultery and the shared meanings of the act between husband and wife are drastically different than they are among ordinary couples who do not view any form of adultery as socially acceptable. Most swinging husbands and wives similarly do regard *conventional* adultery as unacceptable and potentially threatening to a marriage. But the *consensual* adultery that is sexual mate sharing is a very different matter to them; it is not seen as being similar to conventional adultery because it is practiced honestly, openly, and with the husband and wife doing it and sharing it together as a marital unit. Because of these considerations, the conventional adultery of the controls is clearly associated statistically with unhappiness and dissatisfaction in marriage while the adultery of swingers is mildly associated with marital happiness and satisfaction. This is in spite of the fact that swingers practice their form of adultery far more often than the controls practice conventional adultery.

For most women in swinging relationships it took time and considerable stress and difficulty before they were able to undergo this transformation of meaning from their original concept of adultery to their current one. Many women never make the complete transformation and remain behind at the resistance or resignation stages. In order for the transformation of meanings to be complete, it must occur on an emotional as well as on a purely intellectual level. People always accept new ideas faster on an intellectual level than they do on a deeper emotional or "gut" level. Women who were able to make this transformation had, like their husbands, been emotionally detached from their relatives and kin and had always been strongly interested in social-heterosexual interaction. It is significant too that when asked (on the privately filled-in questionnaires) whether or not they felt becoming a swinger was worth whatever difficulties it had involved, only 6 percent of swinging wives answered "no" and only an additional 14 percent responded "uncertain." On the other hand, 35 percent of these wives responded "emphatically yes" and 45 percent responded "mostly yes."

Swinging wives do not seem discontented with the amount of emotional satisfaction they get from their sexual expression. Forty-six percent of swinging wives answered "emphatically yes" and another 45 percent answered "mostly yes" to the question: "Do you feel you derive enough emotional satisfaction and relatedness out of your sexual expression?" Among control women only 38 percent answered "emphatically yes" and 42 percent answered "mostly yes." These differences were significant beyond the .01 level of confidence. It may be that women who become socialized into the world of sexual mate sharing are likely to derive even greater satisfactions out of sexual intercourse than do conventional women their age.

Swingers also report more frequent intercourse with their own legal spouses than do nonswingers. Despite their involvement at sexual mate sharing festivities roughly once in two weeks, 23 percent of swinging couples reported having sexual intercourse with each other six or more times per week, compared to only 2 percent of nonswinging husbands and wives. Thirty-two percent of swinging couples reported intercourse with their legal spouses four or five times weekly, compared to only 14 percent of nonswinging couples. On the other hand, 48 percent of nonswinging couples averaged only zero or one conjugal copulation per week, compared to 11 percent of the swingers. These differences are particularly noteworthy in that there were no significant differences in the ages of swinging and control couples.

It is of further interest that *the control group demonstrated more boredom than did the swingers.* This may be related to the fact that the chief form of recreation for swingers is usually swinging—an activity the couple does together. Shared experiences for a couple seem to be more important than nonshared experiences in developing and maintaining a positive relationship. Yet, the main recreational pursuits in our society (and presumably for the controls) are usually participated in by just one sex.

Divorce statistics might be another reflection of the relative happiness of swinging versus nonswinging couples. It is widely assumed that sexual mate sharing leads to marital discord, family disorganization, and divorce. And in fact, 49 percent of swinging husbands and 34 percent of swinging wives had at some time been divorced, in comparison to only 15 percent of nonswinging husbands and 14 percent of nonswinging wives. Yet it cannot be concluded that swinging and divorce go hand in hand. In this study, *none of the divorces occurred after a man or woman became active with either a present or former spouse in comarital sexual behavior.* Factors other than swinging seem more useful in explaining the higher rate of divorce for swingers. For example, the swinging men contracted their first marriage at an unusually early age. They tended to enter first marriages with women to whom they had felt a strong physical attraction, and they first married after very short courtships. Another factor hurting these marriages could be that swingers mostly led stormier youths than did controls.

It is not possible to give any composite and encompassing statement on the effect of swinging on the conjugal relationship, on family life, and on happiness. Bartell (1971) suggested that swinging is likely to be very good for some couples and very bad for others; but he did not elaborate. I conclude that swinging cannot in and of itself precipitate negative consequences for any couple or person. The consequences of swinging depend on the social and cultural context within which it occurs.

The main purpose of this article was to present some empirically based insights into the process by which middle-class suburban couples become attracted to and socialized into the sexual-mate-sharing subculture. Major predisposing factors were outlined and the reasons for their importance were examined. The author's data were obtained from one hundred California mate-sharing couples and from a comparison group of one hundred nonswinging couples who reside in the same neighborhoods as the swinging couples.

If the swingers in this research are reasonably typical of American swingers, it would certainly appear that three main factors do much to push middle-class couples toward sexual mate sharing. These include: (1) long-term alienation from the family system; (2) an early and sustained tendency to view heterosexual-social interaction as providing strong emotional gratification; and (3) the availability of a literature (fictionalized or otherwise) and services providing direction and ideological supports for becoming involved in comarital sex.

The data also documented the comparative alienation of swingers from the major conventional social institutions, particularly organized religion and politics. It was pointed out, however, that the influence of religion for most people is mediated mainly through the family. But since their relationships with their parents had not been very emotionally gratifying, the swingers had long confined their interaction with their parents and kin to a minimum and were little influenced by them.

On the other hand, swingers were not in any sense socially isolated or without good friends. Despite a failure to build warm parent-child relationships, the swingers' parents provided good sociability models. Good social skills and an absence of interpersonal anxiety are major prerequisites and preconditions for becoming a swinger. People without such skills might develop an interest in sexual mate sharing, but they are not likely to become actively involved.

So, while swingers were found to be emotionally alienated from kin and neighbors, they were even more actively involved with their chosen friends than were the controls. Even in terms of involvement with nonswinging clubs and community social organizations the swingers registered a higher level of active participation than did the controls.

Finally, husbands who successfully entered and remained active within the sexual-mate-sharing community for at least six months had wives whose backgrounds were not too dissimilar from their own backgrounds in terms of the major factors discussed earlier. Not all of these wives were able to accept the idea of sexual mate sharing when their husbands first suggested it. But with increasing exposure to the idea from the husband, the literature, and friends (and provided that the quality of the conjugal relationship up to that time had been good), they were able to gradually and effectively internalize the crucial aspects of the swinging ideology. In short, in order for a husband and a wife to successfully practice this form of consensual adultery, they must come to share similar meanings about extramarital sex. For wives this usually required a greater amount of time than it did for husbands; but some of the husbands, too, had to grapple at the beginning of their involvement in comarital sex with feelings of jealousy and to deal with these feelings in a manner congruent with the swinging ideology.

Even with all the predisposing factors favoring involvement in comarital sexual activity, a deep internalization of the swinging ideology on an emotional "gut" level as well as on an intellectual level would seem to be a basic prerequisite for any long-term involvement. Similarly, while swinging seems to have benefited the marriages of many, it seems quite clear that positive outcomes will befall a couple if and only if there is an honest and thorough-going congruency between the internalized proswinging values of both wife and husband.

In conclusion, sexual mate sharing by itself cannot either help or harm a marital relationship. *What is of vital importance is how the partners view their behavior.* If both partners can be mentally and emotionally satisfied in a swinging situation, then this type of sexual expression will not do any harm to their relationship. If both partners see swinging as an essential part of their relationship, then swinging is right for them.

Comarital sex should be viewed as an alternative unconventional marital life-style in the contemporary United States. It can be seen as constituting one of several marital and nonmarital alternatives to ordering the sexual drive of adult members of society. If the participants all share similar definitions and expectations for their mutual behavior, there is no reason why their behavior should not coexist with more traditional marriage forms.

11.
Sexual Aspects of Group Marriage

Larry L. Constantine and Joan M. Constantine

The authors use both psychological and anthropological viewpoints to discuss motives for entering group marriage. They describe the various patternings of sex life in marital groups they have studied and find that personal growth is often a primary consideration in joining a group. Although sexual reasons for joining a group marriage are important, sexual jealousy poses less of a problem in the dynamics of group marriage than does the fact that a complex and difficult range of interpersonal problems must be worked out in a nonsupportive cultural environment. Although group marriage is unlikely to cure existing marital problems, in many instances the group can and does give significant support for individual growth. As in conventional marriages, sex in group marriage often tends to become the arena in which other problems are fought out—the visible sign that something is wrong. Sexual problems were not significant in the breakup of groups, although groups did tend to break up after relatively short periods. The authors conclude that there are many important lessons to be learned from group marriage that have implications for other types of marriage, particularly open marriage of the future.

From three years of multidisciplinary research (1973), we have found contemporary group marriage to encompass a variety of complex, multidimensional relationships. The group marriages we studied included anywhere from three to six conjugal partners, each of whom considered himself or herself to be married to at least two partners.[1] The average group consisted of four adult partners and three children (usually the children of the couples' preexisting conventional marriages). Without exception, the group marriages we have studied have involved far more than sexual exchanges; yet, in the final analysis, concurrent sexual relationships with more than one partner is one of the chief characteristics of group marriage. In this article we will use concepts as well as data to focus on the sexual aspects of group marriage.

Often reporters, writers, and family scientists want most of all to know the details of the group marriage's sex life, although sex is but one of many aspects of the relationships in a group marriage. So common is the insistence on sexual details that participants frequently react with a defensive posture which downplays the importance of sex in the relationships.[2]

From presentations to college and professional audiences, we have learned that group marriage is surprisingly threatening to many people. The readers of *Life* magazine (Flaherty, 1972) were more than twice as likely to approve of premarital cohabitation as to approve of group marriage, but four times as likely to accept group living without sex. Nine readers out of ten disapproved of group marriage. However, it is apparent that more educated and professional groups are more approving of or interested in group marriage, as more than a fourth of the 20,000 respondents in the *Psychology Today* survey (Athanasiou, 1970) were interested in or in favor of group marriage.

The issue *is* sex, but not sex per se. Rather, the issue is sex in a group, which means the maintenance and acknowledgment of more than one sexually intimate relationship at a time.

An Explanatory Model

If 90 percent of the public disapprove of group marriage, then the few who find the idea personally attractive and the even smaller proportion who actually create such relationships are of singular interest. Our research focused on the motivations for participation in group marriage. As we extended our formal understanding of the reasons why some people strive to develop these relationships, we also added to our informal understanding of why many more people are opposed to group marriage. In the end, the answers seemed in many respects to be covered by a single concept of human sexuality.

Group marriage evokes strong positive and negative reactions because it is related to very basic and nearly universal human desires—desires as operant in the antagonists as in the advocates.

In the course of our research we formulated an elementary model of human sexuality—a model based on diverse anthropological, ethological, and psychological evidence. Sexual attraction between individuals, of course, is largely a function of cultural conditioning and individual socialization with some degree of innate genetic input. The desire for sex is mediated by social factors, such as status and opportunity. In addition, two factors act to amplify or generate sexual attraction—novelty and intimacy. We postulated a human tendency both to seek new and different partners and to sexualize relationships of established proximity, propinquity, and interpersonal intimacy.

It is our contention that an impartial review of the cross-cultural evidence must lead to the conclusion that humans are probably polysexual by nature (that is, preferring sexual relations with a variety of partners without necessarily separating them in time). Some data strongly suggest that polysexuality is an inherent propensity. For example, even in the most restrictive and punitive monogamous societies, both men and women engage in nonmarital sex, resisting cultural counterconditioning and risking grave consequences. It seems equally evident that the desire for sex in the context of ongoing intimacy is both strong and widespread, if not universal.

In the end then, group marriage presents a profound threat because nearly everyone has the desire for sexual intimacy with those with whom they are interpersonally intimate—a best friend's spouse, the good neighbors across the street, and members of the immediate family. It is acknowledged in diverse disciplines from anthropology to psychology that incestuous desires are nearly universal. We believe this applies not only in quasi-family environments, such as communes and extended family groups, but in the nuclear family as well. The ubiquity of the incest taboo attests to the commonness of the underlying link between sexual desires and intimacy. The strength and generality of the incest taboo make strong reactions against group marriage more understandable; most people will be close to a number of people but will have few individuals (likely only one) with whom they can be openly sexual.

But societies more often taboo than approve open multiple relationships. One explanation lies in the ways in which the emotional energy vested in human polysexuality becomes channeled. Multiple relationships are more complex than simple paired relationships. Where multiple relationships are sanctioned, those conflicts in time and space which arise will be visible and open, becoming part of the social process of the group which validates them. On the other hand, the group which prohibits multiple sexual relations transforms the consequences from social effects into internal conflicts within individuals; sexual attractions and desires, however, will be present nonetheless. Societies tend to condone or promote those behaviors which appear to have few undesirable social consequences. Thus, taboos on multiple sexual relations are likely because the negative consequences of the taboos are intrapsychic and less obvious (or perhaps more deferred) than are the consequences of open multiple sexuality.

If common propensities are involved, we do not then expect that those who participate in group marriage will fundamentally differ from the great masses of people who reject it.

The Participants

The people who formed group marriages were found to come from a wide range of backgrounds spanning from lower to upper social classes. They were somewhat better educated and somewhat younger than the national average. Their religious upbringings varied, but an unexpectedly high percentage claimed an ethical-humanist background and an even higher percentage accepted that label at the time of the study. In most cases their childhoods were unexceptional. Most were married and entered the group relationship with their spouses. Those marriages were for the most part happy. On a standard measure of marital adjustment,[3] participants' scores were average but significantly more clustered than the normative population. For the most part, we studied urban and suburban group marriages, but some were agrarian and small town. Politically, participants leaned somewhat toward the left, but there were also conservatives and revolutionaries among them.

The prior sexual experience of our participants did not distinguish them. Almost all had had premarital intercourse. They had experimented with a variety of sexual practices. Consistent with the Kinsey averages, somewhat over half had been involved extramaritally *before* the group marriage experience. Quite a few of these earlier extramarital experiences had been open and shared with spouses, which is probably unusual. About half had experimented with mate swapping, believing it to be based on more than sexual exchange. Most of these were disappointed, however, and dropped out of swinging.

Frequently the group marriage began with very early cross-marital sexual involvement, and in a number of cases participants felt that sex had occurred too soon in the group marriage.

Motivation and Personality

Sex is among the reasons for people entering group marriage. Of the participants we studied, 88 percent said that a variety of sexual partners was among their reasons, but sex was not the most important motivation. Only 18 percent said it was an important motivation; among the other more important motivations, *personal growth* is most noteworthy. Indeed, an interest in genuinely intimate interpersonal relations and the personality growth potential in interpersonal processes is characteristic of group marriage participants.

We also undertook a study of the personality characteristics of participants as an indicator of possible deeper motivation for group marriage participation. If a desire for multiple intimacy is simply human, then we would expect the few who participate in group marriage to be more in touch with their human needs and desires. Since the unstated taboo on multiple intimacy seems to be quite strong, we would expect those who violate it to show less need to conform or defer to such social pressures. It is plausible that both their sexual needs and their needs for variety are above average. In that sex is only one means of expressing the multiple intimacy of a group marriage, we would suspect that participants would have a capacity for intimacy in a broad sense.

To explore our hypotheses, we employed two widely used standard psychological instruments, the Edwards Personal Preference Schedule (EPPS), purporting to measure the levels of fifteen normal personality needs, and the Personal Orientation Inventory (POI), consisting of two scales and ten subscales which are elements of self-actualization or high-level emotional functioning. The POI is generally considered a measure of psychological health. From the scales on which participants differed significantly from established norms, we constructed a composite picture of personality structure as motivation. [4]

In simplest form we hypothesized certain basic *needs* which the individual must be *aware* of and must be capable of carrying over into *behavior*. Three elements are required: needs, awareness, and the ability to actualize in behavior. The three basic needs or drives stem from the model discussed above: sex, variety, and intimacy. The EPPS scores of participants did reveal a significantly high need for change (and a complementary low need for order) plus high needs for heterosexuality and for intraception. The need for intraception includes the need to know and understand other people, which is related to the need for intimacy. The POI results of participants also showed exceptionally high capacities for intimacy and a high awareness of their own needs and feelings. As for satisfying these needs in the face of social counterforces, participants were inner-directed (rather than other-directed), high in the need for autonomy, flexible in application of their values (high existentiality), spontaneous and freely expressive of their needs and feelings, very low in the need for deference to others and to norms, and low in any need for feeling guilty.

The elevated scores on eleven of the twelve POI scales suggests that participants were normally healthy psychologically. Thus, for our participants, emotional problems were ruled out as motivations for entering group marriage.

Sexual Life in a Group Marriage

What is the sex life of a participant in a group marriage like? At first, the multiple sexual involvement and the process of building new intimacy was for some participants all-consuming. While this first flush of a new relationship inevitably receded, participants reported that both their frequency of sexual relations and their enjoyment of them remained at a higher level than before they entered the group relationship. An element of this continued enthusiasm was undoubtedly the fact that sexual pairings were changed often within the groups. Early in the history of most groups, the change of partners was fixed by a schedule of rotation, typically allotting three to four days with each partner. In theory, rotation equalized sexual opportunity, forestalled jealousy and possible incidental rejection, and saved the energy and anxiety that might otherwise be invested in a repeated decision-making process. In practice, only the last held true, and most groups moved gradually toward more flexible and informal means of pairing as their interpersonal skills grew.

Along the way, many strategies for pairing were tried, with even an occasional resort to a deck of cards. One group created a scheme whereby women controlled the sleeping arrangements one month and men controlled them the next. Bedroom arrangements varied, from each person having a bed and personal room to all participants in a single bed (as in some triads). Since the mode was four people (two men and two women), the most prevalent arrangement was one bedroom and one bed per two people. Space was a factor; there may have only been three bedrooms for six adults, and it was much easier to fit three in a bed than five or six.

Infrequently, some or all of the partners in a group marriage went to bed together. Their experiences with group sexual encounters did not form a single pattern. Rarely did a group attempt to share sex communally as a steady diet; more commonly, group sex was an occasional result of particularly strong group feelings. Characteristically, participants reported their group sexual experiences to be profoundly moving, though occasionally tinged with competition or anxiety. With one or two exceptions, sexual contact between members of the same sex only occurred in the group context.

This last finding is especially significant in that participants as a group considered same-sex physical expression of affection to be natural and desirable. There was a phenomenological difference in the way participants perceived the experience of ambisexual encounter in a group and homosexual encounter in a pair. Since they held consistently liberal attitudes on homosexuality and seemed to accept this component in themselves, we conclude that the phenomenological distinction between ambisexual and homosexual experiences is meaningful and significant.

Sexual Problems and Sexual Jealousy

A minority of the group marriages were motivated by sexual and interpersonal problems in the existing conventional marriages of the participating couples. The troubled couples often believed that multiple intimacy would help solve their problems, but usually the problems were exacerbated. At the very least, multiple intimacy is a setting in which the submerged elements of relationships—the hidden contracts and unexamined patterns of all marriages—are likely to surface in ways that invite and may even demand creative resolution. The highly motivated couple generally uses the situation and the emerging material as part of a process to reinforce their relationship. When known or significant difficulties lead people into group marriage, they are unlikely to either make a success of the group relationship or solve their problems.

In a couple of instances, the motivation for group marriage was the inability of a couple to time their climaxes satisfactorily. These couples hoped that relationships with more sexually sophisticated couples would teach them how to achieve mutual sexual satisfaction. Both husband and wife found they could achieve sexual satisfaction with their new partners, but were unable to carry this success into their existing marriage, in part because each interpreted their new success as evidence that the problem lay with their original partner. Group marriage now appears to be inappropriate as blanket security to cover an insecure partnership, as a committee solution to communications problems, or as a sexually highlighted solution to economic difficulties.

Group marriage participants, like all marriage partners, can have problems even where the relationships are basically sound. Some of these problems have been manifestly sexual. Participants have experienced isolated bouts with temporary impotence, vaginal pain, premature ejaculation, monilial infections, and even an occasional lack of passion. But to date, we have found no specifically sexual problem which seems unusually (in comparison to monogamous marriages) prevalent in group marriages, except in that sex is the arena in which relationship issues are so commonly presented.

Quite often, sexual encounters provide the trigger or releasing mechanism for jealous behavior. In society at large, the absence of a jealous reaction would be suspect in a situation where a spouse becomes sexually intimate with another person. Of course, sex is not the only trigger for jealous behavior, but sex does appear to most people to be unusually important in this context. What makes sex important is that people believe it to be important, seeing it as signifying crucial elements of a relationship—especially deep (perhaps total) involvement and exclusive commitment.

Through jealous behavior, people signal their fear that they might lose something they value. Many elements of a relationship may be valued, such as companionship, intellectual stimulation, support, and sex. Anxiety results from situations that appear to someone to carry the potential for ultimate loss of these valued aspects of a relationship. But anxiety is only the primary feeling and is often transformed into anger, rage, despondency, and other feelings which give rise to the behavior we all know as jealousy.

For a person for whom sex is symbolic of an entire relationship or a sign of a commitment which can only apply to one partner, sexual "infidelity" portends not merely the loss of one opportunity for sexual encounter or even simply the changing of the sexual element of a relationship, but the loss of the whole relationship that sex symbolizes for that person. Given the traditional symbolic meaning ascribed to sex, jealousy is the expected outcome of multiple sexual intimacy.

Group marriage participants also experience problems with jealousy; 80 percent considered jealousy to be a problem, although jealousy was rarely regarded as serious, becoming significantly less of a problem as individuals and groups matured. Many participants learned creative ways to deal with jealousy, accepting jealous behavior as signaling the need for exploration of what might be at stake in their relationships at that time. They see sex primarily as communication, as one of many means of expressing themselves with each other, and as a natural concomitant to intimacy rather than as a token of fidelity or an exclusive privilege. For all these reasons—maturation, interpersonal skills, and a nontraditional interpretation of sex—jealousy has generally been more manageable for group marriage participants than for conventional spouses.

The Open Pair

Human sexuality has been linked with the formation of durable paired relationships or pair bonds.[5] It has not been unequivocally established that humans form pair bonds in the same sense that many other animals do. The existence of human pair bonds does not preclude the possibility that lasting and meaningful bonds with other partners can also be formed. In the group marriages we studied, the pair-bond relationships in which participants were involved at the outset of their group marriages continued to be distinguishable both by outside observers and by participants in even the oldest groups (about five years). That is, prior marriages continued to be special or carry primacy in some sense long after the establishment of multiple intimacy. In nearly all cases, prior marriages survived group dissolution; only a few couples separated in the process or as a result of group breakup.

The pair bonds of group marriage participants are unusual in that they are not exclusive; they are open to both alternate sexual and interpersonal intimacy. The same is true of the group bonds, for most of the groups were found to permit and validate further intimacy outside the group marriage. Thus the group marriage itself was often an open marriage in which partners could, if they desired, form and maintain significant relationships with people outside the group without the group necessarily regarding this as disruptive or a violation of faith. We believe this will be the prevailing pattern for group marriages, since the motivating factors in forming the group do not disappear after formation.

Of the possible bonds in a group marriage, the bonds between same-sex members appear to be especially salient in determining group success. Comfort with simple physical expressions of affection, though not necessarily overtly sexual expression, may contribute substantially to the quality of same-sex bonds. For example, two men who can express anger, distrust, or frustration but cannot communicate simple affection are likely to have difficulties sharing a household. In general, women have formed good same-sex relationships more readily than have men, in part due to greater opportunity and because women have usually been less severely socialized against same-sex affection than have men. As an extension of this, more women than men in group marriages have resolved their ambisexuality, which is also true in other emerging sexual life-styles.[6] Most group marriages studied had broken up by the conclusion of our research. Sex was rarely a significant problem while the groups remained intact; and the longer a group lasted, the less likely they were to report sex-related problems. Nor did sexual issues figure prominently in the breakup of groups. Others have reported findings supporting the view that sex is not really a problem in group marriage as many might expect it to be.[7] Indeed, sex may be one of the positive elements in an otherwise difficult relationship.

Implications for the Future

We believe that our research has important implications for the future, especially for the future of conventional marriage. The needs for sexual experience, variety, and intimacy that motivate group marriage are present in everyone, even if to lesser degrees. There also appears to be a fundamental link between interpersonal involvement and a human propensity to sexualize relationships. With greater individual and collective awareness of this propensity to sexualize relationships, there is likely to be more extensive experimentation with a variety of marriage and family life-styles permitting multiple intimacy. In view of the current trend toward a pluralistic society that is more tolerant of alternate life-styles, translation of awareness into behavior should prove very easy for many people in the future. Thus, many of the special problems of today's group marriages may soon be quite general and unspecial. Coping with relationship complexity and the allotment of time and energy are part of close multiple friendships even where sex is not involved. Furthermore, the reduction of jealousy and development of productive ways of dealing with jealous behavior could be of great value, even for couples having conventional, closed relationships.

It seems clear from our research that a group of people can become deeply mutually involved in each other's lives and even extend their intimacy to include sex and yet remain friends. Open, multiple sexual relationships can be handled by individuals and the group in which they occur, just as these individuals and the group can handle the jealous behavior that may accompany the early stages of such relationships. While this may not appear startling for those who have experienced such relationships, the potential impact of such a discovery on conventional society could be profound.

Reference Notes

1. Three-person marriages are not group marriages by traditional definition. The correct term for the relationships studied is "multilateral marriage," but this is a technical issue beyond the scope of this article. See Constantine and Constantine, 1971, p. 10.

2. See, for example, Stein, 1970, p. 19.

3. An adaptation of the Burgess-Cottrell Marital Adjustment Form. See Burgess and Wallin, 1953, and Burgess and Cottrell, 1939.

4. The complete report is found in Constantine and Constantine, 1973.

5. For a detailed discussion of the role of sex in bond formation, see Duyckaert, 1970, and Ramey, 1972.

6. Gilbert Bartell, *Group Sex*. New York: Peter H. Wyden, 1971.

7. Reese D. Kilgo, "Can Group Marriage Work?" *Sexual Behavior*, 1972, vol. 6, p. 2.

12.
Notes on Marriages in the Counterculture

John S. Kafka and Robert G. Ryder

*Selected examples of unconventional marriages are discussed with inter-
pretations of their potential meanings for conventional marriages. The authors describe not only the process of separation from conventionality, but
how some couples drift back into conventional life-styles. An important aspect of the article is the authors' discussion of altered conceptions of sexuality in the counterculture. The comparison with more conventional marriages is also useful in describing differences in the approach to or avoidance
of tension.*

*A portion of this article is devoted to changing sociosexual relations in a
society characterized by a psychology of plenty. New sharing norms, considered an outgrowth of societal change, are considered as part of an emergent
ideology of the counterculture which may create further changes in male-
female relationships. It appears to the authors that young people with a
countercultural orientation tend to face difficulty and complexity in relationships with others because of their different views of themselves and the
world around them. While the indicators of change are easy enough to perceive, the strength of the trends and their ultimate meanings for men and
women of the future remain more obscure.*

In the course of an extensive study of early marriage (Raush, Goodrich,
& Campbell, 1963; Ryder, 1970a; Ryder, 1970b; Ryder, Kafka, & Olson,
1971), the authors located a small minority of couples (less than 1 percent)
who seemed to have serious allegiance to what has been called (Roszak, 1968)
the counterculture or, more recently, alternative culture or hip culture, the
characteristics of which will be described below.* These and other couples located by a variety of ad hoc means were interviewed in either individual or

"Notes on Marriages in the Counterculture" by John S. Kafka and Robert G. Ryder reproduced
by special permission from *Journal of Applied & Behavioral Science* Vol. 9, No. 2/3, 1973, pp.
321-330, published by NTL Institute.

The writers wish to acknowledge their debt to the various colleagues who have contributed
ideas, information, and critical commentary in the course of completing this paper, and particularly to David H. Olson, who has been closely associated with this project and who has made
many substantial and valuable contributions. We also wish to express our thanks to Raymond
K. Yankg, whose comments on various drafts of this paper have been most helpful.

*ED. NOTE : The proportion of relationships and marriages which are countercultural is
probably larger than the proportion found in this study. One reason is that the sampling took
place prior to 1970 and so does not reflect later trends. Second, the method of locating and identifying counterculture couples was imperfect: Some and perhaps many actual counterculture
couples may not have been identified. However, neither of these limitations should be seen as
reflecting on the excellent description of such couples in this article.

joint sessions; some of the joint sessions were quite informal with interviewees casually entering and leaving while the interview was in progress.
The kind of interview procedure employed makes it impossible to arrive at a
well-defined figure for sample size, but we estimate that we each spoke with
upwards of forty persons (Total N thus above eighty) located mostly on the
East and West Coasts, in particular around Washington, D.C., and San Francisco. To a certain extent participants were treated more like informants, in
the anthropological sense, than like subjects, i.e., we were as interested in reports about other families known to an interviewee as in self-reports. Most of
the persons in our sample were in their middle twenties, with a range from
the late teens to the late forties.

There can be little doubt that, as Roszak (1968) has emphasized, the expression *counterculture* refers to a poorly defined, heterogeneous, and
changeable set of phenomena; and yet, as Roszak also points out, it is a set of
phenomena with a slippery but insistent reality. For a couple to be included
in our study, they had to explicitly intend to avoid the hang-ups of conventional marriage; to maximize intimacy; to minimize utilitarian aspects of their
relationship (cf. Cuber & Harroff, 1965); and to eschew possessiveness and
loyalty to conventionally acceptable cultural roles. The importance of money
was generally minimized. Boundaries, as in separating what is inside a marriage or out of it, or inside one's living quarters or out of them, were
deemphasized. Geographical mobility seemed high. Most participants used
soft drugs and often indicated that they were comfortable with drug use.
Many participants, but by no means all, wore their hair long, dressed casually, and presented a manifestly hippie appearance.

All of the participants shared one anomaly in terms of a thoroughgoing
countercultural orientation: They were all legally married and were involved
in primarily dyadic relationships.[1]

This group of couples and the others described by them seemed im-
pressionistically to manifest several notable central tendencies. Briefly, these
central tendencies were as follows:

1. While there was substantial overt unconventionality, there was also a
   consistent tendency, sometimes covert, to return to the conventional.
2. While sexual activity was prominent in the lives of these people, there is a
   sense in which sexuality was given a reduced role; one contemporary way
   of putting it is that sexuality was demystified.
3. The demystification of sexuality was related to the tendency of some
   couples to actively approach emotional tension and sometimes to go out of
   their way to create it.
4. Finally, there is the possibility that a psychology of plenty, as it were, led
   some couples to altered affectional and sexual patterns.

Return to the Conventional

John and Sally[2] lived downtown in a small flat. Sally and her family
were somewhat more affluent and better educated than John. He was a poet;

he generally slept during the day, spent the evening with his wife, and stayed up all night writing and playing with the couple's six-month-old baby. Sally had a regular office job with a major insurance company and was the family's sole source of income. Certainly this was not a stereotypically conventional middle-class couple, even setting aside the fact that they lived downtown rather than in the suburbs. Conventionally, husbands have higher socioeconomic status than wives, wives provide more baby care than husbands, and husbands provide income while wives stay home. There was even a role reversal in the skills John and Sally attributed to each other, with Sally seen as having practical, instrumental abilities and John seen as being good with feelings and emotional matters. Yet there is a sense in which all this overt unconventionality did not prevent the emergence of conventional sex roles. John was not a male housewife; he was a poet or a guru, i.e., the performer of a highly valued activity. Sally was not seen as the head or the mainstay of the family; she was the performer of meaningless work, i.e., earning money at a straight job. John was the socioemotional *expert*, while Sally performed the *merely* instrumental activities. In short, to the extent that sex-role conventionality means that the husband has the higher family status and performs more valued activities, this couple and others like them were quite conventional.

Another indicator of unintended conventionality appeared over time. John and Sally eventually rented a house in the suburbs, which they shared with several other people. John took a part-time job in the records section of a local hospital and supplemented his income by occasionally stealing his friends' records. They bought a Volkswagen bus. For one reason or another, the several companions in the house moved out. Sally became pregnant again and was forced to leave her job. At this point they had become a nuclear family living alone in the suburbs with the wife staying home and the husband wondering how he could earn enough money to make the house and car payments.

Conventional patterns also sometimes reappeared suddenly and surprisingly and caused interpersonal problems, most notably in the case of jealousy. Sometimes the wife, but more often the husband, was an articulate advocate of nonpossessiveness, including sexual nonpossessiveness. John and Sally boasted that they put a great deal of energy into honestly sharing their feelings and beliefs with each other. It turned out that this sharing largely consisted of John telling Sally about the various women he would like to sleep with and advocating a permissive attitude toward sexual sharing without jealousy. Jealousy, however, emerged abruptly and intensely when Sally told John that she had been putting his ideas into practice.

There are two serious qualifications which we must make with regard to the unexpected appearance of jealousy. First, there do appear to be couples who are either not plagued by serious jealousy or who easily resolve the problem of jealousy.[3] Second, while jealousy itself is a conventional enough feeling, the attitude taken toward jealousy by John and Sally is not. One might expect in a conventional marriage, one in which John is jealous because of Sally's sleeping with another man, that Sally would be seen as misbehaving. If she kept it up, Sally might be perceived as having a problem. In our sample, however, it was the jealous affect, not the sexual behavior, which was seen as the source of difficulty. It was John who was seen as having the problem and who was faced with the task of somehow dealing with his unpleasant feelings. There was no question of Sally's right to sleep with whomever she wished.

Connotative Changes in Sexuality

One feature of the counterculture that has received much public attention has been its permissive, open, and forward attitude toward sex and related matters. Among those who believe we are in the midst of a sexual revolution, it is probable that the counterculture is perceived to be in the revolutionary vanguard. Marcuse (1969) speaks in terms of *desublimation* and suggests that overt and blatant sexuality has a political effect, subverting not only conventional sexuality but also the psychic defensive structures which help to support contemporary political forms. It is perhaps in such a context that we can understand newspaper reports of pornography in which performers insist on being identified by their correct (and well-known) family names and such publications as *Zap Comix* in which obscenity and violence are played for laughs. One would expect that those who live in the context of overt and desublimated or demystified sexuality would not esteem sexual behavior in quite the same way as people in a more conventional context, and such seems in fact to have been the case in our sample.

Harrison (1965) has suggested that technological innovations alter our experience of awe. Vast mountain ranges and oceans, for example, are seen in a more matter of fact way because of the invention of the airplane. Certain uncanny bodily sensations are no longer experienced by those who have grown up used to riding in elevators. We would suggest that by a similar process a certain awesomeness which used to accompany the reality and the fantasy of sexual behavior has been much attenuated for persons like those in our sample.

Members of our sample appeared to be more sexually involved than conventional persons, but to esteem their involvement less highly, at least in the sense that sex was not regarded reverentially or fearfully. On the other hand, our participant couples' social lives did not revolve around sex in the way that seems true for couples referred to as swingers (Bartell, 1971; Denfield & Gordon, 1970). [4] Awe and related feelings seemed to be found more in connection with mystical belief systems, soft drug use, and other similar ways of altering one's conscious experience of the world.

Approaching Tension

Many persons in our sample seemed to feel almost an obligation to approach and face up to tension. The stance taken vis-à-vis jealousy was related to this approach to tension in that there was a greater tendency to deal with jealousy as such rather than to terminate jealousy by ending extramarital sex.

For example, Donald and Connie joined together in trying to help one of Connie's girl friends. When Connie discovered that Donald's helping included sexual intercourse, she became furious. She "yelled and threw things." The extramarital sex continued, but Connie claimed to have largely mastered her jealousy and even found pleasurable excitement in her husband's sexual sharing.

George and Betty traveled around the country a great deal. They used to hitchhike and seemed to enjoy the adventure of not knowing whom they would meet on the road. After their baby was born, they acquired a small van for their travels. They emphasized that at the beginning of each trip they would be quite uncertain as to whether they would be coming back at all or coming back together. George and Betty seemed to enjoy the thrill of not knowing what would become of them.

Susan lived alone and was therefore not really part of this sample, but her attitude toward her way of living is illustrative of the positive evaluation of tension. Susan felt guilty about living alone because living alone was comfortable for her. She could be with people when she enjoyed it and avoid them when she wished and thereby avoid the possibility of being caught in a difficult interpersonal situation. She therefore feared her behavior to be a cop-out in the sense that it would prevent her from "growing."

On a more public level, encounter groups and related activities appear to be popular in alternative culture. In political confrontations, other than racial ones, the more dangerous barricades, so to speak, tend to be peopled by individuals from the counterculture. Even the valued ability to remain cool often is shorthand for the ability to remain comfortable in a situation of potentially disabling stress.

A conceptual connection is possible between the tendency to approach tension and the demystification of sexuality. Lichtenstein (1970) suggests that the problem of "how to affirm human beings in the emotional conviction of their existence" is central to the "alienation of our youth." While he states that "sexuality is . . . the most basic way . . . to experience an affirmation of the reality of . . . existence," he adds that "in the course of ontogenesis, other methods, as yet poorly understood, of feeling affirmed . . . develop . . . ." We wish to suggest that in couples like those in our sample the self-confirmatory function of overtly sexual experience may be replaced in part by the search for drug-related and other ecstatic experiences, and the general valuing of tension and intensity as such. That is, tension and intensity as such are valued because they serve the need for self-confirmatory experience.

A Psychology of Plenty

The idea of limited resources—of scarcity—seemed alien to many of the people we interviewed. Husbanding one's resources, saving up for the distant future, and in general denying oneself in the present for the sake of one's own long-term benefit were not popular ideas. While one orientation toward the future was expressed in the saying, which seemed to achieve popularity for a while, that "When you are sailing on the *Lusitania*, you might as well go first class," there was at the same time an implicit sense that in the foreseeable future satisfaction of one's wants would be readily available without a great deal of difficulty. In financial terms there was realistic support for this view in the form of money from parents, in the receipt of welfare checks, and in the claimed discovery of some couples that they could be comfortable on $100 or $200 a month. One couple calculated that they needed to work for money on no more than one day out of thirteen in order to be self-supporting.[5]

A psychology of plenty seemed if anything to be more accepted in social than in material terms. At one time, people like those in our sample seemed to believe, with some apparent accuracy, that they could wander into certain neighborhoods in almost any major city or hitchhike across country and feel assured of being befriended and treated as comrades by nominal strangers. If not love, at least warmth, friendliness, and comradeship were felt to be available on any street corner. This rosy world view was not so widely held currently in our sample as it once was, or at least it was not held in such an extreme form. But it was still believed that, for a prudent and "together" person, companionship is plentiful and easily available. Sexual satisfaction as well was seen by many persons to be plentifully available with a minimum of effort.

To summarize, a psychology of plenty in terms of goods and services was supported by a dramatic attenuation of felt needs. A psychology of plenty in social terms was supported by social arrangements which in effect partially abrogated conventional boundaries between friends and strangers, and between spouses and nonspouses.

Plentiful social resources were seen by some as making possessiveness irrelevant. It was one explanation offered for reduced jealousy in the face of extramarital sexuality or affection. In at least quasi-psychoanalytic terminology, one aspect of this point of view was that an anal-genital basis for object relations was partially supplanted by an oral-genital basis, i.e., affectional ties became less controlled and more diffuse. Some participants put it in terms of a capitalistic model of relationship being replaced by a communitarian model. Still another way to put it, again in quasi-psychoanalytic terminology, might be in terms of relationships being, descriptively, less similar to an oedipal model in which gratification is primarily dependent on one particular person and more similar to a sibling model in which many "siblings" may have some functional equivalence.

While it has been noted that the retention of pregenital capabilities may be adaptive (Kris, 1952; Weisman, 1966, 1967; Novey, 1955), the basic psychoanalytic position traces a hierarchical and more or less linear development of object relations. Object choices progress from anaclitic to nonanaclitic, from part to whole object, from pregenital to genital phases, and from pre-oedipal to oedipal (or part oedipal); each shift along this developmental scale represents a partial supplanting of primitive characteristics by advanced characteristics. Some of the participants in our study would regard any such hierarchical scheme as restrictive and might suggest that in a situation of plentiful resources supplanting one relationship form with another might be senseless self-denial—one can have both.[6] Whether on this kind of basis or some other, it did seem to be true that in some of our couples various perverse relationship aspects seemed to be tolerated or even valued in a dedifferentiation of the usual developmental phases.

Overview

The several aspects of ideology and living patterns upon which we have commented fit together with a certain degree of consistency. The idea of plentiful resources supports and in turn is supported by a sharing orientation, which some of our participants would call communitarian. That aspect of sharing which is affectional or sexual directly creates bountiful resources (cf. Slater, 1970, ch. 4). It also tends to remove from sexuality a certain tinge of awe, a certain transcendental quality.[7] Perhaps this more matter-of-fact attitude toward sex leaves unfulfilled a need for self-affirmation, which contributes to a generally high evaluation of tension and intensity in relation to drug use, interpersonal relationships, and confrontational politics. It also means that sometimes people are to put up with potentially upsetting interpersonal events without simply changing their behavior so as to avoid them.

There are, however, flaws in this ideological-behavioral configuration, even apart from the degree to which it may oversimplify an extremely heterogeneous and complex set of phenomena. It is not true that the people in our sample were so confident of gratification that they eschewed all arrangements which might bring them security. They did, after all, get legally married; and their marriages did tend to include a return to the conventional in the form of traditional sex-role attitudes masked by overt sex-role reversals, occasional concern with middle-class economic security, and in the disvalued but real appearance of jealousy. One possible view, which we sometimes heard, is that these returns to the conventional merely represented unfinished business. Heightened awareness could gradually diminish sex-role bias, and the disvaluation of jealousy along with increased appreciation of the availability of affection and sex could gradually eliminate jealousy. An alternative view might be that the character structure of people in our society simply does not support, for example, radically nonpossessive affection. It may also be that our society is simply not bountiful enough and is getting less so, and that the mutual relationship between sharing and plentiful resources is in the direction of less sharing leading to less plentiful resources.[8] Obviously we do not know which if any of these interpretations have any validity. We do not even know whether our small sample of couples is representative of some significant portion of the vague entity called the counterculture or whether our sample only illustrates aberrant and ephemeral phenomena; we lean toward the former view. We do believe, however, that the ideologies, attitudes, and living patterns observed in our participant couples provide useful and suggestive information as to what is possible in changing patterns of close personal relationships and some idea of the complications which such changes might involve.

Reference Notes

1. While nondyadic relationships occurred in this group, none was primarily nondyadic, and there were no multilateral marriages of the sort described by Constantine and Constantine (1970).

2. Case material is presented to illustrate the writers' impressions rather than to provide evidence for them. Any given "case" may include a selection of material from several actual couples and is in all instances disguised to protect couples' confidentiality.

3. We are deliberately refraining from discussing here various defensive, including counter-phobic, considerations, although information obtained often reached to some extent below a merely descriptive level (cf. Ryder, 1972).

4. Young children of these couples also tended to be exposed to open and matter-of-fact sexuality, with consequences that are as yet unclear.

5. Compare the centrality of money and money problems among conventional couples suggested by Mitchell, Bullard, and Mudd (1962).

6. Perhaps the plentiful resources ethos may be in more conflict with hierarchical formulations than with less linear formulations, such as that of Lichtenstein (1970).

7. For a more extended consideration of the implications of this kind of affect, see Kafka (1969) and Kafka (1971).

8. One is reminded in this context of the words of Mack the Knife, the pertinence of whom is emphasized in a different but not unrelated context by Smith (1972): "Erst kommt das Fressen, dann kommt die Morale."

Part 3.

Alternatives for Whom?

This part of the book discusses alternative life-styles in light of who may be living them; it also looks at what effect social trends have had on the selection of nontraditional options. The subject matter of the articles and the authors' viewpoints range widely, but the common thread running through each selection is the notion that we are still grappling with the question of what alternatives may mean for various groups today and in the future—even including children.

In an article about "people's liberation," Ronald Mazur discusses the Western tendency to neatly dichotomize and polarize categories of people in order to avoid real analytical thinking that goes beyond stereotypes. The double standards strongly influence our thinking about the sexuality of singles and marrieds, men and women, parents and children, husbands and wives, and heterosexuals and homosexuals. Mazur's analysis is liberating in that he exposes the needlessness of accepting stereotypes and double standards. In terms of Mazur's thesis, alternatives may thus be open to everyone if we can abandon preconceptions and expand our notions about intimacy.

Sandra Coyner's hard-hitting article deals not only with the history of women's sexual and social subordination, but also points to modes of adaptation for women to get in touch with their own needs and gain mastery over their lives. Coyner's first concern is freeing women, and then to understand how men may fit into the prospective futures of liberated women. This involves greater sensitivity and concern on the part of men and women to the needs and desires of women. For Coyner, then, the viability of alternatives is directly related to the potential for women to grow beyond traditional roles and for people of both sexes to raise their consciousnesses regarding sex roles and sexuality.

A different but sympathetic view to the one offered by Coyner is developed by Pepper Schwartz in her article on female sexuality and monogamy. Schwartz examines the powerful myths surrounding female sexuality and shows how these continue to bind women into a belief system that precludes their liberation. Schwartz is an advocate of radical restructuring of sexual intimacy, family life, and female self-identity. She emphasizes the need for a feminist-humanist ideological base to underlie and direct "women's liberation," if the movement is to be more than an insignificant flirtation with hedonism and hollowness.

The Martin Duberman article on bisexuality with Roger Libby's commentary on recent bisexuality studies provides a broad perspective for viewing an apparently increasingly common psychosexual adaptation. If not common now as an activity, bisexuality is more frequently discussed as an open option or alternative; thus it is crucial to try to understand directions and potentials. Duberman and Libby have helped us do this by bringing together the insights available from biological, historical, anthropological, and other social science analyses of the phenomenon.

In the next article, Larry Constantine proposes a radical form of family organization—the open family—in which all the members participate fully as voluntary members. In such families, role structures are such that few expectations are imposed as to what is proper for adults or children to do. Rather, tasks and orientations develop from the needs, responses, and reactions to the unique individuals—not from the a priori role-scheme imposed by the outside and based on an old socialization model. Constantine discusses the potential for both a new style of intimacy in the open family and for "kidsex" that could occur at ages as young as children themselves see fit. This of course is threatening to all but the most radical adult thinkers. What we do with this issue in the future is likely to be in part a reflection of the current trend toward greater consideration of children's rights. The equality revolution being what it is, we must anticipate further inroads into ways of thinking about children.

These next five articles present either new or altered modes of thinking about who participates in relationships, families, and life-style arrangements other than monogamous, lifetime-exclusive patterns. The significance in social-psychological terms is undoubtedly great; whether the alternatives will become important as statistical aggregates in this society in the future remains to be seen.

13.
The Double Standard and People's Liberation

Ronald Mazur

Mazur rejects the double standard as the sole guide for sexual behavior in our society. He proposes pluralism as a substitute for it, with various standards of sexual conduct being acceptable for varied people. The author also examines the relationship of the double standard to such common dichotomies as males versus females, parents versus children, and heterosexuals versus homosexuals. He argues that the double standard underlies many such dichotomies and that these have a dehumanizing influence on our society. In the quest for "people's liberation," Mazur concludes, we must reject the tyranny of any one ideology and allow individuals the freedom to determine their own standards and sexual life-styles.

The term *double standard* is commonly applied to a specific area of the human condition—namely, to sexual, and even more specifically, to premarital sexual behavior and standards. Sociological analysis keeps the public preoccupied with the number of people, or the percentage of a prescribed population, which may be classified according to a given behavior, opinion, change, or relationship. The focus on quantitative factors is central to the lively (and sometimes ridiculous) controversy among professionals as to whether the contemporary sexual scene should be classified as revolutionary, evolutionary, or status quo—maintaining. Our obsession with charting incidences of sexual behavior and counting orgasms is a kind of cultural voyeurism. Since we are not about to expose ourselves in honest behavior we would rather peek into other people's lives and live vicariously. We can also have fun by condemning or shaming others who challenge our particular version of decency. And finally, after we count enough heads and watch cautiously until the creative becomes commonplace, we can then safely leap into our cipher in the mass and enjoy a new experience. In the expression of our sexual desires, hopes, and needs, most of us are moral cowards.

The double standard as such is not necessarily cowardly. To the contrary, it is a *standard* which many men and women willingly accept, if not choose. But what we fail to realize is that there is in fact a multiplicity of sexual standards operating in America. The major issue is not the quantitative weight of any one standard over another, but the quality of interpersonal relationships to be realized within any one of the standards. In our society, which is struggling to provide greater freedom for a broad variety of sexual standards and life-styles (sexual pluralism), it is any person's privilege and right to live by the double standard. What must be rejected, however, is the tyranny of the standard when it is imposed upon those who repudiate it for their own lives and who see its destructive effect on those young men and women who are kept ignorant of other options for contemporary man-woman relationships.

Although there are indications that the double standard is on the decline, it is by no means dead and it continues to provide, for better or for worse, countless young people with both the ground rules for sexual behavior and the framework for masculine and feminine roles. Speaking of present-day premarital sexual standards, sociologist Ira Reiss (1970, p. 40) believes that there are four major types: abstinence for both sexes; the double standard, defined as the Western world's oldest standard which allows males to have greater access to coitus than females; permissiveness with affection, an increasingly wide acceptance of intercourse for both sexes when a warm and stable relationship prevails; and permissiveness without affection, which allows both sexes equal sexual experience even in relationships which require only mutual consent without emotional strings attached. Regardless of how influential other standards may become, and no matter how many creative variations may be developed, it is likely that the double standard will continue to shape relationships for a large number of people in the foreseeable future.

In addition to providing sex-role models and defining the privileges and penalties for the behavior of both sexes, the double standard is tacitly condoned by both Judaism and Christianity. Social institutions provide for its perpetuation; the education establishment promotes it; and a host of myths reinforce it. The double standard rests on the assumption that sex pleasure is not for everyone and that men need it more and know best how to enjoy it while protecting their women from its hazards. Such protection is, of course, "necessary" to uphold the moral order, to make women happy, and to preserve the family. These are the deeply held convictions of many men and women who see the double standard as a small price to pay for the sake of such worthy goals.

Again, the problem essentially is not that there are people who hold to the double standard: It is that our society incorporates and sanctions it and persecutes in various ways those who conscientiously hold other standards and seek to live alternative or nonconventional life-styles. It is also important to recognize that the double standard of sexual morality permeates vital areas of intimate relationships other than just the premarital. Consequently, the person who repudiates double standardism finds that a web of conformity creates sticky problems in several areas of interpersonal encounter.

Single Men Versus Single Women

As has been noted, premarital sexual behavior draws a great deal of attention and concern in our society. It is almost as if men and women are embarrassed to seem interested in sexual pleasure once they are married. It is much safer to use the children as the focal point for adult interest in sex. True, there are obvious legitimate concerns such as pregnancy, venereal disease, and social ostracism. We also make a tremendous emotional and financial investment in our children and dread the "ruination" of their lives through sexual folly. But the hazards of premarital sex go beyond these fears and even beyond the traditional risks of the double standard penalties.

The ground rules of the double standard are shifting in a gradual but devastating way, with the female being trapped in a double bind. If she is sexually inexperienced, she is "out of it"; if she takes her sexual freedom seriously, she is "trash," or, at best, not "the kind of a woman that I'd want to be the mother of my children." The usual penalties imposed upon the female under the double standard result in higher incidences of guilt among women on the occasion of the first intimacy; lower incidences of masturbation; and the indictment of "promiscuity" applied almost exclusively to their activities while corresponding male behavior is considered "adventure," "experience," "conquest," and "a sign of virility." Now the shifting double standard really begins to destroy male-female communication and compatible mutual game-playing *after* the period of engagement. Whereas previously engagement signalized permission for sexual exploration and experimentation, males are now using it to claim exclusive rights to a female who, in turn, is required to end her intimate relationships with all other male friends and lovers in order to devote herself solely to the "winner" of her body. It is becoming more common for young men not to be at all bothered by or about the premarital sexual experience of their girl friends, but they are still playing a game of conquest and possession. With great cool, gentleness, and *joie de vivre*, the pseudoliberated single male relates sympathetically to the single female who is struggling for autonomous identity and sexual freedom. This promising communion between the sexes is, however, shortlived, for as soon as that emancipated young woman consents to a primary one-to-one commitment, the double-standard heart of the male beats mightily and he suffocates the flame of love with possessiveness and jealousy. This is not to say that only males are possessive and jealous, but in the premarital stage they are becoming more devious about it, victims of their own con game.

With justifiable bitterness, Shulamith Firestone, in *Dialectic of Sex*, (1970,pp.160-61), excoriates the deceptions of male-designed sexual freedom which does nothing more than provide the men with a greater supply of free lays: "The rhetoric of the sexual revolution, if it brought no improvement for women, proved to have great value for men. By convincing women that the usual female games and demands were despicable, unfair, prudish, old-fashioned, puritanical, and self-destructive, a new reservoir of available females was created to expand the tight supply of goods available for traditional sexual exploitation, disarming women of even the little protection they had so painfully acquired . . . even the hippest want an 'old lady' who is relatively unused."

The above kind of delayed double-standard double-cross is not yet common in our culture and is more likely to occur in urban colleges than among other young adult populations in this country. Indeed, young adults in certain geographical regions and social classes would still consider the old-fashioned prerogative of sex-with-engagement (permissiveness with affection) as being daring and radical. There is also another population of young men and women, small but growing in number, who are sexually liberated and doing a new thing together as they develop an equalitarian standard of sexual morality. But it is disheartening to see how adaptable the destructive aspects of the premarital double standard can be. The value of virginity is being rejected, only to be replaced by the delayed arbitrary judgment and possessiveness of the male, and young adults of both sexes still face the bleak prospect of continued mutual manipulation.

Parents Versus Children

Another form of the sexual double standard which can be destructive is embodied in the myth which declares that sex is only for adults. There is assumed to be a magical moment of maturity beyond which sex is mentionable and before which it is simply not acknowledged as an essential human experience. Though parents by and large favor some form of sex education in public and religious schools, their naiveté is nevertheless incredible. Too little is offered much too late: It is as if parents refuse to recognize their children as sexual and sensual beings. Children, of course, tend to reciprocate the insult and find it hard to believe that their parents, and adults in general, can participate in and enjoy sexual intimacy. It is sad when children lack adult models who express emotional warmth and playful physical closeness, who admit to a lively interest in sex. Too many parents not only conceal their earthiness, but even worry about their children or make them feel ashamed when they exhibit or acknowledge an interest in sex. Parents tend to feel uncomfortable talking to their children about sex unless they can tell jokes on the one hand, or, on the other, speak in ethereal, poetic, or religious terms.

Fortunately, some progress has been made in sex education in the last generation or two. It is now undoubtedly rare for parents to conduct a bedcheck to make sure their children are sleeping on their backs with arms outside the blankets lest the unspeakable vice be committed in the unguarded moments of sleep. Masturbation is generally understood and accepted as a natural process of self-discovery and self-enjoyment, and children today are spared the shame and hangups which not too long ago were the horrendous heritage of most men and women. Curiously, however, parents and educators consider the lack of condemnation of masturbation sufficient to the educational needs of young people. This is still a negative approach to the subject, for a more honest and helpful service to children would be to make sure that all girls and boys, by the end of the seventh grade at least, were made aware of the positive and beneficial aspects of masturbation: benefits such as relaxation of physical and psychic tension, comfortableness with sensuality, self-knowledge and self-acceptance, and empathy with the sexual need of the other sex.[1] Even at the present time, this is still too much to ask of most parents because it is so difficult for adults to accept and feel comfortable with the sexual needs and development of children. It is amazing how much can be blocked out of adult memories! If parents themselves did not initiate a double standard which creates a make-believe world of nonsexual children, they would experience less anxiety about their children's behavior and would be privileged with greater sharing from young people who, regardless of new attitudes toward sex, are still searching for honest and creative relationships.

To be sure, the problems of sex education and permissible sexual behavior for young people are complex and involve more than the parental double standard. But a start must be made somewhere with realistic and forthright education for human sexuality—education which adults need as much as children. How this will be accomplished on a wide social scale is yet unclear and even a controversial issue. One interesting proposal came from Harriet F. Pilpel. Writing as general counsel for Planned Parenthood—World Population, she proposed that the sex-education needs and civil rights of children be protected by law and be taken as seriously as the rights of parents and society. She suggested that ombudsmen be appointed to speak for children and argued that "adequately serving children's needs also serves the best interests of their parents and community" (Sex Information and Education Council of the United States Newsletter, October 1970). Perhaps we wouldn't need some official to speak on behalf of children if parents and educators had the courage and sensitivity to help children appreciate without fear their own being—genitals included.

Husbands Versus Wives

In light of the fact that the overwhelming majority of men and women marry, it may seem preposterous for serious scholars of family life to wonder if marriage has a future. Yet, a long-time observer of man-woman relationships, sociologist Jessie Bernard (1970, pp. 41-3) states frankly that marriage is a poor status for women, and she offers the startling proposal that celibacy be considered as an honorable alternate status for women. And in almost every major popular family magazine today, there are articles detailing the troubled condition of the institution of marriage.

One of the major forces in the reevaluation and reformulation of the marital relationship is the women's liberation movement—a resurgence of the feminist movement which won the voting franchise and then seemingly dissipated by 1930. The new movement, though diffuse and eclectic, has a cohesive and radical cutting edge which will not be blunted in its effectiveness until human relationships and society are reshaped to allow all women full self-realization as persons.

Because of the work of the women's liberation movement, the double standardism of male chauvinists and their co-opted female victims has been exposed. The scholars and leaders of the movement have amassed a devastating indictment of the male's total cultural and personal ego trip—a trip made on the free-to-all-men ticket of the double standard.[2]

It is remarkable how sensitive most aware adults are to the issues of the double standard, considering the fact that it is only within the last several years [i.e., since the mid-1960s] that women in any significant number have renewed the struggle against their inane condition. As recently as 1964, sociologist Alice S. Rossi could say in her comprehensive analysis of the status of women (p. 608), "There is no overt antifeminism in our society in 1964, not because sex equality has been achieved, but because there is practically no feminist spark left among American women." Soon afterwards, though, Betty Friedan's *The Feminine Mystique* (1963) made its impact, and it didn't take long for the awakening of the American woman. Nevertheless, six turbulent and eventful years after Rossi's understated challenge, two male sociologists would claim that "the role of women has changed very little, and today they are even more committed to the home and children than they were in the 1930s during the last gasp of feminism" (Gagnon & Simon, 1970).

Feminism did not, however, die in the 1930s. It merely smoldered until the secret spark was bellowed into a roaring and hot movement by Friedan and her colleagues. After handling hot steel during the war years of the 1940s, women again were faced with a bitter reality. Men determined the purposes and structure of social institutions, defined sex roles, judged sexual behavior, set the conditions for economic independence, committed all physical and human resources to national priorities which they determined, and on top of it all evaluated the sanity of women. It is no wonder that almost all men know in their hearts at least one prayer: "I thank thee, Lord (ol' Buddy), that I was not born a woman!"

One of the critical questions about the movement concerns the impact it will have upon husband-wife relationships. No definitive answer is yet possible, but a reasonable guess is that the movement will cause more trouble than peace, at least for a transitional period. The number of divorces and unhappy marriages is evidence that husband-wife warfare is rampant, and consciousness-raising sessions aren't going to make women any happier with their predicaments. Ultimately, the movement will contribute to the humanization of both sexes, but for the time being it must risk the opening of festering hates and resentments in marital relations. Men have been the exclusive objects of devotion by mothers who knew no better, and adult males unconsciously expect to occupy the place of the deity in the lives of their wives. There are even a sufficient number of wives who exalt this juvenile expectation to the status of "true love." Men and women who accept the double-standard marriage can share a common value framework and make each other content within that context. But even this is becoming more difficult to accomplish, for the traditional uneasy truce which suffers adulterous cheating on the part of the husband is about to break down; women are weary of the hypocrisy and are more willing to face the consequences of painful marital confrontation. Husbands do continue to have the upper hand, for all the world loves a lover (male), whereas the wife who is so crass as to object is a "bitch," and the wife who is independent enough to have her own male friends and night out is a "whore." Women who are relatively happy with the way things are will bitterly resent the movement for raising issues they would rather not confront. Not all women seek the same kind of liberation, and it will be important for the movement not to alienate needlessly those women who choose to maintain the status quo for their lives and their marriages.

In addition to the women's movement, there is in our society another movement which repudiates the double standard of sexual morality. This is the movement for alternative life-styles. Smaller, more amorphous, and more eclectic than the women's liberation movement, the movement for alternative life-styles is attempting to change the lives of individuals and to make permanent changes in American social institutions. This movement includes such experiments in sexual freedom and interpersonal relations as (1) *noncontractual cohabitation*, or so-called trial marriages, a version of which is finding an accepted place in coed dormitories on various campuses; (2) *group marriage*, in which three or more persons create a marital covenant with every other member of the group; (3) *communes*, in which married couples and/or single persons share living resources and also accept mutual responsibilities for community but without necessarily permitting group sex or partner sharing; and (4) *swinging*, so-called spouse swapping, which promotes the kind of group sex which couples participate in together but with a minimum of emotional commitment to the other couples. Styles can, of course, be combined into several variations. Another less well-known option or alternative in marital patterns is (5) *open-ended marriage*.

Fundamental to all of the new options is the conviction that women have an equal right to sexual experimentation, satisfaction, and freedom. And where single-standard restrictions are valued, voluntarily accepted, and self-disciplined, the male also has an equal responsibility to maintain the same values and behavior as his partner. Ultimately, it is a profound yet joyful quality of sexual intimacy and interpersonal sharing which husbands and wives are seeking for themselves, each other, and for their friends through new life-styles.

Heterosexuals Versus Homosexuals

In no other aspect of sexual behavior is the double standard more vicious than in the conflict between heterosexuals and homosexuals. This conflict is commonly presented in terms of normalcy versus deviancy, but this framework itself is a propaganda success of heterosexuals. What is universal or normal in human sexual behavior is for two persons to need each other for mutual sensual enjoyment. Nothing in human nature requires that two persons engaged in such pleasure be of different sexes. Human beings are human beings, and however they may please, comfort, support, inspire, or love each other is of human value. Though it is unusual in our culture for persons to direct sexual passion, with or without love, to members of the same sex, such behavior and relationships can contribute to the mental and physical well-being of both persons involved. Wherever and however two people touch across their loneliness to satisfy their needs, a human event takes place. Heterosexuals may set for themselves exceedingly high expectations and standards of sexual fulfillment, but they deny homosexuals the same rights and opportunities. Because of customary religious condemnation, cultural conditioning, the threat of the unusual, and personal hangups, we prefer to assign homosexuality to the realm of the perverse and the pathological. It is ironic that the prejudice against homosexuals should provide common ground for some clergymen and psychiatrists who otherwise would have little to say to each other. The Victorian moralizing of a few psychiatrists makes them sound like preachers and anti-homosexuality crusaders. Even the modern "apostle of sane sex," Dr. David Reuben (1969), writes on the subject of homosexuality with a pseudoscientific moralism. Though his opinions are expressed with sarcastic humor rather than Victorian self-righteousness, Reuben presents a distorted view of same-sex behavior. His generalizations about the character and motivation of homosexuals are based on his selection of case studies, second-hand reports, and medical gossip, all of which involve bizarre behavior or psychopathology to begin with, and he completely omits any discussion of homosexuals who are emotionally healthy and creative.

One of the experiments in sexual freedom which will eventually bridge the tensions and distinctions between homosexuals and heterosexuals is the phenomenon of group sex as a form of play. The John Birch Society and the Christian Crusade evangelicals were perceptive when they shifted their coordinated and massive attack against sex education in the schools to a campaign against sensitivity training in the schools. When significant numbers of people become involved with the widespread encounter/sensitivity training movement, unpredictable changes are bound to occur in people and society. If men and women shed inhibitions, risk openness and intimacy through touching, and discover the pleasures of shameless sensuality, then all of the familiar protocol of sexual behavior soon becomes questioned and challenged. In effect, people become less afraid to exhibit and receive physical affection. That such a cultural development can be considered dangerous to established morality and American civilization is a commentary on the impoverishment and fragility of our venerable values—or at least on the way in which those values are being interpreted. The ultraconservatives are at least more prophetic in their alarm than are the liberals, who in their analytical coolness, quibble about the precise degree of social change. The encounter/sensitivity movement, in spite of its potential dangers to any unwary individual who cannot cope with its personalized impact, is creating a new class of sensually adventurous persons; men and women who rejoice in their flesh-and-bloodness; who delight in mutual exchanges of being-with-you-in-the-flesh pleasure; who affirm their sensual condition without shame. Sexual playfulness for such persons is a more creative and zestful way of living than the self-stultification which so many people face as their fate. Instead of the overbearing ogling of males or the come-on twittering of frustrated females, a more honest delight in mutual sensual exploration is possible. The essence of the sexual revolution is not revealed in the statistics of who-does-what-to-whom-how-many-times; it is in the new attitude of sex as play and the willingness of people to act accordingly.

It is probable that only a very small percent of those who have had "growth group" experience will experiment with group sex. Of that number there will be those who decide that this type of activity is not their thing. Others, however, will discover that they have a capacity for sensual enjoyment with members of the same sex as well as with those of the different sex. It can be a discovery which is mind expanding and spirit freeing—a dazzling escape from emotional captivity which leads to sweet freedom in a new world. Suddenly, the sexual population is no longer divided into only two types, heterosexuals and homosexuals, with their respective stereotyped roles. To become a *bisexual* is to discover the joy of relating with sensual affection to those of one's own sex; astonishingly, those people who were once impersonal competitors are now potentially personal friends. It is to discover the other half of humanity of which the self is part. And by experiencing one's own homosexual potential, homosexuals no longer seem queer, for now we can empathize with their feelings without threatening our own masculinity or femininity. The variety of sexual patterns increases and enriches all. Instead of only two styles in opposition to each other, we have a range of behaviors:

1. exclusive heterosexuality,
2. bisexuality with dominant heterosexuality,
3. bisexuality with dominant homosexuality,
4. exclusive homosexuality.

These categories could undoubtedly be refined. Are there, for example, people who are bisexual with equal preferences? Is it possible for individuals to move through two or all of these categories at different phases of their lives? As usual, the language of sex becomes a problem, and descriptive phrases can sound awkward. Even definitions are not uniform. The term *bisexual*, for instance, can refer to a hermaphrodite, a person born with both male and female organs. Its use here, of course, refers to a person who experiences sexual intimacy with persons of each sex.

Beyond the Double Standard

The double standard of morality has lost its preeminent status in contemporary human relationships, but it will long exist to some degree in some form or other. Perhaps no other standard will take its place, for the present challenge is not so much to replace it with one ideal substitute, but to create a social climate which fosters pluralism in sex standards and allows for experimentation in life-style. The varieties of sexual expression and the meanings individuals attach to their experiences are incalculable. Tension between standards will not be eradicated and people will continue to feel conflict with each other, but the tension can be creative and the conflicts can be growth opportunities if we learn to value differences and to appreciate each other's humanity. Even sexual freedom can rigidify and become oppressive if the people who consider themselves liberated become pridefully intolerant of the values, preferences, and conditions of others. British psychologist Derek Wright raised a valid issue in a *Life* magazine editorial (November 6, 1970) when he wrote on "The New Tyranny of Sexual 'Liberation.' " In that provocative article he warns:

We begin to grade our sexual partners, as they us, though we do not talk about it. And standards are rising. Too often for the sex experts, the merely possible is instantly the optimal, and tomorrow, for the rest of us, the normal. How we pity or scorn the impotent and the frigid! While, absurdly, some people use sex to exorcise their insecurities, others who find it difficult, distasteful or merely dull conclude that they are odd, outcast and, most desolating of all, inadequate. It is so easy to build a prison around a man by convincing him he is a prisoner.

Even among the supposedly sexually enlightened the grading often takes place. It is dismaying how persons who are sensitive, informed, and experienced will nevertheless have stereotyped expectations of the sexual responses of a partner. If technical performance does not conform to textbook standards or does not measure up to prior encounters of memorable climax, then disappointment, doubt, or analytical probing ruin the pleasure of the experience. The sheer delight in being naked together and appreciating the specialness of the moment, the joy of intimacy, the sharing of sensuality can be entirely missed by those who are preoccupied with the end result of the "Big O." Yes, there is tremendous value in being knowledgeable about the usual sexual responses of men and women. It is important to anticipate the needs and desires of your partner and to bring him/her to complete satisfaction when possible and desired. But this type of expertise need not be the focus of the experience—it can be the background which enriches the pleasure and value of two (or more) persons creating a beautiful time of affirmation and affection. The combinations and varieties of level of lust, genital intensity, orgasmic patterns, physiological endowments, mood on the occasion, etc., are endless, and every act of intimacy is unique, never to be precisely duplicated. Enjoyable sex requires relaxed humor and the ability to appreciate the wonder of the moment on whatever level it can honestly be felt.

To go beyond the double standard, then, it is required of us that we be autonomous, stand on our own values, resist enslavement by any sex ideology, and focus on whole persons as well as on genitals. Of society, it is required that the conditions for, and rights of, sexual freedom be established and upheld in order that all standards and life-styles may be practiced as long as they do no violence to individuals or interfere with the civil rights of others. This task is overwhelming but possible to accomplish if enough people work to shape a social order which places a high priority on human well-being and community. The quality of personal lives cannot be enriched within a dehumanizing social environment; society cannot be radically reformed without men and women who are willing to act with courage. Sociologist Arnold Birenbaum (1970, p. 266) captures the interdependence of self and society in relation to sexuality with the observation that

The failure to achieve an independent sexual life, as part of an independent personality, is the result of the absence of any society-wide effort to bring about the removal of the fragmenting character of modern society. To create the autonomous personality, we must put an end to conditions which produce self-estrangement. The effort itself must involve the self in all its complexity, otherwise the sexual revolution only serves to continue the sense of helplessness, bewilderment, loneliness, and self-estrangement. It cannot be done for us but only by us.

In other words, the issues of sexual values, relationships, and behavior cannot be isolated from the political, economic, racial, and other critical issues of our time. The search for happy sex is ultimately self-destructive if it is not related to the context of total human sexuality and the search for the meaning of life. The social action of homosexuals and lesbians, for example, is redeeming for them as human beings and redeeming for society, which is humanized in the process of response and change. Their sexuality is affirmed ("I am a whole male/female person!") and the restoration of dignity gives them greater meaning in life ("I will not hide in shame, I can contribute to society!"). The humane and reconciling approach and the constructive recommendations of the final report on homosexuality of the National Institute of Mental Health (October 1969) is an encouraging example of the fact that sexual prejudice and myths can be overcome and social policy transformed, once enlightened women and men apply themselves to the task. Of course, the implementation of that report remains to be accomplished.

In any case, before we can achieve a national condition of liberated people—men, women, and children—the hard issues raised by the women's liberation movement will have to be faced and resolved honestly and directly. There is no getting around it. The movement is serious and will not fade away, and all people will benefit from its reformation of human communion and community.

Reference Notes

1. For more on this subject, see Ronald Mazur, *Commonsense Sex*, pp. 31-4 (Beacon Press, 1968).
2. It is interesting to note that discussion of the double standard by psychologists, sociologists, and other professionals has mostly been confined to premarital behavior and rarely analyzed in any depth. The *Encyclopedia of Sexual Behavior* (Ellis & Abarbanal, 1961), for example, includes no article on the subject and cites only three minor references to the double standard in the index.

14.
Women's Liberation and Sexual Liberation
Sandra Coyner

In the following article, one feminist scholar offers an interpretation of the meaning of sexual liberation for women. She relates sexual liberation to other issues and recent directions of the women's movement, and concludes that the thorough questioning of social roles and concepts of womanhood, femininity, masculinity, and sexuality, is the most important new direction that contemporary feminism has taken.

A social scientist and historian, Coyner discusses the women's movement from a sociohistorical perspective; as she traces the trends and issues, she relates these to concurrent social developments including the "sexual revolution" and political radicalism of the Sixties and the changing understanding of female sexuality following the publication of the Kinsey and Masters and Johnson research.

In reviewing the struggle for women's social and sexual liberation, Coyner particularly focuses on the need for women to control their own lives and define for themselves what their needs, desires, and potentials may be. In terms of sexual experiences, Coyner sees this translating into less preoccupation with intercourse and simultaneous orgasm, and more concern for women achieving sexual satisfaction by focusing on clitoral stimulation. Coyner also raises the question as to whether new attitudes toward female sexuality threaten heterosexuality. She concludes that this need not be the case if men can learn to accept women's sexuality, needs, and desires as being equally important to their own.

Women's liberation,[1] a movement embracing many groups and individuals, has seemed to speak ambiguously about the politics of women's sexuality. Some feminist voices have appeared to call for *less sex*. Major complaints have been about the image of women as sex objects, the demands of men for sex strictly on male terms, and the inability of many men to view women as whole persons rather than just as sexual playmates. As women increasingly attacked and withdrew from traditional male-centered sexual behavior and relationships, they seemed to be abandoning both men and sex itself. Other feminist voices, however, have seemed to call for *more sex*. Attacking the double standard of sexual taboos which restricted women's sexual behavior more than men's, and developing woman's potential for repeatable clitoral orgasms, for relative sexual insatiability, and for nontraditional behaviors such as masturbation and bisexual activity, all suggest that women's liberation is pushing female sexuality toward a quantum increase.

In reality, the complaints and promises of the women's liberation movement have all revolved around one central theme: As women, we want our own sexuality under our own control. We no longer will allow our sexual behavior, capacities, rights, and relationships to be defined or limited for us by men, whether as individuals or in the context of social institutions; for our experience has been that men will define us for their own purposes and pleasures. Our emphasis is on self-determination. Significantly, this implies not only the absence of male domination over female sexuality, but also the freedom of individual women to differ from whatever norms or averages may be discovered or postulated.

Identifying Oppression

The first phase of any movement for social change is to identify the conditions that are oppressive and must therefore be changed. Even in its earliest manifestations, the women's movement has spoken in many voices because it speaks for many women who come from varying backgrounds and identify different problems. In the 1960s, when the movement was very new and still comparatively small, it consisted of numerous small groups which largely developed critiques and ideology independently of each other. In historical retrospect, however, most people now distinguish two broad strands of early development: the radicals and the moderates. [2]

The moderate wing is generally identified with the National Organization for Women (NOW), which has not been centrally concerned with sexuality and intimate relationships except as related to abortion rights and issues of childbearing and childraising. Moderates have been more concerned with social issues, especially the narrowness of the traditional role assigned to women, and with the discrimination that has kept women from developing other options. Moderates sometimes criticized radicals for dragging in personal issues of sexuality which have seemed distractions from the real work of securing equal rights. On the other hand, radicals, and especially lesbians, have accused moderates of incomplete dedication to the women's cause when they are unwilling to question or abandon their personal intimate identification with men. There may be some truth to the charge in that moderates might find it hard to label their intimate lives "problematic." The women's movement was born in an era when a woman faced a profound sense of personal failure if she had to admit she had no good relationship with a man.

But the women's movement was also born into the climate of the "sexual revolution" of the 1960s. Changes in sexual behavior had begun to occur before women's new consciousness began to develop, and independently of that. To some extent the differences between moderates and radicals reflected the differences between older and younger women. For the moderates, sex was if anything overemphasized in our culture. Betty Friedan's pioneering book *The Feminine Mystique* (1963) noted that women were led to expect too much from sex—it was supposed somehow to produce "fulfillment," generally through motherhood. Her chapter on women who abandon monogamy portrays them as desperately, joylessly searching to fill the emptiness of their lives with sex, but doomed to dissatisfaction because the problem, as she saw it, was not sexual. Good intimate relationships would come easily enough when woman's horizons were broadened beyond the home. [3]

On the other hand, many of the younger radical feminists were participants in the sexual revolution. Political leftists practiced the "free love" which, in its disdain for sexual conservatism, paralleled the rising attack on establishment politics and economics. Sex was less private, more speakable. What the radical feminists discovered, with considerable resentment, was that the sexual revolution (like the political revolution in progress) had not brought significant positive changes for women. Certainly an old era was just about gone. Social restrictions that had severely limited the sexual behavior open to women were falling. Women were no longer expected to maintain their virginity intact in order to purchase economic security through marriage. Sexual exclusiveness was not viewed as the sine qua non of an orderly society. Because they were no longer required to set the limits on sexual activity by being responsible for saying no, women were supposedly freed to be sexy, to have sex. But radical women found that this freedom was in fact just a new set of duties. They were expected to perform sexually or lose their status as "hip, groovy chicks." The *freedom from* societal restrictions could not become a *freedom to* be sexual because female sexuality remained undefined, misunderstood, and seen only from a male perspective. The trivialization of woman's sexuality is reflected in the not uncommon male response to woman's serious demands: "All *she* needs . . . ," suggesting that sexual woman still has no brains.

Thus it was the personal discovery of many radical women that, after all their work for political and social movements, they were expected to be as constantly available for sex as for cooking and mimeographing. Their sexuality was exploited just as their personhood and leadership abilities were ignored. Stokely Carmichael's comment that the only position for women in SNCC is "prone" (which means stomach down) has been infinitely requoted because it was trenchantly true, as well as insulting. Radical feminism evolved as radical women began talking to each other about feminist social issues, but also about the way they were treated personally and individually within the movement and by the men with whom they lived. Consciousness raising was born. From these experiences came the realization that public exploitation is paralleled in private, and male domination occurs even in intimate situations. And because these frustrations were experienced in *personal* relationships, with *radical* men, it is not surprising that many radical feminists blamed *men as men* for these failures, nor that some came to believe that no men could be trusted.

The "manhating" tone of the radical feminists clearly put off many of the moderates. Some of their actions did too. Perhaps the polarizing event of the early women's liberation movement was the demonstration by New York Radical Women at the Miss America Pageant of 1968. The tactics were certainly seen as radical: demonstrating, picketing, leafletting, crowning a sheep. The image of "bra burning" was attached to radical women's liberation, even though no bra was actually burned in Atlantic City. But beyond tactical questions, the critique was also too personal for many women to identify with. The entire construct of American feminine beauty was attacked—and hence the fantasies and hopes of many an American woman. A number of women who supported the movement on economic issues—equal pay for equal work being the most inarguable—could not accept the personal issues, probably because they believed themselves successful in the universal beauty and mancatching contest, or had invested too much in it already to admit that they had been duped. Attitudes toward woman's sexuality remain today one key contrast between feminists and the antifeminist backlash—proponents of so-called total womanhood. Women in the backlash want to be regarded as sex objects; they may appear at the front door dressed in Saran Wrap, because receiving sexual attention from a man is still seen as a kind of fulfillment.

Unliberated Orgasm

Much of the specific feminist critique of sexual behavior is now generally accepted in the conventional wisdom, probably because it developed in interaction with rather scholarly sex research which brought new understanding of female sexual response. Masters and Johnson remain for most feminists reliable authorities deserving gratitude; their work is the basis of much feminist analysis of what kind of sex women want. [4]

Feminists wanted women to get pleasure from sex. Certainly the idea had been afoot throughout the twentieth century. The Kinsey study (1953) showed that a surprising number of women regularly experienced orgasm, or that a surprising number didn't, depending on how you looked at it. But feminists wanted to maximize female pleasure, and armed with Masters and Johnson's (1966) findings they identified male-oriented sexual practices as hindering it. Specifically attacked were neglect of the clitoris, overemphasis of the vagina, and the "myth of the vaginal orgasm." [5] Freud had decreed that, though little girls found sexual pleasure from stroking the clitoris, unless a woman transferred the center of her orgasm to her vagina she was psychosexually immature. However, most of the vagina has so few nerve endings that many women cannot feel any touch there—and medical science knew this even before Masters and Johnson stated definitively that there was simply no such thing as an anatomically separate (much less superior) vaginal orgasm. But many women who couldn't experience orgasm from vaginal stimulation alone were routinely diagnosed as "frigid," and sent for routine treatment—psychotherapy, not for the man or for the couple, but for the woman, since it was her problem and its cause was in her head, not in sexual technique. Perhaps she had not accepted her feminine role. Given conventional sexual practices, it is no wonder that Freud and his successors were somewhat amazed at the prevalence of this "problem."

American sex practices were simply too male-oriented, and this orientation was perpetuated through marriage manuals and other conventional wisdom. [6] Direct clitoral stimulation was relegated to the status of foreplay, part of the necessary routine of slow female arousal; the clitoris was treated just like breasts or feet or any other erogenous zone, and attention to it was cut off before her orgasm in favor of intercourse, which was "real sex." Simultaneous orgasm was a great ideal; but since it would have to come during intercourse, which might not bring the woman to climax, it seemed that her "failures" prevented it. Woman's ability to achieve satisfaction was further hindered by the "missionary position," in which the man is on top, greatly restricting the woman's ability to move. Since orgasm was difficult for her under these conditions, popular wisdom assumed that she was just "naturally" not as sexy as men. Women were often not expected to achieve regular orgasm; they were assumed to derive sufficient satisfaction, at least some of the time, from knowing that they had afforded a man *his* orgasm. Woman's sexuality could apparently be a matter of vicarious enjoyment. Or perhaps it was just emotional. Security, loving a man, and feeling loved were supposed to be ultimately more important than any physiological responses, desires, or needs. Furthermore, since women supposedly derived no pleasure from sex without love, a double standard was justified emphasizing greater male freedom. A husband's affairs and playing around were not as abnormal as a wife's. Pornography and erotica were thought less stimulating for women; these were produced for men, anyway.

Thus, at the same time that radical feminists were being pressured by radical men to be "good in bed" and always ready for it, they discovered that sexual activity was not responsive to their own needs and desires. Women were not permitted to experience their own sexuality on their own terms. Her orgasm was important for *his* pleasure; bringing a woman to orgasm became a mark of a man's masculinity and virility. A woman's orgasm was seen as something he did to her or for her, playing her like an instrument; but the blame was hers alone if the music didn't come out right. Failing to reach climax could bring down on her accusations of frigidity or prudery. It is no wonder that so many women have admitted to themselves and to others, under the new protection of the women's movement, that they faked orgasm to avoid criticism and a feeling of inadequacy.

Finding a Better Way

Such was the critique made by women's liberation of unequal and male-oriented sex. In the women's movement, this negative phase has been critically important. It has led to some of the most important innovations—the technique of the consciousness-raising group, the new willingness of women to talk to each other about private feelings, the identification as political or social problems of what many women had hitherto felt only as personal failure.

But identifying oppression is never in itself enough; any movement must go beyond, suggesting and building a better way to live. It is at this point that the women's movement finds itself still divided, though no longer painfully so. To forge a newer world, many must experiment with suggested new directions. Only with time will we learn which options work best, and only each woman can decide for herself, individually, which to follow. The last few years have seen many promising new directions opening up. All emphasize the underlying principles of the women's movement: self-determination for women as individuals and as a class. To change from sex objects into sexual subjects, we must define our sexual experiences in our own terms, from our own perspective—not only in comparison to a male norm. We must be guided by our own feelings, and learn sensitivity to our own bodies. We must respect our own needs and desires and become independent enough of male approval to withstand criticism and to occasionally—not always—put our own pleasures ahead of others'. In short, we must learn to know what we want, and then how to get it.

Thus, although sex is generally thought of as an interpersonal activity, most of the exciting and fundamental work by women concerns woman alone. Celibacy, redefined with a connotation of autoeroticism, has developed a new significance as a positive experience which a woman may choose for good and serious reasons. [7] Formerly, many women without an active love relationship with a man felt that they had failed in some important way and were burdened with self-doubt and loneliness. But in the context of woman's growth, women's liberation sees celibacy as an important period for self-exploration and recuperation. Being free from the conflicts and struggles which often characterize intimate relationships can give a woman a lot of growing space.

Thus, changing attitudes toward sexuality means changing our own attitudes about ourselves, particularly attitudes about the female body: Self-esteem begins with respecting and liking our own anatomy. Old attitudes have implied that parts of a woman's body and bodily functions were dirty or ugly. But feminist artists have now given us portraits of female genitals dressed up as beautiful flowers, and the women's health movement approaches the body as a storehouse of health and pleasure, not just propensity to disease. Much discussion of female sexuality occurs in feminist literature about health, as in the excellent *Our Bodies, Ourselves* and the briefer *Circle One.* [8] "Self-help," or encouraging women to see their own cervixes with speculum and mirror, is part of the movement to give women increased awareness and control over their own physiology. Knowledge about our bodies can help us conquer fear, ignorance, shame, and mistreatment by the medical profession. All this includes understanding our sexual responses as well.

Another forum for learning about sexuality is "body therapy," such as that described in the excellent book *Getting Clear* by Anne Kent Rush. [9] The objective is to help women know what they want by teaching body awareness, with specific exercises to help us focus on different areas and sensations. The therapy draws on sources ranging from yoga to belly dancing, including touch therapy developed for overcoming sexual dysfunctions. Body work for women emphasizes two complementary attitudes: openness and centeredness. A woman must be open to feelings, able to receive and understand them: but she must also feel centered in herself. Rush emphasizes that in sex, woman turns *herself* on. This first, crucial step in understanding female sexuality from the woman's viewpoint is that sex is not something done *to* her; it is something she controls and feels in and for herself.

Body therapy produces an awareness of self which naturally spills over into awareness of others, and two people in tune with themselves can more easily tune in to each other. As feminists search for a better way, learning to relate to another person as a sexual equal becomes less a matter of men giving up power than of women reclaiming our own power over ourselves. Women are learning to stop the games and attitudes by which we have made ourselves subservient or helpless, and to get in touch with our own strength. Whereas identifying oppression seems to pit man against woman, building a better way challenges women as well as men to find something different.

Nevertheless, the most exciting feminist emphasis on sexual self-knowledge leads away from men, and specifically to masturbation.[10] Through experimentation with herself, a woman can learn what her sexual capacity is, and what kinds of touches she enjoys. What she learns can be transferred to interpersonal activity—but even more important, she can masturbate just for the fun of it, for herself. Women want to teach each other, in a supportive atmosphere, about the physiology of sex and about specific masturbatory techniques; and women encourage each other to regard masturbation not just as a second-rate sexual outlet, but as a first-rate way to cherish and love one's own body. Masturbation is an important step in ceasing to be somebody else's sex object, and becoming a sexual being. Giving one's own body pleasure is advocated in the same context as keeping it healthy.

Sexual Equals

It would seem a simple matter to revise heterosexual sex to produce more female pleasure. We would expect de-emphasis of intercourse and simultaneous orgasm during intercourse as the only suitable "goals" of sexual activity. Clitoral stimulation, manual or oral, increases in importance when it is seen as central to woman's pleasure. No longer merely a prelude for "the real thing," it might *be* the real thing. Women will also take advantage of findings about the repeatable female orgasm, which can be continued until exhaustion. Since a woman can have many orgasms during a period when a man may have only one or few, the typical female-male orgasm ratio will tend to be unbalanced in her favor. The potential of variety—since a woman can be pleasured and satisfied in so many ways—suggests that there will be more emphasis on oral sex, manual sex, and electrical sex (with vibrators) than ever before. In all this activity, the liberated woman is no longer expected to be passive or merely responsive in sexual activity. She can be the initiator, seeking either verbally or through her movements the kinds of touches and activities she wants. It may turn out to be as difficult for women to become assertive in sex as it is in public life, but women's groups can organize assertiveness workshops in this as in other areas.

Many of these directions may also be seen as tending to threaten heterosexuality. Since the clitoris is the center of woman's sexuality, and a vagina may need a penis (or a penis-substitute) but a clitoris surely doesn't, why does a woman need a man? Certainly not just for sex. Hence the recent changes in the size and shape of vibrators used for sex. Old vibrators were trembling penis-substitutes. Some new vibrators are designed specifically to stimulate the clitoris.[11]

Whether or not sexually liberated women will want heterosexual relationships will probably depend on whether men can learn to relate to women as equals—in sex as in everything else. Lesbian feminism derives much of its strength from its emphasis on the energy lost when women put it into individual struggles with men. Surely, in fact, in view of the usual heterosexual experience, some rejection of men is understandable. Why continue having sex with men if it's no fun, if it's a constant struggle, if one feels left out or not taken seriously? Much of the content of lesbian feminism is anti-man; and lesbians sometimes claim to be the only true feminists because they alone refuse to sleep with the enemy. This decision is justified politically, even more than personally.[12]

But there is another side to lesbianism: loving women. The women's movement has produced a substantial literature by women who recount their relationships with other women, and a definition of the lesbian as the "woman-identified woman" in a positive sense. Lesbian love does not necessarily arise only after, or as part of, a thorough rejection of men. A woman may find that sexual expression is part of the new affection that women have discovered for each other, or she may discover that sex with another woman is astonishingly more rewarding than her previous heterosexual activities. Women are expected to be more likely than men to understand how a woman partner feels and reacts, to know how to please her, and certainly to relate to her as an equal, not as an adversary in a power struggle. She knows, because she's a woman too. There are unfortunately no data to tell us whether the women's movement has raised the proportion of women who identify themselves as lesbians (or just permitted them to do so in public). It would be equally interesting to see how much of today's lesbianism is a temporary phenomenon, which might yield to heterosexuality if men can learn how to relate to sexually liberated women.

It is surely as pretentious for a woman to write about how a man might feel as it is for men to pretend to understand female sexuality, but it is also important to try to define what it means to relate as "sexual equals." To love with a sexually liberated woman, a man must accept her sexuality, her needs, and her desires as just as important as his own. This does not mean that their sexual responses will be *the same*. Men and women may have somewhat different patterns and tempos of response, particularly when the repeatability of her orgasm is emphasized. Even more important, however, *each individual's* sexuality is at least potentially different; and in order to relate freely to a sexually liberated woman, a man will have to be prepared to observe her, to be sensitive to her, and to respond to her. It will not do for men to renounce their roles as sexual initiators and lie back passively, waiting for the liberated woman to make love. They must learn the difficult parts of the old feminine role: Responsiveness and sensitivity are necessary for both partners, not just the woman, and are certainly not outmoded qualities.

Sex between equals can perhaps help people stop using each other in sex. Old-fashioned standard sex between an active man and a passive woman, with emphasis on intercourse, has sometimes resembled solitary masturbation inside a vagina. Clitoral stimulation, like old-style foreplay, can be the same if the emphasis is simply on achieving certain physiological goals—no matter who is active and who is passive. Sex between equals could go beyond just "me doing this to you" and vice versa to an emphasis on moving together. People who respect and love each other can develop styles of interaction, besides subject-object action. And the key to this interaction is communication—which means talking to each other, taking nothing for granted, learning to read one's own feelings and to trust another's. And it involves a lot more than sex.

Female Sexuality Is More Than Sex

Woman's sexuality involves far more than intercourse and orgasm. The uniquely female reproductive functions—pregnancy, childbearing, and lactation—are also part of our sexuality. Recent research has shown that birth and breast-feeding can be sensuous and even erotic experiences, physiologically resembling and in some cases including orgasm.[13] At some phases of the women's movement, it must have seemed that feminists wanted childbearing functions and responsibilities to be removed from women. Shulamith Firestone claimed that total liberation from childbearing, through test-tube reproduction, was necessary for the liberation of women.[14] But by now the movement can concentrate on distinguishing between the valuable experiences and the drudgery, and minimizing or at least spreading the burdens. Collective and social approaches to childraising replace the emphasis on successful housekeeping and mothering as the only ways a woman can prove her worth. A woman's right to bear and raise a child without the restrictions imposed by a relationship with a man may come to be seen as part of her feminine birthright. We may see a renovation of male envy of woman's childbearing *powers*. But the obverse of this argument remains a critical and demanding struggle for the movement: A woman must not be *forced* to bear a child, either by her husband or by society. She must control her own body.

Women's liberation has also complained about birth control methods. The demand for a "male pill" reflects the fact that almost all attempts to control births work by controlling the woman; conception is to be stopped somewhere in her body. But all the inconveniences and dangers associated with contraception also take place within her body. Most under attack is the contraceptive pill, because the side effects are not only uncomfortable for many women, but downright lethal for some. Why has so much research been directed at developing this type of contraceptive, instead of stopping conception before the sperm leave the penis? Is there an anti-woman bias?

On the other hand, sexually liberated women have also wondered whether they wish to trust men with the important business of contraception.

If a man claims to have had a vasectomy, would you believe him? In view of the dangers of the pill and intrauterine device, some feminists recommend the diaphragm as superior and totally under woman's control. It can be inserted early in an evening, whether or not sexual activity develops. The epidemic of venereal disease, however, suggests another solution. The nonmonogamous woman might insist that her lovers wear condoms, and never go without her own supply.

Though sex is usually a private event, it has in our culture a public face as well; for women this usually means vulnerability to male hostility. Rape is a crime against woman's sexuality, founded on male hostility and sadism, which are attitudes that have been condoned by society. Women have been assumed to enjoy not only street attention—which expresses the same attitudes—but probably also rape, at least after the struggle. The passivity and subordination which women were expected to display for their husbands were also expected for rapists: Don't resist; relax and enjoy it; now, admit it, wasn't that fun? Women in rape crisis centers contradict these approaches. They say resistance—a display of force—may be sufficient to deter many rapists who specifically want to attack a helpless female. Women can fight off or run from many attacks; and women who have killed their rapists are considered heroic by many feminists who collect funds and demonstrate to try to keep these women out of jail. More broadly, feminists have been surprised at the prevalence of sadistic themes in most male-oriented pornography. [15] A woman submitting to sex while protesting against it is seen as a great turn-on. Why has sex been made into such a power trip? No wonder self-defense, like self-help, is part of the feminist arsenal.

Monogamy and Other Relationships

Since sexual activity is usually interpersonal activity, liberating women sexually must have implications for the kinds of relationships they will have. The potential for celibacy, bisexuality, and lesbianism have been mentioned. But even within a heterosexual context, we might well wonder whether traditional monogamous and long-lasting relationships will continue to exist. It is clear that the traditional limits on female sexuality have all had the effect—and perhaps the intent—of reinforcing monogamy. A woman who expected less than her due of satisfaction from sex, and who suffered severe social criticism for violating monogamous norms, was effectively constrained from threatening the monogamous institution. Lack of varied premarital sexual experience made a woman less likely to recognize dissatisfaction with her husband, and less likely to seek remedies outside marriage. Woman's responsibilities for childbearing and childraising also became her limits. But a sexually liberated woman, whether single or married, may by the very nature of her immense sexual potential find herself increasingly attracted to multiple sexual relationships. Whether reasonably permanent heterosexual relationships can endure may depend on whether men can relinquish their possessiveness and jealousy—if men cannot sustain a loving relationship with a nonexclusive woman, there may be fewer such relationships.

Many of these speculations revolve around a basic question: How much sex do women want? There is little hope at present of answering such a question, for we cannot conduct much research or even analysis without having our observations colored by our cultural norms. Kinsey, for example, found that men reached their "sexual peak" at an earlier age than did women; but the report describes sexual *behavior*, and it is misinterpreted when people think it says something about sexual *potential*. How can we distinguish sexual behavior—conditioned by society's rules—from sexual desires? Studies of women's reactions to pornography and erotica have suffered similarly. Until devices were invented to measure women's *physiological* responses to erotica (that is, vaginal blood pressure), studies relied on women's *statements* about their feelings. But women taught that they shouldn't react to erotica apparently have difficulty in recognizing their own reactions or admitting them. In fact, women react as strongly to erotica as men do.[16]

So in trying to estimate how much sex women want, we are confronted by the conflicting social pressures which have, on the one hand, repressed women's sexual drives by making women responsible for setting the limits on sexual behavior; and on the other hand, the "sexual revolutions" which have made an unnaturally strong sex drive seem necessary for the *true* woman. Women have claimed both that they wanted more sex than the old restrictive norms permitted, but less sex than the sexual revolutions seemed to require. What data exist, however, suggest that the dominant trends are toward more sex. Premarital sexual behavior has certainly increased, and the trend is toward equal amounts of experience for males and females. There are still many double standards to be broken—women with many lovers, or with extramarital affairs, are still viewed as violating standards. And older women may find cultural restrictions blocking them from all the sexual activity which we now know they are capable of. Knowing that both men and women can prolong their active sex lives as long as they want to is not enough; our culture, which has put a premium on the sexual attractiveness of young women, must also see the older woman as strong and attractive in her own right.

Women's liberation involves every level of woman's social interaction—from her private relationship with herself to the broadest social institutions. Sexuality is basic to the most intimate relationships, particularly self-love and primary bonds with the most important others. Sexual relations are at the foundation of family relations, and the family remains an important unit in our society. If women's liberation tends toward destroying the family, as some critics have alleged, it certainly has not done so yet. Indeed, increasing emphasis on bonds between mothers and children, and between women and their intimate partners, show that women's liberation will probably increase the strength of these primary ties rather than weakening them. Sexual and intimate ralationships between equals, who love and respect each other equally, can be much more rewarding, whole, and stable than relationships based on the coercion of limited choice. Women's liberation has seemed to coincide with a wave of breakups and divorces which probably antedates the movement and may even have contributed to the need for it. We may find that the new relationships established by sexually liberated people last longer.

Liberating sexuality may not be the most obvious result of women's liberation. The major accomplishments of legal reform—equalizing economic opportunities by requiring enforcement of civil rights law and affirmative action guidelines, securing passage of the Equal Rights Amendment, and protecting the only recently acknowledged right to a safe legal abortion—will probably be marked as the most historic and memorable achievements of the young movement. But these are merely continuations of old feminist struggles. The Equal Rights Amendment was first introduced in the 1920s by the victors in the fight for suffrage; educational and economic struggles are even older. What is so startlingly new about contemporary feminism is the thorough way in which it has questioned the social roles allocated to women, and thereby the very concepts of womanhood, femininity, and ultimately sexuality and even masculinity. The struggle to increase women's opportunities and participation in the "man's world" of politics, economy, and society is but the flipside of the attack on the traditional roles assigned to women within the family as wives, mothers, supporters of men. To challenge so much tradition, to challenge the very concepts and assumptions on which a whole society is constructed, requires a deep and intense search beneath the layers of socialization and male domination for woman herself. In this quest, and in the search for new forms of relationships between people, our sexuality is no less than fundamental.

Reference Notes

1. In this paper the terms *women's liberation*, *women's movement*, and *feminism* will be used essentially interchangeably, even though some analysts have tried to define the terms to distinguish separate parts of the overall movement.
2. The best and most recent history of feminism is Jo Freeman, *The Politics of Women's Liberation* (New York: McKay, 1975). Others are Judith Hole and Ellen Levine, *Rebirth of Feminism* (New York: Quadrangle, 1971) and Cellestine Ware, *Woman Power: The Movement for Women's Liberation* (New York: Tower, 1970).
3. Betty Friedan, *The Feminine Mystique* (New York: Dell, 1963,1973). See especially chapters 11 and 13.
4. Some of the best feminist analyses of female sexuality are Barbara Seaman, *Free and Female* (New York: Coward, McCann, & Geoghegan, 1972); Lonnie Garfield Barbach, *For Yourself: The Fulfillment of Female Sexuality, a Guide to Orgasmic Response* (New York: Doubleday, 1975); and Mary Jane Sherfey, *The Nature and Evolution of Female Sexuality* (New York: Random House/Vintage, 1972).
5. The three classic articles on this subject are: Anne Koedt, "The Myth of the Vaginal Orgasm," first printed in *Notes from the Second Year* in 1970, reprinted in Anne Koedt, Ellen Levine, and Anita Rapone, eds., *Radical Feminism*, (New York: Quadrangle, 1974); Susan Lydon, "The Politics of Orgasm," first printed in *Ramparts* in 1968, reprinted in Robin Morgan, ed., *Sisterhood Is Powerful* (New York: Random House/Vintage, 1970); and Alix Shulman, "Organs and Orgasms," in Vivian Gornick and Barbara K. Moran, eds., *Woman in Sexist Society* (New York: Basic Books, 1971).
6. See Michael Gordon and Penelope J. Shankweiler, "Different Equals Less: Female Sexuality in Recent Marriage Manuals," *Journal of Marriage and the Family*, August 1971.
7. See for example the article "Living Without Them" in *Ms.* magazine's "Special Issue on Men," October 1975.
8. Boston Women's Health Book Collective, *Our Bodies, Ourselves* (New York: Simon & Schuster, 1973); Elizabeth L. Campbell and Vicki Ziegler, eds., *Circle One—A Woman's Beginning Guide to Self-Health and Sexuality* (Colorado Springs: Colorado University Press, 1975).

9. Anne Kent Rush, *Getting Clear: Body Work for Women* (Berkeley and New York: Random House/Bookworks, 1973).

10. See especially Betty Dodson, *Liberating Masturbation: A Meditation on Self Love* (New York, Bodysex Designs, 1974); also Ossa Harmon, "Masturbation," *Issues in Radical Therapy* (Oakland, Calif.), and articles in *Circle One*. Masturbation is the principal technique used in women's bodysex and preorgasmic workshops.

11. As noted by Eve's Garden, a mail-order house at 115 West 57th Street in New York City.

12. On lesbian political feminism, see Nancy Myron and Charlotte Bunch, eds., *Lesbianism and the Women's Movement* (Baltimore: Diana Press, 1975); Jill Johnston, *Lesbian Nation: The Feminist Solution* (New York: Simon & Schuster, 1973); Del Martin and Phyllis Lyon, *Lesbian/Woman* (New York: Bantam, 1972); Sidney Abbott and Barbara Love, *Sappho Was a Right-On Woman* (New York: Stein & Day, 1972).

13. Niles Newton, "Trebly Sensuous Woman," and Deborah Tanzer, "Natural Childbirth: Pain or Peak Experience?" in *The Female Experience*, by the editors of *Psychology Today* (1973).

14. Shulamith Firestone, *The Dialectic of Sex* (New York: Bantam, 1971).

15. Linda Phelps, "Female Sexual Alienation," in *Liberation* (May 1971) and reprinted in Jo Freeman, ed., *Women: A Feminist Perspective* (Palo Alto, Calif.: Mayfield, 1975); and Elizabeth Ferber, "Sado-Masochism," in *Circle One*.

16. Julia R. Heiman, "The Physiology of Erotica: Women's Sexual Arousal," *Psychology Today*, April 1975, pp. 90-94.

15.
Female Sexuality and Monogamy

Pepper Schwartz

In discussing female sexuality as related to monogamy, Schwartz points out the many and complex ways in which the double standard continues to keep females in a sexually subordinated position. She develops a case for the consideration of female sexuality as much more akin to that of some males who are liberated, sensitive, and relatively free. The problem of lack of opportunity to disengage oneself as a female from older sexual ethics raises interesting questions about the implications a new attitude would have for men as well as for women.

Schwartz examines three popular myths in regard to female sexual behavior. After exploding these myths through an analysis of current data she turns to implications for the individual and society at large. When and if sexual independence is gained for women, what is likely to be the outcome? According to the author, many difficulties will have to be faced by the woman who attempts to act out a sexually liberated role, even though there are potential rewards in strengthening identity and independence. Still Schwartz admonishes women for just "taking what they get" from men and asks them to examine the context of give-and-take in their sex lives. Insofar as women and men together can reevaluate alternatives in sexual relationships, all stand to gain from the kind of perspective and critical analysis developed in this article.

Current research on female sexual capability (Masters & Johnson, 1966) and recent ponderings on the possible effects of a "sexual revolution" (Davis, 1970; Smith & Smith, 1971) make it incumbent on sociologists to comment on the effects these changes will have on life-styles and interpersonal relationships.

While the sexual revolution has supposedly made sexual experimentation and alternate marital styles possible (Whitehurst, Chapter 21; Wells & Christie, 1970), it seems clear that traditional values of monogamous marriage prevail for the vast majority of people in western society. Extramarital sex may be tolerated (Neubeck, 1962) or adapted to the structure of the relationship (Cuber & Harroff, 1965) but at least at the level of ideology (if not practice) the monogamous nuclear family model is still safely ensconced in the mainstream of American life.

This, of course, is not to deny that some behavior patterns have changed and attitudes toward them have been modified. Premarital sexuality among

---

the young has liberalized and negative sanctions for this behavior are increasingly rare (Davis, 1970). Nevertheless, liberalized behavior patterns do not indicate great changes of consciousness. For example, it is still true that premarital sex, except for the small minority, is normative only when it falls under permissiveness with affection (Reiss, 1971) or "sex with meaning" (Lever & Schwartz, 1971). "Sex as play," or "recreational sex" is only seen as reasonable behavior by a small group of men and a smaller group of women (Lever & Schwartz, 1971, and Vreeland, 1972; Kinsey et al., 1953; Bell & Peltz, 1972). And, while 50 percent of all men and 26 percent of all women engage in extramarital sexual relations, few families try to integrate it into a consciously evolved philosophy of the marital relationship. The double standard, to make this point another way, still exists in the same form it used to, only with slightly more liberal dimensions. The male may take pride in his numerous affairs and regard them as proof of his desirability and his talent— but his female counterpart has no legitimate way to use her own experience as self-affirming. The word *stud* or the adjective sexually *accomplished* sounds awkward, misplaced, or, at best, exotic for a woman. A woman who has had a hundred lovers is an unknown and somewhat frightening figure to men who have thought of women as sexually inexperienced persons who achieve sexual maturity in a "committed relationship" and who then settle down to the primary roles of wife and mother. The imagery of womanhood is nurturance and sensuality: Only "bad" women are lustful and disassociate sex and love. Thus, as some women become sexually aggressive and challenge the norms for female sexual activity, confusion, resentment, and conflict in male-female relationships can be expected. In order to understand this friction and why it may occur, we should look closer at the traditions that are being violated.

Perspectives on a Historical Inheritance

Professional literature (psychological, sociological, medical, etc.) still defines female sexuality in terms of its adjustment to marital (and thus, jointly agreed upon) behavior, rather than discussing what is uniquely female (Gordon & Shankweiler, 1971; Laws, 1971). Sexuality as it is constructed in marriage, and less often, as it is constructed during the courtship, is seen as normative and "normal"; the breadth of female capacity suggested by Masters and Johnson's research is disregarded. Women for the most part accept the idea that their sexual experience will be taught to them and defined for them by men. If their own needs seem to be incongruent with what they expect (i.e., they are still unsatisfied after one act of intercourse), they generally *will* themselves to conform to what they can expect. Failure to be satisfied, or desire for a different pattern of interaction, is most often taken as personal failure or failure of the couple. The question of what the woman desires—or of the appropriateness of the arena of interaction (i.e., marriage) is not often seriously questioned.[1]

It is not surprising that the questioning is narrow in focus, for what happens in bed is generally reflective of the greater social system of the partners.

As Kate Millet says: "Coitus can scarcely be said to take place in a vacuum. . . . It serves as a charged microcosm of the variety of attitudes and values to which the culture subscribes" (1970, p. 23). Thus we have only to look at interpretations of female sexuality at various points in history to note how amazingly congruent the definitions of female sexual "possibility" have been with the actual structure of female interaction in the family and in the state. A couple of examples chosen from a myriad of possibilities may serve to illustrate. For example, it has been hypothesized that before the transfer of property to blood relatives and before the male's role in reproduction was completely understood, women were considered sexually insatiable and allowed considerable sexual freedom with a variety of partners. On the other hand, when transfer of property to the eldest male became a cornerstone of English common law, female sexual freedom was considered dangerous and fear of confusing lineage and the transfer of property caused the image of woman to be reinterpreted and her sexual proclivities to be curbed. Suddenly woman was seen as having distinctly repressible needs and laws were passed to punish anyone who might transgress the new morality (Sherfey, 1966).

Closer to home, when the "feminine mystique" of the 1950s exhorted women to be better homemakers and mothers and to stay out of the labor market (Friedan, 1963), it also began to create ways to make home more exciting and enticing. Sex was used as a "lure to marriage" (Laws, 1971), and marriage manuals were written exhorting women to be exciting for their husbands after the long day at the office. Sex was seen as another marketable item that a woman should develop to give her husband as a reward for providing a wonderful home—and for the purpose of inducing him to stay in it. Sex was respectable again for women—but only in a specific and "blessed" state, the monogamous marital dyad. The husband was seen as the "needy" partner and the orchestrator of sexual moves. The woman was to be the instrument that brought out his true artistry (Gordon & Shankweiler, 1971).

Her own needs were not discussed very well. If she was a good and mature wife, which meant, at least during this time, being able to have vaginal orgasms—and even better—simultaneous vaginal orgasm with her husband, she would be happy and satisfied. Those women who had sex in other contexts or, as in the language of *True Romances* articles, had "urges" that they acted upon in the "heat of passion," were doomed to disrespectability, illegitimate children, and ultimate degradation. They would be denied anything more than a short, and probably unfulfilling, night of sin.

Lest we feel that the 1950s are now ancient history, one must add that present day sexual mystiques follow this model surprisingly closely. While female sexuality has some legitimacy outside of the marital framework (Bell & Chaskes, 1970), there is still no sexual model equivalent to the male's. Men are still seen as entitled to some "random" sexual experience and women who approximate the same activity are considered "problematic" if not clinically ill. The *"Cosmopolitan* girl" or the "sensuous woman" have a certain leeway, but it is questionable how much. At what age does the unmarried, highly experienced playgirl begin to get disreputable? Is it earlier or later than for her male counterpart? Is the unmarried woman somehow seen as more pitiable than the unmarried man? And what about the woman who is unfaithful to her husband? Is she viewed as a bit more bizarre than the man who exhibits the same behavior? It seems reasonable to hypothesize that women are still associated with the sanctity of home and family. Despite the titillating options hinted at by *Cosmopolitan* and like magazines, the same message is before us: Sexual fulfillment is through one man and through one institution, the monogamous marriage. Even among those who will consider living together as an option, the monogamous model remains. If a woman fantasizes about sex with many men she has no model that tells her this is a reasonable option to actualize. Women are accustomed to modifying that desire to fit their more important needs: food, shelter, protection, and security. It is luxurious to be analytical about one's sexual situation. Even when the situation arises that makes them independent of such considerations (personal wealth, a successful career and a bevy of admirers, etc.), lack of societal permission, fear of disapproval and loss of love, and ignorance about how to construct a new life-style often inhibits experimentation. And women often believe the myths they have heard about their emotional and sexual needs.

Reconsidering Some Questionable Hypotheses (Sexual Mythology)

What are these myths that anchor female sexuality within the context of restricted sexual experience and monogamous marriage? Let us look at three that have had great impact:

Myth One: *Women need a committed (love) relationship for sexual satisfaction.*
Myth Two: *The best sexual relationships occur in the marital framework.*
Myth Three: *The marital dyad cannot tolerate any additional sexual access by third parties.*

Myth One: Women need a committed (love) relationship for sexual satisfaction

The idea that women cannot function sexually outside a love relationship is not supported by available evidence. While it is true that Kinsey and others (Kinsey et al., 1953; Masters & Johnson, 1966) found women were *used to* and *trained to* need emotional commitment to justify sexuality by being in love, it is not true that women are incapable of acting otherwise. Given the appropriate socialization women can enjoy sex for sex's sake. Indeed, there is biological and sociological evidence that love and sex *are* separable for women.

On the biological question, Waxenberg (1969) has demonstrated that when a woman's ovaries are removed and the source of androgen cut off, the erotic component is damaged, but the affectional response remains. This implies that *physiologically* love and sex are separable for a woman and that it is the experiential world, not the biological inheritance, that determines how she combines the two.

In reviewing other research on the interaction of hormones and behavior, there is further evidence that sex drive may vary according to the ratio of androgen to estrogen in the body. A high androgen to estrogen ratio indicates a more aggressive sexual nature—a low ratio indicates readiness for a more passive response (Money, 1965). While this raises the possibility that hormone levels may have something to do with sexual appetite, it also might lead us to believe that this sexual appetite might be identified with "androgen" types or "estrogen" types—and not according to sex. In any case, before we could get too enthusiastic about this new definition of "capability" we would have to take into account studies of transsexuals that show, *regardless* of the genetic inheritance, the sense of sexual self (even about something as basic as what gender one is) is more dependent on the individual's psychosexual development than on one's biological inheritance or even the outward appearance of sex roles (Money, 1968). The work on transsexuals and gender reassignment indicates that while hormones and hormonal changes may significantly affect sexual appetite, it is still the social script that gives direction and intensity to individual sexual patterns (Simon & Gagnon, 1970). Therefore, while we need more information on the effects of body on behavior, we are justified in explaining a great deal of sexual activity by understanding how the individual is socialized, the individual's access to information, and the context in which socialization and access to information take place.

Socialization. An overwhelming theme of a woman's life is that she is responsible for her sexual activity. She is the one who gets pregnant, she is the one to bear any social stigma, and she is the one who gets devalued by giving sexual favors too casually. In order to cope with these considerations, and in order to be a "successful woman," she learns a very important lesson: She must always be the partner *in control.* Control becomes an important value.

Of course, by becoming successful as a "controller," the girl or woman also becomes somewhat alienated. She begins, as Simone de Beauvoir (1953) notes, to see herself as an object—a fascinating object, an object that can be used cleverly and to advantage, but nevertheless, less than a real person acting freely. A teenage girl, if she is to keep her social standing in her community, had better keep her wits about her. So, if she is necking in a car, there are three people in the back seat: herself, the boy she is necking with, and herself watching herself. She must be somehow removed from the action.

The girl must be aware of her market value. This tells her how much she can get away with, how much pleasure she can give (or receive), and how much credibility she will develop among her peer group (i.e., what she can claim or deny and be believed). "Reputation" is no minor value. It ranks women both with men and with other women. Knowing this, the girl learns to control her emotions under the most sensual and desirable of interactions.

Even as she outgrows the demanding social network of adolescence, the female cannot forget the lessons of her teenage years. While for those whose education is not over, college will be much different—she will meet more liberal men and her female friends will be more supportive and less willing to judge her (Lever & Schwartz, 1971)—there will still be enough exceptions to that rule to make life harrowing. For most women, the price of gaining sexual freedom is losing the respect of a large group of her "field of eligibles."

When a woman gets older, or gets involved in "committed" relationships, she will probably receive cues that at last she can be sexually free and responsive without incurring negative sanctions. Unfortunately, she may find that she still has trouble "letting go." Mere permission is not enough to change learned behavior. Internalized restrictions carry on, even against the person's conscious state. Her ability to control her emotions and desires have protected her status among her peers, her image in the community, and her potential in the dating and marriage market. Having reaped the benefits of being in control, she is likely to be unable to function in any situation that makes her at all insecure or in doubt of the other's motives. She no longer finds herself attracted to people until her role is defined as worthy and dignified. And she may devalue women who act in any other way.

On the other hand, if we look at women who deviate from this model, we know that not *all* women require either respect or security to function sexually. There are women who are sexually free, able to hold their own in their community, able to justify their acts, and able to attract people who can accept them and respect their idiosyncratic life-style. We know little about the contemporary counterparts of Isadora Duncan, George Sand, and other "free spirits." We do not know how such women fashion their sexual lifestyle in opposition to the norms of society. Do they receive a different socialization than other women? Are they neglected by parents and therefore more free to experiment without punishment? Or are they well loved and secure and less worried about personal and societal rejection? We need to know more about the women who trespass sexual norms as well as those who accede to prescribed boundaries. In particular, it is important to differentiate those who take on "deviant identities" from those who do not. Not every "promiscuous" woman is a professional prostitute or social pariah. In order to understand the rules of sexual availability, we need to know more about those individuals who can bend the rules without being personally punished in the process.

Access to Information. It is not only socialization and peer-group experiences, however, that make a woman feel that love and sex must go together. A woman has no other kind of model for female sexual response. Texts on family, courtship, and mental health all say that the natural expression of sexuality for a woman lies in her capability for monogamous love. "Sex as play," sex as experimentation, and sex as a way of learning about oneself in a friendly, but "not serious" manner, is rarely encouraged by family counselors and therapists. Some professionals, notably feminists, have begun to write about new ways of organizing relationships, but this material is only beginning to be available to the average woman. What might the effect be, for example, if "nonmonogamous sex" was given equal time in all the texts and manuals that women read? Laws (1970) hypothesizes that men help define their identity from a variety of sexual experiences and that similar behavior by females might be valuable for the construction of an independent assessment of self and a strong sexual identity. If this were given sociological credence and if it were researched, offered in professional discussions of courtship, and seriously considered by counselors and advisors, more women might opt for a different pattern of learning about their sexuality. People accept the idea that the individual matures through interactions with others in a variety of social experiences. What might be the effect of offering this simple analysis of interpersonal relations and extending it to the sexual arena? If such a model received serious consideration by professionals it might also receive consideration—and validation—from a variety of women trying to decipher their sexual code and identity.

The Social Construction of Female Sexuality. In our culture it is assumed that the family is the integrative mechanism that ties the individual to the greater society (Goode, 1964). Thus, it is to be expected that sexual patterns are oriented to helping stabilize the family as the basic societal unit. To this end, it is inconvenient to have a population of sexually free women with emotional attachments, "illegitimate" progeny, free-thinking ideology, or independence of livelihood, undermining the family's status. If women do not attach sex to marriage, do not need to get married, and therefore make the family a less identifiable unit of society, society would be less immediately controllable and organizable. Thus, unwilling to cope with changing the value of "kinde, Kuche, and Kirche," the society values all characteristics that tie the individual to the home. In this sense, it has proved efficacious to make the female dependent on long-term relationships for her sexual release. Marriage—as the only healthy place for sexual expression—is validated by governmental, institutional, and professional spokesmen. The family is to be woman's great contribution to society, her anchoring point in life and her focus of identity. Whatever freedoms she may achieve in the job market or elsewhere are not to infringe upon or change her dedication to her children and her monogamous marriage. Otherwise woman's liberation will have "gone too far." Reform, such as with child care, can be understood, but new freedoms, such as sex outside of marriage, are destructive and the work of "radicals." If the family cannot be preserved as it is, then the woman's movement is dangerous. It is no wonder then, that feminists see the family as the major barrier to rethinking sexual roles, sexual identity, and power relationships (Millet, 1970; Firestone, 1971; Greer, 1971, etc.), while antifeminists (Mailer, 1971; Decter, 1972) raise an outcry at anything that threatens to reevaluate either its sexual or sex-role organization.

There is evidence that women can function quite well without emotional or marital commitment in sexual relations for long periods of time—and sometimes indefinitely. The literature on swingers shows that women can enjoy sex much the same way men do, with little or no attachment (Bartell, 1970), or with varying degrees of affection depending on what partner they are with (Palsons, 1972). The NOW questionnaire on sexuality elicited frequent comments from women who mentioned having fantasies of having sex at their own leisure without the demands of a deep relationship (Hite, 1975). Women who have had committed or emotional relationships often state that there are periods of time in their life where a minimum of involvement with a sexual partner is desirable (such as right after getting out of a draining relationship or during a period when one's career is demanding much of one's time and energy) (Schwartz, 1972). Admittedly, these women are most often able to be independent on other grounds—they can support themselves, they are generally highly educated, and they often have unusual socialization patterns (such as a mother who encouraged sexual freedom). Nevertheless, the fact that women exist who do not need a committed relationship for sexual satisfaction indicates that the context of sexual engagement is more open to choice than the myths about female sexuality would have us believe.

Myth Two: The best sexual relationships occur in the marital framework

It is difficult to know what the "best" kind of sexual relationship is. We do not have much data on the subjective meaning of female sexual experience (i.e., a woman's own interpretation of "vaginally" versus "clitorally" stimulated orgasm, or how she enjoys sex with her lover as opposed to her husband). We do have, however, some data to evaluate women's objective performances. For example, we know that all women are physically capable of multiple orgasms yet most women have only one orgasm in a single sexual encounter (Bell, 1972). Masters and Johnson's experiments indicated that the average woman's *capacity* is much greater than presupposed. A woman's actual *performance*, however, depended on her desire, her general physical condition—and, of course, the ability of her partner to satisfy her if the orgasms were to be achieved through intercourse.

The discovery of female capability, that women can come to orgasm many more times than the male, and that each orgasm becomes more and more intense (at least clinically, if not always subjectively) (Masters & Johnson, 1966), is potentially important data. For one thing, it affects female expectations about the sex act and about individual satisfaction. Previously, if a woman felt that she was nonorgasmic, she believed it was her physical or emotional problem. Now, if a woman is nonorgasmic she might be less inclined to blame herself; indeed, she might feel bitter about being deprived of something she has been told she can achieve. Likewise, if she has been heretofore satisfied with one orgasm during intercourse, she may want to know why she shouldn't have three or four. The imagery of the sexual "animal" has been somewhat reversed.

For most women, however, the issue of multiple orgasm is primarily theoretical. The average woman is involved with one man and has had only a few other experiences. She may not be able to evaluate her lover's performance because she has no basis for comparison. Most women take what they get, blame many or most of the inadequacies of the relationship on themselves, and are unsure about how to demand more for themselves or give more to the other person. Generally, whatever the male brings into the sexual relationship determines its boundaries. If he is sexually demanding, the woman is sexually active; if he is not, the relationship usually remains at that level. Since women are not supposed to be the sexual aggressors, they often feel powerless to change the dimensions of the sexual relationship.

Supposing, however, that a woman was fortunate enough to be in a relationship where she could help determine the amount of activity and satisfaction she received, and that her lover was talented in her eyes, one might still argue that this was not the best of all possible worlds for female sexual fulfillment. It could be argued that given female sexual capacity, monogamous marriage does not admit sexual variety or sexual privacy from one's spouse. If a partner is deficient in some area, there is nothing to be done except accept the fact that one "can't have everything." Men often solve this problem by going to prostitutes and paying for services they can't get at home. Women do not have the same institutionalized outlet. Thus, if the male needs less sex than the female, is unable to thrust long enough for her to experiment with her orgasmic capacity, doesn't like oral-genital contact, etc., monogamous marriage inhibits sexual fulfillment.

Of course, nonmonogamy is impossible in marriage as it is now constructed. It is an upsetting idea to most women and men who fear being compared, being seen as inferior, and losing their husband or wife or lover, and such fears are not without foundation. What *would* it mean if we accepted the idea that no person could sexually fulfill the other? There are a number of possible ramifications, both positive and problematic. First, it seems likely that a new kind of sexual self would emerge—one created by self-definition instead of definition by the other. This would mean individuals would learn their own needs, know when they were satisfied or unsatisfied, and negotiate a sexual pattern that would be responsive to a number of partners. This could eclipse the original relationship or support it, but it would almost necessarily mean interpersonal ferment and some risk to existing intimacies. Second, by allowing sexual variety, possessiveness and jealousy would have to be renegotiated. *Commitment* would have to be defined and the importance of sexual access be redefined. Third, sexuality itself could be downplayed in importance by making it a less scarce resource. Love and sex would be even more separable and recreational sex more common and expected.

Of course, this is all conjecture, depending on several kinds of conditional hypotheses. Right now, it is enough to say that, at least at a physical level, we can conclude that marriage may not be the best outlet for the physical possibilities of female sexuality. The emotional and subjective considerations may be more subtle to discern. The critical question is, can a relationship be sustained under such conditions? Can a woman and man share such intimacies and still have a satisfactory life together? Can the family be sexually modified, or must sexual liberation completely destroy the committed dyadic relationship? This leads to Myth Three.

Myth Three: The marital dyad cannot tolerate any additional sexual access by third parties

Or another way of looking at this: Is a woman's utilization of her complete sexual capacity inimical to monogamous marriage and if so, is it anomalous with any kind of dyadic construction? The proposed answer is yes, third-party affairs are probably antithetical to monogamy—but probably not to other kinds of marital or dyadic organization. There will have to be adjustments, however, and the family structure will become more vulnerable.

While some women's sexual appetites—even when fully awakened—may be easily satisfied and many women will have long periods when sexual appetite is dulled, it is hypothesized that there will be a group of sexually liberated women who will generally desire more sexual activity than most monogamous, long-term relationships can provide. Since their sexual needs will transcend what marriage offers, the link between sex and marriage will be altered. These women will be more hesitant to get married since they will face more than a general restriction of freedom; they will face the possible loss of sexual satisfaction. If they cannot negotiate a different kind of marriage, they may choose to defer legal or even interpersonal commitment until their needs for security, children, etc., change their priorities. They may desire to put off marriage until their thirties, while men, having sexual needs that are more easily satisfied and desiring the traditional advantages of having a wife (cook, mother, housekeeper, etc.) may press for earlier marriages. However, if other expected reforms accompany this change in female consciousness (such as equality in the job market, access to prestige positions in society, child care, etc.) both men and women may see advantages in either staying single or having more open kinds of relationships. Certainly, there is the possibility that the roles of "pursuer" and "pursued" would change.

Definitions of relationship and affection might also change, probably enough to allow nonmonogamous, affectional relationships. Sexual intercourse would not necessarily be the ultimate expression of affection and closeness. Some women, in fact, might start looking at men as conquests and sex objects in much the same way men have often regarded females, especially when they had noncommitted sexual relationships. Women will suddenly have new standards with which to judge sexual performance, and technique and talent will now be evaluated in relative terms. The possibilities are numerous and though they may lead in different directions, it seems inevitable that the impact on marriage will be profound.

Thus, the scene would be set so that a new, nonmonogamous construction of the marital dyad would seem reasonable and appropriate. Since the sexual act would have new meaning and probably be seen as less "all-defining" to its participants, nonmarital sexuality would be a less disruptive act than in families operating under traditional expectations and norms. Indeed, it might be much harder to conduct the totally monogamous marriage since sexual restriction, especially if it became "counter-normative," might result in frustration, creating a hostile and tense marital environment. When expectations change, it is hard to rely on old and unresponsive institutions.

Nonetheless, we already know that marriages, even operating as deviant structures in a monogamous system, can tolerate nonmarital sex and still maintain their continuity. Traditionally, only men have been allowed the liberty of relating sexually to persons outside the marriage and they have rationalized their actions by saying that they "can handle it" while their wives would become "too emotionally involved." Under a more egalitarian model, nonmarital sex can exist when adequate rules, ideology, and trust have been established to protect the original couple. This does not mean, however, that such rules totally solve questions on the control of jealousy, loss of romanticism, and possibility of romantic attachment to the outside. Many open marriages have been dismantled because of loss of trust in the partner, falling in love with a third party, or a general feeling of disenfranchisement. The non-monogamous model of sexuality and relationships brings with it its own problems and disillusionment. Nevertheless, the literature on comarital sex and swinging indicates such a model does not automatically signal the end of the marital relationship. Invention may exert strains on the couple, and certain retrenching and dissolution will take place, but marriage or emotional attachments are not impossible. There is no reason to believe that even though people may practice sexual intercourse outside of marriage this makes them any less desirous of a long-term, stable, loving, and committed relationship in their lives. In fact, it is entirely possible that the mercurial nature of affairs and the elation which comes from arousal states (Walster, 1971), infuses all ongoing interaction, and makes one continuing relationship even more attractive to the interactants.

The Importance of an Ideology

It is useful to note at this point that the liberation of female sexuality and its concomitant effect on family structure is not seen as a mere phase in a sexual freedom movement. Rather, female sexual freedom and reorientation of marital patterns is seen here as part of a significant chain of events well within the matrix envisioned by feminists as liberating all peoples from conditions that do not augment human potential. Liberation without ideology, in this case, without a feminist, humanist ideology, is merely so much hedonism that will only flourish when historical conditions and economic exigencies are lush enough to afford the individual such "frivolities." What is being suggested here is a much more important personal and sociological question: We are concerned here with the redefinition and reorganization of sexual intimacy and family life. If female sexuality is no longer tied to home, marriage, and family, it means a higher likelihood of independent women, less need for marriage, and perhaps more freedom for dissolution of relationships. It is difficult now to estimate the effect this will have on intimate dyads, but we should expect this to have an impact on society now and for the foreseeable future. If the family has been the "building block of society," women have been the cornerstone of that construction. If their sexuality has tied them to that position, and if it no longer does, then the organization of courtship, marriage, and family will necessarily be altered. Female sexuality, monogamy, and its alternatives remain issues that will concern us all.

Reference Notes

1. Sensitive therapists like Masters and Johnson try to counsel couples to find out what they need and communicate it to their partner. However, some psychiatrists and counselors (Rosenthal & Rosenthal, 1973; Haley, 1973) have indicated that female demands threaten the male ego and are risky for the relationship. While sex is listed as one of the most common problem areas for married couples, studies indicate women find communicating their needs to men extremely difficult (Rubin, 1975).

16.
The Bisexual Debate

Martin Duberman

Debate continues about the existence and extent of bisexuality. Historian and playwright Martin Duberman offers first some personal comments on contemporary bisexuality, and then he explores the biological, anthropological, and historical perspectives and theories on bisexuality. In an addendum following Duberman's discussion, Roger Libby extends this analysis by reviewing and critiquing the recent sociological data on the subject; he also proposes some refinements in the study of bisexuality. As both Duberman and Libby point out, conclusions and generalizations about bisexuality can be only tentative and incomplete at this point. Keeping this in mind, Duberman suggests that bisexuality seems to be largely culturally dependent—and that the future will see many more Americans relating bisexually than has ever been the case in the past.

About a year ago I made this entry in a sporadic journal I keep:

"Bisexuals seem to be popping up all over. Until recently, I knew very few, and none well. I could relegate them to some distant category of indecision. Now I know many—and tend to romanticize them as the embodiment of the brave new world struggling into being. They're already acting, one part of me says, on the rhetoric most of us are spouting—that warmth between two individuals should eventuate in physical expression, regardless of the genders involved. But is "physical expression" the same as "genital contact"? . . .

When I hear in *detail* about the lives of [Phil] or [Wally], their bisexuality seems less a function of their free "polymorphous perversity" than of their delayed recognition that they prefer sex with men. They continue to maintain a bisexual life because they're trapped in marriage obligations, or continue to need the security and support of a "home life," or remain unwilling to take on the still onerous image of being homosexual.

I remember [Carol] telling me she'd "passed through" her bisexual "phase," that she thought the current pressures to be bisexual were to be resisted as a cop-out, as a failure of nerve.

I don't know. I think it may be the central—and largely ignored—issue in "gay liberation." If, as Freud thought, we all have (or originally had) bisexual capacities, the injunction should be to discover and utilize them. If, as Carol feels, we are *either* homo- or heterosexual, then those who mix the two become cowards and póseurs . . . but that kind of patronization may be *our* way of refusing to come to grips with our bisexuality.

"The Bisexual Debate" by Martin Duberman originally appeared as an article in *New Times* (June 28, 1974). Reprinted by permission of the author.

Now, a year after writing that diary entry, the bisexual ideal has come increasingly to be touted as the standard against which all who aspire to be *bona fide* members of the Sexual Revolution must measure themselves. The psychiatrist Robert E. Gould, speaking as a heterosexual, has recently declared his new-found conviction that "if there were no social restrictions on sexual object choice, most humans would be functioning bisexuals." Phil Mullen, speaking as a homosexual in a recent issue of *The Gay Alternative*, has expressed a view heard increasingly within homosexual circles: ". . . we gay people . . . have often been heard to argue that the lives of straights would be richer if they could only respond sexually and emotionally to others of their own gender. *Our* gay lives, by the same token, would be richer if we could open up to . . . heterosexual love . . . . Now that we're finally learning that gay is good, we'll have to start learning that gay isn't good enough. . . ."

Probably. But I'm less sure than they of everyone's "innate" bisexual nature, and I'm worried that that assumption—though seemingly on the side of liberation—could prove tyrannical, could become the latest in a long series of "scientific" party lines used to whip deviants—in this case exclusive homosexuals *or* heterosexuals—into line. The recent reading I've done in the scanty literature on bisexuality, along with my proliferating personal contact with practicing bisexuals, has deepened rather than resolved the doubts and questions I expressed in my journal a year ago.

But before exploring the theory and practice of bisexuality, I should make one thing perfectly clear: I am not now and have never been a bisexual. To anyone alive in the Nixon Era, it's obvious that the preceding statement is probably untrue. My sexual activities (not to be equated with desires or fantasies) have always been—give or take a few clouded teenage experiences—exclusively homosexual. For most of my forty years, I was made to feel guilty about my homosexuality; now, under the sting of new cultural imperatives, I'm learning to feel guilty about my exclusivity. Since guilt is the common denominator (and since I'm Jewish), one might conclude that no shift in social attitudes will appease my unquenchable instinct for self-castigation.

Among my many exclusively homosexual friends, some resent my espousal of the bisexual theme. At first they thought I'd found a new tactic for asserting superiority. After I explained that bisexuality was an aspiration and not an actuality for me, they settled for the view that I'm a latter-day Horatio Alger, fixated on some version of insatiable Self-Improvement. To which I respond—the nerve having been hit—that they're fixated on self-congratulation (all the while calling it self-affirmation). So the argument stands. And will stand for a long time to come. For we seem a space age away from accumulating the data—theoretical and personal—that might resolve it.

The "objective" data to date derive from three main sources: biology, anthropology, and history. The evidence from all three areas is remarkably thin and often contradictory, either very new (biology) and therefore unreplicated, or very old (history) and therefore incapable of replication. First, biology—the argument, as it were, from "nature," from the genetic, chromosomal, and hormonal "givens."

Biology

The genetic sex of the individual embryo is established at the time of fertilization, but sexual differentiation in the fetus doesn't manifest itself until the fifth to sixth week of pregnancy. Freud (and until recently almost everyone else) referred to the undifferentiated genital system of the embryo during these early weeks as a "bisexual" one. Recent research—and especially that of Mary Jane Sherfey—suggests that it would be more accurate to say that mammalian embryos (unlike those of fish and amphibia) are *female* during the first few weeks of life; the strong intervention of the male hormone, androgen, is necessary to "overcome" what would otherwise be a straight-line development of ovarian reproductive organs. [1]

Freud believed bisexuality was a biological universal—a potential inherent in all cells, tissues, organs, creatures. Since Freud also believed that psychology reflects biology, he assumed that bisexuality is present in the thought/feeling processes of all human beings—even if not in their overt behavior. Some thirty-five years ago, the distinguished analyst Sandor Rado issued what has become the classic attack on Freud's concept of bisexuality. Rado concentrated his fire on the sloppiness of Freud's conceptualization. "Bipotentiality of differentiation" in the early embryonic stages, Rado argued, had been confused with hermaphroditism, the possession of two complete reproductive systems in the mature organism; and only true hermaphroditism, he insisted, could properly be called *bisexuality*.

But the absence of a dual reproductive system in human beings has not kept them from seeking pleasure (or relatedness) wherever their psyches cue them to find it. Strict linguistic definitions of bisexuality have as little to do with the *fact* of bisexual behavior as they do with the everyday vocabulary used to describe the phenomenon. In common usage, a bisexual is simply a person sexually attracted to people of both genders. Less often, the term is used to describe someone who identifies with *behavioral* traits of the opposite sex—someone who apes presumed "masculine" or "feminine" mannerisms or dress.

Thus the narrow semantic point can be conceded to Rado without any other conclusions about bisexuality necessarily following. Rado is correct that "true hermaphroditism"—a bisexual breeding capacity—is never found in human beings. (Well, almost never: a few rare conditions are known that are marked by genital ambiguity—a mixture of ovarian and testicular structures—or, in the male, by degeneration of the testes.) It is also true that this is in decided contrast with other creatures. A garden worm, for example, produces both eggs and sperm—a condition Money and Ehrhardt call "simultaneous bisexuality." In certain species of fish, bisexuality is sequential rather than simultaneous: The Mexican swordtail, for example, "spends part of its life as a male making sperms, and part of its life as a female making eggs." The only process even remotely comparable in human beings may be that fleeting moment during the gradual buildup in the production of androgen in the male fetus at which, in Mary Jane Sherfey's words, "female and male hormonal influences are equal."

Higher in the phyletic scale, among birds and mammals, we do not find the capacity for hermaphroditic reproduction, but in subhuman mammals we do decidedly find bisexual behavior. The zoologist and physiologist R. H. Denniston has written categorically that "frequent homosexual activity has been described for all species of mammals of which careful observations have been made . . . it has little relation to hormonal or structural abnormality." Whether it relates, however, to "dominance behavior" or to what (if apes were humans) we might call "indiscriminate responsiveness to genital stimulation" has long been a point of argument. And in that argument, the "dominance" theoreticians have long been in the ascendance—with some of them denying that anal intromission (let alone orgasm) actually takes place.

But the balance in the argument is rapidly shifting. A convenient summary of that shift can be found in the work of Suzanne Chevalier-Skolnikoff. (The arrival of women scientists on the scene, less frightened—like women everywhere—of homosexuality than their male counterparts, will, I believe, produce a wide variety of reevaluations of supposed scientific truths.) In her study of the stumptail monkey, Chevalier-Skolnikoff has come up with some very unambiguous findings:

Homosexual encounters were numerous . . . the term "homosexual" . . . refers to interactions between individuals of the same sex that involve prolonged (15 sec. or more) intensive genital stimulation of at least one of the animals. This definition excludes most mountings that function mainly as dominance behavior, since these mountings rarely involve prolonged genital stimulation . . . four of the five females in the group were involved in homosexual behavior. . . . Male homosexual interactions were more varied in form. . . . Eight different methods of stimulation were observed. They include extensive manual genital stimulation (which was often mutual), oral genital stimulation or fellatio (also often mutual), as well as dorsal mountings with pelvic thrusts and anal intromission. . . .[2]

Orgasms were observed during female, but not male, encounters; homosexual intercourse took place in essentially the same position assumed in the common heterosexual pattern, and even though heterosexual options for sex were available.

As we've learned from the works of Lorenz, Ardrey, and Desmond Morris, there's great danger in using animal studies to draw simplistic analogies about human behavior. We can tell plainly enough when two male stumptail monkeys are pleasuring each other (in eight observable positions, no less), but we can't be sure whether the incidence or quality is affected by the artificial environment of the laboratory; whether and how the *feelings* of the monkeys relate to their behavior (and thus to our own); whether and how the feelings of scientists watching those prodigies of fellatio affect their "objective" reporting of the material; whether—most basically—the behavior of stumptail monkeys, in or out of the lab, has much of anything to do with that of, say, macaque baboons—let alone the inhabitants of Manhattan Island.

Though the evidence from biology and from animal studies suggests the possibility that genes and hormones play a role in programming patterns of sexual behavior, it suggests far more emphatically that such behavior results from the *interaction* between genetic "predispositions" and the models, cues, and injunctions provided by the social environment—with social learning playing much the more significant role. The latter point has been made incontrovertibly by John Money in his work on transsexuals: Though the anatomical and chromosomal equipment of a given transsexual is entirely intact—it checks out as "correct" against every scientific measurement of gender—the psychological conviction of the individual that he or she has in fact been misassigned overwhelms all the supposed mandates of biology. "I am a woman trapped in a man's body" takes precedence in male transsexuals over all the seeming logic of XY chromosomes, testicles and penis, prostate gland and gonads, androgen levels and hairy chest. Neither psychotherapy nor electric shock, neither the insistence of healers nor the pleas of friends, has ever made the slightest dent in the determination of a transsexual to convert his or her anatomy to conform to the inner conviction that they *were meant to be* the opposite of what their internal biology and external anatomy suggest they are.

Anthropology

The anthropologists have given us additional evidence that our sexual behavior results largely from cultural, not biological, imperatives. Even a cursory glance at the psychosexual patterns of other cultures confirms how much our own are dependent on parochial social dictates.

More than twenty years ago, Clellan S. Ford and Frank A. Beach, in their classic work *Patterns of Sexual Behavior*, revealed that forty-nine of the seventy-six societies (64 percent) they surveyed regarded homosexuality as a normal variable. (They mean male homosexuality; seventeen of the societies did sanction female homosexuality, but in anthropological research—as in everything else—female behavior is less visible, less studied.) The forty-nine cultures vary considerably in the kind of homosexual behavior sanctioned, the degree to which it is formally institutionalized and the extent to which it is merely encouraged, casually accepted, or actually prescribed.

Among the fierce Kukukuku people of the New Guinea highlands, the ingesting of semen is magically endowed, considered essential to virile growth—and accordingly prescribed for all preadolescent and adolescent males. Among the Keraki of New Guinea, the prescription for health and character in the growing boy is regularized anal intercourse with an older man. Among the Crow Indians, sodomy is entirely absent—but there is frequent oral-genital contact. Among the Batak people of northern Sumatra, adolescent boys are expected to have anal intercourse with one another—but fellatio is taboo.

Among the Koniag of Alaska and the Tanala of Madagascar, transvestite males *(berdaches)* are usually regarded as shamans, persons in possession of supernatural power; and sexual contact with a berdache is thought to confer a variety of blessings. They become wives of other men—though the husband may have another, heterosexual wife, and the berdache sometimes has a female mistress. In Davenport's study of a Melanesian people of the Southwest Pacific, transvestitism is unknown; but acceptable sexual practices include homosexual partnerships between adolescent friends and even brothers, and between adolescents and older men—including their fathers' friends.

It's important to remember that in all these examples—and they could be multiplied many times—we're discussing bisexual behavior. The expected, approved, even prescribed homosexuality in these cultures is never found to the exclusion of heterosexuality. It is always expected (the berdache or shaman may be a partial exception) that if there is same gender sex there will also be opposite gender sex—sometimes simultaneously, sometimes alternately, sometimes progressively (that is, gender choice shifting completely from adolescence to adulthood).

The anthropological data allow for many *near*-generalizations in regard to same gender sex. We can say, for example, that it is *usually* connected with puberty rites and/or religious significance; that it *usually* involves anal intercourse rather than oral-genital contact; that it *usually* occurs prior to marriage and breeding; that a considerable age differential is *usually* present between the partners. But the only complete generalization we can make, the one universal we can point to, is that homosexuality is never found *in opposition to* heterosexuality. The same universal is true in all nonhuman animal studies.

There is but one exception: the Judeo-Christian culture of the West. If exclusive homosexuality is to be found only among human beings, the only human beings among whom it is found are those in our own culture. Even within our own culture, moreover, exclusivity is a relatively recent phenomenon; though known at least as far back as ancient Greece, it was considered a rarity and a subject for mockery (for example, in the plays of Aristophanes and Menander). It's important to keep in mind that the converse is also true: Probably more people are exclusively *heterosexual* in our culture than at any previous time in recorded history—and within our culture, the exclusivity (especially for males) is more pronounced now than in earlier epochs.

If this conclusion is correct—and the evidence is sketchy enough (we may, for example, associate exclusive homosexuality with the West simply because the phenomenon has been little studied in Eastern cultures)—it requires explanation, and that in turn requires a closer look at our past.

History

The history of sexual mores in the West is, for the most part, poorly documented—and therefore susceptible to a wide difference in interpretation. (I've often thought "philosophy" is contingent on limited data.) As the anthropologist Steve Weinstock has remarked, "Incidences are easily demonstrated, but attitudes can only be surmised."

There are but two books in English that survey the subject with any competence: G. Rattray Taylor's pioneering *Sex in History* (first published in the mid-'50s), and Arno Karlen's far more comprehensive *Sexuality and Homosexuality* (published in 1971). Taylor's book, gracefully written and often witty, is burdened with a theoretical superstructure derived from the rigid categories of psychoanalysis (the Oedipal complex, etc.) and to that degree now seems overinterpreted and outdated. Taylor's inquiry, moreover, is pretty much limited to England, an island not as narrow in its range of sexual expression as generations of exposure to the royal hand-wave might suggest.

Karlen's book, though its tone is a little prudish and more than a little homophobic, is remarkable for its scrupulous detailing and its sophisticated analysis, its blend of a scholar's precision with a journalist's concern with communication. Among Karlen's most firmly held views is that "we must scrap the biologically rooted concepts of bisexuality and latency." Taylor, on the same theme, waffles strangely; not once, but twice in his book, he states that "homosexual elements are present in everyone." Yet he constantly equates homosexuality with "abnormality." How a quality present in everyone can be considered abnormal is never clarified—though the whimsical implications of the converse are certainly tempting: "Normality is that quality which can be recognized by its absence in everyone."

It's possible, obviously, for a behavioral pattern to be commonplace and yet not biologically determined: Driving a car is one example. Such behavior, we say, is *learned*. Very well. But why through time have human beings been so available for "learning" bisexual behavior? If biology has not been the cause, it has not been a deterrent, either; apparently no biological mechanism has ever existed sufficient to inhibit the capacity to take physical pleasure with people of either gender. "Nature" would seem to be neutral on the subject; we are or we aren't bisexual depending on whether our culture does or does not encourage the activity.

Karlen provides ample evidence for arguing that bisexuality has been so integral an element in human history that statistically speaking we would have to rank it among the few constants of "human nature"—on a par with waging war or using intoxicants. Though Karlen is the first to warn us how scanty the evidence is about the sexuality of early peoples, he does insist that on one matter "with confidence we can say this: for centuries or even millennia before the Greeks, many peoples from the eastern Mediterranean to Sumeria worshiped a goddess whose rites included both heterosexual and homosexual intercourse." He then names the goddess in her various incarnations—Artemis in Ephesus, Aphrodite in Corinth, Astarte in Phoenicia, Ishtar in Babylon, Isis in Egypt . . . Anitis in Persia . . . Cybele in Phrygia . . . Bendis in Thrace. . . .

Even Sandor Rado—like Karlen, unsympathetic to Freud's notion of a biologically rooted bisexuality—agrees with Karlen that as far back as we have records of human behavior, evidence of bisexuality exists. (We only have records, of course, for about 1 percent of our history—the last ten thousand years; before that, human beings lived in nonliterate hunting and gathering societies.) Rado finds traces of bisexuality in the Upanishads and the Old Testament, and he refers to certain Egyptian gods as being "notoriously bisexual." Curiously—in light of his vigorous argument against biological bisexuality—Rado locates the source of persistent bisexual behavior through history in "primeval, emotional needs of animalistic man." Confusing, to say the least. If "primeval emotions" bear no relation to biology, perhaps biology should no longer be looked to as the source of our "instincts."

Our scattered sources suggest that before 500 B.C. sexual activity was more uninhibited and homosexuality more acceptable than thereafter. In her

fine book, *Woman Plus Woman: Attitudes Toward Lesbianism* (1974), Do-
lores Klaich argues persuasively that in Sappho's day (c. 612-558 B.C.) her
poems were celebrated throughout the Greek world, coins were minted with
her image, statues erected in her honor: In other words, no opprobrium of
any kind was attached to her lesbianism (or perhaps, bisexuality—the existence of a husband and—more probable—a daughter, are disputed). It was
not until Emperor Theodosius the Great (the Christian hero who massa-
cred seven thousand people at Thessalonica) and the Council of Con-
stantinople that edicts were issued declaring homosexuality a crime
punishable by death, and that Sappho's poems were consigned to the flames
(A.D. 390).

Any attempt to generalize about Greek or Roman sexuality involves an
absurd compression of a variety of life-styles spread over some thousand
years of human history. Even at any given moment in time, the extent and
shape of bisexual behavior is disputed among scholars. Though Rattray Taylor, for example, agrees with other scholars that among the aristocratic class
in classical Greece "every man was expected to take to himself a boy" and a
boy not chosen by anyone was a boy disgraced, he disagrees with them in
confining the relationship to the kind of quaint Victorian roles of Inspirer
and Listener that I very much doubt Socrates and Alcibiades would have
recognized.

To avoid excessive absurdity in the compression of complex historical
data, it's perhaps best to content ourselves with scattered glimpses of the assorted styles of bisexual identification in antiquity.

In the 4th century B.C. a picked band of male lovers fought against Philip
of Macedon at Chaeronea and died to a man. In Sparta a boy who had no
lover was punished—and a boy who picked a poor lover over a rich one was
fined. Julius Caesar's diversity of sexual tastes earned him the reputation as
"the husband of every woman and the wife of every man"; but even Caesar
was scandalized by the harem of both sexes Mark Antony kept in
Rome—perhaps because Caesar did not believe pleasure should be institutionalized.

Though female homosexuality was practiced in Greece, no one knows
how widely; among the few bits of extant evidence are the fragments of Sappho's poetry, Plato's comment in the *Symposium* that the existence of lesbians, like that of male homosexuals, was to be explained naturally, as part of
bisexual creation, and Plutarch's remark that "at Sparta love was held in such
honor that even the most respectable women became infatuated with girls."

If the definition of bisexuality is broadened beyond "sexual desire for
the same sex" to include nonsexual identification with the opposite sex, the
phenomenon of cross-dressing also becomes a matter of historical interest.
Philip Slater (in *The Glory of Hera*) describes "the prevalence, in puberty ini-
tiations and other *rites de passage*, of exchange of clothes between the sexes."
Among such *rites* was the nuptial ceremony. In both Greek myths and practice we find cross-dressing associated with the wedding night, with a desire,
perhaps, to ensure potency. At Argos brides donned false beards on the wedding night; in Sparta the bride's head was shaved and she put on men's cloth-

ing; at Cos the procedure was reversed: The husband put on women's clothing to receive his bride.

The Greeks, as Rattray Taylor puts it, "were deeply preoccupied with understanding the experiences of the other sex." The story of Teresias—the male seer who spent seven years as a woman—is merely the best-known of many legends depicting men and women who changed sex during the course of their lives. The Greek deities also numbered several bisexual or androgynous figures, the most famous being Hermaphroditos.

In Rome, too, cross-dressing was a familiar practice. Will Durant (in *Caesar and Christ*) describes the sons of the rich in the 1st century B.C. who "dressed and walked like courtesans, wore frilled robes and women's sandals, decked themselves with jewelry, sprinkled themselves with perfume, deferred marriage or avoided parentage, and emulated the bisexual impartiality of the Greeks." (Alas for the pansexual swingers of Le Jardin and Max's, for David Bowie and Alice Cooper, for all those pioneers of the new who, in thinking that they are inventing a world, may be merely representing another shift in an age-old cycle—a shift so long delayed, this last time around, that those applying weight to the edge are perhaps entitled to their claims of originality.)

Otto Kiefer, in his book *Sexual Life in Ancient Rome*, comments that "everything relating to sex was regarded as completely natural, and was approached far more simply and innocently than it is now." The comment is suspiciously sweeping and bland, but Kiefer does draw the needed contrast between the acceptance of diverse sexuality in the ancient world and the repression of it—even of the inner wish for it—in the Christian era that followed, and continues to linger.

By the time of Leviticus, homosexuality had come to be associated with heresy and was made (for males) a capital offense. (It was disapproved for females, too, but penalties were affixed only later.) As Rattray Taylor summarizes the evidence: "a remarkable psychological change" emerged as early as 500 B.C., marked by an increased repression of sexuality and a heightened sense of guilt. The growing homophobia of the Hebraic view eventually overpowered the bisexual ambiance of the Greek and Roman periods.

This is not to say that the Christianized West came merely to exemplify sexual repression; the bawdiness of Chaucer's poetry is alone enough to remind us that official disapproval failed to persuade humanity against the pleasures of the sensual life. But the disapproval was fierce, obsessional—as exemplified in the "penitential books" and in the ferocious punishments ordained during the Inquisition. (Its official handbook, the *Malleus Malleficarum* explicitly stated that "all witchcraft comes from carnal lust.") And the triumph of Christianity did mark, in Karlen's phrase, "the West's full transformation from a shame culture to a guilt culture, in which prohibitions are fully internalized and man is ruled by conscience rather than by others' disapproval."

It hardly needs demonstrating that the guilt, the internalization of sexual prohibitions, remains very much a part of our culture—despite the hopeful signs of a countermovement. Both the continuing repression and the dawning liberation from it are exemplified in a recent controversy in one of our specialized papers, *The Chronicle of Higher Education*. Back in February of this year [1974], the *Chronicle* printed an article by English Professor Louie Crew in which he described his sense of heightened freedom and joy since decloseting himself as a gay person. Two months later the *Chronicle* printed the outraged response of Albert J. Maier, Comptroller of Marquette University in Milwaukee. Maier, in the thunderous tones of the *Malleus*, denounced the publication of Crew's article as "a blunder of unforgivable magnitude . . . a sign of the general moral decadence." Maier went on to characterize homosexuality as "one of the most vile blasphemies against God," and then, with the understatement of a papal bull, warned Louie Crew that "someday he will be called upon to give an accounting of the stewardship entrusted to him by our Creator." Maier left no doubt as to the Lord's verdict: "a one-way ticket to hell."

The ravings of an isolated nut? Not when a recent poll reveals that 85 percent (I can't put my hand on the clipping; the figure was perhaps a little higher) of the country disapproves of homosexuals teaching at any level of our school system, and a still higher percentage disapproves of sex between adult members of the same gender even when in private and even within the context of a love relationship. I have no poll to back my hunch that at this particular moment in time there is still less acceptance of bisexuality than of homosexuality. But I do have a personal anecdote.

In the summer of 1972, an evening of my one act plays was being performed at the John Drew Theater in East Hampton. During rehearsals, I stayed in the home of a couple well known in New York for their philanthropic activities and their liberal attitudes. Though we'd known each other a long time, I'd never discussed my sex or love life with "Joan" and "Don"; it was clear they knew I was gay and equally clear they didn't want to talk about it. I was in love at the time with a bisexual man whom I'd been seeing about a year. He wanted to come out to East Hampton for opening night, and I very much wanted him to. I asked Joan if it was all right if "Bob" stayed overnight. (I should add that they lived in a 30-room mansion, lest the false issue of overcrowding arise in anyone's mind.) Initially Joan said "yes," but on the morning of opening night, with Bob on his way out to East Hampton, she told me that Don had called from Manhattan to say "it might be better" if Bob went to a hotel.

I told Joan I couldn't let it go at that, and wanted to talk things out. She made some reference to their teenage sons—a vague hint of possible seduction, an explicit avowal that she and Don believed the "wrong" influences at a critical juncture could turn youngsters down the "wrong" path. Stupefied more than angry, and still afflicted with "old gay" apologetics, I volunteered the information that Bob had never before been involved with a man, that his earlier love affairs had been with women, that he was—well, bisexual. "Oh my God!" Joan blurted out, "That's *much* worse. Don has trouble enough accepting someone who's homosexual, but someone who crosses back and forth—!!"

Those dangling exclamation points say a lot about "liberal" sexual attitudes in this country. (Not to withhold the punchline: Bob came to East Hampton; we stayed in a motel; the friendship with Joan and Don is ruptured.) It's easier, I believe, for exclusive heterosexuals to tolerate (and that's the word) exclusive homosexuals than those who, rejecting exclusivity, sleep with people not genders. It's easier because in the Cartesian West we've long been taught to think in either/or categories, to believe that one is male *or* female, boss *or* worker, teacher *or* student, child *or* adult, gay *or* straight. To suggest, as practicing bisexuals do, that each of us may contain within ourselves all those supposed diametric opposites we've been taught to divide humanity into is to suggest that we might not know ourselves as well as we like to pretend. It's to suggest, too, that the roles through which most of us define ourselves—"Me, Tarzan"; "Me, Jane"—represent transient and even foolish social values.

Such suggestions are discomforting. Few people welcome discomfort. And that includes most gay people. In the eighteen months or so that I've been active in "movement" politics I've heard considerable disparagement among exclusively homosexual people of the "confusion" and "cowardice" of their bisexual brothers and sisters. Gay people, struggling to accept their self-worth, do not like hearing that once one mountain's been scaled, another may lie directly ahead.

Bisexuals, in short, seem at the moment very much between the devil and the deep blue sea. And in their struggle for the right to their own lifestyle, there isn't much legitimizing comfort to be drawn from the blurred data of the social sciences. Biology, as I've tried to argue, is neutral on the subject. History and anthropology do provide considerable evidence of the widespread incidence of bisexuality through time and across cultures; but it also provides evidence that most people have been predominantly heterosexual.

The safest conclusion to be drawn from these assorted arguments seems to be that human beings will behave sexually as their culture tells them they should behave—and both the social cues and the behavior have varied wildly through time. *Why* societies have differed so radically in their programming is almost as mysterious as why people have almost always accepted that parochial programming as the equivalent of universal truth. I don't mean that answers to these conundrums are impossible to come by—Freudians, Marxists, feminists, and others have all had their say—but only that the answers to date seem partial and polemical. At any rate, as any good utopian knows, evidence from the past—what has been—is no necessary guide to the future—what might be. Even if it can be conclusively demonstrated that sexual dimorphism has been the dominant pattern in history, that does not mean it will or should remain so. Not, that is, unless the argument from biology clarifies and consolidates. Even then, there would be many who would oppose biological determinism—in the name of the continuing evolution of the species, and conscious that in the evolutionary process deliberate human intervention—building cities, inventing a flying machine—has always been salient. Besides, as psychologist Pamela Oline has put it, "What if more *were* known about connections between body chemistry and certain predispositions? Would that knowledge tell us automatically how to behave?"

As regards our own country, it seems beyond dispute that bisexuality is currently more visible and assertive than at any previous time. And in tight little circles within tight little islands like Manhattan, bisexuals are even being hailed as the exemplars of a brave new world. Faced with crosscurrents of adulation and contempt, it's not surprising that bisexuals can sometimes exhibit an incipient chauvinism of their own. I think here of an ex-student of mine (male) who went to live in a small commune after graduating from college. Its members were paired heterosexually, but the women in the commune were also sleeping with each other. They began increasingly to bait the men as "hung-up Puritans" for their reluctance to do likewise—finally driving the man I knew, desperate to get his credentials in the counterculture, to a homosexual experience that was entirely unsatisfying and has kept him, to date, from further experimentation. "Well," someone might say, "that's the way it has to be for a while, as we try out, often disastrously, possibilities that in the long run will prove enriching." Okay, but the long run is a difficult hike to get started on, and pointing a gun in someone's face may not be the optimal way to get him to put on his track suit. It's possible to argue, moreover, that sexual orientation becomes fixed at so early an age—the homo- or heterosexual pattern so thoroughly imprinted—that most adults, even if they had the will, would be unable to activate their bisexual potential. Why *some* adults can and do is one of the many mysteries.

Besides, the long run, if we're lucky, will allow for more not less diversity; we don't want to exchange one set of harnesses for another—not, that is, if we believe the rhetoric many of us are currently spouting about the mysterious specialness of every human creature. I myself feel that the future will see many more people relating bisexually—at least in the minimal sense that some day, and perhaps within another generation, most people will more or less regularly enjoy the pleasures of having sex with someone of their own (or opposite) gender, even though they may still prefer their "core" relationship to be heterosexual (or homosexual).

But the words D. H. Lawrence wrote fifty years ago (*Studies in Classic American Literature*) probably have more value than any prediction—and they are certainly more humane than some of the current ones we're hearing:

That I am I.
That my soul is a dark forest.
That my known self will never be more than a little clearing in the forest.
That gods, strange gods, come forth from the forest into the clearing of my known self, and then go back.
That I must have the courage to let them come and go.
That I will never let mankind put anything over me, but that I will try always to recognize and submit to the gods in me and the gods in other men and women.*

---

*From STUDIES IN CLASSIC AMERICAN LITERATURE by D. H. Lawrence. Copyright 1923, 1950 by Frieda Lawrence. Copyright © 1961 by The Estate of the late Mrs. Frieda Lawrence. All rights reserved. Reprinted by permission of The Viking Press, Inc. and Laurence Pollinger Ltd.

Reference Notes

1. For much of this discussion I'm indebted to John Money and Anke A. Ehrhardt, *Man & Woman, Boy & Girl*, and to Robert J. Stoller, "Facts and Fancies: An Examination of Freud's Concept of Bisexuality," in Jean Strouse, ed., *Women & Analysis* (New York: Dell, 1975).
2. *Archives of Sexual Behavior*, Vol. 3, No. 2, March 1974.

Addendum

As Duberman (above) has emphasized, there is indeed a "scanty literature" on bisexuality, and we may well be "a space age away from accumulating the data" but one would hope not. While Duberman has discussed data from biology, anthropology, and history, it will also be useful to look at the contributions of researchers in other disciplines. Since Duberman's analysis there have been a few exploratory studies which offer tentative insights (but no real theory) into bisexuality from sociological, social-psychological, and psychiatric points of view. The contribution of Kinsey et al. (1948, 1953) is also significant.

Kinsey and his associates developed a now-famous scale for measuring self-identification and reported sexual behavior on a continuum ranging from zero (exclusive heterosexual) to six (exclusive homosexual). A three on the Kinsey Scale indicates a bisexual in the sense of a person who identifies and relates equally to either sex. Very few people in the Kinsey samples were bisexuals in this sense.

Kinsey observed that the definition of bisexuality will vary according to how one groups the individuals in each of the seven categories on his scale. If one classifies only people who are three on the scale as bisexual, then only about 2 − 5 percent would be bisexual. If one includes all who are from one to five on the scale, nearly half of his sample of males would be called bisexuals based on their sexual histories (1948, p. 656). Similarly, if one were to look at the female data, a sample observation follows:

Between 4 and 11 per cent of the unmarried females . . . and 1 to 2 per cent of the married females, had made homosexual responses, and/or had heterosexual experience—*i.e.*, *rated 3 to 6*—in each of the years between twenty and thirty-five years of age. Among the previously married females, 5 to 7 percent were in that category . . . (1953, p. 473).

Kinsey and his associates lamented the use of terms such as *bisexual, heterosexual,* and *homosexual* to describe the overall identity of a person, because such labels confused the relative psychological identification, overt sexual acts, and sex role definitions (masculine and feminine). Kinsey criticized the tendency to pigeonhole people into broad categories such as black or white, homosexual or heterosexual, and preferred indicating sexual identity in terms of specific continua of internal feelings and overt behaviors. In spite of Kinsey's concern over the ambiguities of defining sexual identity, no theory underlies the Kinsey Scale of psychosexual orientation and few conclusions can be drawn.

Blumstein and Schwartz (1974, 1976) carried out an interview study on bisexuality utilizing a sample of 156 males and females. Respondents classified themselves on the Kinsey Scale according to both their self-identity and their overt behavior. Three-hour interviews were carried out with both investigators present in Seattle, New York, Chicago, and San Francisco primarily from 1973 to 1975. The sample was a volunteer, nonrandom "snowball" type, utilizing friends of the investigators, their friends, people in bars and other public settings, and volunteers located through advertisements in straight and gay publications.

Basing their generalizations on a sample with an age range of seventeen to sixty-two, with equal proportions by sex, and different socioeconomic groups (the age and socioeconomic breakdowns are not presented in papers as yet available), the investigators state that 61 percent of males and 32 percent of females reported some homosexual experience before adulthood (1976, p. 5). Childhood and adolescence did not seem to be the final determinants of adult sexual identity; rather, the plasticity of sex object preference was apparent. Sexual communities were shown to be important (1974, 1976) in that social labeling and social support were related to self-identity as heterosexual, bisexual, or homosexual. However, these sexual communities were rather loosely defined in the study (e.g., gay, straight, an emerging bisexual community, libertarian community as a subgroup of the heterosexual community, etc.). The various sexual communities differed in their definitions of and reactions to bisexuals. For example, gays often viewed bisexuality as a "cop-out" and did not fully accept those who labeled themselves as bisexual; heterosexuals typically labeled someone as gay if they were aware that they had experienced homosexual relationships.

Blumstein and Schwartz (1976) found differences in the histories of male and female subjects. Males were more likely to have a first sexual experience (whether heterosexual or homosexual) with strangers, while females were more likely to experience sex with a close friend as an extension of an emotional attachment. Males had more trouble coping with homosexual behavior and developing a homosexual identification than did females; homosexuality implied emasculation for males, while females seemed to accept lesbian identities and behavior as more consistent with their sex role definitions. The authors feel that bisexuality has increased more for females than for males since the Kinsey studies, and that if they are correct, this would reflect the increase in all sexual activity for females. They predict that bisexuality as a lifestyle will be increasingly experimented with as a bisexual community emerges (1974).

The Blumstein and Schwartz research offers some useful descriptive information about bisexuality. However, the relationship between self-identity, behavior, social labeling, and other components of sexual identity (such as erotic attraction, affection, ideological identification, situational variation, and variations in identity over time) is not clarified; these elements are never linked into a systematic theory of sexual identity. Similarly, although sex role and gender concepts were used, they were not tied together with psychosexual orientation in the form of a theory. Blumstein and Schwartz acknowledge the need for "a systematic scheme for understanding the various combinations of identity and behavior," but they feel that "no such scheme can exist without seriously distorting the evidence, and . . . any attempt to create such a system could ignore many of the important variations . . . observed" (1974, p. 280). This is an important consideration, but a theory could help make sense out of the ambiguous combinations of components of sexual identity and behavior.

In addition to Blumstein and Schwartz's bisexual study, five other studies offer tentative clues about bisexuality. Hedbloom (1973) studied sixty-five female homosexuals, about half of whom were married, ranging in age from eighteen to fifty-five. The sampling was done from 1964 to 1970. About nine out of ten had at some time dated males and more than half had had sexual experience with a male. Most lesbians limited their sexual relationships to a few women (1973, p. 329). The small sample and lack of a theory make generalizations very difficult.

Schaefer (1976) studied 151 lesbians aged eighteen to forty in West Germany in 1972. Reviewing the literature and generalizing from her own data, Schaefer indicated that three-fifths to four-fifths of all lesbians have experienced heterosexual intercourse (1976, p. 55). Most of the lesbians in her sample had their first heterosexual experience *before* their first homosexual experience. Schaefer also stated:

As a rule: if heterosexual experiences have not started prior to the first homosexual intercourse, then they will generally not take place at all. On the other hand, women who have had heterosexual experiences prior to their first homosexual intercourse, tend to continue their sexual relations with men even afterwards (1976, p. 55).

Schaefer suggests that homosexual men have easier adjustments than homosexual women, as "they recognize their sexual needs at an earlier age and therefore interrupt the process of heterosexual socialization at an earlier age or they enter into their homosexual career . . . at an earlier age" (1976, p. 57). Schaefer's interpretation of much lesbian bisexuality follows:

. . . many lesbians tend to overestimate their own partial heterosexual reactivity. Social discrimination compels them to utilize and exploit this reactivity, the norms of society cause them to engage in heterosexual experimentation again and again. The "bisexual capacity" . . . (or more accurately: non-exclusiveness of sexual preference) has a completely different significance for lesbians than it has for heterosexual women: Bisexual behavior provides a path *out* of deviance for the homosexual woman, for the heterosexual woman, however, it opens the path *into* deviance (1976, p. 57).

Schaefer's concept of situational heterosexuality or partial bisexuality is reinforced by the observations of Blumstein and Schwartz and Saghir and Robins (1973). Schaefer reasons that self-acceptance and self-esteem are developed by avoiding negative social sanctions; she views partial bisexuality as a behavioral pattern that is developed in order to maintain self-acceptance and self-esteem.

Saghir and Robins (1973), two psychiatrists, carried out extensive interviews with volunteer samples of homosexuals secured through homophile organizations and by referral similar to the sampling of Blumstein and Schwartz. There was also a control group of heterosexuals. The homosexual sample included eighty-nine males and fifty-seven females from San Francisco and Chicago, while the heterosexual sample included forty men and forty-four women. Following are some of the relevant findings that contribute to an understanding of the range of homosexual to heterosexual behavior and psychological responses.

Forty-four percent of the homosexual women and over half of the homosexual men had had at least one stable heterosexual relationship compared to 72 percent of the heterosexual control women and two-thirds of the control men (1973, pp. 250, 99). About 18 percent of the homosexual men and 26 percent of the homosexual women had been married, but all but about 2 percent were divorced or separated at the time of the interview (1973, p. 95). Homosexual women were much more likely to report heterosexual involvements than were homosexual men, but the authors feel it is unreasonable to conclude that this means that homosexual women are more bisexual or more heterosexual than are homosexual men (1973, p. 263). Additionally, about 25 percent of homosexual women report that the major reason for breakups in their affairs was that the other woman was basically heterosexual. Since homosexual men are more likely than homosexual women to have casual encounters instead of extended affairs, this problem of opposing sexual orientations interfering with sexual relationships is less common with homosexual men (1973, pp. 238-9). Saghir and Robins conclude that situational heterosexuality or limited heterosexual responsiveness is more a reality than actual bisexuality for the majority of homosexuals who experiment with heterosexuals, but that for about a third of homosexuals a kind of "limited" heterosexuality exists where intermittent heterosexuality is "persistent and genuine" (1973, pp. 262-3.)

Laud Humphreys' (1975) sociological study of casual male homosexual encounters in men's rooms (called *tearooms*) included one hundred homosexuals of various types. Fifty-four percent of Humphreys' sample were married. Humphreys reported that there was no evidence that the marriages of these men were unstable, and the wives were not aware of their husbands' tearoom activities (1975, p. 105).

Warren's (1974) research involved an ethnographic and interview study of a gay community. She reports that gays view bisexuality as "a state of being so profoundly ambiguous that it precludes action. Furthermore, bisexuality is seen not just as bad faith but as actually impossible, since nobody, in gay folklore, could fail to make the choice between the man and the woman . . ." (1974, p. 153).

Warren comments further on the definition or labeling of individuals in terms of sexual identity:

The identity of the gay individual (or any other, I believe) is *not determined*, either by social stigma or the labels of the gay community. Identity is an existential choice belonging to the self, using the available social meanings in a unique and personal way (1974, p. 155).

However, Warren contends that ". . . stigmatization or public labeling tends to be less significant in the choice of gay identity than interaction with the gay community" (1974, p. 156).

Few, if any, hard conclusions can be drawn from the research on bisexuality. This is because sexual identity is complex; too little research has as yet been undertaken; and the available data are not fit into any consistent theoretical framework. The piecemeal efforts of sex researchers from several disciplines have not resulted in a unified body of knowledge as a basis for a theory of sexual identity. The descriptive counting of orgasms, the heavy emphasis on self-report data, and the disparate treatment of sex role, gender identity, sex object preference, and sexual life-style have not led to any valuable theory or set of hypotheses.

As Laws (1973) has stressed, we must go beyond a focus on genitals and orgasm to a person-centered conception of sex. This would take us beyond the minimal model of sexual functioning to a fuller theoretical model of sexual identity. Social scientists need to develop an understanding of the range of sexual and nonsexual life-styles and to relate various concepts of marriage to the alternatives to marriage. Sex role, gender identity, and psychosexual orientation will have to be integrated together and related to broader identity concepts as well as to the larger social context of intimacy and interpersonal relationships. An investigation of bisexuality and homosexuality and the range of life-styles that are expressions of these sexual orientations is an essential step toward the broader understanding of sexual identity.

—*Roger W. Libby*

17.
Where Are the Kids?
Children in Alternative Life-Styles

Larry L. Constantine

As the author points out in the following article, few children have had the freedom to choose an alternate or a traditional life-style. In addition, the role of children in alternative life-styles is often confused, and some evaluation is needed. To put this issue into perspective, the author describes the two prevailing models of parenting—restrictive and permissive—and presents a countercultural alternative differing from both models.

The ideas Constantine proposes will prompt varying responses from readers since the notion that families should be open and membership strictly voluntary does not fit with conventional wisdom about families. The author argues that children can handle a much greater range of decision making on their own. Children also can contribute uniquely to families and foster learning in ways unanticipated by most adults.

Some advantages of an open family structure become evident only if a new perception of the roles of children is introduced. The author advocates such a shift in the definition of children's roles. Concepts like punishment and obedience lose their significance in this new setting as children begin to take charge of their own lives—even to the point of deciding whether or not sexuality is for them. As the author indicates, this one issue, free sexuality for children, probably remains the most difficult and divisive one for many adults.

In the established American family way, minors have few life-style options. Generally, they live as their parents choose for them to live unless they elect such "alternatives" as detention homes or foster care in a setting virtually indistinguishable from the original home. Even running away may only substitute one set of limited, unattractive choices for another. For most children, the alternative relationships described in this book are not available options. Ironically, some of the same adults who have so staunchly advocated pluralism and freedom of choice in family life-style have entered into alternative family arrangements without even consulting the children they took with them. Communal families, to take one example, are often highly child-oriented, yet rarely do they offer children the alternative of a conventional family life-style. Some new patterns, swinging for example, are strictly "adults only." Most swinging couples do not even tell their children about their involvement in a nonconventional marriage. Even in those alternatives such as communal families and group marriages which include multiple parents, the argued benefits to children can seem to be an afterthought or rationalization for a foregone conclusion.

Parenting Styles

If we are to speak meaningfully of alternatives in relation to children, then we must establish the point of reference. To many Americans, the permissiveness of liberal families is "countercultural." There are really two established norms in relation to children and the child's place in the world: These are termed *traditional* and *rational* by Berger (1972). In the *traditional* view, children are in effect small and inadequate extensions of their parents, totally subject to the traditional and arbitrary authority of parents who must impress upon them the "proper" values and attitudes. Kids who are bad are bad simply because that's the way they are. By contrast, in the *rational* view children become a distinct social category with their own special psychology and rational rules of development by which parents are guided in bringing them up correctly. If some children "turn out" poorly, then it is the fault of parents. Traditional parenting is paternalistic and authoritarian; rational parenting is didactic and hortatory or advisory. To a limited extent these views are held by distinct social classes.

With this dichotomy goes another polarization of parenting, that of *restrictiveness* versus *permissiveness*. Restrictive parents are dominant and authoritarian. They promote dependency and obedience through punishment and encouragement of approval seeking. The child is a blank slate upon which parents imprint their own expectations. At the other extreme are permissive parents who lack expectations and place few if any limitations on children, even for their own integrity and comfort. They provide little supervision or assistance, disallow dependency, and administer neither rewards nor punishment extensively or consistently. Most modern people see these two poles as the only options. If rational permissiveness has "not worked," then we must return to tradition and authority. Even the eminent psychiatrist Robert Cole (1976), seeing no further than this binary choice, has predicted a return to traditional authoritarian parenting. Certainly these two models represent the mainstream patterns of Western families today.

The alternative or "countercultural" view is one which characterizes children as independent of parents and family, as persons rather than a separate social class, as worthy of love, respect, and affection more than attention. The parental role is exemplary or charismatic. Corresponding to this countercultural view of children are so-called *free* parenting practices. Neither restrictive nor permissive, they allow for the unique individuality of particular children with acceptance of their innermost selves and facilitation of their own expectations for themselves. While setting limitations for their own personal rights and interests, parents support growth, autonomy, and self-expression, allowing for both dependence and independence in children as well as in themselves. The parents are not seen as responsible for the outcome of the process—neither to be blamed nor credited for what their children become

—since the responsibilities and results, as in all interpersonal processes, are shared. The essence of such "no-fault parenting" is freedom but not license.

Structural variations such as a communal life-style or the presence of multiple parents may ultimately be less important when assessing alternatives from the point of view of children than is the nature of whatever basic model characterizes the parent-child relationships. A structurally ordinary family operating on a countercultural or free childrearing model offers a genuine alternative life-style for children; similarities in the impact on children have been noted between such "altered ordinary" families and structurally unconventional alternative families (Eiduson et al., 1973).

Children in Communes and Group Marriages

Where, then, are the children and how do they fare in those alternative families which do have unconventional structures? Although studies of children in alternative life-styles are few, enough data have accumulated for some tentative conclusions. The most careful and complete research has been on children in communal families (Smith & Sternfield, 1969; Berger et al., 1972; Johnston & Deisher, 1973) and children of group marriages (Constantine & Constantine, 1973; Hunt, 1972; Salsberg, 1973). In a comprehensive review and summary (Constantine & Constantine, 1976) of seven separate studies involving more than 150 communal and group marriage families, a remarkably clear and consistent picture emerged of the mutual impact of children and new patterns of intimate relationships on one another.

All the studies found that children in communal and group marriage families enjoyed the advantages of multiple parents, even though parenting was not usually fully collectivized. In most cases the children had a strong identification and especially secure relationship with a natural parent, usually the mother, plus a generalized trust in many adults as alternative parents. The parents usually set high standards of freedom from sex-role stereotypes for themselves—standards which they approached, but did not always achieve.

The modal pattern was that of "free" childrearing. In general, children were regarded as full-fledged members of the community or family with essentially the same rights and responsibilities as adults. They were expected to work out their own interpersonal difficulties and contribute to the common good according to their abilities, and were accordingly granted the same respect and freedom as adult members. The guidance provided by adults was mostly positive and supportive; negative discipline was rare and physical punishment almost nonexistent. In all cases the most important features of the childrearing environment were that it gave children greater personal freedom and more immediate access to more adults in a larger variety of roles.

And what were the kids like? Spoiled brats? Model citizens? A variety of clinical and field research techniques, including psychological testing, were employed in these studies to assess the outcome. Contrary to alarmist predictions and not really surprisingly, the children growing up in these expanded families proved to be self-reliant but cooperative, competent more than competitive, friendly, robust, and self-confident. They were happy, with positive, realistic images of themselves. With few exceptions, children have fared uncommonly well in these families; fears of major emotional damage can be laid to rest, at least. One preschool teacher once even singled out a child for a case study of a representative "healthy, normal child," not knowing that this particular four-year-old came from a group marriage family.

Open Family: An Alternative for Kids (and Other People)

One alternative, the *open family* (Constantine, 1975), is specifically predicated on an altered status for children. An open family is a voluntary association of people—children and adults—into a family unit with a single standard of conduct and membership. Regardless of age, sex, or biological relationship, members of an open family regard each other as having equal rights. In *choosing* to live together, open-family members pledge to respect, defend, and promote the rights of all members, including their right to leave.

The law and society work differently, of course, and in maintaining that children have the same rights as adults, the open family relies on perceptions of their situation at variance with those of the outside world. If they are committed to the open-family life-style, adults may have to use their own power to increase that of children, limit their own use of power, or intercede with outsiders and outside institutions.

The open-family and open-marriage models are structurally and ideologically related. Open marriage has often been misconstrued to be a license for comarital sex, but its principal architects, Mazur (1970, 1973) and the O'Neills (1972), had more in mind. In the working open marriage, partners have equal freedom, independent identities, mutual regard, and flexibility in roles.

The open family goes a step further in extending these perquisites to children. Not only are arbitrary prescriptions for appropriate male and female roles eliminated, but so are preconceptions of what is "adult," what is "childish," and what is expected of parents and of offspring.

All families need the *functions* associated with the traditional roles for men and women, mothers, father, and children, but in open families these options are open to everyone. Gentleness, assertiveness, tender caretaking, guiding, teaching, playfulness, dependence, responsibility, frivolity, task direction, nonsense, and logic, all these traits and functions can be learned and shared among all members.

In a visit to an open family one might find a seven-year-old doing some solicitous caretaking of an adult, or negotiating a change in an older person's behavior. Or things might reverse a few minutes later. No one has the full burden or the trap of any one role. For kids this means freedom to make real choices, to experiment with many behaviors, and to assume real joint responsibility. For grown-ups it means freedom from the impossible burden of always being grown-up or right. But open families differ from the long-familiar "liberal democratic family" in which adults step down and become friends—just friends—to their children, leaving all members stuck in a single role prescription rather than free also to parent and be parented as fits the mood and moment.

The single standard for males and females, adults and children, sometimes even extends to economic matters; one open family has instituted uniform wages for all work contributed for the common good.[1]

The more open internal and external boundaries of an open family give members greater access to each other and to significant others outside the family, even across generational boundaries. This is not to be confused with over-involvement or with enmeshment (Minuchin, 1974), as when a traditional parent forces a child to eat his spinach or a rational parent probes demandingly into an adolescent daughter's love life. The open family respects rather than denies privacy and individual differences.

Openness also enables the open family to get more internal feedback on the functioning of its own structures, that is, on its operating rules and definitions of relationships. Structures in all families change—through changing developmental demands, collapse, decay, even revolution. In the open family, input and monitoring by all members make the evolution and adaptation of operating rules and relationships open, purposive, and more or less continuous. Where traditional families value fidelity, unity, and stability, and more permissive families stress creativity, individuality, and spontaneity, open families operate on authenticity, diversity, and adaptivity.

This kind of open reevaluation and adaptation may be institutionalized within open families through such structures as a family meeting or the list that one family kept on its refrigerator, with headings like "Gripe of the Week" and "Joy of the Week."

In developing a typology of families seen in a major field study, Kantor and Lehr (1975) typified the experience within open families quite well. Members were affectionate and emotionally responsive to each other, sharing authentically all feelings, rather than withholding them. The overall result was an emotional climate that fluctuated within a wide latitude. Power structures tended to be lateral and equalitarian rather than vertical and authoritarian. But instead of being "democratic" or tending to anarchy, decision making was normally consensual and "teleocratic" (functionally guided), relying on persuasion, rational dialogue, and dialectical process to reach "no-lose" decisions (Gordon, 1970; cf. Constantine & Constantine, 1973, pp. 137–47). Such a family is based on affinity and commitment among diverse individuals who recognize their interdependence.

Children and Sex

More than a half century after Freud shocked his colleagues by suggesting that childhood was not asexual, it can still be imprudent folly to link children with sex. While most adults and certainly all professionals would acknowledge the sexuality of children, many become uncomfortable with its expression in behavior. Fear and open hostility greet such open and casual approaches as represented by McBride and Fleischhauer-Hardt's (1975) picture book of sex for kids. Even that great liberator A. S. Neill, with rationalizations of jeopardy to the school, apologetically drew the line at sexual free-dom for Summerhill residents.

More recent advocates of children's rights (Farson, 1974; Holt, 1975) have been more daring in suggesting that freedom of sexual expression is an essential right of children. A new humanistic "Sexual Bill of Rights and Responsibilities" (Kirkendall, 1976) cosigned by thirty-four world-renowned professionals has affirmed the joy of sex as "the right of everyone through-out life."

So many alternatives involve nontraditional sexual patterns that we would be remiss if we did not address the relationship of children to new *sexual* life-styles. How do the sexual aspects of open marriages and other multiple relationship styles affect children? What happens to children whose parents relate sexually to other adults?

Troner (1973) suggests that the key is that children of an open marriage do not learn to equate love and friendship for others with desertion, denial, and rejection. Rather, seeing that extramarital relationships do not threaten their parents' relationship, they may develop an exceptional sense of security which mirrors the trust and confidence their parents show in each other. Generally, we find that children are comfortable with their parents' multiple sexual relationships, so long as these are open and comfortable to the adults, and can be openly discussed between adults and children. Children do some-times become aware of what they see to be slights or imbalances, as did one seven-year-old who said she liked how affectionate her daddy was with his new friend but wished he would also do that more with mommy. In our re-search and therapy we did see a few preschoolers and adolescents who ex-pressed transient discomfort over a recent parental shift toward multiple rela-tionships, parroting back the moral stance earlier drummed into them by those very parents.

Dare we ask about open sexual relationships for children? In the course of an excellent ethnographic study of childrearing in communes, Johnston and Deisher (1973) found that in all but a few religious communes inhibi-tions about nudity were minimal and sexuality was approached openly and matter-of-factly. In those communes with older children, physical contact and mutual body exploration were freely engaged in by kids. In two groups, actual sexual intercourse had taken place between most children by the ages of five or six.[2] To these children, sex was "interesting and enjoyable, but not of central importance." They would alternate between periods of enjoying sexual exploration and times when sexual activities were of little interest. There was no evidence that early genital sexuality interfered with educational progress or personality development or was in any way contradictory with traditional childhood pursuits. Their parents felt that, in being freed of the moral structures that have prevented so many in our society from enjoying fulfilling sexual lives, these children have a great personal asset for happiness and will be spared much of the adolescent conflict between physical maturity and social prohibition.

In an extensively researched manuscript on childhood sexuality, Martin-son (1973) reports on sexual experiences of children in sexually open as well as traditional families. Even in traditional settings, a high percentage of children engage in various forms of sex play and have sexual encounters with other children and adults, but a key difference is that these encounters are much more likely to produce guilt or anxiety or otherwise be disturbing than the same experiences among children in a sexually open and accepting family.

While not to be confused with sexual openness, even in cases of sexual abuse of children by adults, numerous studies have documented that early sexual experience is not in itself harmful and that parental attitudes are the key. Upset parents who moralize or threaten may traumatize children more than the sexual abuse itself, while calm and accepting parents have an opposite effect.

If the Israeli kibbutzim are fair indicators, alternative childrearing environments can be expected to have marked effects on the personality and behavior of offspring when they reach adulthood. Only retrospective studies far in the future or costly long-term studies will approach final answers, but the early indications are both promising and provocative.

The children who grow up within the prevailing countercultural ethic or in open families or under free parenting tend to be unusually independent, self-assured, and competent without being excessively competitive; to find varieties of activities and relationships satisfying; to not put too many eggs in too few baskets; and to find no conflict between personal autonomy and integration with the group.

Like generations before them, they are apt to emerge well equipped to live in families like those in which they grew up. *Unlike* their predecessors, these interpersonally adept and adaptable people could also be well equipped for much more than just the same life-style. When the children of alternative life-styles begin to map out their own alternatives, the textbooks may have to be rewritten!

Reference Notes

1. The scheme has been explained in the author's syndicated column on alternatives, *Crunch!* (no. 5), appearing in *Synergy* (Family Synergy, P.O. Box 30103, Terminal Annex, Los Angeles, California 90030) and elsewhere.
2. This may seem a startling finding. Little hard data are available on the ages at which children are first able to consummate the sexual act or, for that matter, to experience orgasm. A number of pediatricians and medical authorities who were approached on this question could offer nothing substantive. Anthropologists have reported on societies with few virgins over the ages of eight to ten. Even in America, one in eight twelve-year-olds is a nonvirgin (Sorensen, 1973). From a growing file of anecdotal data, it appears that most children are capable of coitus with age mates by five or six, while girls first become capable of coitus with adult males at about age eight or nine.

Part 4.

Exploring the Future of Intimate Relationships

Kieffer's article about intimacy develops an analogy which helps us define the parameters of intimacy. She shows that today there are in fact many ways to satisfy the basic need for intimacy and that the patchwork notion of meeting needs describes the network of complementary relationships that satisfies many people's need for intimacy. Kieffer's article serves as a broad and provocative introduction to the subject of today's search for intimacy—and the directions in which that search may lead us in the future.

Whitehurst, in his article involving data about how youth view marriages of the future, takes the speculation about new directions one step further. Both Whitehurst and Kieffer note that Americans have a very high expectation of return from the intimate relationships they pursue. Although the future of intimate relationships is not entirely clear from the articles in this part of the book, a number of clues are given that provide novel ways of thinking about intimacy, that give examples of various means to explore intimacy, and that point to alternatives for those desiring better guidelines.

Also pondering the future in relation to present trends, Anna and Robert Francoeur postulate that a diffused and low-key style of sexuality may replace today's more genitally focused, highly defined approach to sexuality.

The Francoeurs borrow McLuhan's "hot" and "cool" terms from his analysis of the media and apply these to sexual changes they see in the offing. The Francoeur analysis shows how the Playboy mentality and macho outlook fall neatly into the hot-sex category, while the trend in the counterculture to emphasize tribal togetherness and sensuality is more typical of the cool-sex mentality of the future. Whether cool sex will actually be more prevalent in the future or not, the Francoeurs' perspective is useful in examining change and testing current changes against the oncoming realities.

The potential for change in future intimacies is examined by Whitehurst in his article about changing ground rules and emergent life-styles. Whitehurst provides a model for forecasting probable alternatives and rates of "leakage" or fallout from the conventional marital system. He suggests that, insofar as (1) alternatives resemble former models, (2) the economic and political climates are accepting, and (3) opportunities are perceived for entering alternative life-styles, people will be likely to adopt other living situations than lifetime monogamous marriage. The most popular of these in the near future may be modified open marriage, singlehood, and triads.

An alternative to traditional monogamy that carries with it the potential for continued intimacy with the spouse—while introducing outside others as potential sources of satisfaction—is outlined by Myers in her article dealing with the "fourth compartment" style of marriage. Myers maintains that, in addition to meeting the demands of one's spouse, children, and community and job, there is a need for a fourth compartment in which one is accountable only to oneself and one's conscience. The fourth compartment allows a person private time and personal breathing space in which to develop independently and do whatever he or she chooses. Myers emphasizes the necessity for honesty to oneself and individual responsibility.

The causes and functions of jealousy in intimate relationships and the implications of jealous feelings provide the focus for the Mazur article in this part of the book. His religious and social science orientation provides insights that go beyond the normal acceptance of jealousy as a fact of modern relationships. Mazur's discussion of types of jealousy clarifies the bases of jealous feelings. In discussing particular kinds of jealousy—such as jealousy stemming from envy, possessiveness, exclusion, competition, egotism, or fear—he provides guidelines for understanding and beginning to cope with jealousy as a relationship problem. Mazur's assumption is that jealousy, being learned in a social context, can be unlearned and deprogrammed by emotionally supportive groups of people.

The last article in the book is a summary and extension of the work of Robert Rimmer, whose novels have excited the imagination of a great following. His vision of a future that is more humane on the subject of intimacy and sex is pluralistic; it draws attention to the issue of qualitative versus quantitative aspects of intimacy. Rimmer's conclusion is that people are not basically monogamous and that every person deserves a chance to explore the meanings of at least dual intimacies. His overall concern is for the quasi-spiritual sense of togetherness that comes from people sharing not only bodies but a more complete sense of what life is all about.

18.
New Depths in Intimacy

Carolynne Kieffer

As Kieffer points out in this article, Americans are deeply involved in the search for intimacy—primarily because it is so elusive and ephemeral today for a great many people. Whether young or old, married or single, the search for intimacy consumes a large amount of the daily efforts of a good number of us in the contemporary world.

Kieffer suggests that for many people intimacy needs are met by a patchwork of intimate relationships—that is, by a combination of complementary intimate relationships of different types with different individuals. She feels this patchwork model of intimate relationships is more descriptive of reality and perhaps more viable than the traditional model of a single one-to-one relationship in a conventional marriage.

In addition to proposing her patchwork model in this article, Kieffer attacks the issue of a definition for intimacy, making useful distinctions between the intellectual, physical, and emotional levels of intimate interaction and discussing the dimensions of breadth, openness, and depth that are major variables in intimate relationships. Other issues Kieffer raises include the possibility of planning rewarding intimate relationships and the need to be aware of ethical considerations in one's closest relationships.

The Search for Intimacy

Intimacy—the goal of hippies, housewives, and businessmen alike—is not a recent phenomenon. The quest for intimacy is one of the oldest themes of western civilization; the continuous search for intimacy with another human being is evident in western literature from the time of Plato. Intimacy—defined here as the experiencing of the essence of one's self in intense intellectual, physical, and/or emotional communion with another human being—has a past and a present. Unlike the individual in the earlier community *(Gemeinschaft)* environment who was more or less born into a ready-made set of close acquaintances, an individual living in the modern urban society *(Gesellschaft)* must search selectively and deliberately for those persons who are to become his/her close acquaintances and intimates (Davis, 1973; DeLora & DeLora, 1975). The quest for intimacy has taken certain apparently modern forms; the linking of romantic love with marriage is a recent manifestation of this need for intimate experience with another human being (Murstein, 1974). Fromm (1963) has placed this human search for intimacy in the context of the individual's response to the existential awareness of his or her essential separateness and aloneness in the world.

The search for intimacy pervades the literature, music, and media of

The author wishes to express her appreciation to Bruce J. Biddle and Roger Libby for their constructive comments on earlier drafts of this article.

western society. A stranger to our land might well conclude, after being exposed to a fair sampling of our songs and of our product advertising, that it is life, liberty, and the pursuit of *intimacy* that propel our politico-economic and social system. The need for intimacy stimulates many individuals to go about attempting to splice intimate episodes of sufficient quantity and quality into their lives so that they may experience excitement, ego-enhancement, and a sense of meaning. For some persons the search ends in fulfillment of an enduring type; for others it goes on forever, with one disappointing episode after another ultimately totaling a lifetime of searching. Others eventually give up the search and resign themselves to living without intimacy.

The search for intimacy encompasses more of the life span of contemporary individuals than has been reflected in the literature of family sociology. While males and females are waiting longer to enter marriage for the first time, there has also been a dramatic upswing in divorce rates in America. With these trends and no doubt other factors as well, the current situation shows an increasing number of single adults in the U.S. population (see Libby, Chapter 4). Not only is the search for intimacy a phenomenon of the adolescent and young adult years (Erikson, 1959), but it also characterizes the lives of the many intermittently single persons who return time after time to the married state. Authors Whitehurst, Libby, Cole, and others have discussed emergent facets of this search among persons who are cohabiting or married; many couples are experiencing extramarital and comarital relationships, satellite relationships (Francoeur & Francoeur), or other multiple sexually intimate liaisons. The body of family literature for many years has upheld the sequence of engagement, marriage, child-bearing, parenthood, retirement, and widowhood. While this model does fit the situation of many couples, it provides only a vaguely accurate description of the marital and family careers of a significant proportion of American families.

The intimacy system is presently in a state of flux. The traditional model for attaining intimacy (referred to by Libby as the "primrose path," Chapter 4) presented in the courtship-marriage-and-family literature has been a simple one, and the situation is no longer (if it ever was) that simple. New patterns and intimacy cycles are developing in young adulthood and in the middle years. Additionally, persons are living longer, and there is a continued need for intimacy in the later part of life (Avant, 1976). This is, however, a time when many persons are at a loss to achieve "normal" intimate relationships (Kassel, 1970). While many people think of the later years as a period of "reverse intimacy" (Pineo, 1961; Burr, 1970) with disengagement from intimate relationships being normal or expected behavior, Lowenthal and Haven (1968) have supported through research findings the crucial need for intimate relationships in the lives of older persons. As Angyal (1965) has contended, the maintenance of closeness with another human being is the center of one's existence until the very end of life.

The need for intimacy is a basic human need (Fromm, 1963; Maslow, 1971; Morris, 1971). This need underlies much of our present societal structure—courtship, marriage and the accompanying rituals, product advertising, religion, and many of the helping professions. Furthermore, Goode (1973) has noted that the societal importance of love (and, presumably, of intimacy) is reflected in the social constraints designed to control it. Yet needs for intimacy have received so little attention from sociologists, psychiatrists, psychologists, legislators, and educators that nature has been left to run its course—whatever that might be. Today, however, in the midst of a new and general awareness of and attention to human potential, sensitivity, and actualization, we find at last an awakening of interest in intimacy in both the popular and professional literature.

The present book, *Marriage and Alternatives: Exploring Intimate Relationships*, provides an examination of certain modern forms of the search for intimacy. Its tone of support for the honest investigation of alternatives provides a climate for the individual's inquiry into the intellectual, emotional, and ethical issues involved in intimate interpersonal relationships and alternatives. Hopefully, this article will provide some perspective on the *why* of alternatives, whether we are speaking of marriage, comarital arrangements, consensual cohabitation, or creative singlehood. The *why* of alternate life-styles—and the *why* of marriage as well—are questions that are seldom answered; the question, in fact, is seldom raised. The various life-styles discussed in this volume must now be regarded in their proper context, i.e., as part of the human search for intimate union with other human beings.

Defining Intimacy

How do I love thee? Let me count the ways.
I love thee to the depth and breadth and height
My soul can reach . . . .
—Elizabeth Barrett Browning*

A definition of intimacy is every bit as elusive as the search for intimacy itself. The term *intimacy* has been used intermittently by social scientists for over half a century. Early references to intimacy included Cooley's (1909) discussion of intimate aspects of primary groups, Simmel's (1908) discussion of intimate processes, Lewin's (1936) delineation of the self into peripheral and central regions, and Freud's (1922) treatment of narcissism and the transcendence of self. Contemporary social scientists, however, have only begun to raise questions regarding intimate processes and have made few attempts to integrate the work of these earlier writers. Furthermore, intimacy is an often-used euphemism for sexual behavior, and family specialists have tended to equate intimacy with sexual behavior and sexuality. Those who have written about intimate life-styles actually have been referring to a variety of emergent sexual life-styles. Furthermore, there are obvious operational problems in defining and then conducting empirical investigations of intimate processes.

Harlow (1958) has noted that *love* (a word often used interchangeably with intimacy) is regarded by some as an improper topic for experimental research because of its very personal nature. Davis (1973) has pointed out that

---

*From SONNETS FROM THE PORTUGUESE by Elizabeth Barrett Browning.

many individuals would hold that it is impossible to develop a "sociology of intimacy" because of their ideas of the uniqueness of their individual experience with love or intimacy. It is perhaps because of its transcending, almost mystical, aspects that intimacy is often viewed as existing on the "sacred" end of the sacred-versus-secular distinction that has existed in human thought for several millennia. As Biddle (1976) has stated, serious investigators have been "remarkably hesitant to conceive [of] love in researchable terms or to study the ways in which people learn to love and live with one another."

One of the difficulties of developing a consistent definition of intimacy is its subjective character. To paraphrase Coutts (1973), one can only understand aspects of intimacy to the extent that he or she has been privileged to experience them. For example, for some individuals privacy and confidentiality are indispensable in an intimate relationship; others place little priority on this matter and cannot understand its importance to their partner. In the final analysis, as Biddle (1976) has noted, only those who have experienced an aspect of intimacy will understand what another is talking about.

There is a long western philosophic, poetic, and religious tradition of viewing intimacy and intimate processes in the mystical context of the human search for union with another human being (Brown, 1972). Davis (1973) presented a condensed version of Plato's tongue-in-cheek discussion of the origin of lovers. Early humans existed, wrote Plato, as literal "twin-packs"—round individuals with four arms, four legs, one trunk, one neck, one head, two faces, two sets of genitals, and other parts to match. The transformation came in the form of bisection:

> Now when the work of bisection was complete it left each half with a desperate yearning for the other, and they ran together and flung their arms around each other's necks, and asked for nothing better than to be rolled into one . . . . And so all this to-do [the search for intimacy] is a relic of that original state of ours, when we were whole, and now, when we are longing for and following after that primeval wholeness, we say we are in love (Plato, 1937, pp. 316-19; cited in Davis, 1973, pp. 173-4).

Many other subjective references to intimacy as a sense of fusion and oneness with another human being have appeared throughout the ages. The philosopher Spinoza (1941) noted that one property of love is to will a union with the object of one's love. The psychoanalytic tradition has viewed the perfection of the individual as being achieved in his or her union with the world through the experience of pleasure (Brown, 1972). Freud regarded the inability to transcend self or excessive preoccupation with self (narcissism) as neurotic. From the time of Freud's writing of *Beyond the Pleasure Principle* (1922), he regarded the goal of Eros as the seeking of union with another human entity beyond the self (Brown, 1972). Maslow (1971, p. 271) has referred to elements of self-actualization inherent in the "transcendence of 'self' " and in the "mystic fusion . . . with another person or with the whole cosmos or with anything in between." References to intimacy as the transcendence of two individuals to form a common whole have been presented by Cooley (1909), Simmel (1908) and numerous social scientists.

Biddle (1976) has presented an integrative approach to the analysis of intimate relationships. Numerous writers have discussed and some have researched one or several facets of intimate relationships (Huston, 1974; Laing et al., 1966; Thibaut & Kelley, 1959; Winch, 1958); Biddle has developed a three-dimensional conceptual approach to "love relationships" and has suggested its use in the analysis of the processual aspects of such relationships. In his social psychology text written from a role theory perspective, Biddle identified three dimensions—*breadth, openness, and depth*—of the role of each of the partners in an intimate dyad (or, conceivably, in a triad or larger group).

Biddle (1976) noted that intimacy is both a state and a process; in this sense, one must make a distinction between *intimate experiences* (encounters that involve some degree of intensity) and *intimate relationships* (recurring encounters that involve the maintenance within a dyad of a degree of intensity or intimacy over time). Biddle defined *intimacy* as the degree of intensity on any or all of three dimensions—*breadth, openness, and depth.* Breadth, briefly defined, is the range of activities shared by the partners. The openness dimension includes facets of disclosure of "self" in the Jourardian (1968) sense, while depth refers to the extent to which core or essential features of the identities of each partner are shared. Biddle's processual approach to intimate relationships has gone beyond the traditional dichotomous view of love and intimacy (either you have it or you don't) to focus upon multiple dimensions and gradations of intimacy. His schema is a basic and innovative contribution to the analysis of intimate relationships. As Biddle has reminded us, however, there is a need to go beyond these three dimensions and to incorporate other components of intimate processes in future theoretical and empirical work. We will need to develop a multidimensional approach as we attempt to learn more about the complex phenomenon of intimacy.

Breadth, Openness, and Depth

The breadth, openness, and depth dimensions identified by Biddle (1976) provide a framework for analyzing intimate relationships with a degree of conceptual clarity and thoroughness. For our present purposes, I would like to discuss these three dimensions of intimacy in a more specific manner by viewing each dimension in reference to the intellectual, physical, and emotional bases of interaction. The degree of openness in any relationship, for example, can be described more precisely if intellectual disclosure (e.g., describing one's family background) can be distinguished from physical (nudity) or emotional (showing anger) disclosure. Also, there is a difference between shared activities (breadth) that are physical (e.g., caressing) and those that are intellectual (watching educational television) or emotional (sharing grief in a family tragedy, or witnessing with pride a daughter's graduation from college). Discussion of the depth dimension also may be made more precise by viewing it in its intellectual, physical, or emotional manifestations.

The application of intellectual, physical, and emotional bases of inter-action to Biddle's three dimensions allows for greater specificity in discussing the nature of the activities, openness, and depth that characterize an intimate relationship. The trichotomous view of the human person as intellectual, physical, and emotional has its origin in the work of Plato, who started the tradition of viewing the individual as consisting of three faculties: (1) that comprised of thought and reasoning (the intellectual), (2) that consisting of the active or behavioral (the physical) and (3) that composed of dimensions of feeling (the emotional). A number of recent writers on intimacy, including Coutts (1973) and Dahms (1972, 1976) have referred to these three elements as the "bases" of intimate relationships. For Dahms, the intellectual, physi-cal, and emotional bases exist as levels in a hierarchy; he viewed emotional intimacy as the most difficult level to achieve. I will now proceed to discuss each of Biddle's (1976) dimensions of intimacy with reference to their in-tellectual, physical, and emotional manifestations.

In an attempt to graphically describe the two-dimensional approach to intimacy that I will be discussing, I have combined the various dimensions in matrix form in Figure 1. Each of the nine cells in the matrix represents a po-tential dimension of involvement between the partners in an intimate rela-tionship. Using this matrix, one may analyze any intimate relationship (or any less intense relationship) and plot the various dimensions of involvement in the appropriate cells. Since there is a range of degrees of intimacy, some re-lationships are more intense or more intimate than others. The entries in the cells in Figure 1 depict a highly intense relationship; the partners have be-come involved with each other in a broad range of activities and appear to relate to each other with a considerable amount of openness and depth. Since intimacy is a state as well as a process, the Intensity Matrix presents an ana-lytic cross-section of an intimate relationship at one point in time. The rela-tionship depicted in Figure 1, for example, may have been more open at some other times than it was in the period this matrix represents.

The intensity matrix represents one approach to the analysis of intimate relationships. It is not a complex model; it does not include the numerous so-cial psychological processes that characterize the interaction of the partners or that brought them to their present level of involvement. The matrix does provide a model that has utility in the description and analysis of intimate relationships. An individual may use this matrix to analyze his/her own in-timate relationships or to compare levels of involvement or discern patterns among his/her various relationships. Let us now discuss the dimensions of intimacy and the intellectual, physical, and emotional manifestations of each.

Breadth

Every interpersonal relationship, whether or not it is an "intimate" one, has its own degree of breadth. In a broad relationship, the partners spend a considerable amount of time together and solve a major portion of life's problems collectively. In a narrow relationship, the interaction is confined to some restricted areas of the partners' lives (Biddle, 1976).

Figure 1.

Intensity Matrix for the Analysis of an Intimate Relationship

	Intellectual	Physical	Emotional
Breadth (range of shared activities)	✓ *T, MBA, HMR* Telling of the meaningful events in one's day; Participating in a political rally; *HMR* Years of interaction resulting in the sharing of meanings (phrases, gestures, etc.) understood only by the partners; Decision making regarding management of household	Dancing *HMR*; Caressing *HMR*; Swimming; Doing laundry; Tennis; Shopping; Gardening; Sexual intercourse *AMK MAT*; Other sensual/sexual activities	Phone calls providing *MBA* emotional support *HMR* when separated; Experiencing grief in a family tragedy; Witnessing with pride a daughter's graduation from college; Resolving conflict in occasional arguments *HMR MBA AMK*
Openness (disclosure of self)	*HMR MBA* Disclosing one's values and goals; Discussing controversial aspects of politics, ethics, etc.; *HMR, MBA* *HMR* Using familiar language; Not feeling a need to lie to the partner; Sharing of secrets with the partner, and discretion regarding the secrets of the partner	Feeling free to wear old *MBA* clothes; Grooming in presence *MBA* of the other; Bathroom behavior (elimination, etc.) in presence of the other; Nudity; Few limitations placed upon exploration of one's body by the partner; Sharing of physical space (area, possessions, etc.) with few signs of territoriality	Describing one's *HMR, MBA* dreams and daydreams; Feeling free to call for "time out" or for togetherness; Maintaining openness *HMR* (disclosure) *MBA* regarding one's emotional involvement with other intimates; Telling of daily joys *HMR* and frustrations *AMK*; Emotional honesty in resolving conflict; Expressing anger, *MBA* resentment, and other positive and negative emotions
Depth (sharing of core aspects of self)	*MBA HMR* "Knowing" of the partner; *HMR MBA* Having faith in the partner's reliability and in his/her love; *HMR MBA* Occasional experiencing of the essence of one's self in transcendental union; Working collectively to change certain core characteristics of the self, and of the partner	*MAT, HMR, MBA* Physical relaxation, sense of contentment and well-being in the presence of the other	Committing oneself without guarantee, in the hope that one's love will be returned; Caring as much about the partner as about oneself; Nonjealous supportiveness toward the other *MBA* intimate relationships of the partner

NOTE: The matrix represents an analytic cross-section of an intimate relationship at one point in time. Entries in the cells are examples of activities (breadth), freedoms (openness), and qualities (depth) characteristic of one highly intense relationship. The relationship depicted in this figure shows high intensity on each of the three dimensions of breadth, openness, and depth.

Some couples share an occupational involvement as well as a range of other intellectual, physical, and emotive activities. A relationship in which the interaction is largely restricted to sensual/sexual sharing is, of course, a narrow one. While many individuals have equated sex with intimacy, the sexual and other physical aspects of a relationship compose only a portion of the breadth (and also of the openness and depth) of relationship (see Figure 1). Other relationships, for example clandestine ones, are necessarily limited in breadth due to situational and other constraints. All intimate relationships, however, require a minimum of breadth to develop or maintain a certain amount of openness and depth. Breadth, then, is the interactional arena in which the sharing of activities makes possible a degree of intensity of openness and of depth.

Openness

The dimension of openness approximates the nature of intimacy more closely than does breadth. Partners may spend a great deal of time in a relationship and share a broad range of activities and still engage in very little self-disclosure. Openness, then, is the *mutual disclosure of the intellectual, physical, and/or emotional identities of each partner in the process of their interaction.* There is a close and dynamic relationship between the openness dimension and that of depth; an increase in self-disclosure, for example, is likely to facilitate an increase in the depth of the interaction. It should become obvious that the dimensions of breadth, openness, and depth are highly interdependent; change in one of these dimensions is likely to bring about a change in one or both of the other dimensions.

Disclosure in an intimate relationship is not a one-time affair, but a series of minor and major exposures of self in a process which is not linear but which ebbs and flows and cycles and recycles through various levels of exchange (Altman & Taylor, 1973). A highly intense relationship includes a considerable amount of mutual self-disclosure. The process of gradual and reciprocal openness serves a continuous and increasingly rewarding function for intimates. Disclosure is an essential element in the escalation of intimacy.

The process of disclosure proceeds from the more peripheral to the more private aspects of the personalities of each partner (Lewin, 1936; Simmel, 1908; Altman & Taylor, 1973). The progression of the relationship entails reciprocal disclosure by the partners in a fashion that, if not arrested, involves increasingly greater risk-taking and rewards. One partner risks the potential rejection or betrayal of the other by disclosing certain information, and in the process of interaction the other reciprocates (Jourard, 1968; Rubin, 1973; Derlega & Chaikin, 1975). This process continues, with each partner taking increasingly greater risks in a gradual process of mutual openness and trust. Mutual acceptance and liking are early rewards for such disclosure (Altman & Taylor, 1973). Later rewards include increasingly greater levels of commitment and affect which are associated with the depth dimension of intimate relationships.

Some of the openness that occurs in an intimate relationship takes place as verbal disclosure. As Berger and Kellner (1970) have observed, in day-to-day life an individual is dependent upon the regular and daily conversations with his or her intimates. It is this regular dialogue that provides not only a basis for sustaining one's sense of reality but also the validation of one's identity and place in the world. An individual who is without a "buffer-buddy" (Bach & Wyden, 1970) with whom s/he can maintain such a continual dialogue may experience the feelings of anomie that are typical of persons who live such a nonintimate existence. The verbal aspects of intimate disclosure are not to be underestimated.

Rimmer (see Chapter 24) has discussed aspects of physical openness in intimate relationships. As soon becomes evident in his discussion, however, the openness that he describes is actually a blending of elements of intellectual, physical, and emotional disclosure. Jourard (1968) has discussed the confirming and validating aspects of being able to engage in the "authentic disclosure of self" with another person. For Jourard, such disclosure takes the form of intellectual, physical, and/or emotional openness. Whatever form it takes, however, successful self-exposure depends upon, and also encourages, the willingness of the partners to trust one another (Biddle, 1976).

Depth

Of the three dimensions of intimacy, depth is the most difficult to achieve and it is the most difficult to describe and understand. It might be helpful to imagine here the layers of an onion, and to let that onion represent the self. This self, then, has many layers, some more peripheral and easily accessible, and others more central and less accessible. Simmel (1908) and Lewin (1936) used this general idea of central and peripheral regions of the self and observed that the normal progression of intimate relationships proceeds from involvement in superficial areas of the self to interaction that incorporates the central or core areas.

Lewin (1936, p. 126) defined intimacy as an individual's sharing with certain but not all other persons that which "distinguishes him from others, that which is individual in a qualitative sense, as the core, value and chief matter of his existence." This definition approaches the meaning of "depth" as it is used in this article. Depth is defined here as the *degree to which an intimate relationship incorporates identities that are central to the partners* (Biddle, 1976).

The depth dimension of intimacy can be described as a "going beyond the self" in the process of intimate fusion with another person. For Turner, intimacy is the "invasion of the usual boundaries set in interaction and exposure of the self normally concealed" (1970, p. 229). Turner's definition seems more correctly addressed to the openness dimension than to the general concept of intimacy; however, its importance lies in the emphasis on the removal of normal boundaries to interaction. Through self-disclosure the individuals are able to interact at deeper levels than before; this deeper level of interaction incorporates more central aspects or identities of each of the partners than is possible or even desirable in a less intimate relationship. In the process of intimacy and through the facilitative effects of self-disclosure, each of the partners is able to proceed beyond the normal boundaries of the day-to-day self or "ego" and to interact at a level that allows each to be "more" him- or herself than is possible in a less intimate environment. Couples whose interaction is characterized and facilitated by such intense openness and who are able to transcend their individual egos in a deep level of involvement are rare. For these individuals, each is able to transcend individual concerns and regard the needs of the partner as highly and as conscientiously as those of the self. Fromm (1963) has referred to this state of selfless involvement as being one of *love*.

The mystical component of intimacy is perhaps best viewed in conjunction with another or third level of transcendence. In this level of sharing, the individuals experience the state of intimacy even more existentially than has been described thus far. In a relationship that is characterized by intense depth, the self of each of the partners is able in a truly mystical sense to be even more purely him- or herself as s/he partakes of an egoless fusion with another person. For Maslow, the "peak experience" of such union is an experience in self-actualization; in this egoless state we find the "greatest attainment of identity, autonomy [and] self-hood" (1968, p. 105). In the deepest intimate experiences are found love, autonomy and, for Maslow, the source of the greatest potential for individual growth and actualization.

Many modern individuals tend to approach love as a process of mutual exchange in which each of the partners attempts to derive affective rewards for minimal costs (Thibaut & Kelley, 1959). For many of us, this description of love is an accurate portrayal of our ability to love. Most modern individuals fail to achieve the depths in intimacy that enable them to go beyond this equity model of caring (Fromm, 1963). We fail to arrive at a depth in intimacy which would enable us to transcend self and to say with all sincerity that "I am as concerned about you as I am about me." As Fromm (1963) has reminded us, most of us who attempt to love are incapable of committing ourselves without any guarantees in the hope that love will be returned. We say in our actions and perhaps in so many words, "I will be as concerned about you as you are about me." Perhaps we as individuals are so much a product of capitalistic society that we cannot transcend the utilitarian "self" of exchange theory.

In this definitional discussion of intimacy, I have presented one approach that appears to possess a great deal of potential in conceptualizing intimacy and intimate processes. In my discussion of the three dimensions I have generally assumed that, while each intimate relationship is unique, there is a normal progression of intensity that involves increasingly greater depth in a relationship as the dimensions of breadth and especially of openness become more intense. While emotional intimacy may well be a higher level of intimacy than intellectual and physical intimacy (Dahms, 1972, 1976), it is essentially within the *depths* of intimacy that the greatest of rewards are to be found. It is perhaps in the emotional component of depth (see Figure 1) that we find love and the other aspects that are so highly prized by individuals and so difficult to achieve.

The conceptualization of intimacy is a difficult task, as the reader is by now aware. While the dimensions of breadth, openness, and depth appear to offer a great deal of assistance in the analysis of intimate relationships, it would be far too easy to become enamored with the apparent simplicity of this model and the analytic and descriptive power that it provides. The reader must realize that the three dimensions to intimacy can be limiting if one adheres inflexibly to this model. There is undoubtedly much more to be discovered. I would encourage each reader to become quite introspective in his/her future experiences with intimacy. He or she may well discover that intellectual breadth, for example, or physical openness or emotional depth are not nearly as specific and capable of separation as they might appear. Within the experience of intimacy he or she may discover once again, at least for a few moments, that intimacy is a mystery that defies explanation.

Patchwork Intimacy

The traditional model for the meeting of needs for intimacy is generally a restrictive one. The courtship-and-marriage-for-a-lifetime model seems to be meeting the needs of a significant but limited number of adults. This model may be said to be restrictive if for no other reason than the fact that many persons are temporarily and some perhaps permanently *unable* to achieve the status of marriage. There are today millions of Americans who are not married (see Libby, Chapter 4). Still, these individuals are creating for themselves viable life-styles; their needs for intimate relationships are being at least minimally fulfilled. Today's singles encounter, negotiate, and develop a plethora of intimate relationships. The patterns are difficult to detect, perhaps because there are so many. What these singles have in common is the variety, versatility, and elasticity of the arrangements they have contrived for the meeting of their needs for intimacy with another or a number of other human beings.

Most, if not all, married persons also are involved in a multitude of intimate relationships of various degrees of intensity. Many married persons have their own active network of intimates that span beyond spouses and other family members to include a collection of other individuals (work associates and a variety of other intimate contacts) of the same or other[1] sex with whom they share certain understandings, support, and concern. The need for intimacy is met by a *combination* of intimate relationships rather than by one individual. This is not to deny the importance of a central relationship in one's life; however, for an increasing number of individuals a combination of intimate relationships is the mechanism that enables them to meet or to approximate the meeting of their needs for close human contact and for intimate involvement.

I use the term *patchwork intimacy* to refer to this *rather common arrangement of multiple ties to meet one's needs for intimate relationships of different degrees of breadth, openness, and depth that together yield a whole, a rather complex and variegated pattern or conglomerate of intimate relationships and experiences.* In order to maintain a state of mental health and *joie de vivre*, nearly all individuals need a core of persons with whom to consort more or less intimately on a regular basis. The needs of most individuals for intimate relationships and experiences must be met consistently, not sporadically; for more and more individuals these needs are being met through a carefully or not so carefully developed patchwork of intimate relationships. One's patchwork for meeting needs for intimacy may consist of individuals of the same or other sex or of both sexes, of married, ever- and never-married status, of similar or disparate ages, and of many or few relationships of high or low intensity. Intimate partnerships in which there is a good deal of breadth (range of activities) somehow may lack the openness that comes with disclosure or the affective and commitment aspects of the depth dimension. Even the "deepest" of relationships may not provide much in the way of breadth or shared activities, hence other relationships are needed. Again, the most "open" of relationships—those relationships in which there is the greatest amount of disclosure—may be lacking in still other aspects or dimensions and may stimulate the individual to develop additional intimate relationships or arrange for further intimate experiences that meet these needs.

Intimate relationships not only vary in intensity, but they also take different *forms*. An individual's patchwork may include a marital relationship and/or a number of same-sex relationships and/or one or more comarital or extramarital relationships. Likewise, the patchwork of the single person is comprised of intimate relationships which may include consensual cohabitation (see Cole, Chapter 5) and/or a number of same-sex relationships and/or other forms of life-styles discussed in this volume.

The patchwork of most individuals includes a marital relationship; for some, this relationship is permanent while for others it is not so durable. Marriage plays a major role in what Libby has referred to as the intimacy *career* of most modern individuals. Nearly all persons choose sooner or later to attempt to share their intimate and other resources with an other-sex individual in marriage. As Rimmer (1965) and O'Neill and O'Neill (1972) have maintained, however, one cannot realistically expect a spouse or other person to fulfill all of his/her needs. The limitations of time, if nothing else, curtail the benefits to be gained from any relationship. As Davis (1973, pp. 219-20) has aptly phrased it:

All intimates satisfy each other in many ways, but not in all ways. In fact, the more ways in which they satisfy each other, the more their dissatisfactions with each other seem to stand out phenomenologically. In this situation, each intimate is continually confronted with the choice of either ending their relationship in the hope of finding elsewhere the pleasures he is presently enjoying (e.g., sexual) or of attempting to iron out the other's irritating habits or to fill in the other's exasperating deficiencies (e.g., by getting the other to read more) . . . intimates must choose between destroying or reforming their relationships. . . .

Davis does not make explicit a third option—that of meeting needs that are unmet in one relationship through intimate experiences and relationships with other persons.

The patchwork of some individuals includes one sexual relationship; for others it includes several or many, while still others have no current source of sensual/sexual sharing. Even the individual who has a sexually exclusive or monogamous relationship has a number of other nonsexual sources of intimacy; this whole or *gestalt* of intimate relationships and experiences comprises his or her patchwork. *Many* intimate relationships and experiences express this overall approach to meeting intimacy needs. This is not to suggest that patchwork intimacy is a "scavenger" approach to meeting needs for intimacy; for some individuals it may amount to that, but for others it represents an attempt to creatively structure their coexistence with other human beings by responding to specific needs for intimate experiences and relationships in such a way as to foster maximal personal development and growth (as an example of one such creative approach to meeting needs for intimacy, see Libby, Chapter 4).

The patchwork of intimates consists of one or several primary relationships and/or a number of quasi-primary relationships. Primary relationships are highly intense relationships. They are *holistic* in Davis' (1973) sense in that they involve whole persons and encompass to a great extent the lives and aspirations of the participants (Stone, 1954). Other relationships are quasi-primary in that, strictly speaking, they are not primary relationships and yet they do not fit into Cooley's (1909) residual category of secondary relationships. These may be less intense relationships or may be highly intense relationships in which interaction is infrequent or sporadic due to situational or other constraints. An example is that of individuals who see each other only once a year but whose interaction on each occasion seems to enthusiastically and intensely resume where they left off. As Stone (1954) has noted, many relationships exist which bear many of the qualities of primary relationships and yet are neither primary, or secondary in the strict Cooley (1909) sense. Stone has suggested the use of the term *quasi-primary* to refer to such relationships.

Stone (1954; 1976) has suggested that primary as well as quasi-primary relationships serve functions of building individual identities and of integrating the individual into the larger society. Ramey (1975) noted that both primary and secondary relationships comprise his intimate groups and networks; however, the term *quasi-primary* would seem to be more appropriate than the term *secondary* in Ramey's analysis. Also the Francoeurs' satellite relationships (see Chapter 20) are quasi-primary relationships.

Stoller (1970) identified the emerging tendency for more than one nuclear family to share emotional (including facets of intimacy) and other resources (e.g., babysitting services, laundry, and other equipment) on a day-to-day basis that would provide for some needs that were met in somewhat similar ways by the extended family. Stoller predicted an increasing incidence of such networks; this phenomenon is one aspect of the patchwork of intimacy for some individuals and families.

Some of one's intimate relationships are more important than others. I use the term *salience* to refer to the relative value or importance that any of one's relationships holds for the individual. A relationship that has a great deal of salience assumes relatively high priority in the day-to-day life of the individual. Salience can be seen in the amount of time one spends thinking about the intimate partner and about matters having to do with that relationship. Daydreams and fantasies are manifestations of salience, as are dreams that take place during sleep and other signs of mental preoccupation with the partner in his or her absence. The time that one spends dwelling on past interaction, whether pleasant or unpleasant, with one's intimate partner or anticipating future interaction is an indication of salience. Some relationships mean more to the individual than do others. Five minutes with one intimate may be as valuable as half a day spent with another. Furthermore, relationships may assume a great deal of salience at one point in time (e.g., the extramarital "affair," or, for that matter, a marital relationship) and then perhaps fade or diminish in importance. When one takes leave of some intimates, they seem to reside in the mind and provide a continuous referent with whom one keeps more or less a running dialogue. Other intimates leave and, as far as the individual is concerned, are out of his/her life. It is likely that there is a close association between the salience and the intensity of a relationship. Not all highly salient relationships are highly intense ones; moreover, a relationship is unlikely to become a highly intense one unless it has salience for both individuals. The salience of a relationship differs from the actual behavior that is shared. One may spend a great deal of time in a relationship—in fact, it may be a broad relationship—and yet the interaction may have relatively little meaning or importance for the individual. The salience of one's various intimate relationships is an overlooked variable in the family literature.

Each person has his/her own arrangement for meeting individual needs for intimacy. Some have a much greater need and appreciation for intense openness in intimate relationships than do others. Some persons value intensity in the *depth* dimension in a major relationship while others wish to avoid that level of involvement. A patchwork design is a static representation of one's collective relationships. Some intimates are temporary while others remain for a lifetime. The "monogamous ideal" is another static model; however, as divorce rates and other realities have shown, intimates come and they go (see Libby's discussion of transitions in role bonding, Chapter 4). Some relationships increase in intensity and salience, and others diminish or disappear. Furthermore, intimate *experiences*—brief episodes of intense intellectual, physical, and/or emotional sharing—may also be represented in such a static diagram. A patchwork *model* has its horizontal or concurrent dimensions; one's patchwork, however, is continuously changing in kaleidoscopic fashion—this is the vertical aspect of an ongoing process through time. Hopefully, however, the individual assumes more control over his/her intimate "patches" than is possible in the chance occurrences of kaleidoscopic change.

The composition and arrangement of one's patchwork of intimates have implications that are still relatively unexamined by most aspiring intimates and by professionals. For example, some persons have one individual who serves as a major source of intimacy and their relationship is a broad one that meets at least minimal requirements for openness and depth. One of the implications for an individual in such a situation is that he/she is likely to do most of his/her disclosure of "self" and of daily concerns with that one intimate and likely will share less or shallower information with his/her other intimates. On the other hand, an individual who has many intimates but is without a major source of intimacy will be likely to have a lower threshold for disclosure with his/her various intimates. Such an individual will share more information with more people, hence taking more risks in disclosing and being perhaps more likely to suffer repercussions for such disclosures (e.g., disclosing information about his/her other intimate relationships or frustrations experienced with his/her employer). Obviously, there are numerous possible patchwork combinations, and each has implications for openness and depth potentialities or rewards. Individual preferences and capabilities and environmental opportunities and constraints are some factors that determine the composition and design of one's patchwork of intimacy (Biddle, 1976).

Each intimate relationship in a patchwork is unique. One intimate may be available to provide company in lonely moments, while another may provide a welcome sounding-board for ideas. Another may provide a sensuous environment in which one can appreciate and even celebrate one's femininity or masculinity. If one has a spouse, he or she may share in affective and sexual ways, in the mutuality of financial and possibly child-rearing roles, and perhaps in the provision to the other of a sense of security and stability not to be derived from any or all of the other relationships. Another way of saying this is that some relationships are broad because the partners share a majority of life's problems collectively. As a professional in his late forties stated in a recent interview: "One may have a *cerebral* relationship with one person, a largely *physical* relationship with another, and an *emotional* rapport or supportiveness with another. With some individuals you would 'tune in' on a particular wavelength, but beyond that there is not a bit of reception." As is becoming obvious, the patchwork of intimacy is predicated upon different strokes from different folks; the result is a combination of relationships that provide a more stimulating intellectual existence, a more rewarding physical or sexual relationship(s), and a richer emotional life than is likely or possible when only one intimate partner is involved.

While the norm of monogamous intimacy has gone largely unquestioned until recently, *in practice* an individual's intimacy needs are more often met today in diffuse fashion. While most persons equate monogamy with sexual exclusiveness, most individuals (married or not) who have a primary relationship are involved in a variety of intimate experiences and relationships that involve intellectual, physical (which may or may not include sexual), or emotional sharing or a dynamic blending of all three. Perhaps the ideal of monogamy as a model of exclusive (sexual) sharing has placed excessive emphasis upon the physical aspects of intimacy.

Marriage is no guarantee of year-round or round-the-clock intimacy even though the marital relationship provides for a major share of the emotional needs of millions of individuals. It offers security, stability, and convenience in the fulfilling of daily needs and desires. No other living arrangement yet devised has provided so well for so many personal needs and desires of so many individuals, males and females. As newlyweds discover, however, after marriage certain problems remain unresolved; certain needs for intimacy are yet unfulfilled. Even when one's spouse is physically available, he or she may not be *intimately* available when one needs or desires closeness. S/he may be preoccupied with work, studies, or children, or may simply need to be alone or psychologically apart for a while. The butt of many jokes has been the young woman's maintenance of close ties with her mother after her marriage; aside from the daughter's feelings of love, concern, and responsibility, there is also her realization that her mother meets certain needs that are not met by her new husband and probably never will be. While not all married persons maintain a lively patchwork of intimates and some male and female spouses are so isolated by work conditions that they have failed to develop a number of other close interpersonal contacts, many marriages would probably be more rewarding for both partners if each had a more active and meaningful patchwork of intimates.

A good portion of the patchwork of many individuals takes place as work-world intimacy with coworkers and colleagues in the form of emotional and/or intellectual interaction associated with the activities of work and perhaps as physical "behind-closed-doors" intimacy in office buildings or as conference and motel-room behavior. Many of these work-world relationships turn out to be quite broad or deep because of shared activities and interests and perhaps similar values and educational levels. Other relationships have their origin in more casual settings that are leisure-oriented. An example is a relationship in which most of the interaction (breadth) of the relationship takes the form of sensual/sexual sharing. Coutts (1973, p. 72) has suggested that "The intimacy of work is much more durable, is often more rewarding, has more facets and challenges and is more flexible than sexual intimacy."

Patchwork arrangements exist among older persons as well as among those in the young adult and middle years. In an ongoing investigation of emotional support systems among older persons conducted by Habenstein and Biddle (1976), the case history of a widower in his seventies revealed a diffuse patchwork of relationships, all of low intensity. Most of this individual's relationships were with males. He ate breakfast each morning with a group of older men, lunch with a second set of men who gathered in another eating establishment, and dinner with a third group. He had still other contacts at a country club. All his living relatives resided in distant parts of the country. After he described his daily activities in one two-hour interview, this man concluded that the interviewer knew more about his life than anyone else in town. He shared a number of different activities with many different individuals, but his separate relationships were lacking not only in breadth but also in openness and depth. This case history suggests that the "concentrated," exclusive, one-intimate-partner model for meeting needs for intimacy is not a totally accurate or realistic one.

Some patchwork intimacy arrangements include what might be termed *make-do* relationships. Habenstein (personal communication, 1976) used the term *make-do* to refer to relationships that are noninstitutionalized adaptations of an individual to current constraints in his or her life situation. An example of a make-do relationship is that of a 26-year-old single female with a master's degree who developed an intimate relationship with a 29-year-old single male for whom she had difficulty feeling much respect and affection. She told an interviewer that she felt that, while this male was not her intellectual or social equal, he was the only single male of her approximate age in the small town in which she was employed. In exchange theory terms, an individual would follow such a make-do course of action because there are no alternatives equal or superior to the present one (Thibaut & Kelley, 1959). A make-do intimate exchange is one that is for the individual the most expeditious choice among limited options. A single female student nurse said that her sexual relationship with her female roommate was for both of them a make-do arrangement or adaptation to their present situation. She and her roommate would have preferred a heterosexual relationship, but neither had the time or the opportunity to meet eligible male intimates.

Habenstein (1976) has conducted an investigation of make-do arrangements for meeting needs for interpersonal closeness and intimacy among older persons. He noted that intimate make-do exchanges are not at all uncommon among older males and females. An example is the case of two widows, ages seventy-one and seventy-five, who live near each other and spend nearly every evening together because without their mutual company they experience a great deal of loneliness. Make-do relationships represent part of the patchwork of intimacy of many single individuals and also of many married persons, particularly those whose marriages are not "vital" or "total" ones (Cuber & Harroff, 1965). Make-do relationships that are temporary or that compose only a minor part of one's patchwork can provide a viable supplement in meeting one's needs for intimacy. If one's major relationships happen to be make-do, however, and this solution promises to be a long-term one, the situation can be less than desirable. The limited possibilities for growth in such a situation lie in marked contrast to the rich potentialities that inhere in the transcendental processes of intimate union.

The potential for personal growth that exists in a highly intense relationship can be supplemented by a well-chosen patchwork of other intimate relationships. An intimate partner provides an audience for the self. An individual has as many intimate selves as he or she has intimates. The specificity of sharing of different core aspects of the self with one's various intimates provides for growth not possible in the confines of a single relationship. This multiple and concurrent sharing provides a greater flexibility for the self; in several relationships one is able to develop facets of the self that cannot be shared in a single relationship. The development of a reliable patchwork of intimates is an invitation to growth, assuming, of course, that one's intimates have the capability of extending themselves in such a growth-enhancing way.

In the introduction to this article, intimacy was defined as the "experiencing of the essence of one's self in intense intellectual, physical, and/or emotional communion with another human being." For Maslow (1968, 1971), such "experiencing" constitutes growth. Maslow and O'Neill and O'Neill (1972) have discussed the *synergistic* effects of intimate relationships. The concept of *synergy* implies an arrangement of beneficial interaction in which the growth of each of the partners is enhanced and augmented by the growth, pleasure, and fulfillment of the other (O'Neill &

O'Neill, 1972). As Coutts (1973) has noted, for intimate partners, *a* plus *b* equals *ab* plus *ba*. In the context of an intimate relationship, the concept of synergy implies that "through our union, each of us is greater than s/he could be alone." Applied to a patchwork of intimates, synergy involves reaching new heights in personal development that are not possible alone, nor in a single relationship. Not all dyads manage to achieve or maintain a synergistic state of affairs. Some relationships have diminishing rather than synergistic effects; for partners in such relationships, interaction is a zero-sum game in which "I win or you win." The more intense the relationship, however, and the greater the depth that characterizes the interaction, the greater the rewards for each partner. For Maslow, the ego-transcending and synergistic effects of intimate union bring the partners farther along the path toward actualization.

The patchwork configuration can describe the various relationships in the life of an individual, the "whole" or combination of these relationships, and the deficits or gaps, i.e., the extent to which one's needs for intimacy are not being met. The patchwork of relationships could be seen as a mental picture of the *gestalt* of the various intimate relationships in which one shares— the manner in which each of these is related to each other and to the whole. An understanding or gestalt of one's intimate relationships necessarily includes a refined awareness of one's needs for intimacy and the ways in which these needs are being met. It also includes a cognizance of the meaning and value of each of one's relationships and an awareness of the totality of the present situation. An individual who has a mental grasp of his/her "intimate gestalt" is likely to be able to respond to needs for intimacy in a more enlightened manner than otherwise. Such an individual not only feels but also is in greater control of his/her own intimate destiny.

In concluding this section on patchwork intimacy, I wish to emphasize that this concept has been set out here not in an attempt to establish another "ideal," but rather as an attempt to realistically describe today's reality of variation in meeting needs for intimacy. If this concept proves useful in the search for intimacy of any individual, this growth will come only through an increased ability to analyze his/her intimate gestalt and, perhaps, in a greater comfort in designing an intimate environment. Rather than trying to approximate any of the arrangements discussed here, it is hoped that individuals will become the conscious designers of their own patchworks through self-awareness and sensitive planning. The following section presents certain practical aspects of the modern search for intimacy.

Planning for Intimate Relationships

Planning for intimacy is somewhat of a paradox because of what our society regards as a contradiction between *planning* (which implies a calculated, rational approach to decision making) and *intimacy* (which we like to think of as spontaneous, noncalculated behavior not particularly guided by rationality). There is a definite societal bias toward the spontaneous and noncalculated when it comes to intimacy. One example of this is the carefree approach to episodes of sexual intimacy in movies or in novels; such issues as contraception and commitment are not mentioned—heaven forbid—in favor of the "light 'n lively" approach to sexual love. If either of the partners is planning or even anticipating, it is the male; the female is to be interested but passive as a new relationship, a new sexual experience, or a new opportunity for growth is cast her way.

We cannot afford to stand by and let intimacy happen! In a world in which most of us have more than one intimate relationship and numerous opportunities for intellectual, physical, or emotional intimacy, the choice of one's intimate(s) is important. Because of the crucial function that intimacy plays in one's life and because of the difficulties that occur in its absence (Lowenthal & Haven, 1968; Maslow, 1971), it behooves each of us to get the most out of our intimate relationships. In the heterosexual context, females have tended to stand by and wait rather than act upon their needs and desires for intimate relationships and experiences; also, some males have claimed that they are "turned off" by an "aggressive" woman who takes initiative in developing relationships. There are certainly greater limitations placed upon females than upon males in the search for an intimate; still many males and females continue to follow the dictum of tradition rather than daring to act upon what they know in their hearts to be right. Both sexes obviously have a great deal to ponder in helping to set the stage for interaction between males and females that is not only spontaneous and honest but also fair. We must move beyond what Libby has called the "primrose path" of heterosexual relating if we are to experience equality of opportunity for males and females in the realm of intimate relationships.

Beginning a new relationship is difficult indeed. It is easier to continue in one's present situation than to begin anew, retracking old issues long-resolved in one's established relationships. Furthermore, one tends to expect new relationships to come quickly to depths once achieved or maintained in an earlier (or concurrent) relationship. However, the individual who uses initiative and assertiveness in the maintenance of his/her patchwork of intimates will receive greater satisfaction from these relationships. An intimate may, in the words of Dahms (1972, p. 90) serve as a "passive pawn" or an "active origin" of what he or she is to become. In my recent interviews, persons who felt their needs for intimacy were not being met described their feeling of standing with their face pressed against the window pane, desirous of the intimacy that others seemed to have. Females and males have much to gain from becoming actively involved in the search for intimacy. The conscious designing of intimate relationships is an idea in need of fruition!

The plurality of life-styles available today offers for many of us the potential for satisfying needs for intimacy. The means for meeting these needs are becoming freer and less stylized; today the challenge is for each person to work out as best s/he can the patchwork for meeting his or her needs for intimacy. Not everyone will come to experiment or to rest comfortably with these alternatives. Each individual must come to some joint decision(s) with his or her intimate(s) regarding the form that their own intimate relationship will take. Partners who plan on having a long-term relationship may decide whether to marry or to have the relationship take some other form. Intimates in a short-term relationship (e.g., one partner must leave town at the completion of a temporary job assignment) must also engage in joint planning if they are to satisfy the needs of each of them. Individuals who have an open relationship must communicate the plan with each other regarding how much disclosure there will be of sensual/sexual experiences with other partners, and each must then work out his or her arrangements with his/her other intimates as well.

For many persons the notion of multiple intimate relationships evokes concern regarding jealousy. How to deal intellectually and emotionally with the various intimate relationships in one's life and in the life of one's major intimate(s) can be a puzzling issue. Stone has observed that intimacy is essentially the sharing of an individual in the identity of the "other"; he or she "feels with" the self of the partner and in acting takes into account this mutual reality rather than his or her individual or "single" one (personal communication, 1976). His view is consistent with the definition of intimacy presented in this article. One who is capable of sharing in the identity of an intimate may also share his/her "intimate gestalt"; the individual, in other words, is able to sense the value and the meaning of the other relationships in which the partner is involved. Furthermore, as the partner grows in these various relationships, so does the individual him- or herself; such is the nature of synergy. Such, also, is the nature of loving and nonjealous sharing. Jealousy is out of place in an environment of empathetic and generally selfless sharing, with the possible exception of pangs of jealousy that appear during occasional trying times in the relationship or as a result of temporary personal difficulties of one of the partners.

In relationships that are highly intense on dimensions of openness and depth, intimate sharing may include mutual planning for the other relationships of each. In such relationships, the individual's major concern is that the partner receive proper and fair treatment in his/her various relationships and that each of these liaisons be growth-producing and not destructive. In some very intense relationships the partners approach a new or developing relationship of either of them with a perspective of "Let us talk about whether or not this other intimate relationship is going to be a good one for you (or me)." In other relationships that are deep but not especially open, each partner may encourage the involvement of the other in a patchwork of intimate relationships but not wish to know any more than is necessary about these relationships. Many of these individuals experience very little jealousy surrounding the other intimate involvements of the partner. Other couples are not able to achieve the depths of intimacy that would enable them to grow beyond jealousy; still others wish to confine the intimate expressions of each of them as much as possible to the relationship (see, for example, Cuber & Harroff's 1965 description of "total" marriages). While we usually think of jealousy as being confined to one's major intimate relationship(s), the theoretical model of a highly intense relationship that involves depths of loving and a rather persistent "feeling with" the other generally precludes jealousy. Perhaps, in reality, relationships that involve intense and persistent feelings of jealousy are those in which the partners have not reached sufficient depths in intimacy to grow beyond such concern with self; perhaps jealousy is a symptom of a lesser love.

Jealousy and possessiveness are sometimes confused with feelings of anger over the failure of an intimate to meet one's needs for intimacy. An absence which occurs when one is most in need of a major intimate may cause one to feel emotionally, physically, and/or intellectually stranded. One's partner may be involved in activities with his/her other intimates, or in work or other activities that prevent him/her from being physically and/or intimately available. In the course of an intimate relationship, there are times when the performance of one's partner does not approximate what the two have agreed upon or what one has grown to expect. When these incidents coincide with periods of stress or emotional need (for example, the lengthy absence of a spouse during an important series of exams or during a pregnancy), the feelings of abandonment and resentment can be dramatic. Such feelings may be experienced by partners in the closest of relationships or between persons who are no longer intimates; recently divorced and recently widowed individuals also occasionally experience such resentment or anger. There is a difference between the several types of jealousy described by Mazur (Chapter 23) and the feelings of resentment that have their origin in numerous experiences of "when I need this person most, s/he is not here." Intimate partners may certainly attempt through mutual openness and planning to avoid stranding their intimates, but sometimes, in spite of the best of planning, an individual finds herself or himself alone and without the much-needed comforts of an intimate environment.

To be genuinely acquainted with intimacy, we must know what it is to be without it! Each of us must come to grips with the existential fact of our aloneness if we are to be intimate. Fromm (1963) and Moustakas (1972) have asserted that the ability to be alone is a precondition to the ability to love. In other words, married or not, each of us is single to some extent. We are born single and we will die singly. Furthermore, as Erikson (1959) has maintained, it is only after an individual has achieved a sense of identity that he or she is ready to commit him- or herself to an intimate relationship.

Although few are fortunate enough to have the joys of intimacy throughout their lifetime, nearly all of the models are for *having* intimacy. There are *proscriptive* norms for sexual intimacy for singles and for the widowed, and persons smile knowingly or wink at the thought of the divorcee's needs for sexual intimacy. Also, for many persons the thought of intimacy (sexual or other) for the older person is somehow found to be disgusting or ridiculous. Advertising has helped to reinforce this nonsexual, nonintimate stereotype of the older person; according to numerous ads, only the youthful and youthful-appearing individual is eligible for intimacy. Normative limitations for developing intimate relationships have had a constraining influence on the search for intimacy for each of us; constraints, however, have been the greatest for females, the unmarried, and the aged. A considerable portion of the family literature has demonstrated this same myopic view of life-style: I am married—isn't everyone? Furthermore, the fact of one's being married and living in a family situation does not assure the satisfaction of one's needs for intimacy.

"Know thyself" may well be the first step for the aspiring intimate. By carefully analyzing one's needs, preferences, assets, and past experience in forming intimate dyads, one can come a long way in developing insight into his or her own search for intimacy. It would, however, be foolhardy to hold that one's needs for intimacy can always be met in a conscious or rational manner. Some element of the irrational is always there. In a series of recent interviews conducted by this author in a midwestern city among a random sample of approximately two hundred professionals and blue-collar workers from age twenty-two to seventy-three, respondents described the various short and long-term arrangements they had worked out for meeting their needs for intimacy and some of the frustrations and difficulties they experienced in the search for intimacy. One female interviewee revealed that every male she had gotten seriously involved with in the past three years had turned out to be a homosexual. She was eventually able to resolve this difficulty and to attract and relate to males who were not homosexual. A common example of the irrational in meeting needs for intimacy is the substitution of food for intimacy; dieters may be well aware of the meaning of their excessive eating but still unable to change their behavior. However, as Maslow (1968) has pointed out, the more insight one has into his/her behavior, the greater the potential for growth. Knowledge of self is a genuine asset for the aspiring intimate, whether s/he be young, old, or middle aged.

The choice of an intimate is an important one. If one is to grow in the various ways he or she considers desirable, s/he must choose as intimates persons with whom such growth is possible. Achieving "goodness of fit" with another person in an intimate relationship that is maximally growth-producing is a challenge that is not easily met! An individual who is in great need of an intimate, a "soul-mate" or "buffer-buddy" (Bach & Wyden, 1970), can rush into the first relationship that comes along, or can with deliberation take into account his or her own situation, needs, and options, and then attempt to make the best decision possible. A person who is aware of his or her needs for intimacy and who is sensitive to the needs of others is in an excellent position to develop or construct the kind of intimate relationships that he or she would like.

As most persons and certainly all experienced intimates are aware, some intimate relationships are more rewarding than others. Some "intimate" partners share an existence (or, hopefully, only a relationship) of mundane quality. Realistically, some relationships serve only as "filler" in the daily absence of a soul-mate or until some other better relationship comes along. Other intimate pairs enjoy the closest of sharing, the closest of mutual coexistence, that is possible between two persons: They are truly soul-mates and buffer-buddies and have the greatest appreciation for the union they have shared. Cuber and Harroff (1965) have described the intensity of mutual involvement of partners in "vital" and "total" marriages; their typology is appropriate not only with regard to marriage but to other intimate relationships as well.

The *total* relationship described by Cuber and Harroff (1965) is the equivalent of the most intense of relationships in the Biddle (1976) schema. *Vital* relationships exist between partners who share intense psychological closeness and who experience excitement in the mutuality of their sharing of most important life matters. The total relationship is similar to the vital one but is more multifaceted; in some cases all of the important life foci are shared. The partners find their central satisfaction in the life they live with and through each other; these total relationships approximate the monogamous ideal of forsaking all others. Cuber and Harroff have noted that there is virtually no infidelity in these total relationships; they have also pointed out that in some respects these relationships are more readily disrupted because the partners have become adjusted to such rich and intense sharing that a breach which would be considered quite normal in another relationship is regarded as almost unbearable between such total partners.

An aspiring intimate must be aware of the criteria that he or she requires of an intimate partner. One who is looking for an intimate with long-range possibilities will quite likely have different criteria than one who is more concerned about immediate possibilities. One who is very aware of and concerned about his or her own values may demand quite similar values in an intimate. A person who insists that his/her intimate relationships be growth-producing will be more cautious in the choice of an intimate than will others. Persons with social-worker tendencies (females are probably more "guilty" of this than males) often have trouble saying "no" at the outset or in the course of an intimate relationship and may find themselves becoming tramped upon by a horde of intimates or—more likely—exploiters. It goes without saying that an individual must use discretion in establishing intimate relationships for the short and long range, for his/her personal welfare and, yes, even for the sake of his/her reputation! Even the most gregarious individual must use some prudence in developing intimate relationships.

It is not easy to maintain a number of intimate relationships. In a series of recent interviews, both females and males described the "numbers racket" in which they sometimes have found themselves. One divorced male, age sixty-two, told me of his having been involved within the past year in "too many, too superficial" heterosexual relationships until he discovered that for him one highly intense, very intimate relationship was more rewarding. Wiseman (1975) has referred to this phenomenon as the "candy store phase" of developing intimate relationships; this phase of experimentation with a number of intimate relationships lacking in depth and commitment is not uncommon among recently divorced individuals. The maintenance of an intimate relationship takes time, energy, and money. Taking the time to know and to continue to know a number of intimate partners may be rewarding, or may place major constraints on an already busy schedule. From an exchange theory perspective, the rewards that accrue from any of the various intimate relationships that comprise one's patchwork are to be balanced not only against the costs (in time, energy, money, and so on) of maintaining that relationship, but also against the potential costs and rewards associated with one's alternatives.

As one contemplates the initiation of a new relationship, one might ask her- or himself the following questions: Will this relationship allow for the continued development of a sense of identity? How much compromise will be necessary as far as one's values, goals, and needs are concerned? Will the relationship allow for two to become one only when that *one* is the male—or, perhaps the female? Is the relationship to be handled in an open manner or in a clandestine way? If clandestine, can both partners maturely handle the arrangement? Whether the relationship promises long- or short-range opportunities for mutual intimacy, these concerns are valid and probably should be considered and discussed. While some may question the utility of such an approach, an experienced intimate will recognize the validity of these issues. *The world of alternate life-styles is no place for naive people!*

Other questions must be faced regarding the probable potential for *breadth*, *openness*, and *depth* in a new relationship. As far as *breadth* is concerned, what activities does one desire to share—emotional expression, study, writing or designing projects, travel, recreation? Is sex to be a part of the relationship? How available will this person be? How available do I want him or her to be? How much *openness* or mutual disclosure does one see as desirable in this relationship, and how much will be possible? Can the partners agree on the value they place upon confidentiality in an intimate relationship and on the degree of confidentiality that each can expect? Can there be trust between the partners? How much potential for *depth* does this individual appear to offer? How much commitment and genuine caring does one wish to give and to receive? These are some of the issues to be considered in planning for new relationships or in evaluating the merits of present relationships.

In spite of insightful planning for intimate relationships, intimacy doesn't always come when one needs it. Each of us has experienced times when there was no one there to help us meet our needs. As Davis (1973, p. 31) has stated, "It is an essential characteristic of *loneliness* that an individual is unable to pass the time by himself and has no intimate available to help him do so." Here is an excerpt from an interview with a twenty-seven-year-old female who has a fairly active patchwork of intimates:

Last night I was terribly lonely. . . . I would have liked very much to have been with someone. Not just anyone—for that is easy enough—although last night I didn't know where any of the friends that I normally rely on were. My closest, most intimate friend was out of town . . . and I knew that he would not be calling. It was a difficult period. I was very lonely, more lonely than I have been in a long while. Television, the radio—none of these things helped. I would have called someone, but right then there was no one to call. Finally about 10 o'clock I went to bed and tried to sleep. . . . I couldn't fall asleep all that easily; normally I am asleep in five minutes. I cried a few quiet whimpering tears, wanting to give expression to the alone-ness that I felt, and finally went to sleep.

Some creative persons who live alone and some who are periodically alone have learned to work out as best they can their needs for intimate contact. A person who is alone might well develop unique and personal "make-do" arrangements to get through lonely periods when intimacy with others is not possible.

The search for intimacy, when guided by planning that involves knowledge of self and of intimate processes, can bring one to new levels of experiencing the "self" and, ultimately, to new depths in intimacy. As Fromm (1963, p. 24) has reminded us, the search for intimacy stems from a basic and existential human need to fuse with another person in order to transcend the "prison of one's separateness." Both Fromm and Slater (1970), however, have called to our attention the fleeting nature of such transcendence. While one may experience such intimate escape, one cannot hold onto it; one can never "arrive" at intimacy. In the book *Loneliness and Love* (1972, p. 146), Moustakas has provided some perspective on this dual reality of intimacy and loneliness and the potential that inheres in each of them:

> The experience of love is the spark and energy of excitement and joy; it is what makes friendship a lifetime value and what makes activity purposeful. . . . The lonely experience gives a person back to himself, affirms his identity, and enables him to take steps toward new life. . . . A balance is essential. Exaggeration of either loneliness or love leads to self-denial and despair. Love has no meaning without loneliness; loneliness becomes real only as a response to love.

The Pursuit of Intimacy

As I mentioned earlier in this article, intimacy is an issue of great concern to citizens of our time. The steady popularity of "intimate" themes in the various media, the "pop intimacy" of encounter groups, and, for some, the restless moving in and out of "alternate" life-styles and marriages suggest the need of modern individuals for encounter, for understanding, for self-discovery, and for intimate union. The stresses of modern living—those that bring ulcers, heart attacks, and suicides—are thought to be soluble in the medium of the intimate experience. For many individuals, intimacy has become the new religion.

The age-old attempt of human beings to resolve the separateness of individual existence has for many modern individuals become the frantic *pursuit* of intimacy. Millions of desperate individuals are "pursuing" intimacy in ways that bring rewards that are certainly less than optimal. There are, of course, the sordid aspects of the search for intimacy: Prostitution, rape, and other manifestations of this type exist today and perhaps always will. Beyond this negative aspect, however, is the more common situation of the pursuit of an *ersatz intimacy* that provides few rewards and little or none of the growth potential that genuine intimacy offers to individuals. Many persons have sought this ersatz or false intimacy in alcohol or in drugs. Many others have resorted to "intimacy surrogates" or nonhuman substitutes for interpersonal closeness; the adult who must always have a radio or television playing when s/he is alone and the teen who keeps a blaring transistor radio strapped to his/her belt are examples of the modern dependence upon intimacy surrogates. Other contemporary individuals find ersatz intimacy in "scavenger" forms of pursuit. The person who frequently visits the prostitute, the male or female who derives all or nearly all of his/her interpersonal closeness from "pick-ups" or "one-night-stands," and the "social leech" who attempts to derive intimacy from others while giving little in return are examples of this not-infrequent phenomenon.

Many of the difficulties experienced by modern individuals in the search for intimacy are the result of larger structural conditions (Fromm, 1963). Certain values underlying our capitalistic social system and certain practices such as product advertising have affected the modern search for intimacy. Furthermore, as psychologist Donald Campbell (1975) has called to our attention, our standards and expectations for rewards from intimacy have been rising. Also, as Davis (1973) has maintained, in the modern age we tend to expect that all of our individual and social problems can be solved; we tend to think that our needs for intimacy can be resolved in much the same manner as our technological needs can.

In Continuous Pursuit . . .

As the various articles in this book attest, one of the issues surrounding the contemporary pursuit of intimacy is what form or forms this search should take. If indeed certain forms of life-styles are confining, if indeed certain forms restrict individual possibilities for growth, the issue of intimate life-styles should be considered carefully. It is particularly important to have a broader historical perspective on the forms that the search for intimacy takes today. As we attempt to deal with issues and make choices in our own lives, we will do well to recognize that both old and new forms are with us today—and generations to come will be continuing the search for intimacy in their own fashionable way.

Another issue is the ethical one. I find it extremely disconcerting that many modern writers on alternate life-styles have raised other issues regarding these life-styles but have failed to raise perhaps larger questions such as the *why* of alternate life-styles—which would seem to be the need for intimacy—and other issues regarding the ethical concerns surrounding these or any other intimate life-styles.

An ethic for intimates must be given more attention as individuals attempt to meet their needs for intimacy in nontraditional and individualistic ways. With the exception of issues of fidelity, most writers have been remarkably silent regarding the ethical responsibilities of intimates; furthermore, discussions of fidelity have focused almost completely upon fidelity with regard to one's spouse. While some legal responsibilities to a contractual partner are obvious, one's less obvious responsibilities to his or her "other" in consensual and other nontraditional arrangements also merit consideration. For example, the casual attitude taken by many modern intimates toward disclosure of information "gleaned" within their intimate relationships is alarming. Such issues are ethical ones, and perhaps too few of us are aware of the issues. The recent "Humanist Statement" entitled "A New Bill of Sexual Rights and Responsibilities" (Kirkendall et al., 1976) is certainly a step in the right direction. Perhaps what is needed is a new bill of *intimate* rights and responsibilities.

Still another issue to consider is that, for many modern individuals, the *pursuit* of intimacy amounts to little more than an attempt to resolve personality problems of dependency. Unfortunately, for many of us the need to "have someone to call our own" represents a very basic problem of needing to depend upon and cling to another person. The individual who comes to an intimate relationship with the need to "find" him- or herself in another person has very little to offer or to gain in the relationship. Once again, we must realize that the ability to be alone is one of the most important characteristics in a potential intimate. As Fromm (1968, p. 94) has stated, "If I am attached to another person because I cannot stand on my own feet, he or she may be a lifesaver, but the relationship is not one of love."

Mature intimate relationships are not the proper home for dependent people! On the other hand, one of the first steps in the development of the ability to be intimate is the realization that none of us is independent. We must be able to be alone, and yet none of us can survive very well in isolation.

It is, then, in our *interdependence* as human beings that the greatest rewards and the greatest potential for individual development are to be found. The realization of our basic *inter*dependence is one of the basic insights that comes with maturity. The individual who has made great progress in learning to be alone and in learning to be intimate is a person to be admired. Of all of our personal and nonbiological human needs, it would seem that the need for intimacy and the complementary need for self-hood and autonomy comprise our most basic and most unheralded of needs. The need to be alone and the ability to be intimate are two challenges facing modern individuals and modern societies. Each person must have satisfying experiences with each if s/he is to realize his/her potential as a human being. Vive intimacy! Vive autonomy as well!

Reference Notes

1. The phrase "opposite sex" connotes a situation of diametrically different conditions or traits, which is not generally the case between the sexes. The blending of "masculine" and "feminine" traits in both males and females is well documented; hence, the term *other* is used throughout this article.

19.
Youth Views Marriage: Awareness of Present and Future Potentials in Relationships

Robert N. Whitehurst

This article presents results of a survey of university student attitudes toward marriage. Three hundred first-year college students were asked about weaknesses in the marriages of their parents' generation and about aspirations for their own male-female relationships. Respondents to the survey, all students in social science classes in a southern Ontario university, are probably not much different from the average college student across North America. They expressed an interest in a variety of life-styles and the hope to construct adult relationships that would avoid some of the pitfalls observed in marriages of the preceding generation.

In many ways student concerns were not as radical as they were innovative. Students recognized that love may not last, that one can love more than one person, and that we are living in an age where openness is becoming the norm. It is not clear how these changed attitudes toward alternative life-styles will actually shape life-styles of the respondents. The author concludes that the radicalism of the Seventies and economic change are among factors that will shape life-style choices and suggests that a mix of life-styles —alternatives that borrow from the old and add the new—may be the outcome.

This chapter explores attitudes of university students toward marriages of their parents' generation as contrasted with their own marital expectations. The thesis is threefold: There are some changes in the offing, these may be of importance, and it is useful to discover how college students feel about such matters. The data from three hundred introductory social science students allow some exploratory-nonrandom hypotheses to be drawn about the possibilities for changes in the near future.[1] Although it is likely that no sweeping or revolutionary changes will soon occur, changes that do evolve will probably have an impact on many marriages, and more people may be making changes in the older monolithic, conventional system of marriage.

In general the survey findings are consistent with other information about changes in youth attitudes toward established ways of doing things. They suggest that there will be less emphasis on institutionalized styles of life, more on personal and existential meanings, and less blatant materialism, all accompanied by somewhat changing economic outlooks and concerns about the future (Whitehurst & Plant, 1971, pp. 1-8). The paragraphs below, a discussion of what is wrong with parental (i.e., the previous generation's) marriages—as seen by youth—will be followed by some themes and patterns which appear as alternatives to the problems prevalent in marriages of the previous generation. Before summarizing, some of the discriminating variables in the student sample will be discussed in terms of factors relevant to understanding marital change.

What Is Wrong with Parental Marriages?

Of the three hundred respondents to the survey questionnaire nearly 84 percent gave some kind of answer to the two open-ended questions at the end of the structured portion. The first asked students to describe what is wrong with marriages in the generation of their parents. Three dominant themes recurred: Nothing is wrong (22 percent of those answering); marriage is too materialistic; and there is too little communication. About 12 percent complained that marriage was too tradition-bound, 7 percent said it was dull, and fewer said there was too little freedom, females were subordinated, and people who married had too little in common.

It is fairly obvious that these middle-class students did feel negatively toward some things in marriages in their parents' generation. Just as obviously, many felt that "nothing" was wrong. We might interpret their answers to mean that very large numbers of people have no plans (at least in their first college year) to depart from the model provided by the preceding generation. This is indeed the only explanation consistent with other findings on this topic. Despite all we hear about pot and free sex on college campuses, most youth are still essentially conventional. This does not mean that they are "pure" in the sense of the Protestant ethic, but that they are following the role models of their predecessors. They are continuing the double standard and preparing for conventional family roles, including "normal" extramarital ventures, in spite of increased strength of norms on campuses about honesty, growth, and openness in sexual and other relations. This author's tentative conclusion is that marriage will not change for most people. Even when considering minor variations on current themes fostered by new technology, *slightly* better sex education for the next generation, and perhaps more sexual freedom for a *few* more, there is little promise of much that is really new.

But what about those who did find real faults in their parents' system of marriage? We can only speculate about the effects on their lives of heavy resistance to parental materialism. One result (when coupled with increased leisure) could be a future of increased involvement in home rituals with more craft items produced and fewer items purchased. Perhaps life in general could be enriched and simplified, while family life becomes more meaningful. Such a satisfactory outcome may be too much to expect, though, as most fathers and husbands seem to use increased leisure time for sports, male pastimes, or deeper involvement in their jobs. A generation of new-style, involved-at-home fathers is not yet in the offing. A functionalist view of the sentiments expressed by the antimaterialists in our sample might suggest that this norm may facilitate adjustment to the future. If the world becomes a place in which less productive work per person is adaptive, then the new sentiment may well become a universal norm, rather than a passing fad of university students. It remains to be seen, however, whether the strong antimaterialist sentiments supported by youthful peers may not be altered when the practical exigencies of married life occur. In this day-to-day coping they may find that they need other definitions of reality.

As for problems of communication in marriage, just calling for more communication between the partners is somewhat similar to the old saw about education being the answer to nearly all social problems. In one sense it is correct to see communication as the key to better relationships, but merely emphasizing the importance of "communicating" is a simpleminded approach. Few of us question the functionality of noncommunication in marriage. If values in a relationship are very dissonant, communication can only make things worse unless there is some realistic basis for resolution of newly opened areas (or reopening already touchy sore spots). A little communication can be a good thing, but expecting it to serve as the nexus of marriage problem-solution is naive. Lack of communication can be seen as a solution or as a problem. An example might include the wife who becomes intrigued with joining a women's liberation group. If she has an average husband (even one whose lip-service loyalty is on her side), she is much more likely to get flak than her husband's understanding if she tries to communicate each detail of her newly emerging consciousness and anger to him. However, if the conflict persists long enough (assuming both partners are no more neurotic than average), they may ultimately "get it together" as a couple. There is of course little chance of their really succeeding because often problems are walled off. Situations may be circumscribed by silent contracts to not discuss the thorny issues because everyone knows there will be conflict. There are extremely few couples who can resolve their own differences, in spite of books to the contrary.[2] The pair who really want to "get it together" and seek outside help and find someone competent to give them realistic assistance is also a rarity. But while really adequately communicating pairs in this society are scarce, this does not change the social fact that people see lack of communication as a problem and wish it would not be so in their own marriages. Wishing does not make it so, and in this structuralists' view it cannot become so without basic restructuring of the socialization experiences of both men and women.

If male-female relationships are to improve notably, means will have to be found to help men deal with their fears of women in more openly threat-free, communicative ways. Only the barest beginnings have been made in this direction, and the presumed improvement is slight in impact for most males. Most males do not like to admit they are emotional cowards. The following survey results show the disparity of views held by the sexes concerning the present low levels of communication.

Females in the sample were about two times more likely than males to cite marital communication as a problem in the older generation. In the same ratio, women were more likely than men to consider marriage as dull and were three times more likely to register the feeling that marriage was unfair because it subordinated women. It should also be noted that no men in the sample wanted to strive for greater equality in their marriages. Of those who said marriage was not for them, the respondents were more likely to be females than males (39 percent male, 62 percent female). Whether these are rumblings stirred by liberationist sentiments or whether these same differences would be revealed if there were no women's liberation movement is hard to say. We do know that women have always registered different feelings and expectations about marriage, but the complaints may be relatively new.

Consistent with other information on conventionality, social controls, and marriage, none of the respondents who were from ethnic backgrounds (self-identified) or considered themselves as "very religious" said that females were subordinated by men in marriage.

Although responses from the strongly religious and ethnics were predictably very conventional, about 12 percent of those finding things wrong with marriages of their parents' generation claimed they were too tradition-bound. Without further probing it is difficult to interpret just what they meant by this. A general feeling is that older marriages tend to get in a rut and become just too predictable. Let us turn to an evaluation of what youth hope to change in their own marriages to correct the problems they see in older marriages—that is, how they hope to capture the intimacy and romance they believe should exist.

Making a Good Marriage

Of those answering the open-ended item dealing with things to do to make their own lives or marriages better and to avoid the pitfalls seen in older marriages, an overwhelming majority (73 percent) claimed they would stay single longer. The missing empirical referent here is a specific definition of what constitutes "longer." A general impression suggests that most people feel it would be better to wait until they are twenty-five or thirty years old before they marry. One possible interpretation of this datum is that since (if) sex of the premarital variety seems no longer to be a large hangup, people will not become propelled as often into hasty sex-driven marriage relationships. With the instant impact of the morning-after pill to negate any potential pregnancy, and greater availability of abortion, there is a likelihood of far fewer "shotgun" weddings. All this supports change; whether the responses in this sample are already reflecting some of these changes or not is as yet unknowable.

There is also a factor which may need some explaining in terms of the frequency of registering sentiments as to how to make one's marriage better. After the above-mentioned 73 percent of those responding to "stay single longer," the next categories had no more than 7 percent of respondents making any further suggestions. Among the most important of these recurring themes (7 percent each) were the expressed desire to live for the day (not to worry about the future), to work out more open marriages, and to engage in better family planning. Existential themes stressing spontaneous decisions, spur of the moment arrangements, and keeping an open mind were all mentioned. This is no doubt a reaction to youth's feeling that their elders live in an overstructured, rigid, overcontrolled, and overpredictable world. The "hang-loose" ethic has made its mark on most phases of the youth culture, although there are limits to its application. Again, it may be that life in the university atmosphere more easily lends itself to this kind of life-style. If a student misses classes for a day, the consequences are not equivalent to those faced by a father with a mortgage and outstanding bills who misses a day's work. The hang-loose approach may be a response to a world held to be non-manipulatable, ready to be snuffed out at any time by wars, bombs, or pollution—if not by death from automobiles or violence in other forms. Insofar as these threats are seen as real, the adaptation is relevant. However, carrying the hang-loose ethic into all aspects of life from college on undoubtedly will have interesting corollaries both for the individual and for our society's future.

A minority of those surveyed appear to be affected by talk of open marriages and to actively feel that they should be working toward making this a more viable choice. Of those seeing more open marriages as desirable, women were four times as likely to support this goal as men. This lends some small support to the thesis developed by Jessie Bernard in her recent work on marriage and women.[3] Women were also about three times as likely as men to claim they would solve their future marital problems by more careful mate selection. There were again striking variations in the frequency of awareness of certain problems and solutions between the sexes. "Better family planning" may mean little more than avoiding premarital pregnancy and/or too-early pregnancy and having fewer children than most families that serve as current role models.

Marriage Attitudes

A series of questions tapped feelings about current topics and some changes occurring in marriage and sexual relationships. The data are at times unclear and apparently contradictory in places. They need further clarification in future research. The following items were scaled on Likert-type scales and will be discussed here as percentages either agreeing (two categories of choices) or disagreeing (two categories—strongly disagree or disagree).

Twelve percent of the total sample agreed that monogamy is dying. This percentage appears to include an unknown number who regret its presumed impending death, as well as those who are happy about it. Of those who agree, twice as many singles responded this way as marrieds. Possibly the most striking single piece of information about which there was consensus was the item dealing with the notion that a good marriage is possible to develop. An overwhelming 96 percent of the respondents felt that they were capable of doing it. Perhaps this should not be surprising in a culture that provides so few alternatives for the expression of adult identity outside of marriage. It might be the ultimate personal affront to be forced to recognize that one is not really capable of having a successful marriage. The possibility of a successful marriage is nearly universally accepted as an idea—that is, all the respondents felt *they* could do it; it is interesting that prior data tended to emphasize sentiments that quite often people married who were not personally mature or otherwise not ready for it (Whitehurst & Plant, 1971, pp. 1-8). Few of our respondents seemed to regard themselves as incapable of contracting a good marriage.

Of the total, 18 percent said they would seriously consider a group living situation for themselves, although there were more singles than marrieds who were positive toward group living. That 13 percent of the marrieds said they would live in a group setting might be seen as a larger than expected proportion.

In a similar 1973 survey, White and Wells found that 43 percent of their sample expressed some interest in communal living (54 percent of the males, 33 percent of the females). Their sample was geographically different (more rural) and their question was posed differently than in the current study. However, they found an unexpectedly high proportion of their sample expressing interest in alternatives or expressing a desire to organize their lives quite differently than their parents. White and Wells also noted that there were significant differences in the rates of expressed interest in various life-styles by sex (for example, males were more interested in complex multiple relationships than females, while females were more interested in homosexual marriage). The same authors also found an unexpectedly large range of acceptance of life-styles at variance with standard monogamy, even if practiced by their family members (White & Wells, 1973, pp. 280-95).

Returning to the present study, a striking 58 percent agreed that it is possible to love (including sexually) more than one person at a time. Maybe not surprisingly, more marrieds than singles subscribed to this belief. If beliefs are increasingly followed by consistent actions, we can predict a continued trend toward more extramarital involvements in the near future. To try to make this datum consistent with some other, more conventional, attitudes, it may be necessary to note that pure motives, attitudes, and feelings are indeed rare and that people do hold beliefs tentatively that are not consistent with each other. It is fairly clear that stronger pressures to adapt new thinking about monogamy are afoot. Having agreed with the premise does not mean that all these people will have affairs, group marriages, or multiple sexual contacts. Holding the belief does, however, materially enhance the possibility of further considering the behavior for themselves—given the relatively free social context of a pluralistic society. As the end of the 20th century draws ever nearer, it appears that the certainties of life once experienced by North Americans no longer operate at the same level of surety.

One of the consequences of this decreased certainty in life may be increasing ease of relativization of those things once called "sin." Over the last couple of decades there has been an ever growing frankness among people from all spheres to admit the ease with which they do things they once categorized as wrong, sinful, or evil. This changed attitude toward sin can be seen in part as a response to adult realities; we learn to work the system and avoid compulsive conforming habits when they have little or no relevance in the bureaucracies which rule our lives. It is also in part a growing sense of disease within a system which is being redefined as less morally right and therefore less morally relevant. Sexual interaction has not escaped the notice of those involved in this onsweep of moral relativizing.

Conclusions

This sample of university students provides several indications of change affecting potential man-woman relationships, in and out of marriage. In rank order of most to least frequently occurring responses, these items and their evaluations follow: A large majority of the sample (96 percent) felt that they were capable of contracting a good marriage, even though some of them claimed they did not intend to do so. Nearly 60 percent of the sample claimed they were capable of loving (including sexually) more than one person at a time. The meaning and interpretation of this is a bit unclear. The proportion is much higher than expected, especially in the conservative area of the survey where many ethnics and Roman Catholics reside. It may be no more than a momentary consensus when campus life is making its normative mood felt; it may, however, be much deeper and longer lasting than that. If so, this kind of normative change will be felt in succeeding behavior of large numbers of people in their own marriages. Over half of those in the sample claimed they would follow marital and sexual life-styles at variance from their parents'. The range of perceived potential here runs all the way from developing anti-materialist attitudes to entering into group marriages and communal life-styles. It is clear at any rate that there is awareness of some *need to change*, but how much, how fast, and the implications of the directions of change are not too clear.

Of the total sample, 19 percent said they would be willing to try group living arrangements. This proportion is higher than expected, and may in part be attributed to a local tendency for males and females to structure off-campus co-op housing. This is no doubt already an advanced social-sexual arrangement on many campuses and will grow in the near future. The popularity of single-sex dormitory housing is declining. Campus norms tend to downgrade those who persist with traditional housing arrangements. Whether this means more sexual activity among university youth is also unclear.

Among the discriminating variables associated with divergent views of marriage or of monogamy and its future, ethnicity and religiosity together are still probably the most powerful predictors of conventionality. A very small minority of those who considered themselves as religious or ethnically identified or both, held attitudes favorable to group living, multiple love partners, or other alternatives to monogamy. Religion or ethnicity may provide positive emotional support for good marriages in some cases, and it is clear that insofar as these forces operate forcefully and with real threat of negative sanctions, they will continue in their effect. If changes in identification with ethnicity and religion continue, as most of the literature suggests, there will be fewer people willing to settle for the confining life-style of conventional monogamous marriage.

The most important differentiating variable for this (as for most samples) was sex. Women have come to view their own hopes, destinies, and fears in recent years in much more clearly articulated ways so that their views have become more differentiated from the views of men. Their concerns are clearly indicated in the data: equality, openness of marriage, better planning of families, more careful mate selection, and maintaining adequate communication. Until and unless men and women come to share views as to what are problems and solutions, the disparity of these nonconverging worlds will continue to create hardships for both (Bernard, 1972, pp. 46-9).

One further comment is in order from the vantage point of sociology and social controls. Although the data herein may be construed to indicate very real changes on the part of some university people at a particular point in their life cycles, we do not know how much real effect these changes will have in the years ahead. Rather significant proportions indicated a willingness to try life-styles at variance with their elders', but we must not overlook the intrusion of real negative sanctions that tend to delay the pursuit of change. Although it is true that many young people find a positive sense of reward, pioneership, and camaraderie in the pursuit of new life-styles, these are by and large a hardy bunch who do not represent anything like the majority. Most of us will still find the threats of being shunned, ostracized, and in other ways threatened (mostly economically) too high a price to pay for engaging in a "deviant" life-style. Job and community security are just too important for most to risk by openly living in an alternative marriage pattern. Until we can open up the system to truly democratic and optional life-styles and remove the negative sanctions for living other than monogamous lives, we can expect only minor social changes. Most will still continue to opt for clandestine affairs. Even though the costs here may be high, they are not perceived as being as high as those exacted by an openly "deviant" alternative lifestyle. In this sense, as a culture we are continuing to foster a schizoid response in people. There is no way to eliminate sex outside of marriage in our open society. We can either face it squarely and seek answers that make sense to us now, or we can continue to act with duplicity, and carry on with the patterns that have helped create a world that is inhumane in its effects on so many people. If persistence of the system is what it is all about, let us no longer talk of people as important. If, in fact, people and their needs are important, let us proceed with the realignment of mores affecting the social and legal definition of marriage.

Reference Notes

1. The survey of a sample of three hundred first-year students in social science classes was conducted in a southern Ontario university, characterized by recent immigration; some students were marginals, many were educated in their pre-university training in separate schools (essentially Catholic). Thus the population is likely to be overrepresented by those with conservative parental backgrounds (which may be reacted to by many degrees of rejection or acceptance by university youth).
2. Several books of recent vintage which make marriage appear as a readily soluble problem would include: Nena and George O'Neill, *Open Marriage*, 1972; George R. Bach & Ronald M. Deutsch, *Pairing*, 1970; Julius Fast, *The Incompatibility of Men and Women*, 1972.
3. Jessie Bernard, *The Future of Marriage*, World Publishing Co., New York: 1972. Or see excerpts in Bernard, "Marriage, Hers and His" in *Ms.* magazine, Dec. 1972, pp. 46-9, 110-13.

20.
Hot and Cool Sex: Fidelity in Marriage

Robert T. Francoeur and Anna K. Francoeur

Borrowing the terms hot *and* cool *from Marshall McLuhan, Robert and Anna Francoeur look at the evolution of the social meanings of sex. They propose that a sensual wholeness of expression, typical of our tribal forebears, be described as* cool *sex, and that the contemporary style of sexuality, which is more genitally focused and highly specific in its definition and expectations, be termed* hot *sex. Cool sex is defined as involved, intimate, and embracing rather than exclusive, possessive, and jealous. The meanings of intimacy, fidelity, and comarital relationships are considered in the context of both hot and cool sexual relationships.*

The Francoeurs go on to examine the possibility of a retribalization of sensuality and the recapture of the cool sex experience. The authors hypothesize that hot sex is destructive, tending to minimize awareness of total selfhood and to imprison people in restrictive social roles. The Francoeurs advocate a more sensual and degenitalized cool sex approach to life as a means of becoming more fully human.

Four and a half million Americans get married each year. Roughly a hundred and fifty million Americans are married today.

Yet most professional observers and laymen will agree that the traditional American marriage is in serious trouble. Countless sociologists, psychologists, theologians, and other experts have focused our attention on some fairly obvious external factors, suggesting that economic shifts, contraception, women's liberation, and social mobility are the key factors in the changed state of marriage in our society. Undoubtedly such developments have been very influential, but the real problem, we are convinced, remains mostly unexplored. It rests in the shadows of human consciousness.

This basic issue, which we try to explore here, is *a radical shift in our understanding and appreciation of ourselves and others as sexual persons.* External factors have produced a tense, still unresolved revolution in consciousness, a great shift in our sexual images. Along with our basic understanding of femininity and masculinity, the revolution wreaks havoc with our traditional appreciation of intimacy, responsibility, and fidelity in our human relations. The eye of the storm is a *new* way in which sexual persons, men and women, relate to each other.

The difficulty we face in pinning down this shift in consciousness does not mean the shift is imaginary. Every married couple in this country lives the tensions between the traditional and new sexual images and relations. Each married couple gives unique flesh to this tension, though the basic nucleus remains the same in all marriages. These tensions seem to come closest to the surface in young people looking forward to marriage and in marriages in their seventh and twentieth years.

Regardless of age, regardless of educational background, regardless of social strata and condition, most Americans breathe an atmosphere which, however unrealistically, still conditions each of us to picture married life as being conducted along very specific lines with definite expectations. *The fact of being married automatically defines a person.* It confers a definite status and set of social obligations on both husband and wife.

Expanding life expectancies, social mobility, contraception, the separation of sexual intercourse from procreation, the recognition of female sexual responses and needs, and the education and emergence of women as persons in the mainstream of life are crucial *external* factors. But their real importance is the echo and response they create in the consciousness of individual men and women. We cannot zero in on the conflicting polarity of sexual images which today threaten to tear apart every marriage in this country unless we face the issues honestly and openly.

Sex and Communications

Marshall McLuhan, the much idolized and disputed analyst of communications, loves to wreak havoc with our traditional images by twisting words that were once assumed to have clear definitions into new shapes and meanings. His message is that communications media have become even more important than their content. A major revolution in communications media—the advent of electronics—signals an even more radical revolution in our culture and social attitudes.

In one of his earlier and more substantial works, *Understanding Media: The Extensions of Man*, McLuhan explains the difference between hot and cool communications media (McLuhan, 1964, p. 22).

A hot medium is one that extends one single sense in "high definition." High definition is the state of being well filled with data. A photograph is, visually, "high definition." A cartoon is "low definition," simply because very little visual information is provided.

The viewer is *excluded* from the photograph he looks at because the complete picture rules out any contribution or participation other than passive observation. The cartoon, on the other hand, invites participation. Its rough outline sketches provide a minimum of data and urge the viewer to fill in the image for himself. Printed books and lectures are hot media because they do not invite and encourage participation. A seminar is a cool media because it is based on involvement and participation. Television, for McLuhan, is the ultimate in cool media because it is so involving, as witnessed in the public reaction to the Kennedy funerals, or the first lunar landing.

Many critics have bristled at McLuhan's wrenched usage of simple words like *hot* and *cool*. Admittedly, this is a novel use of traditional words, provocative to some but confusing to others, especially people who love books and the clarity of the printed word. For book addicts and literate people *hot* invariably carries all the overtones of vital, stimulating, vigorous, and lively, while the traditional usage of *cool* leaves one with a picture that is passionless, uninspiring, dull, and lifeless.

In a brief but provoking article on "The Future of Sex" for *Look Magazine* in 1967 (Leonard, 1970), McLuhan and George B. Leonard suggested an even more controversial twist for our traditional terms hot and cool. They applied the adjectives to our sexual images and consciousness, speaking of hot and cool sex. Applied to our changing awareness of human sexuality and the retribalization of sexual and marital mores, hot and cool sex are virgin, untried, and undefined concepts.

One basic unmentioned problem is that when *McLuhan and Leonard speak of hot and cool communications, they are concerned with the media rather than with the content.* "The medium is the message." But when they move into sexual consciousness, most of their emphasis is on hot and cool consciousness—on content, rather than on media. As modes of communicating different sexual images, one can say that the well-defined images of Racquel Welch, Ursula Andress, or the *Playboy/Penthouse* centerfold are hot sex media while Twiggy, unisex fashions and hair styles are cool sex media because they lack definition and leave much to the imagination and speculation of the observer. But one can hardly speak of other equally concrete media of hot and cool sex. It is somewhat awkward and unuseful to say motels, drive-in theaters, affairs, and mistresses are hot sex while water beds, Woodstock festivals, and group marriages are cool sex.

Despite these limitations—and because we have not yet coined a more satisfactory label—we are not completely unhappy with the concept of hot sex. The same cannot be said for the term cool sex because of its traditionally negative connotations—really the opposite of what McLuhan and Leonard hint at in discussing the future of human sexuality. Despite all the explanations and descriptions one can offer, the term *cool sex* still carries with it far too many overtones of passionless, uninvolved, dull, lifeless relations between men and women. But until some inspired etymologist or linguist solves our label problem, we are left with the seminal concepts of hot and cool sex.

A decade ago, when McLuhan and Leonard first hinted at the contrast between hot and cool sexual perceptions, the concept struck us as very promising. But they have not developed the potential of this cultural perspective. Thus we would like to explore in some depth this imagery, and pursue its application to the conflicting images of male/female relations hidden in the miniature portraits we presented earlier. In other words, we would like to attempt a portrait of hot and cool sex attitudes, and then view this in the realities of two common forms of marriage today, closed and open marriages, where the meaning of intimacy, responsibility, and fidelity are set in sharp contrast. Finally we will explore a practical solution to the tension and conflict.

Hot Sex

The sexual consciousness of most Americans, and, in fact, of most Europeans today, is a fascinating and disturbingly adolescent complex.

Hot sex may be a bit caustic as a label for this consciousness, but you will likely agree that it is quite appropriate after we look at many obvious facets of our traditional sexual consciousness in an abstract composite portrait. This composite may appear distorted *if* you try to see *all* our details in the behavior of one person you know well, be he friend, enemy, spouse . . . or closer home. No one person could have all the traits we give here as characteristic of the hot sex mentality. By the same token of honesty, we should be able to recognize a variety of these traits in our own awareness as well as in the behavior of others we know.

Hot sex, like hot media, has a "high delineation." The blown-up Playmate or Pet of the Month, with her outsized breasts, buttocks, and genitals in full view, offers a vivid image of the ideal hot sex female.

Hot sex today has a circus of obsessions, a whole variety of anxieties flowing from the segregation of sex and its reduction to the genitals. Hot sex is the American fascination with what appears to be an unlimited variety of "perfect" sexual techniques, positions, and combinations, all of which must be experienced. Hot sex is the worried quest for mutual orgasm at all costs, the anxious frantic search for the "perfect" partner, or rather the perfect organ. Hot sex is casual in its impersonalism: In the dark, one partner is the same as another, and often the same even in the light of day.

When human sexuality is segmented from life and highly defined in terms of genitals, it naturally has to be scheduled, arranged, planned, both in time and place: the bedroom, night, the motel, a plotted pursued affair. In this atmosphere sex holds only an explosive, volatile, tenuous place in everyday life.

Hot sex is fucking or—more accurately, when you appreciate the Teutonic celebrational meaning of "fucking"—screwing in the most depersonalized sex-object way. In the curiously anonymous underground pornographic novels of Victorian England for instance, heroes and heroines parade their lusty adventures with no attention to the personalities involved—only an occasional mention of names, circumstances, or situations occurs but with an all-engrossing tyrannic monomania for the interlocking of genitals. Of course, such hot sex is male-dominated, guided by a double standard, and patriarchal. Playmates and pets must be totally submissive to the male whim.

In a hot sex culture there is also a figleafed obsession with nudity and with the naked female figure. Nudity, even in private or with one's spouse, is frowned on, for nudity exposes the "private parts" of the body and that means sex—genital sex.

Hot sex is entropic, self-destructive because it lives by possessing and conquering sex objects. But entropic also because of its vital pressures to perform: the destructive compulsion of the male to screw every chance he gets and the equal pressure on the female to satisfy the male ego with the blessing of a mutual orgasm.

Genital, hot sex becomes an end unto itself: sex for fun, for ego satisfaction, for ego building. In hot sex one can escape the unbearable burden of time and aging simply by multiplying experiences. A good scorecard, with ever mounting conquests, assures one of eternal youth.

Hot sex is the forbidden fruit, the thrill of cheating, the escape from the boredom and routine of everyday relations into the romantic wonderland of the affair. Even in the modern socially accepted infidelity, the swinger and spouseswapper reduce human sexuality to screwing. The swinger often evades real intimacy, real involvement. The swinger allows genital infidelity, provided one does not become "involved." The swinger does not solve his or her jealousy, which can accept a temporary safety valve swing while still viewing real intimacy as a threat and potential competition.

In a hot sex culture, marital fidelity becomes synonymous with genital exclusivity, and intimacy can only mean sexual intimacy. For a hot sex culture such as America has had for decades, every sexually mature single person is a threat. The unmarried, the widowed, the divorced—all are *obviously* sex-starved. Intimacy of any kind with them must be resolved as soon as possible by marriage. An affair must lead to a divorce and remarriage, so all single persons are a threat to married couples.

In a hot sex culture such as ours, *couples* exist—not individual, sexually mature persons who also happen to be married. Couples go everywhere together. It is often even unthinkable for a married person to go anywhere without his or her spouse, unless excused by business, housewife/motherly errands, or the safe bachelor's night out for poker, bowling, bridge, or Weight Watchers.

In a hot sex culture, a wife is a female you marry to take out of circulation so she can provide you with a family: A wife belongs to her husband, her identity is drawn from him. Hence monogamy—life-long, and sexually exclusive—must obviously be maintained as *the sole way of adult life,* and everyone must be urged or even compelled (subtly and not so subtly) to marry as soon as possible. The slightest thought of an alternative to traditional monogamy is taboo. In a hot sex culture, adult sex life is based on the premise of an inviolable monolithic monogamy.

Hot sex is dualistic, agnostic. It really despises—or at best tolerates—the body, and despite all its protestations to the contrary, ultimately enshrouds the body with countless taboos that restrict touching and body contact to only the most "innocent" type. As a result, hot sex is basically sterile, antiseptic, and antisensual. Like the fabled *Love Machine* and the *Valley of the Dolls,* hot sex is cut off from the whole person as well as isolated from nature and the cosmos. In place of the earthly cosmic myths of primitive cultures, the hot sex mentality can substitute only the frail treacherous lure of the great orgasm hunt, the Parsifalian quest of the perfect partner with the perfect organ and technique, the *Love Story* myth, and the belief that despite its segregation from life—in fact, because of this segregation—hot sex, genital sex, is *IT.*

In a few words, *hot sex is male-dominated, double-standard, intercourse-obsessed, and property-oriented.*

Cool Sex

Many of the common tensions surrounding sexual concepts can be traced to the inevitable conflicts our generations and culture must experience because we are in the process of transition. After centuries of gently brewing beneath the surface, a new consciousness of human sexuality is finally surfacing—not just among the young, but more vitally among those married couples in their thirties and forties.

Degenitalized in part, the relationship of man and woman can be validly expressed as a relationship of peers, between two evolving, developing, maturing, and unique sexual persons, between two unique, distinct persons. In this emerging cool sex tradition, men—and especially women—have to become conscious of themselves as individuals with a real existence outside their socially imposed stereotyped roles. Men and women must realize that in the Biblical tradition, creation is an ongoing process of becoming. In many respects, as Paul Klee put it, "Becoming is superior to being." Masculinity and femininity, in a cool sex culture, lack clear definition. They are fluid, constantly changing with each individual sexual person, constantly evolving and constantly being created not as eternal archetypes, but as process incarnations, each with a unique value.

Yet for most people, even today, and more so for men than for women, the delineation of sexual intercourse has remained the dominant obsession. Even when we accept physical expression of the relationship between a woman and a man which is not limited to genital intercourse, we find our hot sex obsession with intercourse creeping into the picture.

Yet the medieval and renaissance recognition of women as persons in their own right brought an acceptance of the possibility that a woman and a man can cross-fertilize something besides egg and sperm. The emergence of woman as a peer, particularly in the American patterns of courtship over the past hundred years, has made a major contribution to the transformation of hot sex. With petting and "making out" increasingly accepted by adolescents as a way of discovering sex images, relating, and communicating, the physical spotlight on sexual intercourse continued to diffuse into all phases of life to the point where some critics accuse youth of claiming they discovered sex. In some ways, they have indeed discovered sex. At least they seem to be revitalizing some very desirable aspects of tribal cool sex.

The result of this uneven transformation is today's volatile, bewildering amalgam of hot and cool sexual attitudes. It is the conflict we all experience as we face the impossible contradictions involved in our own personal combination of hot sex attitudes from our culture and the varying degrees of accommodation we have made with the emerging cool sex mentality of our emerging global tribe.

The consciousness of cool sex requires a certain strength of self-identity. Men and women must first of all be somewhat secure in their self-images, without relying on the blessing of society's stereotypes. In Maslow's language, they must be self-actualizing and not always turning to society or another person for approval, direction, and borrowed identity. Some real degree of psychological and emotional maturity—the ability to stand alone—is essential to a cool sex mentality.

Given the low definition of masculinity in cool sex, it is no longer possible for men to judge masculinity and identity in terms of multiple conquests and (male) progeny. Nor can a woman continue to sum up her identity as a person in the phrases "his wife" and "their mother," or in the number of times she has produced pattering feet for the nursery.

Cool sex means considering and accepting *for others and for oneself* the possibility of real alternatives to the traditional hot sex stereotypes of breadwinner, housewife, parent, married couple, fair white maiden (the sexless school teacher), dark lady (seduceable secretary), and double standards. Sexual persons in a cool sex society cannot be defined in terms of roles. Every individual, each man and woman, must be free to explore and express his or her personality, with as little role playing as possible and with a minimum of imperatives other than the basic rule of not exploiting others in any way, especially by using them as objects, sexual or otherwise.

Cool sexuality is expressed in integrated, holistic behavior that accepts the human body wholeheartedly and fully. It is not disturbed by nudity, or scandalized by "immodesty" as was Michal when David danced before the ark. Cool sexual consciousness celebrates the body in the tradition of Solomon's "Song of Songs." It is involved and intimate, and simultaneously inclusive and embracing rather than exclusive, possessive, and jealous. It takes into consideration all the needs and responsibilities of *all* the persons involved in or affected by a relationship. It removes the spotlight from genital intercourse and tends to integrate a whole range of bodily intimacies, touching, nudity, and sensuality along with intercourse into the total framework of daily living.

Human relations guided by a cool sex consciousness are synergistic, rather than entropic. Cool sex does not mean the end or lack of emotion, intense feeling, concern, or warmth. What it does mean is that relations are not taken in terms of possession or competition. A married couple will look upon their relationship in terms of (it is to be hoped) a lifelong commitment. But these pair-bonds will be set as primary relationships within the realistic context of today's life with its increasing mobility, life expectancies approaching a hundred years, contraceptives, and the liberation of women as persons in all areas of life. In a tribal culture, the nuclear family and exclusive couple in time become secure in their primary relationship and come to accept an openness and flexibility unheard of and unthinkable in a hot sex culture. This openness would accept intimate relations on all levels, including the sexual genital, within the orbit of the primary relationship. This flexible multilateral pluralism would be far more functional than the rigid couple pattern of past generations, but it would involve necessary risks. Comarital or, as we call them, *satellite relations*, are based on the premise that given the complexities of today's life, the varieties of educational backgrounds and personal expectations, we can no longer expect a spouse to totally and completely satisfy all one's needs. *The comarital or satellite relation becomes possible only when one is secure in one's own self-identity and in one's pair-bond relation, when one does not consider his or her partner property that cannot be shared without being lost.* The satellite relation is not the explosive affair, but a constructive complementary relation open to married and single persons, husbands and wives alike, in a context where relations are synergistic, reinforcing, and strengthening, rather than entropic and competitive.

This expansion of human relations to integrate new modes and expressions of intimacy within the couple marriage seems to recapture a consciousness that appeared in the earliest Biblical tradition but was quickly lost. The Jewish people had no word for sex, or for sexual intercourse, until they borrowed these fragmenting terms from the "more civilized" urban thinkers of Persia, Greece, and Rome. The authentic Biblical tradition speaks of the engaging, pleasuring, person-integrating relationship between a man and woman not as "making love" or as sexual (genital) intercourse, but as *yahda*, "knowing." This is no Victorian euphemism. It is indicative rather of a holistic approach to human relations uncommon in western consciousness and probably traceable to the tribal origins of Israel.

Few modern writers have been able to capture this cool sex consciousness. Many of them cannot even deal with the present tensions of ordinary people. Witness for instance the inability of John Updike, in both *Couples* and *Rabbit Redux,* to deal with questions of extramarital intimacies and relationships in anything but the totally negative threatened hot sex framework (see Clanton, Chapter 7).

Only in science fiction, or the utopian essay/novels of Robert Rimmer, does one see real success in depicting cool sex attitudes (see Rimmer, Chapter 24). One outstanding example is Robert Heinlein's haunting science-fiction novel *Stranger in a Strange Land.* Heinlein uses satire, humor, and fantasy to tell the story of Valentine Michael Smith, son of the first humans to land on Mars, who is raised and educated by Martians after his parents die. Valentine returns to Earth with a later expedition, only to be shocked by the hot sex mentality of earthlings. The Martian pattern of male/female relations is communal and multisensual, with no sharp cultural distinction between male and female roles. What earthlings call sexual intercourse and reduce to a matter of mere genital coupling, Valentine sees as "groking" or "growing closer," a kind of semierotic relating and interpersonal knowing in the original Biblical sense.

A similar verbal awareness is evident in most tribal cultures even today where a simple unsophisticated form of cool sex consciousness prevails. Most tribal cultures, for instance, have no word for illegitimacy, because all children are young persons in their own right and not the property of a particular set of parents. Often, too, because of the parity of men and women in tribal cultures, there is no word for adultery. Social taboos do limit sexual behavior for the good of the community, but not because the wife or daughter is the property of some male.

Cool sex, then, is egalitarian, single-standard, sensually diffused, and oriented towards intimacy and open relations with persons.

Marriage—Serial Monogamy

The question now is how the conflict and tensions of hot/cool sex are affecting marital patterns in our obviously changing society.

Two factors deserve comment. Our divorce and remarriage rate alone would demolish the myth that traditional lifelong sexually exclusive monogamy is the American way of marriage. If we are honest, we would have to admit that a more common American practice is serial monogamy, with a large segment of our population having two or more spouses in their lifetime. A second fact undercuts the sexually exclusive character of our traditional monogamy myth. Marriage experts today commonly estimate that 60 percent of the married men and over a third of America's married women engage in extramarital relations sometime during their married life. Morton Hunt, author of *The Affair* (Hunt, 1969, p. 289), is more sanguine: "Within another generation, based on present trends, four of five husbands and two of three wives whose marriages last more than several years will have at least a few extramarital involvements." Apparently, then, traditional monogamy has already yielded to serial monogamy and some sort of nonexclusive marriage.

We can go further in response, as we did in *Eve's New Rib* (R. Francoeur, 1972), and offer evidence that we are a very pluralistic society in our marital patterns. An exciting variety of male/female relationships has been gaining more open acceptance, or at least toleration, in our culture: single parents, trial marriages and premarital cohabitation, gay unions, triangle and multilateral marriages, group marriages, mate-exchanges (swinging) and a variety of communal situations. Marriage and male/female relations in America today have at least twenty basic styles, even though serial monogamy and nonexclusive couple marriages are more acceptable and prevalent.

Serial monogamy is the least radical deviation from the traditional American marriage. It changes only one factor—the lifelong character of marriage—and then the modification is more often in reluctant practice than in aspirations and expectations. Otherwise, serial monogamy is very traditional. In most cases it is strongly rooted in hot sex attitudes and expectations. This fact, we believe, is the reason why the lifelong character is untenable, and why a series of spouses becomes essential.

The image of marriage, both traditional and in its serial monogamy form, portrays the ideal, typical, average married couple as an inseparable romantic pair, drifting on the bright cloud of eternal youth and passing on at some imperceptible point to blissful old age as grandparents of a devoted clan. So perfectly matched is this couple that *they can expect to satisfy totally and completely all the varied complex needs and desires of their spouse.* All the high definition stereotypes of the traditional myth are maintained.

Few husbands and wives today accept the fact early in their marriages that they cannot possibly meet all their spouse's needs. Furthermore, most women in the beginning of their marriages do not consider their own needs. Why should they, for that matter? The culture women grow up in is male-dominated and guided. In the traditional myth women are taught from childhood to love, honor, and obey. Most women are conditioned to enter marriage fully convinced that they will be happy "serving" their husbands—though we seldom express it that bluntly.

In the exclusivity of hot sex and traditional marriage, two adults are expected to avoid all intimate relations with members of the opposite sex, even at the cost of considerable denial and isolation, since such relations could prove dangerous to the mythic character of the traditional marriage. The couple then is forced to live a symbiotic existence, an inseparable pair, together as much as possible, sharing everything. In this exclusive relationship the *expectation* is that two unique and individual persons will continue to grow on completely parallel tracks for fifty, sixty, or more years. To achieve this goal, the wife can of course, and often does, submerge her personal development in that of her husband and children. Even when parallel growth is attempted on an equal basis, the end result is frustration and divorce *if* the expectation is that the husband and wife can and must find all their needs met by their spouse.

Woven through this question of exclusivity is another inflammable expectation. The traditional myth, expressed in books like *The Sensuous Couple* (Chartham, 1971), argues that the sexual relationship must always retain the passion and romance of the courtship and honeymoon period. In every other area of human behavior, we accept average performances. Lovemaking, to the contrary, must always be an earth-shaking orgasmic high—every time! And when it is not, something is assumed to be wrong with the marriage. The instinct then is to look elsewhere. Result: an affair, guilt-ridden because it must inevitably mean the end of the existing marriage, divorce, and remarriage.

The nuclear problem in serial monogamy is that it remains based on the highly defined sex roles, status, expectations, and obligations of the hot sex mentality. It produces a common type of marriage: closed, inflexible, highly structured. Given our highly mobile society where cultures and subcultures are constantly mixing and influencing each other, the rigidity and high definition of the traditional marriage is impossible to maintain for long.

In the early years of marriage, most women today are still willing to play the traditional roles. Wives find joy in bolstering their husbands' egos, doting on them, scurrying about the kitchen and new home. In later years the role playing wears thin and the wife begins to rebel. "I'm a human being too. What about my ego, my growth as a human being, my fulfillment as an individual?" The male response is typical: "She's a ballbreaker, a nag, castrating me every chance she gets." And then, "Who needs that kind of marriage?" Divorce occurs and for the male a search for a new spouse—a sweet, very feminine woman. But is she really basically different—sweet, feminine, and docile? Or is she just a novice and willing to play the assigned role for a while?

The romantic honeymoon may last a year or two, and then the appearance of a child or two gives new focus to the relationship and distracts the couple from their changing relationship. The explosive periods for closed marriages come in two peak periods: when the last child is off to school and the wife is left home alone and when the children leave home for college or marriage and suddenly the couple is left face-to-face with nothing to say to each other because their whole world has been their offspring.

In *Future Shock* (1970), Alvin Toffler maintains that serial polygamy with several mates will be the dominant pattern of marriage in coming generations. We agree, reluctantly, because the average divorce and remarriage *does not come to grips with the basic problems of human relations* and our needs for intimacy and fidelity in a mobile society. It is a frustrating impossible search for a mythic ideal, for the high definition stereotyped roles and expectations of the traditional American marriage, and the hot sex mentality can exist only in the unreality of a never-never land.

Open Marriage—Flexible Monogamy

Our definition of flexible monogamy very much coincides with the description of "open marriage" offered by anthropologists George and Nena O'Neill in their best-seller *Open Marriage* (O'Neill & O'Neill, 1972). Our approaches were totally independent of each other, ours working from a biological/historical/technological starting point while the O'Neills worked from the areas of anthropology and sociology. Hence the correlation is most interesting.

In a composite description of open marriage we might begin by stating that an open marriage is an honest relationship between two people who accept each other as equals, friends, and partners. It is a nonmanipulative, nonexploitive relationship with equal freedom and identity for both partners. There is no need for dominance and submission on either side, no arbitrary one-sided restrictions or stifling jealous possessiveness. Neither partner is locked into a stereotyped role provided from the outside by society, relatives, or the local community. Domestic chores are shared, as are other obligations in the marriage according to real convenience and talent rather than according to some predetermined role, rule, or fifty-fifty agreement. Each partner has interests and friends which the other may or may not share. An open marriage therefore allows and encourages the partners to enrich their primary pair-bond relationship with a variety of relationships that complement and reinforce the marriage.

Open marriages are custom-made and highly individual. There is no single unchanging archetype, as there is for the closed marriage. And furthermore, each unique open marriage is made more unique because it is constantly growing and evolving. No couple can say they have an open marriage, because if they believe that, in complacent satisfaction the status quo of their relationship at that moment will be extended into an unchanging pattern that is only a modified form of closed marriage. At best a couple can say they are working towards an open marriage (see O'Neills' *Open Marriage* for a discussion of guidelines to achieve this goal, pp. 67-77).

Obviously much more can and should be said of the contrast between open and closed marriage patterns, but what we have said here indicates two critical concerns. One is to develop the means of evolving more easily into the social consciousness everything indicates we are headed for, a tribal culture with a cool sex mentality. The other is the more philosophical/theological question of the new meaning of fidelity, intimacy, and commitment.

Moving from Hot to Cool

Few Americans living today will ever be able to shuck off completely the hot sex atmosphere in which we were born. Yet, hopefully, more and more Americans will be able to face the problems of human relations today and accept the challenges of self-identity, maturity, and growth that inevitably accompany the tribalization of our culture on a global scale. The question then becomes clear. How can we learn to shift into the new patterns of thought, how can we learn to accept and live the new patterns of relating, when our culture is predominantly in the opposite stream?

Logically, the answer is obvious: *Create a transitional tribal environment to which men and women can retreat for short periods of time, where they can learn to relate in more human and intimate ways and gain self-identity.* Then they can hopefully return to our hot sex transitional society with a new perspective.

Currently there are a number of quite varied and differently motivated experiments in cool tribal sex which all seem to share one feature in common: In the vast majority of cases they are all blind groping experiments entered into by people who are often psychologically and emotionally unprepared for the demands of their new relations and unequipped in terms of guidelines from society or past experiments. This, fortunately, is changing as society comes to recognize and tolerate more openly alternate patterns of marriage. Communications networks are developing between different groups across the country.

Fidelity, Intimacy, and Commitment

Not far beneath the surface of diffused sensuality, open sexuality, and multilateral relationships of today is the very serious ethical and theological question posed by hot and cool sex concepts. What is the real nature of fidelity? What is the relation between marital fidelity and intimacy which is so linked with personal growth?

Is the type of fidelity and commitment treasured by a monogamous couple in our hot sex culture the same kind of fidelity and commitment shared by a primary pair bond couple with a tribal cool sex mentality? Obviously, from what we have seen so far, the answer is a resounding negative. Fidelity, according to hot sex, is crystal clear. It is exclusive and outlaws any participation or intimacy outside the marital union. Fidelity, according to cool sex, is open, inclusive, and invites participation.

Nearly two thousand years before Christ, Abraham was called by Yahweh to leave his kinsfolk and his father's house with faith that the Lord would show him a new land. This was Yahweh's covenant, that Abraham would become father of a host of nations and dwell in a promised land. Years later, when the aged patriarch was commanded by Yahweh to sacrifice his only son, his only hope of future descendants, Abraham again responded with absolute fidelity to the covenant.

Fidelity in the Biblical tradition is a very complex concept. It can be first seen as a major attribute of God: faithfulness or 'emet (Exodus 34:6). Its two Hebraic roots can be traced to āman which suggests solidity and sureness and to bātah, suggesting security and confidence. Greek roots which were later incorporated into the Biblical tradition are less certain since the Greek religion allowed practically no place for faith as such. Even so, the related Greek concepts are helpful, bringing in aspects of hope, confidence, loyalty, belief, truth, and reliability.

The fidelity of Yahweh ('emet) is frequently linked with his paternal concern and goodness (hesed, or in the Septuagent eleos). Yahweh's commitment to his chosen people required in turn fidelity from the people. Fidelity then involved the whole person, every aspect of life. It is commitment, loving concern, unconditioned loyalty. It should permeate all aspects of human life, beginning with one's commitment to the Supreme Being and flowing through the mutual relationships binding relatives (Genesis 47:29), friends (Samuel 20:8), and allies (Genesis 21:23).

How then did this broad humane concept of fidelity as "loving concern" become restricted to sexual exclusivity in the domain of marital fidelity? Cause and effect relations are difficult, if not impossible, to trace in the history of ideas and attitudes, but we feel that something can be said in favor of one specific Biblical influence. Central to the Jewish religion, and quite in contrast to most of their neighbors, was the belief in one supreme God and the rejection of all other gods. Very early in the old covenant, the patriarchs and prophets began using one common human experience as an example, an illustration of the relationship between Yahweh and his chosen people. To explain this divine covenant and especially the fidelity of Yahweh in spite of the infidelity of his chosen people, the patriarchs and prophets spoke often of the covenant between a husband and wife.

When the prophet Osee denounced the idolatrous Israelites of his day, he drew his imagery from his own personal experiences, his tragic marriage to the unfaithful Gomer. Despite all her perfidious affairs, Osee never failed to love Gomer and seek her return to the purity and tenderness of their early love. Marital infidelity then became a useful symbol and analogy of all forms of covenant infidelity, especially idolatry. Sometime later though this imagery was inverted, and the symbol became a reality in its own right wrapped in all the sinfulness of idolatry. Instead of concentrating on the fidelity and loving concern of Osee for the unfaithful Gomer as a good symbol of Yahweh's paternal concern for his unfaithful people, we somehow began to focus. all our attention on the infidelity of the chosen people and use the proscriptions against their idolatry to condemn extramarital activity.

Marriage has always had an economic basis in society. Economics is usually tightly woven into the fabric of marriage. In many simple societies marriage has been primarily an economic arrangement between two families or tribes. Love between two young people was seldom its justifying motive. In this context marital fidelity could hardly be defined in terms of selfless commitment and loving concern for the human development and fulfillment of another person. The primacy of economics in the marriage contract focused attention on the legal contract concerned with property exchange, community responsibilities, and production of progeny to continue the family line or inherit certain estates. Marriage consequently became a legal exchange of goods, the mutual exchange of the right to another's body for those acts conducive to procreation. Sexual intercourse became "the marital debt." A spontaneous person-involving act became something a wife put up with to keep her husband from sowing his seed in some other incubator—paying the marital debt. Ultimately the strength and validity of the marriage contract became totally dependent on the delivery of goods. A marriage ceremony in church was not sufficient to create an indissoluble union. Bodies had to be delivered and exchanged at least once to consummate the contract.

Sexual relations outside marriage also took on this aspect of property obsession, especially for the moralist and lawyer. Sexual intercourse for an unmarried woman was an injustice to her father or guardian who was deprived of the proper bride-price due a virgin. The unfaithful wife likewise did an injustice to her husband by depriving him of the certainty that the child she bore was his legitimate blood heir with legal right to inherit his property. For the unfaithful man there was the injustice of putting his hands on another man's exclusive property. Marital fidelity then became, in the neat definition of the Reverend Robert Capon, "what I did not do in Dubuque."

When economic considerations were primary in the marriage relationship, premarital and extramarital relations were seen and often condemned on the economic base of injustice. But they did not pose an emotional threat to the marriage. The economics of injustice could be worked out to the mutual satisfaction of the aggrieved male party and the male trespasser. But this situation began to change radically around the 1880s in western Europe and America. Like some menopausal offspring of the courtly love tradition, a new sentimental model for familial relationships was born. One prime component of this new image was the fantastic notion that one man and one woman should mate and henceforth be responsible for satisfying all of the other's significant *emotional* needs. Prior to this time the emotional relationship of husband and wife was not very important. It might develop, and often did. But whether or not it ever appeared in a marriage, the husband was under no social constraint to relate to his wife either as lover or as friend. Marriage in fact was often seen as the last place one would expect to find an emotional loving relationship. With the advent of the sentimental-romantic model for marriage, there arose a new definition of the proper relationship between husband and wife based on the necessity of an exclusive emotional union of two parties. From this time on the extramarital affair became a real threat to every ideal marriage. The economic injustices of premarital and extramarital relations can be eliminated with contraceptives and the disappearance of the family as a self-sustaining unit of society, but there remains the romantic-sentimental myth and model.

In Biblical times, with pestilence, war, famine, and a dreadful rate of infant and maternal deaths, the average human barely survived 22 years. By the Middle Ages the average European could look forward to a life expectancy of about 33 years. A century ago the average life span was inching up over the forty-year mark. In 1900 the average American had a life expectancy of 47 years. Today the average American woman can expect to live 74.6 years, and the average American male 67.1 years. These last two figures are, of course, below the life expectancy of middle- and upper-class Americans who have easy access to the benefits of modern medicine. Yet the United States ranks twenty-fourth among the nations of the world for average male life span and ninth for women. On the eastern shore of the Black Sea the peasants of Abkhasian and the Caucasian Mountains often live well beyond a hundred years.

These statistics are important because they highlight the fact that the lifelong sexually exclusive monogamous marriage evolved over a period of some two or three thousand years when the average life expectancy slowly climbed from twenty to forty years. We should also recall the frequency with which women died in childbirth, a fact which allowed most men to bury two or three wives in their lifetime and consequently be bound to sexual exclusivity with one particular woman for only a few years before death and remarriage brought a new woman on the scene. A concept of fidelity which allowed a double standard with some freedom for the male and chattel status for the woman thus posed little psychological or emotional opposition to the reduction of marital fidelity to sexual exclusivity.

Until recently most married couples judged the success of their marriage in terms of two hot sex components: (1) how faithfully does the husband meet the stereotyped role of the good breadwinner and the wife her stereotyped role as mother/housekeeper? and (2) are they both, at least the wife, sexually faithful? True, these criteria are losing their popularity and essentialness somewhat, but they still remain for many—perhaps even for most—the criteria of a good marriage.

Along with this distorted idea of what constitutes marital fidelity has come a very disastrous consequence: the inhumane restriction and limitations we must place on all interpersonal relations in a hot sex society where all single people, especially the young single girl and the "sex-starved" divorcee and widow, are viewed only as a threat to all happily married couples.

Sadly, our society with its hot sex consciousness dogmatically assumes that any and all personal relations between men and women, married or unmarried, at any age beyond puberty, will inevitably end up in bed if they get any deeper than the most superficial level. This assumption makes all personal relations highly dangerous, forbidden fruit, to be shunned even at the cost of cramping and drastically reducing our potential for growth as human persons. We grow by relating and sharing with others. Yet we try to maintain, at all costs, a society in which we relate intimately only with our spouse, and then as some sort of desexed androgynous pair with other equally desexed individuals, single and married.

Once on a New York television interview with two charming women, one in her mid-twenties and single, the other probably in her fifties and happily married, the older woman frankly admitted that whenever any female acquaintance indicates anything more than a superficial interest in her husband, they simply never see that person again. Jokingly, the younger woman asked if she kept some poison in her cupboard for emergencies. The implication is clear: Our concepts of fidelity and intimacy are horribly distorted on all levels.

In today's emerging tribal culture, conferred adulthood and sexual identity no longer work as usual. Initiation comes by experimentation, by learning, and by knowing personally. Youth must explore a variety of experiences and then choose their own adult and sexual identity. The American adolescent takes a vacation from life after puberty, withdrawing from the main stream into high school and college, where he or she can explore and experience, seeking to be faithful to himself.

Faithfulness, as Erik Erikson suggests, is essential to one's growth as an autonomous, independent, mature person. One must gain the strength to remain faithful to oneself, a power to define oneself from within and to remain constant to that self-definition whatever outside pressures one encounters, whether from the entrenched older adult establishment or from the tyrannical conformism of the peer group. One of the most devastating forms of the latter appears on college campuses when virginity for anyone over eighteen may be ridiculed as puritan frigidity or an unnatural hang-up.

One of the crucial factors in developing the virtue of fidelity is a growing competence and ability to integrate the personal and the sexual aspects of one's life. The whole practice of courting and "making out" can be very useful and function in this process. The American pattern of courtship helps young people develop their own sexual identity, their own sense of fidelity, by encouraging them to engage in limited, though progressively more intimate and involving relationships. In this process, adolescents can explore the meaning of fidelity. They may learn the meaning of mutual responsibility and sharing in growth-oriented relationships. They often learn what it means to be committed and to commit oneself. Group dating, couple dating, going steady, "pinning"—even the American engagement, which is more flexible and tentative than the European engagement—encourage an exploration of the meaning of fidelity by allowing young people to work their way through a variety of intimate relationships and commitments, pacing themselves and learning by mistakes as well as by good experiences.

In a very real sense then, the Biblical concept of sexual intercourse as *yahda*, knowing, today embraces the whole range of interpersonal relationships between sexual persons. Dating, courtship, making out, sexual intercourse, all are forms of knowing which require fidelity and demand a progressively more responsible sense of intimacy and mutual responsibility for each other's continued growth as sexual persons. Loving concern (*hesed*), a solid self-identity (*'emet*), and a confidence in one's ability to handle new levels of intimacy and commitment when the right time comes (*bātah*) are the three essential characteristics of a modern concept of fidelity in the Biblical tradition. Obviously, this concept of fidelity has much to say about the possibility of an intimate, even sexual relationship complementing and reinforcing the primary bond relationship of a married couple: the possibility of a co-marital or satellite relationship. It also has much to say about the "premarital" sexual experiences of young people. But its focus is on the *quality and intent* of the relationship, not on whether or not it goes beyond a certain black and white line, be this making out, French kissing, mutual orgasm by masturbation, or genital penetration.

Both fidelity and intimacy have *new meanings* in today's emerging tribal culture. This new meaning exists between a husband and wife, among married couples, between married and single persons, and among single persons, young and old.

Myths

A final closing word must be said about the mythic reality of both hot and cool sex. Both indeed exist, but both also do not exist. The hot sex traditional romantic marriage was an ideal, a myth which guided generations in their married lives. Equally so, now that we are rejecting and destroying this hot sex myth, we feel compelled to create a new myth, a new pattern, which we have called cool or tribal sex. But the cool sex consciousness we describe here is an unreal composite drawn from certain real elements in various tribal cultures of the past and present, the Marquesan Islanders, Samoans, Hindus, North American Indians, and others. Marshall McLuhan suggested once that we ride into the future looking into a rear view mirror—history. Just at the time modern technology and civilization are turning primitive cultures into fossils, modern man seems compelled to romanticize their sexual attitudes and consciousness, weaving them into a new mythic pattern for the future. It can present a new danger if we merely substitute for what we have had, the glorification of a nonexistent synthesis of cool sex distilled from a variety of tribal cultures, and turn this into a mythic symbol of new patterns of relating in and around the husband/wife/family constellation.

21.
Changing Ground Rules and Emergent Life-Styles

Robert N. Whitehurst

Sexually open life-styles have enjoyed varying popularity over the years; however, their current status is problematic. Questions concerning their description, understanding, and legitimacy persist. In this article Whitehurst uses what he calls the "fallout" model to explore the conditions which prompt one to enter any form of intimate relationship.

Whitehurst identifies a range of probable alternative life-styles relating to intimacy. He concludes that much about intimacy (marriage and its budding alternatives) can be understood in terms of the way in which individuals balance their feelings of security and autonomy needs. He includes modified open marriage, postmarital singlehood, and extended intimate networks among the most likely alternatives. He also considers swinging, communes, triads, and group marriage. Whitehurst also examines changing ground rules in emerging life-styles. Here he focuses on attitudes toward love, sex, jealousy, privacy, and children.

This article is an attempt to evaluate some of the changes now occurring in relationships which involve the problems and joys of intimacy. Our concern will be to develop some ideas about what male-female relationships will be like in the future based on the observation of general indicators of survey data. We shall use the fallout model as a way of examining variables which affect choice of life-styles.

Conclusions presented here are speculative, but they represent an inductive effort to make some tentative predictions of change on the basis of limited knowledge. All futurists must do the same. So, without further apology, but remembering the tentativeness of it all, let us look at what is happening now.

My approach to emergent life-styles in this paper is based on the notion that instability, change, and conflicts are enduring aspects of social life. Let us start with the fallout model and conceptualize what may happen to relationships as people seek continued solutions to their personal, identity, and intimacy needs—especially needs not fulfilled in the conventional arenas of marriage and family.

The Fallout Model

The fallout model is a means of examining how alternative life-style choices occur in the process of fallout or "leakage" from social controls that keep most people tracked into conventional marriages. Before we use this model in our prediction of trends let us look at some underlying assumptions. The first assumption may become altered in the future and thus cast suspicion or absolute error into the forecast: I will assume that basic economic and political stability will support the development of trends of the recent past. Having enough money, leisure, and freedom to vary one's life-style seems to be a necessary precondition of exploring alternatives. Although these preconditions have varied greatly in the past ten years, there is at least minimal stability in both economic and political systems, and barring major ecological, political, and economic upheavals, the way is smoothed for further life-style explorations.

Another assumption involves early socialization. People learn to accept the conventional typical monogamous marriage and family in early socialization. Only a minority will defy conventional mores and enter into nonmonogamous relationships or collective arrangements. Thus the first tentative conclusion is that alternatives *are* not and most likely *will not* be for the masses. But this brings me to the beginning of the model and the hypothesis that grows out of it.

Most people are reared conventionally, believing that marriage involves only two people monogamously tied for life to their own or adopted children. However, an increased amount of fallout occurs in this system of conventional thought as people get divorces or become disillusioned with the promise of monogamy, and for other reasons not considered here. There is a fairly large market for alternative life-styles today—a market fed by a number of factors. Along with the assumption that a fairly liberal political and economic climate must exist in order for alternatives to flourish, certain other assumptions must also be considered. These can act as facilitating or intervening variables.

Divorce rates, for example, are influenced by social-structural variables and thus fluctuate widely. Whether people divorce when their marriages are not positive and productive depends on social variables as well as psychological ones—such as the partners' feelings of personal security, sense of self, and autonomy needs. How these major influences feed into the potential for alternatives is shown in Figure 1. When political and economic climates are right, when divorce rates are high, and when persons experience a sense of high personal security and high autonomy needs, one or more of the described alternate life-styles may appear.

The appearance of a given life-style depends on a set of intervening variables: similarity to former life-style and former experience (but with a greater promise of fulfillment), perceived opportunity to engage in a new and different life-style, and support systems for entry. These support systems may vary. That is, there may be a *significant other* in a close relationship, a special reference group which supports a new life-style, or larger social networks which aid in establishing another life-style. The social networks involve a number of items ranging from family to special organizations (such as the Sexual Freedom League, swingers' organizations, or other specialized groups) and including the more general influence of the media.

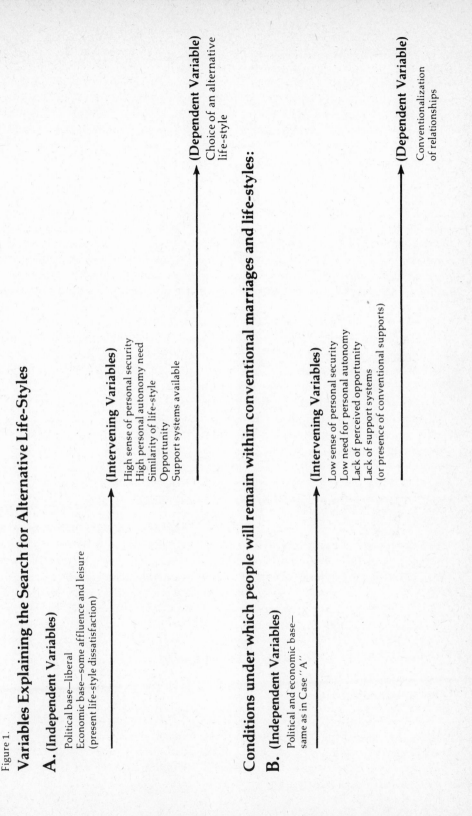

Figure 1.

Variables Explaining the Search for Alternative Life-Styles

A. (Independent Variables)

Political base—liberal
Economic base—some affluence and leisure
(present life-style dissatisfaction)

(Intervening Variables)

High sense of personal security
High personal autonomy need
Similarity of life-style
Opportunity
Support systems available

(Dependent Variable)

Choice of an alternative
life-style

Conditions under which people will remain within conventional marriages and life-styles:

B. (Independent Variables)

Political and economic base—
same as in Case "A"

(Intervening Variables)

Low sense of personal security
Low need for personal autonomy
Lack of perceived opportunity
Lack of support systems
(or presence of conventional supports)

(Dependent Variable)

Conventionalization
of relationships

Although it is impossible to predict the appearance of life-styles based on these variables, we can hazard some guesses about variations from the conventional monogamous marriage. Figure 2 shows hypothetical fallout from more conventional life-styles and marriages and how it leads to other adaptations. These adaptations are listed in decreasing rank order. However, there are complications. We must recognize the important difference between appearances and reality. For example, Cuber and Harroff (1965) showed that people may present a conventional appearance to the community but may practice very different life-styles. Similarly, people may at times maintain a private part of their lives much like that described by Myers' Fourth Compartment style of adaptation (see Chapter 22), not shared with their spouses. Some triads, gay relationships, and quasi-kin networks may also have this cloak of secrecy about them to maintain an air of respectability in the community. Figure 3 predicts the degree of sexual involvement outside the basic life-style of marriage or status as presented to the community. The hypothetical data are arranged with portions of the adult population in the future arrayed on the vertical axis and the range of sexual involvement on the horizontal.

There are several problems with such a hypothetical model. One involves the nature of extramarital involvement (EMI) in any particular adaptation. For example, although it is hypothesized that roughly 65 percent of the adult population may appear conventionally monogamous, they may be intermittently or sporadically adulterous. These relationships may be even more problematic for modified open marriages, which can easily lead to a variety of other experimental life-styles. The following tries to clarify some of the relationships between changing norms and ground rules and sexual patterns in various life-styles.

Emergent Life-Styles

Although by no means an exhaustive coverage of alternatives open to people today, the following list includes life-styles that will be among those frequently encountered in the future. Because long-range forecasting of such behaviors is almost impossible, I have simply extended current normative notions to suggest ways in which they may affect relationships. There is no rank order of preference or model development implied in this listing. However, current trends suggest that modified open marriage, some forms of singlehood, extended intimate networks, and triads or group collectives will serve as the more widely used alternatives.

Modified Open Marriage

There is little evidence that many people can stand the emotional pressures (jealousy, time problems, and loss of control over spouses) that accompany sexually open marriage. Thus, modified open marriage may become one of the more usual forms of openness, in which freedom, trust, and diminution of sexism on the part of partners is evident.

Figure 2.

Hypothetical Distribution of "Fallout" from Conventional to Alternate Systems

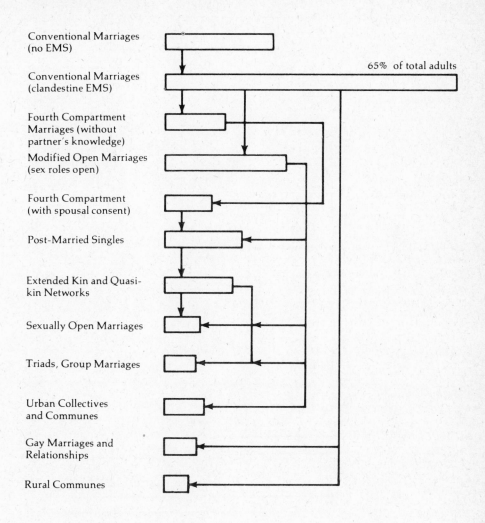

Conventional Marriages
(no EMS)

Conventional Marriages
(clandestine EMS)

65% of total adults

Fourth Compartment
Marriages (without
partner's knowledge)

Modified Open Marriages
(sex roles open)

Fourth Compartment
(with spousal consent)

Post-Married Singles

Extended Kin and Quasi-
kin Networks

Sexually Open Marriages

Triads, Group Marriages

Urban Collectives
and Communes

Gay Marriages and
Relationships

Rural Communes

Arrows indicate directions of flow from conventional marriages and other adaptations most likely to follow
from the preceding life-style.

NOTE:
The assumption is that most are socialized in early years to be conventional—then some of the
forces described herein take effect and create a certain amount of fallout into other relationship
categories. Note that the percentages add to more than 100. This is due to the nonexclusivity
of categories—some people may belong simultaneously to more than one: for example, a person
may be in a gay triad, or a single in a quasi-kin group, or be a fourth compartment person with
a modified open marriage and so forth.

Figure 3.

Hypothetical Distribution of Alternative Life-Styles by Degree of EMI Sexual Involvement

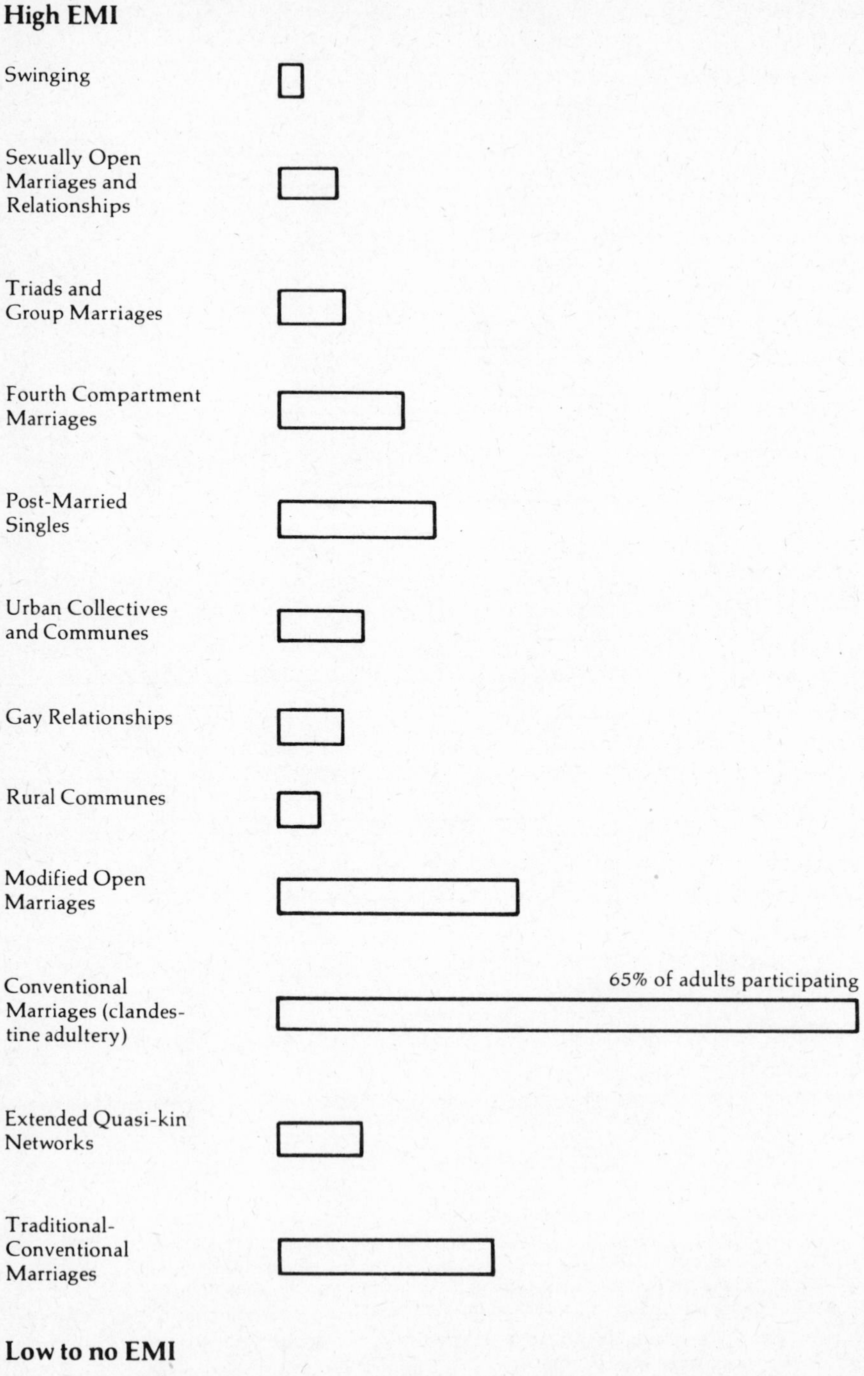

High EMI

Swinging

Sexually Open
Marriages and
Relationships

Triads and
Group Marriages

Fourth Compartment
Marriages

Post-Married
Singles

Urban Collectives
and Communes

Gay Relationships

Rural Communes

Modified Open
Marriages

Conventional
Marriages (clandes-
tine adultery)

65% of adults participating

Extended Quasi-kin
Networks

Traditional-
Conventional
Marriages

Low to no EMI

Since its publication, the O'Neills' *Open Marriage* (1972) has become a classic and a best-seller, no doubt a reflection of the doubt and near desperation associated with a number of marriages. Its popularity may also reflect the adventuresome spirit of Americans constantly on the watch for something "more" in life. At the same time it seems to show how we do seek something more than many have. The O'Neills' work is aimed at producing more openness, honesty, and trust while simultaneously developing more autonomy and personal expression within a marriage. This concept has been somewhat foreign to marriage. We primarily think of marriage as sacrifice and loss of autonomy rather than as the beginning of selfhood and autonomy. The O'Neills did not solve the problem of how, in an open marriage, one may have tennis and cocktails with an interesting outside person and not engage in sexual activity. In this respect, the open marriage concept seems an arbitrary and unnatural adaptation—but then so is monogamous marriage with conventional rules applied. The area of sexuality outside of marriage is still a gray one which may create anxiety, sense of loss, and complex problems for spouses.

In open marriage the focus is on equality and the partners' increased freedom to define themselves and their interests. Probably sexuality outside of marriage will intrude itself many times. Whether this comes to be seen as destructive or constructive must be viewed in light of the relationship. As Myers suggests in Chapter 22, there are many varieties.

The church, extended family, and community no longer maintain their sanctioning power over marriages as effectively as they once did. As a result, higher divorce rates, looser control over spouses, and more freedom for both men and women will increasingly place adults on their own in potentially sexual settings. The outcome will be unparalleled opportunities for expansion of sexuality and intimacy.

"Leakage" from conventional marriages is more likely to affect people in the choice of modified open marriage than other forms. Open marriage is the more likely choice because it is so similar in both form and norms to conventional marriage, and also because it does not immediately threaten the relationship with outside sexuality. This form will probably become the preferred alternative life-style. Although modified open marriage may lead to more separations and divorces, it may also lead to new, more stable, and satisfying forms of marriage.

Postmarital Singlehood

At the time of this writing, Morton Hunt is revising his book *World of the Formerly Married*—a book that has remained popular since it appeared in 1966. Increasing numbers of young adults are taking Bertrand Russell's advice and getting their divorces while they are young. Also it appears that more people are becoming wary of hasty second marriages when so many appear not to be great improvements over the first ones. The old folklore suggested that mismatched partners caused a marriage to fail. Today increasing numbers of people see their marital problems as inherent in the relationship rather than as the fault of one of the partners. More openness in jobs for women creates a climate of relative independence from men and further adds to the singlehood potential.

Singlehood as a more general category has several other adaptations. These are discussed by Libby in Chapter 4. Although separation from an impermanent singles relationship is not easy, it is generally less traumatic than divorce. A new style of singles adaptation may be coming into view with the current discussion of roommates. This style simply acknowledges the heterosexual pair as having no more or less power and control over each other than do other kinds of roommates. While both are free to construct their lives autonomously, sexuality among roommates is there when both want it. Of course this life-style is not problem-free since people tend to become differentially involved through time. Both roommates should have a relatively mature approach to this life-style, sources of autonomy, and strong needs for individual lives. When tempered with togetherness this life-style can work. The implications for the development of intimacy are problematic. Probably only a few are suited by temperament to this kind of life.

Singles are also taken on occasion into extended family or quasi-kin networks which serve as important socioemotional support units. In short, the range of singles behavior is broad and complex. It involves a great number of adaptations which will probably be expanded as more singles search for means to satisfy family and intimacy needs without turning to marriage.

Extended Family Networks

When singles are taken into extended or quasi-kin networks without extramarital sexual involvement, they will probably be like those described by Stoller in 1970. In networks of non-kin intimates, activities will often involve children and weekend recreation. Families will sometimes cooperate in solving economic problems, and in some cases will share housing. Families with common problems with children, seeking a clear sense of community, and with a need to cooperate with others outside of their nuclear family unit will be most likely to try this alternative. This is an area that has been investigated in terms of child-care services and recreational patterns, but these "families" could well expand to include a variety of singles, marrieds, old, and young in unexpected combinations—designed to yield a more satisfactory sense of social-emotional cooperation as well as sexual solidarity.

There are not many widespread adaptations designed for sharing cars, household goods, and other goods and services not commonly shared between nuclear families. The extent and direction of this trend have not yet been determined and its implications for more radical forms of family sharing are unclear. This life-style could become a radical alternative if families shared cars, televisions, vacations, and other commodities formerly held to be the domain of the single nuclear family. In addition the implications for sexual sharing are certainly present in any arrangement which involves intimacy and sharing of so many *other* aspects of one's personal life. Since this kind of arrangement involves so many factors, it may be unrealistic to view it as a viable alternative for many families.

Swinging

Swinging can probably be dismissed as a nonradical activity in North American society since it does not affect the nuclear structure of the family in any way. Children are usually brought up conventionally in families of swingers, thus the implications for change are minimal. The fears of becoming affectionately involved, a current norm of swinging, do not enhance the probability of creating true alternatives to the conventional marriage. It tends instead to simply translate the old-fashioned ephemeral affair into a game for everyone. This is not to suggest that swinging is a simple social phenomenon or easily understood. As Gilmartin (Chapter 10) shows, there are some implications to this sexual behavior that are important to understanding other relationships.

As is true in other alternative life-styles, swinging is not all of a piece; apparently some groups tend to evolve true intimacy in multiple relationships, even though their number may not be large. However, economic, occupational, and other hazards of becoming known as a swinger seem to have decreased the ranks of swingers over the past several years. Most people will not risk endangering their careers or jobs by having the wrong people become aware of their activities. Unless times of super affluence and leisure are once more thrust upon us, swinging seems doomed to an unimportant role—a marginal life-style affecting 1 − 4 percent of all marrieds.

Triads and Group Marriages

Although the topic of group marriage has been discussed by the Constantines (see Chapter 11), little professional work has been done on triads. This may be due in part to the relatively conventional appearance of most triads from the outside. To the casual observer they may not look too unusual. Triads have a characteristic of harboring people who appear to have no particular desire to look "deviant." Thus, they enjoy the best of both worlds— seeming "normal" yet enjoying an alternative to monogamy.

An unbalanced sex ratio in cities tends to favor men in many triads, although two men sharing companionship and one wife may also be common. We simply lack data to understand how the sex ratios in triads actually occur. Local norms, the bisexuality emphasis, and the simple availability of surplus females in cities are among factors that enter into the sex-ratio choice in a triad. Thus, there are various forms of triads, some nonsexual, some closed families in respect to sexuality, and others that look like open marriage with sexuality shared inside and outside the triad.

Rationales for triads are not difficult to find. First, they are much less complicated in terms of the number of relationships. (A dyad is the simplest form with only two relationships; in a triad there are four potential sets of relationships; in a four-person group there are a possible twenty-six.) Obvi-

ously then, triads have the greatest potential of success on the basis of minimizing complexity while maintaining the "extra" involvement seen as desirable. A second reason why people form triads is that triads offer social,
economic, and household division-of-labor advantages not found in the dyadic union. Triads offer a larger range of adult models for children and more
flexible sitting services for children, and they also function as socioemotional
support units. The problem of being the odd person is of course present in
the triadic relationship. Therefore, triads tend to be successful when all partners have at least a genuine respect, tolerance, and liking for each other.

New data in process of analysis in California (LaFollette, 1976), suggest
that triads may be one of the most stable alternative life-style forms.

Group marriage seems to have attracted few long-term adherents, but an
adapted version may also be in the making as a more usual form. Some variant of it is likely to become popular. This version involves an organization
that is not quite a group marriage, nor a commune. It is a collective where
members share work, recreation, and household benefits and duties but have
few marriage-type obligations to any particular person(s). These collectives
are most often found in fairly large cities where housing, social isolation, and
the economics of single life are often a problem. The collective solution to
these problems involves no formal rules about sexuality; dyads do seem to
form and break up, only without the usual problems of divorce.

Communes—Urban and Rural

At some point in any continuum of social organization, urban collectives
(groups of individuals living together and untied to dyads or other interpersonal commitments, but joined only by the commitment to make the
house a friendly and peaceable place to live) blend into and become communes. One way to envision the basic difference is to view communes as
being more deeply involved and committed: Members must abide by rules of
interpersonal conduct and try to fulfill expectations about loving, caring, and
maintaining in-depth relationships with the others. From this vantage point,
urban communes occur less often than collectives, but like collectives may
seem to resemble the roommate idea expanded to include many people.
Among the several typologies of communes and collectives, Millar's (1973) is
useful. He makes distinctions among these groups in terms of variations in
social cohesion and sexual expression.

Millar uses the Hare Krishna as an example of close-knit, cohesive
and Apollonian sexual orientations (as contrasted with the Manson family, a
tight-knit, cohesive Dionysian cult).[1] There is no necessary sexual connection between forms of social organization in any particular collective,
whether it is called a commune or not.

Thus, the number of communes one sees in urban areas is in part a matter of the way communes and collectives are defined. The potential for tight-
knit Dionysian (sexually open) communes seems extremely limited and their
numbers appear to be on the decline (Ruth, 1976). This may not be true for

urban collectives of various sorts, given further inflation, shortages (including housing), and other ecological considerations which make collective sharing of some aspects of life desirable. The potential also seems delimited because of the failure in our culture to prepare people for such sharing. Much of the whole scripting of women and men relies heavily on building the ideal family model—one with two parents and few children. When this idea is violated, it is mostly by liberated, avant-garde types. The rampant individualism in this culture generally militates against commune life, which is seen as taking away more personal freedoms than are offset by perceived awards.

In his book *Earthwalk* (1974), Slater developed a variation on the theme of Jonathan Livingston Seagull. His story, which centers around Jonathan Livingston Strangelove, in fact portrays our penchant for the extremes of achievement through individualism and competition. Slater's view of this Strangelove adaptation to achievement, individualism, and competition is that it has helped create the present isolation, loneliness, and failure of community which has no counterpart in human history. The relative failure of the commune movement to capture the fancy of Americans seems to indicate a wariness toward having any collective impose either its tyranny or helpfulness on us. Slater's view of the future is that if we do not find ways to recapture community in America, we will have even worse social chaos. Of course, the commune movement cannot be viewed as the only indicator of community, but its rejection by people in general offers some verification of Slater's thesis.

Among the reasons for the probable decline of communes in rural areas is the fact that people with farming expertise and land are very conventional and are therefore unlikely to see communes as offering viable life-styles. Those with ideological orientations to farm-subsistence commune life, on the other hand, ordinarily do not realize how hard the life can be. Rural-subsistence communes require an intensity of commitment, work, and cooperation that is seldom sustained. Of course, this generalization is subject to qualifications (Kanter, 1972; Conover, 1975). In many cases rural communes are more radical than most other forms of alternate life-styles; they reject almost the entire consumer package, jobs, and even sexuality. They are much less likely either to form or to last than other styles, in spite of a certain romantic-nostalgic attraction in the idea of getting back to the farm.

The question of whether the commune is in a state of growth or decline is a matter for open debate. Perhaps part of the confusion lies in our lack of understanding of what constitutes a commune (as discussed earlier in this section). The classic form of commune, in which the members pull away from "society" and engage in a farm-subsistence life-style, is waning. Religious-spiritual communes and those with a solid economic base tend to be more lasting.

At the moment, skimpy evidence would lead to the suggestion that perhaps communes are increasing in the Boston area and in some places in California, where triads seem to be increasing. These observations may be nothing more than the artifact of researcher interest in these areas; this, though, is unlikely. It is more likely that communes are scattered in numerous places, with their density being heavier on either coast.

As for sexual arrangements in communes, we know that they are diverse. Something like free sexuality (but not license) is encouraged at Twin Oaks in Virginia (Kincade, 1973), while the varieties of sexual freedom or restrictions are less well known in other places. Given current conditions, the best prediction for the near future would be potentially more collectives and sharing arrangements. Perhaps we will see more urban communes, fewer rural ones, and variations on monogamous life-styles in all these forms, with serial monogamy probably being the most frequent style. The supportive context of collectives and communes, however, lends itself to a number of potentials.

Changing Ground Rules

Some evidence suggests that norms are being restructured in specific areas of intimate relationships. Among the important norms that are changing, the following are more likely than some others to figure in a greater awareness of alternate life-styles and possibly to support experimentation.

Love

The meaning of a loving relationship as an empathic response between individuals is dramatically changing. No longer do so many people believe in a lifetime monogamous true love as a possibility, even though they think it desirable. Many feel that love, by its very nature, tends to be impermanent, but life-giving, and so should be enjoyed on those terms. Increasing numbers also feel that love can be shared and that it is possible to love any number of people simultaneously. (See Kieffer, Chapter 18.)

Jealousy

As a culturally induced problem, jealousy tends to be regarded as purely the problem of the person experiencing the feeling, not the person who presumedly produced the state. In marriage, if a husband and wife agree to a nonexclusive relationship, the problem of jealousy is one which each of them can grapple with and work through essentially alone. No longer is jealousy automatically seen as reasonable and a sign that one partner loves the other. Jealousy more frequently is seen as a reaction to one's own immaturity and insecurity. Thus it is a problem to work out the best way one can; it less often means the "offending spouse" stops doing whatever it was that produced the jealous state. (See Mazur, Chapter 23.)

This is not to suggest, however, that jealousy is a simple problem, for it clearly is not. Jealousy is not the same (or even noted) throughout the world; evidence about the mixed nature of the expression of jealousy would lead me to the conclusion that most of it involves cultural learning. There may be some deep-seated need to pair-bond of which we are unaware; but the generally polysexual and polygamous nature of women and men today leave this premise in doubt.

The optimum number of relationships a person can handle simultaneously is another thorny issue currently being debated. There are many unanswered questions, but people are willing to experiment and, we hope, to learn from errors.

Sex

These days sex is coming to be seen as a celebration of one's aliveness with another in a loving relationship or at least in a temporary liaison where exploitation and "gamesmanship" are minimized. Its central importance is receding and the threatening and ominous symbolic meanings once attached to it seem to be diminishing.

Perhaps the central meaning of the sexual revolution is involved with the changing norms of sexuality, rather than with total sexual liberation of everyone. People have become much more accepting of a broader range of sexual expression in others, if not in themselves. As a people we have opted for broader conceptions of sex-roles, dress, and behavior patterns, as well as sexuality. The effects of all these subtle and overt changes which have not yet solidified are a bit hard to assess. Our normatively fluid state seems to be merely changing emphasis with respect to sexuality and not regressing to former and more rigidified codes, as some would suggest. Traditionalism seems to be giving way steadily to more diffuse styles of living, including sexuality. (Libby, Chapter 4.)

As the meanings of our terms change, the threat so often associated with sexual activity changes as well. The overall effect is to tend to make sexual activity a celebrated commonplace, much like eating, which can now have many social connotations and varieties of expression. Sex is somehow becoming legitimized in the face of a still harshly punitive and repressed society. This may be due as much to prurient interests of the majority and to the voyeurism of "the conventionals" as to the efforts of youth to construct new norms and new meanings surrounding sexuality. At least some of the implications of the changed attitudes on sex for marriage are rather obvious, as sex becomes something less than that magic which either makes or breaks a relationship. When it is just one more lovely and loving activity that people do, and as it becomes detached from the old order, we stand to become more humanized.

If we could conceptualize extramarital sex (EMS) as a problem to be understood from the vantage point of role analysis, it might be clearer that more, not less, EMS should be expected. Looking at the respective roles of legal marriage partners, as contrasted with extramarital lovers, it can be seen immediately that role-content does much to explain the glamour of EMS activity (at least in the early stages of the development of EMS relationships).

At the onset of an EMS relationship, there is a flirting period in which the romance of youth is recaptured, even if only for a moment, before the relationship is either consummated or short-circuited. This initial encounter takes people back to more romantic days of their lives—to situations that are often forgotten or downplayed in their daily rituals of living as husband and wife. The role expectations for lovers are very similar to those operating in premarriage dating, where topics of conversation, activities, and body preparation tend to heighten romanticism and escape from reality. Thus it is likely that, given current North American values on newness and experience-seeking, we will continue to see a rise in EMS activity as long as opportunity structures remain open for participants.

After settling into marriage, wives have fewer opportunities (or may make fewer opportunities) to be shown off with husbands under the above-described circumstances. Thus, in some combination of forces that impel males and females to stray from the conjugal bed, the following may be among the more important to understand: Given some doubts about current norms (or feelings of anomie—which means a sense that the rules do not apply to oneself or have no meaning), open opportunity, intelligence enough to engage in moral relativism, and a need for new experience (also aided by the contrast of dull routines), people are likely to seek EMS experiences more frequently. If this listing of predisposing factors is any indication, it is likely that many more North Americans may be ready to consider the game.

A general hypothesis, which may be tested by research, involves the changing nature of touching experiences in marriage. There is probably a decrease over the span of the marriage cycle of the frequency of touching, fondling, and general caressing of partners; it may be that this is what people miss in relationships and are searching for in sexual situations.

The basic content and meaning sought in EMS then may be sensual rather than sexual. However, due to our strong *expectations* of sexuality, much sexual interaction might occur as a substitute for sensuality. After all, in this sex-obsessed culture it would almost be an affront to personal identity to engage in all the processes of beginning an "affair" and then only engage in petting or body fondling. Meanings get sexualized beyond their ordinary significance, and sexual acting-out is one result.

There is an emerging norm which acknowledges that wives and husbands and people in general are not so much better or worse than each other, but are simply different; and that it is enough to experience the difference. However, since we are all extremely conditioned to be competitive about most of our activities, it will probably be some time before this emergent norm about the relative differences in people takes effect. As siblings in families, we are compared favorably and unfavorably—not thought of simply as different human beings. Thus, too, wives and husbands are compared unfavorably (but apparently on second thought more favorably) with paramours. Probably adopting such a norm would be humanizing for all social contacts, but it runs counter to what all North Americans seem to use as a perceptual base of experience—namely, that there are good guys and bad guys, and that one's task is to sort them out, attach labels, and then act on the premise that these categories are reality. Perhaps the norm is, to some extent, changing as a response to a need of so many to avoid the bad-guy label for engaging in EMS. If so, the change is a welcome one.

Children

Offspring are no longer seen as an unalloyed blessing to create the fabric of a solid marriage. They are also less often seen as extensions of parents, as status objects, or as things to manipulate and control to our own liking. Children are, in counterculture families, less often prisoners of the family; they are most likely to be treated as autonomous persons much earlier and to be kept in positions of dependence for shorter periods of time.

The children's rights movement is in its infancy and there are stirrings of awareness for developing conceptions of children at great variance from the standard one of the present day. (See Constantine, Chapter 17.) Constantine's concept of "open family" involves a range of autonomy and potential for children that currently would simply not be understood by most American parents. The fact that the literature on the topic is growing (albeit fostered by adults) is a sign of our continued expansion of awareness of inequities throughout human systems. This equality revolution has diffused and will probably continue in this direction, altering our perception of children's capabilities and limits, much the same as has happened to women in this country. As both men and women take responsibility for contraception, both marriage and children will continue to be redefined in terms of the ecological and economic strategies felt to be appropriate for the coming world. Clearly, the meaning of having and rearing children is not the same as in times past.

Privacy

Bernard (1972) has shown that when people marry, there is a marriage that is *his* and one that is *hers*. Quite obviously, if a woman's work is taken at all seriously, we might conclude that women will soon be demanding something like equal opportunity. This notion will no doubt extend to cover such exigencies as *her* study, *her* conventions attended, and *her* own private sphere in which she can act with impunity and freedom. This does not mean that the home and family, husband-wife, and mother-child relationships will be nonexistent. It simply means that wives and mothers will probably gain the same (or nearly the same) freedoms as men to pursue their own private and personal interests. A reasoned analysis should suggest no reason why this should not be.

Myers (Chapter 22) suggests that partners must become aware of the effects of each other's needs while being honest with themselves. How much one tells a spouse or lover depends on the situation and on one's judgment of what is needed for a productive relationship. Myers claims that self-honesty must be the major criterion of judgment.

Open marriages would obviously be handled differently than a "Fourth-Compartment" style of relationship. The major dimensions of privacy—space, time, and security from psychological invasion—must all be considered. Of course a prime source of frustration and difficulty for people in intimate relationships is struggling with these dimensions as they intersect with the other person's. For example, the needs for privacy are varied and can occur in combinations in any relationship. Accordingly, we might expect relationships to be only accidentally happy and to produce well-being for the partners for only short periods of time

Ramey's (1976) interpretation of husband-wife differences in privacy needs shows how some of our assumptions about privacy as an issue are problematical in two-person marriages. He also maintains that collective living can provide—contrary to the popular stereotype of collectives—some better answers to this problem of privacy.

The changing ground rules for male-female relationships will continue to develop in the alternative life-styles that will be most frequently practiced. The development of these life-style alternatives will depend in part, however, upon economic, political, and opportunity structures, as well as upon personal and interpersonal considerations. Following our fallout model of change, life-styles which are similar to those experienced in the past have a greater probability of successful adaptation. Modified open marriage, post-marital singlehood, and triads are the most frequently found alternatives and will continue to be so.

Open sexuality is more problematic as norms governing jealousy and love, although changing, seem to have made minimal impact.

As alternate life-styles are adopted, relationships at many levels and in many places will be altered. The future of sex, the raising of children, the role of privacy, and the future of love remain to be better understood as further research helps us to get a firmer grasp on the multiple realities at hand.

Reference Notes

1. Apollonian-Dionysian is the dichotomy in the culture of types first developed to describe orientations to life-styles by Benedict in *Patterns of Culture* (1961). The term *Apollonian* refers to the life-style of cooperation, sobriety, and self-restraint (for example the Zuni Indians of the American Southwest) as contrasted with the *Dionysian* style found in the Kwakiutl of Vancouver Island—a hedonistic, emotionally expressive, drunken, and foolhardy people.

22.
A Couple Can Also Be Two People
(Marriage, Honesty, and Personal Growth)

Lonny Myers

In this article, medical sexologist Lonny Myers looks at the possibilities for freedom and growth within marriage. She also addresses the problem of marital honesty and honesty to oneself.

Dr. Myers presents a model of marriage that incorporates a "fourth compartment," or a breathing space in which one is accountable only to oneself. She stresses that at least some part of oneself is not "married" but is a separate person outside of the primary relationship. Given this fact, she suggests that being married and being free need not be opposite poles, but that there can be many sources of fulfillment within a framework of responsible marriage.

The conventional marriage of the twentieth century imposes severe limits on the individual freedom of the marital partners. Because of these limits, many adults find themselves caught between the desire for personal growth and the obligation to live within the restrictions imposed by conventional marriage.

This article will examine the restrictions imposed by marriage, the problem of honesty within such restrictions, and the possibilities for personal growth which exist in various kinds of marriages. I have chosen to discuss honesty and personal growth in juxtaposition to extramarital relationships because extramarital relationships are usually surrounded by maximum restrictions and given the minimum of consideration as a valid option for personal growth. In discussing extramarital relationships, I can establish a principle of freedom and responsibility that will also apply to the less frightening sources of personal growth. I wish to emphasize that personal growth in fact often involves other activities, hobbies, sports, job changes, music, art, travel, and the like.

Marriage: Variables and Options

Marriage takes many forms, some of which are highly defined and rigid while others are loose and flexible. No two marriages are entirely alike, nor are they static over time.

Personalized Definitions

Marriage holds different meanings for different people. Thoughts and tasks connected with marriage can take up 80 percent of the wife's time, energy, and emotion, while taking only 30 percent of the husband's time. One couple might find most of their satisfaction in togetherness and meet all their intimacy requirements within the relationship, thus making the partners' occupational, social, and political lives far less important. Another couple may enjoy their most rewarding experiences outside of the marriage; the relationship between the two is more a matter of comfort than of excitement. There are low-key/low-energy people who do not find life very exciting either inside or outside the marriage. There are high-key/high-energy people who take an exuberant joy in both marriage and outside activities. And there are unlimited possible combinations of these types. There are couples for whom playing traditionally defined social roles is important; the wife does wifely things and the husband does husbandly things. There are couples for whom the basic roles of breadwinner and housekeeper are reversed. There are couples for whom traditional sex roles are unimportant—whoever has the energy does the job. There are highly structured marriages with well-defined rules; there are casual marriages which are defined as they go along. There are marriages with children; marriages without children; marriages with in-laws; marriages with no in-laws; marriages with serious financial problems, serious drinking problems, serious health problems; marriages with no easily identifiable serious problems; and marriages with no apparent problems at all.

Marriage also holds different meanings for the same couple at different times in the relationship. The importance of a good sexual relationship at the age of twenty-five is certainly different from the importance of sex at eighty. Similarly, needs for nonsexual intimacies vary depending on satisfactions from other sources. The importance of doing things together may change greatly as education, jobs, and children influence the activities of each partner. Possessiveness may gradually become far less important after an intense marriage has developed into a comfortable one. And then again, time may have little to do with possessiveness. One couple may remain possessive for forty years while another may not be possessive even at the start.

Extramarital Intimacy

Confusion prevails in most discussions of extramarital relationships because there is a tendency to disregard the different kinds of marriage from which these relationships stem. Obviously, though, in a marriage which is perfectly satisfying and fulfilling without outside relationships, there is not even the impulse to develop them. The type of marriage involved has an important bearing on the question of extramarital intimacy.

However, in many marriages there is a lack of mutual understanding—much less, gratification—of the needs of the marital partners. Although it is possible for some marriage partners to achieve intimate communication and simple joy from being together, it is often much harder to achieve these inside the marriage than outside the marriage. Outside the marriage, interaction and intimacy often flow easily because of the ability to be selective. The person you are relating to need not know about your broken furnace, your mother's major surgery, your son's drug problem. You are free to communicate almost in a vacuum, and you can include only those facts that help you to make the relationship positive. A relationship that brings you a few moments of joy can do great things toward building your strength to cope. However, inside a marriage moments of joy may require complex preparation and dedicated effort. Even when there are mutual respect, love, and admiration within the marriage, many people find that the excitement and freedom possible in an extramarital relationship cannot be duplicated at home. The total picture at home may be quite satisfactory; away may be just a supplement, not a substitute.

Another source of confusion stems from the assumption that most couples enjoy at least a reasonably satisfactory sexual relationship and therefore have no need to find extramarital sexual relationships. The reality is that many couples have miserable sexual relationships, while others make love joyfully and almost daily after twenty-five years of marriage. Whatever the pattern, chances are that one of the partners is having sex either more often or less often than she/he would choose. It would seem exceedingly rare that two people would continually have the same appetite for coitus with each other over a period of twenty years. When the differences are slight, the reasonable adjustments of one's spouse may be made easily. But my guess is that many men and women are forced into a pattern of infrequency or abstinence at times when sex is very important to them. For many persons this means years of frustration with solitary masturbation as the only legitimate sexual outlet, and for some, even this outlet is excluded.

Couples may behave quite "normally" in social situations. They may even seem quite affectionate, but this outward display may bear little resemblance to what happens when they go home to bed. An apparently affectionate couple may not have had coitus in five years while a bickering pair may make passionate love as soon as they arrive home.

These two false assumptions—the idea that extramarital affairs all relate to the same kind of marriage and the idea that all marriages are at least partially satisfactory—are usually implicit in discussions concerning the desirability of intimate relationships outside of marriage. (By "intimate relationships" I mean those that satisfy a need for intimacy. For some this may be sexual, for others it may mean open, good communication without genital sex. The reality is that much sex is nonintimate and much intimacy is nonsexual. From the society we get messages, such as, "Sex is intimate," when the truth is that "We, who are the experts, would like to restrict sex to intimate relationships." The tendency of sex education to ignore nonintimate sex is appalling.)

Textbooks, journals, and magazines tend to depict model marriages that satisfy all intimacy needs and expect marital partners to accommodate themselves to that mold. Paradoxically, the very people who encourage the traditional marriage are usually the ones who emphasize that "marriage is hard work." There is no claim that it is *easy* to satisfy all of one's needs within the marital relationship. The idea presented has been that if marital partners work hard enough, they will be able to recapture at least part of the excitement so noticeable when they were first married.

Time-Out Periods

If indeed marriage is work, won't people need a vacation from time to time? There should be nothing startling or new about this question. Just as getting away from one's children occasionally has become accepted as an option within the category of responsible motherhood (fathers were never expected to be eternally on duty), getting away from one's spouse should be accepted as an option within the category of responsible partnership.

In many marriages, each person enjoys activities without the other, but for the vast majority, there has to be a specific acceptable excuse. If the man is going fishing, the woman may be left at home. If the woman is going to visit her sister, she may leave her husband at home. But there is a tendency to avoid leaving simply for the purpose of being apart for a while. Convention demands that we invent rationalizations to camouflage an honest motivation and need to be separated for a while. Less conventional couples, on the other hand, may allow for separate vacations and talk freely about the usefulness of temporary separation.

What about dating? While it is permissible for a man to choose to go fishing rather than be with his wife, and a woman to choose to go visit her sister rather than be with her husband, neither of them can elect to go out on a date rather than be together. Both of them must sustain the illusion that night after night, year after year, they would prefer each other's company to that of anyone else. Married people are not allowed to go out merely because they seek to relate privately to another person, if that person could be regarded as a potential sex partner.

The ban on extramarital dating is so thoroughly embedded in popular wisdom and "expert" opinion that to challenge it even verbally is to invite retaliation rather than discourse. There are no scientific data to prove that sexually monogamous couples are happier or healthier than couples who have explored extramarital sex, nor is there any scientific proof for the common assumption that extramarital dating is necessarily destructive to marriage.

What evidence has been collected comes mainly from the dating habits of "patients" and "clients" who bring their "problems" to "experts." Professionals apparently feel no obligation to study the extramarital dating habits of people who find dating satisfying. Only when dating becomes a problem does it come to the attention of "experts," who then write about the problems created by extramarital dating! This system of "fact-finding" is tantamount to using patients in a tuberculosis sanitarium to study the effects of hospitalization on respiratory function.

Since the social sanctions against dating are so severe, married people who arrange dates are likely to become both fearful and guilty. Thus an element of self-fulfilling prophecy enters with all but the most secure individuals. A classic example of self-fulfilling prophecy is the guilt associated with masturbation. When all the "experts" condemned masturbation and warned of its horrible consequences, many people suffered agonizing guilt over a harmless, enjoyable, and very human activity. Most marital partners suffer the same kind of guilt, and probably for just as poor reason, when they plan a responsible evening with a "date."

In relationships that remain marriage in name only, i.e., for economic or social reasons other than good companionship, the lack of permission to date is truly pathetic. There are too few marital partners who can face the situation squarely, admit that they do not enjoy each other's company, and allow each other a private life. Even in marriages in which there is no sexual relationship at all, the partners may deny each other the right to enjoy sex with someone else. This restraint may well receive the blessing of the "experts" who equate self-denial with strength.

Open Marriage

The publication in 1972 of the O'Neills' *Open Marriage* was one of the first breakthroughs toward sanity on the subject. The O'Neills specifically accept dating in their concept of open marriage; however, they de-emphasize the role of sex, making the assumption that if the marriage is great (the marital sex both exciting and abundant), there is little need for sex on the outside. They state that one's dating experiences must be of the variety that can be comfortably related to one's spouse. Thus dating can be used to enhance and enrich the lives of two happily married adults, without the complications of romance or coitus.

"Safe" dating that does not threaten the basic romantic one-to-one marital relationship is okay by the O'Neills, but real "turn-ons," exuberant joy, etc., are reserved for home. In our society, a super "high" experience is often associated with sex—but the closeness and sharing are far more significant. Extramarital intimacy means a sharing with someone, with or without sex, when the vibrations flowing between you make you feel very special, very alive, and not in need (at the moment) of your spouse. This may be frightening for many. How can you feel so good with someone else? Many cannot handle this, and they deny the good feelings, pile on the guilt, and return home ashamed. I believe that a more real approach is that one can enjoy intimate satellite relationships that satisfy immediate, here-and-now needs without denying the validity of one's primary relationship.

When the O'Neills do deal with the role of sex in extramarital dating relationships, they concede that these relationships can, on occasion, include coitus and still be helpful rather than harmful to the marriage. Nevertheless, they do not deal with either extramarital sex as fun, or with exciting, deep intimacies as sources of personal enrichment.

The unfortunate aspect of open marriage is that it is limited to an ideal situation. The system is fine for a marriage in which the two partners grow at relatively even rates, but a marriage that starts out as a successful open marriage might come under great strain if one partner begins having much more fun and dating much more than the other. The less popular partner might well decide to close up the marriage and cut off the freedom; this could cause great conflict when the freedom continues to fulfill the other partner.

Ideal marriage is a fine goal, but there is an implication that if one does not attain this state, one is a failure. Since the vast majority of people will never develop an ideal marriage (traditional or open), a model limited to perfect relationships promotes feelings of inadequacy, guilt, and frustration. It is my belief that to impose a sense of failure upon those who cannot attain the ideal is destructive and an obstacle to personal growth. On the other hand, to hold that divorce is the solution for every couple who cannot attain the ideal is to advocate the end of marriage as a dominant social institution. While my special concern is with the personal growth of those who are caught in mediocre marital relationships, it extends further to the enrichment of people lucky enough to enjoy a good marriage.

Honesty

Honesty, like marriage, holds different meanings for different people and for the same people at different times in their lives. For some, honesty means being unashamed to share any fantasy. For others, it means only that they do not knowingly make a false statement. Early in marriage, it may be possible to be almost completely honest, but as the peak of fervent attraction gradually subsides into deep caring, the partners may either consciously or unconsciously put consideration of each other's feelings above "honesty."

There are many times when honesty may be synonymous with cruelty. Should a person pass on gratuitous slander? Isn't it "moral" to leave something that is unimportant unsaid if it would cause pain? Isn't it even possible to confuse revenge with honesty, or inflict punishment under the guise of honesty? My conclusion is that to be always completely honest is a valid concept only when applied to oneself.

To hide an irrelevant truth from a loved one may be good. Even to hide a relevant, but harmful, truth may be acceptable. Many people hide their extramarital experiences from their marriage partners out of kindness. Although they would love to tell their spouse about such experiences, they refrain because they do not believe that such information would be accepted in the same spirit in which it was given. In many couples one partner's intimacy needs are in truth completely satisfied by the marital relationship, but the other partner's are not. The nonparticipating spouse would not understand how extramarital intimacy could possibly be a positive growth experience and would be terribly threatened.

But how can we rationally assume that five, ten, or twenty years after an intimate pair bond is established all intimacy needs will necessarily be met by one's partner? One reaction to unmet needs is quiet desperation. Many choose this route. But how honest are those who suffer in silence? Do these unhappy people openly describe their intense frustration to their spouses? Others who find their needs are not met may be as honest as possible within the limits of the spouse's capacity to understand. This reluctance to be completely open is clearly not hypocrisy. It is remarkably different from the person who agrees that adultery is wicked and then secretly takes a lover.

This introduces a kind of qualified honesty that makes a distinction between feelings and physical behavior. This type of honesty would demand the truth about stolen kisses or actual adultery, but not about fantasies. If confronted by suspicious questions, a person could be honest about her/his physical behavior without describing emotional involvement.

To be completely honest would demand that each person share not only fantasies but all of the conflicts with her/his partner. It would mean admission not only of clandestine meetings but also of consideration of such meetings. It would mean confessing to moments of wishing to be free and single. The cost of stretching honesty that far is often exorbitant. Few persons find the benefits of sharing this kind of conflict even worth thinking about. This is often regarded as a decent departure from honesty; that is, when dealing with inner conflicts, it is generally regarded as unselfish and virtuous to be selective and to keep certain thoughts to oneself. But extramarital relationships are often sacrificed because one cannot admit that one has serious intimate needs beyond the marital relationship. At this point, the question of honesty to oneself is perhaps more the issue than honesty to one's spouse.

Honesty between spouses, however, has usually been regarded as a requisite for a good marriage. The time that departure from honesty is frequently recommended is after the fact. Some professionals may suggest that it is better not to reveal everything about the past, but few endorse embarking on a new venture that demands withholding the truth from a spouse. Withholding the truth about fantasies—out of loving concern—is often acceptable, but to act out the fantasy in order to eliminate the frustration is usually regarded as a weakness and rarely thought of as being honest with oneself.

In many marriages, unshared fantasy, frustration, and dishonesty are already a reality. The idea that one must not deceive one's spouse may then be only a rationalization for not engaging in extramarital intimacies. The more honest reason may be that extramarital intimacy would constitute self-admission that all of one's intimate needs cannot be fulfilled within the marital relationship. It is likely that the obstacle to considering extramarital relationships as a possible enhancer of the marriage is the fear of the clash, the fear of being discovered. The discovery is threatening because it will focus on important real differences that have been masked by polite togetherness. It will become obvious that behavior one partner accepts, the other finds utterly unacceptable. Actually, many marriage partners may have had unshared frustrations and unshared wishful thinking for years, but not all of these have done anything tangible that can be proved against them.

Although the secret wishful fantasies may involve great emotion, occupying hours of daydreaming and even interfering with functioning for a month or more, withholding the truth about such preoccupation is not usually regarded as being dishonest. It may even be regarded as considerate. But to withhold the truth about a fun, exciting date involving only a few hours and not interfering with other responsibilities is usually regarded as "dishonest," "deceptive," and "betraying a trust."

Of course, not all extramarital intimacy is good, nor all self-denial bad, but society tends to be more accepting of irritable behavior provoked by denial than of joyous behavior stemming from extramarital intimacy. Certainly, honesty gets lost in these situations. We are not honest about the possible bad effects of self-denial; and we are not honest about the possible good effects of extramarital intimacy. What we need is a more objective look at extramarital intimacy, an honest evaluation of its risk/benefit ratio. One thing is sure: The risks and benefits will be different for each person depending on the individual's ability to cope, level of confidence, and motivation for self-fulfillment.

Personal Growth

Personal growth may involve big decisions regarding an entire life-style or little decisions about how to make today more meaningful—plus all the variations in between. Much has been written about how marriage robs many women of personal growth (few men must sacrifice medical school plans in order to marry and raise a family), and much more will be written about how the pressure on men to make money and support a family thwarts personal growth.

Social conformity demands that a couple be considered as an institution. For example, in social gatherings, it is expected that both halves of a couple will be invited; such gatherings, therefore, usually end up only including those couples to whom neither the host nor the hostess has any objection. The fascinating Mrs. X and the notorious Mr. Y never get invited because their spouses don't fit in with the other invited guests. Seldom is either member of a couple invited to attend on her/his own merits; she or he must almost always come as half of an institution. This loss of personhood, along with the loss of many opportunities for personal growth, is generally accepted as an inevitable aspect of the institution of marriage.

Whereas some people continue to grow and enjoy life while sharing everything with a spouse, the rules of traditional marriage curtail creative activities for the vast majority. Even the so-called open marriage depends on equal growth and does not deal with the realistic possibility that one partner may have far more imaginative fantasies than the other.

For those who enjoy companionship, loyalty, and a good sex life within their marriage, the sacrifice of extramarital intimacies may well be a good bargain, at least the best one to be made. But for those married persons who do not enjoy comfort and understanding within their marriage, the restriction against extramarital intimacies is an exorbitantly high price to pay for maintaining a proper image.

The traditional ideals make all sex outside of marriage evil and all intimacies outside of marriage irresponsible. These ideals are built into our culture and we get irrational messages about extramarital intimacy throughout our lives. In terms of personal growth, the price of striving for these ideals is often extremely severe. A person in a traditional marriage is forbidden to learn about people, about life, or about sex through extramarital intimacies.

A Proposal: Introducing Independence into Marriage

What choices are open to allow for more personal growth within the institution of marriage?

I suggest that life for the married person can arbitrarily be divided into four compartments. Compartment I is the time/energy spent with one's spouse; Compartment II is the time/energy spent on "family" matters (with or without children) but specifically not with one's spouse. Compartment III is nonfamily time; time/energy given to work, community projects, entertainment with friends, sports, and so on, when one is not accompanied by spouse or children, but time that is completely "open" to inspection; one's spouse can know exactly what one is doing and with whom.

Compartment IV is time/energy allotted to privacy, time when activities are limited only by one's conscience, sense of responsibility, and ability to respond to one's own needs. Big brother is not watching and one need not play show-and-tell afterwards. It is the chance to depart from one's usual role which has attached expected behavior; one is not identified as Mrs. X, president of the bank; or Mr. Y, secretary of the P.T.A.; mother of Jane; or husband of Judge Z. Compartment IV is budgeted time/energy/money that allows for freedom within the structure of marriage.

The important aspect is that one is not proposing to rob one's family of Compartments I and II, or rob one's job or community obligations of Compartment III. Compartment IV entitles one to take private time, to be daring and to explore new experiences instead of being limited to the conventional.

Consider some examples:

—Bill and Mary share their Compartment IV. Both are married, not to each other.

Bill's marriage is an exceptionally satisfying one, but he has for twenty years supplemented sex at home with responsible extramarital relationships. Had he not, he would have resented the restrictions that marriage placed on him; he would not have been able to love his wife as deeply or as long as he has without taking the freedom he needed to meet other women and be with them occasionally. A gentle person with great sensitivity, he has often talked to Mary about enrichment, about responsibility, about remaining concerned with both his wife and Mary's husband. He made it clear from the start that his wife (with whom he still makes love four or five times a week) and children (to whom he is very devoted) have priority; he sincerely cares for Mary and enjoys her companionship. He wanted to be certain that her decision to have extramarital sex was one that she would be able to live with and find helpful.

Mary's marriage, on the other hand, is less satisfying; her husband, although stalwartly faithful to her, is rather cold and domineering. In spite of her apprehension that her husband might find out about her relationship with Bill, she derives a great deal of satisfaction and fulfillment from being with Bill; the warmth and sensitivity that she receives from Bill are carried over to enhance the relationship she has with her husband.

—Dr. Jones is a bisexual surgeon in a small town. His wife is aware of his bisexuality but his patients are not. The fact that he has sex regularly with men in addition to having a good marital sex life in no way decreases his ability to perform surgery. Yet, the confidence of his patients would be shattered if they knew of his bisexuality. The negative fantasies of the patients—not the physical acts of the physician—might damage an otherwise good physician/patient relationship. Similarly, the negative fantasies of the uninvolved spouse often spark the destructive consequences of particular extramarital activities, be they sexual or nonsexual.

—Janet uses her Compartment IV for playing poker, a recreation which her husband, Jim, vehemently opposes. Jim's father was a compulsive gambler whose gambling debts ruined Jim's chance to go to college. When they were first married, Janet had no need to gamble; after thirteen years of nongambling marriage, however, she found a compatible group of friends who enjoyed poker.

Janet is scrupulously careful about the amount she risks, that is, the money to be spent on her Compartment IV evenings; never does she go over the allotted amount. She is not a compulsive gambler; she finds it easy to stay within the limits she has set for herself. Her secret poker games have been going on for several years, with no demonstrable harm to her husband or the marriage. With time, patience, and tremendous skill, Jim might be able to accept her gambling. But until then, what is to be gained by confrontation?

Many of us have our hang-ups and are married to spouses with hang-ups. *Long before we can all become perfect, may we not simply work around each other's hang-ups?* Not all Compartment IV's are used to compensate for hang-ups. In a very good marriage, there is sometimes just the need to be autonomous, the need to make an independent decision and be involved in an independent act with a positive feeling of personhood. Such a spouse *could* tell, but enjoys the feeling of preserving a part of her/his life separate from the marriage, unique and secret.

—Sally loves sex and uses her Compartment IV for sex. Her husband, Jack, enjoys rather routine sex once or twice a week, but does not experiment much and does not like oral sex. Sally reads a great deal about sex, is more imaginative in her sexual fantasies, and truly enjoys oral sex. She supplements her marital sex life with outside sex relationships. Sally is secure in her marriage, which she considers to be exceptionally fine; her appetite for more imaginative sex is fulfilled in her Compartment IV sex life. She is careful to relate to men who are also secure and don't want to hurt their marriages.

—George is an experienced tailor. As a child, George was forced to help his father, who was a tailor. However, George told his wife, Nancy, that he never learned how to sew, he merely helped in the shop. He said this because he did not want to be saddled with mending and alterations, let alone be asked to create new clothes for his family. While he keeps his talent a secret, he occasionally, in semidisguise, goes across town on Saturday mornings and works in a tailor shop. Because he usually spends Saturday mornings out doing errands or working overtime, George has a convenient excuse for the time he is away at the tailor shop.

George gets a big bang out of his Compartment IV although he has never heard that term. Granted that if Nancy and George had perfect communication, the couple could discuss George's sewing talents and see to it that they were not exploited. As it is, George quietly watches Nancy sew and chuckles inside; Nancy likes to sew and is reasonably good at mending and altering hand-me-downs for the children.

Nancy is the more imaginative partner, the one who is creative about ideas for recreation, about how to stretch a budget, about how to remodel the house; George supports her, and they enjoy planning their lives together. That wee bit of independence that George has, however, gives him a feeling of uniqueness, a feeling of nondomination that makes life with Nancy not just bearable but a joy.

Compartment IV is based on the premise that it is possible to remain close, loving, caring, and passionate even when one has secrets from one's marital partner, *providing that one understands that part of oneself did not get married*. With this realization, neither marital partner remains permanently "melted" into an institution (relationship). Who has the authority to demand "all or none" marriages for everyone? Without such a limitation, both partners remain individuals voluntarily teaming up to share most of their lives together and developing a trust that allows each to follow her/his own conscience. Each gives the other the right to a certain amount of time/energy that can be used completely independently; each respects the Compartment IV of the other without censorship. A mature kind of trust is maintained because each remains bound by conscience. Living within rules diminishes the responsibility of conscience; freedom from rules demands the exercise of conscience. Thus, developing an intimate extramarital relationship (or smoking pot, or attending a gay party, or anything else) is not something that one automatically may or may not do. It is a matter for independent decision.

This is an alternative to the traditional dogma that everyone should give up independence in marriage and share everything, making the merger of two persons as complete as possible. This is an alternative to possessiveness in human relationships.

The traditional possessiveness which our society inculcates may remain entrenched for generations, but even now the acceptance of Compartment IV can allow spouses to accept the possibility of extramarital relationships without demanding to know the degree of intimacy or sexual involvement. It can avoid direct confrontation with something that our traditional values uniformly condemn. It can help to eliminate irrational compulsions either to give or withhold information. It can allow each person to decide for herself or himself when everything or nothing may be communicated to the marriage partner.

This changes the level of trust between two people from "I trust you not to do anything I don't approve of," to "I trust you to act according to your conscience. You don't have to pass my list of do's and don'ts when you make a decision. I do not want to restrict your growth. I do not want you to restrict mine. Let us agree to be faithful to our marriage and to remain motivated to help each other achieve maximum fulfillment and growth." The implications of this philosophy for extramarital intimacies are great.

As indicated in the introduction, the use of extramarital intimacy as a source of fulfillment and personal growth depends on available time, energy, and space where discreet meetings can take place. It is also necessary that other obligations and responsibilities be fulfilled. For years, the public has been bombarded with images associating intimacy outside of marriage with irresponsibility. There are enough cases "proving" this statement to keep the campaign going for many more years. But there is another side to the coin. Many responsible people do in fact use extramarital intimacy as a source of personal growth, as was verified by Kinsey over twenty-five years ago. Under most marriage contracts, however, this means that a person must either cheat or go underground.

Cheating occurs when a person feels that she/he is doing something wrong but wants to do it enough so that she/he accepts the guilt; or finds the compulsion so strong that it seems as though she/he cannot help herself or himself. Going underground occurs when persons believe that what they are doing is right but understand that the "occupation army" has power over their jobs, the custody of their children, their standing in the community, and their future opportunities.

Many people are a part of the sexual underground. These people believe that their life-styles are best for them, in spite of the fact that such life-styles may be unacceptable to the community—and quite often, to their spouses. Many homosexuals and bisexuals are in the underground; although not ashamed of their sexual orientation, they must keep their behavior secret or suffer serious consequences. With them are those enjoying intimate extramarital relationships; they consider such experiences as positive, and they feel good about such experiences. I refer to responsible persons who are highly motivated to cause no harm, with the result that often their relationships are either neutral or beneficial to their marriages.

Currently, there is little choice for someone who is far more imaginative than her/his mate and whose needs are not satisfied within the marital relationship. The options are: (1) dissolve the relationship, (2) frustrate personal growth, (3) cheat, or (4) go underground. If the concept of a private compartment were accepted, there would be a built-in escape valve, an opportunity for the conscientious withholding of selected information without breaking the rules. It is a matter of making the rules fit people's needs rather than making people's needs conform to rules already proven inadequate.

Those who enjoy traditional marriages receive ample support from society and have no need for change. For those interested in a less restrictive form of marriage, I suggest the following: (1) accept extramarital intimacy and dating after marriage (with or without sex) on their merits as legitimate sources of personal fulfillment and growth; (2) when contemplating long-term pairing, incorporate the concept of Compartment IV; and (3) if already involved in a bond that prohibits extramarital intimacy and seriously restricts growth, consider putting loving concern above honesty to others and putting honesty to oneself above all.

23.
Beyond Jealousy and Possessiveness

Ronald Mazur

In the following article Mazur analyzes jealousy and shows how sharing can enrich human relationships rather than destroy them. The article begins with a discussion of the foundations of jealousy in Western culture. It moves on to look at the various types of jealousy, at how jealousy tends to make relationships destructive, and at how jealousy reflects the problems of the person having jealous feelings.

Mazur contends that since jealous behaviors are learned, they can, in a supportive setting, be unlearned. He feels further that understanding the various types of jealousy is a first step toward analyzing one's own jealous feelings (or one's partner's) and overcoming them.

"I the Lord your God am a jealous God" (Deut. 5:9, RSV)
"Love is not jealous or boastful" (1 Cor. 13:4, RSV)

To those who are not familiar with the complexities of Jewish and Christian theology, it certainly looks as if St. Paul one-upped God in wisdom. The transposition of the above biblical sentences implies that the boastfully jealous God is without love, and provides an interesting example of the varied and confusing meanings of "jealousy."

It is astonishing that so little has been written in recent years about such a universal and powerful emotion—an emotion which has triggered horrendous violence in human experience. Religious mythology, the theater, and the classics are suffused with themes of jealousy and its consequences. In the ancient Greek pantheon, Hera is the prototype of the jealous bitch who constantly nags husband Zeus about his incurable and outrageous philandering. The second-century Latin writer Apuleius contrives the gripping story of a vengeful mother who is bitterly jealous of Psyche, her son Cupid's lover. And among Shakespeare's gory tragedies, Othello, whose insane jealousy drives him to murder his faithful wife, Desdemona, is an unforgettable characterization. And yet, in works of psychology, sociology, anthropology, and philosophy, scant attention is given to the analysis and significance of jealousy. Perhaps jealousy has simply gone underground to allow a superficial social accommodation of changing marital partners.

Jealousy is a critical clue to models of marriage. It is an emotional response which is situational and learned. Its primary function has been to reinforce the sexually exclusive factor in traditional monogamy. But as models of monogamy change, the expression of jealousy loses its value and may even be considered inappropriate behavior and a sign of emotional immaturity. In 1958, for example, David Mace could write:

Jealousy can be a very destructive force in a marriage. Yet we won't understand it aright unless we recognize at the start that it is essentially quite natural and, in its right place, good and useful. We are all endowed with certain protective emotions. . . . Jealousy [is one of them]—it makes you watchful over the relationships upon which your security and happiness depend. [1]

In 1972, the husband and wife authors of *Open Marriage: A New Life Style for Couples* stated forthrightly: "No matter how little or how much, jealousy is never a good or constructive feeling. It may show you care, but what you are caring for is too much for yourself, and not enough for your mate." [2]

Which viewpoint is correct? Possibly both. Something has happened to marriage in the fourteen-year interval between those two statements. With greater equalitarianism, and new covenantal or contractual options within marriage, the function of jealousy is changing if not disappearing. Sociologist Jessie Bernard clearly understands the process when she asserts: "If monogamous marriage as we have known it in the past is in process of change, there may be less and less need for jealousy to buttress it, and less and less socialization of human beings to experience it or move to control it." [3] In traditional monogamy, jealousy may be attributed a positive value; the lack of it, for example, being interpreted as indifference, uncaring, or unloving. In open-ended marriage, however, jealousy has no positive function and is not valued; it is, at best, a symptom of tension and poor communication in the relationship.

For those who are strongly motivated to outgrow jealousy, three questions are critical: What is the nature of jealousy? Can jealousy be totally and permanently eradicated from a person? And how do persons go about understanding and deconditioning jealous feelings and behavior patterns? Before answering such questions, it is helpful to assume a casual and positive attitude toward jealousy in persons: It's there; it's something to deal with; somebody is experiencing deep feelings, and the task is to understand them in the context of what that person is trying to learn or communicate. Joan Constantine and Larry Constantine, in their research and work with multilateral or group marriages, make observations about jealousy applicable to other alternative life-styles.

If all jealousy is simply rejected as undesirable or immature, the affect goes underground and interferes with group functioning and the exchange of other feelings. If jealousy is lauded or facilely accepted, growth in important dimensions can be hindered. Thus it is necessary for participants in group marriages to differentiate among various forms of jealousy. Jealousy, if approached properly, becomes an opportunity to discover new information about individuals and their relationships.

Jealousy must be recognized, admitted, and worked with if it is to lead to personal growth and relational enrichment.

What, then, is the meaning of jealousy and how can it be recognized?

While nineteenth-century American dictionaries clearly indicated both nega-tive and positive meanings of the word, it is interesting that the 1970 paper-back edition of *The American Heritage Dictionary of the English Language* gives predominantly negative denotations of *jealous*. To be jealous is to be "1. Fearful of loss of position or affection. 2. Resentful in rivalry; envious. 3. Possessively watchful; vigilant." What seems clear is that the word itself has borne the burden of too many meanings; there is a great deal of legitimate difference and semantic confusion surrounding its historical usage. The trend also seems to be to use it only in a negative way. Regardless of how contemporary lexicographers define it, jealousy is more than a word; it is usually a gut-feeling experience filled with anxiety, resentment, threat, fear, and other hurtful emotions. It comes like a flash flood, undoubtedly causing various physiological manifestations. Jealousy is a complex emotion, and perhaps the only way to understand it and to control it—not eliminate it—is to analyze its various forms. Perhaps, if we analyze its various forms, we will find that jealousy can be defused of its demonic potential.

The following is a typology of jealousy which does not include the ar-chaic positive usages, or the classifications of "healthy" or "romantic" jeal-ousy. It is intended for use by all those who are disturbed by unwanted feel-ings of jealousy—who want to work toward eliminating it in relationships. In the open-ended marriage, jealousy has no creative purpose. This is to recog-nize, however, that in a lengthy transitional period, persons conscientiously experimenting with open-ended marriage and other life-styles will already be conditioned to be jealous under various circumstances and will have to re-learn new emotional and behavioral patterns. The task, then, is to recognize, understand, and deal openly and creatively with whatever kind of jealousy is experienced. It must also be emphasized that the forces of jealousy are inter-related with some common causes and consequences.

Envy-Jealousy Versus Reality Living

While some scholars make a case for differentiating *jealousy* from *envy*, it is more fruitful to consider enviousness as a variety of jealousy. The terms are often used synonymously and defined as such in contemporary dictio-naries. Although an 1886 American dictionary states that "Envy is a base passion, and never used, like jealousy, in a good sense," it is quite probable that of all the forms of jealousy, most persons can easily empathize with envy. Early American lexicographers were clergymen or theologically astute scholars who understood and accepted biblical morality. They knew that the "jealous God" of Scripture was zealous for the righteousness of His people, that the quality of that jealousy was commitment and caring. They also knew the biblical commandment against covetousness—desiring wives or cattle not lawfully theirs. To be envious, therefore, was to break the Commandments.

To feel envy, however, is not actually to steal anyone's wife, livestock, or other possessions—it is wishful thinking. Everyone experiences it count-less times. Someone else is always better-looking, more personable, more tal-ented, richer, luckier, more intelligent, more courageous, happier, more lovable or loved, or more valuable for the human race. What one envies reveals not simply what one would like to have, but often what one would like to be. But if envious wishful thinking is not soon transcended by realistic, dedicated work toward desired goals, or by honest, possibly humorous rejection of the specific source of envy, it can lead to crippling resentment and self-pity. A Boston newspaper interview with a young couple living an open-ended relationship probed the difficulties of such a life-style. The young husband was enthusiastic and self-assured but did admit to one difficulty. He admitted to being jealous on occasions when a male friend of his wife's would take her to restaurants he could not afford. Although the husband used the word *jealous*, what he was more specifically feeling was envy-jealousy. He wanted to have the money to provide experiences as enjoyable for his wife as any other male could provide. The nature of envy, as well as other forms of jealousy, is that it always needs *more* to satisfy it. The young man seemed to be able to express his wishes honestly, without rancor or self-defeating pride. But if he had lacked the ability to be in touch with his feelings, to deal with them openly, he would have set conditions for the failure of his marital relationship.

Perhaps certain types of personalities are prone to certain types of jealousy, but everyone at times has reflected on his/her given life situation and looked with envy on greener fields. If one faces the reality of one's own limitations and circumstances, however, anger and/or aspiration will be appropriately directed rather than deflected inwardly causing depression and/or debilitating self-pity.

Possessive-Jealousy Versus Autonomy

Emotional space for each partner to be autonomous is a necessary condition for any type of creative marriage or intimate relationship. For the recognition and growth of our own self—our integrity or wholeness—we need emotional space. Poet Kahlil Gibran advises lovers: "Love one another, but make not a bond of love. Let it rather be a moving sea between the shores of your souls,"* and he speaks of "spaces in togetherness." This is startling for young lovers to hear, for they think of their love as an eternal bond. But Gibran jars the thoughtful into serious consideration of unspoken realities. Very few couples, however, consider the meanings of a traditional pronouncement of marriage: "I now pronounce you man and wife." Man and *wife?* Apparently men, clergy and grooms, are loath to create such a binding role as husband, for why not say "husband and wife"? Clergymen would sound ridiculous saying, "I now pronounce you Man and Woman," though such a declaration has intriguing possibilities. In any case, such a pronouncement would grant the Man nothing—which is not what traditional marriage was created for. It is the woman who is *given* in marriage by her father or other male kinsman. The traditional wedding service, deceptively elegant and

---

*From "On Marriage" in *The Prophet* by Kahlil Gibran. Copyright © 1923 by Kahlil Gibran, renewed 1951. Reprinted by permission of Alfred A. Knopf, Inc.

sentimental, is the ritual wherein the father of the bride pays his property tax and transfers the title of ownership. It is no wonder that people cry at weddings—there are a number of profound reasons why tears are appropriate.

Possessiveness is culturally sanctioned but is nevertheless a dehumanizing process. The possessive person does not know the inherent value or even the identity of the person possessed. The possessor is also possessed by private versions of reality—a reality requiring order, reassurance, and respect from without, and a sense of power and control. This allows for predictability, homage, and manipulation, but negates the qualities of spontaneity, authentic self-esteem, and mutuality of relationship. By perceiving the other merely as an extension of one's own life—even when romantically intended—that other person is deprived of dignity, individuality, and freedom to be and become with integrity. Possessiveness can, of course, be symbiotic in the sense that both spouses build their lives around it and feed off each other. This is so much the case that possessive marriage has superseded religion as the "opiate of the masses"; it is a stupefied security without joy, enthusiasm, or adventure.

The double standard reinforces the sanctions for possessiveness in accordance with the best interests of males. When the male is possessive-jealous, the female is supposed to feel proud and grateful. When the female is possessive-jealous, the male flaunts it as a sign of his desirability and attractiveness as long as the female doesn't push too hard. But when the female becomes too demanding she is demeaned as being nothing but a castrating bitch.

Possessive-jealousy is perhaps the most raging and wrathful form of jealousy, leading to acts of cruel vengeance and even murder. "You belong to me and if you cross me I'll get even with you. If I can't have you nobody is going to have you." That sentiment sounds as if it comes from one of those unbelievably trite movies. Yet, the sentiments of possessive people *are* unfortunately trite, and potentially destructive.

Is it possible to be monogamously committed to someone without possessiveness? We pose the question because many couples seem to confuse *commitment* with *belonging to*. Possessiveness is commitment without trust. Conversely, commitment with trust celebrates the autonomy of the other, rejoices in the uniqueness of the other, is aware of the privacy needs of the other. There need be no contradiction between mutual commitment and the mutual allowance for emotional space.

Exclusion-Jealousy Versus Sharing

The most painful type of jealousy is exclusion-jealousy—being left out of a lovely or critical experience of a loved one. While it's true that *every* experience is unique to the person undergoing or feeling it—since no two persons will ever see, feel, understand, and value a shared experience in precisely the same way—it is nevertheless true that there is something beautiful and important about a couple going through something together. For those who seek to live a joyous open-ended marriage, exclusion-jealousy will be the most difficult interpersonal barrier they must overcome. It is a formidable hurdle which occasions the most sublime exhilaration once cleared. Over the long course, it recurs at intervals but it becomes easier to take and soon becomes a pleasurable challenge.

It's easy to feel jealous when you are excluded. It's not a matter of wanting to deny one's partner a new or enjoyable experience with someone else. Rather one wants to be included in the experience. It is also not a matter of possessiveness as such. For one can be genuinely nonpossessive and yet be overcome by exclusion-jealousy. It can happen for two reasons—being shut out of a good time, and/or not having similar pleasure with another while the spouse is involved elsewhere. It sometimes comes down to a matter of, "Damn it, how come you have all the opportunities while I seem to be stuck in a rut?" Or it could be something like, "Why did you go there with your friend when you never like to go there with me?" Exclusion-jealousy is especially intense when a partner feels—or is—neglected in comparison to the time, finances, interest, and enthusiasm the spouse is lavishing upon someone else. Then there are those inevitable disappointing conflicts in plans when one partner says, "Oh, by the way, I'll be out with so-and-so on next Thursday evening" and the other replies, "Hell, I was hoping we could do something special together that evening." That "something special" is usually quite specific and it means changing plans with the friend or disappointing the spouse. With a little practice, however, couples can avoid such conflicts.

Couples living an open-ended marriage will handle the problems of exclusion-jealousy in various ways, including an attempt never to exclude each other. Some couples, for example, feel strongly that they can always include the spouse, even when the spouse is not present, by sharing their experiences verbally and by having their friends always meet the spouse. This inclusive approach might possibly work for couples with similar needs who are able to verbalize experiences and always enjoy meeting each other's friends. Other couples, however, will not find this a satisfying solution—their needs for privacy and emotional space may be strong, they may find verbal analysis of their experiences superficial. Such couples would rather confront the fact of exclusion directly. They are willing to say, "Yes, it's true we have experiences with others from which our spouse is excluded. We don't experience all of each other's intimate friendships, but we rejoice in the persons we are and in the richness of our relationships. We simply have to learn to live with the freedom to have partially separate lives—and we really wouldn't want it any other way." Ultimately, it is not so much a question of just sharing each other.

Competition-Jealousy Versus Specialness

Marriage partners who are self-actualizing may at times be jealous of each other's achievements and will compete for recognition and success. At its best, this can be creative tension; at its worst, undercutting one-upmanship.

The arena of competition, however, is not restricted to status and success. This is not to say that this contest is unimportant or trivial. On the contrary, it's imperative for women to refuse being consigned to supportive roles, to unleash their full creative potential for the benefit of themselves and for all people. If this kind of competition makes men uncomfortable, that's *their* problem. Women for too long have apologized for bruising frail male egos, and such men are just going to have to grow up and stop expecting their wives to be their mothers.

Negative forms of competition stem from a lack of self-confidence or self-esteem leading to jealousy of the partner's achievements, attractiveness, friends, or sexual performance. Behind competition-jealousy is the attitude: "You think I'm not good enough for you, but I'll show you!" This projection of inadequacy demands constant reassurance from the partner, but the reassurance is always suspected of being mere condescension. What is needed to overcome this form of jealousy is the development of self-esteem in combination with the sense of being essentially *special* to one's lover. This sense of specialness rests on the attitude: "Sure, I'm aware you know some fantastic people who also think you're great, but that makes me happy for you because I also know I'm uniquely special to you, that the quality of our relationship is one of the highest shared values in our lives." To be glad for the other without feeling like a second-rate person does indeed require a high degree of self-esteem. And, ironically, that self-esteem is easier to develop when two people lovingly help each other to be special through mutual respect, sensual pleasuring, admiration, approval, support, and sometimes forgiveness.

Egotism-Jealousy Versus Role Freedom

Role flexibility or interchangeability is a new personal freedom and a new feature of contemporary interpersonal relationships. The rigid stereotypes of masculinity and femininity have already been shattered, opening new avenues for self-realization and interpersonal openness. There are, to be sure, casualties of this shattering of sex stereotypes, and there are those who defensively hide from its impact. A time of transition is confusing and difficult for many. Nevertheless, the change is relentless and there is no turning back to the comforting absurdities of conformist man-woman, woman-woman, or man-man relationships. There is a new role freedom for all persons who will no longer allow themselves and their potentialities to be defined by cultural conformity or the insensitive expectations of others. This freedom also allows problems to surface: men may become enraged or embarrassed because their wives challenge them in public; women may become enraged or embarrassed because their husbands seem openly affectionate to other males. Examples of anger or embarrassment over a conflict in role expectations are endless.

Egotism-jealousy is a denial of role freedom. It is, in a sense, wanting a girl/boy just like the girl/boy that married dear old dad/mom. Rather than see the crisis of role interchangeability as an opportunity for growth, some people are ashamed of their "unfeminine" wives or "unmasculine" (note that the word is usually "effeminate") husbands and are jealous of other people who have "ideal" husbands/wives.

Egotism-jealousy can also be turned against the spouse with the ability for role flexibility who exposes the rigidity of the less flexible partner.

Egotism-jealousy is similar to envy-jealousy but is more specifically related to one's ability or inability to expand one's ego awareness and role flexibility. When both men and women can be persons in whatever ways that make them happiest regardless of what and how tradition defines them sexually, they will invest less of their egos in social roles and status. Can you imagine a time when baby boys and baby girls will be born free?

Fear-Jealousy Versus Security

Jealousy can be just plain fear—fear of losing someone special, fear of being lonely, of being rejected. To the extent that one's own value depends upon a partner's devotion, one will be vulnerable to the fear of desertion. If there is a classic form of jealousy, this probably is it, although an equally strong case can be made for possessive-jealousy. Fear-jealousy doubts the commitment of the other; it breeds on insecurity. It torments with anxiety and anguish. "What if my lover finds someone else better than me? What will happen to me?" Underlying such fearful feelings is the assumption that one is satisfying to the lover only as a desirable product—when something "better" comes along one will be abandoned. It's a hell of a way to live, but fear-jealousy is the foundation on which most marriages precariously endure.

The only security in a healthy relationship is to be a person, not a product. None of us is desirable or enjoyable in every way on every day, and if our relationships depend on the fear of having our lovers discover the attractiveness of others, then we do indeed shape dull and emotionally crippled lovers. Let your lover look at you with all of your blemishes and shortcomings and let your relationship be a dynamic exploration in life and becoming rather than a wedding exchange of personality packages. The strongest and most joyful relationships are those in which partners are not afraid to let each other go; attempting to control the duration of a relationship because of insecurity sacrifices the magnificence of every *now*. Bless and celebrate each moment of joy and loving with thankfulness, and let the future take care of itself.

Jealous behavior continues to be socially sanctioned in "appropriate" forms, but there are reasons to believe it will diminish as it ceases to serve a useful function in interpersonal relationships. Jessie Bernard (1971) believes: "If it is true that marriage is indeed moving away from the old monogamic format in the direction of some as yet unclarified form, jealousy in the classic form would no longer be required to support it and we could expect its gradual diminution. But until we know with more certainty the nature of the model —or models—of marriage we are moving toward, jealousy in some form or other may continue to crop up in the clinician's office." It is probable, also, that even as models of marriage are clarified and become culturally accepted, forms of jealousy will be experienced by most people to some degree some of the time. Whether one believes that jealousy is inevitable or eradicable, normal or neurotic, is ultimately not the most important issue. What is important is to ask the most helpful question: "What *kind* of jealousy affects my relationships?" It is of no practical use to try to decide once and for all whether or not one is a jealous person. But if one understands the various types of jealousy something can be done to control and minimize it—to disarm it if not dissolve it. Simply expressing jealousy is a cop-out in a relationship—it is not being honestly open to one's self or to the special other. So much more of the expectations and satisfactions of a relationship could be understood, communicated, and creatively acted upon, if couples could understand the specifics of jealousy. What is it that you *really* resent? Are you afraid? Envious? Excluded? Competitive? Possessive? Does your ego hurt? What do you *really* want to communicate to each other? It doesn't help merely to say "I'm jealous." Jealous how? Can we *do* something about it? Should we renegotiate our expectations of each other? How can we grow from here?

Jealousy Inventory Exercise

A couple or small group may gain insight into the specific meanings of jealous feelings by analyzing jealousy experiences according to the six types of jealousy described above.

A couple can simply write out or relate to each other their last remembered jealous experience and then try to rephrase the feelings more directly in terms of the six kinds of jealousy.

In a group of six or more, each person could write about a jealousy experience anonymously (without age, name, or sex). Shuffle papers and redistribute with each person reading the paper in hand and offering some possibilities for more direct expression of the experience: e.g., "this person felt left out"; "this person isn't aware of his/her partner's need for privacy"; "this person seems envious and unhappy about what he/she doesn't have"; etc.

If it doesn't feel right or comfortable to share a jealousy experience with a partner or a small group, use the following four examples for discussion. They were obtained in a small group and are shared as written. Were the writers male or female? How could they have expressed themselves directly and honestly to the person who occasioned the jealousy? What could each person do to improve the relationship or situation?

Question: When was the last time you felt jealousy and how do you remember the experience?

Example 1

My last experience with jealousy took place when the person with whom I'm involved chose to spend a weekend vacationing without wanting to have me along. My feelings were very intense because for me there could be no real pleasure in a vacation without bringing this person. I was angry, hurt, rejected totally out of proportion to the occasion.

Example 2

I feel jealousy to a limited extent when my partner or I discover relations *as deep* as ours that were had before our present relationship.

I feel a *twinge* of jealousy when friends in a "family-network" relationship have a tactile relationship with partner.

Example 3

Although I felt, and feel, that the sensual/sexual experience need not be confined exclusively to the mate or partner of the moment, I became extremely jealous, insecure, annihilated when this led to my partner's acute emotional involvement. By losing the partner's primary commitment to me, I was losing much of my identity.

Example 4

When I felt my mate was able to express feelings completely (not necessarily sexual) and I was not able to do so I felt jealous of this ability. This was not a threat on the part of my mate, but rather a feeling of a lacking on my part. My mate's warmth, concerns, fears, and hopes were able to be expressed and experienced but mine were hidden both to me and others.

Reference Notes

1. David Mace, *Success in Marriage* (Abington Press, 1958), p. 11.
2. Nena and George O'Neill, *Open Marriage* (M. Evans Inc., 1972), p. 246.
3. Jessie Bernard, "Jealousy in Marriage," *Medical Aspects of Human Sexuality* (April 1971), p. 209.

24.
Being in Bed Naked with You
Is the Most Important Thing in My Life

Robert H. Rimmer

*In four of his works novelist Robert Rimmer portrays a way of life
where one maximizes joy by becoming open and sexually freed. Placing little
credence in most of our theories of "natural" possessiveness, hostility, and
monogamous exclusivity, Rimmer develops the thesis that people are loving
by nature and that intimacy with two or three people in long-term relationships can be a highly rewarding and satisfying life-style.*

*Rimmer feels multiple intimate relationships in addition to a good mar-
riage are inevitable and contingent only upon our recognizing our needs and
facing love in a more open, receptive, and childlike way. Here his creative
mind formulates the thesis developed in the novels. Rimmer, no utopian
dreamer, claims that it is possible to live and find fulfillment in the life-style
he proposes. He has acquired a large following in the past several years, and
the feedback he has received has helped him in the formulation of the ideas
set forth here.*

As you read the title of this essay are you smiling or frowning? If you're
between sixteen and twenty-five years of age, of either sex, and have had a
reasonably loving and protected early life, I hope you are smiling. Maybe
even in agreement. Because you still have some wonder left in your life, and
the possibility of snuggling—of warm body contact with a loving human
being of the other sex—is high in your order of personal priorities.

But, alas, after thirty the wonder and the joy and the amazement of this
other person, naked in bed with you (Oh hell, I have done this so many
times!) is often replaced by genital priorities, how-to-do-it techniques, or a
complete lack of spontaneity. The sexual merger for many humans has about
the same significance as the singing commercial—"You deserve a treat
today"—and the physical blending and ultimate orgasm is as familiar and
about as inspiring as the one billionth look-alike hamburger. "Now that is
over with—do we turn on television, or do we go to sleep?" For humans who
have arrived at this point in their lives *being naked with you* is more an embarrassment than a joy, and certainly not the most important thing in life!

Because I believe that human sexual loving in simultaneous combination
with mental surrender can induce altered states of consciousness, and that
humans have a need to experience the world in different dimensions—stoned
thinking as distinguished from straight thinking—I have written a quartet of

---

novels which try to convince the reader of this essential premise. *Being naked with you* (the convenient location often being bed, but not necessarily so) is the most important thing in my/your life!

In July 1943, in a paper titled *A Theory of Human Motivation*, Abraham Maslow historically proposed that humans passed through a hierarchy of human needs, and at any epoch in human life on this planet different cultures could simultaneously be on different levels on the ladder of personal development. People can only begin the climb to the next peak when they have their feet firmly placed on the plateau below.

The first needs which must be satisfied are physiological—basically the hunger and sex needs followed by the safety needs (the needs of freedom from pain or fear). Third are the love needs—the necessity of being a part of a world that cares about you, and finally are the needs for esteem, followed by the top of the pyramid—the need for self-actualization—in Maslow's words "the need to become everything one is capable of becoming."

It seems to me that the fourth and fifth needs—all of which make a sharp demarcation between persons in control of their environment and that part of them which is a prey to the unpredictable world—are encapsulated in the third needs—the love needs. Additionally, I am convinced that most human beings can *learn* a complete awareness of their humanity and that these completely human love needs—as distinguished from the primal needs—have no direct connection with our descent from the apes.

If there ever was a "territorial imperative," or if we have innate tendencies toward "human aggression," these childish hedonisms can be easily "conditioned" out of us in the learning and growth process of living.

Men and women who have already arrived at this level of humanity are able to blend their personal selves with others without loss of identity. They may even be able to surrender themselves with deep intimacy with several persons of the other sex, and make the discovery that finding one's self is the ability to lose oneself. Thus the concept of *being naked with you* is both a sexual need and a need for alternate consciousness that becomes the road to Nirvana. It is an almost ineffable peak that can be experienced as one learns to surrender oneself with another human being. And, as a true Buddha, you do not go alone to Nirvana but remain to bring the world of humans with you.

The surrendering, of course, at this time in human history (even for those well advanced in the hierarchy of human needs) is a more daring adventure than most people are capable of, basically because nowhere in the advanced technology of the Western world are our religious or educational systems making any effort to train young people in the vast potential of human interrelationships. In fact, just the opposite. Our strong Judeo-Christian conditionings still motivate our actions and despite the decline of interest in weekend religion, while most of us may agree that we are created in the image of God, few would agree with me that you and I are the only God we will ever know. The split between God out there—(not God as you)—coupled with the Anglo-Saxon certainty that work and Kantian duty are the salvation of man, plus the meritocracy structure of capitalism all combine to destroy our natural childish wonder, and we are afraid to admit the need to experience the world upside down (as youngsters do by looking head-down through their legs, or by whirling). So the average human being, confirmed in the ego-centric behavior of childhood, actually fears self-surrender and is unaware that *being naked with you* could help ward off vast loneliness and the inter-personal muddles most of us live in.

About fifteen years ago—when I was approaching forty and the inward rebellion against the hoked-up morality, ethics, and sheer shuck of my world was only a smoldering fire—I tried to evoke the feeling of *being naked with you* in the form of Ten Commandments which became an integral part of the novel *The Rebellion of Yale Marratt*.

Commandments, of course, is an overblown word for a basic philosophy of life. Like any proselytizer worth his salt, I was trying to convince a largely disinterested world that there was a saner departure point for human rela-tionships. Here are the tenets for a new kind of religion which Yale Marratt tried to introduce into the world via his foundation, Challenge, Inc.

1. Challenge believes that Man is God.
2. Challenge believes that men must be taught to challenge and excoriate any concepts that deny the ultimate divinity of Man.
3. Challenge is not concerned with the immortality of Man. Man must be taught to seek his salvation on this earth and in this lifetime through the Love and Understanding of all men.
4. Challenge believes that the only destiny of Man is the pursuit of knowl-edge, and every Man of sound mind and body should actively pursue his destiny.
5. Challenge believes that no Man is preconditioned to act by metaphysical fate or man-conceived determinism.
6. Challenge believes that Man is the measure of all ethical and moral val-ues, and the test of validity in Man's ethics and morals and written laws should be that they exalt and confirm the dignity of Man.
7. Challenge believes that any human problem (hence, all problems known to Man) can be solved in the atmosphere of Love, and that the existence of hate as an emotion should be extirpated from Man's relationships and be considered the greatest evil confronting civilization.

Now here is the first statement of the *being-naked-with-you* philosophy which I still believe is quite valid.

8. Challenge believes that in the sexual union of Man and Woman, all hu-mans regardless of language, race, or creed become deeply aware of the Beauty and Goodness inherent in each Man and Woman, and that through proper instruction from childhood can learn to transfer this Ul-timate Insight into their daily commerce with each other.
9. Challenge believes that its beliefs are so honestly right for today's civ-ilization that if men everywhere would accept them and teach them to their children for several generations, eventually a crusade would result

that would wipe tyranny and oppression from this world.
10. Challenge will never cease to challenge. No thing . . . no belief, not even the Commandments of Challenge, are sacred or inviolable.

The Tenth Commandment could well be the most important one because, in addition to the Eighth Commandment, it embodies an entire philosophy of life, suggesting that even the ego of the Commander is not sacred, and that human beings with a cosmic consciousness, and hence a sense of humor, can be their own *doppelganger*, and stand aside and chuckle at themselves, and their own pretentiousness.

The story of Yale Marratt is essentially the search of one man (myself) for the roots and meaning of living. Why am I here? What is this life all about? Does it really matter? The potential answers all of us have experienced are either optimistic—God is in heaven, all is well with the world—or a parallel cynicism which uses the daily reality to disprove such foolishness, or a shrugging, hopeless hedonism which seems to be typical of the past few decades in American life.

In this framework, Yale Marratt marries two women and struggles with the meanings of intimacy and love in an unconventional manner. Yale believed in the Sixth Commandment of Challenge—man is the measure of all ethical and moral values. He challenged the law and proclaimed his right to live in a responsible bigamous marriage. The book leaves unanswered the question of whether the people of Connecticut will take action to change the outmoded laws on bigamy.

Twelve years later, Connecticut (as well as 49 other states) has continued to let sleeping dogs lie. But many ménages à trois are flourishing sub rosa. From hundreds of letters I have received I am sure that this form of marriage, whether it be two men and one woman, or two women and one man, because it tends to act out monogamy, by revolving around the lone representative of one sex as the leader, is surprisingly viable and long lasting.* Today, many marriage counselors believe that a legal three-person relationship should be available to older people who could pool their resources and their social security and live much fuller lives. The stress is placed on economics however and not on *being naked with you*.

Many religious leaders, suddenly aware that *being naked with you* can be embraced without the necessity of denying that God is out there somewhere, are now accepting the fact that while monogamy will continue as the prime basic interpersonal encounter, marriage in the future will offer much looser structures in the area of companionship, family, and sexual fidelity.

Group marriage, swinging, and communal living, all quickly popularized by the press in the past few years, are now giving way to what the

---

*Editors' note: Empirical data collected by Patrick LaFollette, a founder of Family Synergy in Los Angeles, support Rimmer's optimism about the existence and viability of triads. LaFollette's data (unpublished as yet) indicate about equal proportions of triadic groups with one woman and two men as with two women and one man. The triads are affiliated with Family Synergy.

O'Neills have labeled "open marriage." They have proceeded to define this panacea solution in terms of better interpersonal relationships in monogamy. But the O'Neills, though they offer the possibility of companionship with the other sex, sidestepped the day-to-day interaction of a monogamously married couple trying to cope with a second or third love relationship.

Many recent books have explored alternatives to traditional marriage. A brief list might include the O'Neills' book, *Open Marriage*; Carl Rogers' fascinating excursion into this area in his book *Becoming Partners: Marriage and Its Alternatives*; John and Mimi Lobell's *John and Mimi* in which a young couple in their twenties use their own names and freely reveal to each other in separate chapters their numerous sexual encounters in their particular brand of open marriage; and my book *Adventures in Loving* which has more than twenty articles by people between twenty-five and forty-five attempting different life-styles from bigamy to group arrangements, orgies, triads, and open marriages. However, the plain truth is that most of these experimenters or adventurers, as I call them, have only the faintest idea of how to make alternate life-styles which incorporate multiple sexual involvements really work on an emotional, interpersonal basis.

Most of the marriage counselors writing books, whether they be Gina Allen and Clement Martin in their book *Intimacy*, or Joyce Brothers in her book *The Brothers' Approach to a Liberated Marriage*, or Jane Mouton and Robert Blake in their work *The Marriage Grid*, or Herbert and Roberta Otto writing in *Total Sex*, give lip service to an unreal, impossible world of sexual freedom coupled with I-gotta-be-me interpersonal relationships. Most of them seem to be unaware that sexual hedonism as a way of life may be possible in the animal world but will not work for human beings.

Typical of the confusion in the minds of many of the sexual popularizers who believe, evidently along with Masters and Johnson, that good sex is physical first and mental second is some of the work by Helen Gurley Brown. Here is a quote from the introduction to *Cosmopolitan* magazine's *Love Guide*, a bedside companion for the confused young female.

> Here we hope is the ultimate *love* book . . . it is not a sex text—although it *will* revolutionize your sex life if you really do all we tell you. Sexuality is *not* a mechanical thing. If an orgasm were your only goal, an electric vibrator would help you achieve that, *technically*. But what any woman *really* wants is so much more . . . more human, more beautiful, more fulfilling, more magical, more supportive. She craves intimate sharing between two people.

The emphasis is Helen Gurley Brown's. Few females or males would disagree with the last two sentences. But do those sentences jibe with the contents of the book? Here are the chapter titles—and the sheer shuck that you get for your money: *Awakening Your Sensuality* . . . *Sexual Muddles and Fallacies* . . . *The Erotic Senses* . . . *Know Your Body Nude* . . . *How to Excite Yourself* . . . *How to Make a Man Want You* . . . *Know His Body Nude* . . . *Losing Your Virginity without Losing Your Cool* . . . *That First Night with a New Man* . . . *Ways to Sustain Passion* . . . *How to Make Him a Better Lover* . . . *Sick Sex* . . . *Continuing to Live Sensuously*. . .topped off with *Your Zodiac Seduction Book*.

Contrast the introduction with the contents and you have the typical guide to what can be the ultimate physical contact any of us can experience in interrelationships. *Being naked with you* as the most important thing in one's life would be regarded by Helen Gurley Brown as sheer pollyannaism. It is obvious that *Cosmopolitan's* advertising revenue and circulation is much higher on her order of priorities. But picking on Helen Gurley Brown is not fair. I am sure even she has once or twice experienced the ultimate sensuality of letting go of her ego . . . surrendering herself. If she or any female would dare to convey the how-to of that mental-sexual involvement in print it would be a more valuable guide than *Sex and the Office Girl.* The first question that needs to be answered is why can't we recapture our childhood wonder?

In *The Rebellion of Yale Marratt* I took the first tentative steps toward identifying the *being naked* approach to life with the following statement that Yale makes to Cynthia, whom he has just married. Previously, Yale has told Cynthia that he is married to Anne, but he doesn't know where she is. On the day of his marriage to Cynthia he discovers that Anne has his child. In a conversation with Yale, Cynthia reviles him and in a defeatist tone wonders why Yale doesn't just leave her alone and go to Anne, whom his father finds more acceptable.

"Listen," Yale said, angrily, "my life, so far, has been conditioned by people making tragedies where there is no tragedy. If you had come to me and told me what Pat had said to you, I would have told him to go to hell. I would have married you. We would have found a way somehow. . . . Cindar, did you ever stop to think of how most people live life with a suicidal complex, a masochistic drive to hurt themselves? That's what I mean by making tragedies where there is no tragedy. Look at my father. He could make a tragedy out of my love for you simply because you are Jewish. He multiplies tragedy by trying to make me something I'm not. My sister is making tragedy where none need exist. Anne has a tragic complex evidently; or else she would have tried to find me. Everywhere you turn people have twisted their lives out of perspective over some human failing."

Now here is the first *being-naked-with-you* approach. Yale continues:

"Some person or persons fail to measure up to some idiotic idea another person has of himself, and boom you have the seeds of self-destruction. Look at the world around you. What is the basis of all the hatred but a deluded idea of the importance of 'self'? Look at the murders in the morning papers, the divorces, the man-made scandals. What does it all amount to but a form of egomania? A feeling that the *I* is so damned important that it must justify itself at all cost. Do you know, I'll wager ninety-five percent of the novels written or the plays produced each year would have no basis for existence if it weren't for making tragedies where no tragedy should ever exist. There is only one tragedy in the world, and that is this terrible delusion with the importance of self."

Cynthia had stopped crying. She listened to him in silent wonder. "What has this to do with us?" she asked, thinking Yale hasn't really changed. He could still run wild with words.

"It means simply, I love you! I love Anne. Your solution for that situation is for you or Anne to withdraw in lonely resignation, wishing the winner good luck in the best jolly-old-cricket tradition—while the unseen audience wipes away the tears; because of course that is the only thing to do. That's the way they want the world to end," Yale said bitterly, "not with a bang . . . but with a whimper. Man must love the idea of whimpering idiots; there are so many of them."

Later in *The Harrad Experiment* I proposed, as an integral part of the Harrad approach to life, entirely new interpersonal experiences based on a self-disclosing style of human interaction. It also proposes that learning a new perspective on one's ego, vis-à-vis other human beings, is possible for most youngsters. Here is an example in a conversation between Phil Tenhausen, the guiding light of Harrad College, and Harry Schacht, an undergraduate student.

"I was never demanding of Beth," Harry said angrily.

Phil chuckled, "You expected because you loved her that she would love you in an identical way, didn't you? That's an extremely demanding idea. It can lead to the following conclusions. You either blame yourself, telling yourself that Beth didn't love you because you are ugly or you are Jewish or any of a host of masochistic ideas that you may dream up to whip yourself with; or you take a more positive approach and tell yourself that Beth is really not a good person because she didn't respond to your good love. The first approach will destroy your identity and probably lead to insanity; the second approach which is more typical, will ultimately bring you to the following: 'I really dislike Beth. She is promiscuous and will never love any one except herself.'

"Depending on how strongly you react, it is a simple step to move from her apparent rejection of you to your rejection of her. This makes life simple. You reduce your problems to black and white. In this case: 'I hate Beth.' All of this is extremely unrealistic thinking. You are planning to be a doctor, aren't you, Harry? In our opinion many of the illnesses that you will encounter will have been triggered by this type of thinking. Hating is a self-indulgence that eventually leads to self-destruction. Where are you at the moment, Harry?"

[Later, Beth tells Harry,] "From each person I've made love with, I've learned something . . . mostly that the act of sexual congress is simply not so damned death-defying, all-encompassing serious. It is not the alpha and omega of love or marriage. It's fun. The really wonderful thing about it is, if you come to the act of love defenseless, willing to give your self to another person, and the other person shares this feeling, then for a few moments in your life it's possible to be wholly and completely the real you. If two people make love this way, and stop playing roles with each other and can enjoy and accept each other for the frightened little people they really are . . . then sexual intercourse becomes a way of saying 'I am for a moment no longer me, I am you!' "

Here Beth is stating the concept of *being naked with you*, expressed as the ultimate key to deeply involved interpersonal relationships. Just in case you think I only mean this figuratively, let me refer you to the quartet of my novels. *Being naked* in these books is a literal way of life, too, and accompanying it is the *continuous wonder of you*—your flesh, your physical processes, your contingency as a human being (you will die) that makes me aware of the unending mystery of life. Thus the literal and figurative acts of *being naked together* combine in a *simultaneous mental-sexual surrender*—a letting go which carries overtones of Eastern philosophies in its restructuring of human values, and lets you, the lover, discover beyond any shadow of a doubt that the third priority of human life is what makes us human.

In *The Natural Mind*, Andrew Weil establishes a potential educational and religious approach to life that is in distinct contrast to the popular philosophy embodied in the songs, "I'll do it my way" and "I gotta be me." It contrasts with a style of hedonism which, ultimately, one can't live with and which has produced the age of the shrink, sensitivity training, and encounter—most of which insist on being true to one's self, doing one's thing, as a much higher priority than *being naked with you.*

In the novel *Proposition 31*, I have suggested many times through the action of the characters that ability to lose one's ego, even to the point of playing at the role of a chameleon and taking on the other person's coloration, will not endanger one's personal identity. Instead it opens the possibility of an exchange for a cosmic identity and a world of warm laughter and objectivity about one's self, and one's petty problems. Corporate marriage (a merger of the lives of two to three families) as proposed in *Proposition 31* or synergamy (two coexisting monogamous marriages) as proposed in *Thursday, My Love*, can exist only if most of the participants achieve this kind of interpersonal interplay.

In *Thursday, My Love*, temporarily putting aside the exploration of a two-couple or three-couple group marriage, I have suggested that a parallel relationship coexisting with the monogamous marriage might be easier to cope with (especially at the outset) than the complications of learning the *being naked with you* approach that is a *sine qua non* of humans interacting in a group relationship.

Most people who have been married for any length of time are aware that the "one-and-only" aspect of monogamous marriage is a romantic concoction of nineteenth-century writers and theologians. At some point in their married lives, many spouses actually discover another human being with whom they might have been just as happy (or miserable?). Why is it inconceivable that this second relationship, which is at present considered adulterous, could be structured into a committed involvement which would be approved by the original spouses? The second relationship would not necessarily be an economic one. The important aspect of it would be that a man or woman involved in this second dyad could adjust to it separately without feeling guilty. Unlike the group or corporate marriage which I have proposed in *Proposition 31*, synergamy (a word I have coined) would allow the learning experience of functioning in two separate relationships to proceed without the additional cross-relationships that make group living under one roof traumatic for those who have had no training in interpersonal relations.

The *being naked with you* aspects of synergamy which ultimately might create the groundwork for a group marriage (but not necessarily so) are expressed in many places throughout the book. Here Father Jesonge Lereve, in *Thursday, My Love*, weds Angela Thomas to Jonathan Adams; they have been married for many years to others.

"Angela and Jonathan . . . as lovers you have come to this humble church to consecrate your love in a form of marriage which has no sanction in the law of the State, nor of the Church. Yet the truth is that the marriage or commitment of two human beings to care for each other has neither strength nor stability because of any divine origin nor sacramental quality, nor pronouncements of man, but rather because the individuals dare to transcend their own ego and in the process be each other. Such a commitment is something one gives out of his own desire. Duty, obligation, responsibility may be contained in the word commitment, but these states of being tend to be outer-induced . . . pressured into existence by society. Such feelings tend to define love in terms that are self-destructive. A marriage of the kind you are entering into, ideally, should be witnessed and approved by your present spouses, and in view of the prior giving of oneself the limitations of the new commitment informally agreed upon. One day we may be able to offer this open strengthening of the family by a responsible process of accretion and blending of existing family units."

Father Lereve smiled as he noted that Angela and Adam were holding hands. "There is no ring in this ceremony. The words I ask you to repeat after me are only as strong as your joy and love for each other as interacting human beings. Repeat after me this synergamous bond you willingly assume. 'I, Angela . . . I, Jonathan . . . with no less love for my present spouse and my family, do accept the commitment to love and to cherish . . . you, Jonathan . . . you . . . Angela. I am aware that my love for you does not modify my prior commitment to my husband . . . to my wife. While our relationship to each other is supportive, it should also grow and gain strength because it reinforces and strengthens and adds perspective to the nature of our love both for each other and for our first spouses and children.' I pronounce you man and wife. May God love you!"

Common to all the life-styles I have proposed and even in the "fun" novels I have written, (That Girl From Boston and The Zolotov Affair) as well as the nonfiction, are six basic beliefs:

First, being naked together is a heterosexual, mental-sexual surrender. The quality of this surrender may be possible in homosexual or lesbian relationships but I am deliberately not going to go into that or even the potential of bisexual surrender.

Second, this mental-sexual surrender is a one-to-one relationship—or to use sociological lingo, it is dyadic. While the insights and the loss of ego experience inherent in such a relationship can be recalled and used to broaden the scope of all interpersonal experience, it cannot be attained in group sex or in casual mate-swapping. My feeling is that these cannot be labeled either good or bad activities, but they might have one advantage—they could provide some experience in learning how to live in a life-style that involves several intimate dyadic experiences occurring alternately in one's life.

This brings me to the third belief that seems to shock more people than anything else I write—that some people are able (and millions could be trained) to maintain several dyadic relationships with members of the other sex on a committed basis over a lifetime, and thus enhance the quality of their lives beyond what would be possible in an exclusively monogamous situation. But such relationships won't work as secret adulterous relationships, nor as post-facto comparison indulgences where the original monogamous couple have separate sexual flings, and then regale each other, presumably to jazz up their own sex lives, with the retelling of their new sexual satisfactions and encounters.

How many of these separate dyadic heterosexual relationships can be maintained in the average person's life? I do not know. Two, I am sure of—three might be even better—particularly if the three couples lived under the same roof, and had common purposes and goal directions for their lives. Of course, if there were a Harrad-type undergraduate training available, the couples who had this training could easily embrace this kind of mental-sexual surrender with more than one member of the other sex.

I doubt whether more than three couples could interrelate their lives on this level, however. The human time factor is against them. And there can be no surrender if you are climaxing with a dozen different human beings. Group sex may be better for you and more fun than jogging, and many medical experts are in full agreement that a really active sex life will keep you in good physical shape. . .but on the other hand since an orgasm only takes as much energy as climbing two flights of stairs, if there isn't mental surrender too it probably won't give you much satisfaction. And it could leave you puffing!

Whenever I categorically state my fourth premise to a live audience it is not long before half the hands are waving in indignation. Many of the younger generation believe that right now they have a kind of Harrad situation, since the dormitories are pretty open, and many couples live together off campus—and as for marriage, why get married? But no matter—the premise is—and I am certain about it—that heterosexual relationships function more effectively when there is commitment—and that commitment, whatever variety it may be, is a defined, accepted part of the social structure. All of our Western social structures have emphasized monogamy. They have tolerated very little premarital experimentation with the exception perhaps of the bundling or hand-fasting mentioned by Sir Walter Scott in his novel *The Betrothed* as a one-year introduction to monogamy without the bells necessarily tolling in a wedding ceremony.

I do not think there will be a Harrad-type premarital education in the 1970s. Nor will there be legal structures that permit bigamous marriages or synergamous marriages. But I believe all of these proposals, including Harrad, will be actualized in the next twenty years. Their acceptance will come because *they are not Utopian*—and, despite Ecclesiastes, all we have to do is dare and there could be something new under the sun.

The fifth belief that I will never cease championing is that this new kind of interpersonal behavior could be taught to young people from birth. However, it is not too late for an effective beginning at seventeen and eighteen, no matter what the person's previous family conditioning has been—*if* the teaching could occur in an undergraduate life-style and environment similar to that I proposed in *The Harrad Experiment*. The nature of the living environment, the opportunity to experience more than one member of the other sex in a deeply involved intimacy, coupled with a continuing seminar in human values taught by teachers who were capable of entirely new approaches to interpersonal relationships embodied in the *being naked with you* approach to life, would be eagerly embraced by young people out of high school, most of whom, amazingly, still hang onto much of their idealism.

And finally, if we dared to consciously condition a new generation and make this approach to education a human birthright in the United States, so that every young person could be exposed to a warm, humorous *deconditioning* from the moral, ethical and shuck values that dominate much of our lives, we would give every human being the opportunity to climb the final steps on Maslow's hierarchy of human needs. The need for self-esteem and the need for self-actualization would emerge like a butterfly from its previous incarnation as the need *to be naked together*.

And the goal can be summed up in Soren Kierkegaard's key to living: "Learn to be objective toward one's self and subjective toward others." *Being naked with you* is the first step.

Epilogue
Roger W. Libby

This book has focused on the nature and implications of sexual and non-sexual intimacy across a variety of life-styles. One of the reasons for the central emphasis on sexual expression is the traditional monogamous model with the limitations it places on sexual and other intimacy within marriage. Until recently, monogamy has been the only relationship where sexual intimacy has been socially and legally approved. The emergence of alternative life-styles provides a variety of options to monogamous marriage for the expression of sexual intimacy. The trend toward the increased visibility and viability of alternative intimate life-styles is at the heart of this book. It has been assumed that some can engage in monogamous, sexually exclusive marriage and merely endure, while others are more happily monogamous. In the spirit of the title of this book, monogamous marriage has been viewed as one of many alternatives rather than as a unidimensional model for everyone to follow. Thus, the exploration of intimacy within and outside of monogamous marriage clearly portrays the human potential for love and intimate friendships in a broad range of relationships. Some will satisfy some aspects of intimacy within one primary relationship, while at the same time being open to emotional and intellectual intimacies beyond their monogamous relationship. Others will attempt to limit all expressions of intimacy to monogamy.

Reconceptualizing Marriage and Alternatives

The variety of definitions and role expectations (or ground rules) for "monogamous" marriage make it difficult to compare the images with the realities of actual marital experiences. McMurtry, Whitehurst, and Roy and Roy make it obvious in their articles that monogamy has not been clearly defined and that it has not met the needs of many who have attempted to model their marital relationships after this so-called ideal. McMurtry indicated that one tenet of monogamy is sexual exclusivity, but that monogamy literally means "one marriage." Sexual exclusivity is commonly included in the definition of monogamy. What once may have been defined as monogamy in terms of ownership and emotional-sexual exclusivity is now simply referred to as "marriage" with the ground rules rarely spelled out further. Without more precise terms to label monogamy and other styles of marriage and life-styles, it is confusing to deal with the variety of intimate life-styles. Precise labeling would force people to deal more insightfully with intimate life-styles, and to be more honest about intimacy.

Redefining a term and/or life-style such as monogamy is a challenge to both the traditional monogamous system and to semanticists who must somehow keep pace with variations of the monogamous model. Are we just redefining a term (*monogamy*), or are we accurately describing a variety of marital and nonmarital life-styles? Both of these options seem relevant—changing terms reflect the increasing range of marriages in a plural sense rather than marriage as monogamy in a restrictedly singular sense.

It is neither precise nor honest to refer to someone as "married" without distinguishing the type of marriage to which that person has agreed at a particular point in time. Marriage, like other relationships, is *a process*. The definition of each marriage is subject to change; this reality must be considered in any reference to a person (or couple) as "married." Cuber and Harroff (1965) developed a typology of marriages from a subsample of 211 of their 427 upper-middle class Americans. Their subsample was limited to those who had never seriously considered divorce. They indicated that their subsample had either intrinsic (intimate) or utilitarian marriages and that these marriages were categorized into five types: (1) *the conflict-habituated*, in which the couple conflicted about many issues unless a major crisis occurred; (2) *the devitalized*, in which the couple was once deeply in love and later the intimacy in their relationship broke down, but they stayed together anyway; (3) *the passive-congenial*, in which the partners always were passive toward each other and never really intimate; (4) *the vital*, in which vitality and mutuality of feelings were strong, but each spouse maintained a separate identity without always appearing as a couple; and (5) *the total marriage*, a rare, multifaceted relationship with constant togetherness and total bliss.

Cuber and Harroff's typology certainly does not indicate a single concept of "marriage." The vital marriages could include spousal agreement for emotional and sexual sharing with others beyond the marriage. It is clear from their study (the sampling took five years, and the analysis another two years) that even among couples who never considered divorce and who were between the ages of thirty-five and fifty-five, a wide range of relationships and ground rules occurred within the structure of "marriage." The authors were aware that they were describing marital rather than personality types. For example, a vital person could have a devitalized marriage. Cuber and Harroff's typology provides for "*different kinds of adjustment and different conceptions of marriage*" (1965, p. 61). An extension of and further testing of the Cuber and Harroff typology with more types of intimate relationships would be a fruitful direction for research.

Gertrude Stein might have said: "Monogamy is monogamy is monogamy." It is clear that semantics help form our perceptions of reality and affect our attitudes, behavioral intentions, and behavior, as well as how we *feel* about our behavior. Monogamy is obviously being redefined to include intimacy with others, even if this does not necessarily include sexual intimacy beyond marriage. Emotional caring, companionship with the other sex, and flexibility for both spouses in the work and leisure worlds provide a basis for expanding one's patchwork of intimates, and for some, the sexual expression of these feelings. In order for the latter reality to be acknowledged, a redefinition of marriage to include more than the limited view of sexually exclusive monogamy is needed.

That language affects our perception of reality has been discussed by Berger and Luckmann (1967) in their treatment of the "social construction of reality." Social scripts and roles are largely defined by language. Roles make up much of scripted behavior (as if we are all actors on a stage in the Shake-spearian sense). An example of the lag between attitudinal and behavioral change in sexual mores and language which accurately depicts emerging life-styles is the term *comarital* which was devised to describe sexual sharing beyond marriage. Such sharing is considered a part of the marital contract by the spouses in a given marriage rather than as "extramarital" in the sense of being extra to or competitive with the marriage (see Chapter 6). Similarly, the double standard of sexual morality has been ratified through the use of tradi-tional language. Kirkendall observed:

The double standard of sexual morality peers through various of our verbal ex-pressions. Thus we speak of one girl as "nice" while another has "gone astray" or has "fallen." We do not think of a boy in the same terms. He has "sown his wild oats" (1966, p. 235).

Arnold and Libby's (1976) study of sexual terms revealed that college students differed by their sex in their evaluation of sexual terms. Males were consistently more accepting of words indicating sex beyond the monogamous script than were women. For example, men were more accepting of both *hus-band* and *wife swapping* as terms than were women. Women were more mor-alistic than men in their use of language and the connotations language had for them. Women more than men reinforced the double standard through their use of sex-related terms. Arnold and Libby concluded that it is difficult to verbalize attitudes, feelings, and desires within the context of traditionally (and often loosely) defined semantics. The Arnold and Libby study provided support for the oft-mentioned Whorf hypothesis that:

. . . linguistic patterns themselves determine what the individual perceives in his world and how he thinks about it. Since these patterns vary widely, the modes of thinking and perceiving in groups utilizing linguistic systems will result in basically different world views. Briefly stated, according to Whorf, language shapes our ideas rather than merely expressing them (Fearing, 1954, p. 47).

Some people are innovative and essentially write their own scripts for relationships, but following Gagnon and Simon (1973), all human sexual ex-perience is scripted behavior. Gecas and Libby (1976) indicated that we per-ceive our world through our symbolic screens, and our use of sexual lan-guage is rarely neutral. Our values and biases show up in our choice of words and in the way we use them. For example, moralists typically use a word such as *promiscuity* to indicate those who are engaging in sex acts with more than one person. Such a word might also refer to someone who is having more sex than the user of the term can accept or is experiencing personally. Often those who speak of "higher morals" usually mean that traditional morals are somehow *better* than morals allowing for the enjoyment of sex beyond monogamy. Similarly, some so-called liberals are moralistic in imposing their values on others (e.g. some bisexuals who contend that people are not fully sexual or "with it" unless they are bisexual).

Some social scientists contribute to confusion about values and con-notations of words through their insistence that the counterculture be ana-lyzed in a "value-free" context. An example of this is Gerald Leslie's (1976,

p. 389) insistence on calling the counterculture the "youth contraculture." Leslie wants to make it clear that he is analyzing rather than identifying with this group. However, it is questionable that *contraculture* is a more socio-logical concept than *counterculture*. This is more than an issue of semantics. Leslie's distinction is an attempt to claim that a sociological term must be value-free (which would seem to assume that subcultural groups such as the youth counterculture can be dealt with as if they were not strongly affecting the larger culture). Every sociological analysis indicates some identification with a value position. Leslie's bias in favor of the traditional model of mar-riage and the family in the name of objective sociology does not escape his readers in spite of his proclamations of being value-free. Unlike Leslie, we make no attempt to be value-free or to analyze without identifying our pref-erences. We believe it is intellectually more honest to identify the bias of a book rather than attempting to claim neutrality. Sociologists and psy-chologists must study and make theoretical sense of alternatives, and it would then be in order to make recommendations based on theory and data for social policy and legal changes. These recommendations must have a real-ity-orientation toward the pluralistic nature of our society.

It is important to recognize that our use of language (as well as even more ambiguous nonverbal cues and gestures) affects our perception of real-ity. It would be helpful to communicate more openly and to define more clearly terms related to intimacy and sex. However, such an attempt at clarity and honesty would militate against many of the games people play. Many games appear to be part of the "primrose path" of monogamous relation-ships.

The State of Sex and Monogamy

The problems of sexually exclusive monogamy are well documented and illustrated by McMurtry, Whitehurst and Roy and Roy in Part One. The le-galistic, Judeo-Christian rules approach to sexual morality, documented by the Roys and such other Christian situation ethicists as Joseph Fletcher (*Situation Ethics*, 1967), has given way to a more rationalistic approach to distin-guishing moral and immoral acts. Situation ethicists are interested in serving love in a humanistic sense rather than adhering to "thou shalt nots" such as thou shalt not commit "adultery." Adultery is redefined to include traditional infidelities rather than all sexual intercourse beyond marriage. In 1964 the British Quakers issued a small book which is consistent with later situation ethics writers; the essence of that book is illustrated in the following:

In seeking to find a truly Christian judgement of this problem, we have again and again been brought to the quality of human relationships as the only final criterion. To base our judgement on whether or not the sex-act has taken place is often to fal-sify that judgement fantastically (1967, p. 51).

The increased acceptance of nonmarital sexuality must be grappled with by traditional moralists who have condemned any kind of extramarital or co-marital sexual intimacies. Roy and Roy strongly urge that the intimacy-sexual needs of single, divorced, and widowed people be incorporated in a view of comarital sex which sanctions sexual intimacies between married and unmarried people. In this regard, McMurtry's "Afterword" suggests that adultery is distinctly different from spousal approval of sex beyond marriage in that the former is not ethical while the latter is often more supportive than detrimental to love within marriage.

In Chapter 2, Whitehurst identifies the wide gaps between monogamous ideals and the realities of extramarital sex. As was stated in the Introduction, we do not live in a behaviorally monogamous society. As early as 1929 in *Marriage and Morals*, Bertrand Russell was critical of sexually exclusive marriage. Russell noted two social trends which he predicted would greatly affect sexual intimacy—namely the liberation of women and the implications of birth control methods for sexual behavior within and beyond marriage. Russell's adamant stand for equal rights for women, including sexual rights, challenged the very basis of patriarchal marriage. Russell was critical of the repressive influence of Christianity (namely St. Paul) on sexual and marital morals, and he recognized the value of sexual variety beyond monogamy. His view was that marriages were happier if neither spouse expected a great deal of happiness from marriage (1966, p. 92). Russell was no anarchist; he supported responsibility in sexual and intimate matters, and he valued intimacy. He stated:

Those who have never known the deep intimacy and the intense companionship of happy mutual love have missed the best thing that life has to give; unconsciously, if not consciously, they feel this, and the resulting disappointment inclines them toward envy, oppression and cruelty (1966, p. 83).

Consistent with Russell's views on marital expectations is an anonymous book published in 1885 entitled *How to Be Happy Though Married*. This book was dedicated to "those brave men and women who have ventured, or who intend to venture, into that state which is 'a blessing to a few, a curse to many, and a great uncertainty to all . . .' " (1885). An example of realism still not very popular with newlyweds appeared later in the book. The author stated:

We expect too much from life in general, and from married life in particular. When castle-building before marriage we imagine a condition never experienced on this side of heaven; and when real life comes with its troubles and cares, the tower of romance falls with a crash, leaving us in the mud-hut of everyday reality. Better to enter the marriage state in the frame of mind of that company of American settlers, who, in naming their new town, called it Dictionary, "because," as they said, "that's the only place where peace, prosperity, and happiness are always to be found" (1885, p. 55).

The state of sex and monogamy is typified in two popular paperback books. Alix Kates Shulman's *Memoirs of an Ex-Prom Queen* (1973) and Erica Jong's *Fear of Flying* (1973) present excellent examples of women who were indoctrinated into the primrose path of dating and sexually exclusive marriage and then became disillusioned with chauvinist ownership by their husbands. These women yearned for adventure and freedom with other men and a sense of peace with themselves as free individuals. A part of this yearning for freedom included sexual freedom and a curiosity about sexual variety with different men. Socialized in a culture which only reinforced female dependence on a male, it was exceedingly difficult for either heroine to break with the custom of patriarchal monogamy. No competing social script offered guidelines clear enough to follow a nontraditional way of life with social support for their new identities.

In contrast with, but consistent with the themes of these two autobiographical novels is an article by Sonya O'Sullivan published in both *Harpers* (1975) and *Cosmopolitan* (1976) magazines. In O' Sullivan's article, the husband leaves home for a younger woman after the wife discovers his infidelities. The wife is totally confused, as she has no script to guide her new single life. She has lived *through* her husband and her children and has no identity of her own. Her self-definition has always been that of part of a *couple* rather than an *individual*. She is horrified, angry, and frightened when her husband levels with her and tells her he wants to leave her. The American dream of permanent monogamous marriage is shattered in a few quick moments. Mrs. is on her way to being single and alone, but she is unprepared for this new life.

The harsh reality of divorce should make more people question marital expectations and ground rules. The competitive, possessive nature of our capitalistic society (as noted by McMurtry, Chapter 1) affects the way we define love, intimacy, and marriage. Without other visible alternatives to monogamy, what *can* a wife do in such a situation except follow the traditional script? The underlying answer in the traditional script is to find another man who is a *better match*, who will not be interested in other women, and who will be a good provider and father as well as the only lover a woman could ever hope for. Such a mythical expectation leaves many women (and men) with the question: "Is this all there is?" If readers have followed this book carefully, the answer is a clear "Of course not!" The oppressive male domination and insensitivity portrayed in *Memoirs of an Ex-Prom Queen* and *Fear of Flying* have led to an increased consciousness among women of male exploitation and increased identification with the goals of the women's liberation movement. The women's liberation movement and other social movements affect attitudes, behaviors, social policies, and laws. In a word, the visibility of alternative life-styles through the interaction of social movements and the mass media is providing a *climate* for living the life-styles presented in this book.

The Women's Liberation Movement and the Climate for Alternatives

The women's liberation movement probably has been the crucial social movement to affect changing sex roles which in turn affect both opposite-sex and same-sex relationships in all life-styles including monogamous marriage. The feminist influence has also been felt by children (see Constantine, Chapter 17); women and children are both moving into a better bargaining position with men, in part because of the women's liberation movement. Mazur, Coyner, and Schwartz all attribute much of the change we have witnessed and the potential for change in sex roles as a part of the emergence of alternative life-styles to feminist ideology. Feminist writings such as Shulamith Firestone's *The Dialectic of Sex* (1972) and the recent documentary analysis of the women's liberation movement as a social movement and its political and social evolvement by Jo Freeman (*The Politics of Women's Liberation,* 1975) have kept feminist ideology on a scholarly basis. Similarly, books such as Joan Roberts' *Beyond Intellectual Sexism* (1976) underscore the importance of our personal and social histories in determining the nature of our perception of reality.

The women's liberation movement has also provided increased support for gay liberation and for lesbian and bisexual life-styles. In particular, the National Organization for Women (NOW) has taken active stands supporting lesbian relationships. As president in 1975 and 1976, Karen DeCrow has called for social acceptance of lesbians, although this has been met with heavy resistance by Betty Friedan, one of the architects of the women's movement in America in the mid-fifties.

To the extent that women succeed in achieving economic, social, and sexual independence, it is probable that they will demand many of the alternatives to monogamy. An excellent example of a feminist choice of alternative open relationships is Simone de Beauvoir's intimate relationship with Jean-Paul Sartre. The forty-five year relationship was discussed in an interview with John Gerassi (1976), in which de Beauvoir revealed that the lack of jealousy in their open relationship was due to their mutual security together, and the reality that others did not play the *same* role in each other's lives. This attitude reflects the same understanding of intimate relationships as is expressed in Kieffer's concept of patchwork intimacy (see Chapter 18). The equality emphasized in feminism was central to the success of the de Beauvoir-Sartre open relationship. As a pioneer feminist, de Beauvoir simply practiced what she preached. Social movements such as the women's liberation movement provide social support and visibility for alternatives to the partriarchal monogamous system most have been socialized to accept as the *only* acceptable life-style. Changing sex roles provide a key basis for the emergence of alternative life-styles which include multiple sexual intimacies as well as emotional sharing beyond the marital dyad.

The interrelationship between social movements such as the women's liberation movement and the alternative life-styles and human potential movements has led to an increased emphasis on the need to analyze and change male roles. A men's liberation movement would appear to be emerging judging from the increasing number of books and other media exposure to men's roles. For example, Marc Feigen Fasteau's book, *The Male Machine* (1974), and Warren Farrell's book, *The Liberated Man* (1974), have been followed by books such as Deborah David's and Robert Brannon's *The Forty-Nine Percent Majority* (1975). But it was Joseph Pleck and Jack Sawyer (*Men and Masculinity,* 1974) who were, along with Myron Brenton (*The American Male,* 1966) the real pioneers in the acknowledgment of male problems and the analysis of the traditional male sex role. The dramatic changes in the female sex role prompted by the women's liberation movement have made it more than clear that male roles would be affected if males wished to relate intimately with women affected by the movement (see Coyner, Chapter 14). Additional implications of men's liberation include support for and understanding of both bisexuality and homosexuality and the range of life-styles possible for those with either of these psychosexual orientations.

Female rites of passage have traditionally differed from male rites of passage—particularly in the realms of careers and sexuality, but this is all changing. Berger and Luckmann (1967, p. 21) have stated that the world consists of multiple realities, and that it is shocking for people to move from one reality to another. Objective reality is constructed by the characterization of people in social roles according to Berger and Luckmann; from this view roles are the mediating links between the social order and beliefs about it. Joan Roberts (1976) points out that the problem with Berger and Luckmann's formulation as it applies to women is that the majority of social roles are allotted to men rather than women, leaving beliefs to be determined mainly by men. Normative role expectations are then defined by men, and women are expected to adhere to these male designs. Roberts' recommendation is the development of a culture of women which is not dependent on the male culture. She states:

. . . a noncontingent woman's culture is needed to offset the culture of men that has become *the* culture of all. Changes in masculist economic and political power will not achieve female autonomy. Even if androgyny is the final goal, it will be reached only when women in independent association have sufficient strength to insist on their own definition of the female component of the unified human psyche. Without their own input into a new imagery, the male version is likely to reform women to act like modified men (p. 47).

Roberts continues:

Individual acts of love, honor, and decency are not uncommon between women and men. In my life and in the life of *every* woman, there are men we like or love or cherish. But the problem is to create a society in which these acts are built into the processes and structures and into the idealized imagery, the belief systems created by both women and men. This is possible only when women assert the strength of their own values and their own beliefs through collective action in a noncontingent culture (p. 59).

The strong impact of women's liberation on female sexual expression has been discussed at length by Schwartz, Coyner, and Mazur. Coyner's perception that reasonably permanent heterosexual relationships will endure only to the extent that men are not possessive and jealous of nonmonogamous sexual behavior of women is probably quite accurate for women who identify with feminist ideology. The continuing sexualization of women would seem to suggest that women will desire more and better sex. Whether the bulk of their sexual contacts will be heterosexual is yet to be determined, but it is safe to predict that feminist women will not relate sexually to antifeminist men. The challenge for men to reexamine their own rather narrow sex roles and to contribute to the changing male role through men's liberation is great. Just as Coyner states that our sexuality is no less than fundamental to the search for new forms of relationships, it is obvious that sex role definitions as a part of our sexuality must become more flexible for alternative life-styles to emerge with the potential for equalitarian and intimate interaction between the sexes as well as between those of the same sex.

Judith Long Laws (1977) has commented that sexual life-styles imply not only alternative social constructions of reality, but a community that supports and reinforces these life-styles. Following Berger and Luckmann, Laws agrees that alternative constructions of reality are *in competition* rather than in coexistence. This would seem to be true, particularly as the sexes and other social groups have something to gain or lose from one life-style over another. It is rather obvious that open marriage is in competition with monogamous marriage for adherents, and that feminists are more likely to support either open marriage or a variation of monogamy which is open and equal in sex role definitions, if not open for both spouses in terms of sexual intimacy beyond marriage. If a marriage is sexually open, feminists of course demand such openness for women as well as men. Similarly, competition between singlehood and monogamous marriage may well increase to the extent that there are more advantages to remaining single. In this regard, the growing proportion of career women who remain single for longer periods of their lives (if not forever), or who demand sexually open marriages, is likely to increase the competition between alternative life-styles and monogamy in the near future.

Much like the competition between various alternative life-styles, the differing segments of the women's movement are often at odds with each other. Although much of the impetus to stress intimacy is coming from humanistic feminism, and even though this major branch of women's liberation is also liberating for men (see Mazur, Chapter 13), women who have rejected all men do not contribute to an increased male consciousness or to improved female-male relationships. In contrast to Joan Roberts' discussion of the need for women to be alone for periods of time to develop a unique culture which is noncontingent on traditional male culture, some separatist "feminists" are not humanists; some of these women have lived through a man (usually a husband) for years, and when they become angry they leave their husbands to live through the women's movement. It must be recognized that the oppressive male system forces some women to go through stages of being with other women and away from men by becoming totally immersed in the movement *before* they can emerge with an identity of their own. The same can be said of men who are tied strongly to the traditional male-competitor-aggressor role. Anti-male separatist women and traditional men are both literally prisoners of their roles, and they are both quick to present their roles as models for others to follow. Alternative life-styles necessitate roles which are more flexible as a basis for individual growth and self-determination. Otherwise, experiments with intimacy will fail just as often as monogamy and other similar rigid arrangements.

In spite of the often conflicting ideologies in the women's liberation movement, much of the increasingly favorable climate for the emergence of alternative life-styles can be linked to this movement. Similarly, the social visibility and support to make alternatives more viable for women as well as men can in part be traced to the activist orientation of those involved with human potential, population, and more recently, alternative life-styles social movements. Alternatives have been supported by and have emerged from social movements and the communication of movement ideologies through the mass media.

The Impact of Social Movements on Alternatives

A general discontent with monogamous limitations on intimacy has led to direct or indirect identification and affiliation with social movements which support alternative views of sex and sexual life-styles. The growth of social movements makes options to traditional sex roles and monogamy more evident to and viable for the masses through the mass media, rap groups, and through changes in social policies and laws. Although it is difficult to directly measure the impact of each social movement or a particular media portrayal on the acceptance and practice of various experiments in intimacy, there is little doubt that the communication of the major issues of social movements such as women's liberation, gay liberation, population, environment, human potential, and alternative life-styles movements has led to an increased awareness of alternatives, and to increased experimentation. Such awareness and experimentation also lead to increased support for the social movements which provided the impetus for such consciousness and experiments in living. Even though social scientists are just beginning to document the impact of social movements on social policies and laws (for an excellent example see Jo Freeman's 1975 in-depth analysis of the women's liberation movement and its relation to the policy process), attitudinal, behavioral, and policy changes are a natural result of such movements. The passage of the ERA will be traced to the women's liberation movement. However, this and other legislative examples may also be traced to complementary social movements. The complementary effect of such related social movements provides social support beyond that of one social movement. In spite of the in-fighting and diffuse nature of the women's liberation movement with its subgroups, it remains the strongest single social movement in recent years. Although the major movement organization (the National Organization for Women) has not developed an overall sexuality statement which would deal effectively with alternative life-styles, the various separate statements and task forces such as the Sexuality and Lesbianism Task Force have provided some contributions to the body of feminist ideology and some guidelines for feminists to deal with discrimination against women due to their sexual orientation.

The impact of the population groups such as Zero Population Growth (ZPG) and the National Organization for Non-Parents (NON) has been to increase awareness about the problems of both overpopulation and the reality that married couples (as well as single people) do not all need children to be fulfilled, and that children often make parents unhappy (this is particularly true of large families from empirical studies reviewed by Nye, Carlson, and Garrett in 1970). In addition, the human potential movement has emphasized the achievement of self-actualization and increased personal and interpersonal growth in the tradition of Maslow and other humanistic psychologists. This emphasis on human potential extends far beyond the meeting of basic needs and mere survival. Similarly, the alternative life-styles movement is concerned with a humanistic approach to expanding emotional, economic, and sexual parameters so that one's expressions of intimacy are not limited to one person. The underlying basis that all of these social movements have in common is a strong belief in the humanist tradition.

The American Humanist Association (AHA) and the Association for Humanistic Psychology (AHP) have contributed to many of the ideological tenets for the women's liberation movement, the gay liberation movement, the population control movement, the human potential movement, the environmental movement, and the alternative life-styles movement. Of course, these movements have also had an ideological impact on humanist groups. The essence of the humanist position on sexuality and sex roles is well-integrated in the Humanist Statement on Sexual Rights and Responsibilities (Kirkendall et al., 1976). Some selections from that important statement follow:

The limitation of sexual expression to conjugal unions or monogamous marriage was perhaps sensible so long as reproduction was still largely a matter of chance, and so long as women were subjugated to men. Although we consider marriage, where viable, a cherished human relationship, we believe that other sexual relationships also are significant. In any case, human beings should have the right to express their sexual desires and enter into relationships as they see fit, as long as they do not harm others or interfere with their rights to sexual expression. This new sense of freedom, however, should be accompanied by a sense of ethical responsibility. . . . Responsible sexuality should now be viewed as an expression of intimacy for women as well as for men, a source of enjoyment and enrichment, in addition to being a way of releasing tension, even where there is no likelihood of procreation (1976, p. 4).

A concern with population control, birth control, abortion, and sterilization with *both* sexes taking responsibility is also strongly emphasized. Sex is viewed as the communication of intimacy and physical pleasure rather than just a means to reproduce. Self-actualization and mutuality of feelings for responsible decisions about sexuality are at the heart of the humanist statement. In contrast to traditional morality, the statement concludes:

For the first time we realize that we own our own bodies. Until now our bodies have been in bondage to church or state, which have dictated how we could express our sexuality . . . (1976, p. 6).

These excerpts from the humanist statement are clearly consistent with and supportive of the essence of similar ideologies of related social movements. Readers are encouraged to consider the humanistic basis of this book and of particular writers. While the personal orientation of each author does not always come through clearly, the commitment each has to the existence of options should be evident. The combined impact of social movements, emerging alternatives to monogamy, and media portrayals of alternative avenues to intimacy make it increasingly clear that monogamy is but one of several choices.

Alternative Life-Style Trends

Since the publication of an earlier version of this book in 1973 (*Renovating Marriage*), the alternative life-styles movement has continued to develop. Contrasting views and predictions concerning the future of intimate life-styles are offered: If one can accept *Time Magazine*'s editorial stand, nonexclusive sexual life-styles are on the decline and monogamous marriage is golden. However, if one is cognizant of social trends toward increased divorce and marriage at later ages, then one must interpret these social trends with some reality orientation as these trends relate to the state of sex, monogamy, and alternatives.

Some trends do seem clear. Swinging is apparently declining along with communal living (although the latter may witness an increase as housing and economic reasons become important in the not-too-distant future), and singlehood, cohabitation, and sexually open marriage appear to be increasing in popularity. Group marriages may be neither increasing nor decreasing, but they too probably will see some growth later along with intended communities (communes). Some group marriages will continue to occur in the context of larger intended communities. Monogamy will remain as the most popular choice, although this does not mean that extramarital sexual relationships will not commonly accompany this marital form. In the Counter-Epilogue, Vera and David Mace discuss the viability of traditional monogamous marriage as an option for the future. However, it is my position that sexually open marriage and various forms of comarital and extramarital sex may often be more beneficial than damaging to marital relationships. This will be more true as more social and legal support develops. Smith and Smith contend that we *assume* extramarital intercourse will harm a marriage, but we rarely ask the obverse question: "What, we should want to know just as fervently, are the effects of *not* expanding one's sexual life?" (1974, p. 32).

My process model in Chapter 4 provides a basis for viewing exchange decisions over a sexual-intimacy career, and Whitehurst's "fall-out" model in Chapter 21 offers additional insight into why more people are opting for alternatives to monogamy. Bernard's comments (Chapter 8) on choosing between exclusivity and permanence in a marriage apply to other dyadic and larger interpersonal groups as well. The real-life implications of literature and movies have been ably demonstrated by Clanton (Chapter 7) and Rimmer (Chapter 24). Rimmer's novels have surely provided the impetus for many to experiment with intimate alternatives. The impact of the mass media on behavioral patterns and on actual sexual experimentation is something we can only speculate about, but it appears that *the media have exposed as well as triggered experiments with intimacy*. Those trying out sexually open marriage (see Knapp & Whitehurst, Chapter 9), swinging (see Gilmartin, Chapter 10) or group marriage (see Constantine & Constantine, Chapter 11) were probably all stimulated to experiment by exposure to ideas in the media and by discussions with friends. The diffusion of innovative life-styles through the media-friend process has been a theory in mass communications for some time, and has received empirical support. There is no reason to believe that such diffusion does not occur in such an exciting area as alternative life-styles. The media are central to the communication of options and to the development of the alternative life-styles movement.

The past three or four years have seen increased visibility of alternative life-styles through the publication of newsletters from various alternative groups and organizations. Family Synergy is one of the oldest alternatives organizations with a well-distributed newsletter, social and educational functions, and a planned journal. Pat LaFollette and Hy Levy were the cofounders of Family Synergy in 1972 in Los Angeles, and since that time regional subgroups of Family Synergy and similar groups have sprung up.

The results of a questionnaire (LaFollette, 1976) included with the membership mailing of Family Synergy indicated that 63 percent of the membership were living in some kind of sexually open relationship. The reasons for joining Family Synergy included a wish to support a movement for social change, to meet others interested in expanded families and for sexual relationships, while a minority joined for professional reasons (such as studying the members' life-styles). Most of the reasons for joining were justified in what members reported receiving from their membership.

Another alternatives organization, Future Families of the World (FFW), was started by Carol and Duane Parsons. The group produces a newsletter, *Joy-Us*, and offers conferences, social functions, and related activities. FFW is located in Washington, D.C. The newest national organization is the Alternative Marriage and Relationship Council of the United States (AMRCUS), founded by Ray Noonan in Philadelphia. Noonan is also developing a new journal to be published privately, *Alternatives in Marriage and the Family*. Of importance to communards and others involved with alternatives is the journal, *Communities*, produced in part by the Twin Oaks Commune in Virginia, and published in Oregon. Finally, several other new groups are being formed such as "Wide World of Singles" in Buena Park, California, to spur social and sexual interaction between singles, along with complementary swingers' groups.[1] Alternative groups are offering rap sessions, encounter groups, workshops, conferences, newsletters, and professional journals. Robert Rimmer and the hippies of the late Sixties can take at least some credit for the impetus which has led to the current wave of organized efforts to deal systematically, humanistically, and academically with alternatives.

The increasingly improved contraceptive technology and the increased openness of the media point to the need for social scientists to delve more deeply into the experiential realities of alternatives, and to determine the process of bonding and disintegration of intimacy in various experiments with different living situations. Comparative studies of monogamous marriage and alternatives to monogamy will require taking seriously changing sex-role definitions and the decreasing social controls on sexual behavior.

A second special issue of *The Family Coordinator* on "Variant Family Forms and Life Styles" (October, 1975), the proliferation of books on various alternatives, and the equally apparent interest on the part of television specials, talk-shows, and the movies indicate that the analysis of contemporary intimacy patterns is a major interest of our ever changing society. The chainlike network of growing interest and involvement in alternatives is truly amazing in light of the unidimensional model of monogamous marriage and the primrose path of dating and courtship which have been held up to us as the only really "normal" way to proceed through life as a sexual being. Functional courses in marriage and the family in colleges and universities are beginning to take on a different glow—they are exploring singlehood, cohabitation, and a range of alternatives to monogamous marriage and parenthood.

The Future of Intimate Life-Styles

Futurism is an exciting profession—futurists speculate, and take risks about projecting into the future. In the area of alternative life-styles, the World Future Society publishes a special studies newsletter called *Life-Styles Tomorrow*. A range of subjects is included—changing concepts of dating (which relates to the social scripting of dating as opposed to "getting together" in Chapter 4), tolerance of gays, sex and singles who are aged, single mothers, marital contracts, and others. The role of women in alternatives is also a focus of the newsletter. This would seem to underline the overlap between the women's liberation movement and the alternative life-styles movement, an overlap which is likely to be increasingly evident in the near future.

Whether one agrees with Firestone's (1971) call for the demise of the family or not, a redefinition of both the marriage relationship as a more equalitarian and open dyad, and of the family to include intimate networks and emotional if not sexual sharing beyond the nuclear family seem likely to be a part of the future. There are many architects for the future of intimate relationships—Nena and George O'Neill (*Open Marriage*, 1972, and *Shifting Gears*, 1975), Ronald Mazur (see Chapters 13 and 23, as well as *The New Intimacy: Open-Ended Marriage*, 1973), Robert Thamm, *Beyond Marriage and the Nuclear Family* (1975), Gordon Clanton and Lynn G. Smith, eds., *Jealousy* (1977), Herb Seal, *Alternative Life Styles* (1975), and of course the early innovator and dreamer, Robert Rimmer, with his many novels including *The Harrad Experiment* (1965), *Thursday, My Love* (1972), and *The Premar Challenge* (1974). In the more distant past, Maslow's theoretical work on synergy and a Eupsychian society (see *The Farther Reaches of Human Nature*, 1972) offers brilliant insights into a self-actualizing society with innovative sexual and emotional life-styles and the merging of pleasure experiences in the work and leisure worlds.

James Ramey (1975) predicts that "intimate friendships" (relationships which are either sexual or *potentially* sexual, which seems to include an almost indefinable group of people) and their extension to intimate networks of people, along with cohabitation will be the most popular alternative to monogamy. Although I have some qualms about defining "intimate friendships" as Ramey and his subjects do (see Chapter 6), it does seem that sexualintimate friendships with both closed and open groups of friends who share intimacy in emotional and sexual ways will experience increased visibility, and that more will opt for these kinds of relationships. Creative singlehood includes this option, as do sexually open marriages and *open* cohabitation arrangements. Even though most cohabitation arrangements are defined as sexually exclusive, it appears likely that more will cohabit with some agreement for other intimate relationships. This is consistent with Ramey's prediction that cohabitation and intimate friendships will be the most prevalent alternative life-styles, since those in single, cohabiting, or married states would qualify if they are potentially available for sexual and emotional sharing beyond the primary relationship (or beyond coprimary relationships for some).

If Philip Slater's analysis of change and progress in *Earthwalk* (1974) is correct, we cannot assume linear progress, nor can we assume we are advancing as a civilization. The relentless pursuit of power in a capitalistic society may make it quite difficult to achieve intimacy in any life-style. Slater's perception is that we too naively feel the future will be better than the present which is better than the past. His challenge is to reexamine our assumptions and perceptions so real progress can be achieved.

Progress generally includes some provision for security and some for adventure. The two values are often at odds, as is indicated by Jessie Bernard. She summarizes her view of human desires and the need for security:

Human beings want incompatible things. They want to eat their cake and have it too. They want excitement and adventure. They also want safety and security. These desiderata are difficult to combine in one relationship. Without a commitment, one has freedom but not security; with a commitment, one has security but little freedom.

In the past the desire for security, though present in both marital partners, has tended to be stronger among women than among men, and the desire for outside—especially sexual—adventure greater among men than among women. There is no assurance that this difference will survive the decline in the importance of motherhood in the future, or in the increase in labor-force participation by women, or the lengthened years of sexual attractiveness in women. My own observation of young people convinces me that in the future the emphasis among both men and women may well be on freedom rather than on security, at least to a far greater extent than today. Conceivably to a too great extent (1972, p. 81).

So the quest for both freedom and security is closely related to the way we approach experiments with new sexual life-styles.

The politics of sex roles and sexual life-styles are ever present, and they affect personal freedom to experiment with intimacy in ways which are at odds with the socially and legally approved monogamous model. The reality of politics hinders scientific research about sexuality (for example, the U.S. Congress decided in 1976 to withdraw federal funding from research at Southern Illinois University which studied the effect of marijuana use on sexual response). The politics of the seventies have not been overly conducive to a legitimization of alternative life-styles. (For further discussion of the politics of sex and sex roles, see Gordon & Libby, eds., *Sexuality Today and Tomorrow*, 1976).

The politics of sex roles shows up clearly in *The Total Woman* (1973) by Marabel Morgan, which is an attempt to counter the impact of the women's liberation movement and reinforce the traditional, monogamous, male-dominant model. The security that Jessie Bernard referred to may well be at the base of such a "counter movement." As Lawrence Casler suggests: "Ordinarily, we are more eager to justify our choices than to change them. Unless we are unusually self-confident, we will seek such confirmation from other people" (1974, pp. 36-7). It is probably accurate to say that most people want some assurance that "the good life" will result from the choices they make about marriage, life-styles, and intimacy.

For many people current legal statutes provide at least the illusion of continuing emotional, sexual, and economic rewards. However, the social visibility and support for various experimental life-styles is likely to be reflected increasingly in new social policies and laws. In the meantime, policies and laws are slow to change and the lag between social change in attitudes and behavior related to intimacy is still not very evident in institutional-legal systems. Sex role definitions and alternative life-styles are certainly prime examples of a large gap between the reality of everyday decisions about ways to express intimacy in a variety of life-styles and relationships, and the moralistic image of "thou shalt not" in legal statutes. Most family law is limited to a narrow conceptualization of monogamous marriage and the nuclear family as the only models for intimacy. Communes, group marriages, various open marriages, creative singlehood, and cohabitation are often viewed as illegal; and, although it is difficult to enforce outmoded sex laws, punitive enforcement for political reasons is not uncommon. Legal contracts without marriage are feasible in many instances (as in writing and renegotiating one's relationship or marital contract, or a cohabitation contract), but few apparently recognize that there are ways of dealing with intimate life-styles within the legal structure beyond the realm of family law. Contractual law may well offer some favorable possibilities for those seeking legal supports for living in an alternative life-style not recognized in family law. In some cases nonlegal contracts serve a useful purpose. Such is the case with negotiating the ground rules (or contracts) for various cohabitation (see Edmund Van Deusen, 1974) and marital arrangements (see Marvin Sussman, 1975).

Kelly Weisberg (1975) identified many of the gaps between alternative family and life-style structures and the law. She stated:

The growing pluralism of marriage styles and family forms, in conjunction with the pervasive belief that love relationships should not be subject to external regulation by the state, has resulted in increased interest in how the legal order affects alternative family styles (1975, p. 549).

Lenore Weitzman (1974, 1975) has been engaged in ongoing research on marriage, divorce, and related laws as they concern alternative life-styles and family forms. Weitzman identifies some problems with marriage contracts. She states:

The marriage contract is unlike most contracts: its provisions are unwritten, its penalties are unspecified, and the terms of the contract are typically unknown to the "contracting parties" (1975, p. 531).

Biases against alternative life-styles can be traced to religious dictates, as is suggested by Weitzman's observations:

The Judeo-Christian ideal embodied in law is one of a monogamous heterosexual union, that is, two single individuals of the opposite sex. The assumption of a heterosexual two-person marriage is so basic that it is rare to find legislation which explicitly excludes homosexual or group marriages (1975, p. 540).

Housing or zoning restrictions affect communes and group marriages, and other legal limitations are reflected by Weitzman as follows:

Plural marriage and communal families suffer from many of the same legal restrictions that homosexual unions face: they are excluded from the economic advantages in filing joint income tax returns; from family benefits under social security; disability, and health insurance programs; from property and tax benefits of inheritance laws; and they may lose custody of their children (1975, p. 541).

Laws are the first order ideal type norms and as such they reflect societal expectations (which usually are more accurately described as hopes and fantasies). As sexual mores change (Libby, 1977), the law must catch up. Despite recent legal decisions making it the right of the state to impose restrictions on sexual behavior between "consenting adults" (for example, the Supreme Court ruled that a Virginia sodomy statute was constitutional), the pursuit of intimacy in its many forms continues. *We cannot legalize intimacy.* Although our often repressive legal and economic-political system makes it more difficult to achieve intimacy, the search for intimacy is likely to be enhanced by social movements identified here, and the law and other traditional institutions will have little impact on genuine feelings and experiences. In fact, the law is diminishing as the first order of sexual mores or taboos in the eyes of those who once felt the law was "right." The law and the church not-withstanding, alternative life-styles are continuing to evolve and to receive social support from the counterculture and from the larger culture as well.

An Approach to Experiments with Intimacy

We have attempted to present an overview of potential life-style concepts in the seventies. There is little doubt but that other variations of the monogamous model will be experimented with in the coming years; we do not know how much social support experimenters will receive from the larger society. Those who take risks to be different must have a protective shell to withstand social pressures to conform to traditional definitions of marriage. It is obvious that adventures in loving and living sexually will initially remain a part of the secret society, but as these styles of interaction become visible through the writing of journalists and the research of social scientists, the social and legal institutions will likely make necessary adjustments.

As has been outlined in detail in this book, there is already a range of alternatives to the exclusively monogamous heterosexual relationship. There is a wide range of ground rules possible within open marriage, from the O'Neills' (1972) rather limited view in terms of sexual freedom, to the views of many of the contributors to this volume. It seems that most of the alternative sexual life-styles are based on equality between the sexes, the encouragement of individual growth, and developing the uniqueness of a private identity.

We have stressed marriage and alternatives as processes, rather than as static entities incapable of change. It seems too much to expect that two individuals will share all of the same interests and needs for an entire lifetime. While this reality is increasingly recognized in many areas of life, the sexual seems to be the last arena of acceptance of change and confrontation.

Sex is, among other complex things, a language, a communication. But, as John Wilson (1965) indicates, it is too often treated as a *possession* in the acquisitive society that stresses materialism and competition. Many fear touching adults of either sex in a loving or a sensual way, conscious that in our culture such gestures are automatically construed as sexual foreplay. Unfortunately, to many women sex is a bargaining point to be used, rather than a natural desire to be expressed. As Wilson indicates, we tend to barter sex for love, or he might have added, for the illusion of love! Wilson contends that we should explore our desires and proceed to obtain them, as he elaborates:

None of us know what we want, or think we know: but we lack the moral courage to try to achieve it, because we are beaten down by life. We over-value things like security, we become timid and resigned, and perhaps we create for ourselves a morality or a metaphysic to prop up our resignation. We compromise too soon. Others of us, uncertain what we want, still lack the courage to try out new experiences and new forms of living . . . (1965, p. 252).

Wilson continues:

Whatever our sexual objectives—and no doubt these will be substitutes for earlier objectives—there are good reasons for saying that we ought to pursue them if only in order to find out the precise nature of our own wants. We may be forced . . . to *work through* certain desires in order to understand our own natures. The tragic side of human sexual activity is that most people seem either to work at satisfying their desires without gaining any understanding, or else to deny themselves satisfaction, equally without any increase in awareness of their own natures (1965, p. 253).

It appears that many parents view maturity as conformity to their values, rather than accepting or tolerating alternative values about sex and marriage, and viewing maturity as whatever is effective for each individual in his or her communication with others. But, since maturity is a value judgment, and since values are facts to each individual, we often have trouble accepting those who are "different." Wilson aptly identifies the meaning of being "sensible" or "reasonable" about sex:

A "sensible" attitude to sex usually means thinking about it but not doing anything. This is directly contrary to the empirical or experimental attitude I . . . advocate. "Don't do anything you may regret" is one of the stupidest pieces of advice ever given. If one took it, one would never learn anything at all; to learn something, you have to start by making mistakes and doing it badly—and of course you will regret this later. But this is how one learns.

On the other hand, you know what some mistakes are already; you have your own criteria of what is sensible. It is not sensible (in this society) to have illegitimate children, seduce minors, bring up children before you know that you and your wife (or husband) can produce a happy family, and so on (1965, pp. 260-61).

A related position is taken by Nena and George O'Neill in *Shifting Gears* (1974) where they discuss the "maturity myth"—that "settling down" will lead to attainment of emotional security and that the future will be manageable. As they emphasize, there are no guarantees for intimacy and emotional-relationship growth; personal and interpersonal growth occur from close communication and being able to "shift gears" to adapt to change in society, in relationships, and in oneself.

In the book we have assumed choice of a life-style to be the legitimate right of each human being. It is important to ask oneself: "Does this relationship make me happy?" (as well as to consider the consequences of the relationship to others). Additionally, one should realize that if one person in a relationship either cares less and/or knows more about the other person's social script (what motivates them, what they fear, how they want to be seen, and the like), that person who cares less and knows more is in a position of power—power which can be used to exploit the other. However, if one does know more about the social scripts in a relationship and also cares about the relationship, that person is also in a position to further the intimate growth potential of that relationship. As Wilson put it, we must say "yes to life," rather than being reluctant to extend ourselves to others, or sitting on the fence and watching life go by while we nurture our security.

A major theme has been the search for intimacy in a variety of life-styles over a lifetime. This search has led to Kieffer's explanation of "patchwork intimacy" (Chapter 18) and my description of role transitions over time (Chapter 4). The perception of rewards and costs in each intimate relationship and in specific life-styles provides a basis for the patchwork concept, which serves as an organizing framework to map the stages and decision points over one's intimacy career. The patchwork conceptualization allows for a depiction of each person's unique configuration of intimate others up to and including present relationships, with a view to the future design of patchwork intimates. Self-analysis based on the patchwork concept should result in an understanding of repeated patterns of forming, developing, dissolving, or changing intimate relationships. It may then be feasible to determine what has aided in the development and continuation of intimate relationships, and what has contributed to the weakening of the bonds in other once intimate relationships. The intent of such a self-analysis of the matrix of intimate others over time is to provide each person with a greater understanding of types of relationships and behaviors which seem to support intimacy and then attempt to focus energy and attention on these relationships and behaviors. While feedback from friends and other intimates may help in such a self-analysis, each person must ultimately come to terms with her or his unique self and the ways in which various life-styles and relationships either support or detract from a strong sense of self and self-intimacy as a basis for intimacy with others. It is more than an intellectual exercise to map out one's patchwork of intimate others over the past and into the present. Graphic portrayals can be discussed with intimate others, and through introspection (as well as other processes such as encounter groups or therapy) one may grow in self-knowledge and then apply such awareness to everyday interaction with intimate others as well as potential intimate others. Graphic portrayals of the configuration of intimate others is simply one way to conceptualize patterned behavior and to understand how habits are learned and sometimes must be unlearned so that personal and interpersonal growth can occur as a basis for the development and maintenance of intimate relationships.

Intimacy within and beyond monogamous marriage does not occur in a vacuum. The constant feedback of others and the images in the mass media contribute to the social scripting of roles and role expectations in intimate relationships. For example, the organized activist orientation of the sixties has changed to an introspective look into the self, resulting for some in increased self-awareness and improved interpersonal relationships. Jerry Rubin's reevaluation of his anger and political activism in the late sixties and Judy Collins' apparent search for her self in her more recent recordings and a movie suggest that the rhetoric and music of the late sixties is being played down in favor of a fresh emphasis on the nature of the self and the potential for self-actualization. Maslow's early emphasis on expanding potential for intimacy is in vogue as a basis for the search for increased emotional caring and acceptance of oneself as a part of the exploration of intimate relationships within and beyond various styles of marriage. Maslow's approach is similar to Rimmer's emphasis on self-disclosure (Chapter 24) as a means to achieve deep intimacy with several others of the opposite sex in sexual relationships. The emphasis on heterosexuality does not preclude intimacy with both sexes, as is discussed by Duberman in Chapter 16.

The changing nature of female sexuality and the probable emergence of a noncontingent culture of women (Roberts, 1976), along with the focus on the self rather than the couple as the unit of analysis when looking at intimacy patterns all point to an approach extending beyond a "couple front" (O'Neill & O'Neill, 1972) to the uniqueness of a stronger sense of self and self-intimacy. In their award-winning paper, Paula Dressel and Virginia Murray (1976) contend that as it becomes more difficult for one person to meet all of one's needs, alternatives will provide more opportunities to meet affectual, sexual, and intellectual needs. In a word, the emphasis on *intimacy* will emerge as the central focus. Dichotomous distinctions about the expression of intimacy along genital lines will be less evident as people realize that limiting sexual intimacy to monogamous marriage is *overemphasizing* the sexual aspect of living, and *underemphasizing* the synergistic potential for intimacy of all kinds within, beyond, and without marriage. The freedom to love and be loved extends beyond the bonds and boundaries of marriage for many, and such a reality is sure to influence others toward new adventures in intimacy. Expanded conceptualizations of the family to include intimate others not related by blood are now emerging. Nuclear families are being redefined to include single people and other married couples who share in the preparation of meals, household tasks, recreation, and for some sexual activities. A stronger sense of community and this expanded concept of what a family is complements the extended kinship functions which are often not satisfied by relatives to the extent that might have been true in the past.

It is largely the increasing visibility and viability of alternatives that has forced a near total revision of the first version of this book with a shift away from a unidimensional focus on marriage toward a broader orientation toward intimacy and relationships, be they marital or nonmarital, exclusive or nonexclusive, heterosexual, homosexual, or bisexual, childless or with children, and so on. The increasingly broad range of options makes this book even more important as a compendium of the most recent developments in the field of interpersonal relationships and the variant forms these relationships take. It is unlikely that alternatives will prove to be a stage in a cycle back to monogamy. It is equally improbable that most people will openly accept multiple sexual relationships in the near future. What is more likely is the growing tolerance for and research about the various alternatives now emerging.

If we have added in any small way to the potential for insight and joy to the reader, we have succeeded. This does not gainsay the fact that potential joys are just that—potentials that must be acted upon and courageously attacked with as much of our own good sense as we can muster. It was nicely put by Jessie Bernard in the summary of *The Sex Game*, her book dealing with communications among the sexes:

There are many casualties in the process of working out relationships suitable for this day and age, many experiments that prove lethal. Coping with challenges new to the human species is, we repeat, not easy. But whoever said the human condition was painless? Whoever said it was easy to be a human being? Of either sex? (1972, p. 332).

Casualties occur in "normal" as well as in unconventional marriage; we cannot help but find life limiting when we refuse to take up the challenge. The attempt to *renovate* marriage may yet be one of the twentieth century's notable achievements—and we are only on the threshold of change.

I feel that humans need more laughter and joy and self-awareness through personal and interpersonal growth from creative experiments in living. This involves taking risks and trying out new things; it involves being in touch, rather than *fearing* touch communication. We need a variety of experiences. We need to be willing to discuss openly, to reappraise our values and our behavior, to introspect, to relate, to care, and to enjoy!

Reference Notes

1. Unlike the groups mentioned above, whose efforts are more holistic and scholarly, groups such as these tend toward the sensational and serve to illustrate the economic and sexist exploitation of the alternative life-styles movement by our capitalistic society. Swinging, which had been on the decline, is apparently branching out into the world of singles and others who might not call themselves swingers but whose behavior breaks down to swinging. Of the alternatives in

this book, swinging—at least the recreational, party type of swinging—is least consistent with the humanistic tenets of the alternative life-styles movement, and most consistent with the super-ficiality and compartmentalization of sex in the larger society.

2. Phyllis Penn also addressed the issue of nontraditional and assertive sex-role definitions for women in her article, "Could You, Would You Make a Pass at a Man?" (*Cosmopolitan*, May 1976, pp. 205-7, 234-5). Penn asserts:

Very few women have ever made the first sexual move toward a man in their lives. *Men* make passes at *us*. We do something else—we behave in ways that provoke them to seduce us—but that's different from our initiating sex, just as waiting for a well-earned promotion is different from laying the groundwork, then *asking* for it.

Women are far more liberated, socially and sexually, than ever before. But seduction—the activity that turns a social relationship into a sexual one—seems to be the last frontier of the revo-lution. . . .

Sex is no longer such a scarce commodity that men will pounce whenever it is offered, how-ever surreptitiously. They are, poor darlings, almost numbed by the availability of women. (We do outnumber them, and we're getting more and more openly sexual.) (p. 205)

Counter-Epilogue

David Mace and Vera Mace

We greatly appreciate and applaud the generous and open-minded gesture of the editors, who have invited us to make a critical evaluation of this book—and to have the last word!

Where shall we begin? We had better introduce ourselves, because the position we adopt can only be understood in terms of our personal and vocational identities.

We are an elderly couple who have been married to each other, very happily, for forty-three years. Like Winston Churchill, we consider that getting married was the best thing we ever did. As we look back together across the years we see that marriage has contributed enormously to our personal growth, our enjoyment of life, our understanding of other people, our willingness to be adventurous and take risks, and our sense of fulfillment.

Our life work has been to promote better marriages, so that others might share our joy. This pursuit has taken us literally to the ends of the earth. We have visited seventy-five countries, and been involved in programs and projects in sixty-one of them. We have studied marriage in all the major human cultures—not simply by reading books, but by living among the people concerned, sitting down with them in their homes, talking with them about their experiences.

Despite all our efforts, we now see marriage widely attacked, abused, ridiculed and reviled. Naturally this distresses us. But it also challenges us, and our response is to try to understand, and to interpret to ourselves and to others, what is happening.

This book embodies the substance of the contemporary attack on marriage, presented by a group of writers whose knowledge of the field matches our own, and whose ability and sincerity are not to be questioned. At least half of them are known to us personally, and counted among our friends. The question that confronts us is: Why have we, confronted by the same facts, arrived at very different conclusions?

There are three possible answers—that our thinking has been biased; that their thinking has been biased; or that the differences between us are not as great as they appear to be.

It would not be appropriate for us to look for bias in others, but we should certainly examine ourselves in this regard. We think we have open minds—as Quakers, we are not committed to the defense of creeds and dogmas. However, we belong to the older generation, and may be suffering mildly from future shock. And we readily admit to judging marriage by its successes, of which we have encountered a great many, rather than by its failures, of which we have also encountered a great many. If it is bias to look for the best that is possible, and then to work to make it possible, we must plead guilty on that account.

We would like, however, to focus on the third possible explanation—that the differences are not as great as they appear to be—and see what can be done to narrow the gap. We have always felt that debate, which seeks to emphasize differences, is a less profitable exercise than dialogue, which minimizes differences by looking for common ground.

We ought to make it clear at the outset that we offer no defense of "traditional" or "conventional" marriage—not because we think there was ever anything inherently wicked about it, but because in our new, open culture it has become anachronistic.

Attacks on marriage, we have noticed, often adopt two procedures which we consider questionable. First, they judge what was done in the past by the very different standards of our contemporary society. Fair play surely demands that we give our ancestors the benefit of the doubt. If human history represents progress (and this may be open to question) we should face the fact that, had we lived in an earlier age, and known only what those around us knew, we would probably have spoken as they spoke and have done what they did. The marriage patterns of the past were probably acceptable in the conditions under which people then lived; and perhaps they even helped to preserve Western culture and to make it possible for us to be alive and enlightened today. *De mortuis nihil nisi bonum* (Speak nothing but good of the dead).

Second, attacks on marriage usually imply that the traditional pattern, with all its rigidities, has passed unchanged into our modern culture. That is far from the truth. Marriage has undergone dramatic change, and is still steadily changing, as it adapts itself to today's world.

Our major complaint about this book, therefore, is that it fails almost completely to identify the "alternative" form of marriage that is most widely practiced, and most widely preferred, in our contemporary society. This failure exists despite the fact that Ernest W. Burgess, the acknowledged "father" of American family sociology, clearly charted the change and identified the new form—a generation ago. His book *The Family—From Institution to Companionship* (Burgess & Locke, 1945) summarized his extensive research. The old institutional marriage is described in such terms as "formal," "authoritarian," "rigid discipline," "elaborate ritual," while the new emerging companionship pattern is delineated in terms of "interpersonal relationships," "mutual affection," "sympathetic understanding," and "comradeship." Surely the first group of terms represents precisely the values in marriage which the counterculture has deplored, and the second group the very values which it has extolled. Yet as early as 1945, the studies of Burgess indicated clearly that the transition was in full swing.

What happened? The significant insights of Burgess were largely ignored. Family specialists—educators, counselors, and researchers alike—continued to accept as their conceptual frame of reference the "static" view of marriage as a "state" or "estate" held together by the joint pressures of religion, law, and public opinion. Meanwhile, a whole generation of young couples set their sights on the new companionship model—more often referred to as the "love" marriage or the "fifty-fifty" marriage. They tried to make it work; but, over and over again, they failed, and became discouraged and disillusioned. Their failure, painfully obvious to their children, led to the open rebellion of today's generation of youth, and the turning away to seek other more palatable "alternatives."

Why did they fail? Burgess warned that, in order to facilitate the difficult transition to the new form of marriage, new kinds of supportive services would need to be provided in our communities. He did not define these very clearly, but others did so later. Nelson Foote (Foote & Cottrell, 1955) coined the term "interpersonal competence." He said, in effect, that the new kind of marriage would not work on the basis of stereotyped roles, which had sufficed for the static traditional marriage. The new companionship model required high levels of flexible skills that would sustain and nurture dynamic interaction. He was saying, in effect, that just as all airplane pilots had to be retrained when we made the changeover from piston-engined planes to the new jets, so all married couples needed to be retrained as we changed from the institutional to the companionship marriage. Otherwise, in both instances, they would soon be crashing all over the place.

The warning of Foote, like that of Burgess, was largely ignored. Only in the last five years or so have we begun to study seriously the complexities of the interaction process in a dynamic dyadic relationship. However, new insights are now coming fast—on sexual fulfillment, on couple communication, on self-disclosure and intimacy, on the creative use of conflict, on the love-anger cycle, on mutual negotiation for complementary rewards. We now stand on the threshold of a promising new era in the facilitation of rewarding, creative dyad interaction.

The possibilities for better marriages are exciting. In what we now call the marriage enrichment movement, we are experimenting with these new tools and getting very encouraging results. In skillfully led couple groups, we are seeing significant and lasting changes taking place in dull, superficial marriages as they break loose and embark on new growth. We are becoming aware that the majority of marriages in North America are functioning far below their potential—Lederer and Jackson (1968) estimated the really successful ones as only 5-10 percent of all. But we now realize that couples need no longer accept this miserable yield. With proper help and guidance they can appropriate the locked-up capacity for depth relationship that has been there all the time, but that no one helped them to actualize.

In short, we are at last beginning to provide the services to marriages which should have been made available a generation ago, when the new alternative companionship style was emerging to replace the traditional marriage.

But meanwhile, a soured and disillusioned generation is off on a quite different quest. Some decision had to be made as to what should replace the no longer functioning institutional marriage. There were two obvious choices—to maintain the monogamous structure, but change completely the mode of functioning within the structure; or to change to a new structure or structures. Burgess saw the first course as obvious and logical. Unfortunately, as we perceive it, the decision to take the second course seems to have commanded more widespread support, and our society has taken off on what, in our personal judgment, may prove to be a false trail.

Since this is a challenging statement to make, let us pause at this point for an elaboration.

Let us make it quite clear that we are not at all opposed to serious and responsible experiments in developing new social interaction patterns and new personal life-styles. We have ourselves, throughout our lives, been involved in a wide variety of "creative experiments in living," as Roger Libby calls them. What disturbs us is the manner in which the current experiments are being reported—particularly the frequently repeated implication that these new patterns are now fully tested and viable options and that their universal adoption is now only a matter of time. In our opinion this claim simply cannot be justified.

As we see it, there is little that is really new in the experimental patterns described in this book. In the main they are older family patterns that were discarded as Western culture adopted the monogamous marriage and the nuclear family—a process which we perceive as evolutionary, and others view as a retrograde step. Group marriage was noted by Julius Caesar among the ancient Britons. Experiments in communal living have been widely reported, in the Acts of the Apostles and elsewhere, throughout recorded history. Polygamy has been extensively practiced in many human cultures. The extended family is a characteristic feature of most landowning, agrarian societies. Arrangements, clandestine or otherwise, to permit sexual variety have been almost universally associated with marriage and family systems.

What *is* new is the attempt to operate these well-known and ancient social arrangements in a different manner and for a different end. The structures are not new—but the hope is that a change at the *functional* level can enable them to serve our needs. Instead of being devices to preserve social order, as they were in the past, it is hoped that they can be made to foster personal and relational growth and development better than traditional family life did.

Something of this kind could happen. We admit we are not too optimistic about adapting multilateral family systems to individual growth goals, because their major function in the past was to preserve the cultural heritage by firmly discouraging and suppressing individual initiative. And while we certainly acknowledge the urgent need to find new forms of community living to replace the hideous impersonality of our present urban culture, it seems very odd to us that in the dedicated effort to devise better ways in which men, women, and children can relate to each other, the basic biological unit—the nuclear family—should be completely ignored, or even written off as a hopeless case. After all, a nucleus is by definition the basic entity which represents the foundation stone, the seminal element, the starting point for all further growth and development. Nuclear families have been the building blocks for most human groupings which have had enduring quality—including extended families and a good many communal experiments. It is interesting to note, for example, that persistent recent reports from Israel indicate the resurgence of the nuclear family unit in the *kibbutzim.*

It has become fashionable in these days to heap calumny upon the nuclear family. Many of the criticisms we have read are based on very slender evidence, and even on quite inaccurate historical interpretations. The nuclear family is indeed in trouble at this time. But that need not surprise us, since marriages are breaking down on an unprecedented scale, and neighborly relations between contiguous families have been gravely eroded in city and suburban complexes. Given a healthy marriage as its base, however, and close and mutually creative links with other families in a cooperative community, the nuclear family could soon leap into vigorous and healthy life. There are plenty of models now available for our inspection—but no one cares to report them, or study them.

What we are saying is that the monogamous marriage and the nuclear family function far better in the companionship mode than they ever did in the institutional pattern; and that they can adapt very easily—much more easily than the more clumsy multilateral structures—to the new emphasis on personal and relational growth and development. They can also provide, in what are now called "family clusters," models of wider social interaction that will stand comparison with the best specimens of communal living in the new experimental extended families.

All this seems to us to be logical and rather obvious, and we have difficulty in understanding why it does not seem so to many of our professional colleagues. Are we stupid, uncomprehending, or naive to see it so? And we would add that this is not merely a theory for us, an intellectually contrived position which we feel obliged to defend. It finds its full validation in our own marriage, in our own family relationships, and in the marriage and family relationships of many of our closest friends, in this and in many other lands.

Even if we are mistaken, and some radical changes in family structures must come in time, we find ourselves deeply disturbed by the present widespread breakdown of marriages—many of which, we are now convinced, could be prevented by making a concerted and sustained effort to give the couples concerned the insights, the tools, and the retraining that they need.

Sweeping social changes, we are convinced, need to be carefully planned and phased. Even if our current family structures leave much to be desired, and must ultimately be discarded, it would be in our judgment irresponsible, and dangerous in the extreme, to allow them to collapse in ruins. Millions of people would then be searching and experimenting in the hope that they could come up with something new that would meet their needs. It makes sense, surely, for people to go on living in the house they have, with all its shortcomings, until a new house is available to which they can make an orderly transition.

There is already evidence in the mounting incidence of social pathology in our culture—crime, delinquency, social maladjustment, personality disorder, loss of respect for others and for the property of others, and much else—that the fabric of our society is eroding. Many causes can be cited for these disturbing manifestations of corporate disintegration; but it seems to us that the primary cause must be the failure of families to fulfill their basic task—to feed out into the community citizens who can build up rather than tear down. Families must provide new citizens who have been given enough emotional security and love to function contributively and creatively.

When we first embarked upon our life work, some forty years ago, we summed up our philosophy in a simple statement, as follows: "You can't achieve a higer quality of relationships in any community than exists in the families that make up that community; and you can't achieve a higher quality of relationships in any family than exists in the marriage on which that family is based." Sustained by these convictions, we have spent our lives in the effort to make marriages warm, loving, and creative—beginning with our own. Today, this seems to us to be a goal no less worthy than it seemed when we began. This, as we see it, is the message we must continue to proclaim, as widely as possible, by precept and by example.

We have tried in our counter-epilogue to respond positively to the attack on monogamous marriage. We recognize, however, that many of the writers of the foregoing chapters have been advocating measures intended to *improve* our marriage system, as well as offering alternatives to those who find it unacceptable. Some of these seem to hold out some promise—others raise questions in our minds. Obviously we do not have the space to take up, one by one, the many concrete proposals that have been offered.

We would like to close with some broad suggestions about the kind of action we consider to be desirable as we all seek workable solutions to the very complex problems our culture faces in the area of intimate relationships between men and women.

1. We need to examine, closely and carefully, our realistic alternatives. To do this we need dialogue rather than debate, responsible planning rather than a crossfire of polemical rhetoric between warring factions. People tend to assume that conservative and radical groups, if brought together, would be unable to listen to each other. Our Quaker heritage suggests to us that this is not necessarily so. We ourselves have frequently made close and lasting friendships with people whose views were very different from our own, and have often learned more from our opponents than from those who shared our opinions.

   The first and only White House Conference on the Family was held in 1948. Perhaps the time has come for another such Conference to be called, and for many divergent views to be heard, in the hope that some degree of consensus may be reached.
2. It would be helpful for a concerted effort to be made to establish criteria, even if some of them had to be highly flexible, to determine what kinds of family groupings should now merit social recognition. Our legal system is in great confusion as to what constitutes a family, and a rather drastic overhaul of our rigid traditional concepts is due, if not overdue. Inequities and injustices abound, and some of them at least can surely be tidied up.
3. Help is urgently required by men and women who, inside and outside marriage, are trying sincerely and earnestly to make their relationships function creatively. Our present counseling services are for the most part

remedially oriented, and often become available only when people are already in serious trouble. They need to be complemented by preventive services which will seek to keep people out of trouble, by training them in interpersonal competence so that they have the skills and insights necessary to use their relational potential for creative growth. We are now convinced that, given the necessary motivation and support on a large scale, this could be done.

In closing, we again express our gratitude for the rare privilege of being allowed, in the final pages of this book, to express views that will not be fully shared by some of the other authors. Such magnanimity is rare, and for this the editors are deserving of the highest praise.

Bibliography

Abbott, S. & B. Love. *Sappho Was a Right-On Woman*. New York: Stein and Day, 1972.

Acock, A. & M. DeFleur. A Configurational Approach to Contingent Consistency in the Attitude-Behavior Relationship. *American Sociological Review 37* (1972): 714-726.

Adams, M. The Single Woman in Today's Society: A Reappraisal. *The American Journal of Orthopsychiatry 41* (1971): 776-786.

Alternative Marriage and Relationship Council of the United States (AMRCUS), publisher of *Alternatives in Marriage and the Family: The Journal of AMRCUS*. P.O. Box 1961, Philadelphia, Pa. 19105.

Altman, I. & D. Taylor. *Social Penetration: The Development of Interpersonal Relationships*. New York: Holt, Rinehart and Winston, Inc., 1973.

Angyal, A. *Neurosis and Treatment: A Holistic Theory*. New York: John Wiley and Sons, 1965.

Anonymous (a graduate in the university of matrimony). *How to Be Happy Though Married*. London, England: T. Fisher Unwin, 1885.

Arafat, I. & B. Yorburg. On Living Together Without Marriage. *Journal of Sex Research 9* (1973): 97-106.

Arnold, W. & R. W. Libby. Semantics of Sex Related Words. *General Semantics Bulletin, 38-40: 1976, 92-96.*

Athanasiou, R., P. Shaver & C. Tavris. Sex. *Psychology Today 4* (1970).

Avant, W. R. Sexuality and Older Persons. Unpublished manuscript, 1976.

Bach, G. & R. Deutsch. *Pairing*. New York: Avon Books, 1970.

Bach, G. & P. Wyden. *The Intimate Enemy*. New York: Avon Books, 1975.

Baker, L. The Personal and Social Adjustment of the Never-Married Woman. *Journal of Marriage and the Family 30* (August 1968): 473-479.

Barbach, L. G. *For Yourself: The Fulfillment of Female Sexuality, a Guide to Orgasmic Response*. New York: Doubleday, 1975.

Bartell, G. Group Sex Among the Mid-Americans. *Journal of Sex Research*. May 1970.

Bartell, G. *Group Sex*. New York: Peter H. Wyden, Inc., 1971.

Bastian, F. *The Enclaves*. Garden City, N.Y. Doubleday, 1965.

Beauvoir, S. de. *The Second Sex*. New York: Alfred G. Knopf, 1953.

Beauvoir, S. de. (in an interview with John Gerassi), The Second Sex 25 Years Later. *Society 13*, Jan.-Feb.: 79-86.

Bell, R. *Marriage and Family Interaction*. Homewood, Illinois: Dorsey Press, 1967. Rev. ed., 1971; 3rd edition, 1975.

Bell, R. *The Sex Survey of Australian Women*. Melbourne, Australia: Sun Books, 1974.

Bell, R. & J. Chaskes. Pre-marital Sexual Experience Among Coeds, 1958 and 1968. *Journal of Marriage and the Family 32* (1970): 81-85.

Bell, R. & D. Peltz, Extra-marital Sex. Unpublished manuscript, 1972.

Bell, R., S. Turner & L. Rosen. A Multivariate Analysis of Female Extramarital Coitus. *Journal of Marriage and the Family 37* (1975): 375-385.

Bell, R. & L. Silvan. Swinging—The Sexual Exchange of Marriage Partners. *Sexual Behavior 1* (1971): 70-79.

Beltz, S. E. Five-Year Effects of Altered Marital Contracts (A Behavioral Analysis of Couples). In G. Neubeck, ed., *Extramarital Relations*. Englewood Cliffs, N.J.: Prentice-Hall, Inc., 1969.

Benedict, R. *Patterns of Culture*. New York: Mentor Books (New American Library), 1949.

Berger, B., B. Hackett, & R. Millar, Childrearing Practices in the Communal Family. In H.P. Dreitzel, ed., *Family, Marriage, and the Struggle of the Sexes*. New York: Macmillan, 1972.

Berger, M. Trial Marriage: Harnessing the Trend Constructively, *Family Coordinator 20* (1971): 38-43.

Berger, P. & H. Kellner. Marriage and the Construction of Reality. In H.P. Dreitzel, ed., *Recent Sociology No. 2*. New York: Macmillan, 1970.

Berger, P. & T. Luckmann. *The Social Construction of Reality*. New York: Anchor Doubleday, 1967.

Bernard, J. Present Demographic Trends and Structural Outcomes in Family Life Today. In J. Peterson, ed., *Marriage and Family Counseling, Perspective and Prospect.* New York: Association Press, 1968.

Bernard, J. *The Sex Game.* Englewood Cliffs, N.J.: Prentice-Hall, 1968.

Bernard, J. Two Clinicians and a Sociologist. In G. Neubeck, ed., *Extramarital Relations.* Englewood Cliffs, N.J.: Prentice-Hall, Inc., 1969.

Bernard, J. Infidelity: Some Moral and Social Issues. In J. H. Masserman, ed., *The Psychodynamics of Work and Marriage,* 1970, and the present book (Chapter 8).

Bernard, J. Women, Marriage, and the Future. *The Futurist* (April 1970): 41-43.

Bernard, J. Jealousy in Marriage. *Medical Aspects of Human Sexuality.* April 1971: 209.

Bernard, J. *The Future of Marriage.* New York: World Publishing Co., 1972.

Bernard, J. Marriage: Hers and His. *MS. 1,* No. 6: December 1972.

Bernard, J. Comments on Glenn's Paper. *Journal of Marriage and the Family 37* (August 1975): 600-601.

Bernard, J. Notes on Changing Life Styles, 1970-1974. *Journal of Marriage and the Family 37* (August 1975): 582-594.

Biddle, B. J. *Role Theory: Expectations, Identities, and Behaviors.* Chicago: Dryden Press, 1976.

Bienvenu, M., Sr. Measurement of Marital Communication. *Family Coordinator 19* (1970): 26-31.

Birenbaum, D. Revolution Without the Revolution: Sex in Contemporary America. *The Journal of Sex Research* (November 1970): 266.

Blau, P. *Exchange and Power in Social Life.* New York: John Wiley, 1964.

Block, D. Unwed Couples: Do They Live Happily Ever After? *Redbook,* (April 1969): 90+.

Blumstein, P. W. & P. Schwartz. Lesbianism and Bisexuality. In E. Goode & R. Troiden, eds., *Sexual Deviance and Sexual Deviants.* New York: William Morrow & Co., 1974.

Blumstein, P. W. & P. Schwartz. Bisexuality. Unpublished manuscript, 1976.

Booth, A. & E. Hess. Cross-Sex Friendship. *Journal of Marriage and the Family 36* (February 1974): 38-47.

Boston Women's Health Book Collective. *Our Bodies, Ourselves.* New York: Simon & Schuster, 1973.

Bower, D. *The Determinants of Dyadic Commitment Among Cohabiting Couples: A Pilot Study.* Unpublished Honors Thesis, Denison University, Granville, Ohio, 1974.

Bower, D. *A Description and Analysis of a Cohabiting Sample in America.* Unpublished Master's Thesis, University of Arizona, Tucson, Arizona, 1975.

Bowman, C. Cultural Ideology and Heterosexual Reality: A Preface to Sociological Research. *American Sociological Review 14* (1949): 624-634.

Brenton, M. *The American Male: A Penetrating Look at the Masculinity Crisis.* New York: Coward-McCann, 1966.

Brewster, M. Graduate student paper. Syracuse University, March 1976.

Broderick, C. Socio-Sexual Development in a Suburban Community. *Journal of Sex Research 2* (April 1966): 1-24.

Broderick, C. Children's Romances. *Sexual Behavior 2* (May 1972): 16-21.

Brown, H.G. *Sex and the Office.* New York: Pocket Books, 1965.

Brown, N. *Life Against Death.* Middletown, Conn.: Wesleyan University Press, 1972.

Burgess, E.W. & L.S. Cottrell. *Predicting Success or Failure in Marriage.* Engle-Wood Cliffs, N.J.: Prentice-Hall, 1939.

Burgess, E.W. & H.J. Locke. *The Family: From Institution to Companionship.* New York: American Book Co., 1945.

Burgess, E.W. & P. Wallin. *Engagement and Marriage.* Philadelphia: J.B. Lippincott, 1953.

Burr, W.R. Satisfaction with Various Aspects of Marriage over the Life Cycle: A Random Middle Class Sample. *Journal of Marriage and the Family 32,* 1970: 29-37.

Cadwallader, M. Marriage as a Wretched Institution. *Atlantic 218* (1966): 62-66.

Campbell, D. On the Conflicts Between Biological and Social Evolution and Between Psychology and Moral Tradition. *American Psychologist 30,* 1975: 1103-1126.

Campbell, E. L. & V. Ziegler, eds., *Circle One—A Woman's Beginning Guide to Self-Health and Sexuality.* Colorado University Press, 1975.

Carlson, J. The Sexual Role. In I. Nye et al.,

Role Structure and Analysis of the Family. Beverly Hills, Cal.: Sage Publications, Inc., National Council on Family Relations Monograph Series, J. Sprey, ed., 1976.

Casler, L. *Is Marriage Necessary?* New York: Human Sciences Press, 1974.

Chartham, R. *The Sensuous Couple.* New York: Ballantine Books, 1971.

Chesser, E. *The Sexual, Marital and Family Relationships of the English Woman.* Watford: Hutchinson's Medical Publications Ltd., 1956.

Christensen, H. T. A Cross-Cultural Comparison of Attitudes Toward Marital Infidelity. *International Journal of Comparative Sociology 3* (1962): 124-138.

Christensen, H. T. Attitudes Toward Marital Infidelity: A Nine-Culture Sampling of University Student Opinion. *Journal of Comparative Family Studies 4* (1973): 197-215.

Christensen, H. T. Letter to Roger W. Libby. January 1975.

Christensen, H. T. & C. F. Gregg. Changing Sex Norms in America and Scandinavia. *Journal of Marriage and the Family 32* (1970): 616-628.

Claesson, A., R. Lindgren, & G. Lindth. The Conscience Marriage and the Law. Unpublished (mimeo.): Uppsala, Sweden, 1973.

Clanton, G. Letter to Roger W. Libby. January 1976.

Clanton, G. & C. Downing, eds. *Face to Face.* New York: E. P. Dutton, 1975, and Ballantine Books,1976.

Clanton, G. & L.G. Smith, eds. *Jealousy.* Englewood Cliffs, N.J.: Prentice-Hall, 1977.

Clatworthy, N.M. Living Together. Chapter 3 in N. Glazer-Malbin, ed., *Old Family/New Family.* New York: Van Nostrand, 1975.

Clavan, S. Changing Female Sexual Behavior and Future Family Structure. *Pacific Sociological Review 15*, No. 3: July 1972.

Coffin, P. Young Unmarrieds: Theresa Pommett and Charles Walsh, College Grads Living Together, *Look*, (January 26, 1971): 634+.

Cole, C.L. *Values and Marital Adjustment: A Test of Homogamy Theory.* Unpublished Dissertation. Iowa State University, Ames, Iowa, 1973.

Cole, C.L. Data Book for 1973 Cohabitation Survey. Unpublished. Department of Sociology, Denison University, Granville, Ohio, 1973.

Cole, C.L. Data Book for 1974 Cohabitation Survey. Unpublished. Department of Sociology, Denison University, Granville, Ohio, 1974.

Cole, C.L. Living Together as an Alternative Lifestyle. *Personnel and Guidance Journal 55* (in press).

Cole, C.L. & D. Bower. Data Book for 1974 Panel Interviews. Unpublished. Department of Sociology, Denison University, Granville, Ohio, 1974.

Cole, C.L. & D. Bower. Role Disparity in the Cohabitation Pair-Bond. Paper presented at the North Central Sociological Association, Windsor, Ont., Canada, May 1974.

Cole, C.L. & G. Spanier. Becoming a Mate Swapper: Some Thoughts on How the Process Works. Paper presented at the Midwest Sociological Society, Kansas City, Missouri, April 21, 1972.

Comfort, A. *The Joy of Sex.* New York: Crown Publishers, 1972.

Comfort, A. *More Joy.* New York: Crown Publishers, 1974.

Comfort, A. Swinging Future (an interview with Alex Comfort). *Time Magazine.* (January 9, 1973), p. 35.

Communities: Journal of Cooperative Living. P.O. Box 117, McMinnville, Oregon 97128.

Conover, P. An Analysis of Communes and Intentional Communities with Particular Attention to Sexual and Gender Relations. *The Family Coordinator 24*, No. 4 (October 1975): 453-464.

Constantine, L. Open Family: a Lifestyle for Kids and Other People. Paper presented at National Council on Family Relations, annual meeting, Salt Lake City, 1975.

Constantine, L. & J. Constantine. *Group Marriage: A Study of Contemporary Multilateral Marriage.* New York: Macmillan, 1973.

Constantine, L. & J. Constantine. Where Is Marriage Going? *The Futurist 4* (1970): 44-46.

Constantine, L. & J. Constantine. Group and Multilateral Marriage: Definitional Notes, Glossary, and Annotated Bibliography. *Family Process 10* (1971): pp. 157-176.

Constantine, L. & J. Constantine. Sexual Aspects of Multilateral Relations. *Journal of Sex Research 7* (1971): 204-226.

Constantine, L. & J. Constantine. *Treasures of the Island: Children in Alternative Families.* Studies of Marriage and Family, Monograph 90-038. Beverly Hills, Cal.: Sage Publications, 1976.

Cooley, C.H. *Social Organizations: A Study of the Larger Mind.* New York: Charles Scribner's Sons, 1909.

Coutts, R. *Love and Intimacy.* San Ramon, Cal.: Consensus Publishers, 1973.

Cuber, J. F. Adultery: Reality Versus Stereotype. Unpublished manuscript, as cited in Bernard, Chapter 8.

Cuber, J. F. Adultery: Reality Versus Stereotype. In G. Neubeck, ed., *Extramarital Relations.* Englewood Cliffs, N.J.: Prentice-Hall, Inc., 1969.

Cuber, J. F. & P. Harroff. *Sex and the Significant Americans.* Baltimore: Penguin Books, Inc., 1965.

Dahms, A. *Emotional Intimacy: Overlooked Requirement for Survival.* Boulder: Pruett Publishing Company, 1972.

Dahms, A. Intimacy Hierarchy. In E.A. Powers & M.W. Lees, eds., *Process in Relationship*, 2nd ed. New York: West Publishing Company, 1976.

Danziger, C. & M. Greenwald. Alternatives: A Look at Unmarried Couples and Communes. New York: Research Services Institute of Life Insurance (pamphlet), 1973.

David, D. & R. Brannon, eds. *The Forty-Nine Percent Majority: The Male Sex Role.* Reading, Mass.: Addison-Wesley, 1976.

Davis, K. Jealousy and Sexual Property. *Social Forces 14* (1936): 395-405.

Davis, K. *Human Society.* New York: Macmillan, 1949.

Davis, K. & G. Katts. The Dynamics of Sexual Behavior of College Students. *Journal of Marriage and the Family 32* (1970): 390-397.

Decter, M. Toward the New Chastity. *The Atlantic Monthly 230* (1972): 42-55.

Delhees, K. & R. Cattell. *Manual for the Clinical Analysis Questionnaire.* Champaign, Ill., 1PAT, 1971.

DeLora, J.R. & J.S. DeLora, eds., *Intimate Life Styles: Marriage and Its Alternatives*, 2nd ed. Pacific Palisades, Calif.: Goodyear Publishing Company, 1975.

Denfeld, D. & M. Gordon. The Sociology of Mate Swapping: Or the Family that Swings Together Clings Together. *Journal of Sex Research 6* (1970): 85-100.

Derlega, V. & A. Chaikin. *Sharing Intimacy: What We Reveal to Others and Why.* Englewood Cliffs, N.J.: Prentice-Hall, Inc., 1975.

Dodson, B. *Liberating Masturbation: A Meditation on Self Love.* (New York: Bodysex Designs, 1974.

Drabkin, R. Living Together . . . And the Law. *Marriage and Divorce 1* (1974): 18-20.

Dressel, P. & V. Murray. A Systems Explanation of Changing Family Behavior. *The Southern Sociologist.* Spring 1976: 11-15.

Dullea, G. "Marriage Tax": It Has Couples in a Rage (and Even Divorcing). *The New York Times* (March 27, 1975): 26.

Duyckaert, F. *The Sexual Bond.* New York: Delacorte Press, 1970.

Easton, B. S. & H. C. Robbins. *The Bond of Honour, A Marriage Handbook.* New York: Macmillan, 1938.

Edmiston, S. How to Write Your Own Marriage Contract. *Ms. Magazine.* Spring, 1972: 66-72.

Edwards, J.N. Extramarital Involvement: Fact and Theory. *Journal of Sex Research 9* (1973): 210-226.

Edwards, J.N. & A. Booth. Sexual Behavior In and out of Marriage: An Assessment of Correlates. *Journal of Marriage and the Family 38* (February 1976): 73-83.

Eiduson, B., J. Cohen, & J. Alexander. Alternatives in Childrearing in the 1970s. *American Journal of Orthopsychiatry 43* (5), October 1973.

Ellis, A. *Sex Without Guilt.* New York: Lyle Stuart, 1958, 1966.

Ellis, A. & A. Abarbanal, eds. *The Encyclopedia of Sexual Behavior.* New York: Hawthorn Books, 1961.

Erikson, E.H. Identity and the Life Cycle: Selected Papers. *Psychological Issues 1*, 1959, whole.

Eshleman, J.R. A Cross Cultural Analysis of Sexual Codes: Beliefs, Behavior, and the Perception of Others. Paper presented at The National Council on Family Relations, Portland, Oregon, November 1972.

Esquire. Room-mates (September 1967): 94-98.

Farber, B. *Family: Organization and Interaction*, San Francisco: Chandler Publishing Co., 1964.

Farrell, W. *The Liberated Man*. New York: Bantam, 1976.

Farson, R. *Birthrights: A Bill of Rights for Children*. New York: Macmillan, 1974.

Fast, J. *The Incompatibility of Men and Women*. New York: Avon Publishing Co., 1972.

Fasteau, M.F. *The Male Machine*. New York: McGraw-Hill, 1974.

Fearing, F. An Examination of the Conceptions of Benjamin Whorf in the Light of Theories of Perception and Cognition. In H. Hoijer, ed., *Language in Culture*. Chicago: University of Chicago Press, 1954, pp. 47-82.

Ferkiss, V. *Technological Man*. New York: George Braziller, Inc., 1969.

Firestone, S. *Dialectic of Sex: The Case for Feminist Revolution*. New York: William Morrow & Co., 1970, Bantam, 1971.

Fishbein, M. & I. Ajzen. *Belief, Attitude, Intention, and Behavior*. Reading, Mass.: Addison-Wesley, 1975.

Fishel, D. & N. Allon. Urban Courting Patterns: Singles' Bars. Paper presented at the American Sociological Association Annual Meeting, Summer 1973.

Flaherty, T. In Defense of Traditional Marriage. *Life*, November 1972.

Fletcher, J. Love is the Only Measure. *Commonweal 83*: 431, 1966.

Fletcher, J. *Situation Ethics: The New Morality*. Philadelphia: Westminster Press, 1967.

Foote, N. Sex as Play. *Social Problems 1* (1954): 159-163.

Foote, N. & L.S. Cottrell. *Identity and Interpersonal Competence*. Chicago: University of Chicago Press, 1955.

Francoeur, R. *Eve's New Rib*. New York: Harcourt Brace Jovanovich, 1972, Delta Books, 1974.

Francoeur, R. & A. Francoeur. *The Future of Sexual Relations*. Englewood Cliffs, N.J.: Prentice-Hall, 1974.

Francoeur, R. & A. Francoeur. *Hot and Cool Sex: Cultures in Conflict*. New York: Harcourt Brace Jovanovich, 1974; Cranbury, N.J.: A.S. Barnes, 1976.

Freeman, H.A. & R.S. Freeman. Senior College Women: Their Sexual Standards and Activity—Part II. Dating: Petting-Coital Practices. *National Association of Women's Deans and Counselors Journal*. Spring 1966: 136-143.

Freeman, J. *The Politics of Women's Liberation*. New York: David McKay & Co., 1975.

French Institute of Public Opinion. *Patterns of Sex and Love: A Study of the French Woman and Her Morals*. New York: Crown Publishers, Inc., 1961.

Freud, S. *Collected Papers IV*. J. Riviere and J. Strachey, eds. New York: The International Psycho-Analytic Press, 1922.

Friedan, B. *The Feminine Mystique*. New York: Dell Books, 1963, 1973.

Friends Home Service Committee. *Towards a Quaker View of Sex*. London, England: Friends House, 1964 (revised edition).

Fromm, E. *The Art of Loving*. New York: Harper & Row, 1956.

Fromm, E. *Revolution of Hope: Toward a Humanized Technology*. New York: Harper & Row, 1974.

Funk and Wagnalls. *Standard Dictionary*. Chicago: Encyclopaedia Britannica, 1966.

Future Families of the World (FFW), Newsletter. *Joy-Us* from FFW. P.O. Box 7574, Washington, D.C. 20044.

Gagnon, J. H. & W. Simon. Unpublished paper, 1969.

Gagnon, J. H. & W. Simon. Prospects for Change in American Sexual Patterns. In H. Lief, ed. *Medical Aspects of Human Sexuality*. Baltimore: Williams & Wilkins, 1975.

Gavin, M. The Living Together Phenomenon. Unpublished Master's Thesis. Washington State University, Pullman, Washington, 1973.

Gebhard, P. In M. Hunt, *The Affair*. New York: World, 1969.

Gecas, V. & R.W. Libby. Sexual Behavior as Symbolic Interaction. *Journal of Sex Research 12*, February 1976: 33-50.

Gilder, G. *Sexual Suicide*. New York: Bantam Books, 1973.

Gilder, G. *Naked Nomads*. New York: Quadrangle, 1974.

Gilmartin, B.G. Social Antecedents and Correlates of Comarital Sexual Behavior. Unpublished Doctoral Dissertation, 1976.

Glenn, N. D. The Contribution of Marriage to the Psychological Well-Being of Males and Females. *Journal of Marriage and the*

Family 37 (August 1975): 594-600.

Glick, P. A Demographer Looks at American Families. *Journal of Marriage and the Family 37* (1975): 15-26.

Glick, P. Some Recent Changes in American Families. *Current Population Reports.* Bureau of the Census, Special Studies, Series P-23, No. 52, U.S. Government Printing Office, 1975.

Glick, P. Personal discussion with Roger Libby. March 1976.

Goode, W. J. *The Family.* Englewood Cliffs, N.J.: Prentice-Hall, 1964.

Goode, W.J. The Theoretical Importance of Love. In W. Goode, *Explorations in Social Theory,* New York: Oxford University Press, 1973.

Gordon, M. & P. J. Shankweiler. Different Equals Less: Female Sexuality in Recent Marriage Manuals. *Journal of Marriage and the Family 33,* No. 3 (August 1971): 459-465.

Gordon, S. & R. Libby, eds. *Sexuality Today and Tomorrow: Contemporary Issues in Human Sexuality.* North Scituate, Mass.: Duxbury Press, 1976.

Gordon, T. *Parent Effectiveness Training: The "No-lose" Program for Raising Responsible Children.* New York: Peter H. Wyden, 1970.

Grant, A. No Rings Attached: A Look at Premarital Marriage on Campus. *Mademoiselle 66* (April 1968): 208+

Greer, G. *The Female Eunuch.* New York: McGraw-Hill, 1970-71.

Guittar, E. & R. Lewis. Self-Concepts Among Some Unmarried Cohabitants. Paper presented at the National Council on Family Relations, St. Louis, Missouri, October 1974.

Habenstein, R. Personal communication to Carolynne Kieffer, 1976.

Habenstein, R. & E. Biddle. Case history from AOA Research Project #90-A-516-01. Local socio-environmental contexts and personal moorings in relation to decision-making and the elderly, 1975-1978 (in progress).

Haley, J. Address at the Annual Meeting of the National Council of Family Relations, Portland, Oregon, 1973.

Hall, L. & N. Wagner. Initial Heterosexual Experience in Sweden and the United States: A Cross-Cultural Survey. Unpublished paper, 1972.

Harlow, H.F. The Nature of Love. *American Psychologist 13,* 1958.

Harmon, O. Masturbation. *Issues in Radical Therapy,* Oakland, Calif.

Harper, R. Extramarital Sex Relations. In A. Ellis and A. Abarbanel, eds., *The Encyclopedia of Sexual Behavior.* New York: Hawthorn Books, 1961, 1967.

Harrison, J. A Reconsideration of Freud's "A Disturbance of Memory on the Acropolis in Relation to Identity Disturbance." *Journal of the American Psychoanalytic Association 13* (1965): 518-527.

Havelock, E. & R.N. Whitehurst. Letter to Roger W. Libby. January 1976.

Hayner, N. *New Patterns in Old Mexico.* New Haven: College & Univ. Press, 1966.

Hedblom, J. H. Dimensions of Lesbian Sexual Experience. *Archives of Sexual Behavior 2* (December 1973): 329-343.

Heiman, J. R. The Physiology of Erotica: Women's Sexual Arousal. *Psychology Today,* April 1975: 90-94.

Hennon, C. Open-Systems Theory and the Analysis of Non-Marital Cohabitation. Paper presented at the Groves Conference on Marriage and the Family, Hot Springs, Arkansas, April 1974.

Henze, L. & J. Hudson. Personal and Family Characteristics of Cohabiting and Non-cohabiting College Students. *Journal of Marriage and the Family 36* (1974): 722-727.

Hickrod, L. Religious Background of College Students and Attitudes Toward Living Together Before Marriage. Paper presented at the National Council on Family Relations, Portland, Oregon, October 1972.

Hite, S. *Sexual Honesty.* Warner Paperbacks, 1974.

Hoffman, M. *The Gay World.* New York: Bantam Books, 1969.

Hole, J. & E. Levine. *Rebirth of Feminism,* New York: Quadrangle, 1971.

Holt, J. *Escape from Childhood,* New York: Ballantine Books, 1975.

Homans, G. *Social Behavior: Its Elementary Forms.* New York: Harcourt Brace Jovanovich, Inc., 1961.

Huang, L. Some Patterns of Non-Exclusive Sexual Relations Among Unmarried Cohabiting Couples. *International Journal of the Review of Sociology 6* (in press).

Hudson, J. & L. Henze. A Note on Cohabitation. *The Family Coordinator* 22 (1973): 495.

Humphreys, L. *Tearoom Trade: Impersonal Sex in Public Places*, 2nd ed. Chicago: Aldine Press, 1975.

Hunt, A. Multilateral Marriage from the Child's Perspective. Unpublished report, Multilateral Relations Study Project (Center for Family Change, Acton, Mass.). February 1972.

Hunt, M. *The World of the Formerly Married.* New York: McGraw-Hill Book Co., 1966.

Hunt, M. *The Affair.* New York: World Publishing Co., 1969.

Hunt, M. The Future of Marriage. *Playboy 18* (August 1971): 116+.

Hunt, M. *Sexual Behavior in the 1970s.* Chicago: Playboy Press, 1974.

Huston, T.L., ed. *Foundations of Interpersonal Attraction.* New York: Academic Press, 1974.

Johnson, M. Courtship and Commitment: A Study on a University Campus. Unpublished Master's Thesis, University of Iowa, Iowa City, 1968.

Johnson, M. Commitment: A Conceptual Structure and Empirical Application. *Sociological Quarterly 14* (1973): 395-406.

Johnson, M. Some Issues in the Area of Courtship and Commitment. Paper presented at the Groves Conference on Marriage and the Family, Myrtle Beach, South Carolina, May 1973.

Johnson, N. The Careening of America. *The Humanist.* July/August 1972: 10-17.

Johnson, R. Some Correlates of Extramarital Coitus. *Journal of Marriage and the Family 32* (1970): 449-456.

Johnston, C. & R. Deisher. Contemporary Communal Childrearing: A First Analysis. *Pediatrics 52* (3), September 1973.

Johnston, J. *Lesbian Nation: The Feminist Solution.* New York: Simon and Schuster, 1973.

Jong, E. *Fear of Flying.* New York: Holt, Rinehart and Winston, Inc., 1973.

Jourard, S.M. *Disclosing Man to Himself.* New York: Van Nostrand Reinhold Co., 1968.

Kaats, G. A. & K. E. Davis. The Dynamics of Sexual Behavior of College Students. *Journal of Marriage and the Family 32* (1970): 390-400.

Kafka, J.S. The Body as Transitional Object: A Psychoanalytic Study of a Self-Mutilating Patient. *British Journal of Medical Psychology 42* (1969): 207-212.

Kafka, J.S. Ambiguity for Individuation; A Critique and Reformulation of Double-Bind Theory. *Archives of General Psychiatry 25* (1971): 232-239.

Kalmback, C. Replication Study of Heterosexual Cohabitation Among Unmarried College Students: Cornell University and Central Michigan University. Unpublished manuscript. Central Michigan. University, 1973.

Kandel, D. & G. S. Lesser. Parent-Adolescent Relationships and Adolescent Independence in the United States and Denmark. *Journal of Marriage and the Family 31* (May 1969): 348-358.

Kanter, R. M. *Commitment and Community.* Cambridge, Mass.: Harvard University Press, 1972.

Karlen, A. The Unmarried Marrieds on Campus. *New York Times Magazine* (January 26, 1969): 29+.

Kassel, V. Polygyny After Sixty. In H. Otto, ed., *The Family in Search of a Future.* New York: Appleton-Century-Crofts, 1970.

Kephart, W. M. *The Family, Society, and the Individual*, 2nd ed. Boston: Houghton Mifflin Co., 1966.

Kieffer, C. Consensual Cohabitation: A Descriptive Study of the Relationships and Sociocultural Characteristics of Eighty Couples in Settings of Two Florida Universities. Unpublished Master's Thesis, Florida State University, Tallahassee, Florida, 1972.

Kieffer, C. Personal communication to Charles Cole, March 1976.

Kilgo, R. D. Can Group Marriage Work? *Sexual Behavior 6* (1972): 2.

Killian, L. Social Movements. *Society Today*, 2nd ed., Del Mar, Cal.: CRM Books, 1973.

Kincade, K. *A Walden Two Experiment.* New York: William Morrow & Co., 1973.

Kinsey, A., W. Pomeroy, & C. Martin. *Sexual Behavior in the Human Male.* Philadelphia: W. B. Saunders Co., 1948.

Kinsey, A., W. Pomeroy, C. Martin, & P. Gebhard. *Sexual Behavior in the Human Female.* Philadelphia: W.B. Saunders Co., 1953.

Kirkendall, L. A. *Premarital Intercourse and Interpersonal Relationships.* New York: Julian Press, 1961.

Kirkendall, L. A. Semantics and Sexual Communication. *ETC: A Review of General Semantics 23,* June 1966: 235-244.

Kirkendall, L. A. & R. W. Libby. Interpersonal Relationships—Crux of the Sexual Renaissance. *The Journal of Social Issues 22* (April 1966): 45-60.

Kirkendall, L. A. et al. A New Bill of Sexual Rights and Responsibilities. *The Humanist 36,* January/February 1976: 4-6.

Knapp, J. Co-Marital Sex and Marriage Counseling: Sexually Open Marriages and Related Attitudes and Practices of Marriage Counselors. Doctoral Dissertation, University of Florida, 1974. Ann Arbor, Mich.: University Microfilms: 79-19, 352.

Knapp, J. The Myers-Briggs Type Indicator as a Basis for Personality Description of Spouses in Sexually Open Marriage. Paper presented at the First National Conference on the Uses of the MBTI. Gainesville, Florida, October 1975b.

Knapp, J. Some Non-Monogamous Marriage Styles and Related Attitudes and Practices of Marriage Counselors. *The Family Coordinator 24* (1975a): 505-514.

Knapp, J. An Exploratory Study of Seventeen Sexually Open Marriages. *Journal of Sex Research* (in press).

Knupfer, G., W. Clark, & R. Room. The Mental Health of the Unmarried. *American Journal of Psychiatry 122* (February 1966): 841-851.

Koedt, A. The Myth of the Vaginal Orgasm. In A. Koedt, E. Levine, & A. Rapone, eds., *Radical Feminism.* New York: Quadrangle, 1974.

Kris, E. *Psychoanalytic Explorations in Art.* New York: International Universities Press, 1952.

Ladies Home Journal. A survey of readership. October 1968.

LaFollette, P. Results of Synergy Study of Its Membership. *Family Synergy Newsletter.* March 1976.

LaFollette, P. Unpublished data from a study of the Family Synergy membership in Los Angeles, Calif.

Laing, R., H. Phillipson, & A. Lee. *Interpersonal Perception: A Theory and a Method of Research.* New York: Springer Publishing Co., 1966.

Lance, L. Reverse Double Standard: A New Concept. Unpublished manuscript. Department of Sociology, University of North Carolina at Charlotte, 1976.

Lautenschlager, S. A Descriptive Study of Consensual Union Among College Students. Unpublished Master's Thesis, California State University at Northridge, Northridge, California, 1972.

Laws, J.L. Toward a Model of Female Sexual Identity. *Midway.* Summer 1970: 39-75.

Laws, J.L. A Feminist Review of the Marital Adjustment Literature: The Rape of the Locke. *Journal of Marriage and the Family 33,* No. 3, August 1971.

Laws, J. L. Exotica-Erotica: A Plea for Continuities in the Study of Human Behavior and Sexual Behavior. Paper presented at the American Psychological Association, August 29, 1973, Montreal, Canada.

Laws, J.L. Chapters 1 and 2 in *The Sexual Scripts: The Social Construction of Female Sexuality.* Co-edited by J. Laws & P. Schwartz. Hinsdale, Illinois: Dryden Press, 1977.

Leach, W.H., ed. *Cokesbury Marriage Manual.* Nashville, Tenn.: Abingdon Press, 1945, 1959.

Lederer, W.J. & D.D. Jackson. *The Mirages of Marriage.* New York: W.W. Norton, 1968.

Leslie, G. *The Family in Social Context,* 3rd ed. New York: Oxford University Press, 1976.

Lever, J. & P. Schwartz. *Women at Yale.* New York: Bobbs-Merrill, 1971.

Levin, R.J. Premarital and Extramarital Sex. *Redbook 145* (October 1975): 38-44 and 90-94.

Levinger, G. Letter to Roger W. Libby. November 1975.

Lewin, K. *Principles of Topological Psychology.* New York: McGraw-Hill, 1936.

Lewis, R., G. Spanier, V. Storm, & C. LeHecka. Commitment in Married and Unmarried Cohabitation. Paper presented at the American Sociological Association, San Francisco, California, August 1975.

Libby, R.W. Replies to Trost. *Journal of Marriage and the Family 36* (1974): 674.

Libby, R.W. A Second Review. *Journal of Marriage and the Family 38* (1976): 195-196.

Libby, R.W. Today's Changing Sexual Mores. In J. Money and H. Muspah, eds., *Hand-*

book of Sexology. Amsterdam, Holland: Elsevier Excerpta Medica Press, 1977.

Libby, R.W. & J. Carlson. Sexual Behavior as Symbolic Exchange: An Integration of Theory. Unpublished manuscript, 1976.

Lichtenstein, H. Changing Implications of the Concept of Psychosexual Dvelopment: An Inquiry Concerning the Validity of Classical Psychoanalytic Assumptions Concerning Sexuality. *Journal of the American Psychoanalytic Association 18* (1970): 300-318.

Life. Coed Dorms: An Ultimate Campus Revolution. (November 20, 1970): 32+.

Limpus, L. Sexual Repression and the Family. *Liberation of Women.* Boston: New England Free Press, 1969.

Lindsey, B. The Companionate Marriage. *Redbook* (October 1926).

Lobell, J. & M. Lobell. *John and Mimi: A Free Marriage.* New York: St. Martin's Press, 1972.

Lobell, J. & M. Lobell. *The Complete Handbook for a Sexually Free Marriage.* New York: Pinnacle Books, 1975.

Lobsenz, N. Marriage vs. Living Together. *Modern Bride* (April/May 1973): 124+.

Lobsenz, N. Living Together: A New Fangled Tango or an Old-Fashioned Waltz. *Redbook* (June 1974): 86+.

Löcsei, P. Syndyasmos in Contemporary Budapest. Unpublished (Mimeo.), Budapest, 1970.

Lowenthal, L. *Literature and the Image of Man.* Boston: Beacon, 1963.

Lowenthal, M. & C. Haven. Interaction and Adaptation: Intimacy as a Critical Variable. *American Sociological Review 33* (February 1968): 20-30.

Luckey, E. Marital Satisfaction and Its Association with Congruence of Perception. *Marriage and Family Living 22* (1960): 49-54.

Lydon, S. The Politics of Orgasm. In R. Morgan, ed., *Sisterhood Is Powerful.* New York: Random House/Vintage, 1970.

Lyness, J., M. Lipetz, & K. Davis. Living Together: An Alternative to Marriage. *Journal of Marriage and the Family 34* (1972): 305-311.

McBride, W. & H. Fleischhauer-Hardt. *Show Me! A Picture Book of Sex for Children and Parents.* New York: St. Martin's Press, 1975.

Mace, D. *Success in Marriage.* Nashville, Tenn.: Abingdon Press, 1958.

Mace, D. & V. Mace. *We Can Have Better Marriages—If We Really Want Them.* Nashville, Tenn.: Abingdon Press, 1974.

McIntosh, J. & G. Nass. Career Orientation and Heterosexual Autonomy Attitudes of Wheelock Students. Paper presented at Wheelock College Colloquium, May 1975.

Macklin, E.D. Heterosexual Cohabitation Among Unmarried College Students. *Family Coordinator 21* (1972): 463-472.

Macklin, E.D. Report from the Workshop on Non-Marital Cohabitation. Paper presented at the Groves Conference on Marriage and the Family, Myrtle Beach, South Carolina, May 1973.

Macklin, E.D. Cohabitation in College: Going Very Steady. *Psychology Today 8* (1974): 53-59.

McLuhan, M. *Understanding Media: The Extensions of Man.* New York: McGraw-Hill Co., 1964.

McLuhan, M. The Future of Sex. In G. Leonard, *The Man and Woman Thing.* New York: Dell, 1970.

McWhirter, W. The Arrangement at College. *Life* (May 31, 1968): 56+.

Mailer, N. The Prisoner of Sex. *Harper's 242* (March 1971).

Marcuse, H. *An Essay on Liberation.* Boston: Beacon Press, 1969.

Martin, D. & P. Lyon. *Lesbian/Woman.* New York: Bantam Books, 1972.

Martin, R.M. & F.L. Marcuse. Characteristics of Volunteers and Nonvolunteers for Hypnosis. *Journal of Clinical and Experimental Hypnosis 5* (October 1957): 176-179.

Martinson, F. *Infant and Child Sexuality.* (Available through The Book Mark, Gustavus Adolphus College, St. Peter, Minn.) St. Peter, Minn.: F.M. Martinson, 1973.

Maslow, A. *Motivation and Personality.* New York: Harper and Row, 1954.

Maslow, A. *Toward a Psychology of Being,* 2nd ed. Princeton, N.J.: D. Van Nostrand Company, Inc., 1968.

Maslow, A. *The Farther Reaches of Human Nature.* New York: Viking Press, 1971.

Maslow, A. & J. Sakoda. Volunteer-Error in the Kinsey Study. In J. Himelhoch & S. Fava, eds. *Sexual Behavior in American Society.* New York: Norton, 1955, pp. 119-125.

Masters, W. & V. Johnson. *Human Sexual Response*. Boston: Little, Brown and Co., 1966.

Masters, W. & V. Johnson. *The Pleasure Bond: A New Look at Sexuality and Commitment*. Boston: Little, Brown and Co., 1975.

Mazur, R. *Commonsense Sex*. Boston: Beacon Press, 1968.

Mazur, R. Beyond Morality: Toward the Humanization of the Sexes. Paper presented at National Council on Family Relations, annual meeting, Chicago, 1970.

Mazur, R. *The New Intimacy: Open-ended Marriages and Alternative Lifestyles*. Boston: Beacon Press, 1973.

Mazur, R. Unpublished notes to Roger W. Libby. October 1975.

Mazursky, P. & L. Tucker. *Bob and Carol and Ted and Alice*. A screenplay.

Mead, M. Marriage in Two Steps. *Redbook* 127 (July 1966): 48-49.

Millar, M. Apollonians and Dionysians: Some Impressions of Sex in the Counter-Culture. In R. Libby & R. Whitehurst, eds., *Renovating Marriage*. Danville, Calif.: Consensus Publishers, 1973.

Millet, K. *Sexual Politics*. New York: Doubleday, 1969.

Minuchin, S. *Families and Family Therapy*. Cambridge, Mass.: Harvard University Press, 1974.

Mitchell, H., J. Bullard, & E. Mudd. Areas of Marital Conflict in Successfully and Unsuccessfully Functioning Families. *Journal of Health and Human Behavior* 3 (1962): 88-93.

Money, J. *Sex Errors of the Body*. Baltimore: Johns Hopkins Press, 1968.

Money, J. & A. Erhardt. Progestin-Induced Hermaphroditism: IQ and Psychosexual Identity in a Study of 10 Girls. *Journal of Sex Research* 3 (1967): 83-100.

Money, J., A. Erhardt, & R. Epstein. Fetal Androgens and Female Gender Identity in the Early Treated Adrenogenital Syndrome. *The Johns Hopkins Medical Journal* 122: March 1968.

Montgomery, J. *Towards an Understanding of Cohabitation*. Unpublished Dissertation, University of Massachusetts, Amherst, Massachusetts, 1972.

Montgomery, J. Commitment and Cohabitation Cohesion. Paper presented at the National Council on Family Relations, Toronto, Ont., Canada, November 1973.

Morgan, M. *The Total Woman*. New York: Revell, 1973.

Morris, D. *Intimate Behavior*. New York: Random House, 1971.

Mosher, J. *Correlates of Attraction to the New Alternatives in Marriage*. Unpublished Dissertation, University of Connecticut, Storrs, Connecticut, 1974.

Moskin, J. R. The New Contraceptive Society. *Look* (Feb. 4, 1969): 50-53.

Moustakas, C. *Loneliness and Love*. Englewood Cliffs, N.J.: Prentice-Hall, 1972.

Murdock, G. *Social Structure*. New York: Macmillan, Inc., 1949.

Murstein, B. I. *Love, Sex, and Marriage Through the Ages*. New York: Springer Publishing Company, 1974.

Myers, I. *Manual for the Myers-Briggs Type Indicator*. Princeton, N.J.: Educational Testing Service, 1962.

Myers, L. & H. Leggitt. A New View of Adultery. *Sexual Behavior*, February 1972.

Myers, L. & H. Leggitt. *Adultery and Other Private Matters: Your Right to Personal Freedom in Marriage*. Chicago: Nelson-Hall, 1975.

Myron, N. & C. Bunch. *Lesbianism and the Women's Movement*. Baltimore: Diana Press, 1975.

Nasholm, A. Married Cohabitation and Unmarried Cohabitation. *SOU* (1972): 41.

Nass, G. Letter to Roger W. Libby. October 1975.

Neubeck, G., ed. *Extramarital Relations*. Englewood Cliffs, N.J.: Prentice-Hall, 1969.

Neubeck, G. The Dimensions of the Extra in Extramarital Relations. Unpublished paper.

Neubeck, G. & V. Schletzer. A Study of Extramarital Relationships. Reprinted in Neubeck (1969). Originally appeared in *Journal of Marriage and the Family* 24 (1962): 279-281.

Newsweek. Unstructured Relationships: Students Living Together. (July 4, 1966): 78.

Newsweek. First Singles' Church. (June 12, 1972).

Newton, N. Trebly Sensuous Woman. In *The Female Experience* by the editors of *Psychology Today*, 1973.

Novey, S. Some Philosophical Speculations About the Concept of the Genital Character. *International Journal of Psychoanalysis* 36 (1955): 88-94.

Nye, I. Personal discussion with Roger W.

Libby. February 1976.

Nye, I. & F. Berardo. *The Family: Its Structure and Interaction.* New York: Macmillan, 1973.

Nye, I., J. Carlson, & F. Berardo. Unpublished paper, 1970.

Nye, I., J. Carlson, & G. Garrett. Family Size, Interaction, Affect and Stress. *Journal of Marriage and the Family 32,* May 1970: 216-227.

O'Neill, N. & G. O'Neill. *Open Marriage: A New Life Style for Couples.* New York: M. Evans Company, 1972, Avon Books, 1973.

O'Neill, N. & G. O'Neill. Open Marriage: A Synergic Model. *Family Coordinator 21* (1972): 403-409.

O'Neill, N. & G. O'Neill. Patterns in Group Sexual Activity. *Journal of Sex Research 6* (May 1970): 101-112.

O'Neill, N. & G. O'Neill. *Shifting Gears: Finding Security in a Changing World.* New York: M. Evans, 1974; Avon, 1975.

O'Sullivan, S. Single Life in a Double Bed. *Harper's Magazine,* Nov. 1975, and *Cosmopolitan Magazine,* April 1976: 140-150 and 160.

Otten, J. Living on Syntax. *Newsweek* (December 30, 1974): 9.

Otto, H., ed. *The Family in Search of a Future.* New York: Appleton-Century-Crofts, 1970.

Packard, V. *The Sexual Wilderness.* New York: David McKay Co., 1968.

Panzer, M. No World for a Single. *Coronet Magazine 37* (April 1955).

Palson, C. & R. Palson. Swinging in Wedlock. *Society 9:* No. 4, February 1972: 28-37.

Peer, E. The Broken Family: Divorce U.S. Style. *Newsweek* (March 12, 1973): 45-57.

Perlman, D. Self-Esteem and Sexual Permissiveness. *Journal of Marriage and the Family 36* (August 1974): 470-473.

Perls, F. The Gestalt Prayer. In *Gestalt Therapy Verbatim.* New York: Bantam, 1969.

Peterman, D., C. Ridley, & S. Anderson. A Comparison of Cohabiting and Noncohabiting College Students. *Journal of Marriage and the Family 36* (1974): 344-354.

Pflaum, J. *Delightism.* Englewood Cliffs, N.J.: Prentice-Hall, 1972.

Phelps, L. Female Sexual Alienation. *Liberation* (May 1971). Reprinted in J. Freeman, ed., *Women: A Feminist Perspective.* Palo Alto, Calif.: Mayfield, 1975.

Phillips, D. L. Mental Health Status, Social Participation and Happiness. *Journal of Health and Social Behavior 8* (December 1967): 285-291.

Pineo, P.C. Disenchantment in the Later Years of Marriage. *Marriage and Family Living 23* (1961): 3-11.

Plato. Symposium. In *The Dialogues of Plato,* Vol. I. Translated into English by B. Jowett. New York: Random House, 1937.

Pleck, J. & J. Sawyer, eds. *Men and Masculinity.* Englewood Cliffs, N.J.: Prentice-Hall, 1974.

Potter, J. Sex Education: An Expert Speaks Out. *American Baby Magazine.* April 1968.

Proulx, C. Sex as Athletics in the Singles Complex. *Saturday Review of the Society 1* (1973): 61-66.

Psychology Today. What Makes You Happy? A *PT* Questionnaire. Vol. 9, No. 5 (October 1975): 66+.

Radloff, L. Sex Differences in Mental Health: The Effects of Marital and Occupational Status. Paper presented before th American Public Health Association, October 1974.

Ramey, J. Emerging Patterns of Behavior in Marriage: Deviations or Innovations. *Journal of Sex Research* (February 1972).

Ramey, J. Intimate Groups and Networks: Frequent Consequences of Sexually Open Marriage. *The Family Coordinator 24* (1975): 515-530.

Ramey, J. Legal Regulation of Personal and Family Lifestyles. Paper presented at the Fourth International Conference on the Unity of the Sciences. New York, November 1975.

Ramey, J. *Intimate Friendships.* Englewood Cliffs, N.J.: Prentice-Hall, 1976.

Raphael, P. Twentieth Century Woman's Dilemma. *Female Forum (Penthouse* Special Edition), 1975.

Raush, H., D. Goodrich, & J. Campbell. Adaptation to the First Years of Marriage. *Psychiatry 26* (1963): 368-380.

Redbook Magazine. Mail Questionnaire Study. October 1975.

Reiss, I. L. *Premarital Sexual Standards in America.* New York: Free Press, 1960.

Reiss, I. L. The Sexual Renaissance in America. *Journal of Social Issues* 22 (April 1966).

Reiss, I. L. *The Social Context of Pre-Marital Sexual Permissiveness*. New York: Holt, Rinehart, and Winston, 1967.

Reiss, I. L. Premarital Sexual Standards. In *Sexuality and Man*. New York: Charles Scribner's Sons, 1970.

Reiss, I. L. *Heterosexual Relationships Inside and Outside of Marriage*. Morristown, N.J.: General Learning Press, 1973.

Reiss, I. L. Letter to Roger W. Libby, January 1976.

Reuben, D. *Everything You Always Wanted to Know About Sex But Were Afraid to Ask*. New York: David McKay Co., 1969.

Rimmer, R. *The Rebellion of Yale Marratt*. New York: Avon Books, 1964.

Rimmer, R. *The Harrad Experiment*. Los Angeles, Calif.: Sherbourne Press, 1966; New York: Bantam Books, 1973.

Rimmer, R. *Proposition 31*. New York: New American Library, 1968.

Rimmer, R. *Thursday, My Love*. New York: New American Library, 1972.

Rimmer, R. *Adventures in Loving*. New York: New American Library, 1973.

Rimmer, R. *The Premar Challenge*. New York: New American Library, 1974.

Roberts, J. *Beyond Intellectual Sexism*. New York: David McKay Co., 1976.

Roebuck, J. & S. Spray. The Cocktail Lounge: A Study of Heterosexual Relations in a Public Organization. *American Journal of Sociology* 72 (1967): 388-395.

Rollin, B. New Hang-Up for Parents: Coed Living. *Look* (September 23, 1969): 22+.

Rosenthal, S. & C. Rosenthal. Men's Reaction to Unresponsive Wives. *Medical Aspects of Human Sexuality* 7, No. 11 (Nov. 1973): 12-32.

Rossi, A. S. Equality Between the Sexes: An Immodest Proposal. In R. J. Lifton (ed.), *The Woman in America*. Boston: Beacon Press Daedalus Library, 1964.

Rossi, A.S. Maternalism, Sexuality, and the New Feminism. Unpublished paper presented at the 61st annual meeting of the American Psychopathological Association, New York, 1971.

Roszak, T. *The Making of a Counter Culture*. New York: Doubleday and Company, 1968.

de Rougement, D. More Love in the Western World. In J. Updike, ed., *Assorted Prose*. New York: Knopf, 1965.

Roy, D. & R. Roy. *Honest Sex*. New York: The New American Library, 1968.

Rubin, L. Unpublished paper on the sexual norms of working class women, 1975.

Rubin, Z. *Liking and Loving: An Invitation to Social Psychology*. New York: Holt, Rinehart and Winston, Inc., 1973.

Rush, A.K. *Getting Clear: Body Work for Women*. Berkeley and New York: Random House/Bookworks, 1973.

Russell, B. *Marriage and Morals*. New York: Bantam Books, 1966 (Liveright edition, 1929).

Ryder, R.G. Dimensions of Early Marriage. *Family Process 9* (1970): 51-68.

Ryder, R.G. A Topography of Early Marriage. *Family Process 9* (1970): 385-402.

Ryder, R.G. Describing Variations Among Marriages. Unpublished paper, 1972.

Ryder, R., J. Kafka, & D. Olson. Separating and Joining Influences in Courtship and Early Marriage. *American Journal of Orthopsychiatry 41* (1971): 450-464.

Safire, W. On Cohabitation. *The New York Times* (September 24, 1973): 31M.

Sagarin, E. On Obscenity and Pornography. In Kirkendall & Whitehurst, eds., *The New Sexual Revolution*. New York: Donald W. Brown, Inc., 1971.

Saghir, M.T. & E. Robins. *Male and Female Homosexuality*. Baltimore, Md.: Williams and Wilkins Co., 1973.

Salisbury, W. & F. Salisbury. Youth and the Search for Intimacy. In Kirkendall & Whitehurst, eds., *The New Sexual Revolution*. New York: Donald W. Brown, Inc., 1971.

Salsberg, S. Is Group Marriage Viable? *Journal of Sex Research 9* (4), November 1973.

Sapirstein, M.R. *Emotional Security*. New York: Crown Press, 1948.

Scanzoni, J. *Sexual Bargaining*. Englewood Cliffs, N.J.: Prentice-Hall, 1972.

Schaefer, S. Sexual and Social Problems of Lesbians. *The Journal of Sex Research 12* (February 1976): 50-69.

Schrag, P. Posse at Generation Gap: Implications of the Linda LeClair Affair. *Saturday Review* (May 18, 1968): 81.

Schwartz, P. The Sexually Liberated Woman. Unpublished paper, 1971.

Seal, H. *Alternative Life Styles*. New York:

McGraw-Hill, 1976.

Seaman, B. *Free and Female.* New York: Coward, McCann, & Geoghegan, 1972.

Secord, P. & C.W. Backman. *Social Psychology,* 2nd ed. New York: McGraw-Hill, 1974.

Secrest, M. *Comparison of Role Expectations of Married and Cohabiting Couples.* Unpublished Master's Thesis, University of Kentucky, Lexington, Kentucky, 1975.

Shakespeare, W. *Othello.* Act III, Scene 3.

Sheehy, G. Living Together: The Stories of Four Young Couples Who Risk the Strains of Non-Marriage and Why. *Glamour* (February 1, 1969): 136+.

Sheppard, E. Sugar Daddy's on the Shelf. *Washington Post.* Feb. 9, 1966.

Sheraton, M. Legalities of Unwedded Bliss. *Couples* (1973): 78-81.

Sherfey, M.J. The Evolution and Nature of Female Sexuality in Relation to Psychoanalytic Theory. *Journal of the American Psychoanalytic Association 14* (1966): 28-128.

Sherfey, M.J. *The Nature and Evolution of Female Sexuality,* New York: Random House/Vintage, 1972.

Shulman, A. Organs and Orgasms. In V. Gornick & B.K. Moran, eds., *Woman in Sexist Society.* New York: Basic Books, 1971.

Shulman, A. *Memoirs of an Ex-Prom Queen.* New York: Bantam Paperbacks, 1973.

Shuttlesworth, G. & G. Thorman. Living Together Unmarried Relationships. Paper presented at the Groves Conference on Marriage and the Family, Hot Springs, Arkansas, April 1974.

Simmel, G. *The Sociology of Georg Simmel.* Translated by Kurt Wolff. (From *Soziologie, Untersuchungen uber die Formen der Vergesellschaftung,* Leipzig: Verlag von Duncker & Humblot, 1908.) New York: The Free Press, 1950.

Simon, W. & J. Gagnon. Pornography: The Social Sources of Sexual Scripts. Paper presented at the 17th annual meeting of the Society for the Study of Social Problems, San Francisco, Cal., August 1967.

Simon, W. & J. Gagnon. Psychosexual Development. *The Sexual Scene.* New Brunswick, N.J.: Transaction Books, 1970.

Skinner, B.F. *Walden Two.* New York: Macmillan, Inc., 1960.

Slater, P. *The Pursuit of Loneliness: American Culture at the Breaking Point.* Boston: Beacon Press, 1970.

Slater, P. *Earthwalk.* Garden City, N.Y.: Anchor Doubleday Books, 1974.

Smith, D. & J. Sternfield. Natural Childbirth and Cooperative Childrearing in Psychedelic Communes. *Excerpta Medica,* International Congress Series, No. 207, April 1969.

Smith, J. & L. Smith. Co-marital Sex and the Sexual Freedom Movement. *Journal of Sex Research 6* (1970): 131-142.

Smith, J. & L. Smith, eds. *Beyond Monogamy.* Baltimore: Johns Hopkins University Press, 1974.

Smith, M.B. Ethical Implications of Population Policies: A Psychologist's View. *American Psychologist 27* (1972): 11-15.

Smith, P. & K. Kimmel. Student-Parent Reactions to Off-Campus Cohabitation. *Journal of College Student Personnel* (May 1970): 188-193.

Sontag, S. The Double Standard of Aging. *Saturday Review* (September 23, 1972): 29-38.

Sorensen, R.C. *Adolescent Sexuality in Contemporary America.* New York: World Publishing, 1973.

Spinoza, B. de. *Ethics.* New York: E. P. Dutton & Co., Inc., 1941.

Spreitzer, E. & L. Riley. Factors Associated with Singlehood. *Journal of Marriage and the Family 36* (1974): 533-542.

Sprey, J. On the Institutionalization of Sexuality. *Journal of Marriage and the Family 31* (1969): 432-441.

Starr, J. & D. Carns. Singles in the City. In *Marriages and Families.* H. Lopata, ed. New York: D. Van Nostrand Company, 1973.

Stein, M. *Lovers, Friends, Slaves.* New York: Berkeley Publishing Corp., 1974.

Stein, P. Changing Attitudes of College Women. Unpublished study, Rutgers University, 1973.

Stein, P. Singlehood: An Alternative to Marriage. *Family Coordinator 24* (October 1975): 489-505.

Stein, P. *Single.* Englewood Cliffs, N.J.: Prentice-Hall, 1976.

Stein, R. Not Just an Ordinary Family. *San Francisco Chronicle.* August 28, 1970, p. 19.

Stein, S. Common-Law Marriage: Its History and Certain Contemporary Problems.

Journal of Family Law 9 (1969): 271-299.

Stoller, F. The Intimate Network of Families as a New Structure. In H. Otto, ed., *The Family in Search of a Future*. New York: Appleton-Century-Crofts, 1970.

Stone, G.P. City Shoppers and Urban Identification: Observations on the Social Psychology of City Life. *American Journal of Sociology* 59 (1954): 36-45.

Stone, G.P. Personal communication to Carolynne Kieffer, 1976.

Storm, V. *Contemporary Cohabitation and the Dating-Marital Continuum*. Unpublished Master's Thesis, University of Georgia, Athens, Georgia, 1973.

Stratton, J. & S. Spitzer. Sexual Permissiveness and Self-Evaluation: A Question of Method. *Journal of Marriage and Family* 29 (August 1967): 434-442.

Straus, M. SIMFAM: A Technique for Observation Measurement and Experimental Study of Families. In J. Aldous et al., eds., *The Family Problem Solving Group*. New York: Dryden, 1971.

Straus, M. Letter to Roger W. Libby, November 1975.

Strodbeck, F. Husband-Wife Interaction Over Revealed Differences. *American Sociological Review* 16 (1951): 468-473.

Stuckert, R. Role Perception and Marital Satisfaction: A Configurational Approach. *Marriage and Family Living* 25 (1963): 415-419.

Sussman, M., B. Cogswell, & T. Marciano, eds. The Second Experience: Variant Family Forms and Life Styles. *Family Coordinator* 24 (special issue), October 1975.

Symonds, C. Pilot Study of the Peripheral Behavior of Sexual Mate Swappers. Unpublished Masters' Thesis, University of California, Riverside, Cal., 1968.

Symonds, C. Sexual Mate Swapping and the Swingers. *Marriage Counseling Quarterly* 6 (1971): 1-12.

Synergy. Newsletter from Family Synergy. P.O. Box 30103, Terminal Annex, Los Angeles, Calif. 90030.

Tanzer, D. Natural Childbirth: Pain or Peak Experience? In *The Female Experience* by the editors of *Psychology Today*, 1973.

Terry, S. Harassing of Black Minister Brings Racism to Vermont. *The Washington Post*. Jan. 2, 1969.

Thamm, R. *Beyond Marriage and the Nuclear Family*. San Francisco: Canfield Press, 1975.

Thibaut, J. & H. Kelley. *The Social Psychology of Groups*. New York: John Wiley and Co., 1959.

Thorman, G. Cohabitation: A Report on the Married-Unmarried Life Style. *Futurist* (December 1973): 250-254.

Time. Trial by Marriage. (April 14, 1968): 110-112.

Toffler, A. *Future Shock*. New York: Bantam Books, 1970.

Troner, S. Open Marriage: A Goal to Reach. *Forum*, No. 2, (Wisconsin Psychiatric Institute, Symposium on Parenting in Alternative Family Forms), 1973.

Trost, J. Adultery in Sweden. Research Report, Uppsala University, Department of Sociology, 1970: 1-7.

Trost, J. On Renovating Marriage. *Journal of Marriage and the Family* 36 (1974): 448-449.

Trost, J. Married and Unmarried Cohabitation: The Case of Sweden, With Some Comparisons. *Journal of Marriage and the Family* 37 (1975): 677-682.

Turner, R.H. *Family Interaction*. New York: John Wiley & Sons, Inc., 1970.

Udry, J. *The Social Context of Marriage*, 2nd ed. Philadelphia: J.B. Lippincott Co., 1971.

Updike, J. *Couples*. Greenwich, Conn.: Fawcett Publications, 1968.

Updike, J. Eros Rampant. *Harper's*. June, 1968.

U.S. Bureau of the Census. *Census of Population, 1960: Persons by Family Characteristics*. Vol. II., 4B, U.S. Government Printing Office, 1964.

U.S. Bureau of the Census. *Census of Population, 1970: Persons by Family Characteristics*. Vol. II., 4B, U.S. Government Printing Office, 1973.

U.S. Bureau of the Census. *Marital Status and Living Arrangements: Current Population Reports*, Series P-20, No. 271, U.S. Government Printing Office, March 1974.

Van Deusen, E. *Contract Cohabitation: An Alternative to Marriage*. New York: Avon Books, 1974.

Varni, C. An Exploratory Study of Spouse Swapping. *Pacific Sociological Review* 15 (1972): 507-522.

Vonnegut, K., Jr. *Mother Night.* New York: Avon Books, 1961.

Vreeland, R. Sex at Harvard. *Sexual Behavior* 2, No. 2: February 1972.

Walster, E. Adrenalin Makes the Heart Grow Fonder. *Psychology Today 5:* June 1971.

Ware, C. *Woman Power: The Movement for Women's Liberation.* New York: Tower Publications, 1970.

Warenberg, S. Psychotherapeutic and Dynamic Implications of Recent Research on Female Sexual Functions. In G. Goldman and S. Milman, eds., *Modern Woman: Her Psychology and Sexuality.* Springfield, Illinois: Charles C Thomas, 1969, 3-24.

Warren, C. A. B. *Identity and Community in the Gay World.* New York: Wiley-Interscience, 1974.

Weisberg, D.K. Alternative Family Structures and the Law. *Family Coordinator 24,* October 1975: 549-561.

Weissman, P. Psychological Concomitants of Ego Functioning in Creativity. *International Journal of Psychoanalysis 49* (1969): 464-469.

Weissman, P. Theoretical Considerations of Ego Regression and Ego Function in Creativity. *The Psychoanalytic Quarterly 36* (1967): 37-50.

Weitzman, L. Legal Regulation of Marriage: Tradition and Change. *California Law Review 62,* July-September 1974: 1169-1288.

Weitzman, L. To Love, Honor, and Obey? Traditional Legal Marriage and Alternative Family Forms. *Family Coordinator 24,* October 1975: 531-549.

Welles, P. *Bob and Carol and Ted and Alice,* New York: Bantam Books, 1969.

Wells, T. & L. Christie. Living Together: An Alternative to Marriage. *The Futurist* (April 1970): 50-57.

Westermarck, E. *The History of Human Marriage.* New York: Allerton, 1922.

White, M. Unpublished study. Department of Sociology, Washington State Univ., Pullman, Washington, 1972.

White, M. & C. Wells. Student Attitudes Toward Alternate Marriage Forms. In R. Libby & R. Whitehurst, eds., *Renovating Marriage: Toward New Sexual Life Styles.* Danville, Calif.: Consensus Publishers, 1973, pp. 280-295.

Whitehurst, R.N. Adultery as an Extension of Normal Behavior: The Case of the American Upper-Middle Class Male. Paper presented at the National Council on Family Relations, Minneapolis, Minnesota, October 1966.

Whitehurst, R.N. Personal communication to R.W. Libby, 1968.

Whitehurst, R.N. Extramarital Sex: Alienation or Extension of Normal Behavior. In G. Neubeck, ed., *Extramarital Relations.* Englewood Cliffs, N.J.: Prentice-Hall, Inc., 1969.

Whitehurst, R.N. The Unmalias on Campus. Paper presented at the annual meeting of the National Council on Family Relations, Washington, D.C., October 1969.

Whitehurst, R.N. Sex: In and Out of Marriage. *The Humanist.* Jan./Feb. 1970: 27-28.

Whitehurst, R.N. American Sexophobia. In L.A. Kirkendall & R.N. Whitehurst, eds., *The New Sexual Revolution.* New York: Donald W. Brown Inc., 1971.

Whitehurst, R.N. Living Together Unmarried: Some Trends and Speculations. Paper presented at the Groves Conference on Marriage and the Family, Myrtle Beach, South Carolina, May 1973.

Whitehurst, R.N. Open Marriage: Problems and Prospects. Paper presented at the annual meeting of the National Council on Family Relations. St. Louis, October 1974.

Whitehurst, R.N. Swinging Into the Future: Some Problems and Prospects for Marriage. In R. Caven, ed. *Marriage and Family in the Modern World,* 4th ed. New York: Thomas Y. Crowell Co., 1974.

Whitehurst, R.N. & B. Plant. A Comparison of Canadian and American University Students' Reference Groups, Alienation and Attitudes Toward Marriage. *International Journal of Sociology of the Family 1* (March 1971): 1-8.

Wide World of Singles, *Emerge,* P.O. Box 5366, Buena Park, Cal. 90622.

Wilson, J. *Logic and Sexual Morality.* Baltimore, Md.: Penguin Books, 1965.

Wilson, T. & E. Meyers. *Wife Swapping: A Complete 8-Year Survey of Morals in North America.* New York: Volitant Press, 1965.

Winch, R.F. *Mate Selection: A Study of Complementary Needs.* New York: Harper, 1958.

Wiseman, R. Crisis Theory and the Process of Divorce. *Social Casework 56* (1975): 205-212.

Wolfe, L. *Playing Around: Women and Extramarital Sex*. New York: William Morrow and Co., 1975.

World Futurist Society. Life-Styles Tomorrow. Newsletter for Special Studies Division, 4916 St. Elmo Ave., Washington, D.C. 20014.

Yankelovich, D. *The Changing Values on Campus*. New York: Washington Square Press, 1972.

Zelnik, M. & J.F. Kantner. The Probability of Premarital Intercourse. *Social Science Research 1* (1972): 335-341.

Zetterberg, H. The Secret Ranking. *Journal of Marriage and the Family 28* (1966): 134-143.

Ziskin, J. & M. Ziskin. *The Extra-marital Sex Contract*. Los Angeles: Nash Publishing Company, 1973.